08

FULLMETAL ALCHEMIST

by HIROMU ARAKAWA

80

FULLMETAL EDITION

FULLMETAL
ALCHEMIST

by HIROMU ARAKAWA

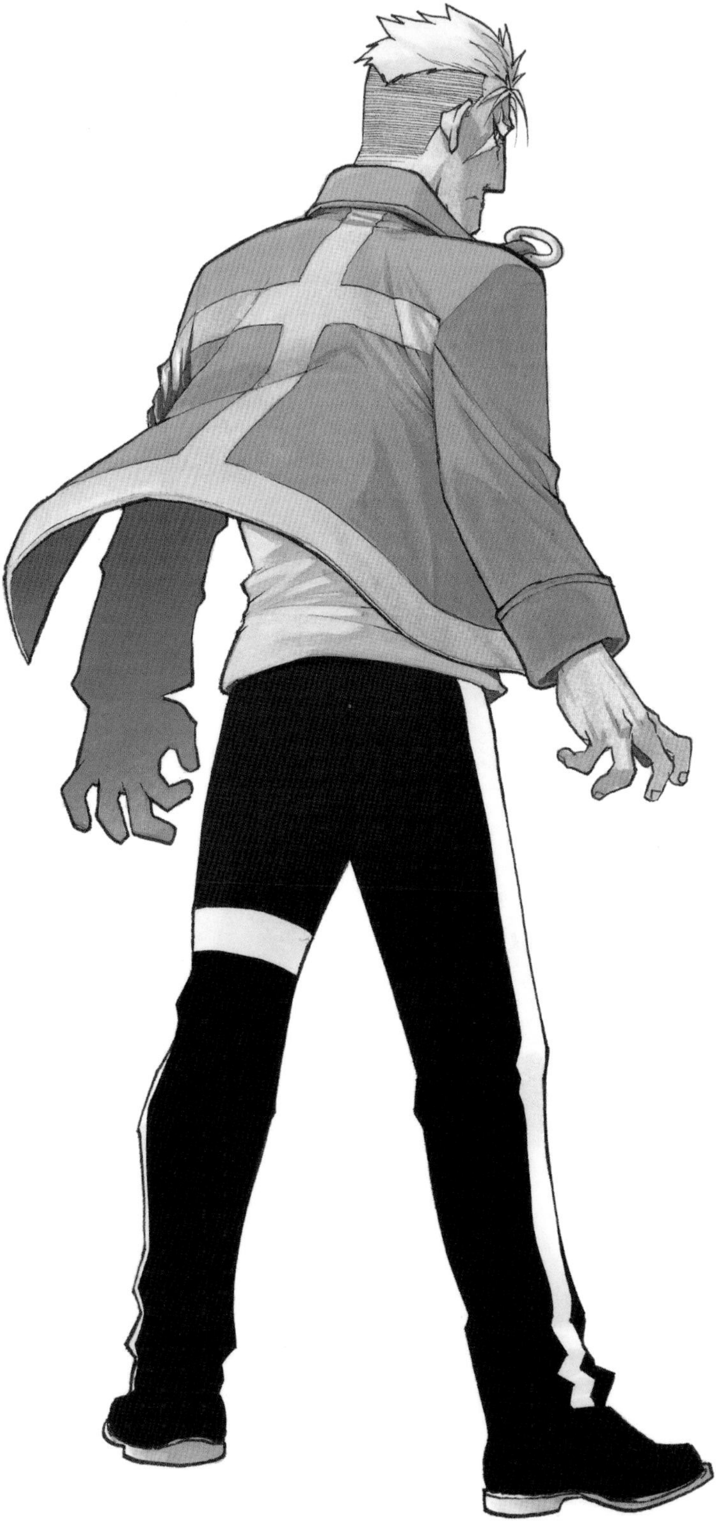

FULLMETAL ALCHEMIST

08
CONTENTS

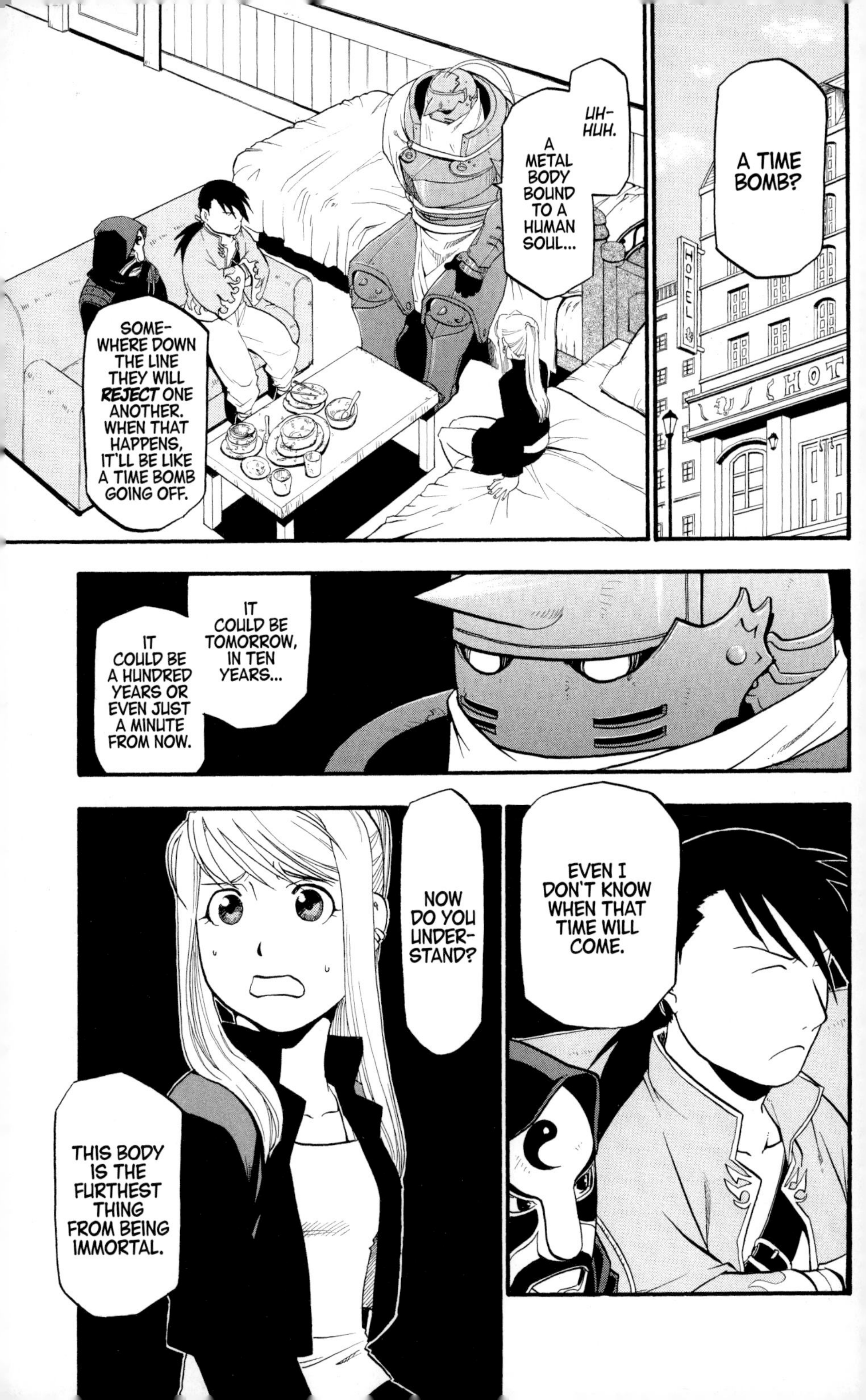
A TIME BOMB?
HOTEL
UH-HUH.
A METAL BODY BOUND TO A HUMAN SOUL...
SOME-WHERE DOWN THE LINE THEY WILL *REJECT* ONE ANOTHER. WHEN THAT HAPPENS, IT'LL BE LIKE A TIME BOMB GOING OFF.
IT COULD BE TOMORROW, IN TEN YEARS...
IT COULD BE A HUNDRED YEARS OR EVEN JUST A MINUTE FROM NOW.
EVEN I DON'T KNOW WHEN THAT TIME WILL COME.
NOW DO YOU UNDER-STAND?
THIS BODY IS THE FURTHEST THING FROM BEING IMMORTAL.

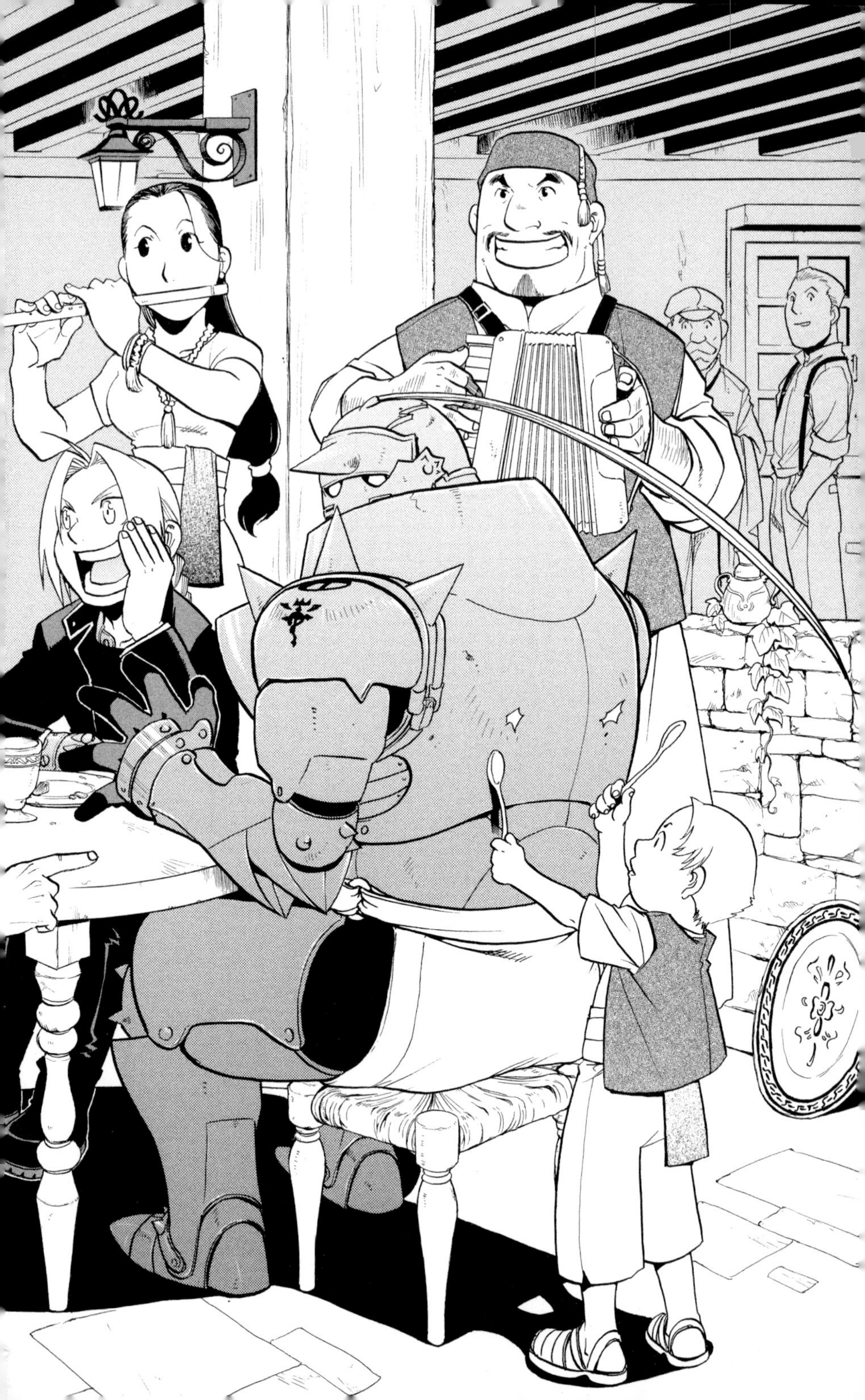

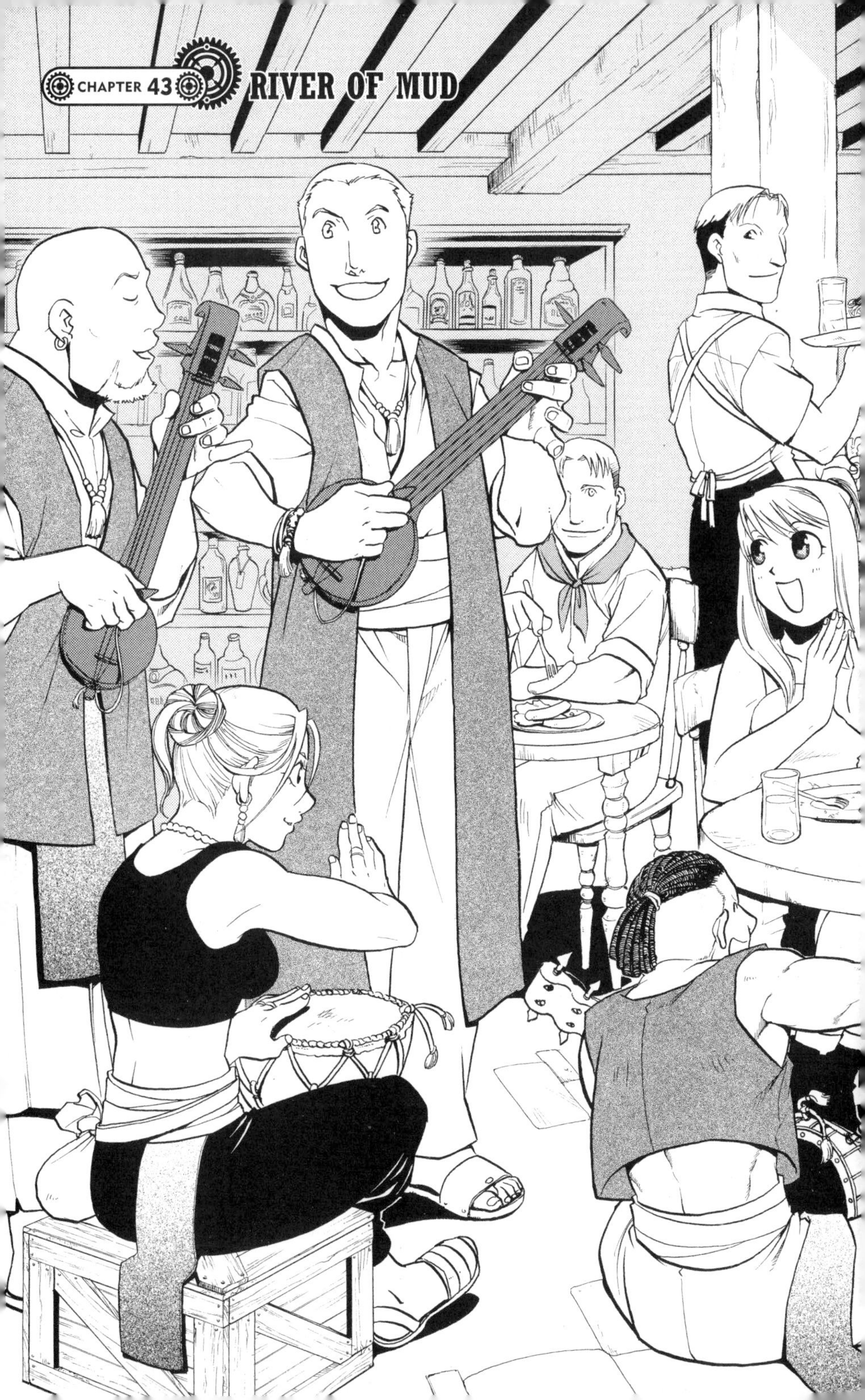
CHAPTER 43
RIVER OF MUD

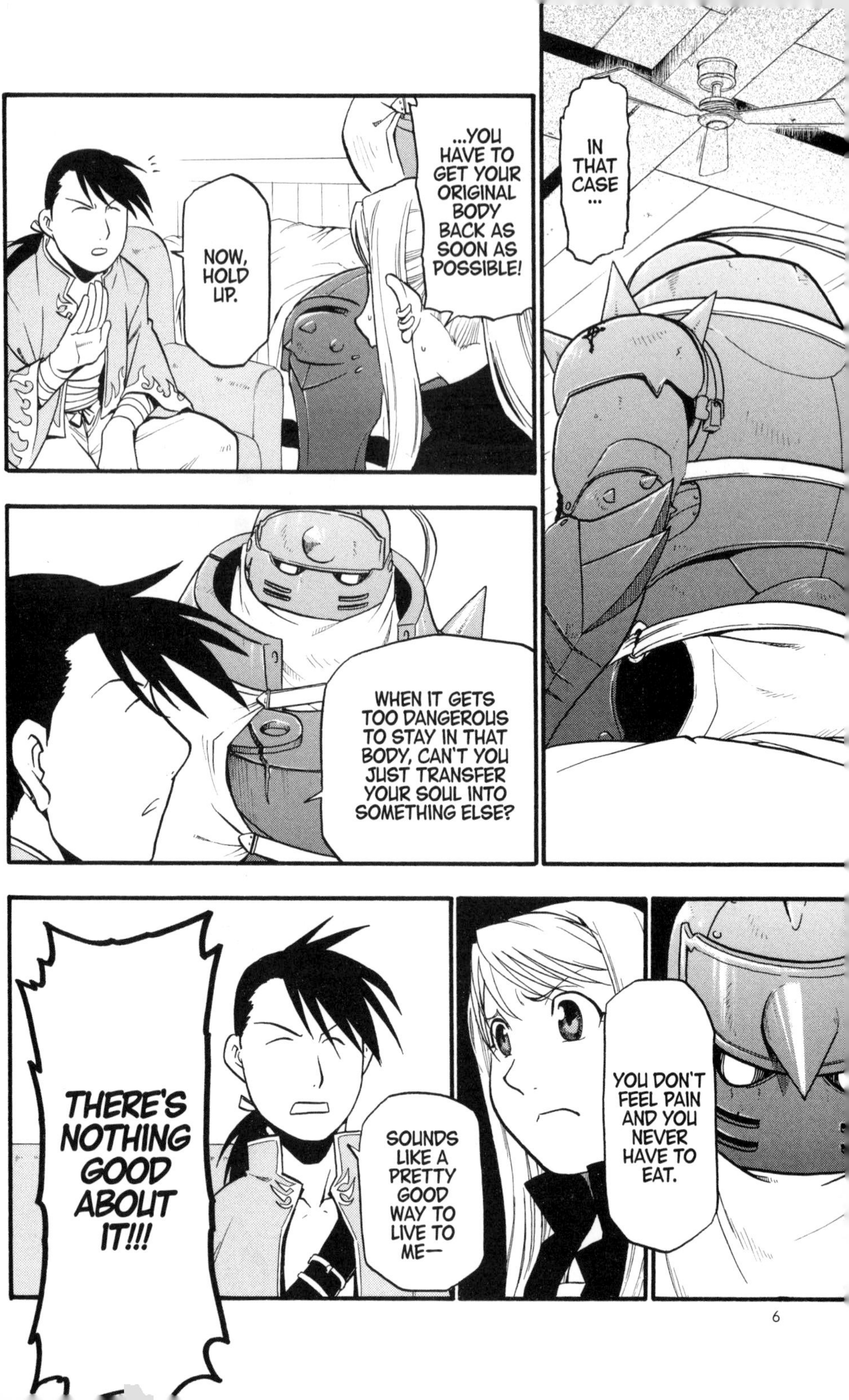
IN THAT CASE...
...YOU HAVE TO GET YOUR ORIGINAL BODY BACK AS SOON AS POSSIBLE!
NOW, HOLD UP.
WHEN IT GETS TOO DANGEROUS TO STAY IN THAT BODY, CAN'T YOU JUST TRANSFER YOUR SOUL INTO SOMETHING ELSE?
YOU DON'T FEEL PAIN AND YOU NEVER HAVE TO EAT.
SOUNDS LIKE A PRETTY GOOD WAY TO LIVE TO ME—
THERE'S NOTHING GOOD ABOUT IT!!!

YOU...

YOU DON'T KNOW ANYTHING!!

SLAM

WINRY!

I'M SORRY...

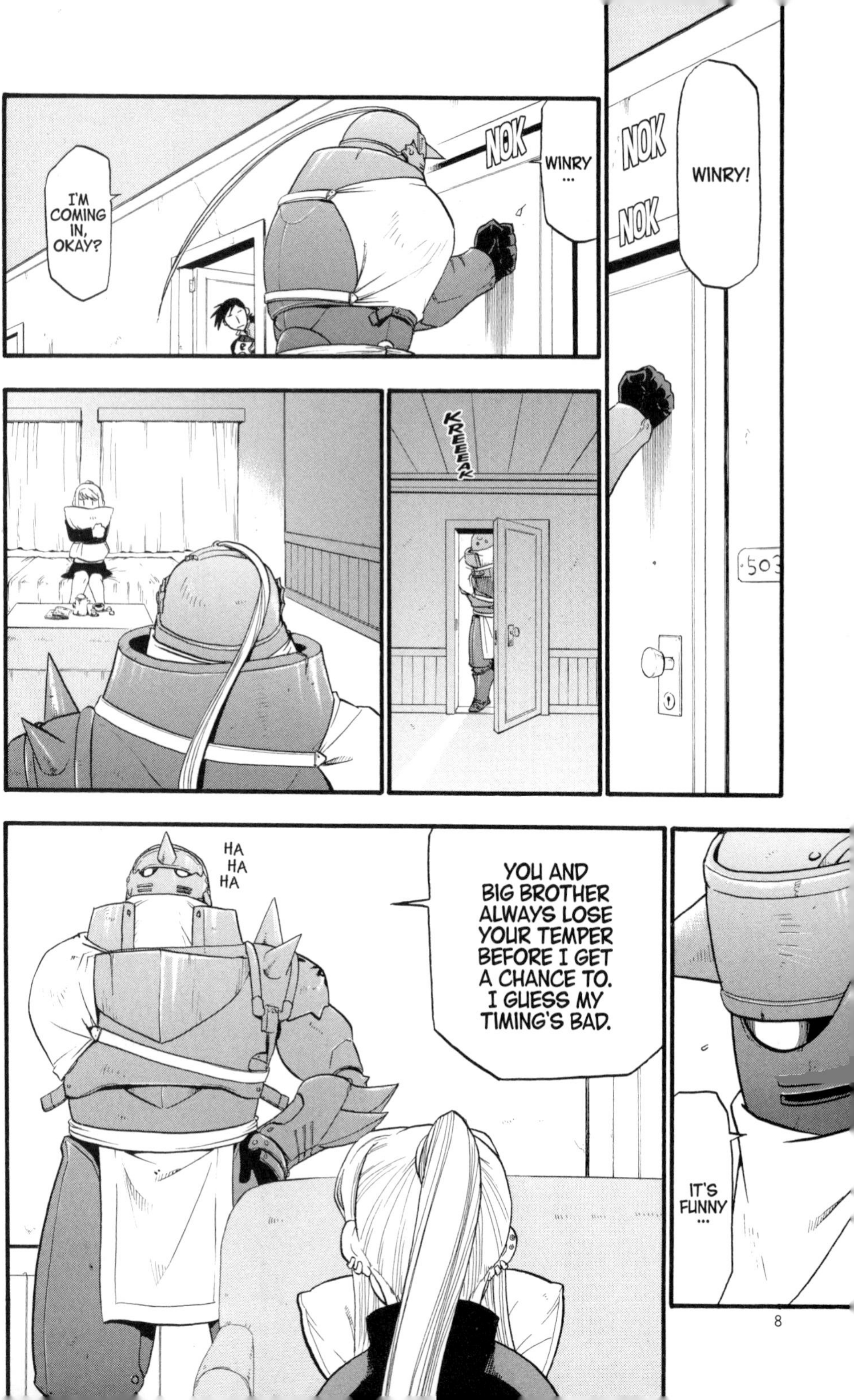
NOK
NOK
WINRY!
NOK
WINRY...
I'M COMING IN, OKAY?
KREEEAK
IT'S FUNNY...
YOU AND BIG BROTHER ALWAYS LOSE YOUR TEMPER BEFORE I GET A CHANCE TO. I GUESS MY TIMING'S BAD.
HA HA HA

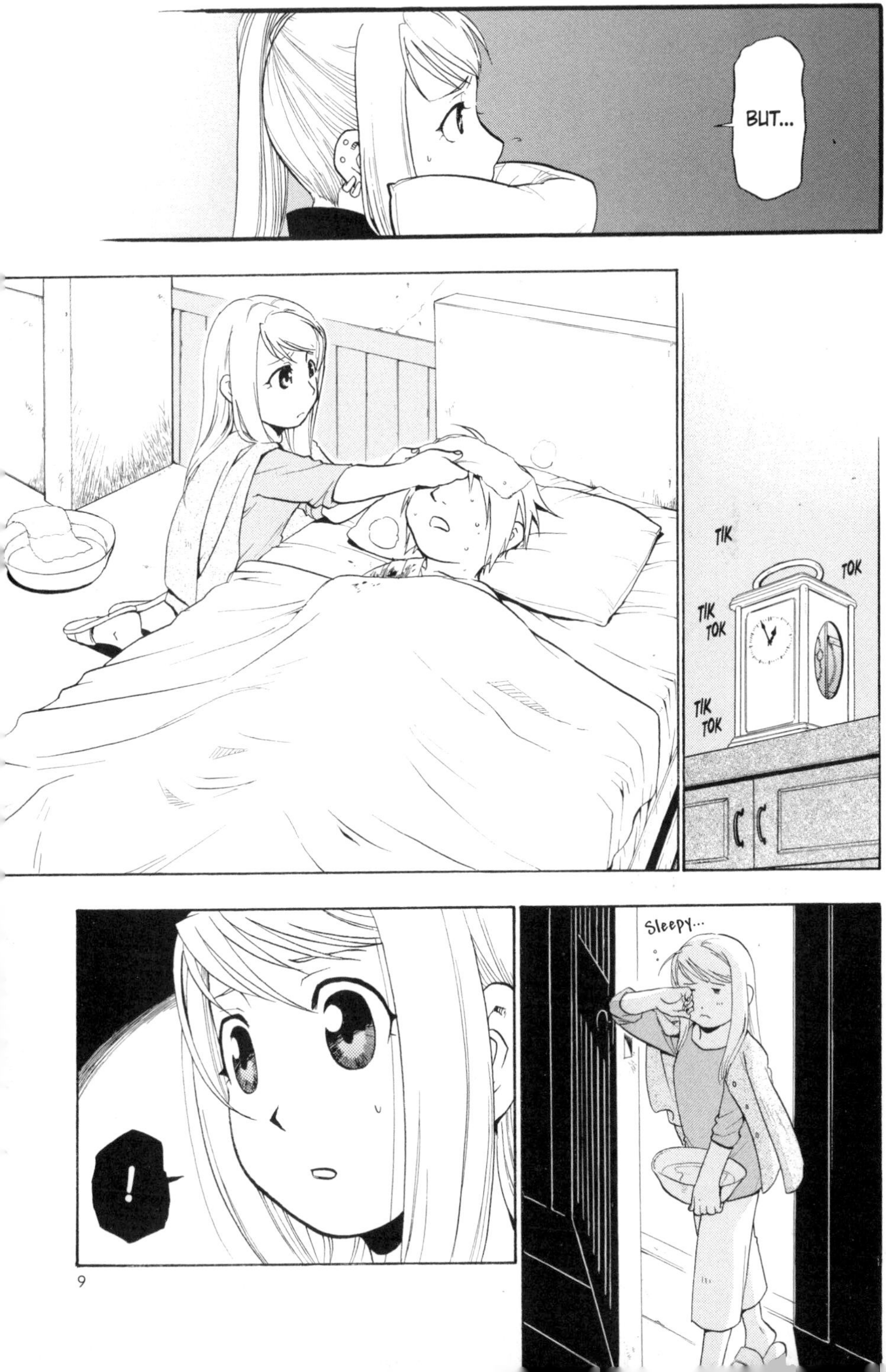
BUT...
TIK
TOK
TIK TOK
TIK TOK
Sleepy...
!

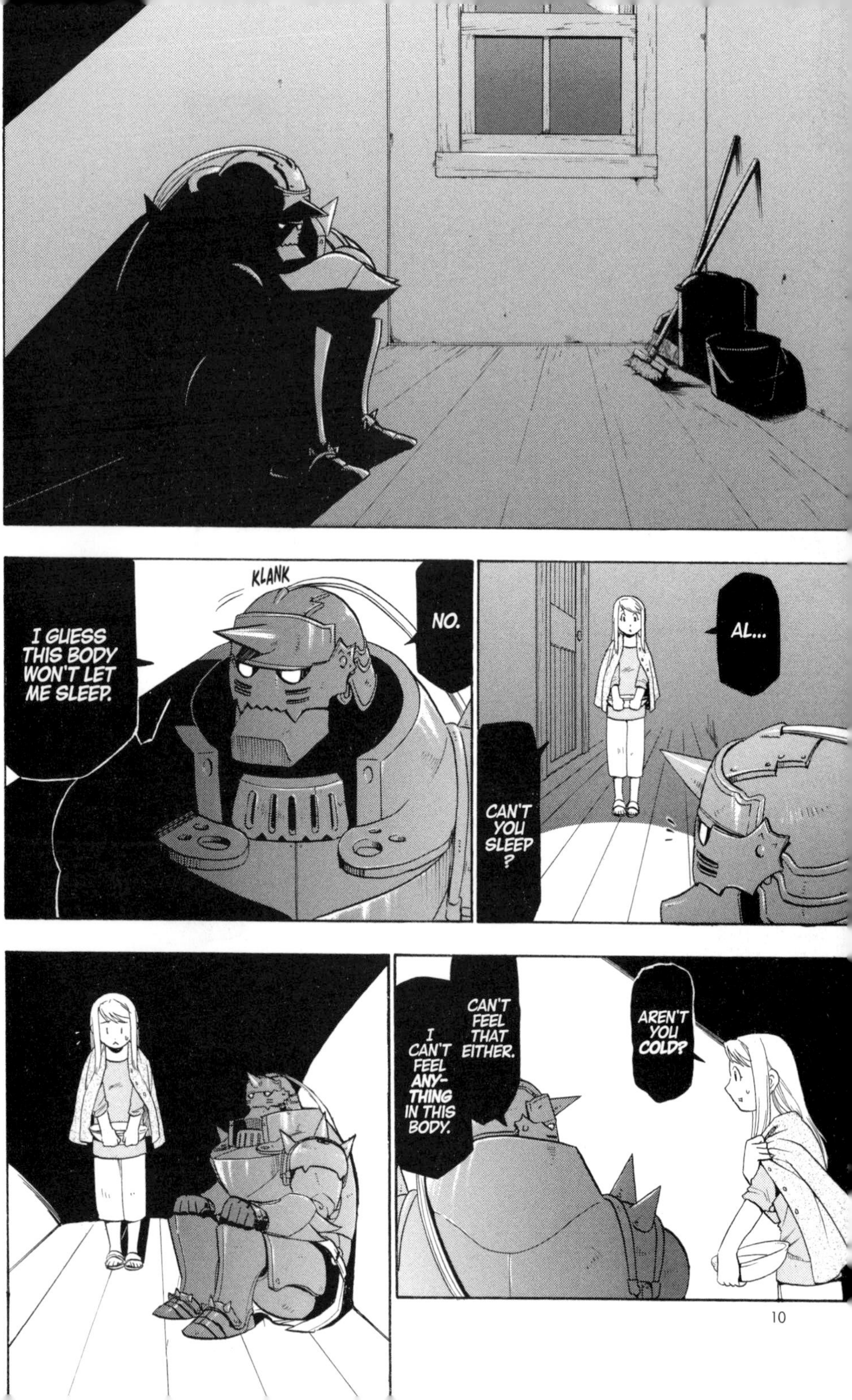
AL...
CAN'T YOU SLEEP?
KLANK
NO.
I GUESS THIS BODY WON'T LET ME SLEEP.
AREN'T YOU COLD?
CAN'T FEEL THAT EITHER.
I CAN'T FEEL ANY-THING IN THIS BODY.

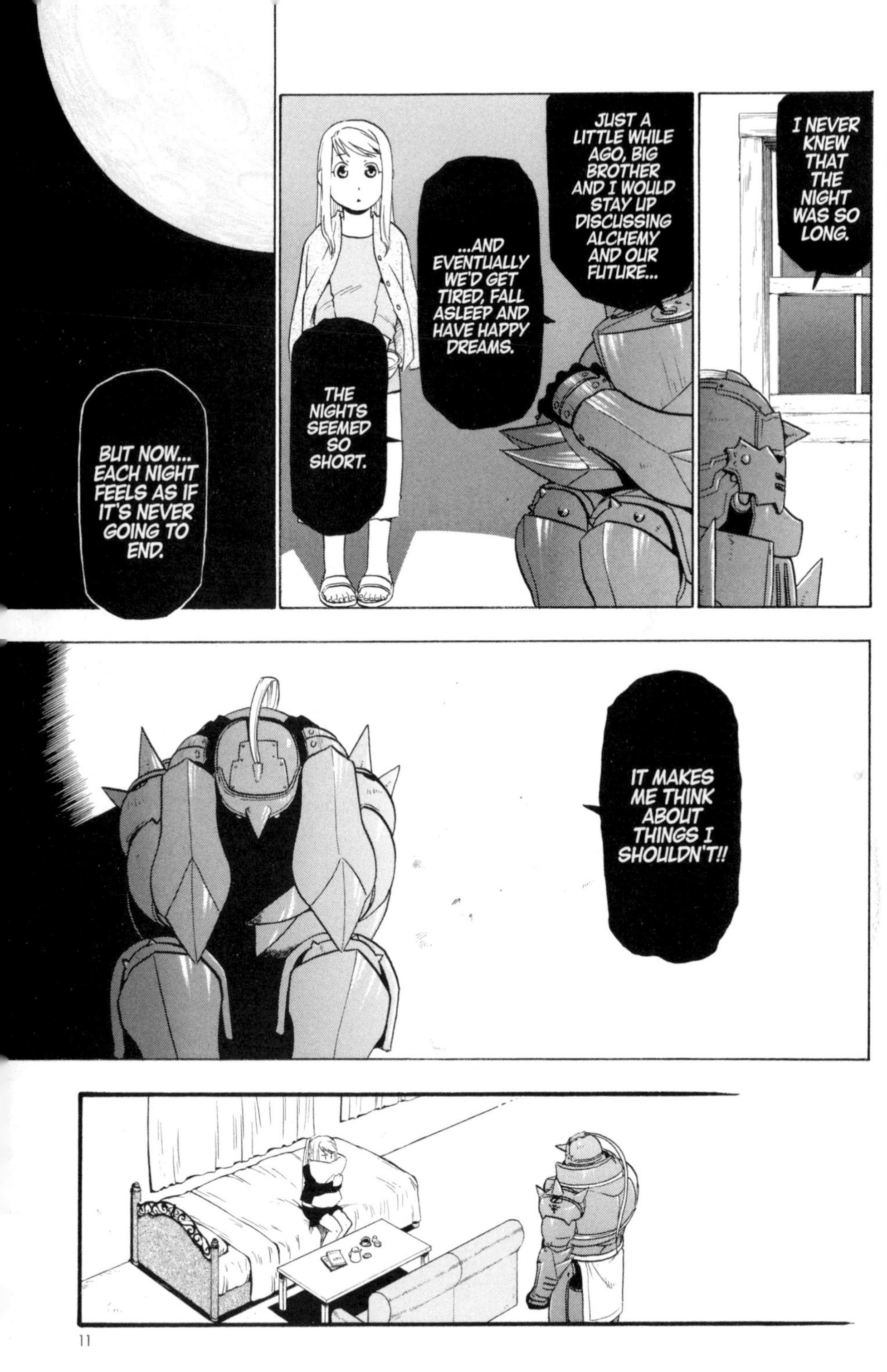
I NEVER KNEW THAT THE NIGHT WAS SO LONG.
JUST A LITTLE WHILE AGO, BIG BROTHER AND I WOULD STAY UP DISCUSSING ALCHEMY AND OUR FUTURE...
...AND EVENTUALLY WE'D GET TIRED, FALL ASLEEP AND HAVE HAPPY DREAMS.
THE NIGHTS SEEMED SO SHORT.
BUT NOW... EACH NIGHT FEELS AS IF IT'S NEVER GOING TO END.
IT MAKES ME THINK ABOUT THINGS I SHOULDN'T!!

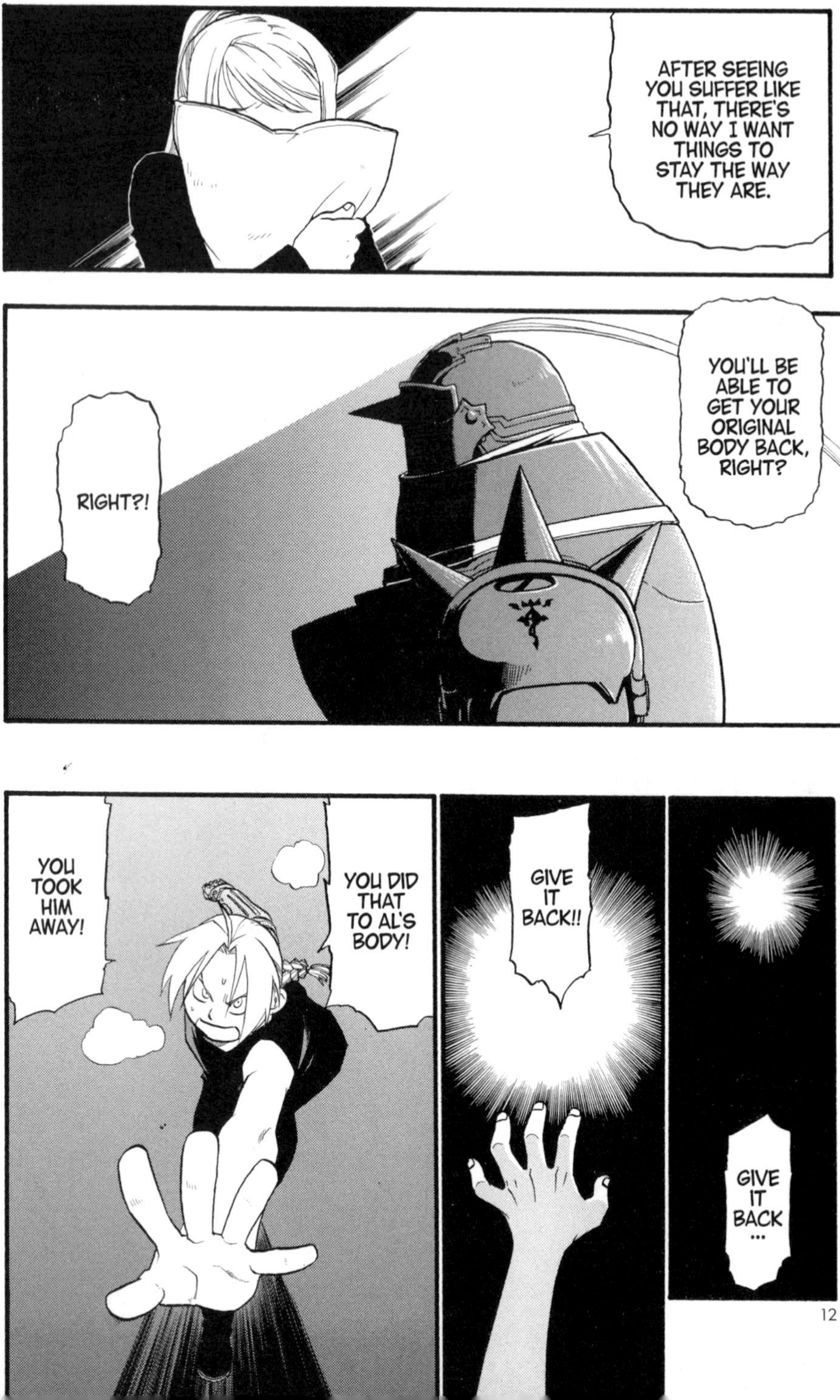
AFTER SEEING YOU SUFFER LIKE THAT, THERE'S NO WAY I WANT THINGS TO STAY THE WAY THEY ARE.
YOU'LL BE ABLE TO GET YOUR ORIGINAL BODY BACK, RIGHT?
RIGHT?!
GIVE IT BACK...
GIVE IT BACK!!
YOU DID THAT TO AL'S BODY!
YOU TOOK HIM AWAY!

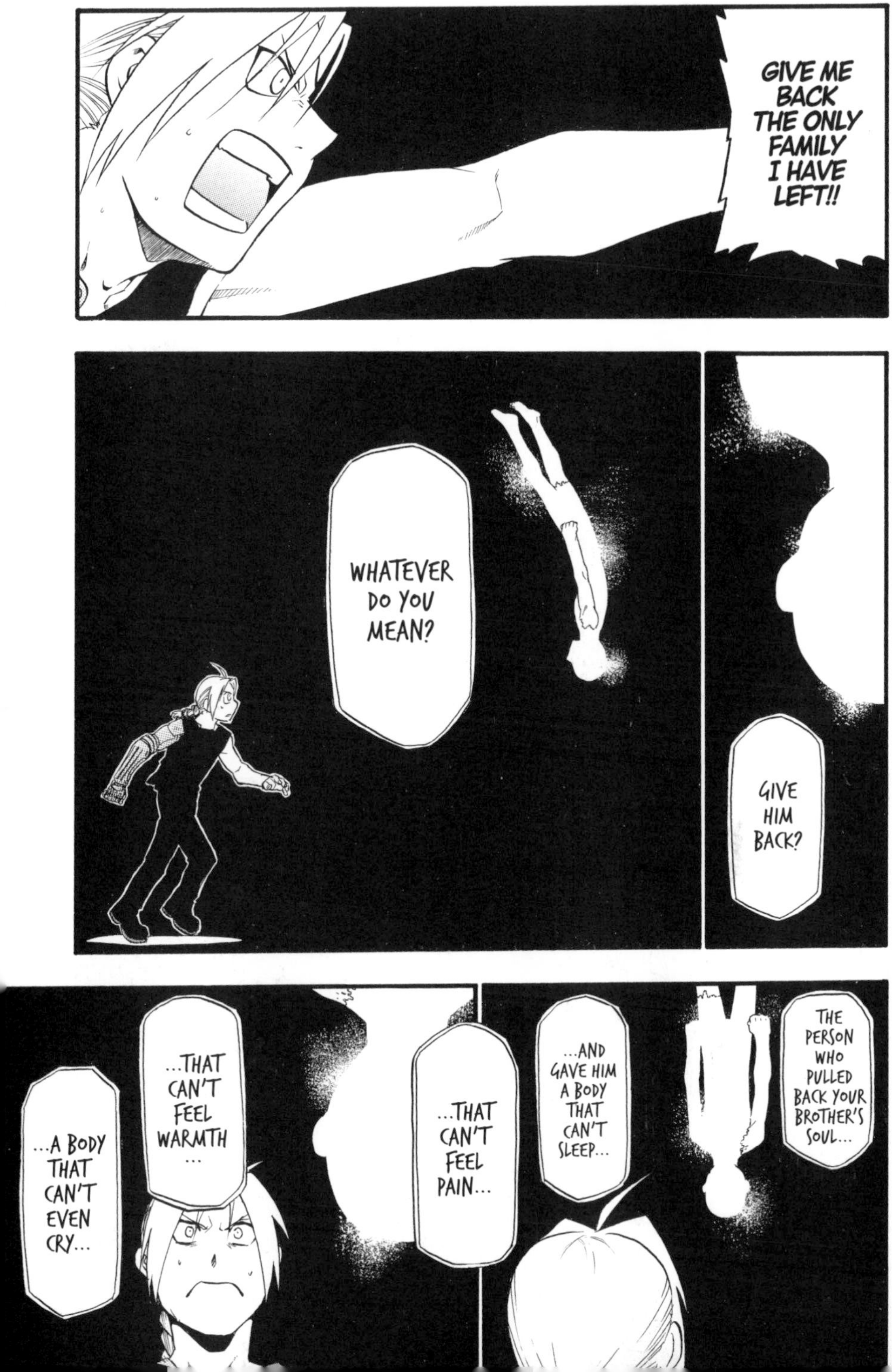
GIVE ME BACK THE ONLY FAMILY I HAVE LEFT!!
GIVE HIM BACK?
WHATEVER DO YOU MEAN?
THE PERSON WHO PULLED BACK YOUR BROTHER'S SOUL...
...AND GAVE HIM A BODY THAT CAN'T SLEEP...
...THAT CAN'T FEEL PAIN...
...THAT CAN'T FEEL WARMTH...
...A BODY THAT CAN'T EVEN CRY...

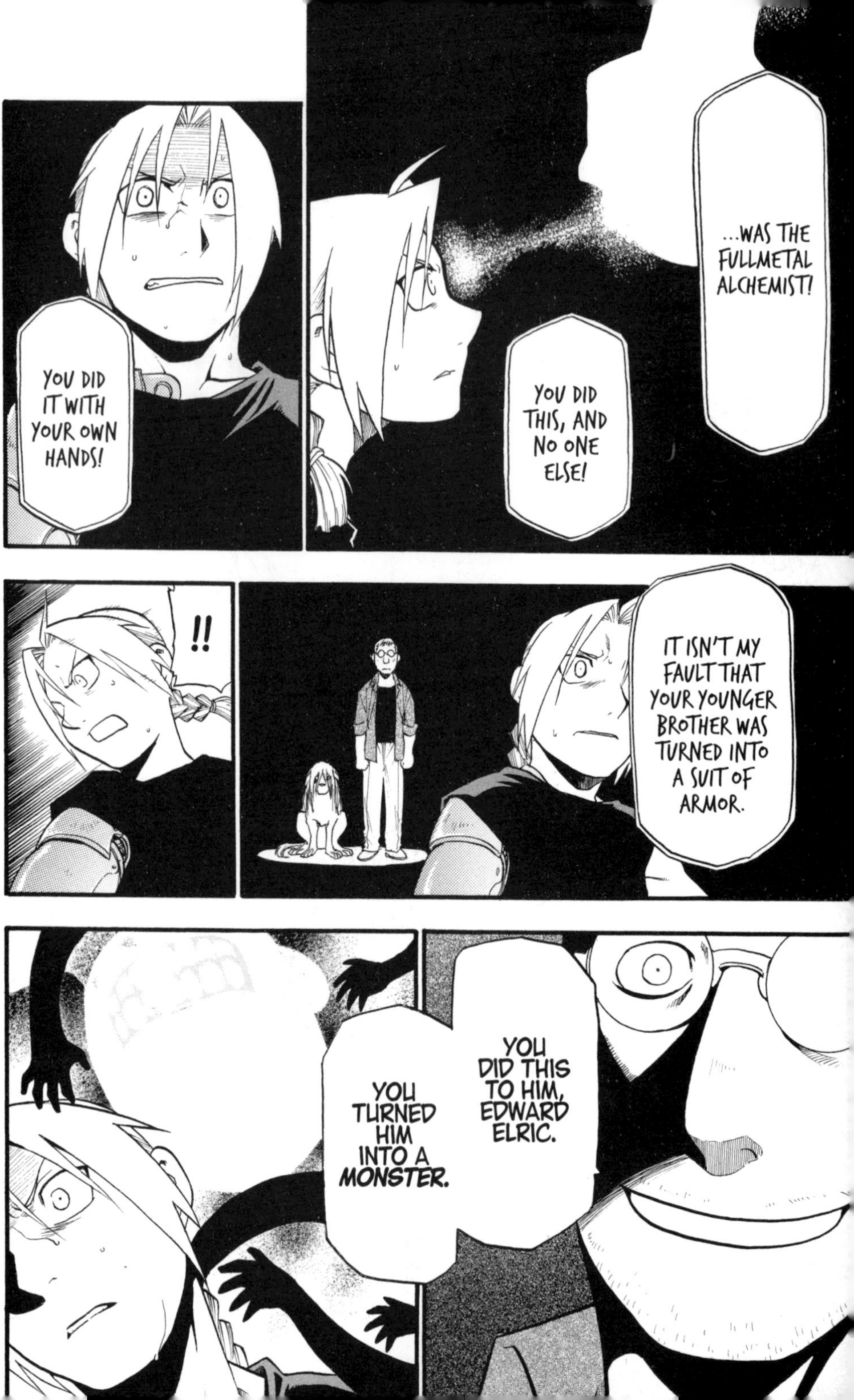
...WAS THE FULLMETAL ALCHEMIST!
YOU DID THIS, AND NO ONE ELSE!
YOU DID IT WITH YOUR OWN HANDS!
IT ISN'T MY FAULT THAT YOUR YOUNGER BROTHER WAS TURNED INTO A SUIT OF ARMOR.
!!
YOU DID THIS TO HIM, EDWARD ELRIC.
YOU TURNED HIM INTO A ***MONSTER.***

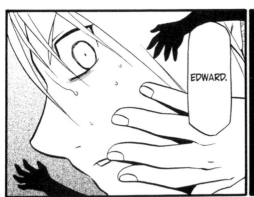

EDWARD.

NO...NOT JUST YOUR BROTHER.

ED.

DON'T LEAVE ME HERE LIKE THIS!

PLEASE BRING ME BACK TO LIFE SOON!

PROM-ISE ME?

ED...

ED...

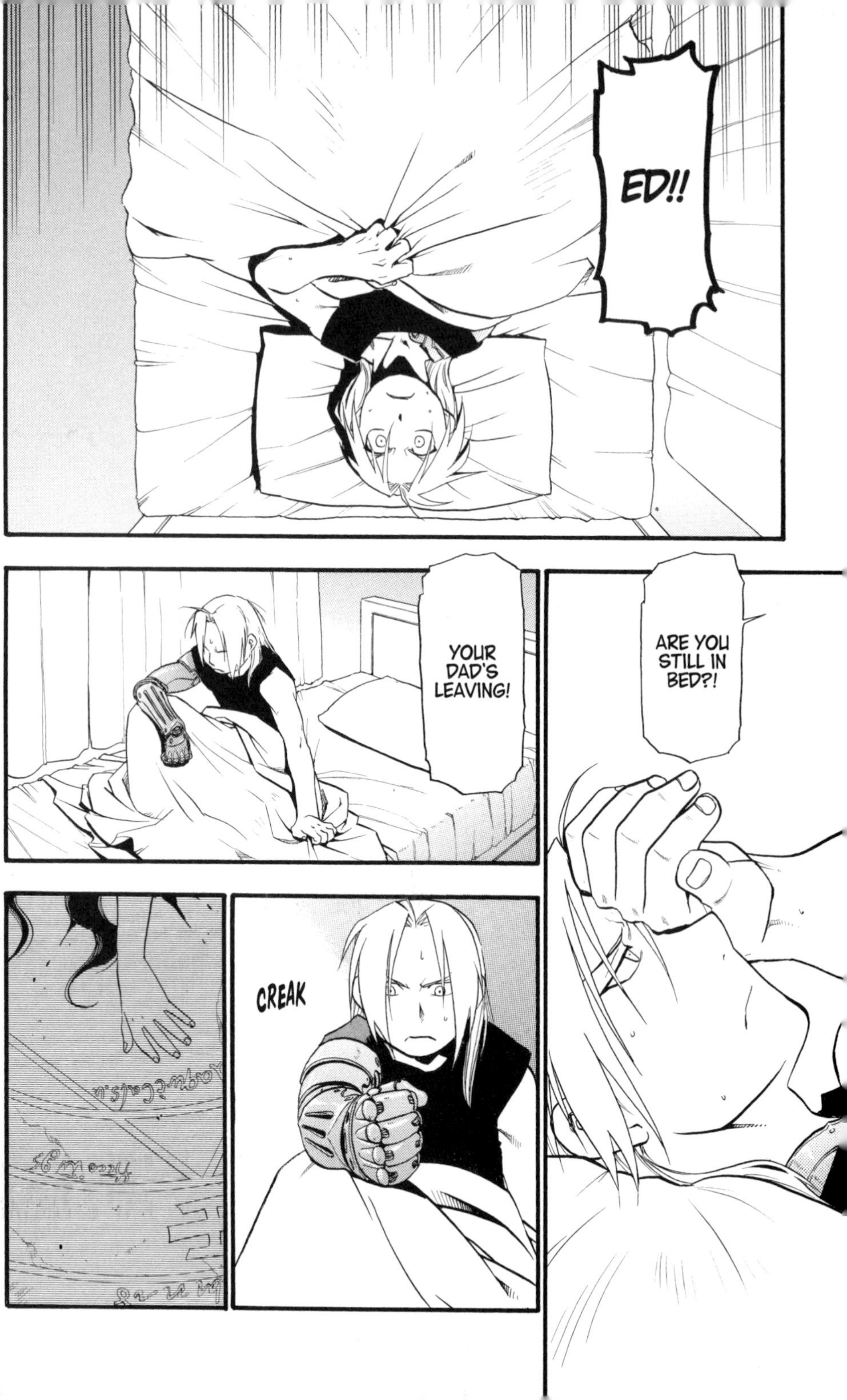
ED!!
ARE YOU STILL IN BED?!
YOUR DAD'S LEAVING!
CREAK

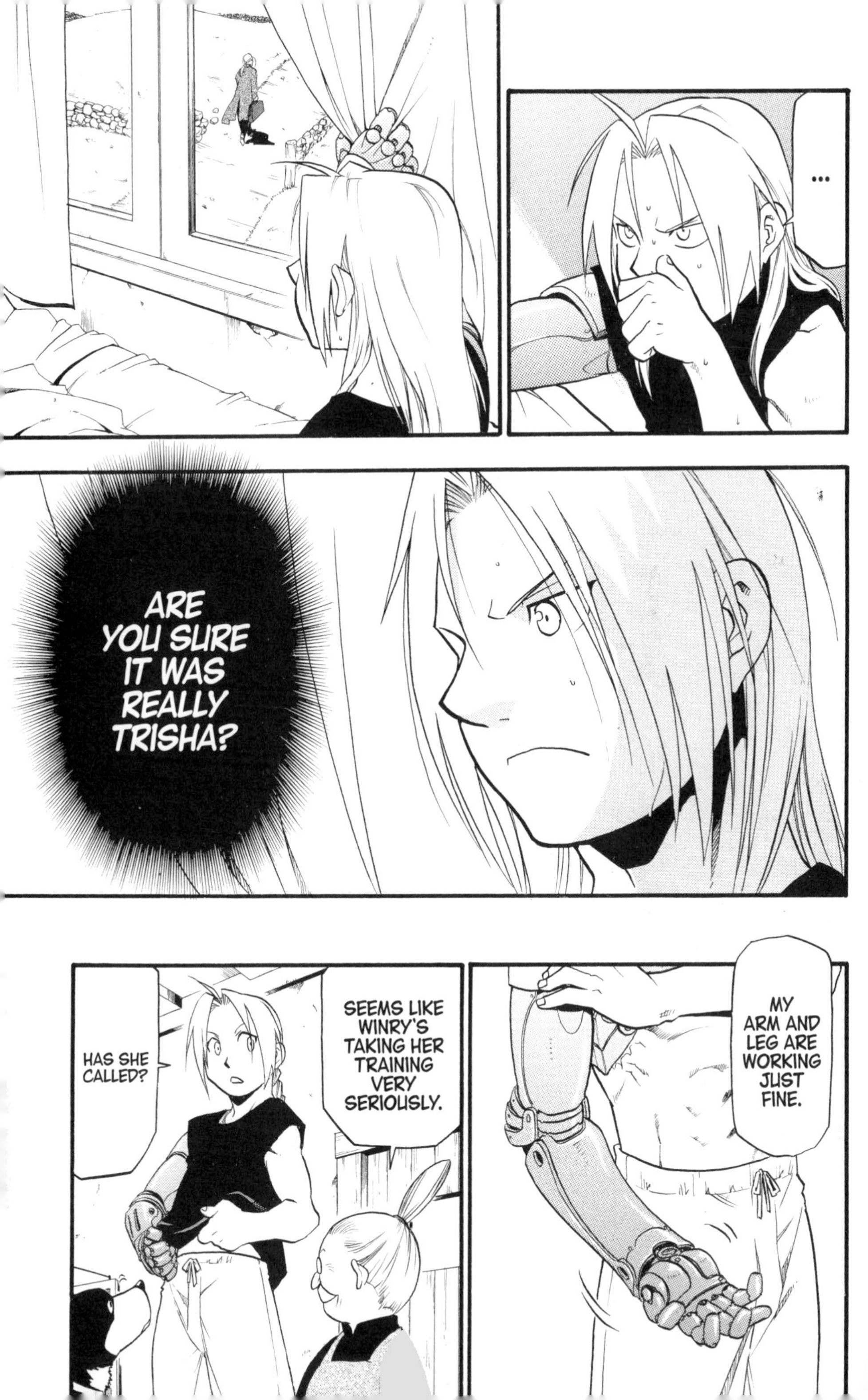
...
ARE YOU SURE IT WAS REALLY TRISHA?
MY ARM AND LEG ARE WORKING JUST FINE.
SEEMS LIKE WINRY'S TAKING HER TRAINING VERY SERIOUSLY.
HAS SHE CALLED?

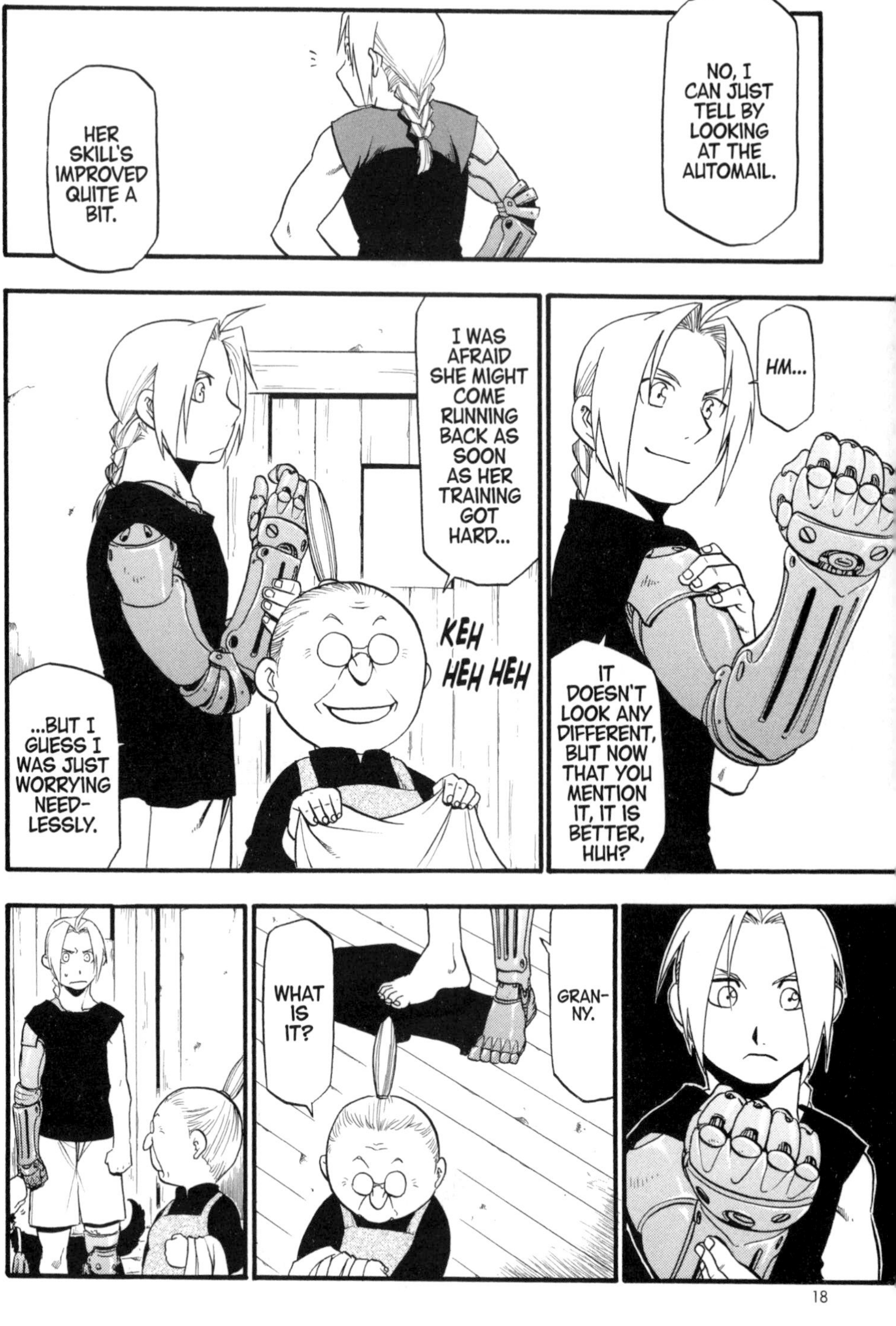
NO, I CAN JUST TELL BY LOOKING AT THE AUTOMAIL.
HER SKILL'S IMPROVED QUITE A BIT.
HM...
IT DOESN'T LOOK ANY DIFFERENT, BUT NOW THAT YOU MENTION IT, IT IS BETTER, HUH?
I WAS AFRAID SHE MIGHT COME RUNNING BACK AS SOON AS HER TRAINING GOT HARD...
KEH HEH HEH
...BUT I GUESS I WAS JUST WORRYING NEED-LESSLY.
GRAN-NY.
WHAT IS IT?

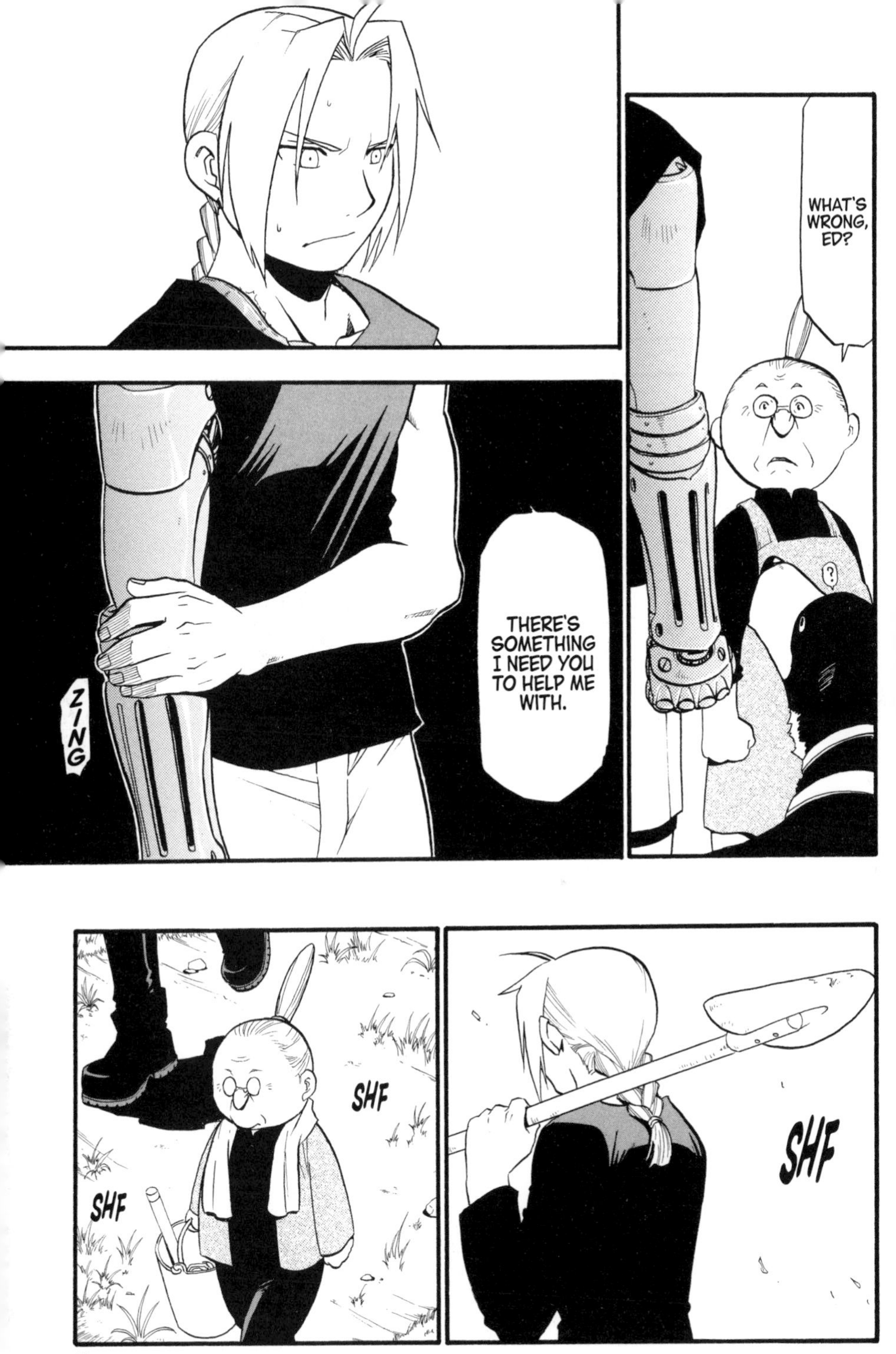
WHAT'S WRONG, ED?
THERE'S SOMETHING I NEED YOU TO HELP ME WITH.
ZING
SHF
SHF
SHF

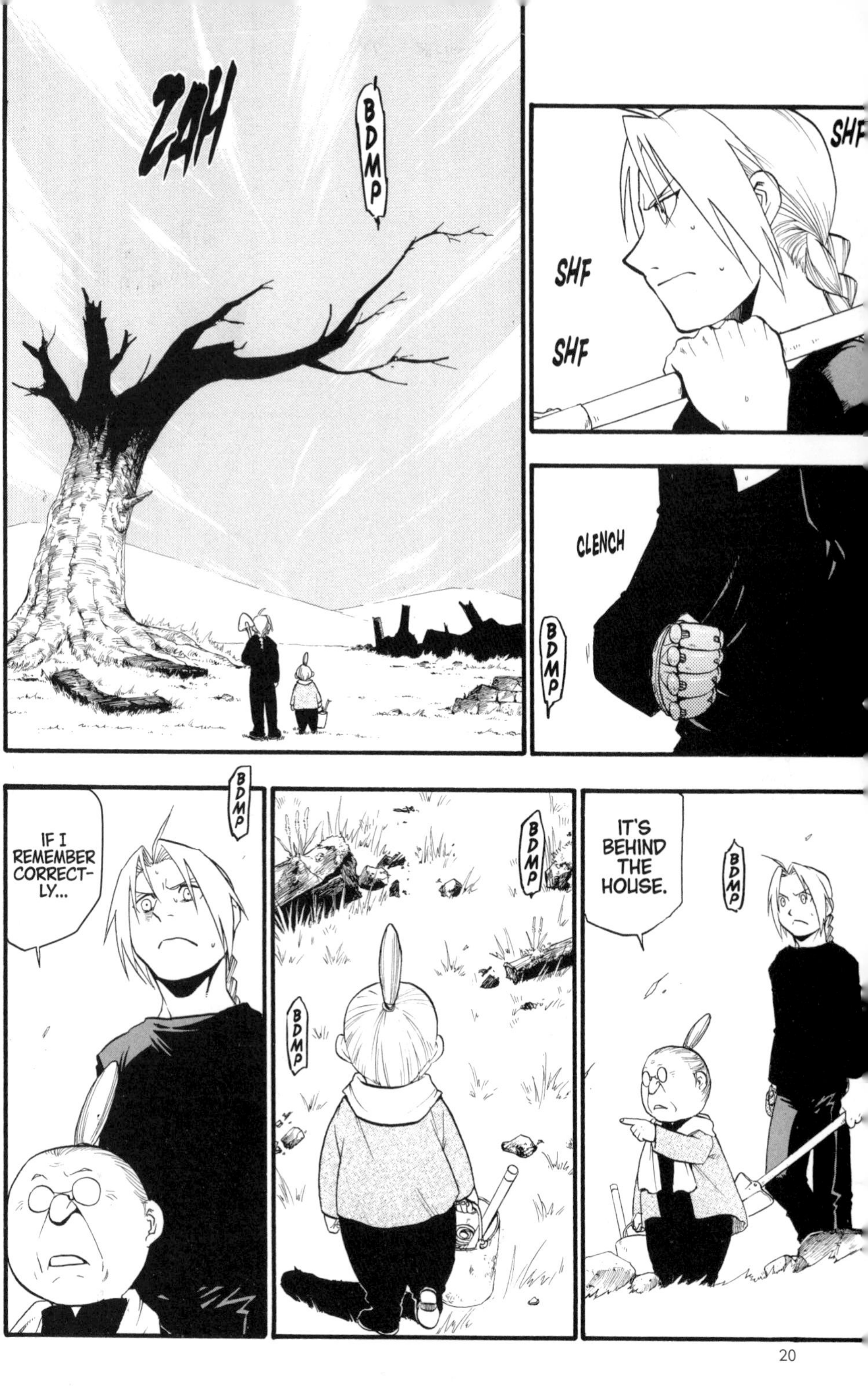
SHF
SHF
SHF
CLENCH
BDMP
ZAH
BDMP
BDMP
IT'S BEHIND THE HOUSE.
BDMP
BDMP
BDMP
IF I REMEMBER CORRECT-LY...

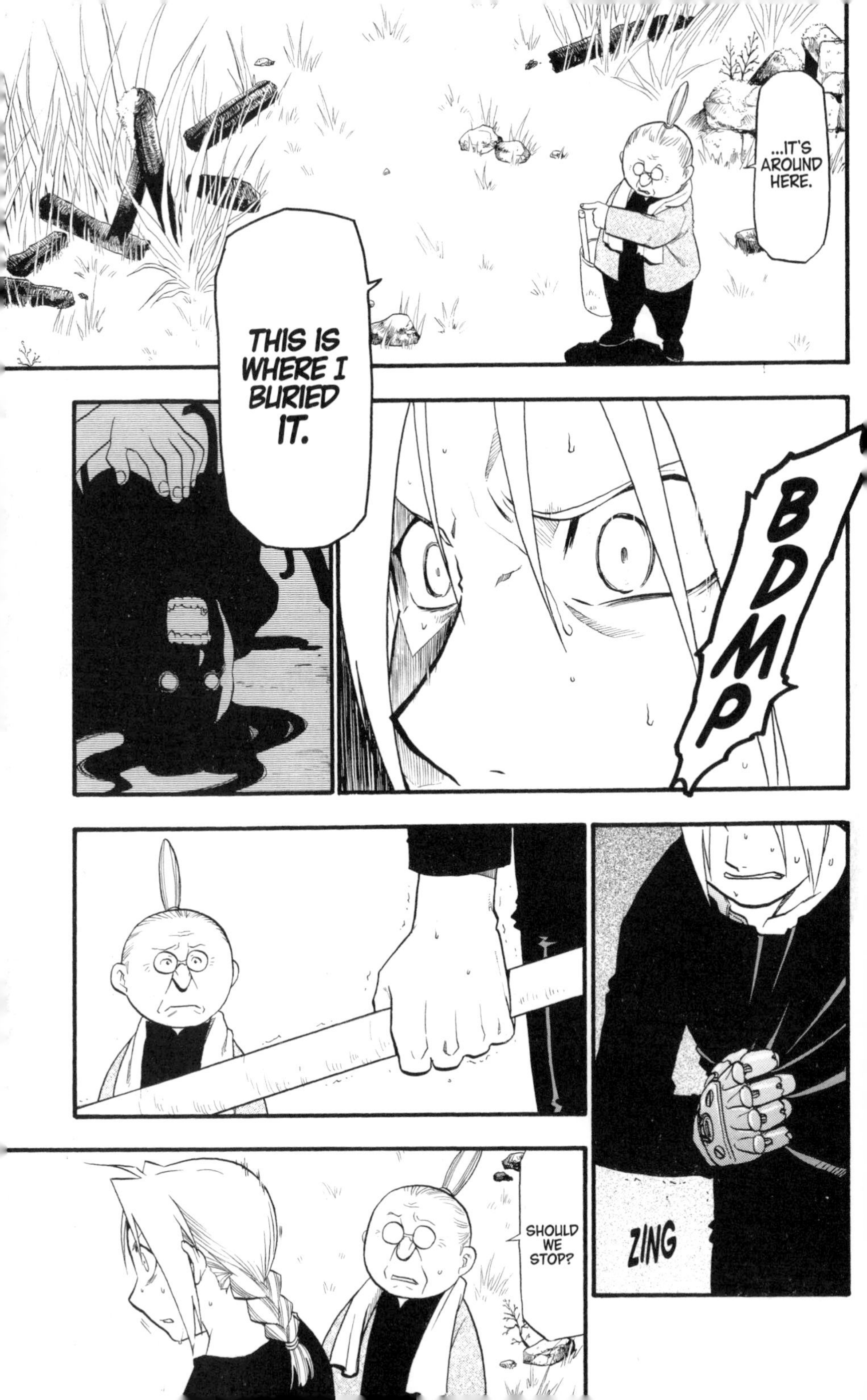
...IT'S AROUND HERE.
THIS IS WHERE I BURIED IT.
BDMP
ZING
SHOULD WE STOP?

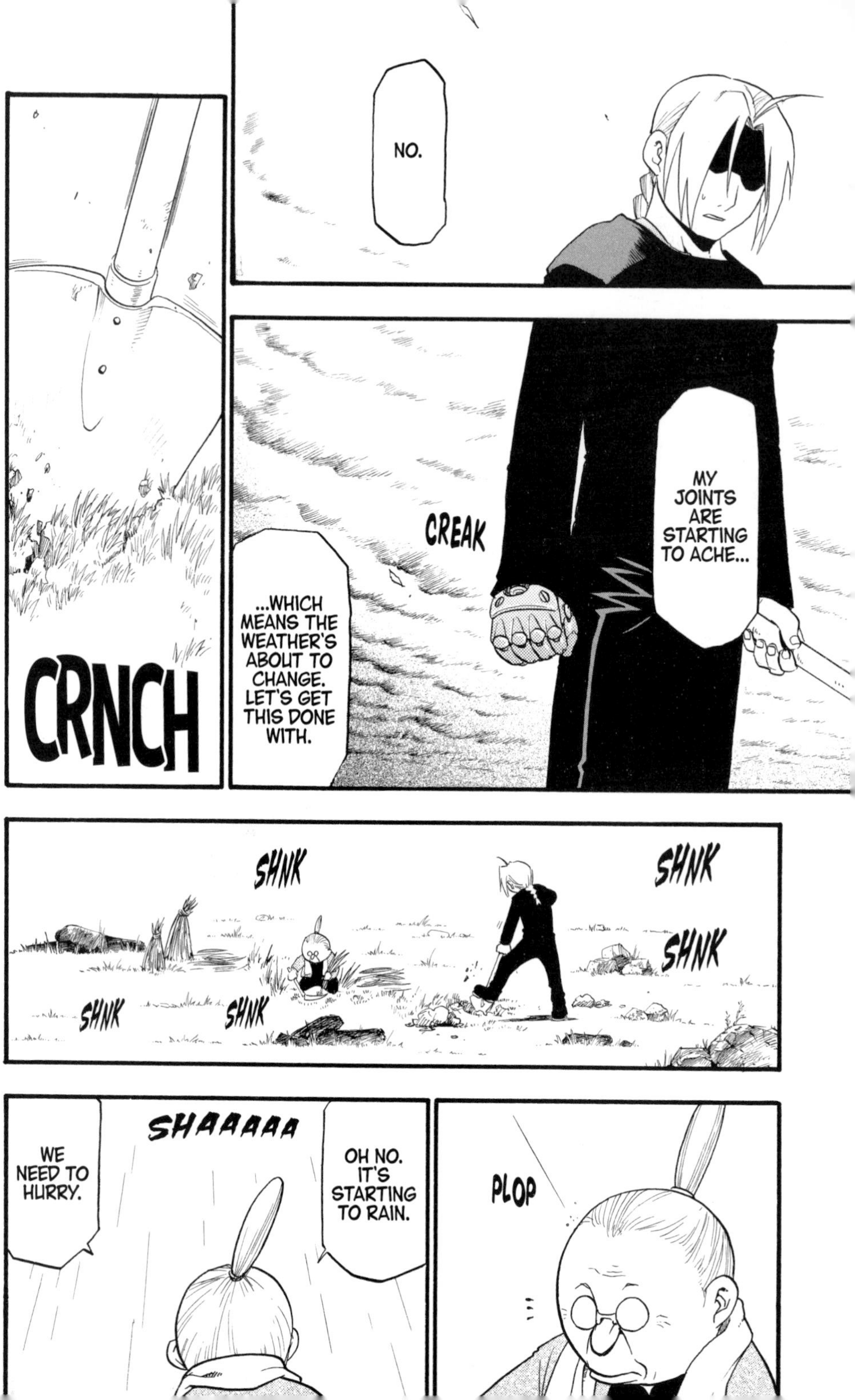
NO.
MY JOINTS ARE STARTING TO ACHE...
CREAK
...WHICH MEANS THE WEATHER'S ABOUT TO CHANGE. LET'S GET THIS DONE WITH.
CRNCH
SHNK
SHNK
SHNK
SHNK
SHNK
PLOP
OH NO. IT'S STARTING TO RAIN.
SHAAAAA
WE NEED TO HURRY.

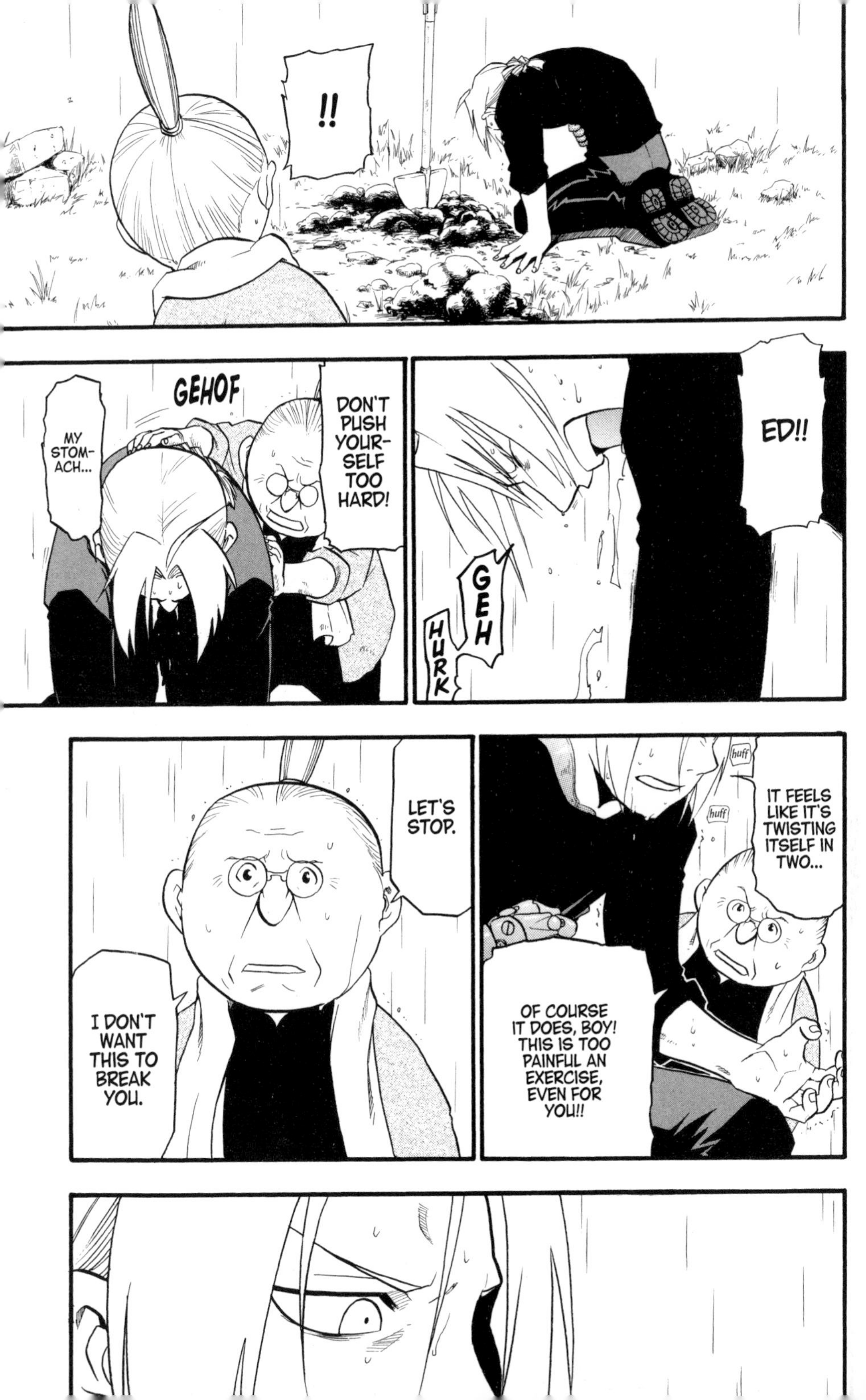
!!
ED!!
GEH
HURK
DON'T PUSH YOUR-SELF TOO HARD!
GEHOF
MY STOM-ACH...
huff
huff
IT FEELS LIKE IT'S TWISTING ITSELF IN TWO...
OF COURSE IT DOES, BOY! THIS IS TOO PAINFUL AN EXERCISE, EVEN FOR YOU!!
LET'S STOP.
I DON'T WANT THIS TO BREAK YOU.

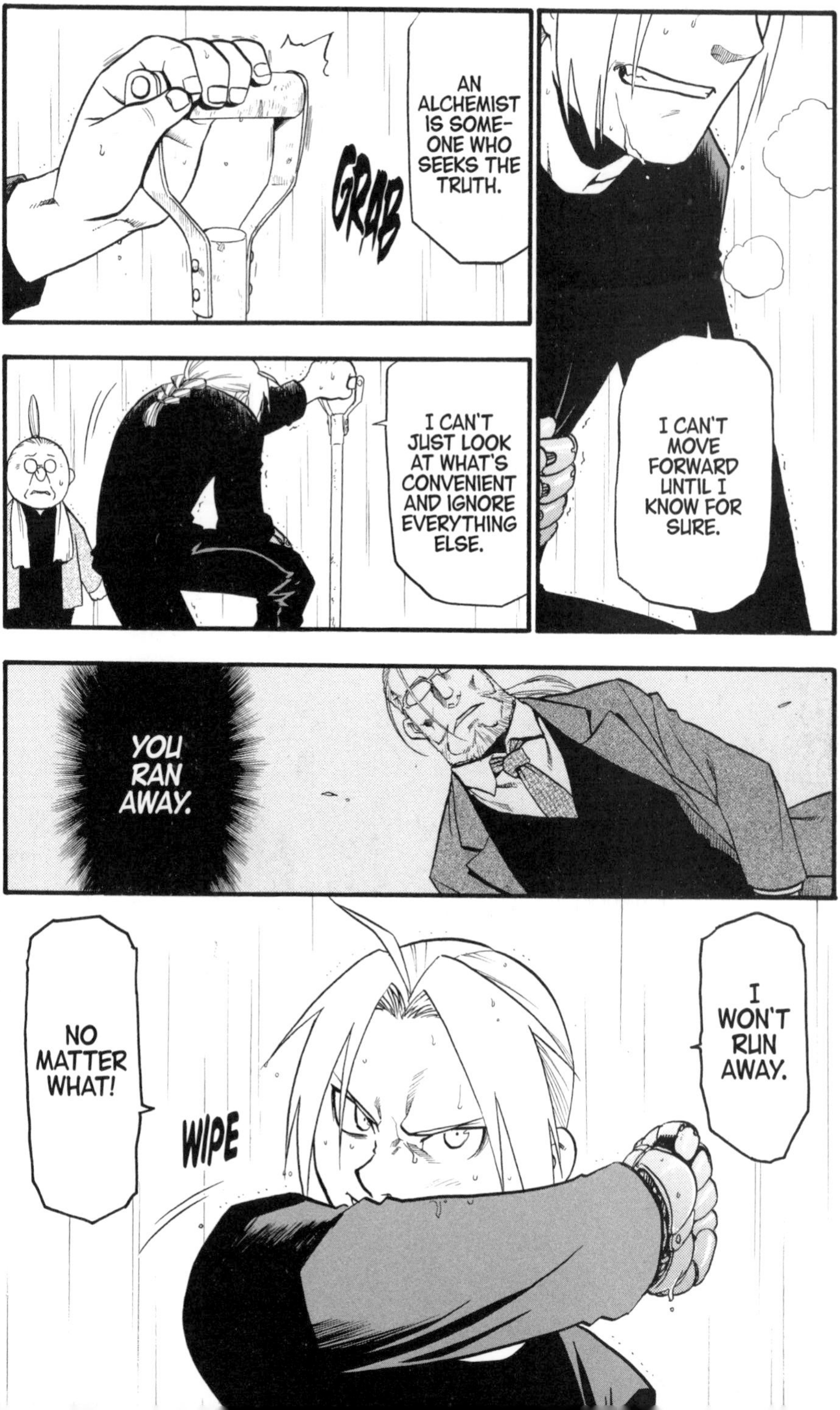
I CAN'T MOVE FORWARD UNTIL I KNOW FOR SURE.
AN ALCHEMIST IS SOME-ONE WHO SEEKS THE TRUTH.
GRAB
I CAN'T JUST LOOK AT WHAT'S CONVENIENT AND IGNORE EVERYTHING ELSE.
YOU RAN AWAY.
I WON'T RUN AWAY.
WIPE
NO MATTER WHAT!

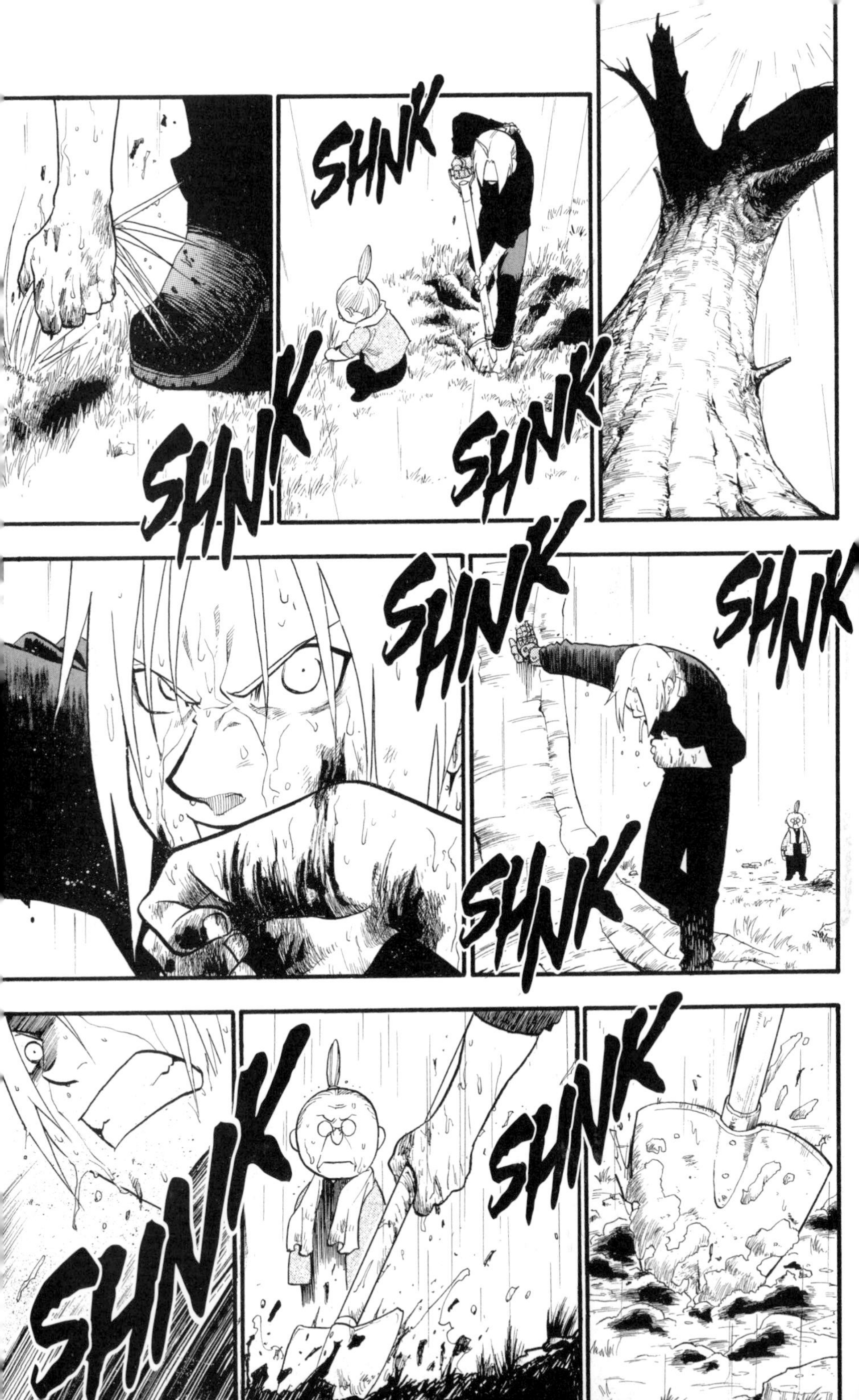
SHNK
SHNK
SHNK
SHNK
SHNK
SHNK
SHNK
SHNK

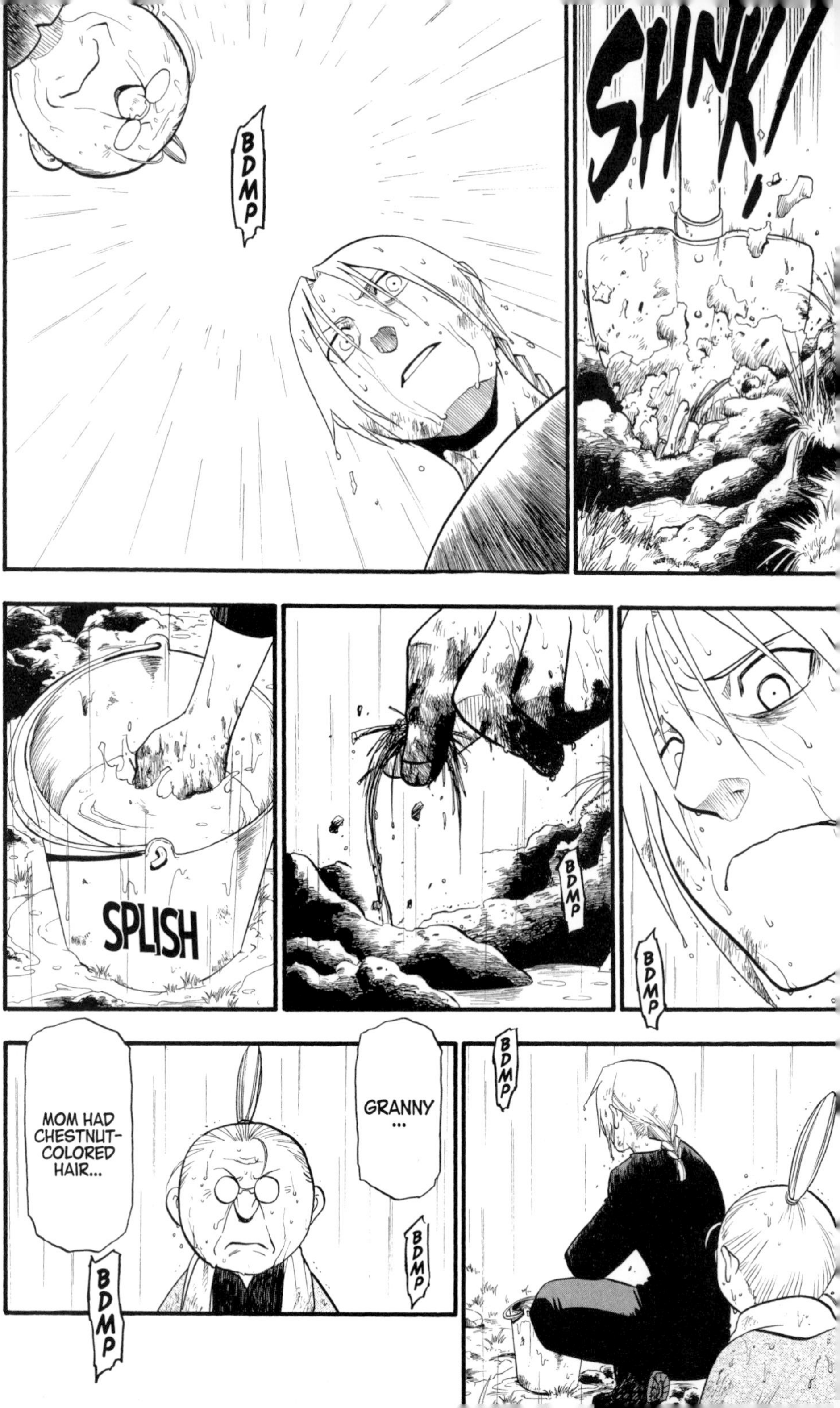
SHNK!
BDMP
BDMP
BDMP
SPLISH
BDMP
GRANNY ...
BDMP
MOM HAD CHESTNUT-COLORED HAIR...
BDMP

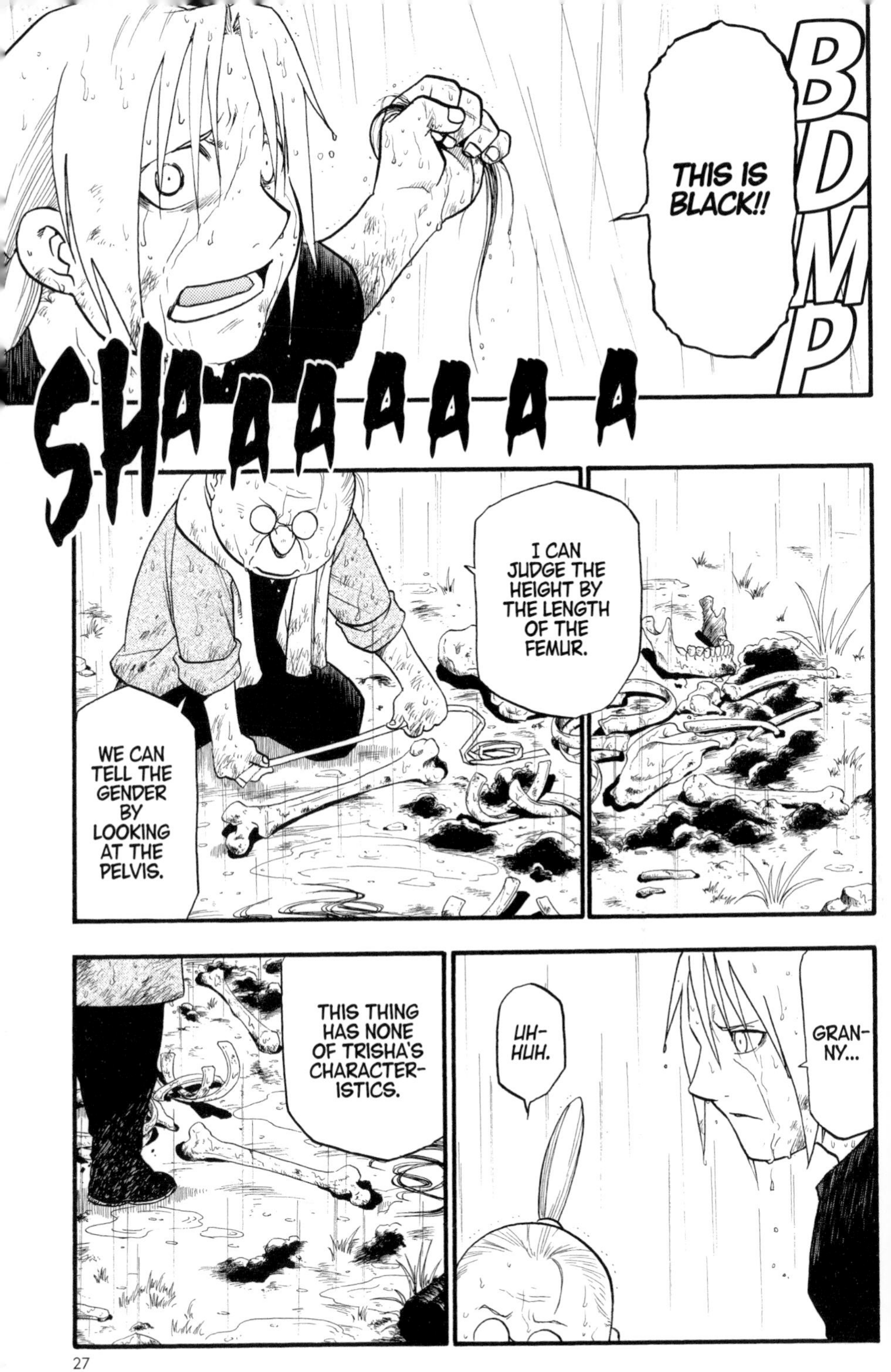
THIS IS BLACK!!
BDMP
SHAAAAAAA
I CAN JUDGE THE HEIGHT BY THE LENGTH OF THE FEMUR.
WE CAN TELL THE GENDER BY LOOKING AT THE PELVIS.
GRANNY...
UH-HUH.
THIS THING HAS NONE OF TRISHA'S CHARACTERISTICS.

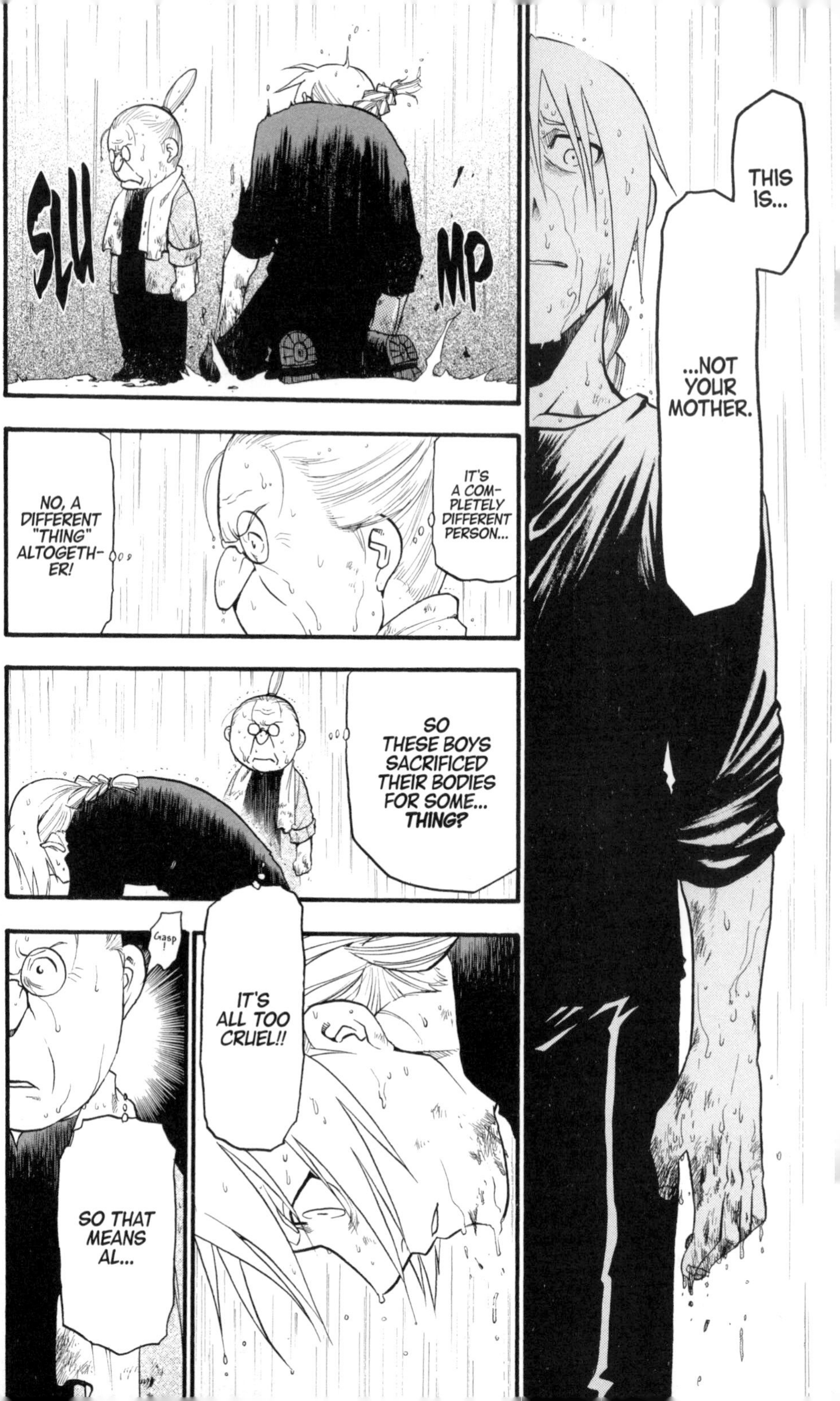
THIS IS...
...NOT YOUR MOTHER.
SLUMP
IT'S A COMPLETELY DIFFERENT PERSON...
NO, A DIFFERENT "THING" ALTOGETHER!
SO THESE BOYS SACRIFICED THEIR BODIES FOR SOME... THING?
IT'S ALL TOO CRUEL!!
Gasp!
SO THAT MEANS AL...

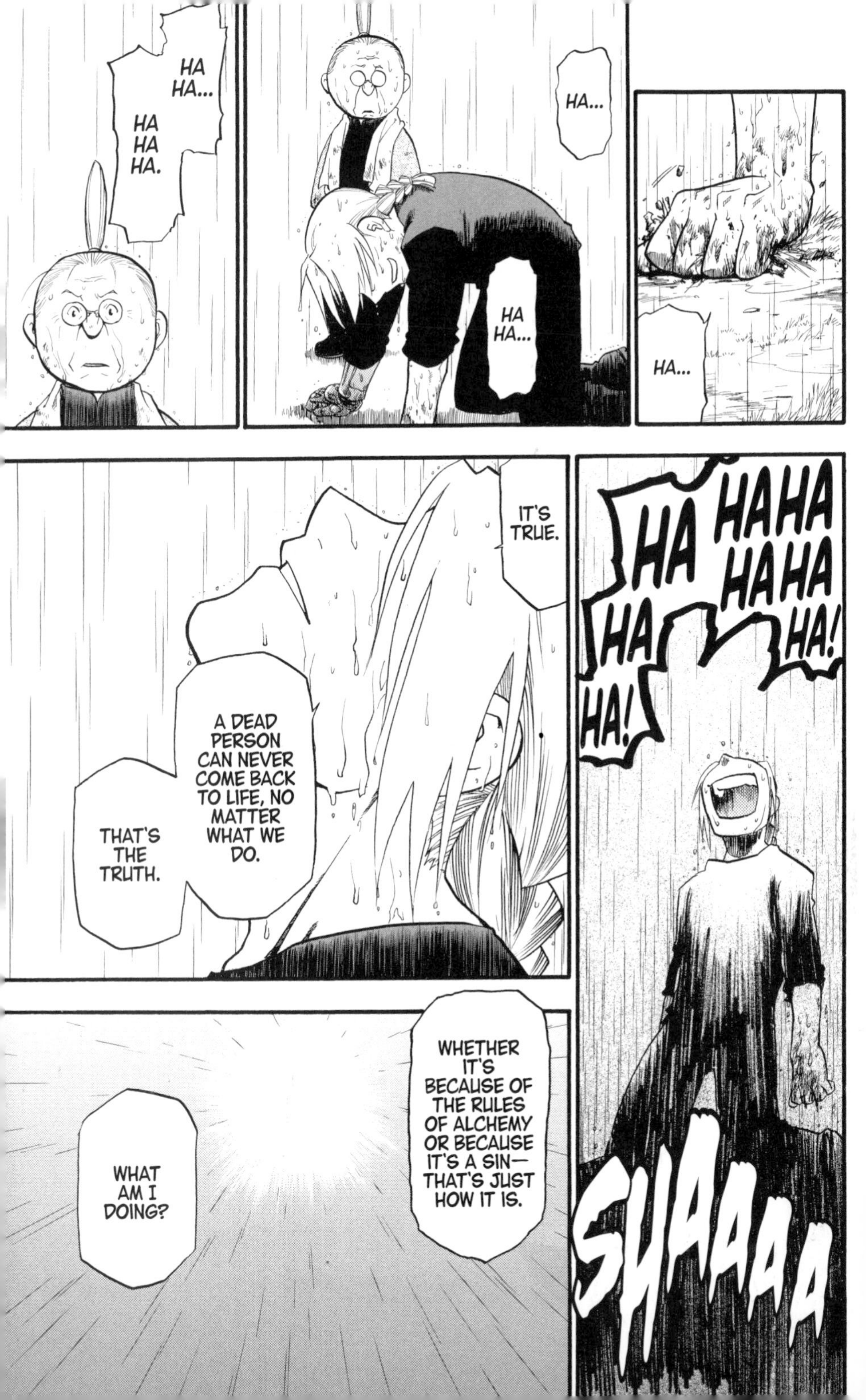
HA...
HA...
HA HA...
HA HA...
HA HA HA.
HAHA HAHA HA! HA HA HA!
SHAAAAA
IT'S TRUE.
A DEAD PERSON CAN NEVER COME BACK TO LIFE, NO MATTER WHAT WE DO.
THAT'S THE TRUTH.
WHETHER IT'S BECAUSE OF THE RULES OF ALCHEMY OR BECAUSE IT'S A SIN—THAT'S JUST HOW IT IS.
WHAT AM I DOING?

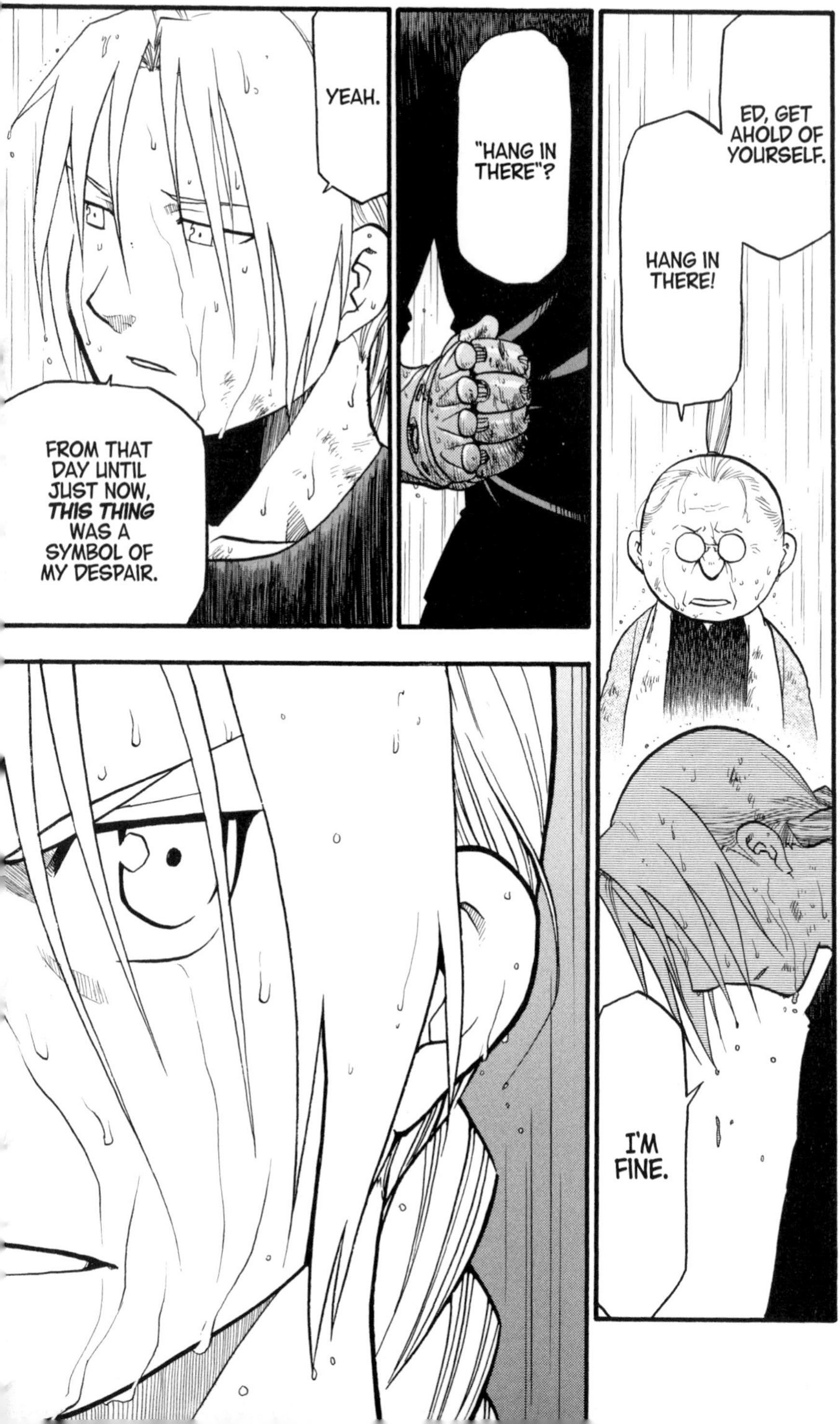
ED, GET AHOLD OF YOURSELF.
HANG IN THERE!
I'M FINE.
"HANG IN THERE"?
YEAH.
FROM THAT DAY UNTIL JUST NOW, ***THIS THING*** WAS A SYMBOL OF MY DESPAIR.

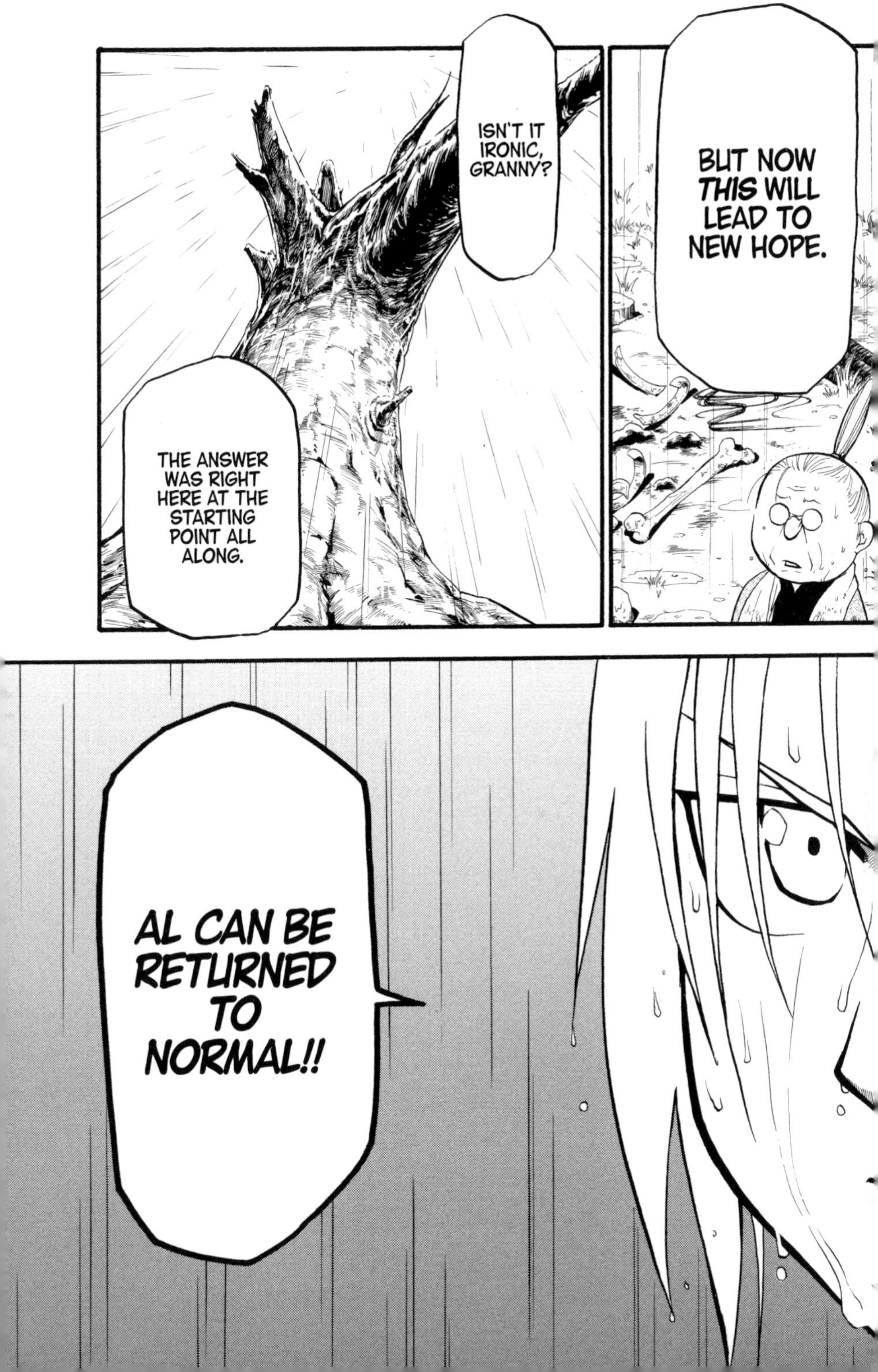
BUT NOW *THIS* WILL LEAD TO NEW HOPE.
ISN'T IT IRONIC, GRANNY?
THE ANSWER WAS RIGHT HERE AT THE STARTING POINT ALL ALONG.
AL CAN BE RETURNED TO NORMAL!!

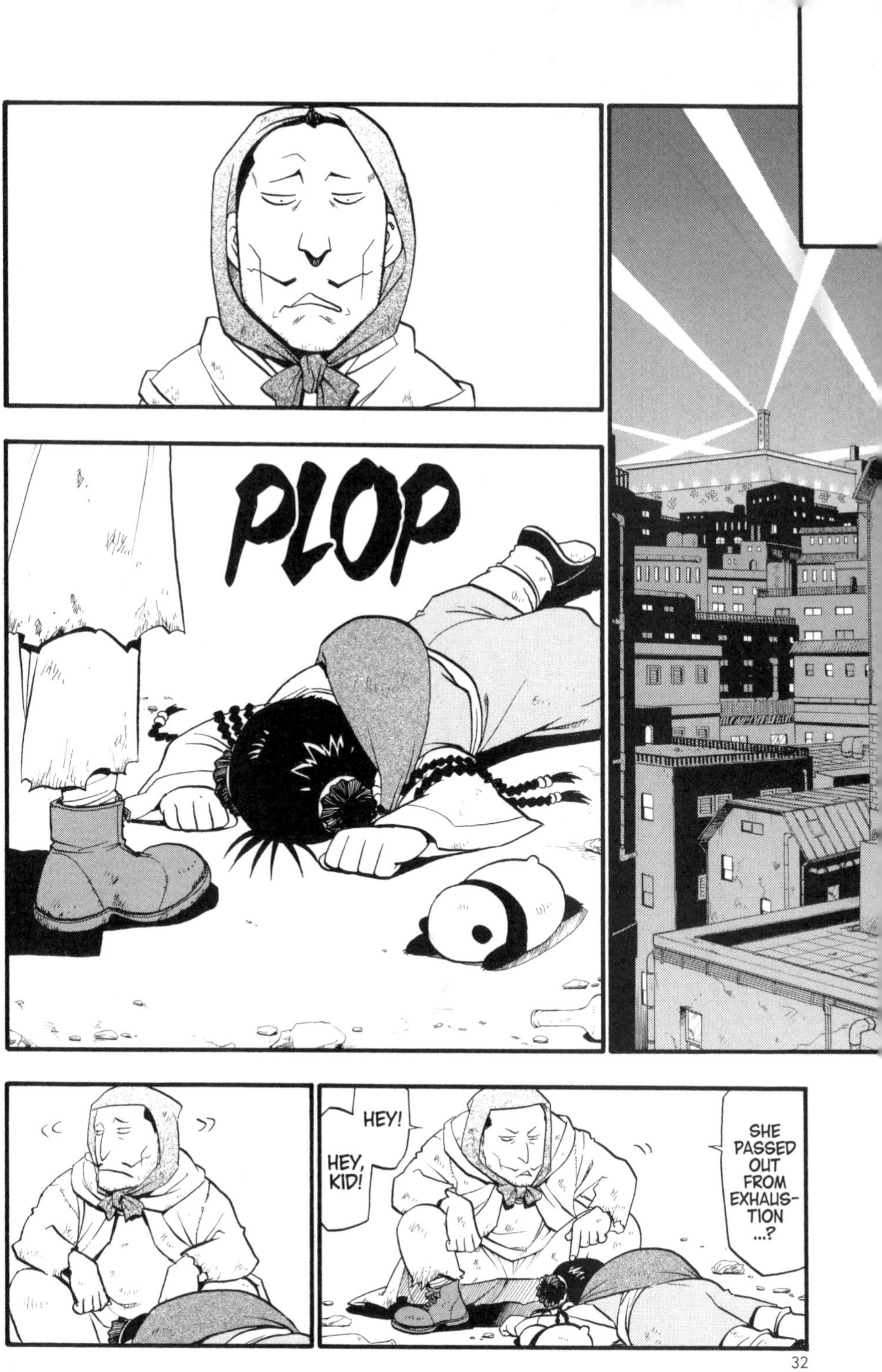
PLOP
SHE PASSED OUT FROM EXHAUSTION ...?
HEY!
HEY, KID!

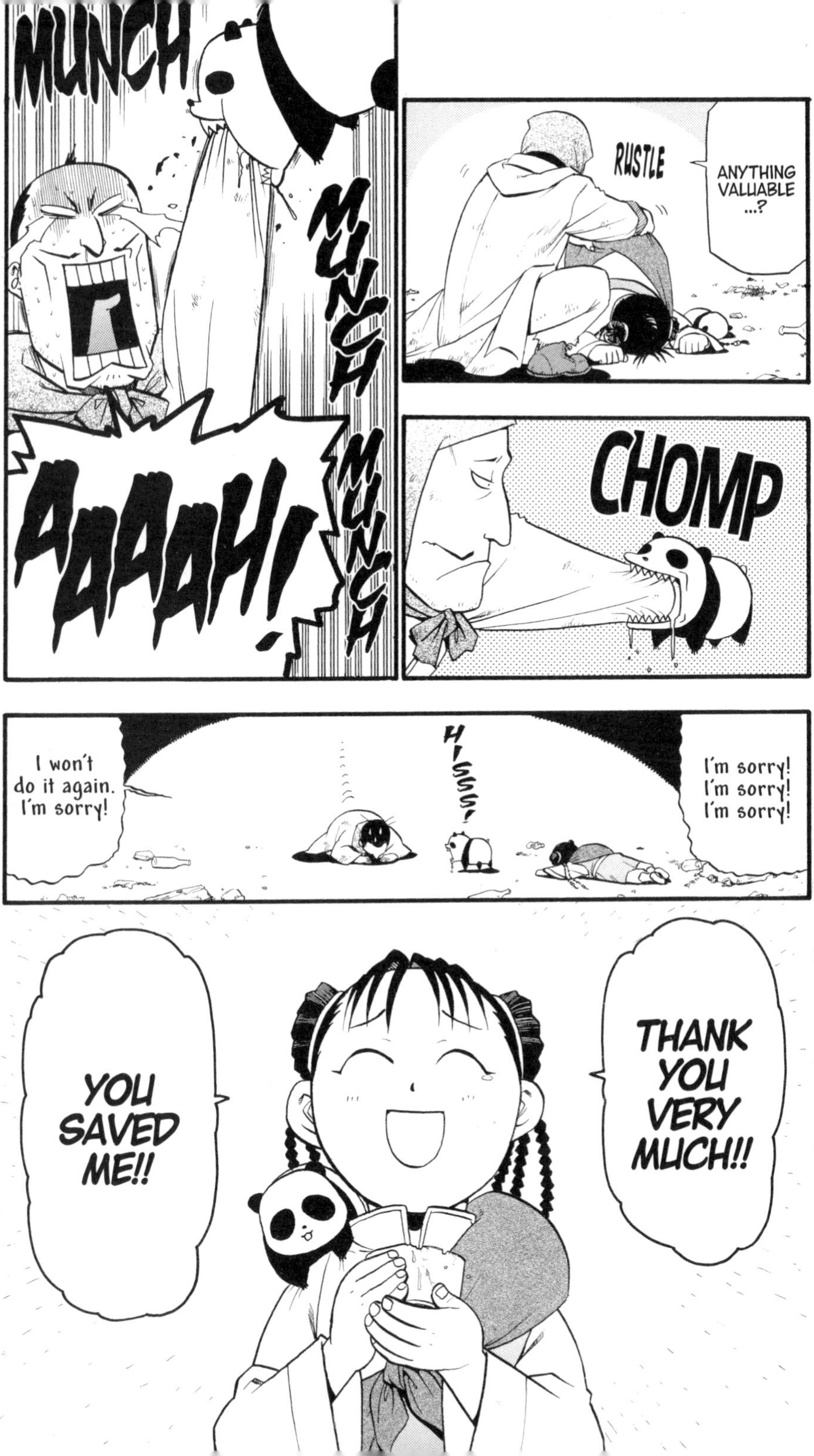
RUSTLE
ANYTHING VALUABLE ...?
CHOMP
MUNCH
MUNCH
MUNCH
AAAAH!
I'm sorry! I'm sorry! I'm sorry!
HISSS!
I won't do it again. I'm sorry!
THANK YOU VERY MUCH!!
YOU SAVED ME!!

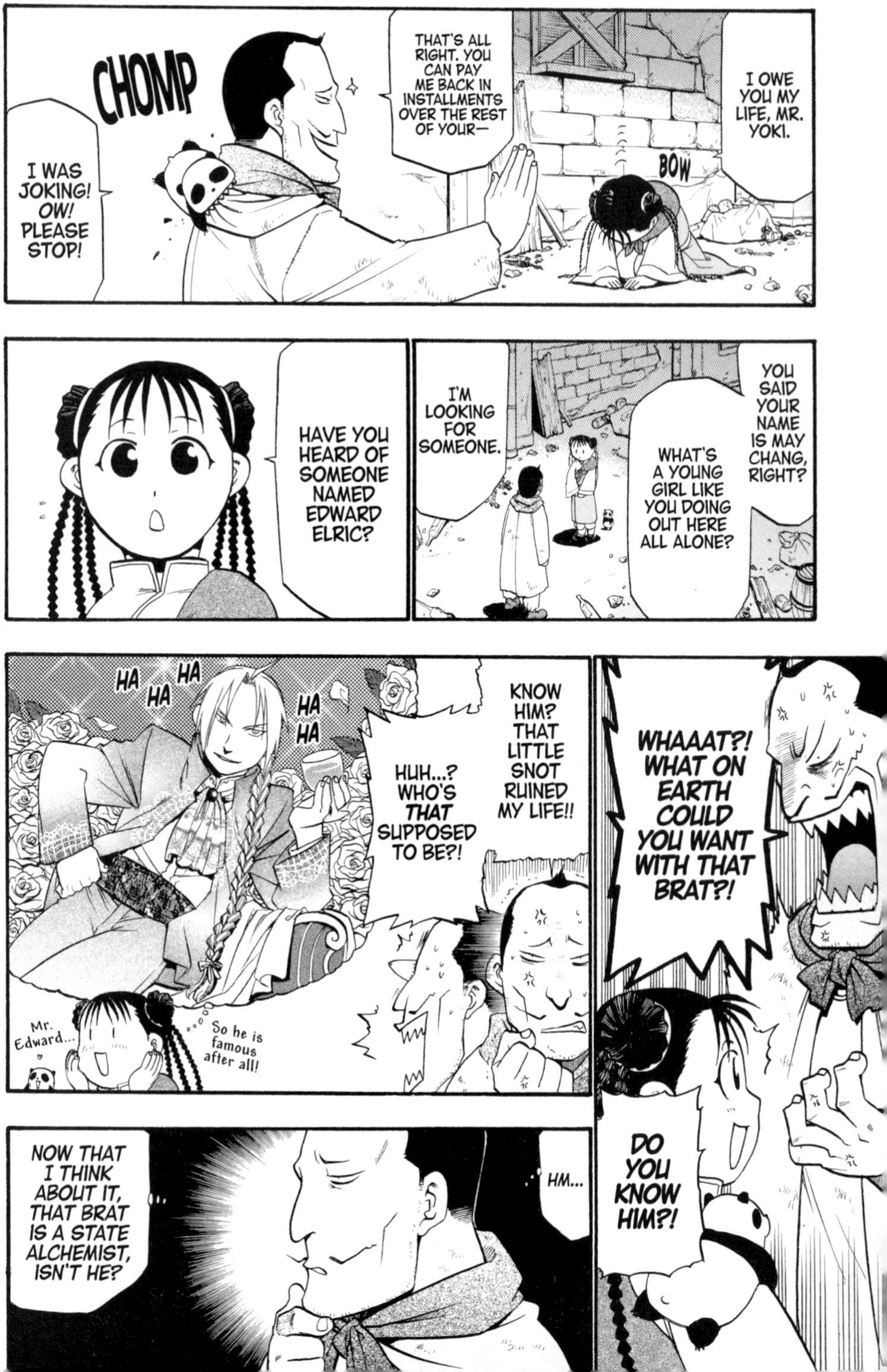
I OWE YOU MY LIFE, MR. YOKI.
BOW
THAT'S ALL RIGHT. YOU CAN PAY ME BACK IN INSTALLMENTS OVER THE REST OF YOUR—
CHOMP
I WAS JOKING! OW! PLEASE STOP!
YOU SAID YOUR NAME IS MAY CHANG, RIGHT?
WHAT'S A YOUNG GIRL LIKE YOU DOING OUT HERE ALL ALONE?
I'M LOOKING FOR SOMEONE.
HAVE YOU HEARD OF SOMEONE NAMED EDWARD ELRIC?
WHAAAT?! WHAT ON EARTH COULD YOU WANT WITH THAT BRAT?!
DO YOU KNOW HIM?!
KNOW HIM? THAT LITTLE SNOT RUINED MY LIFE!!
HUH...? WHO'S THAT SUPPOSED TO BE?!
HA HA HA
HA HA
So he is famous after all!
Mr. Edward...
HM...
NOW THAT I THINK ABOUT IT, THAT BRAT IS A STATE ALCHEMIST, ISN'T HE?

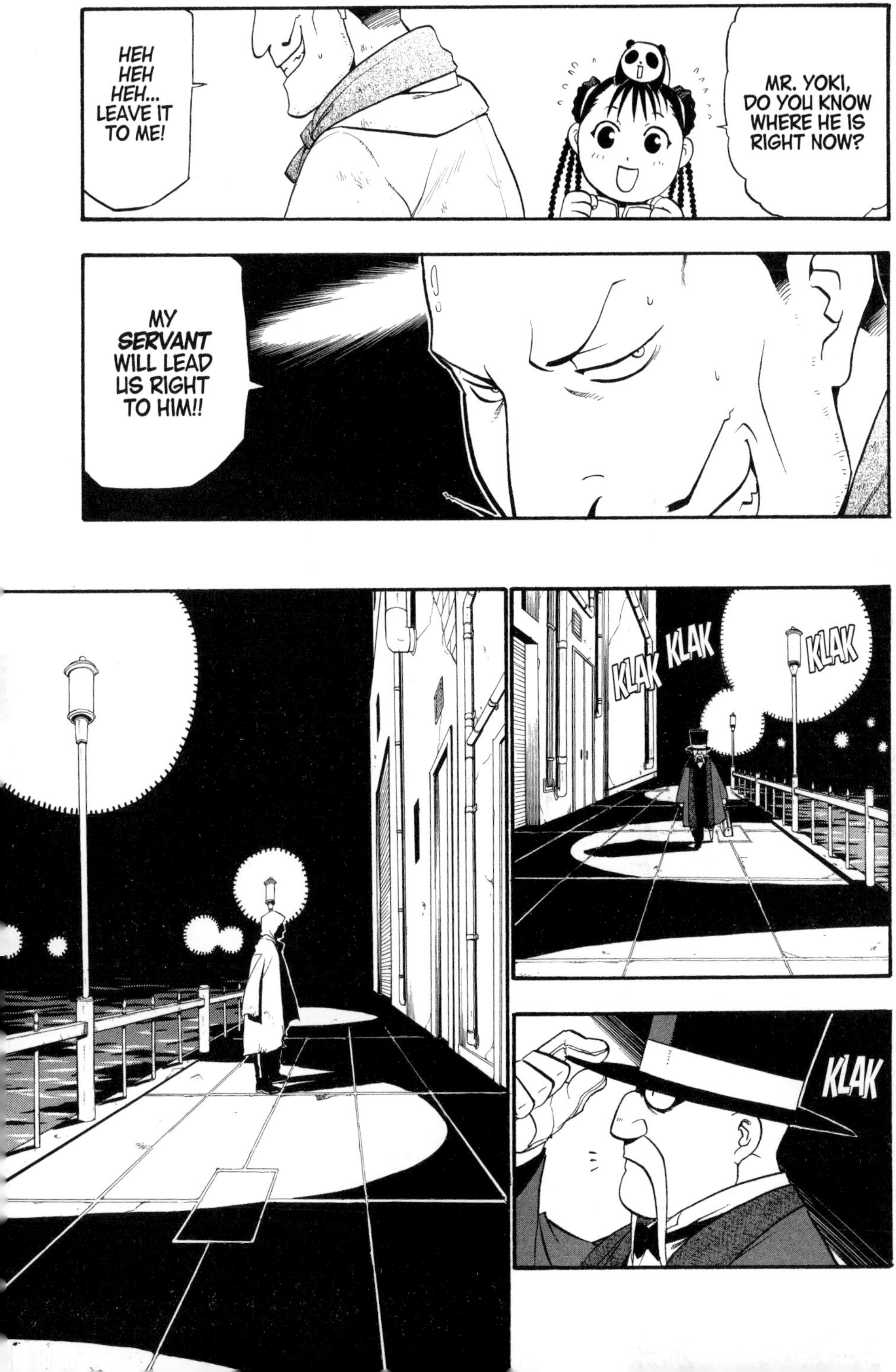
MR. YOKI, DO YOU KNOW WHERE HE IS RIGHT NOW?
HEH HEH HEH... LEAVE IT TO ME!
MY SERVANT WILL LEAD US RIGHT TO HIM!!
KLAK
KLAK KLAK
KLAK
KLAK

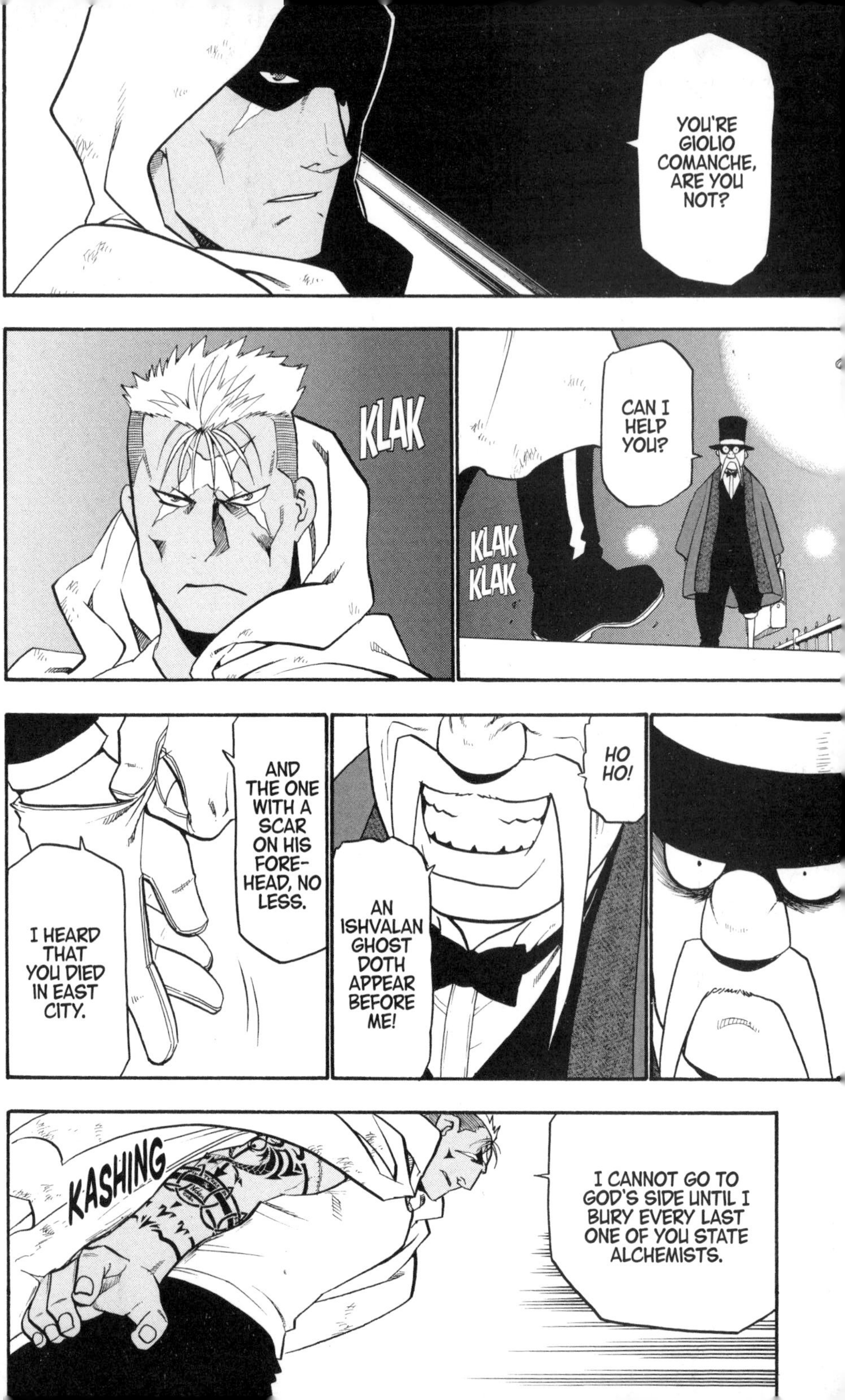
YOU'RE GIOLIO COMANCHE, ARE YOU NOT?
CAN I HELP YOU?
KLAK KLAK
KLAK
HO HO!
AN ISHVALAN GHOST DOTH APPEAR BEFORE ME!
AND THE ONE WITH A SCAR ON HIS FORE-HEAD, NO LESS.
I HEARD THAT YOU DIED IN EAST CITY.
I CANNOT GO TO GOD'S SIDE UNTIL I BURY EVERY LAST ONE OF YOU STATE ALCHEMISTS.
KASHING

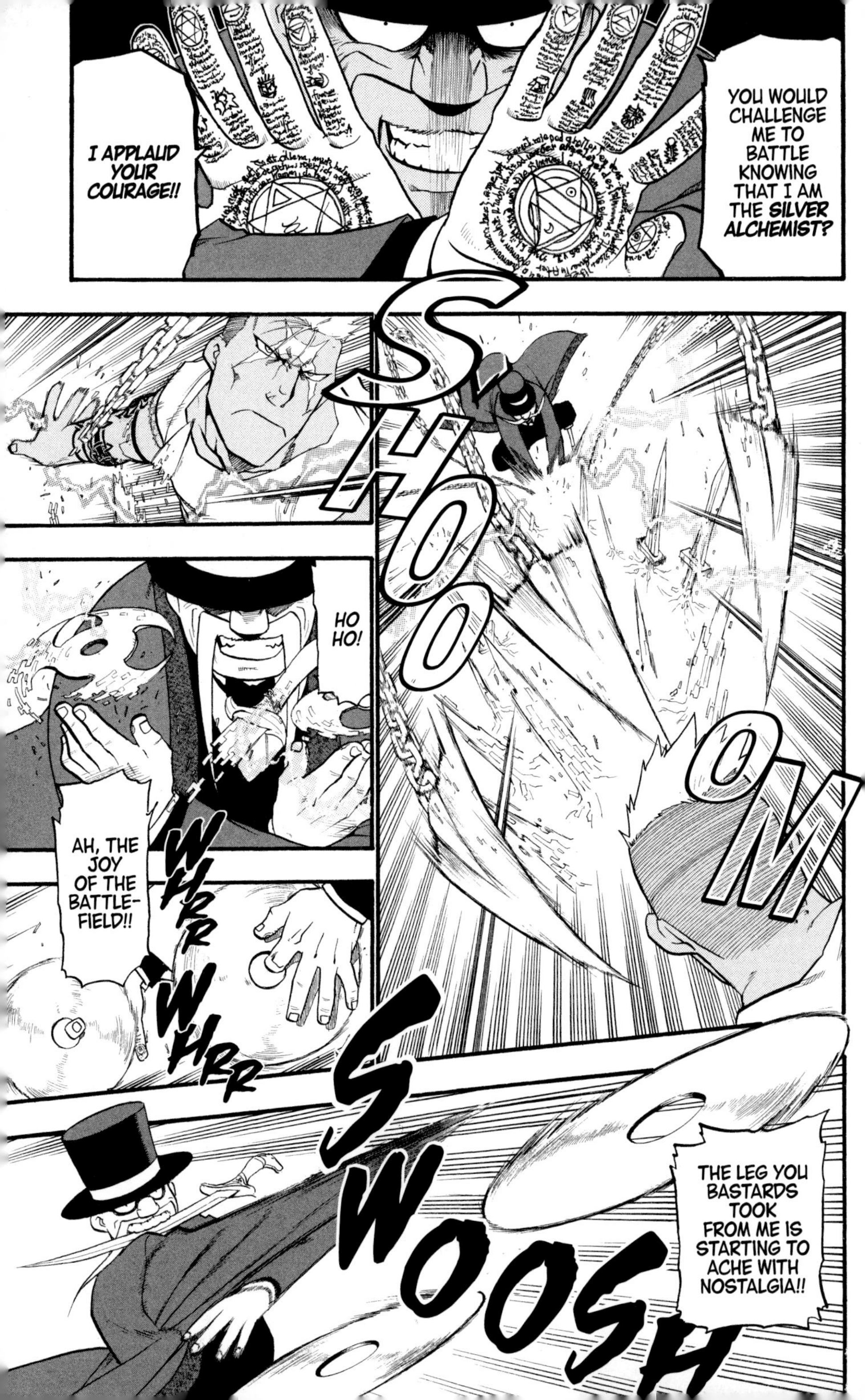
YOU WOULD CHALLENGE ME TO BATTLE KNOWING THAT I AM THE **SILVER ALCHEMIST?**
I APPLAUD YOUR COURAGE!!
SHOOOOM
HO HO!
AH, THE JOY OF THE BATTLE-FIELD!!
WHRR WHRR
THE LEG YOU BASTARDS TOOK FROM ME IS STARTING TO ACHE WITH NOSTALGIA!!
SWOOSH

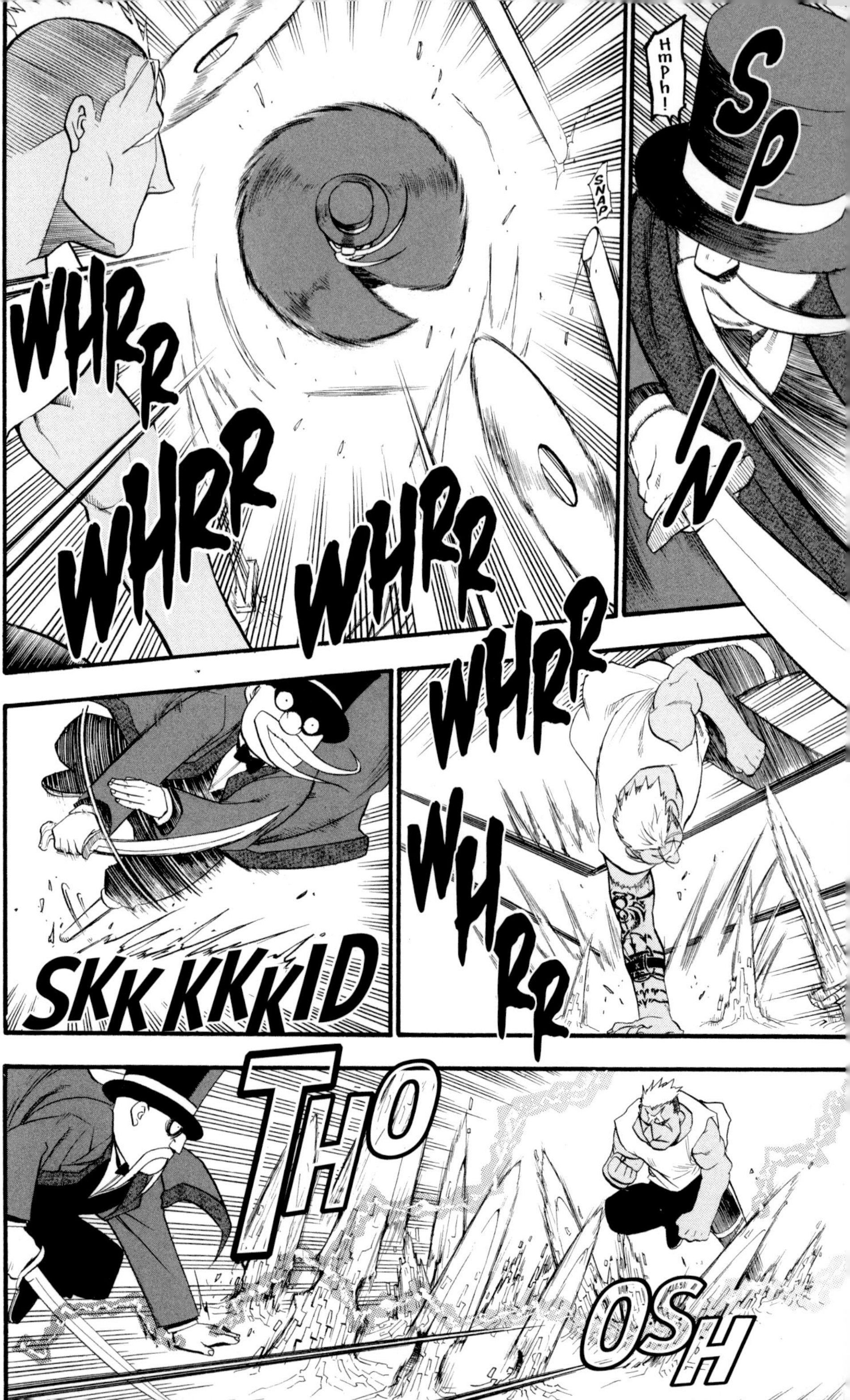

Hmph!
SNAP
SPIN
WHRR
WHRR
WHRR
WHRR
WHURR
SKKKKKID
THOOSH

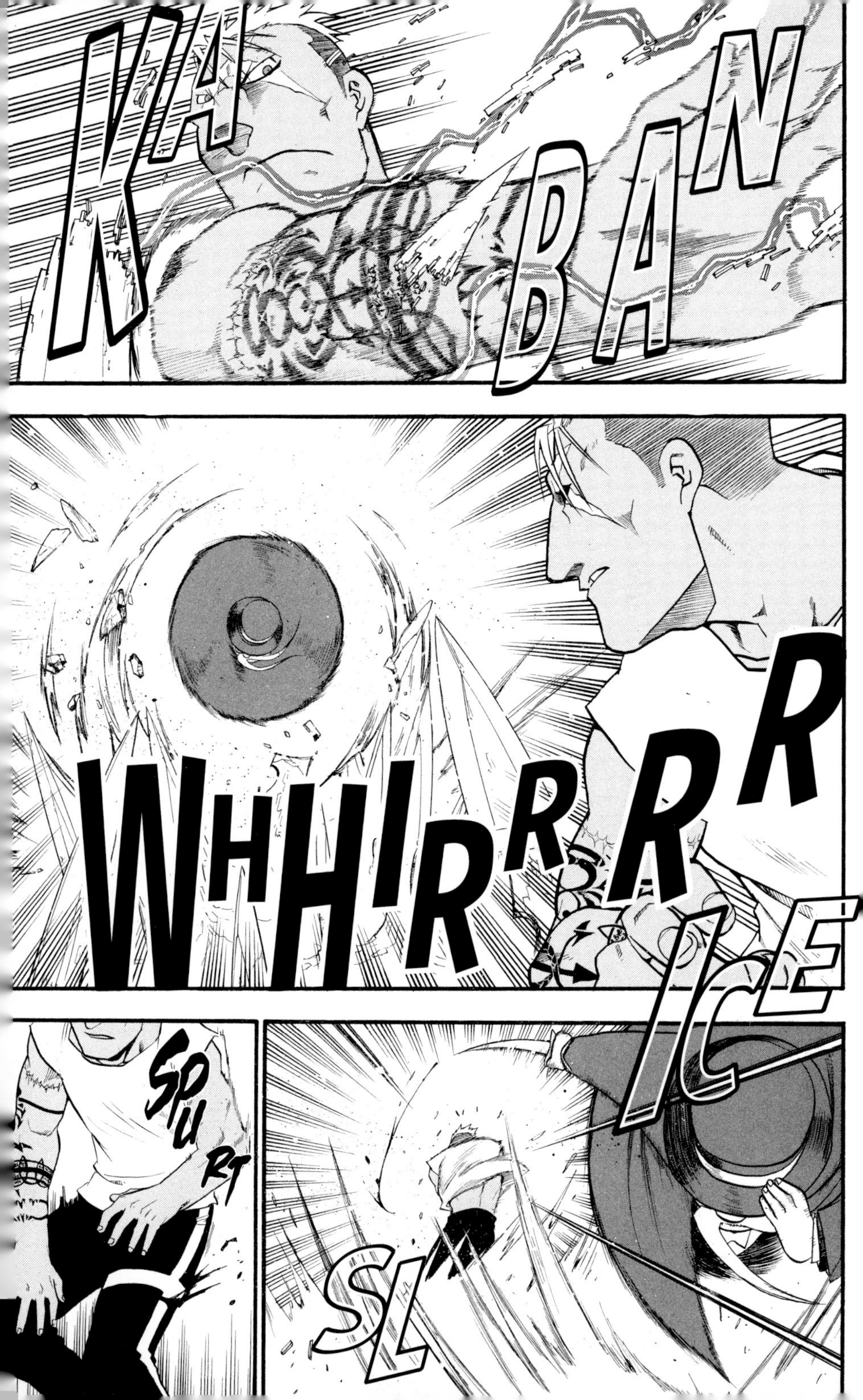
KA
BAN
WHHIRRRRR
SLICE
SPURT

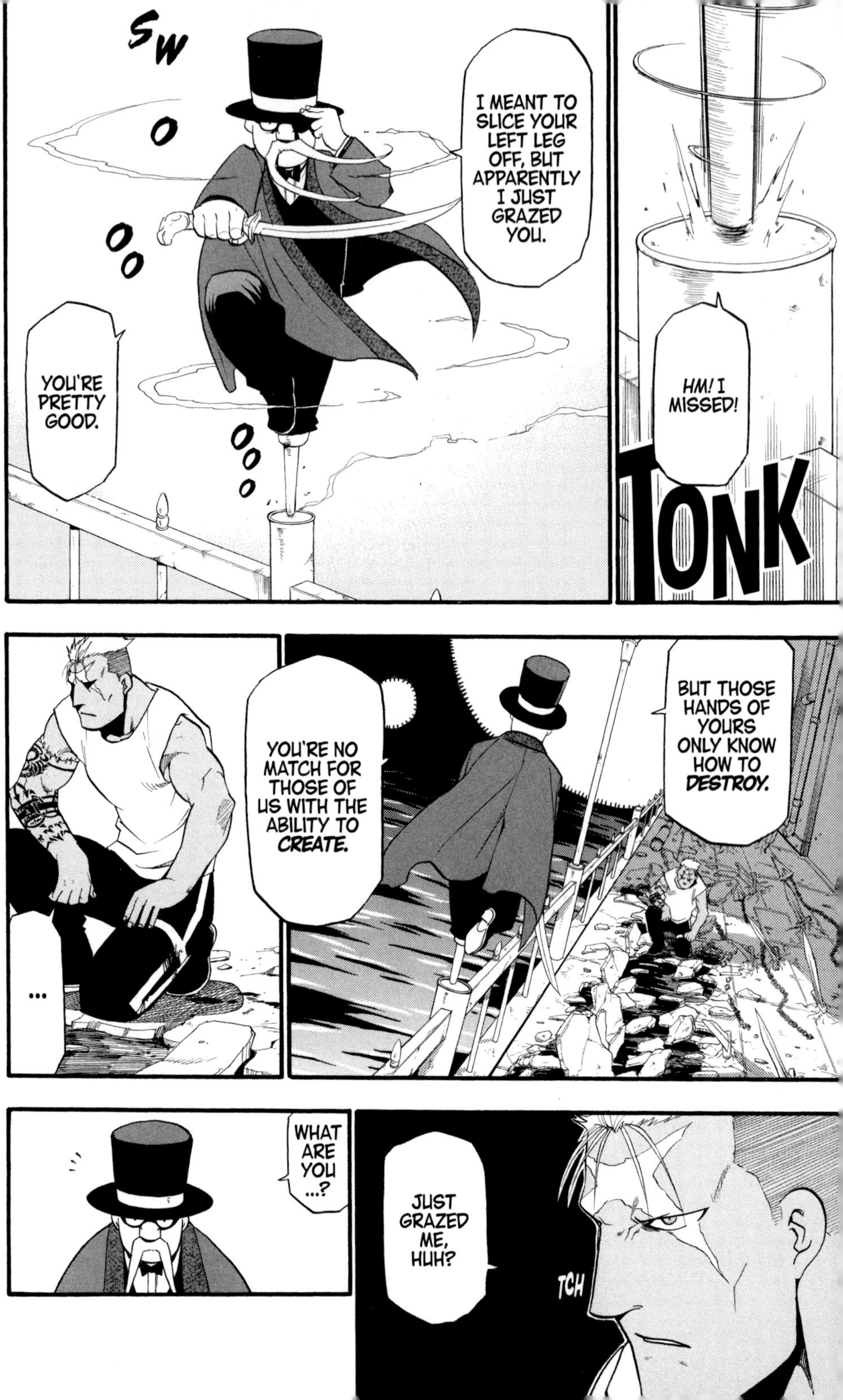
HM! I MISSED!
TONK
I MEANT TO SLICE YOUR LEFT LEG OFF, BUT APPARENTLY I JUST GRAZED YOU.
SWOOOOOO
YOU'RE PRETTY GOOD.
BUT THOSE HANDS OF YOURS ONLY KNOW HOW TO DESTROY.
YOU'RE NO MATCH FOR THOSE OF US WITH THE ABILITY TO CREATE.
...
JUST GRAZED ME, HUH?
TCH
WHAT ARE YOU ...?

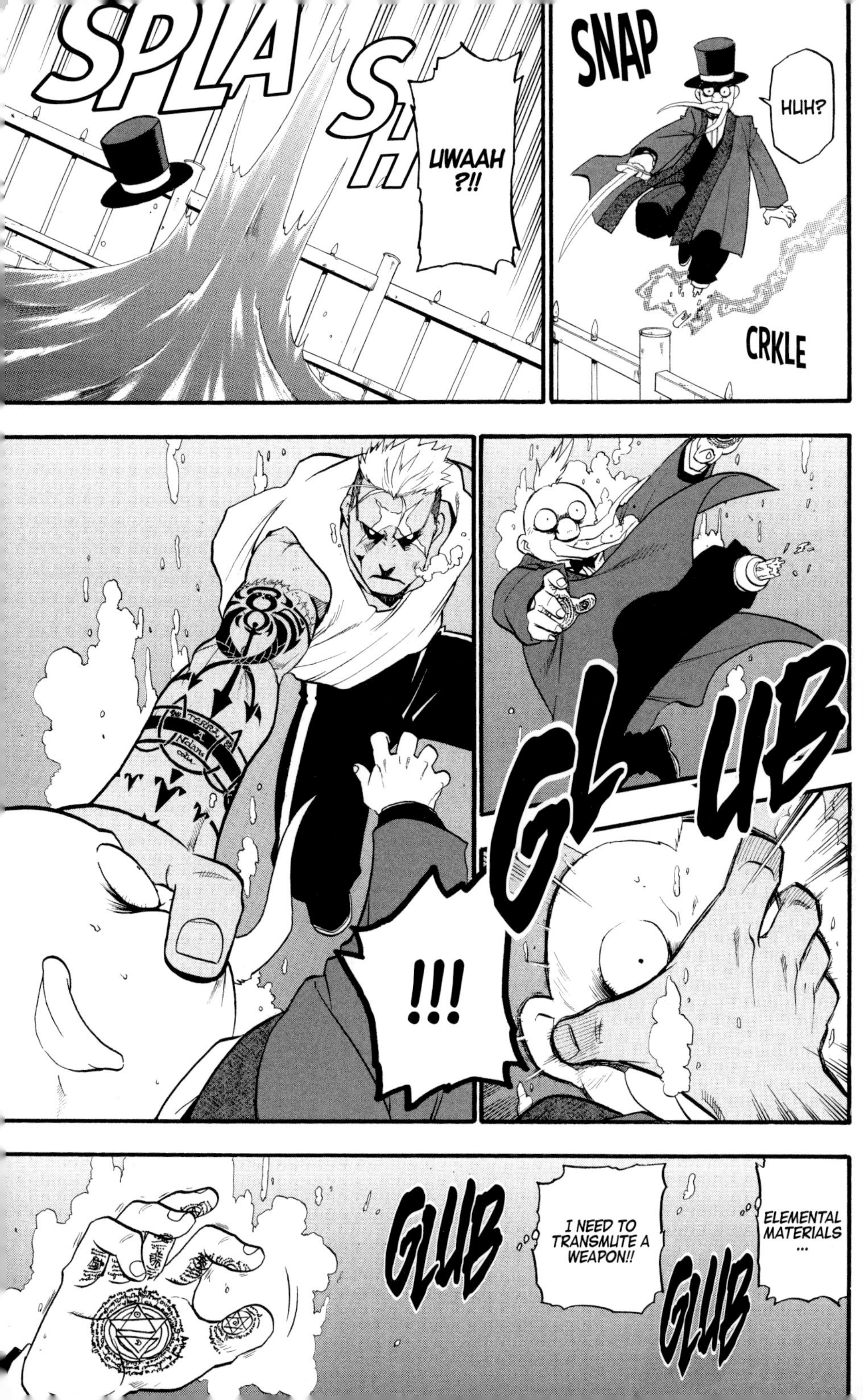
SNAP
HUH?
CRKLE
SPLASH
UWAAH?!!
GLUB
!!!
ELEMENTAL MATERIALS...
GLUB
I NEED TO TRANSMUTE A WEAPON!!
GLUB

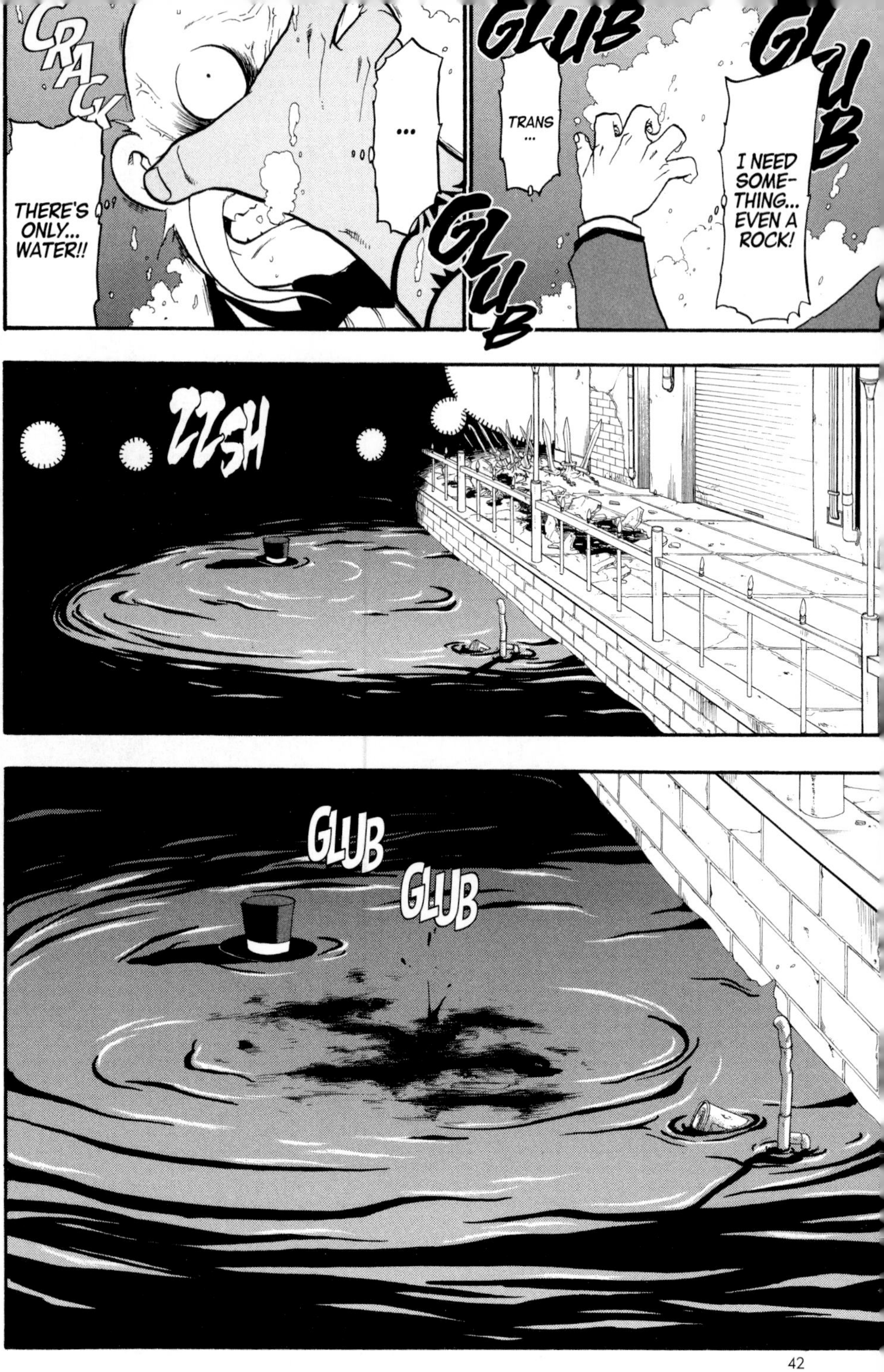
GLUB
GLUB
I NEED SOMETHING... EVEN A ROCK!
TRANS...
...
CRACK
THERE'S ONLY... WATER!!
GLUB
ZZSH
GLUB
GLUB

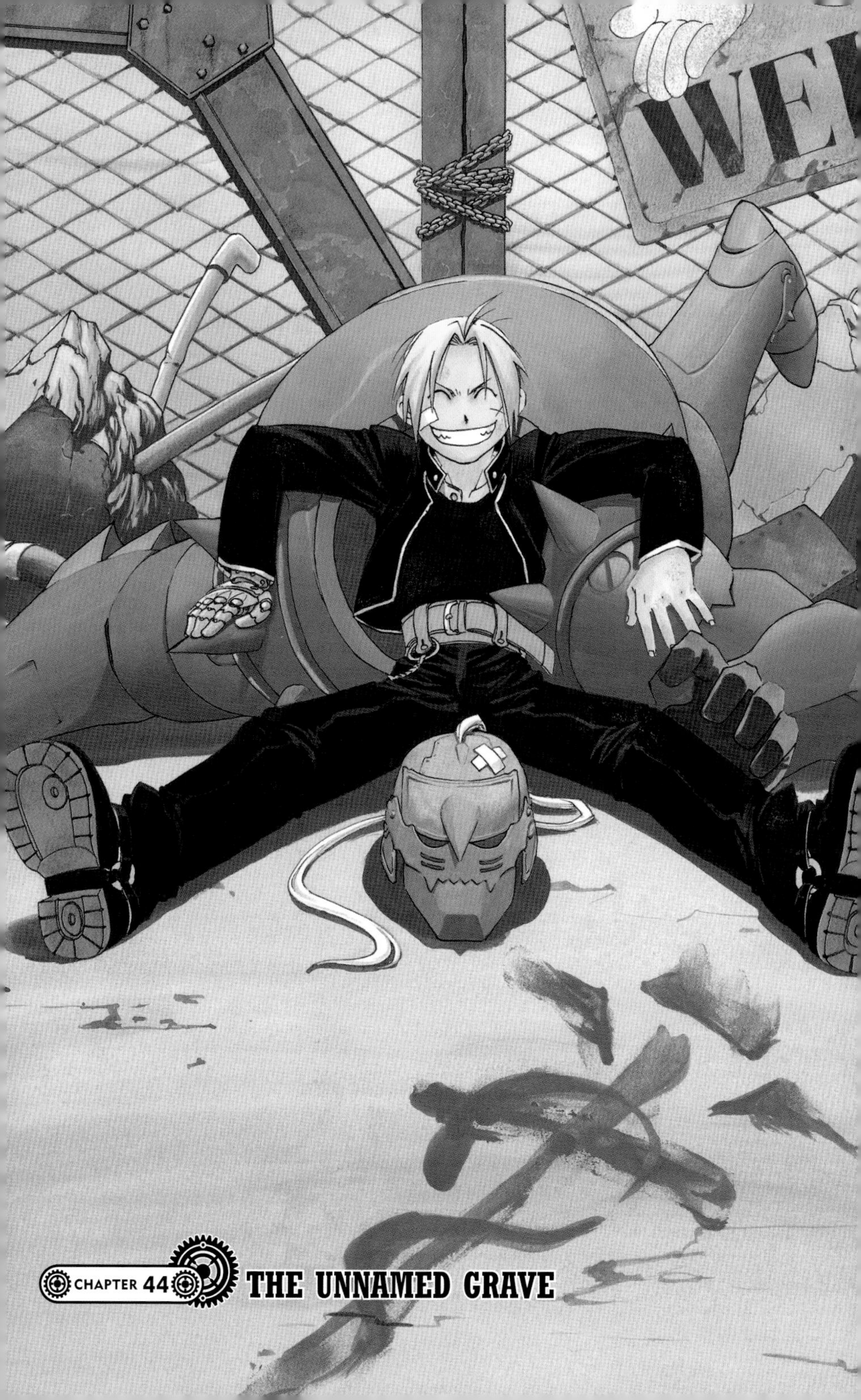
CHAPTER 44
THE UNNAMED GRAVE

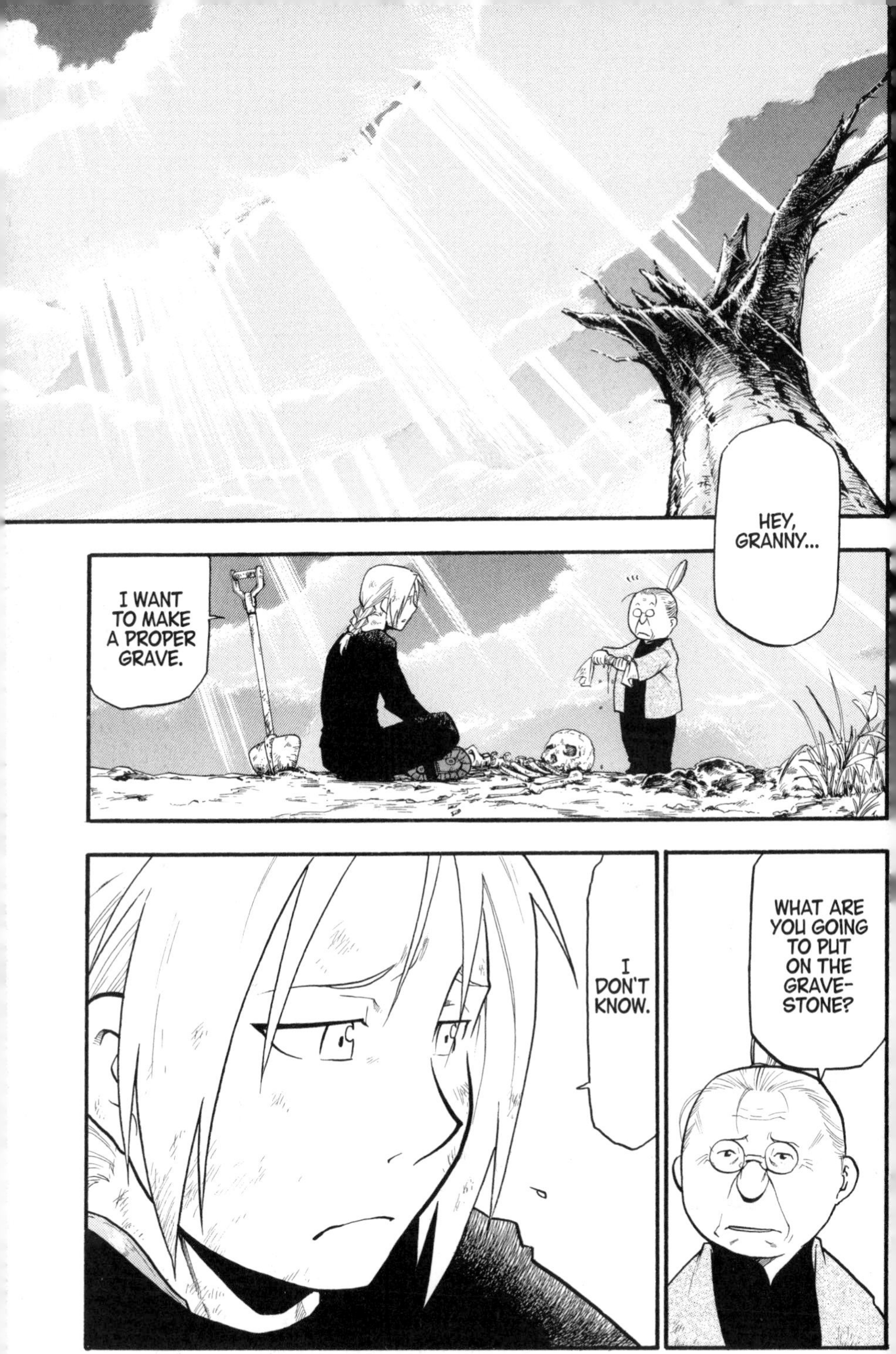
HEY, GRANNY...
I WANT TO MAKE A PROPER GRAVE.
WHAT ARE YOU GOING TO PUT ON THE GRAVE-STONE?
I DON'T KNOW.

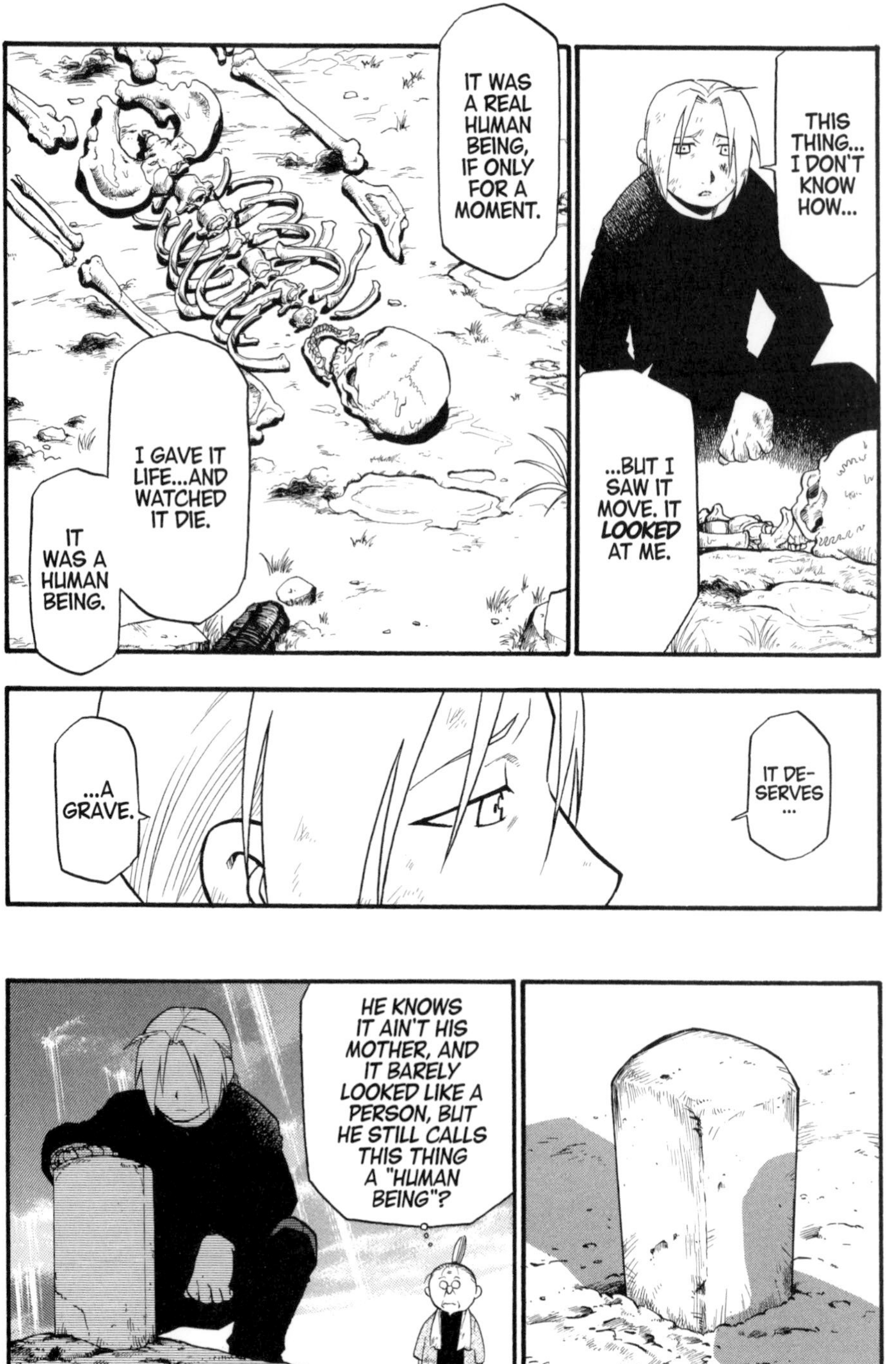
THIS THING... I DON'T KNOW HOW...
...BUT I SAW IT MOVE. IT LOOKED AT ME.
IT WAS A REAL HUMAN BEING, IF ONLY FOR A MOMENT.
I GAVE IT LIFE...AND WATCHED IT DIE.
IT WAS A HUMAN BEING.
IT DE-SERVES...
...A GRAVE.
HE KNOWS IT AIN'T HIS MOTHER, AND IT BARELY LOOKED LIKE A PERSON, BUT HE STILL CALLS THIS THING A "HUMAN BEING"?

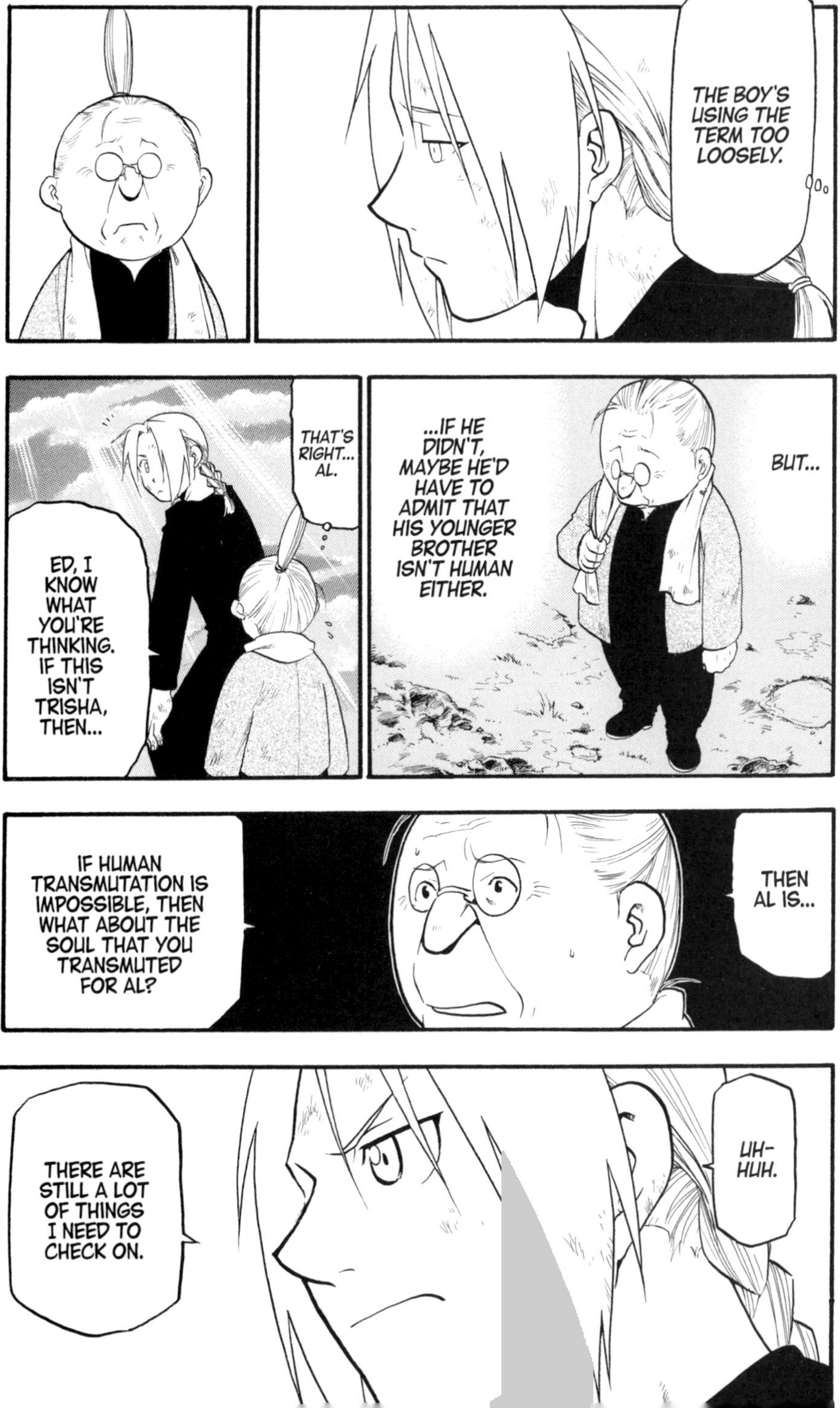
THE BOY'S USING THE TERM TOO LOOSELY.
BUT...
...IF HE DIDN'T, MAYBE HE'D HAVE TO ADMIT THAT HIS YOUNGER BROTHER ISN'T HUMAN EITHER.
THAT'S RIGHT... AL.
ED, I KNOW WHAT YOU'RE THINKING. IF THIS ISN'T TRISHA, THEN...
THEN AL IS...
IF HUMAN TRANSMUTATION IS IMPOSSIBLE, THEN WHAT ABOUT THE SOUL THAT YOU TRANSMUTED FOR AL?
UH-HUH.
THERE ARE STILL A LOT OF THINGS I NEED TO CHECK ON.

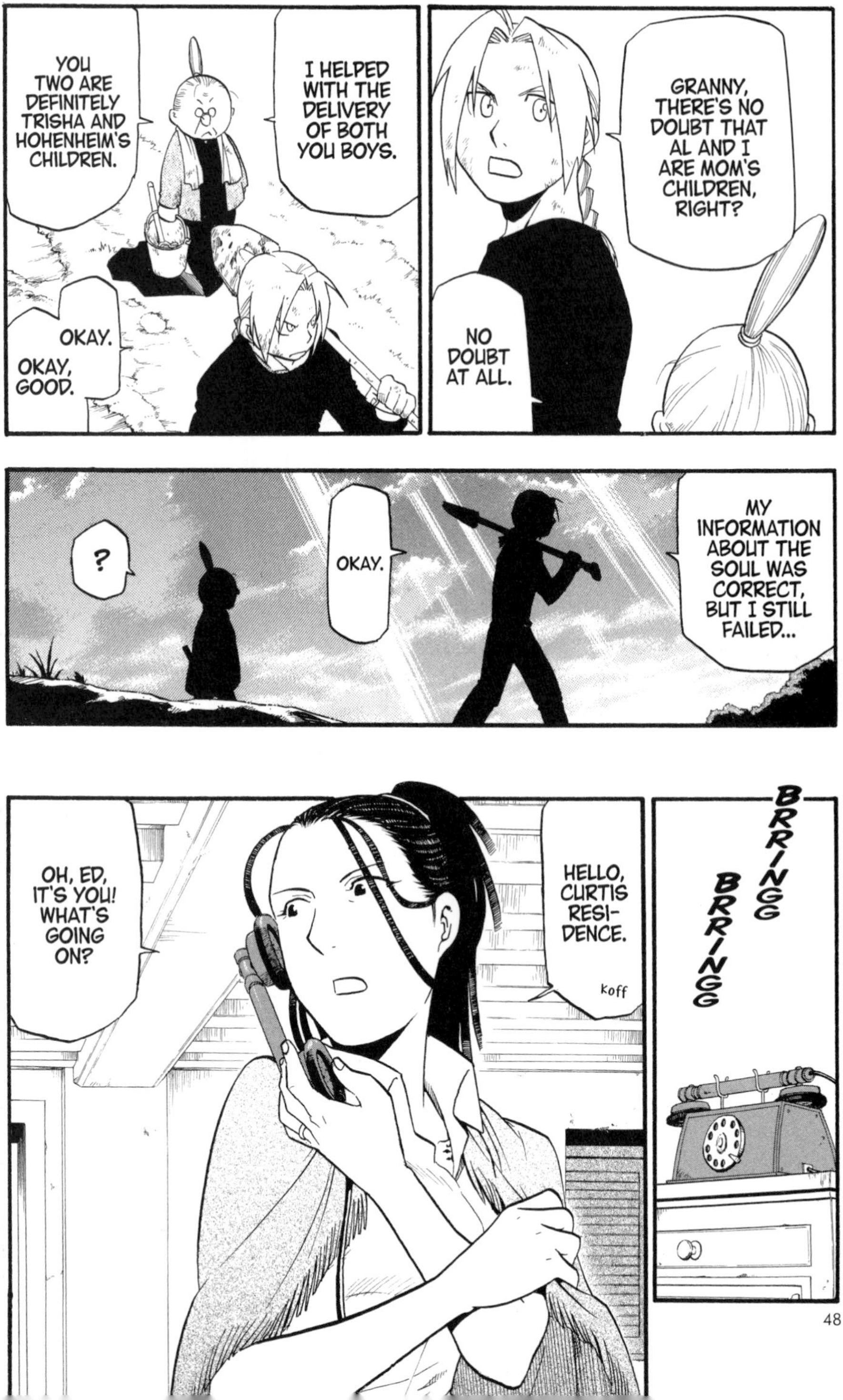
GRANNY, THERE'S NO DOUBT THAT AL AND I ARE MOM'S CHILDREN, RIGHT?
NO DOUBT AT ALL.
I HELPED WITH THE DELIVERY OF BOTH YOU BOYS.
YOU TWO ARE DEFINITELY TRISHA AND HOHENHEIM'S CHILDREN.
OKAY.
OKAY, GOOD.
MY INFORMATION ABOUT THE SOUL WAS CORRECT, BUT I STILL FAILED...
OKAY.
?
BRRINGG
BRRINGG
HELLO, CURTIS RESIDENCE.
koff
OH, ED, IT'S YOU! WHAT'S GOING ON?

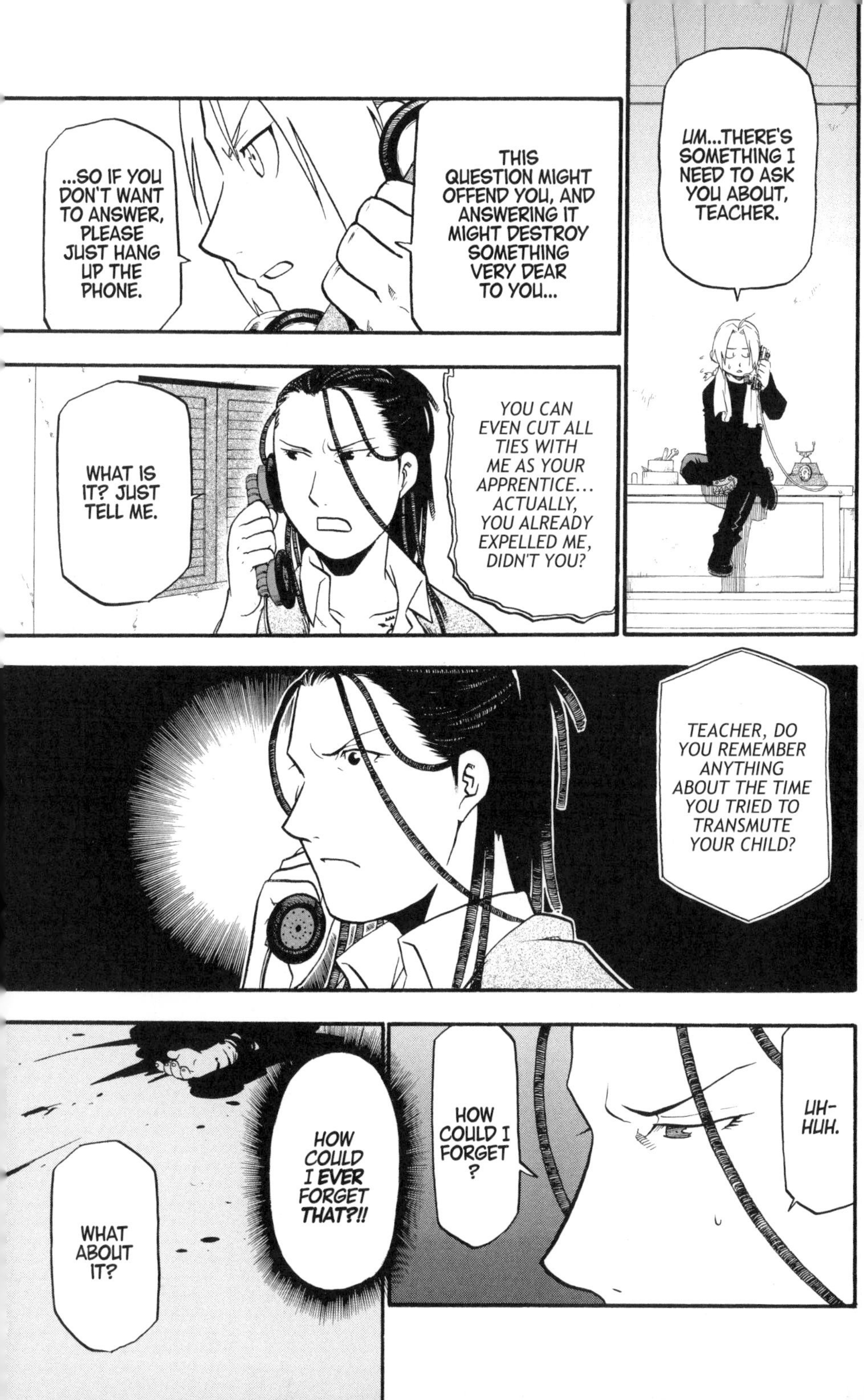
UM...THERE'S SOMETHING I NEED TO ASK YOU ABOUT, TEACHER.
THIS QUESTION MIGHT OFFEND YOU, AND ANSWERING IT MIGHT DESTROY SOMETHING VERY DEAR TO YOU...
...SO IF YOU DON'T WANT TO ANSWER, PLEASE JUST HANG UP THE PHONE.
YOU CAN EVEN CUT ALL TIES WITH ME AS YOUR APPRENTICE... ACTUALLY, YOU ALREADY EXPELLED ME, DIDN'T YOU?
WHAT IS IT? JUST TELL ME.
TEACHER, DO YOU REMEMBER ANYTHING ABOUT THE TIME YOU TRIED TO TRANSMUTE YOUR CHILD?
UH-HUH.
HOW COULD I FORGET?
HOW COULD I EVER FORGET THAT?!!
WHAT ABOUT IT?

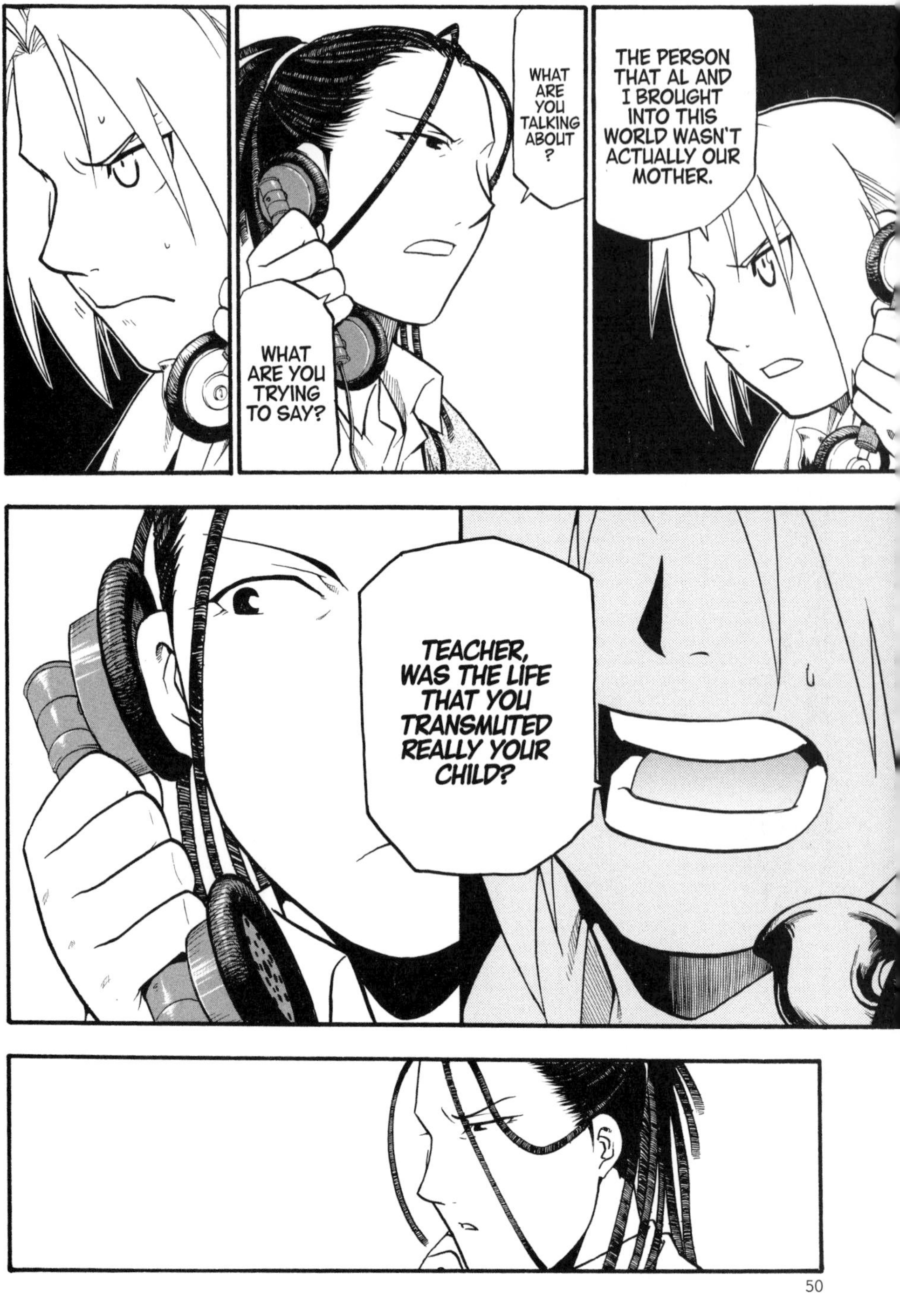
THE PERSON THAT AL AND I BROUGHT INTO THIS WORLD WASN'T ACTUALLY OUR MOTHER.
WHAT ARE YOU TALKING ABOUT?
WHAT ARE YOU TRYING TO SAY?
TEACHER, WAS THE LIFE THAT YOU TRANSMUTED REALLY YOUR CHILD?

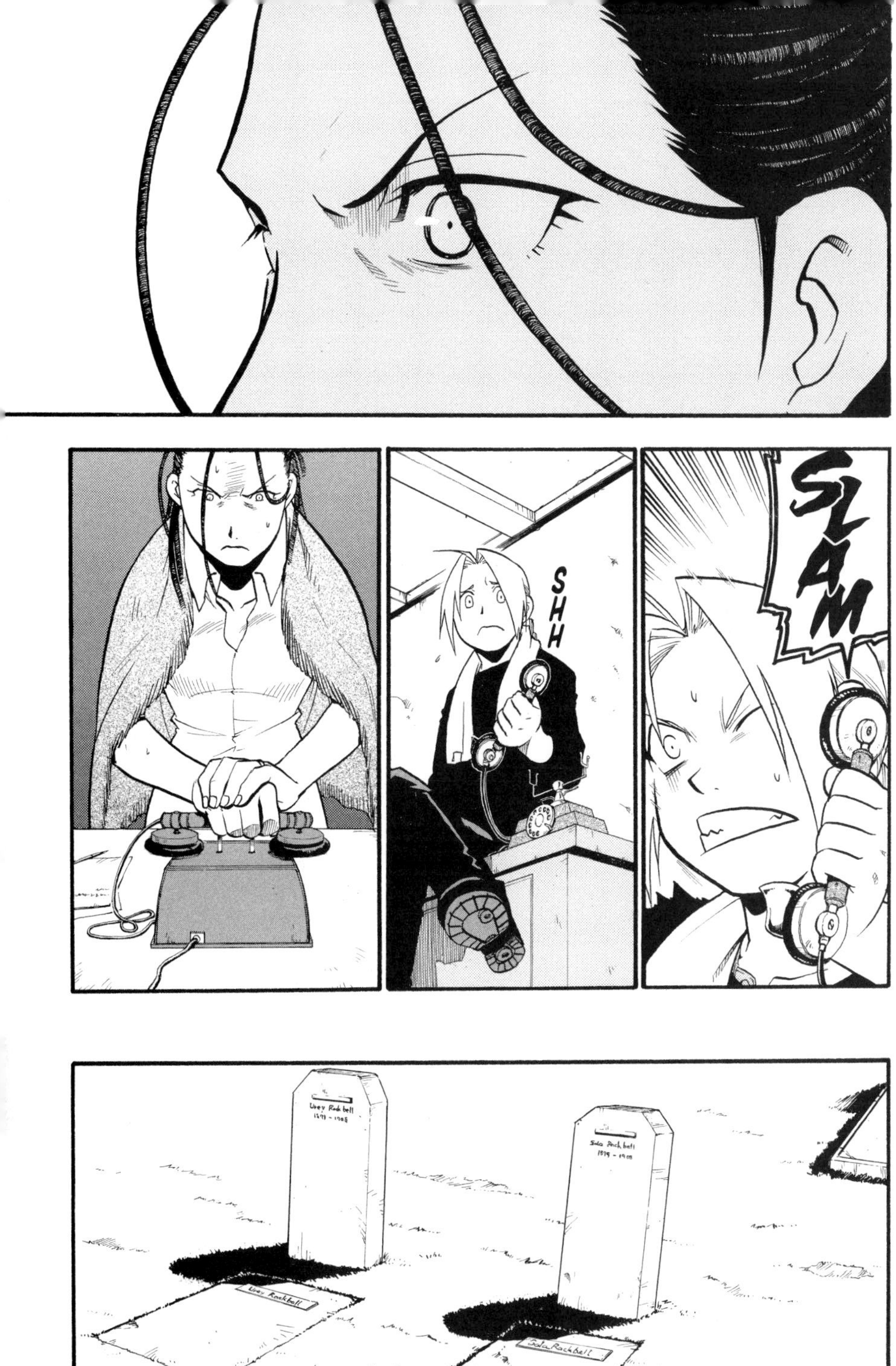
SLAM
SHH
Sara Rockbell
Urey Rockbell
Urey Rockbell

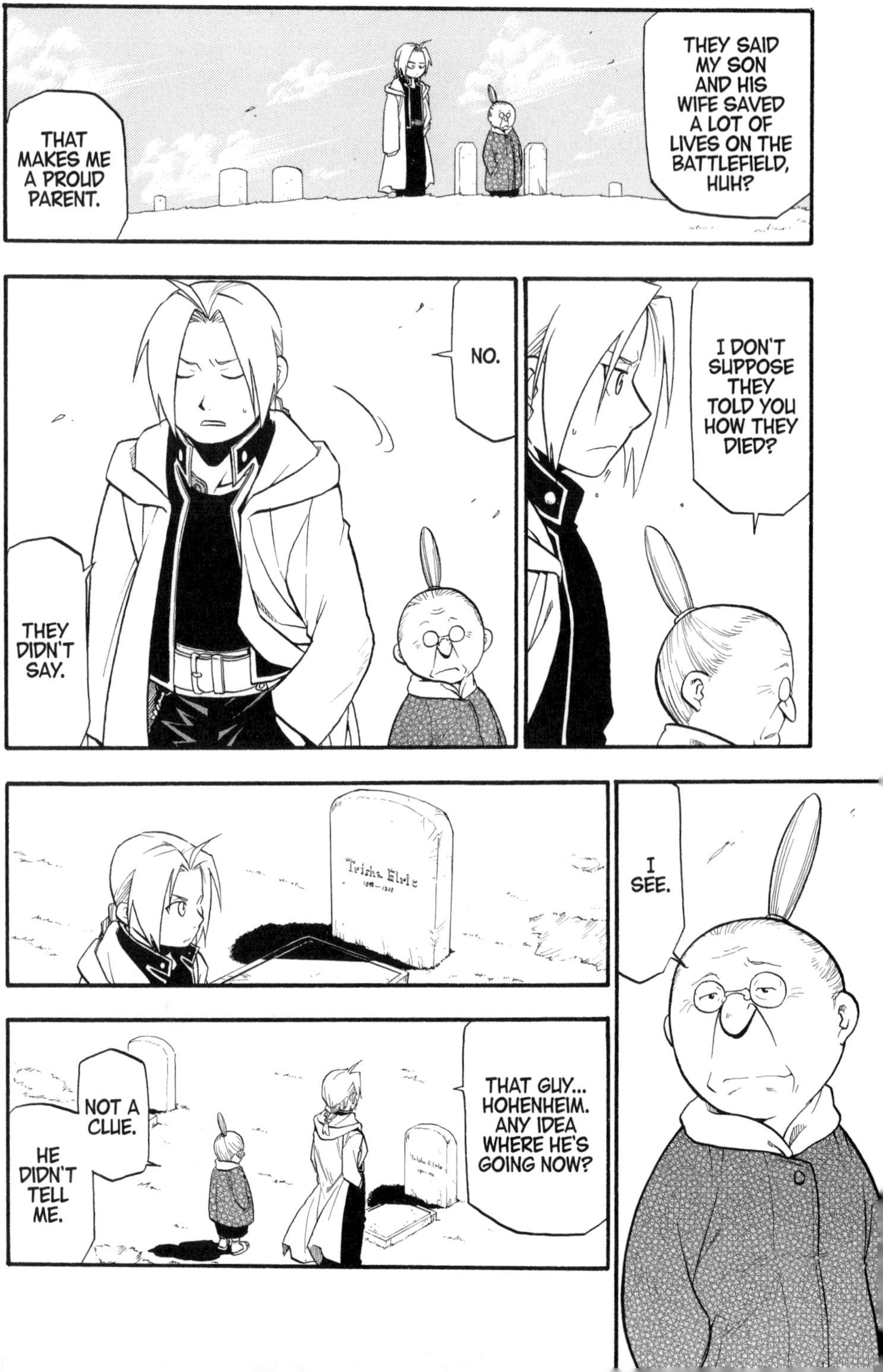
THEY SAID MY SON AND HIS WIFE SAVED A LOT OF LIVES ON THE BATTLEFIELD, HUH?
THAT MAKES ME A PROUD PARENT.
I DON'T SUPPOSE THEY TOLD YOU HOW THEY DIED?
NO.
THEY DIDN'T SAY.
I SEE.
Trisha Elric
THAT GUY... HOHENHEIM. ANY IDEA WHERE HE'S GOING NOW?
NOT A CLUE.
HE DIDN'T TELL ME.

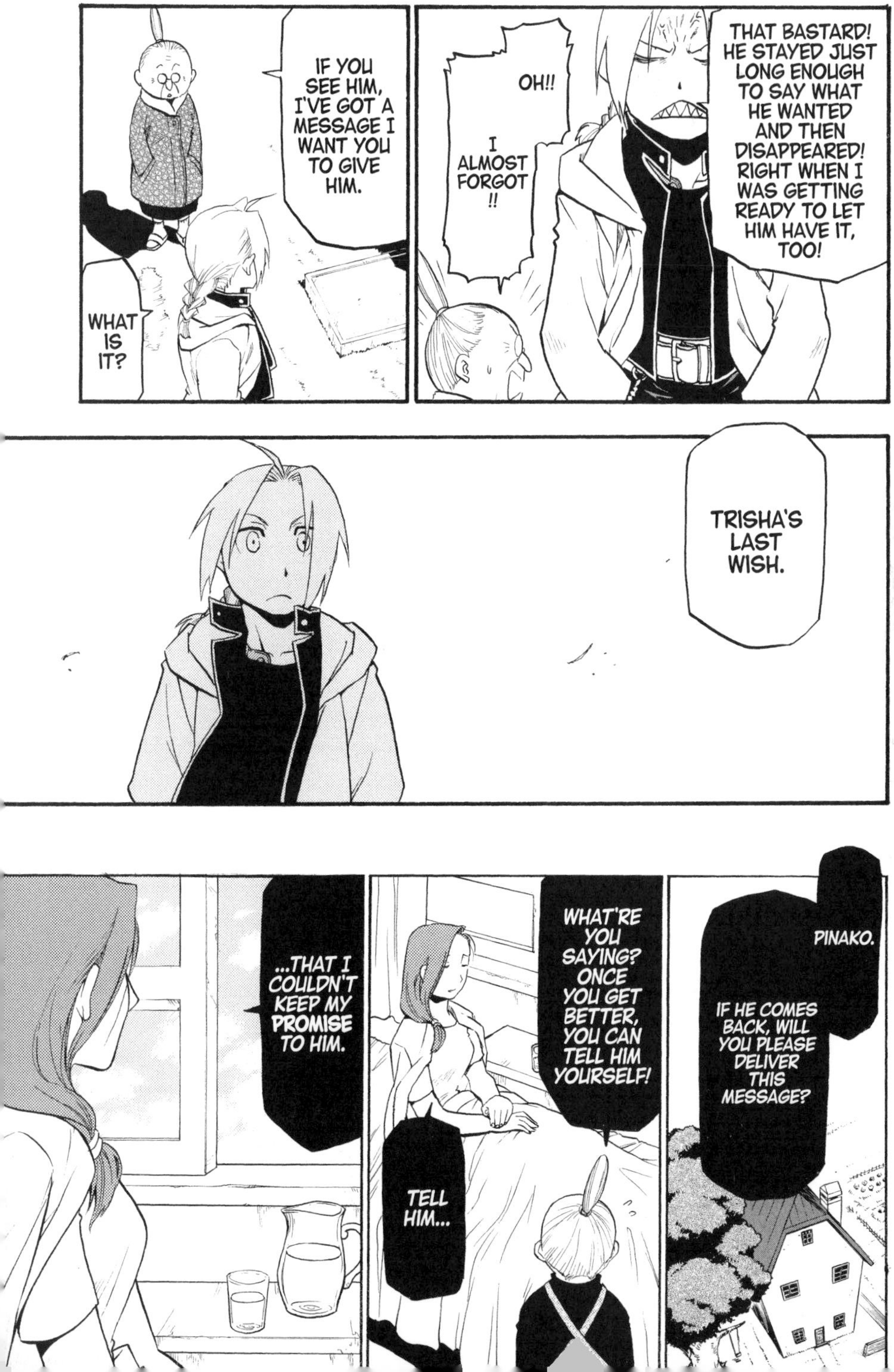
THAT BASTARD! HE STAYED JUST LONG ENOUGH TO SAY WHAT HE WANTED AND THEN DISAPPEARED! RIGHT WHEN I WAS GETTING READY TO LET HIM HAVE IT, TOO!
OH!!
I ALMOST FORGOT!!
IF YOU SEE HIM, I'VE GOT A MESSAGE I WANT YOU TO GIVE HIM.
WHAT IS IT?
TRISHA'S LAST WISH.
PINAKO.
IF HE COMES BACK, WILL YOU PLEASE DELIVER THIS MESSAGE?
WHAT'RE YOU SAYING? ONCE YOU GET BETTER, YOU CAN TELL HIM YOURSELF!
TELL HIM...
...THAT I COULDN'T KEEP MY PROMISE TO HIM.

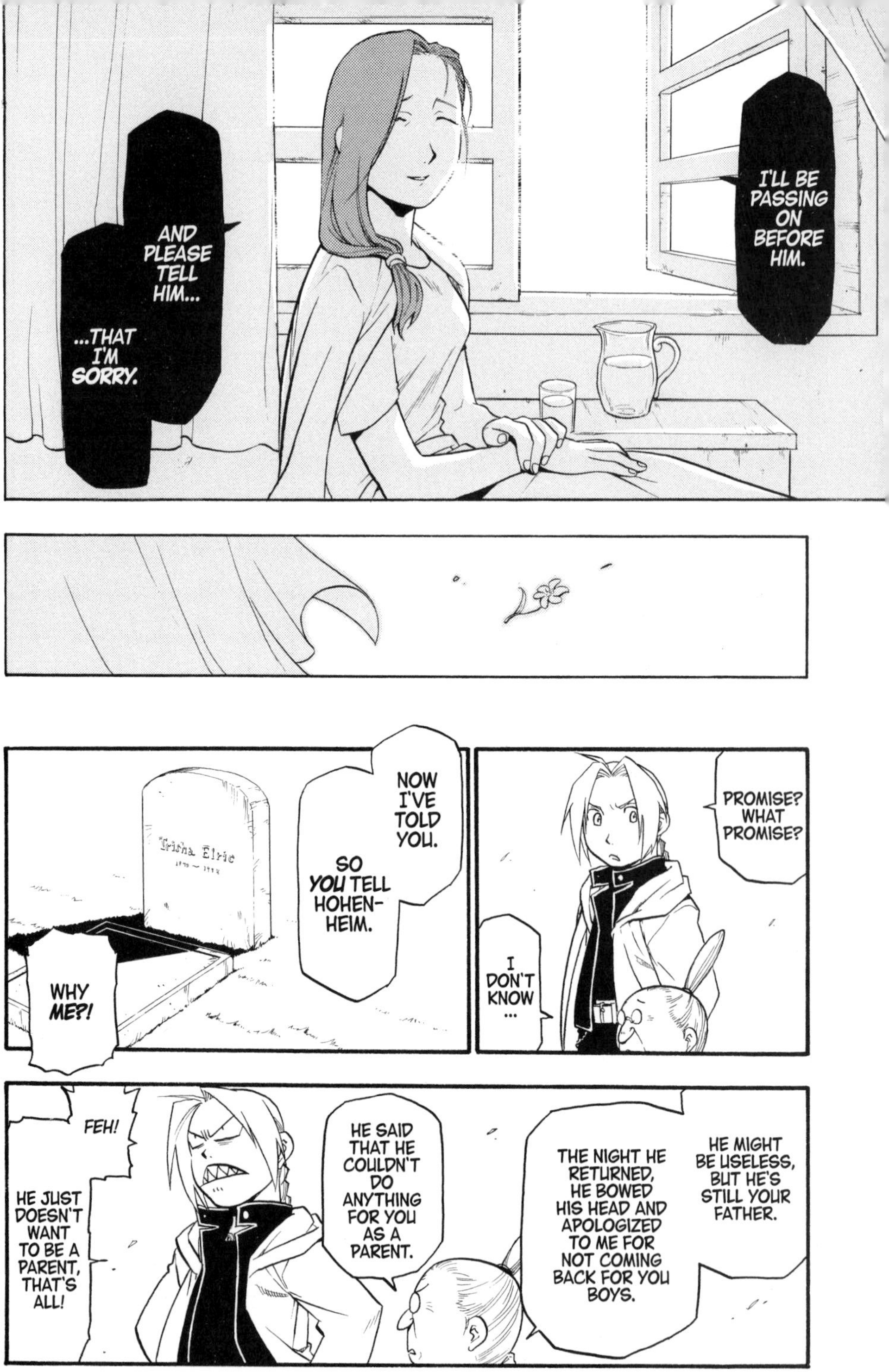
I'LL BE PASSING ON BEFORE HIM.
AND PLEASE TELL HIM...
...THAT I'M SORRY.
Trisha Elric
PROMISE? WHAT PROMISE?
I DON'T KNOW ...
NOW I'VE TOLD YOU.
SO YOU TELL HOHENHEIM.
WHY ME?!
HE MIGHT BE USELESS, BUT HE'S STILL YOUR FATHER.
THE NIGHT HE RETURNED, HE BOWED HIS HEAD AND APOLOGIZED TO ME FOR NOT COMING BACK FOR YOU BOYS.
HE SAID THAT HE COULDN'T DO ANYTHING FOR YOU AS A PARENT.
FEH!
HE JUST DOESN'T WANT TO BE A PARENT, THAT'S ALL!

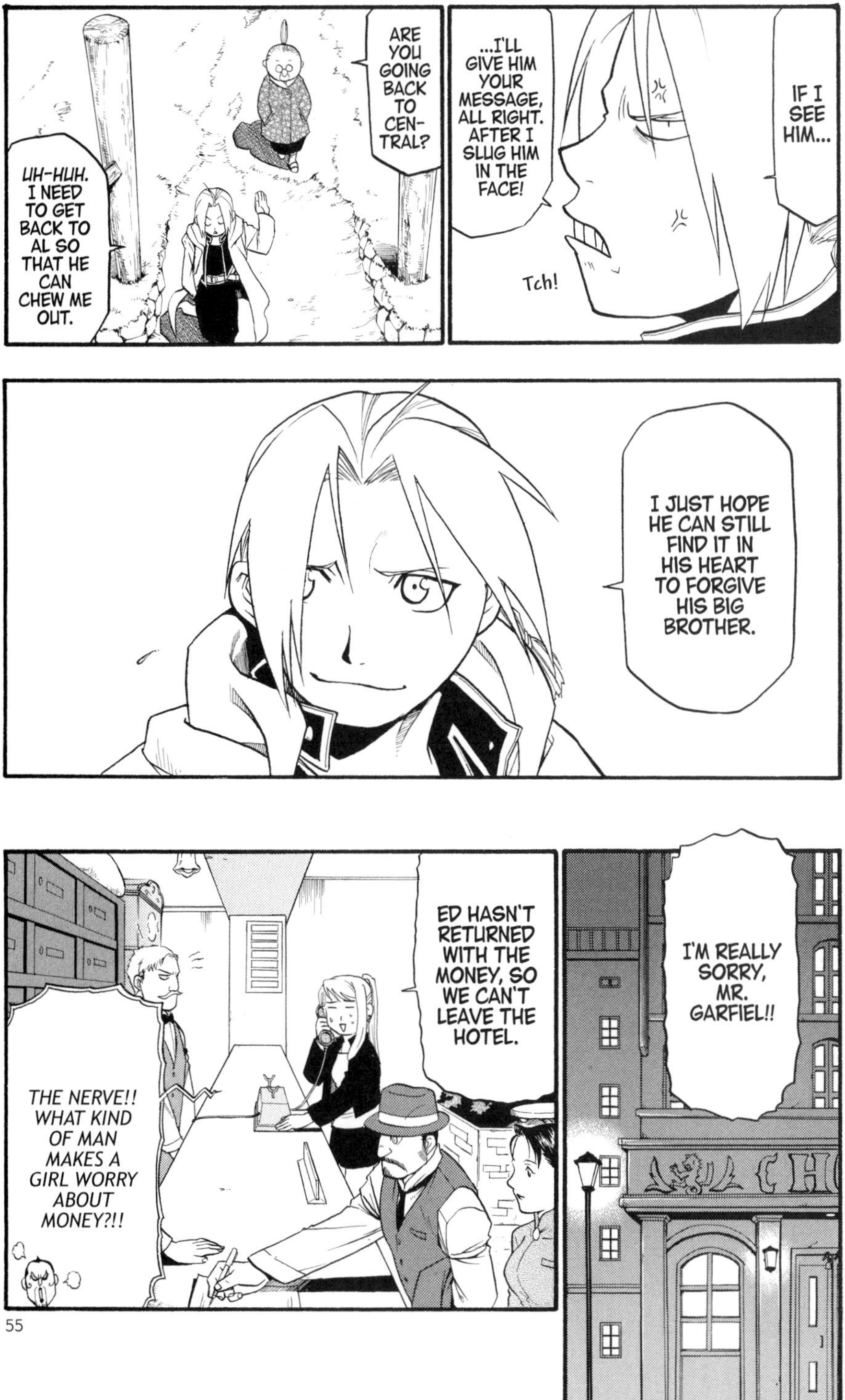
IF I SEE HIM...
...I'LL GIVE HIM YOUR MESSAGE, ALL RIGHT. AFTER I SLUG HIM IN THE FACE!
Tch!
ARE YOU GOING BACK TO CENTRAL?
UH-HUH. I NEED TO GET BACK TO AL SO THAT HE CAN CHEW ME OUT.
I JUST HOPE HE CAN STILL FIND IT IN HIS HEART TO FORGIVE HIS BIG BROTHER.
I'M REALLY SORRY, MR. GARFIEL!!
ED HASN'T RETURNED WITH THE MONEY, SO WE CAN'T LEAVE THE HOTEL.
THE NERVE!! WHAT KIND OF MAN MAKES A GIRL WORRY ABOUT MONEY?!!

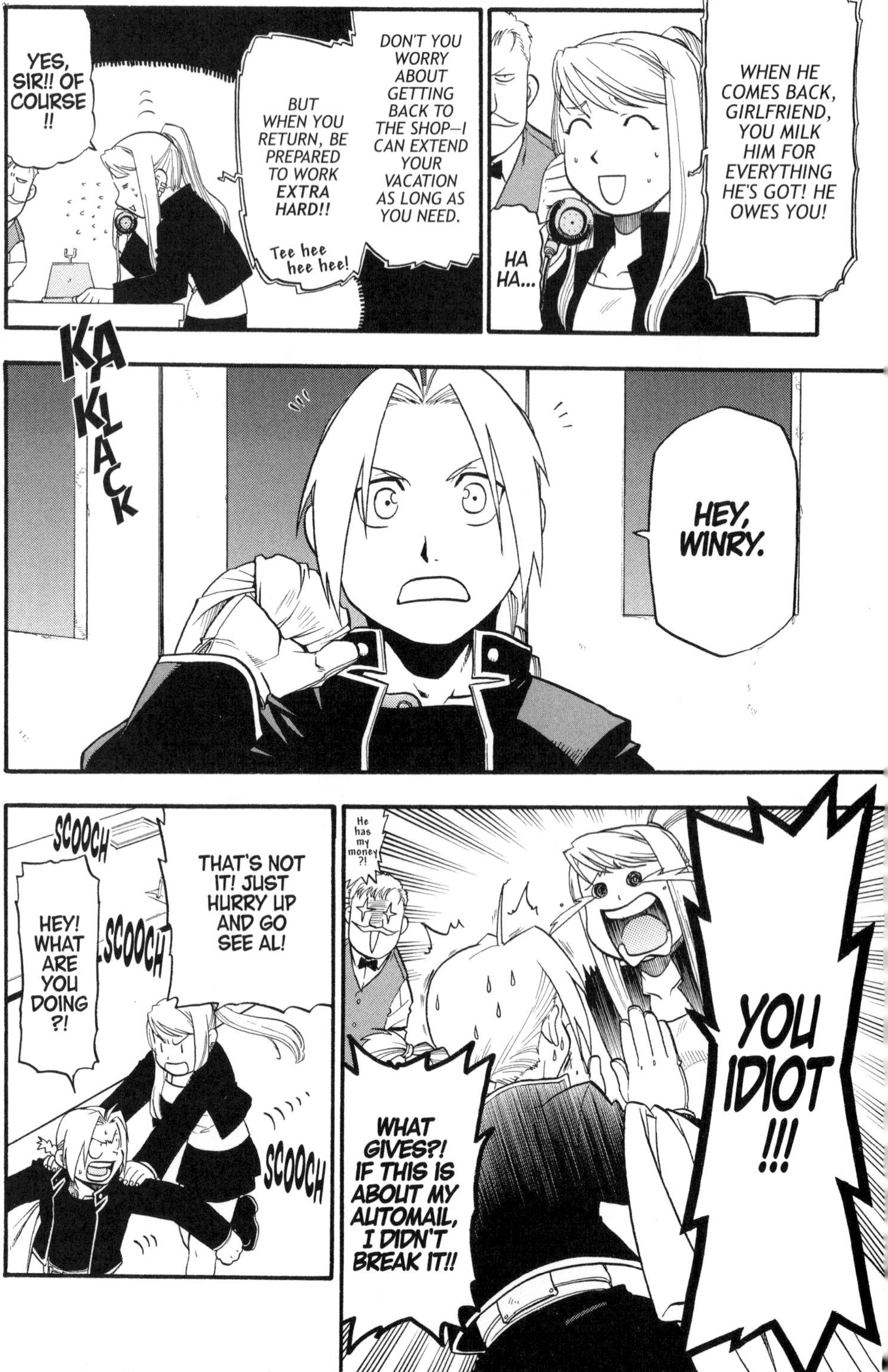
WHEN HE COMES BACK, GIRLFRIEND, YOU MILK HIM FOR EVERYTHING HE'S GOT! HE OWES YOU!
HA HA...
DON'T YOU WORRY ABOUT GETTING BACK TO THE SHOP—I CAN EXTEND YOUR VACATION AS LONG AS YOU NEED.
BUT WHEN YOU RETURN, BE PREPARED TO WORK EXTRA HARD!!
Tee hee hee hee!
YES, SIR!! OF COURSE !!
KA KLACK
HEY, WINRY.
YOU IDIOT !!!
He has my money ?!
WHAT GIVES?! IF THIS IS ABOUT MY AUTOMAIL, I DIDN'T BREAK IT!!
THAT'S NOT IT! JUST HURRY UP AND GO SEE AL!
SCOOCH
HEY! WHAT ARE YOU DOING ?!
SCOOCH
SCOOCH

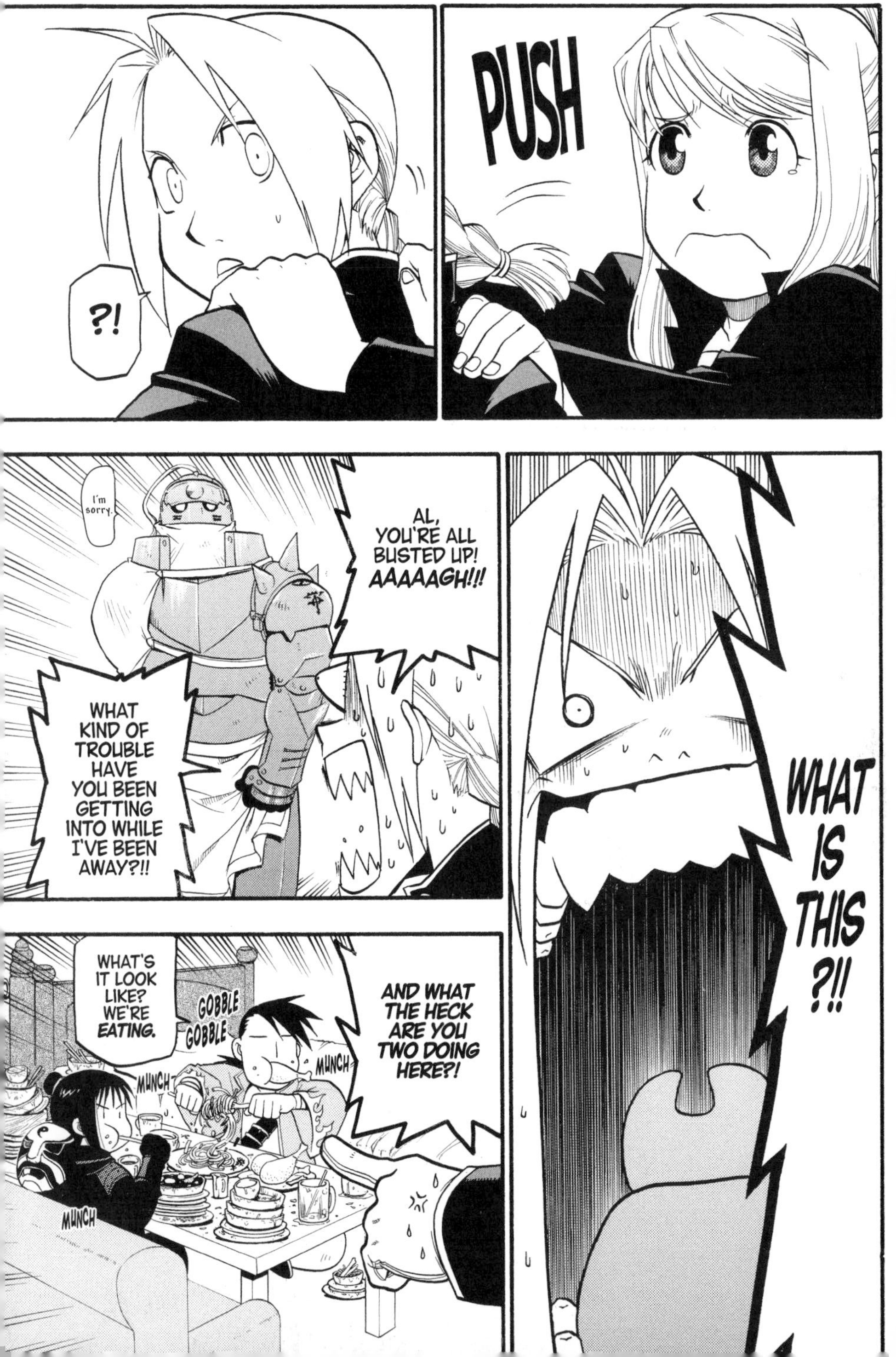
PUSH
?!
WHAT IS THIS?!!
AL, YOU'RE ALL BUSTED UP! AAAAAGH!!!
I'm sorry.
WHAT KIND OF TROUBLE HAVE YOU BEEN GETTING INTO WHILE I'VE BEEN AWAY?!!
AND WHAT THE HECK ARE YOU TWO DOING HERE?!
MUNCH
GOBBLE GOBBLE
WHAT'S IT LOOK LIKE? WE'RE EATING.
MUNCH
MUNCH

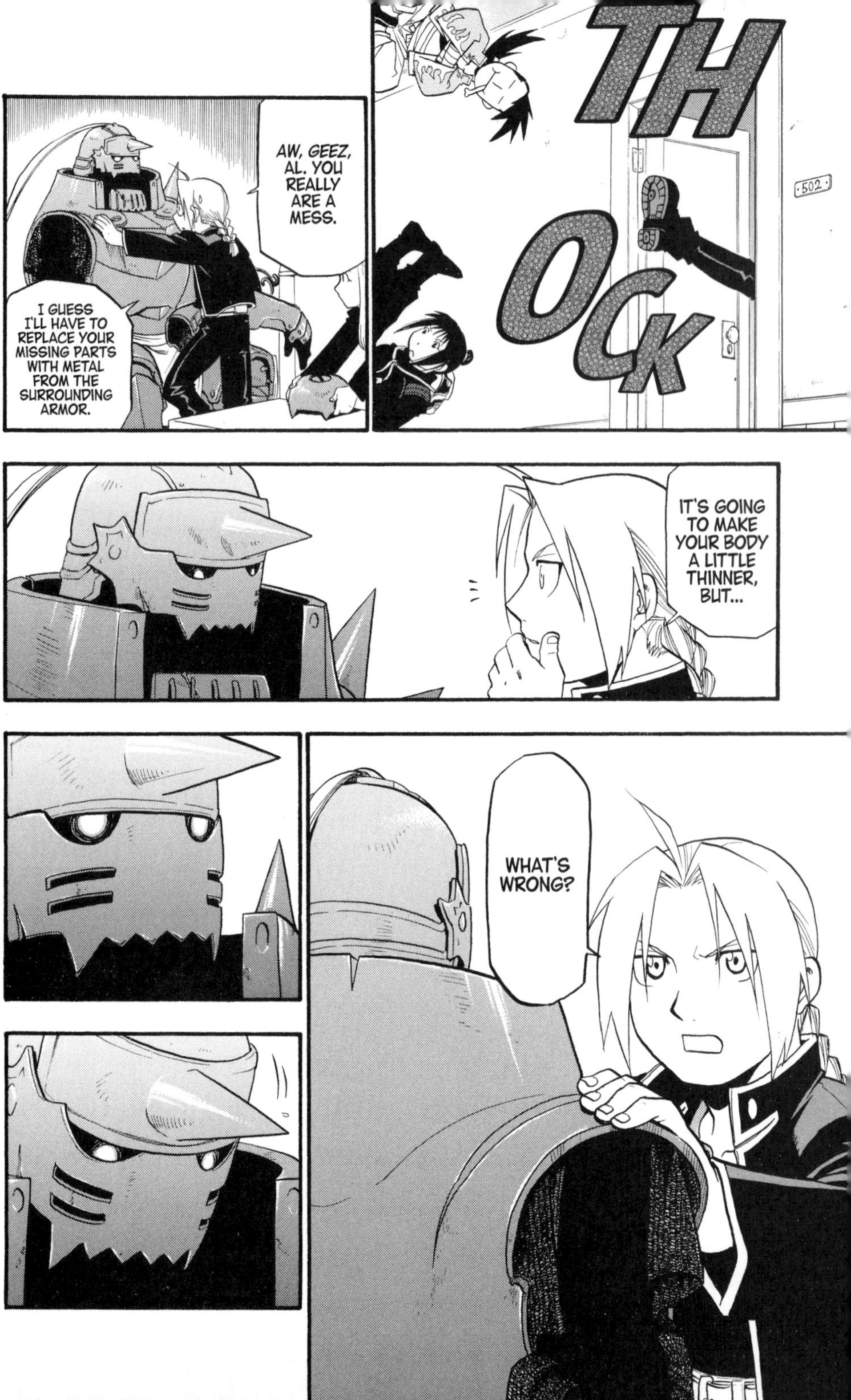
THOCK
502
AW, GEEZ, AL. YOU REALLY ARE A MESS.
I GUESS I'LL HAVE TO REPLACE YOUR MISSING PARTS WITH METAL FROM THE SURROUNDING ARMOR.
IT'S GOING TO MAKE YOUR BODY A LITTLE THINNER, BUT...
WHAT'S WRONG?

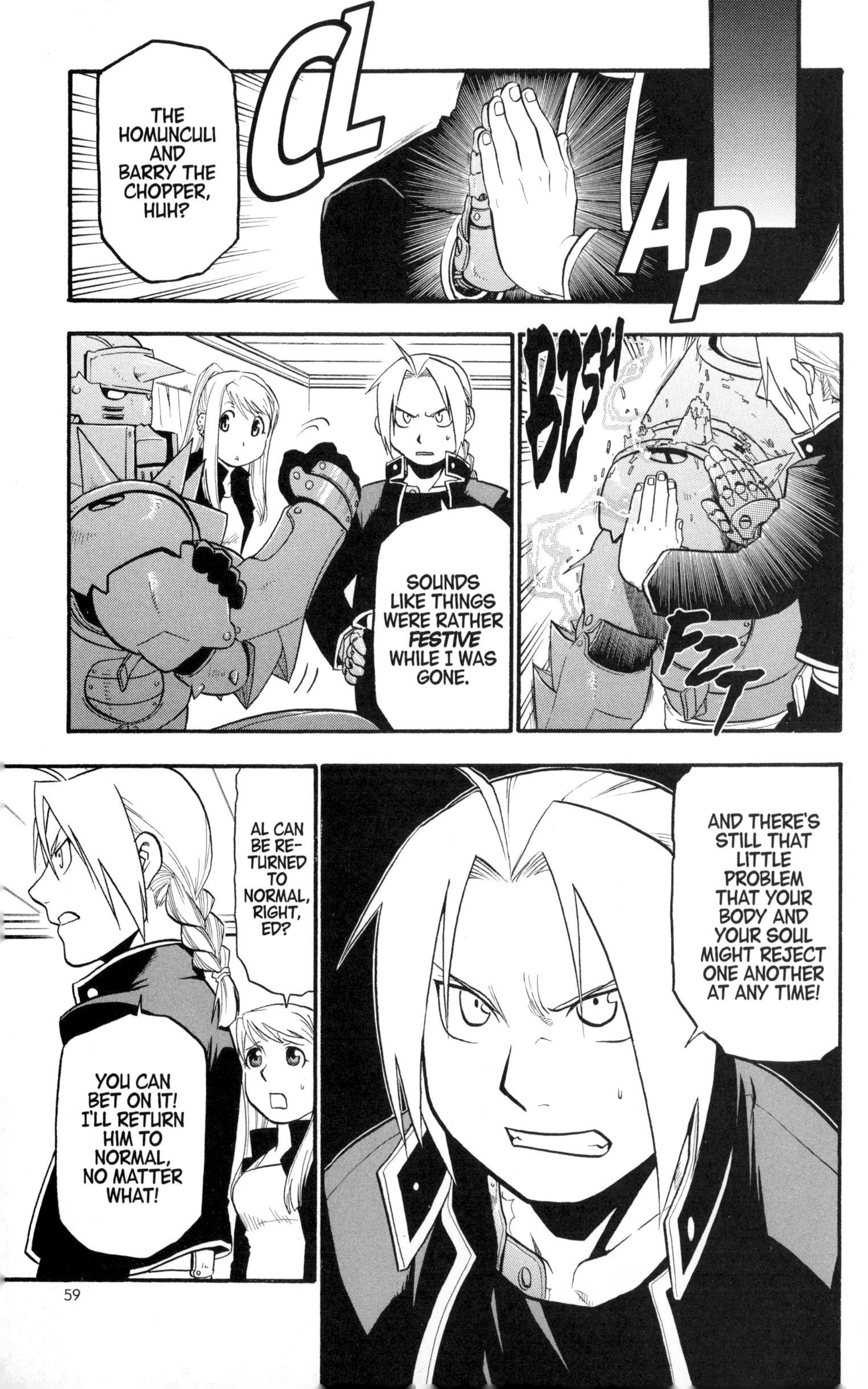

CLAP
THE HOMUNCULI AND BARRY THE CHOPPER, HUH?
BZSH
FZZT
SOUNDS LIKE THINGS WERE RATHER *FESTIVE* WHILE I WAS GONE.
AND THERE'S STILL THAT LITTLE PROBLEM THAT YOUR BODY AND YOUR SOUL MIGHT REJECT ONE ANOTHER AT ANY TIME!
AL CAN BE RE-TURNED TO NORMAL, RIGHT, ED?
YOU CAN BET ON IT! I'LL RETURN HIM TO NORMAL, NO MATTER WHAT!

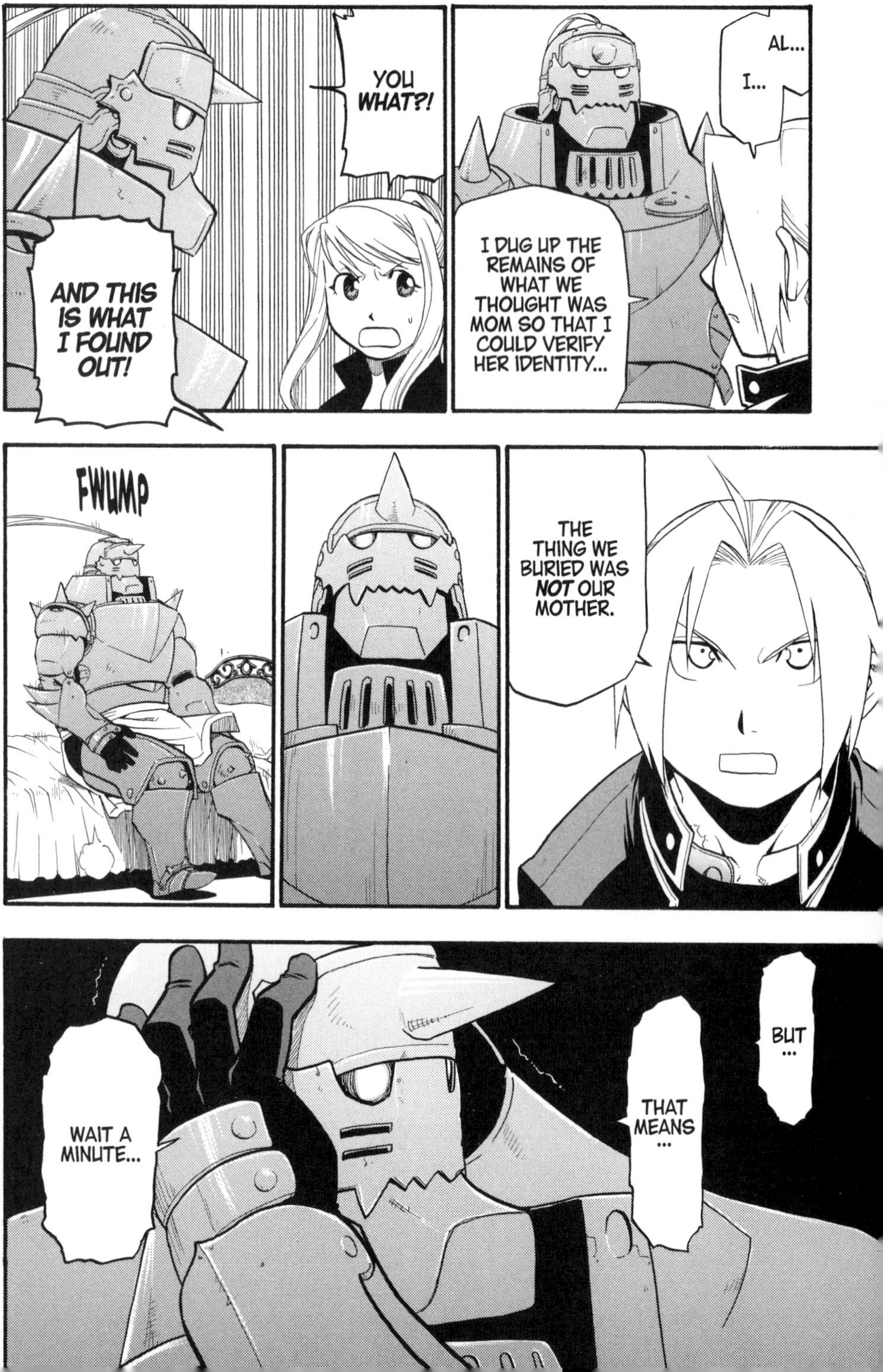
AL...
I...
I DUG UP THE REMAINS OF WHAT WE THOUGHT WAS MOM SO THAT I COULD VERIFY HER IDENTITY...
YOU WHAT?!
AND THIS IS WHAT I FOUND OUT!
THE THING WE BURIED WAS ***NOT*** OUR MOTHER.
FWUMP
BUT...
THAT MEANS...
WAIT A MINUTE...

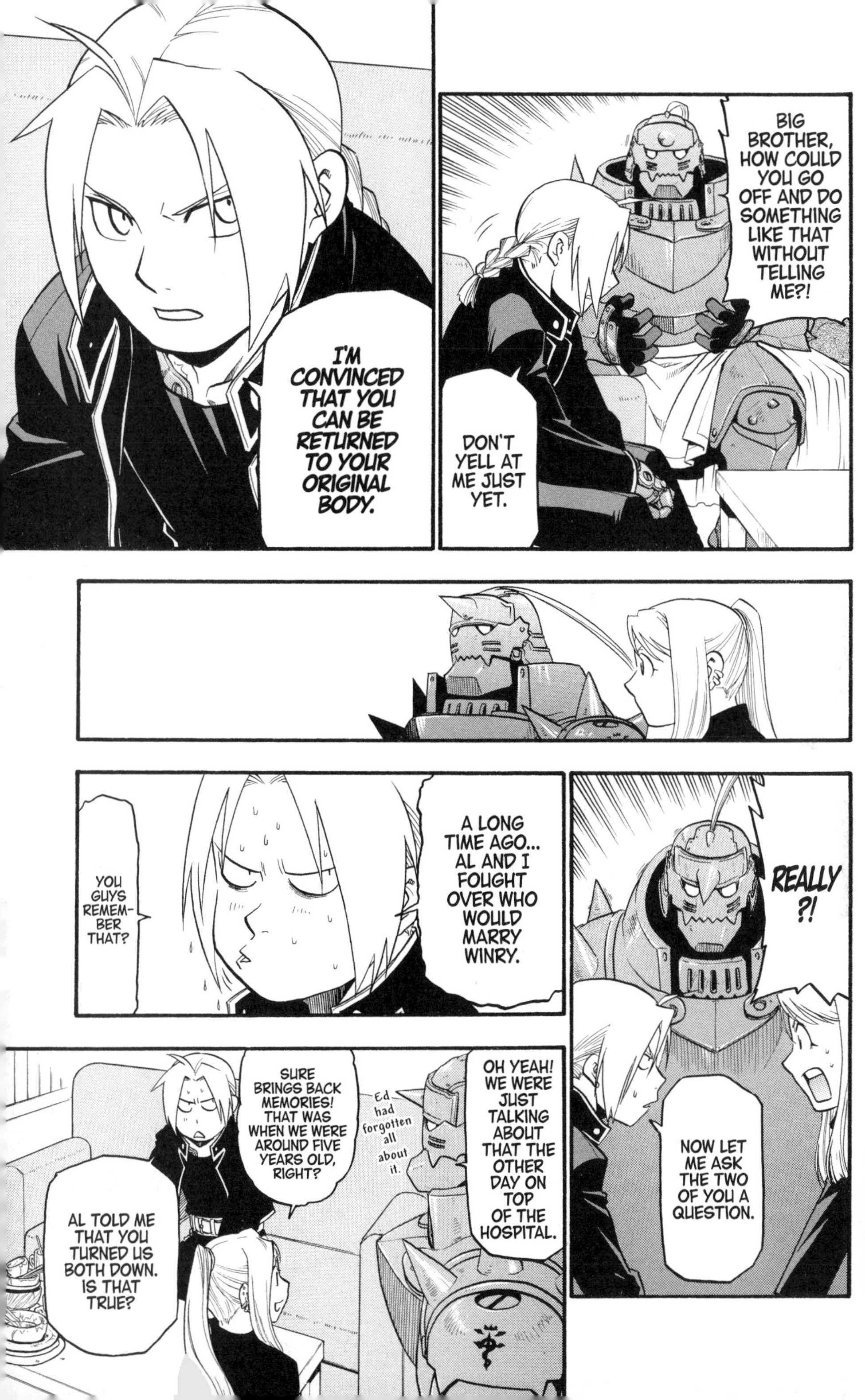
BIG BROTHER, HOW COULD YOU GO OFF AND DO SOMETHING LIKE THAT WITHOUT TELLING ME?!
DON'T YELL AT ME JUST YET.
I'M CONVINCED THAT YOU CAN BE RETURNED TO YOUR ORIGINAL BODY.
REALLY?!
NOW LET ME ASK THE TWO OF YOU A QUESTION.
A LONG TIME AGO... AL AND I FOUGHT OVER WHO WOULD MARRY WINRY.
YOU GUYS REMEMBER THAT?
OH YEAH! WE WERE JUST TALKING ABOUT THAT THE OTHER DAY ON TOP OF THE HOSPITAL.
Ed had forgotten all about it.
SURE BRINGS BACK MEMORIES! THAT WAS WHEN WE WERE AROUND FIVE YEARS OLD, RIGHT?
AL TOLD ME THAT YOU TURNED US BOTH DOWN. IS THAT TRUE?

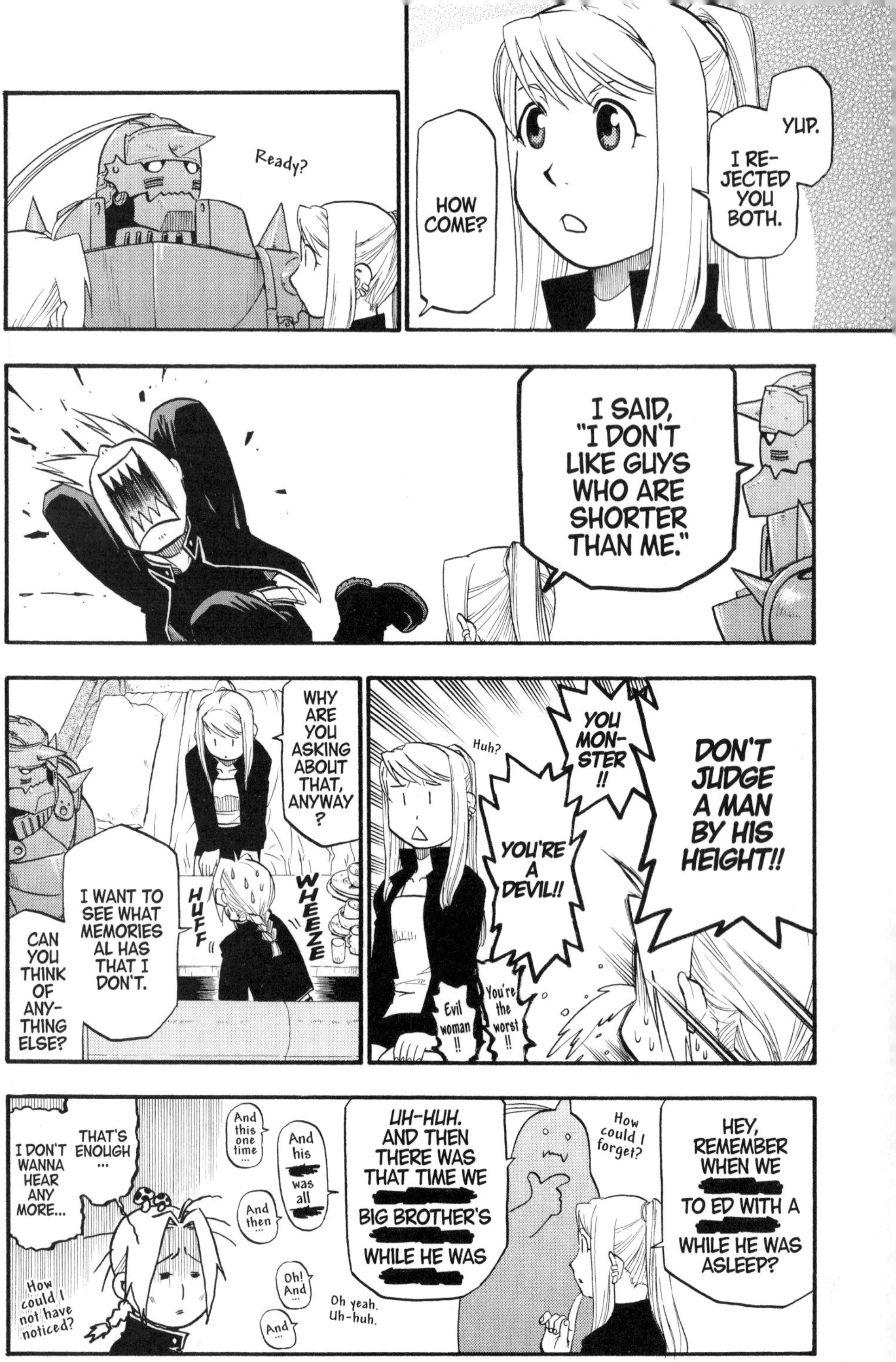
YUP. I RE-JECTED YOU BOTH.
HOW COME?
Ready?
I SAID, "I DON'T LIKE GUYS WHO ARE SHORTER THAN ME."
DON'T JUDGE A MAN BY HIS HEIGHT!!
YOU MON-STER!!
Huh?
YOU'RE A DEVIL!!
You're the worst!!
Evil woman!!
WHY ARE YOU ASKING ABOUT THAT, ANYWAY?
WHEEZE
HUFF
I WANT TO SEE WHAT MEMORIES AL HAS THAT I DON'T.
CAN YOU THINK OF ANY-THING ELSE?
HEY, REMEMBER WHEN WE [redacted] TO ED WITH A [redacted] WHILE HE WAS ASLEEP?
How could I forget?
UH-HUH. AND THEN THERE WAS THAT TIME WE [redacted] BIG BROTHER'S [redacted] WHILE HE WAS [redacted]
Oh yeah. Uh-huh.
And his [redacted] was all [redacted]
And this one time...
And then...
Oh! And...
And...
THAT'S ENOUGH...
I DON'T WANNA HEAR ANY MORE...
How could I not have noticed?

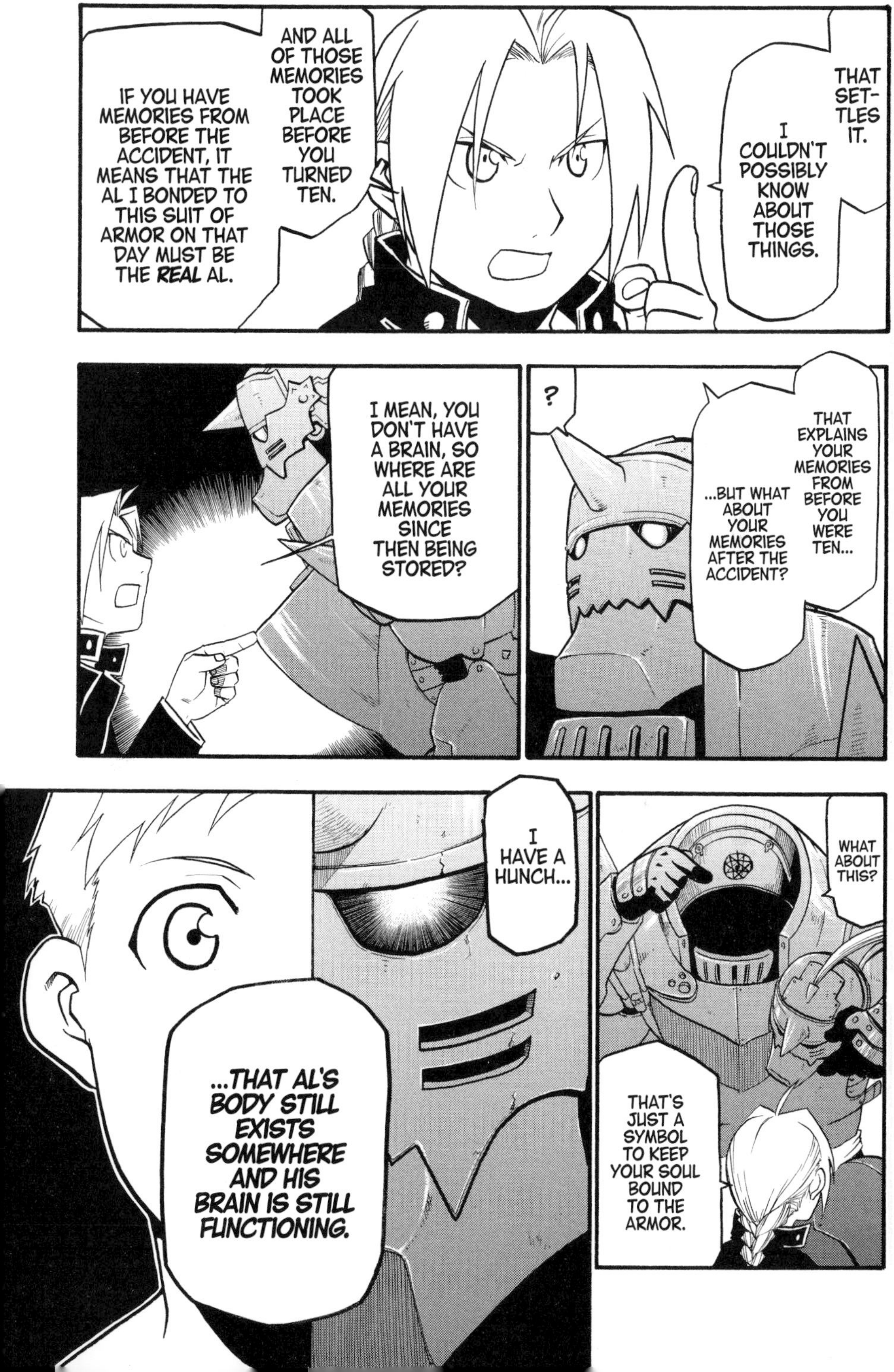
THAT SETTLES IT.
I COULDN'T POSSIBLY KNOW ABOUT THOSE THINGS.
AND ALL OF THOSE MEMORIES TOOK PLACE BEFORE YOU TURNED TEN.
IF YOU HAVE MEMORIES FROM BEFORE THE ACCIDENT, IT MEANS THAT THE AL I BONDED TO THIS SUIT OF ARMOR ON THAT DAY MUST BE THE ***REAL*** AL.
THAT EXPLAINS YOUR MEMORIES FROM BEFORE YOU WERE TEN...
...BUT WHAT ABOUT YOUR MEMORIES AFTER THE ACCIDENT?
?
I MEAN, YOU DON'T HAVE A BRAIN, SO WHERE ARE ALL YOUR MEMORIES SINCE THEN BEING STORED?
WHAT ABOUT THIS?
THAT'S JUST A SYMBOL TO KEEP YOUR SOUL BOUND TO THE ARMOR.
I HAVE A HUNCH...
...THAT AL'S BODY STILL EXISTS SOMEWHERE AND HIS BRAIN IS STILL FUNCTIONING.

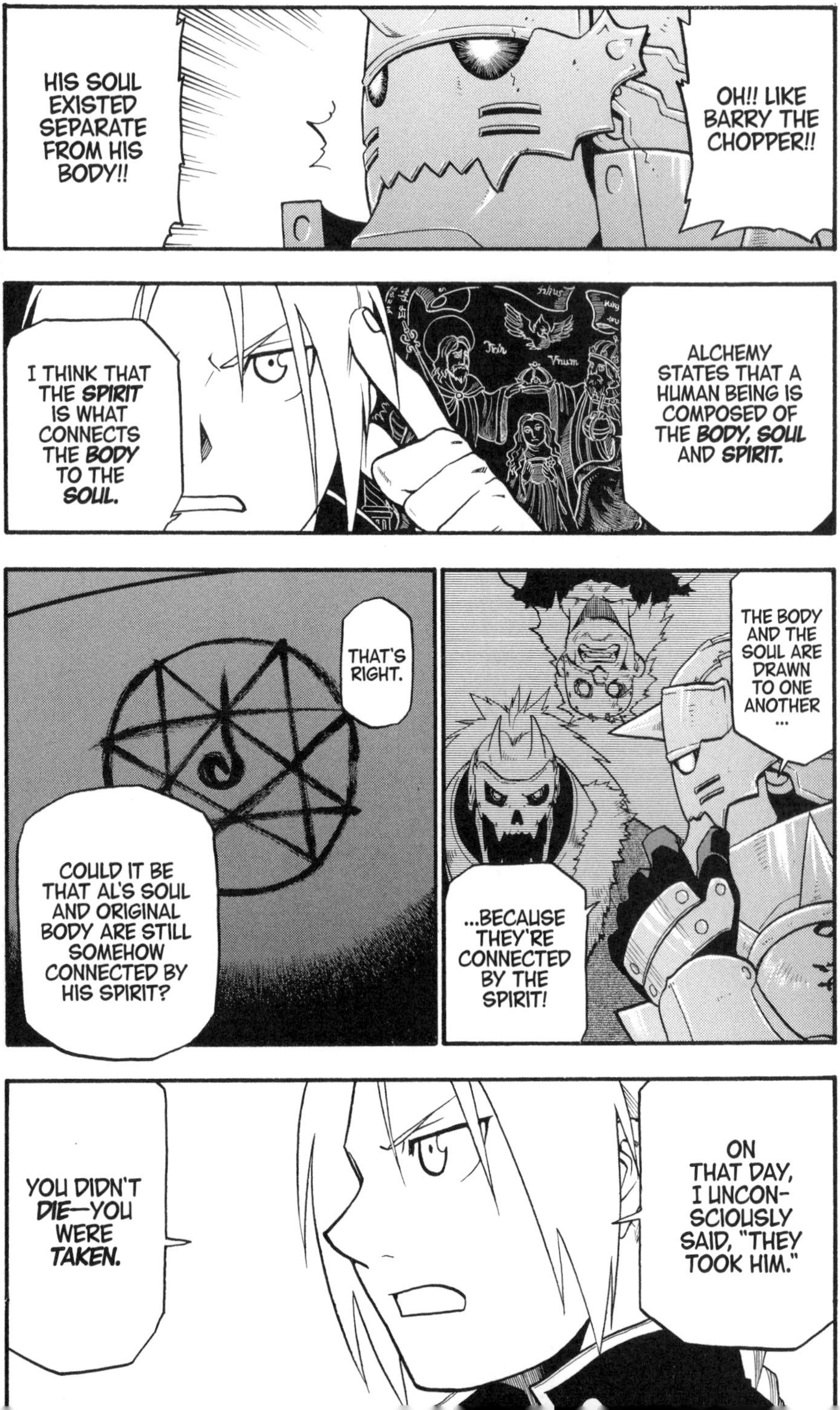
OH!! LIKE BARRY THE CHOPPER!!
HIS SOUL EXISTED SEPARATE FROM HIS BODY!!
ALCHEMY STATES THAT A HUMAN BEING IS COMPOSED OF THE **BODY, SOUL** AND **SPIRIT.**
I THINK THAT THE **SPIRIT** IS WHAT CONNECTS THE **BODY** TO THE **SOUL.**
THE BODY AND THE SOUL ARE DRAWN TO ONE ANOTHER ...
...BECAUSE THEY'RE CONNECTED BY THE SPIRIT!
THAT'S RIGHT.
COULD IT BE THAT AL'S SOUL AND ORIGINAL BODY ARE STILL SOMEHOW CONNECTED BY HIS SPIRIT?
ON THAT DAY, I UNCONSCIOUSLY SAID, "THEY TOOK HIM."
YOU DIDN'T **DIE**—YOU WERE **TAKEN.**

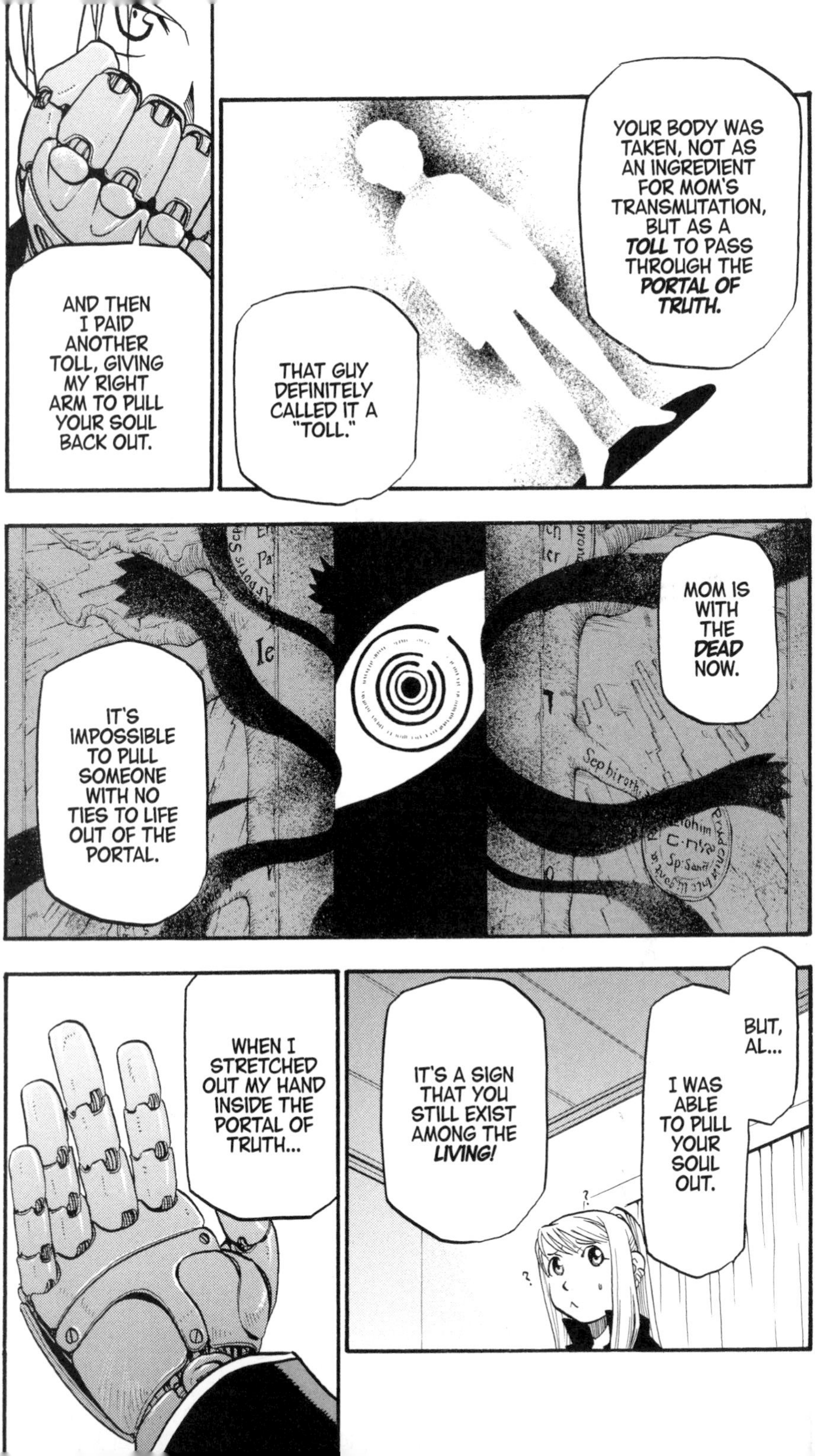
YOUR BODY WAS TAKEN, NOT AS AN INGREDIENT FOR MOM'S TRANSMUTATION, BUT AS A ***TOLL*** TO PASS THROUGH THE ***PORTAL OF TRUTH.***
THAT GUY DEFINITELY CALLED IT A "TOLL."
AND THEN I PAID ANOTHER TOLL, GIVING MY RIGHT ARM TO PULL YOUR SOUL BACK OUT.
MOM IS WITH THE ***DEAD*** NOW.
IT'S IMPOSSIBLE TO PULL SOMEONE WITH NO TIES TO LIFE OUT OF THE PORTAL.
BUT, AL...
I WAS ABLE TO PULL YOUR SOUL OUT.
IT'S A SIGN THAT YOU STILL EXIST AMONG THE ***LIVING!***
WHEN I STRETCHED OUT MY HAND INSIDE THE PORTAL OF TRUTH...

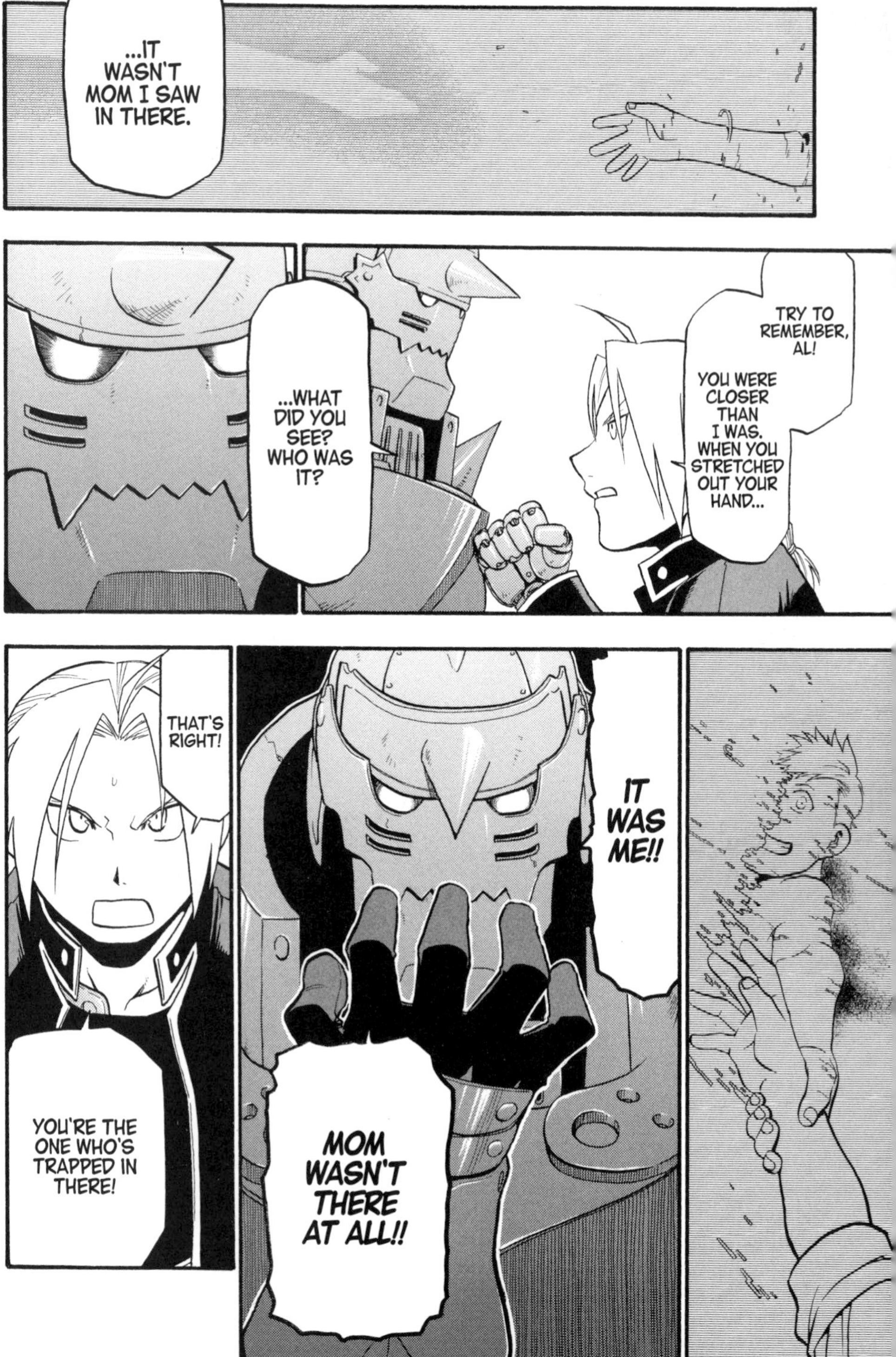
...IT WASN'T MOM I SAW IN THERE.
TRY TO REMEMBER, AL!
YOU WERE CLOSER THAN I WAS. WHEN YOU STRETCHED OUT YOUR HAND...
...WHAT DID YOU SEE? WHO WAS IT?
IT WAS ME!!
MOM WASN'T THERE AT ALL!!
THAT'S RIGHT!
YOU'RE THE ONE WHO'S TRAPPED IN THERE!

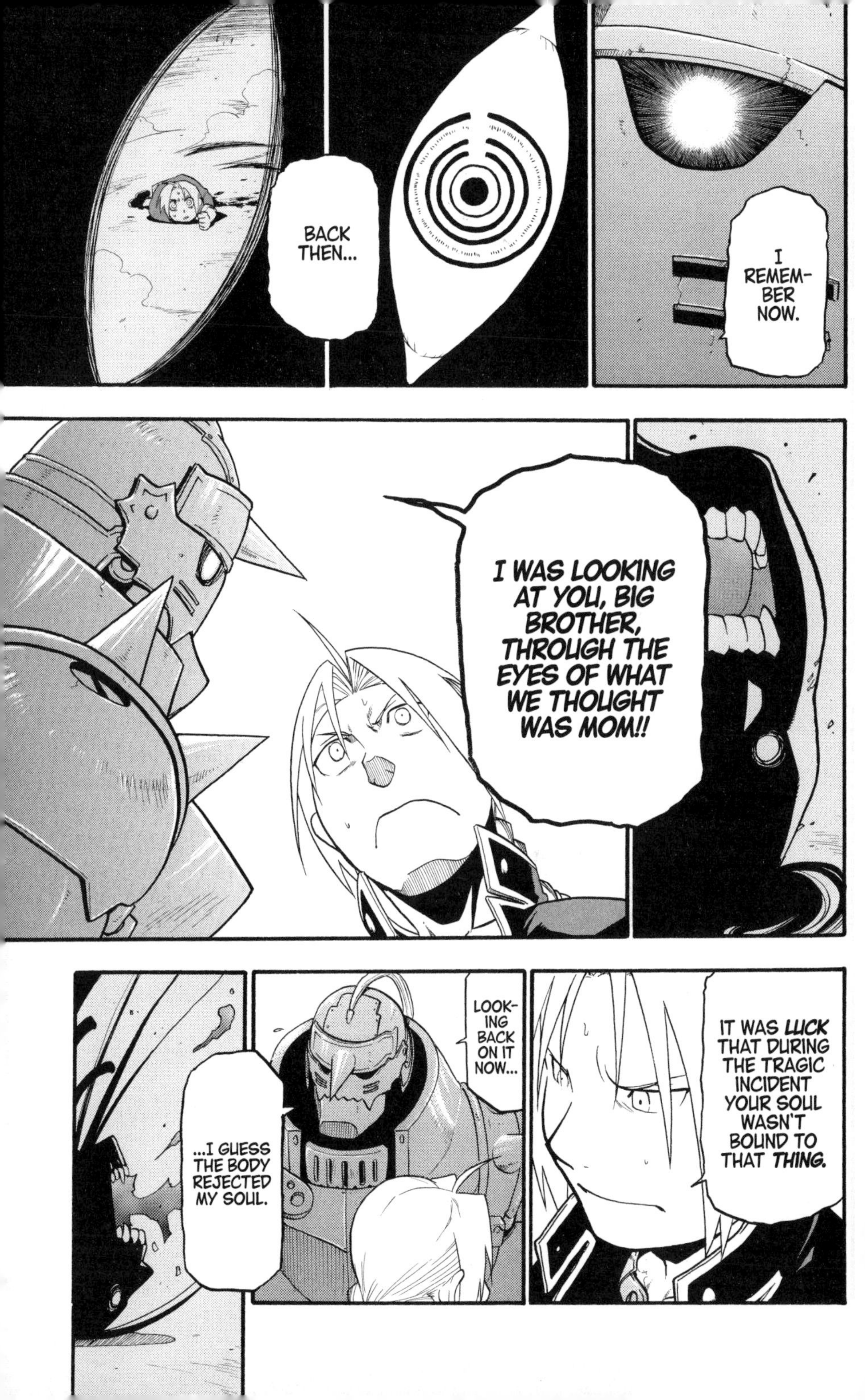
I REMEMBER NOW.
BACK THEN...
I WAS LOOKING AT YOU, BIG BROTHER, THROUGH THE EYES OF WHAT WE THOUGHT WAS MOM!!
IT WAS LUCK THAT DURING THE TRAGIC INCIDENT YOUR SOUL WASN'T BOUND TO THAT THING.
LOOKING BACK ON IT NOW...
...I GUESS THE BODY REJECTED MY SOUL.

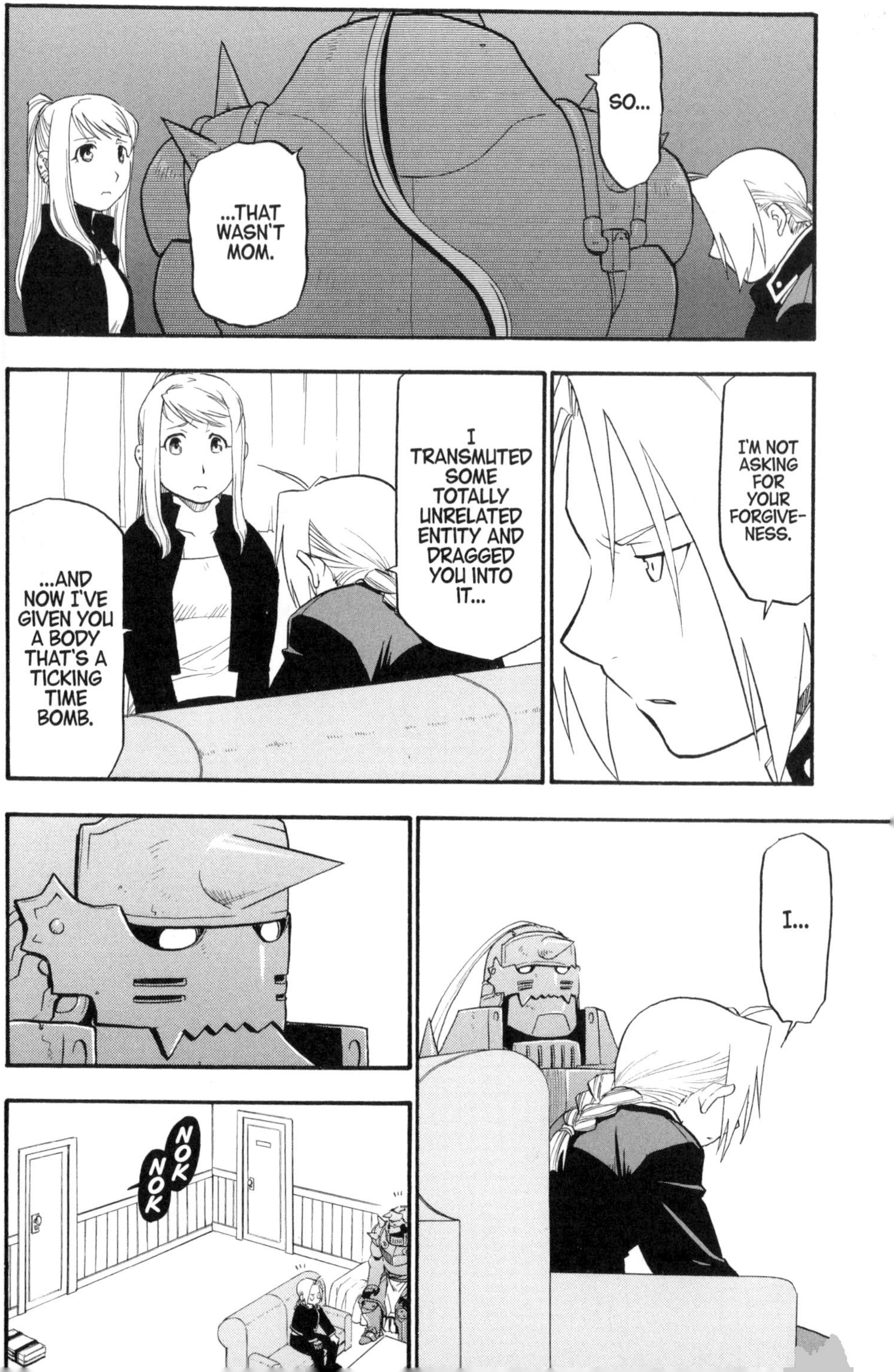
SO...
...THAT WASN'T MOM.
I'M NOT ASKING FOR YOUR FORGIVE-NESS.
I TRANSMUTED SOME TOTALLY UNRELATED ENTITY AND DRAGGED YOU INTO IT...
...AND NOW I'VE GIVEN YOU A BODY THAT'S A TICKING TIME BOMB.
I...
NOK NOK

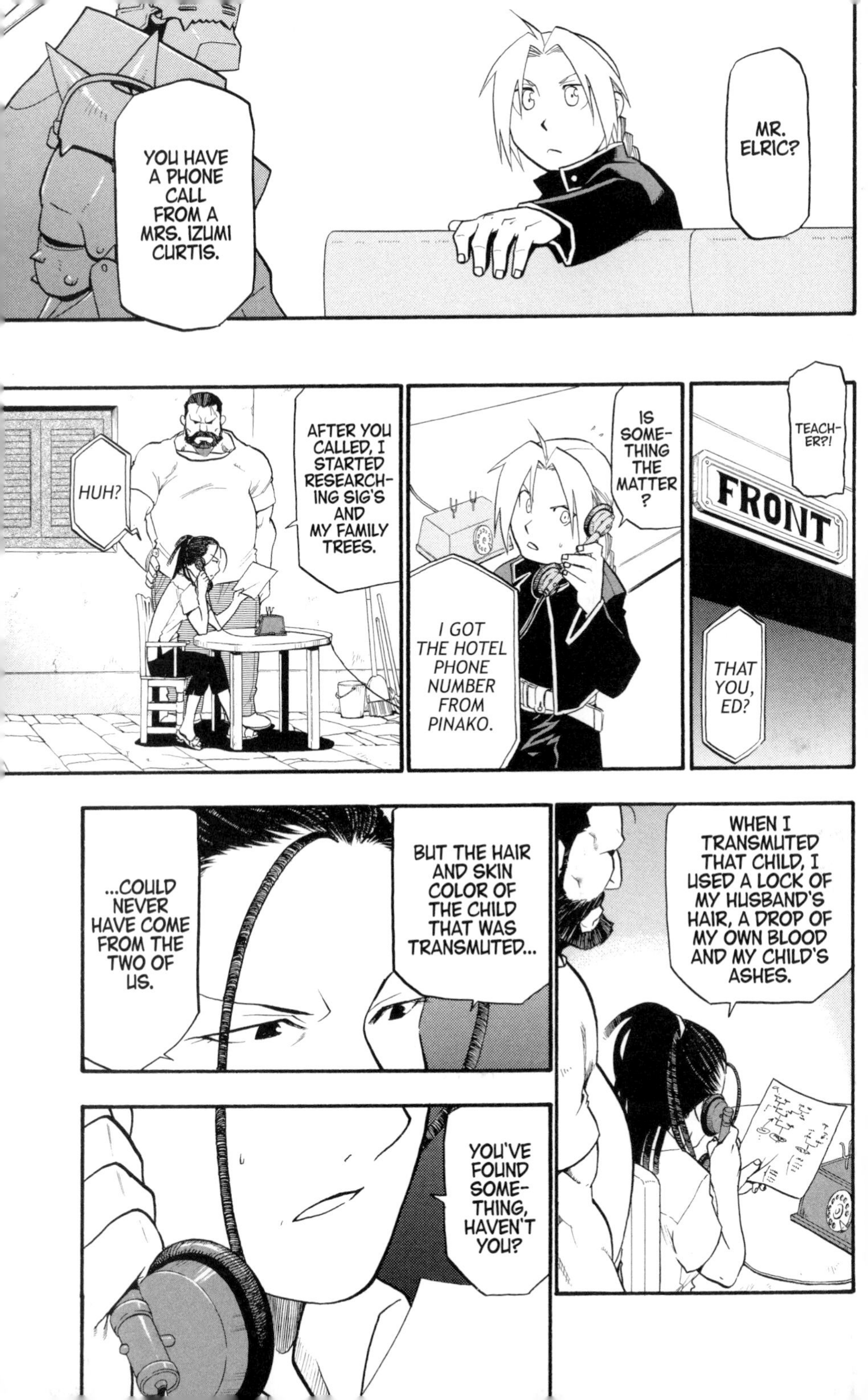
MR. ELRIC?
YOU HAVE A PHONE CALL FROM A MRS. IZUMI CURTIS.
TEACHER?!
FRONT
THAT YOU, ED?
IS SOME-THING THE MATTER?
I GOT THE HOTEL PHONE NUMBER FROM PINAKO.
AFTER YOU CALLED, I STARTED RESEARCH-ING SIG'S AND MY FAMILY TREES.
HUH?
WHEN I TRANSMUTED THAT CHILD, I USED A LOCK OF MY HUSBAND'S HAIR, A DROP OF MY OWN BLOOD AND MY CHILD'S ASHES.
BUT THE HAIR AND SKIN COLOR OF THE CHILD THAT WAS TRANSMUTED...
...COULD NEVER HAVE COME FROM THE TWO OF US.
YOU'VE FOUND SOME-THING, HAVEN'T YOU?

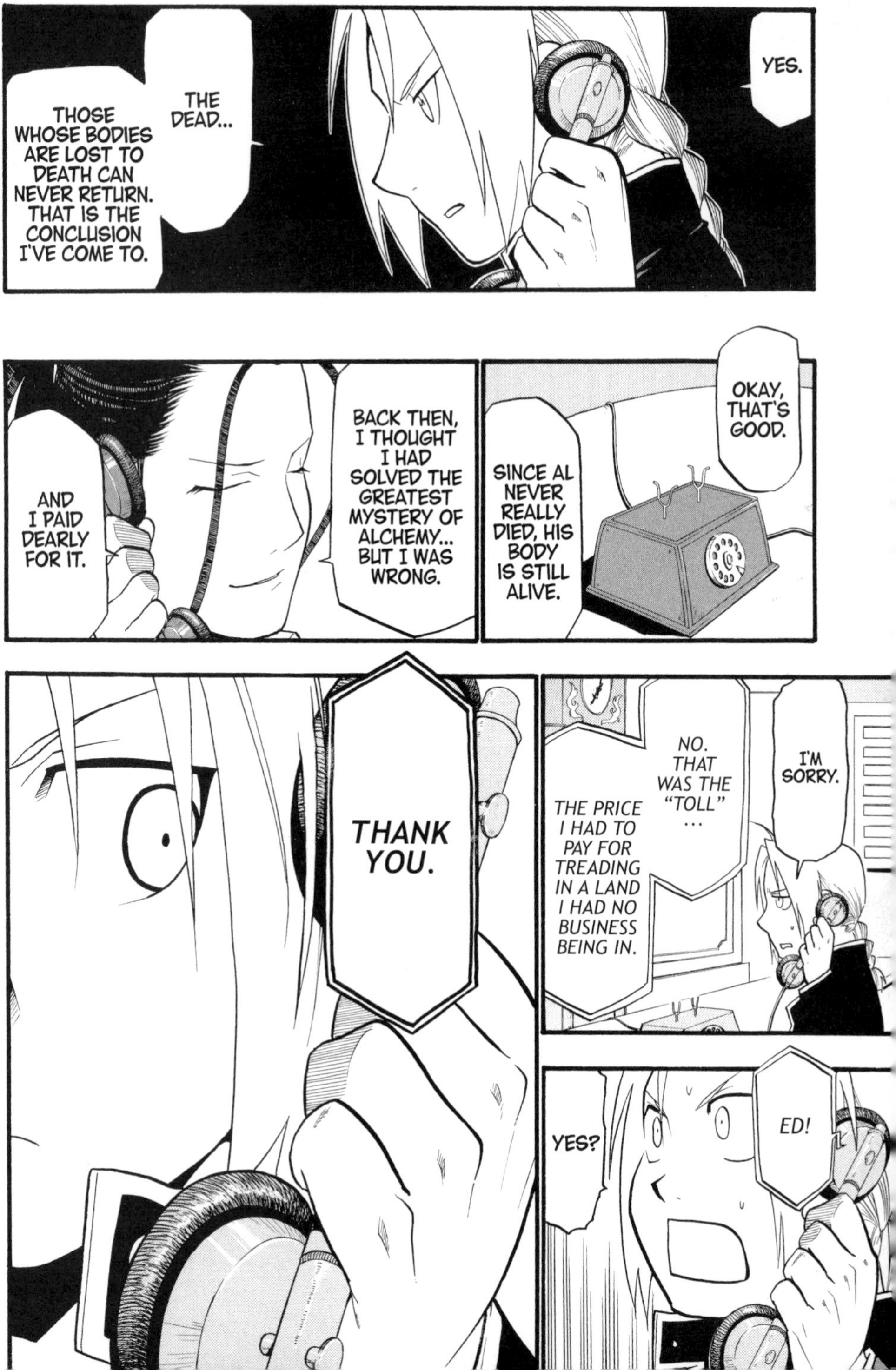
YES.
THE DEAD...
THOSE WHOSE BODIES ARE LOST TO DEATH CAN NEVER RETURN. THAT IS THE CONCLUSION I'VE COME TO.
OKAY, THAT'S GOOD.
SINCE AL NEVER REALLY DIED, HIS BODY IS STILL ALIVE.
BACK THEN, I THOUGHT I HAD SOLVED THE GREATEST MYSTERY OF ALCHEMY... BUT I WAS WRONG.
AND I PAID DEARLY FOR IT.
I'M SORRY.
NO. THAT WAS THE "TOLL"...
THE PRICE I HAD TO PAY FOR TREADING IN A LAND I HAD NO BUSINESS BEING IN.
ED!
YES?
THANK YOU.

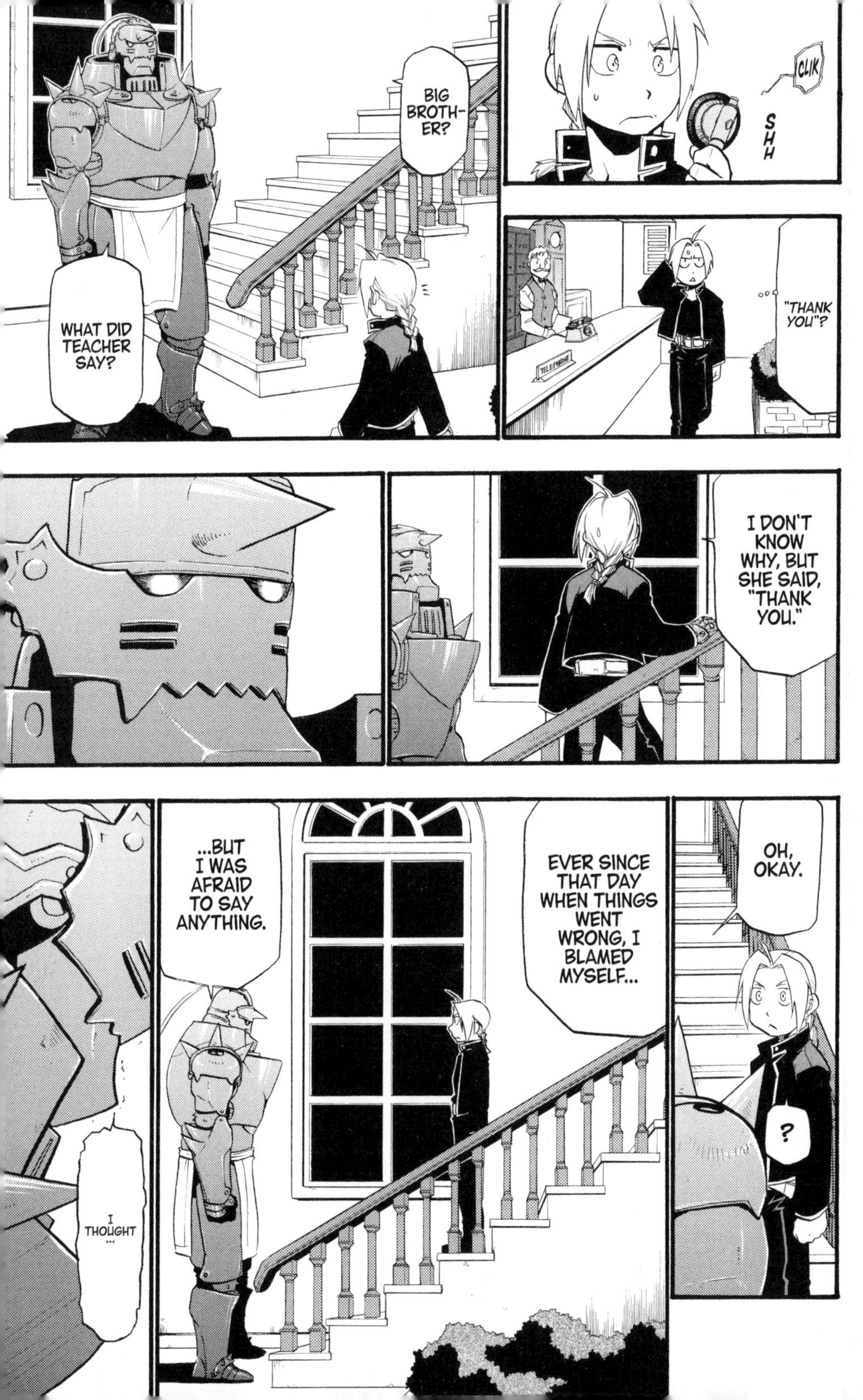
CLIK
SHH
"THANK YOU"?
BIG BROTHER?
WHAT DID TEACHER SAY?
I DON'T KNOW WHY, BUT SHE SAID, "THANK YOU."
OH, OKAY.
?
EVER SINCE THAT DAY WHEN THINGS WENT WRONG, I BLAMED MYSELF...
...BUT I WAS AFRAID TO SAY ANYTHING.
I THOUGHT...

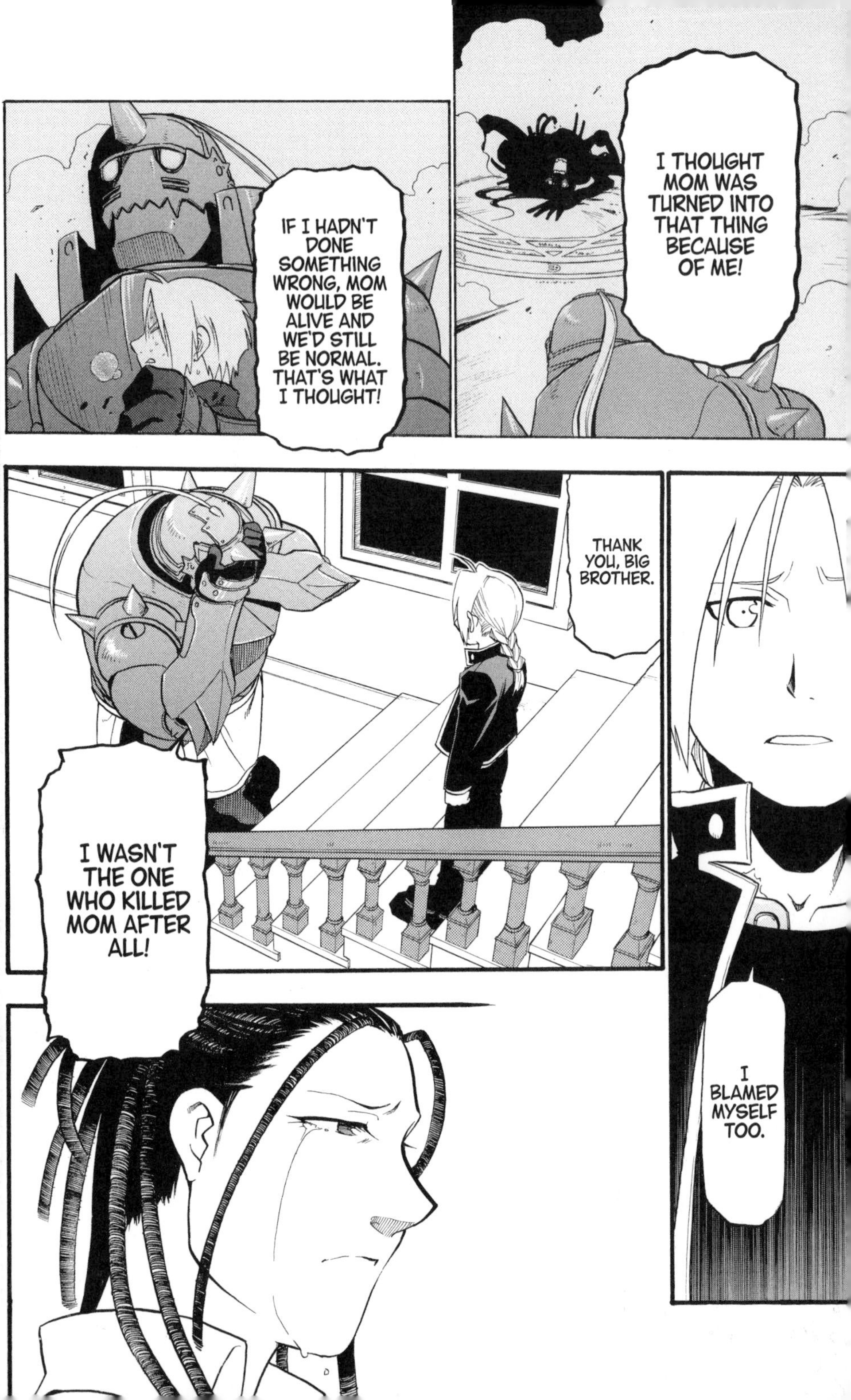
I THOUGHT MOM WAS TURNED INTO THAT THING BECAUSE OF ME!
IF I HADN'T DONE SOMETHING WRONG, MOM WOULD BE ALIVE AND WE'D STILL BE NORMAL. THAT'S WHAT I THOUGHT!
THANK YOU, BIG BROTHER.
I WASN'T THE ONE WHO KILLED MOM AFTER ALL!
I BLAMED MYSELF TOO.

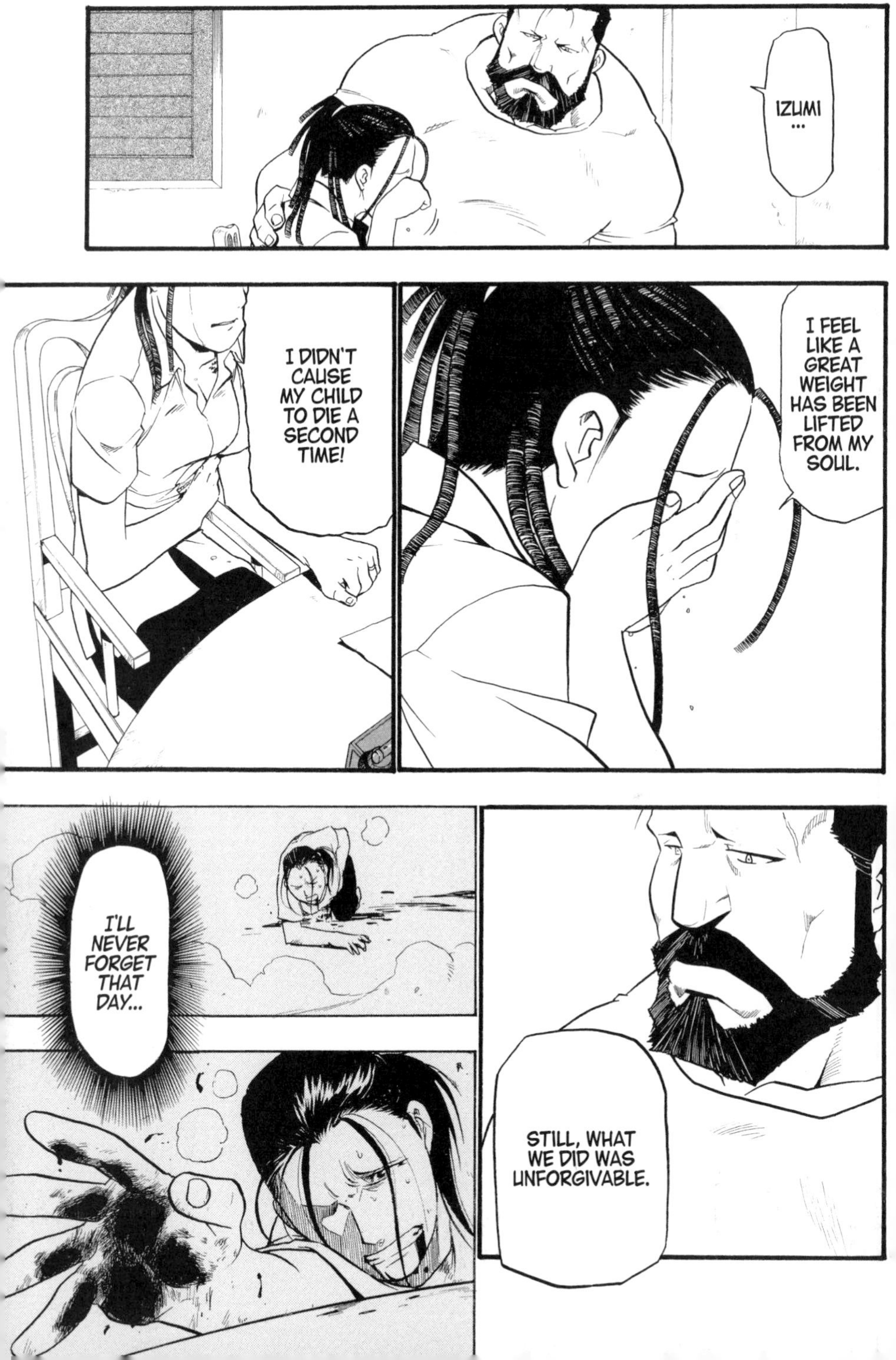
IZUMI ...
I FEEL LIKE A GREAT WEIGHT HAS BEEN LIFTED FROM MY SOUL.
I DIDN'T CAUSE MY CHILD TO DIE A SECOND TIME!
STILL, WHAT WE DID WAS UNFORGIVABLE.
I'LL NEVER FORGET THAT DAY...

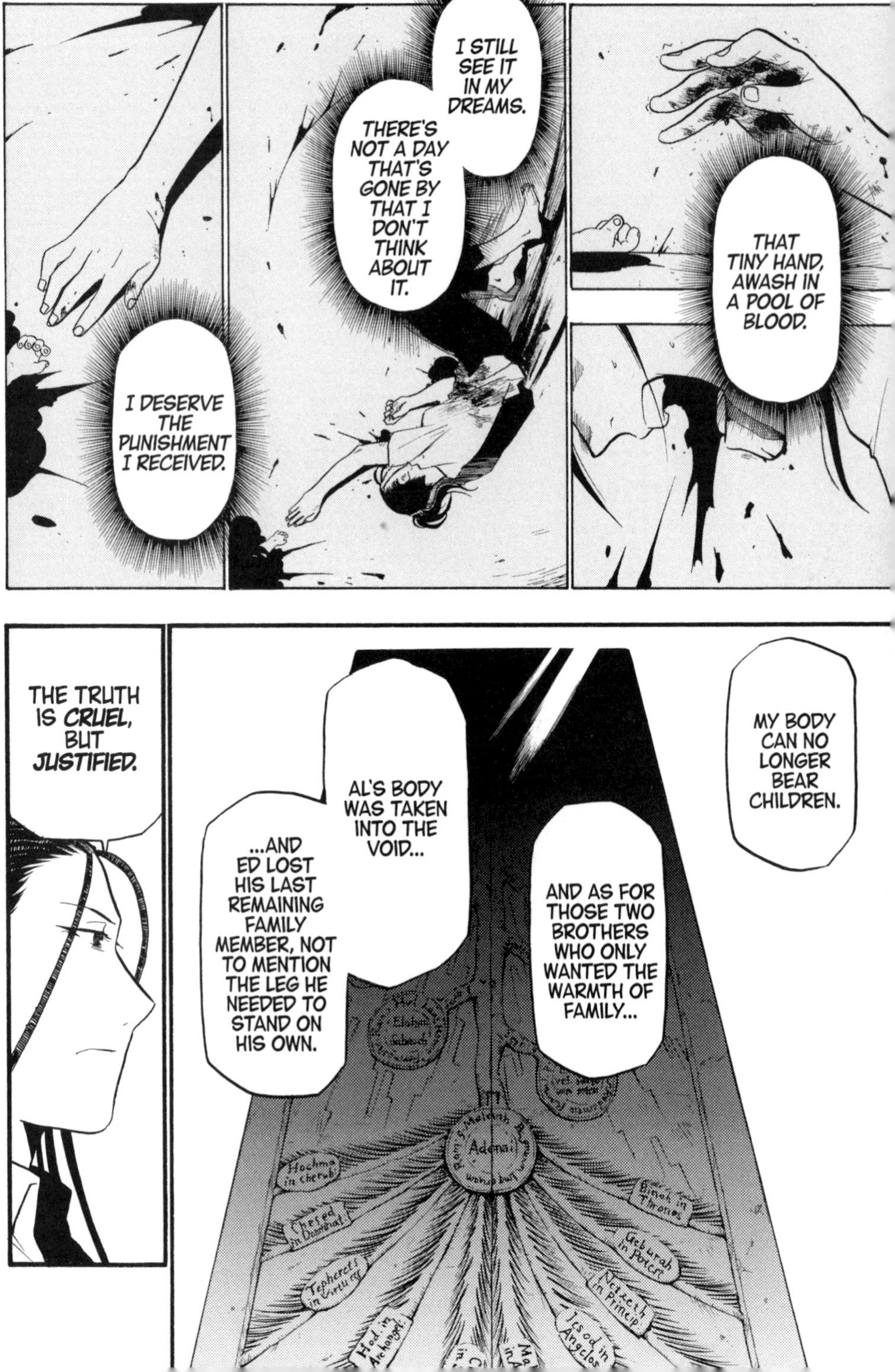
THAT TINY HAND, AWASH IN A POOL OF BLOOD.
I STILL SEE IT IN MY DREAMS.
THERE'S NOT A DAY THAT'S GONE BY THAT I DON'T THINK ABOUT IT.
I DESERVE THE PUNISHMENT I RECEIVED.
MY BODY CAN NO LONGER BEAR CHILDREN.
AND AS FOR THOSE TWO BROTHERS WHO ONLY WANTED THE WARMTH OF FAMILY...
AL'S BODY WAS TAKEN INTO THE VOID...
...AND ED LOST HIS LAST REMAINING FAMILY MEMBER, NOT TO MENTION THE LEG HE NEEDED TO STAND ON HIS OWN.
THE TRUTH IS **CRUEL**, BUT **JUSTIFIED**.

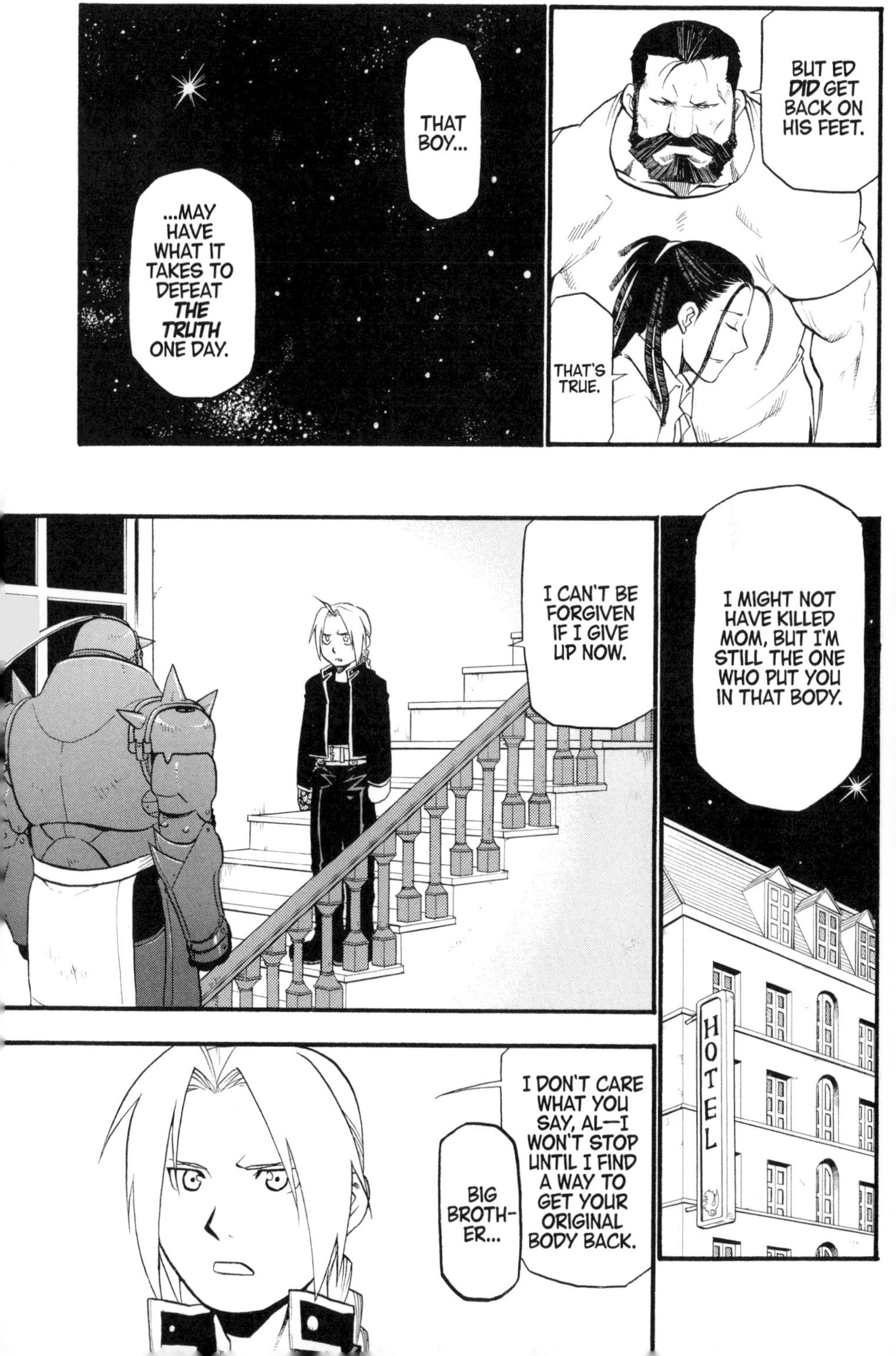
BUT ED DID GET BACK ON HIS FEET.
THAT'S TRUE.
THAT BOY...
...MAY HAVE WHAT IT TAKES TO DEFEAT THE TRUTH ONE DAY.
I MIGHT NOT HAVE KILLED MOM, BUT I'M STILL THE ONE WHO PUT YOU IN THAT BODY.
HOTEL
I CAN'T BE FORGIVEN IF I GIVE UP NOW.
I DON'T CARE WHAT YOU SAY, AL—I WON'T STOP UNTIL I FIND A WAY TO GET YOUR ORIGINAL BODY BACK.
BIG BROTH-ER...

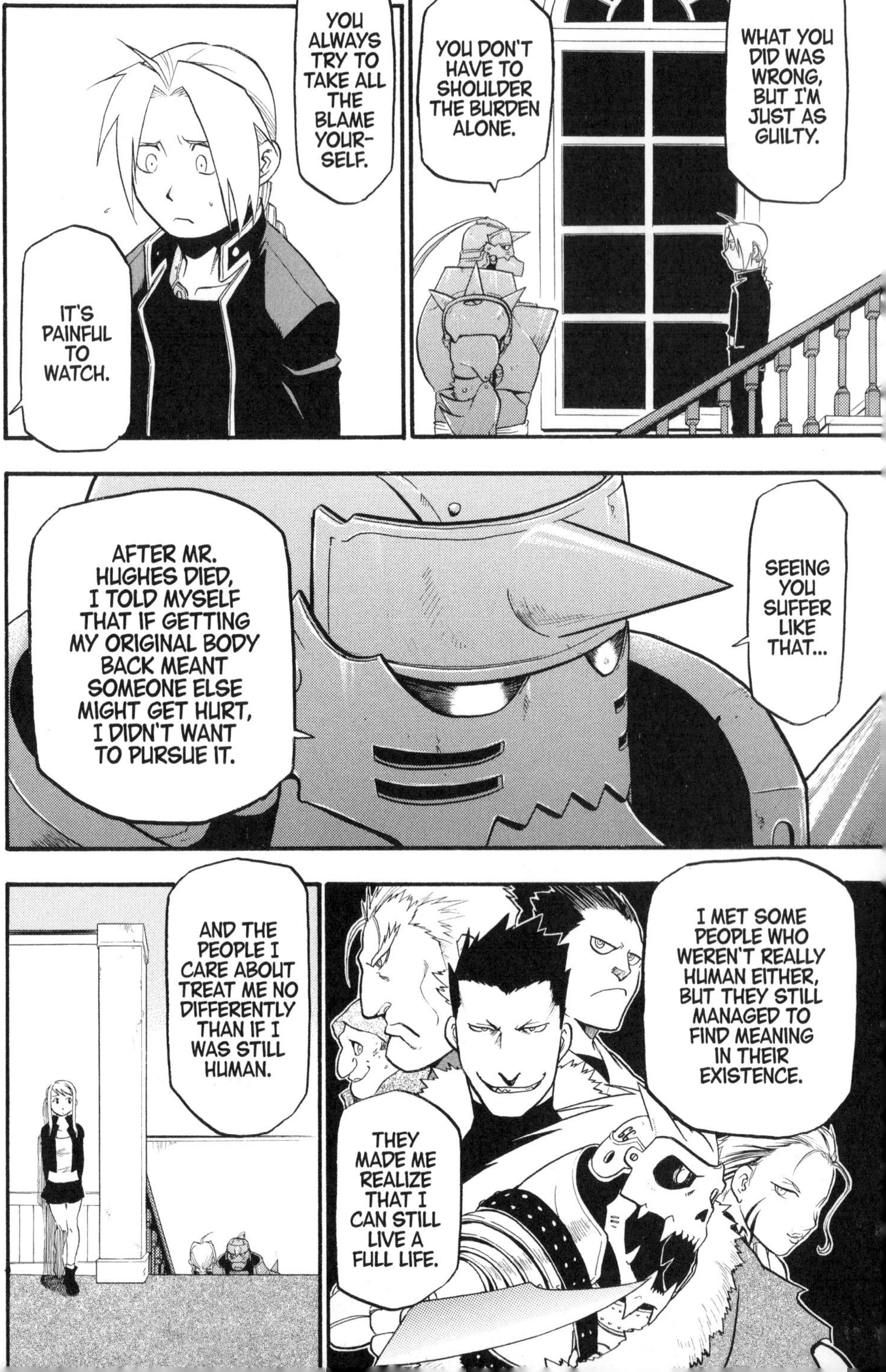
WHAT YOU DID WAS WRONG, BUT I'M JUST AS GUILTY.
YOU DON'T HAVE TO SHOULDER THE BURDEN ALONE.
YOU ALWAYS TRY TO TAKE ALL THE BLAME YOUR-SELF.
IT'S PAINFUL TO WATCH.
SEEING YOU SUFFER LIKE THAT...
AFTER MR. HUGHES DIED, I TOLD MYSELF THAT IF GETTING MY ORIGINAL BODY BACK MEANT SOMEONE ELSE MIGHT GET HURT, I DIDN'T WANT TO PURSUE IT.
I MET SOME PEOPLE WHO WEREN'T REALLY HUMAN EITHER, BUT THEY STILL MANAGED TO FIND MEANING IN THEIR EXISTENCE.
THEY MADE ME REALIZE THAT I CAN STILL LIVE A FULL LIFE.
AND THE PEOPLE I CARE ABOUT TREAT ME NO DIFFERENTLY THAN IF I WAS STILL HUMAN.

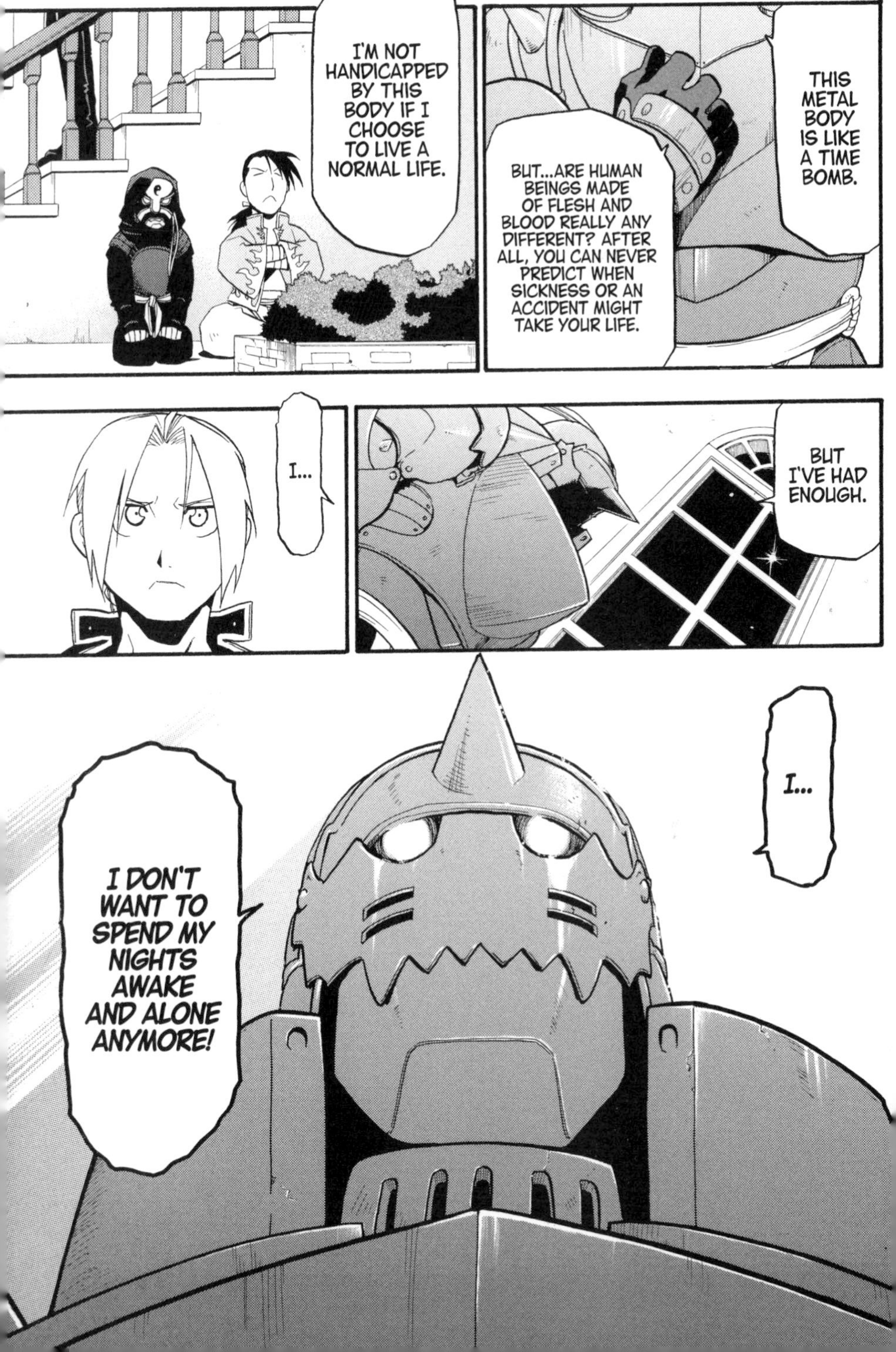
THIS METAL BODY IS LIKE A TIME BOMB.
BUT...ARE HUMAN BEINGS MADE OF FLESH AND BLOOD REALLY ANY DIFFERENT? AFTER ALL, YOU CAN NEVER PREDICT WHEN SICKNESS OR AN ACCIDENT MIGHT TAKE YOUR LIFE.
I'M NOT HANDICAPPED BY THIS BODY IF I CHOOSE TO LIVE A NORMAL LIFE.
BUT I'VE HAD ENOUGH.
I...
I...
I DON'T WANT TO SPEND MY NIGHTS AWAKE AND ALONE ANYMORE!

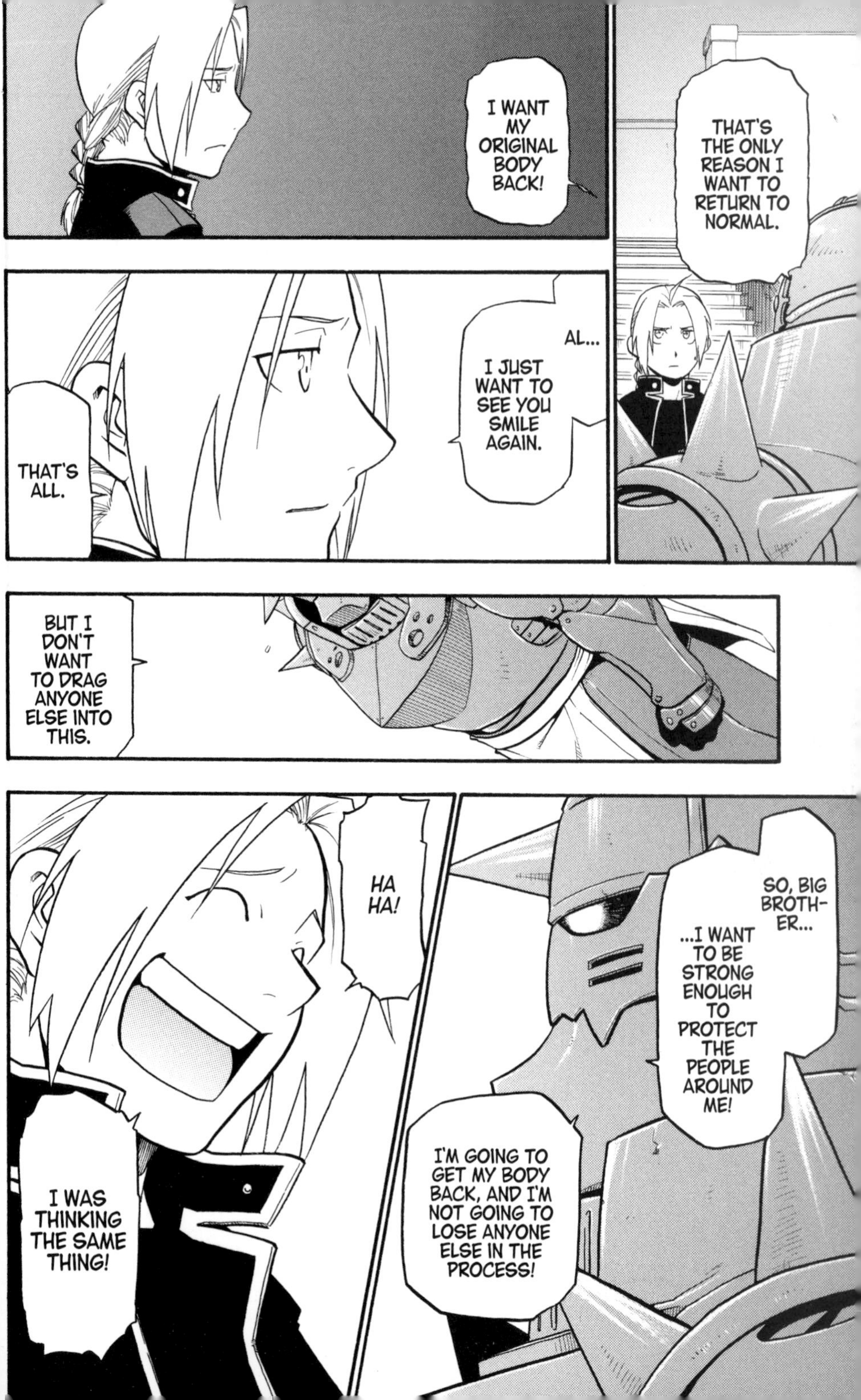
THAT'S THE ONLY REASON I WANT TO RETURN TO NORMAL.
I WANT MY ORIGINAL BODY BACK!
AL...
I JUST WANT TO SEE YOU SMILE AGAIN.
THAT'S ALL.
BUT I DON'T WANT TO DRAG ANYONE ELSE INTO THIS.
SO, BIG BROTH-ER...
...I WANT TO BE STRONG ENOUGH TO PROTECT THE PEOPLE AROUND ME!
I'M GOING TO GET MY BODY BACK, AND I'M NOT GOING TO LOSE ANYONE ELSE IN THE PROCESS!
HA HA!
I WAS THINKING THE SAME THING!

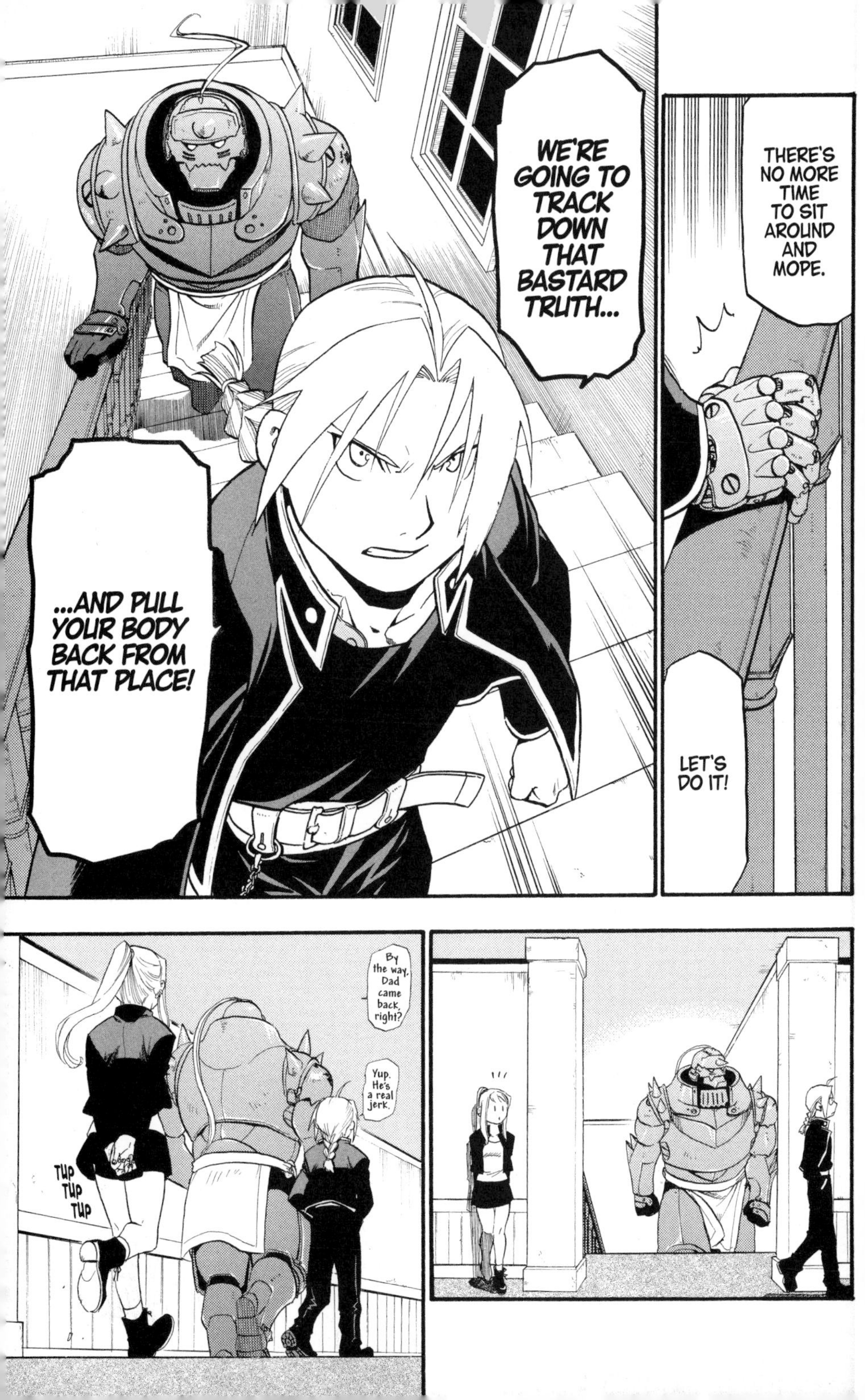
THERE'S NO MORE TIME TO SIT AROUND AND MOPE.
LET'S DO IT!
WE'RE GOING TO TRACK DOWN THAT BASTARD TRUTH...
...AND PULL YOUR BODY BACK FROM THAT PLACE!
By the way, Dad came back, right?
Yup. He's a real jerk.
TUP TUP TUP

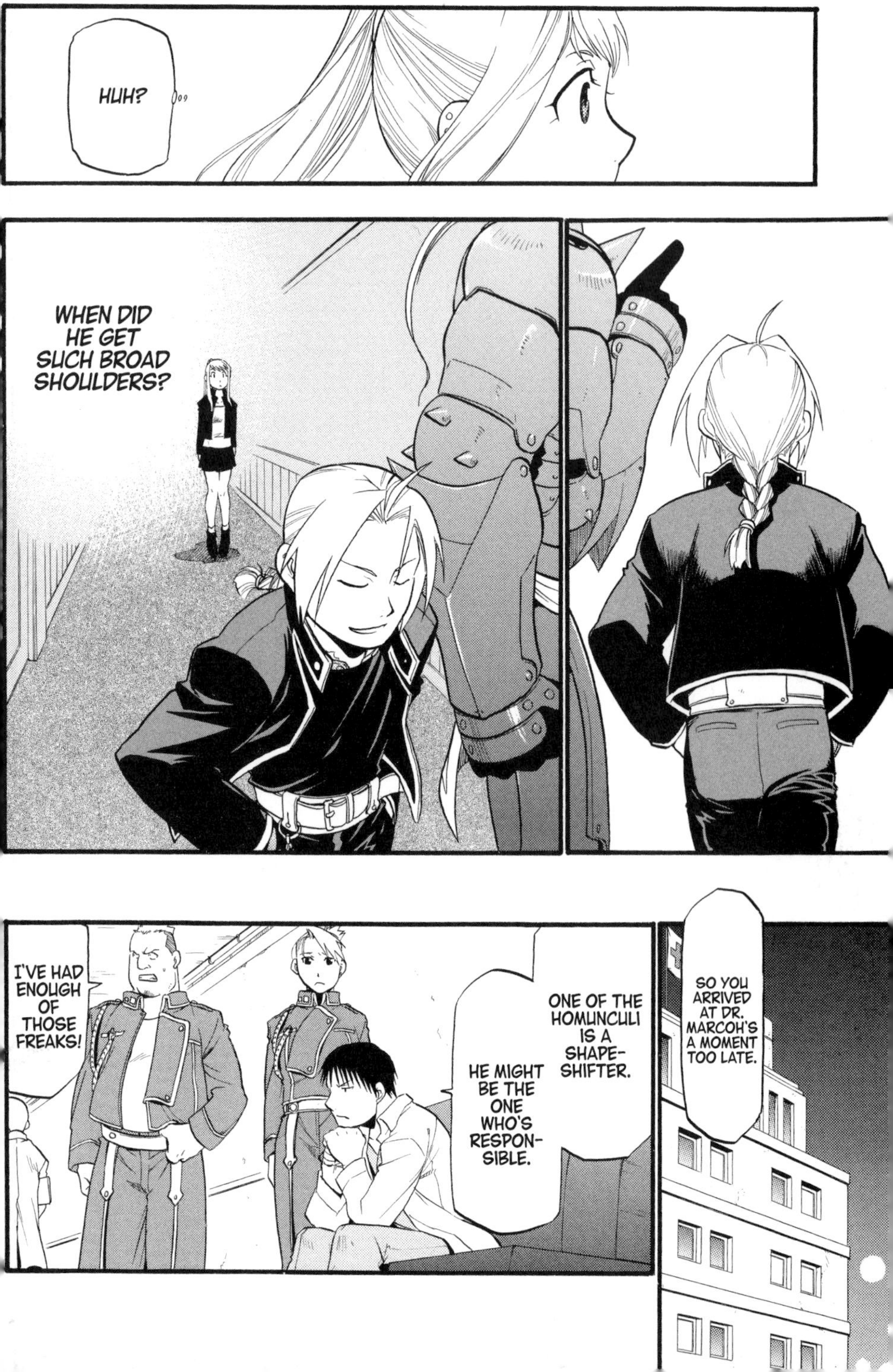
HUH?
WHEN DID HE GET SUCH BROAD SHOULDERS?
SO YOU ARRIVED AT DR. MARCOH'S A MOMENT TOO LATE.
ONE OF THE HOMUNCULI IS A SHAPE-SHIFTER.
HE MIGHT BE THE ONE WHO'S RESPON-SIBLE.
I'VE HAD ENOUGH OF THOSE FREAKS!

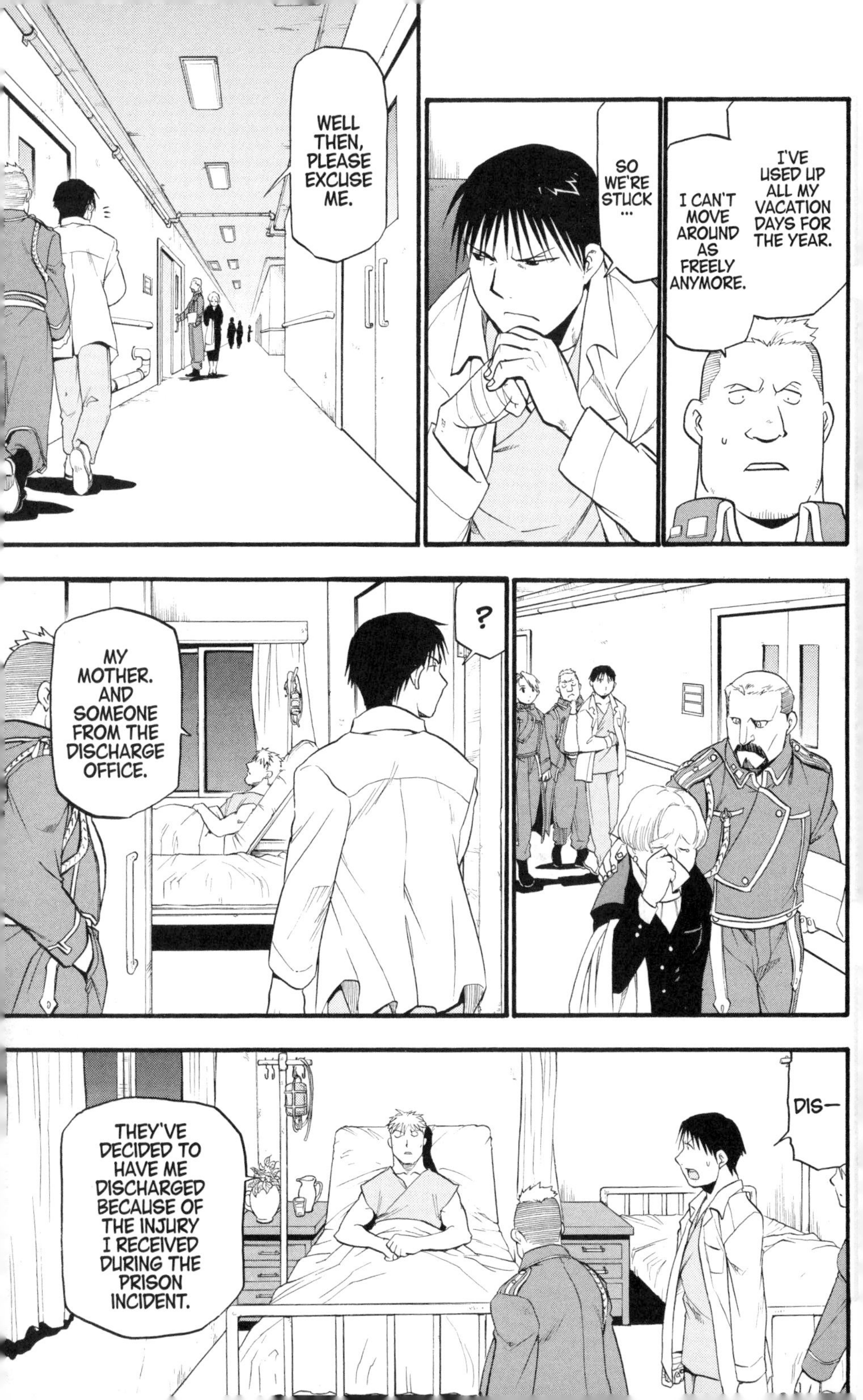
I'VE USED UP ALL MY VACATION DAYS FOR THE YEAR.
I CAN'T MOVE AROUND AS FREELY ANYMORE.
SO WE'RE STUCK ...
WELL THEN, PLEASE EXCUSE ME.
?
MY MOTHER. AND SOMEONE FROM THE DISCHARGE OFFICE.
DIS—
THEY'VE DECIDED TO HAVE ME DISCHARGED BECAUSE OF THE INJURY I RECEIVED DURING THE PRISON INCIDENT.

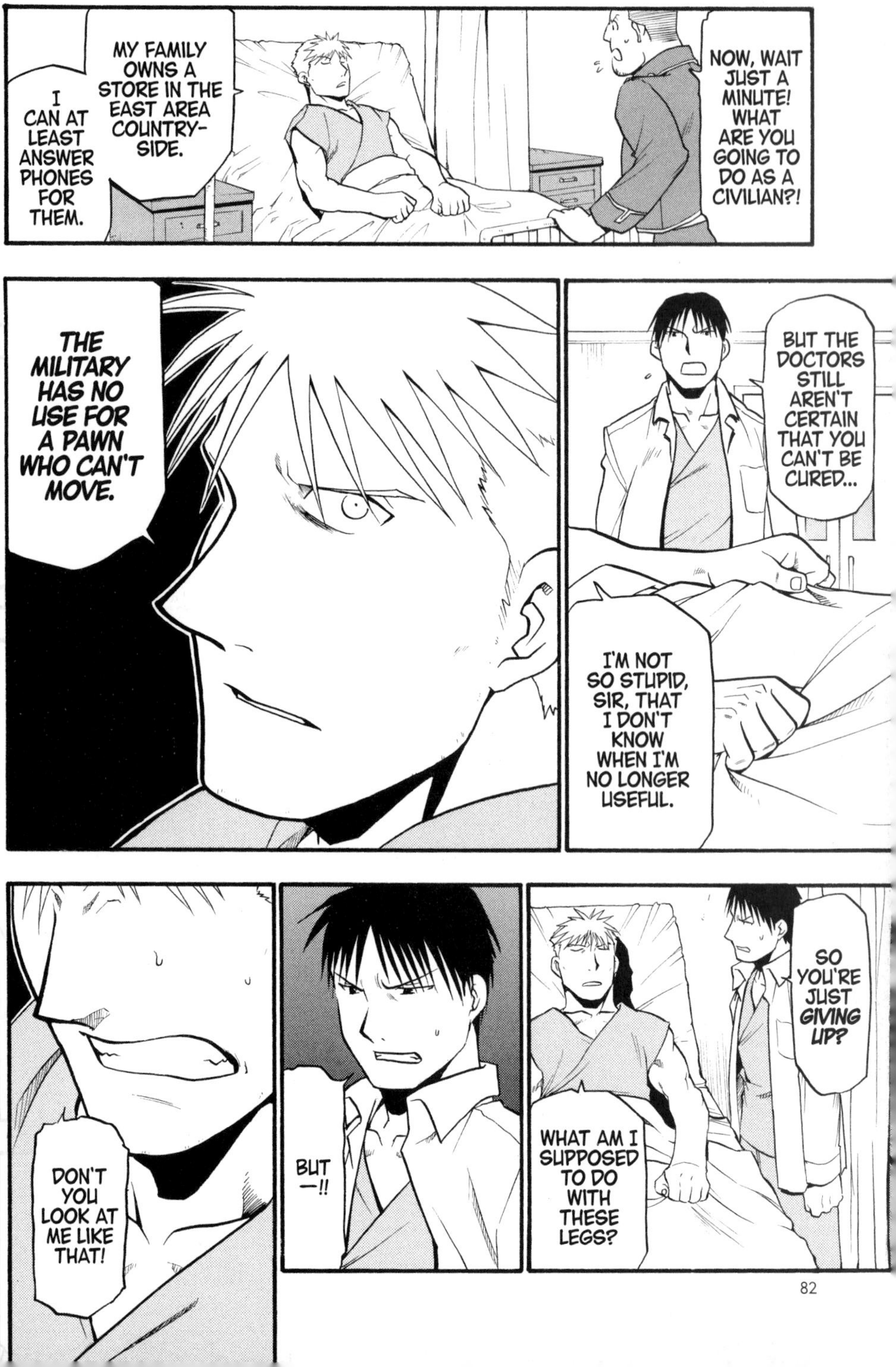
NOW, WAIT JUST A MINUTE! WHAT ARE YOU GOING TO DO AS A CIVILIAN?!
MY FAMILY OWNS A STORE IN THE EAST AREA COUNTRY-SIDE.
I CAN AT LEAST ANSWER PHONES FOR THEM.
BUT THE DOCTORS STILL AREN'T CERTAIN THAT YOU CAN'T BE CURED...
I'M NOT SO STUPID, SIR, THAT I DON'T KNOW WHEN I'M NO LONGER USEFUL.
THE MILITARY HAS NO USE FOR A PAWN WHO CAN'T MOVE.
SO YOU'RE JUST *GIVING UP?*
WHAT AM I SUPPOSED TO DO WITH THESE LEGS?
BUT —!!
DON'T YOU LOOK AT ME LIKE THAT!

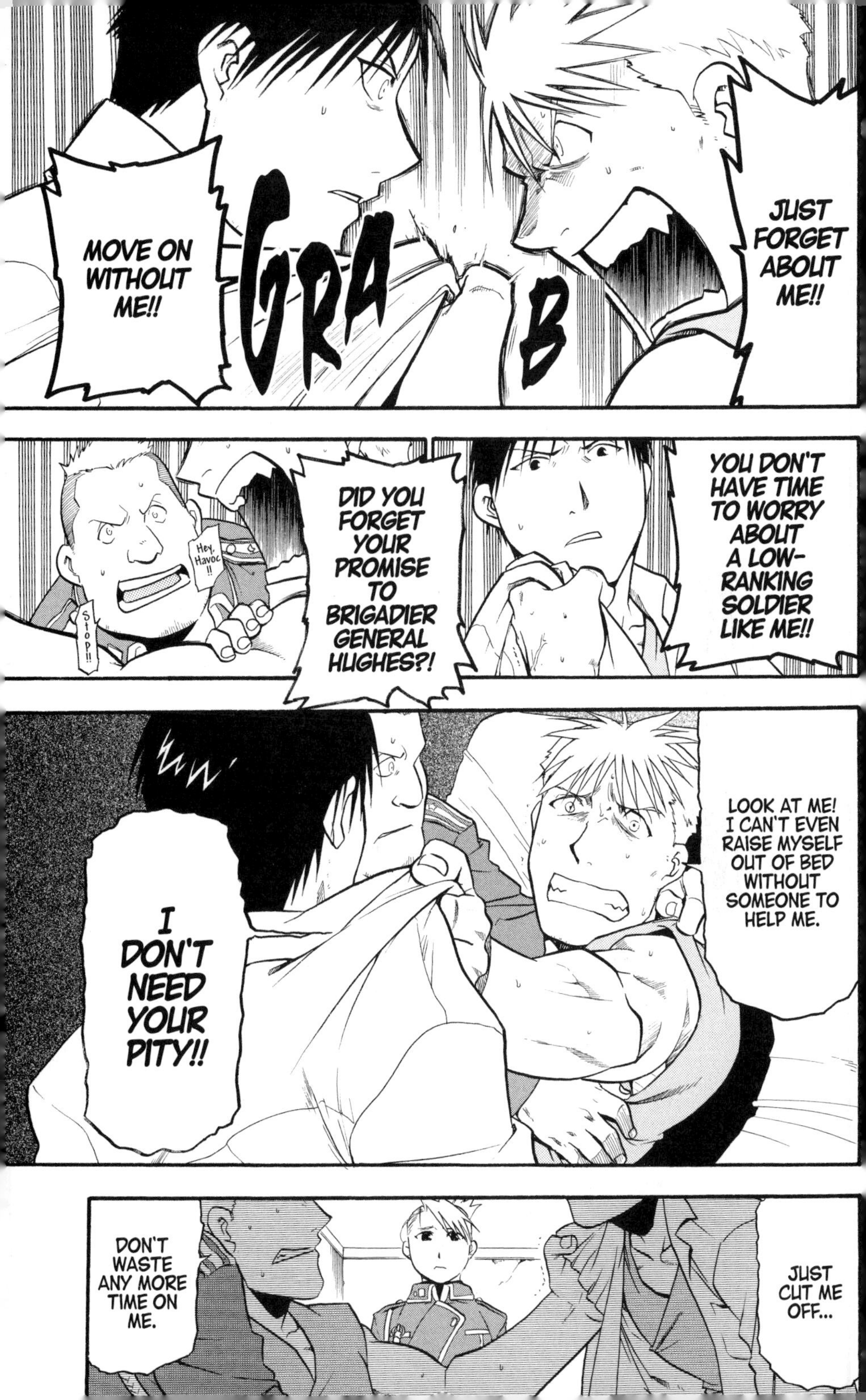
JUST FORGET ABOUT ME!!
GRAB
MOVE ON WITHOUT ME!!
YOU DON'T HAVE TIME TO WORRY ABOUT A LOW-RANKING SOLDIER LIKE ME!!
DID YOU FORGET YOUR PROMISE TO BRIGADIER GENERAL HUGHES?!
Hey, Havoc!!
Stop!!
LOOK AT ME! I CAN'T EVEN RAISE MYSELF OUT OF BED WITHOUT SOMEONE TO HELP ME.
I DON'T NEED YOUR PITY!!
JUST CUT ME OFF...
DON'T WASTE ANY MORE TIME ON ME.

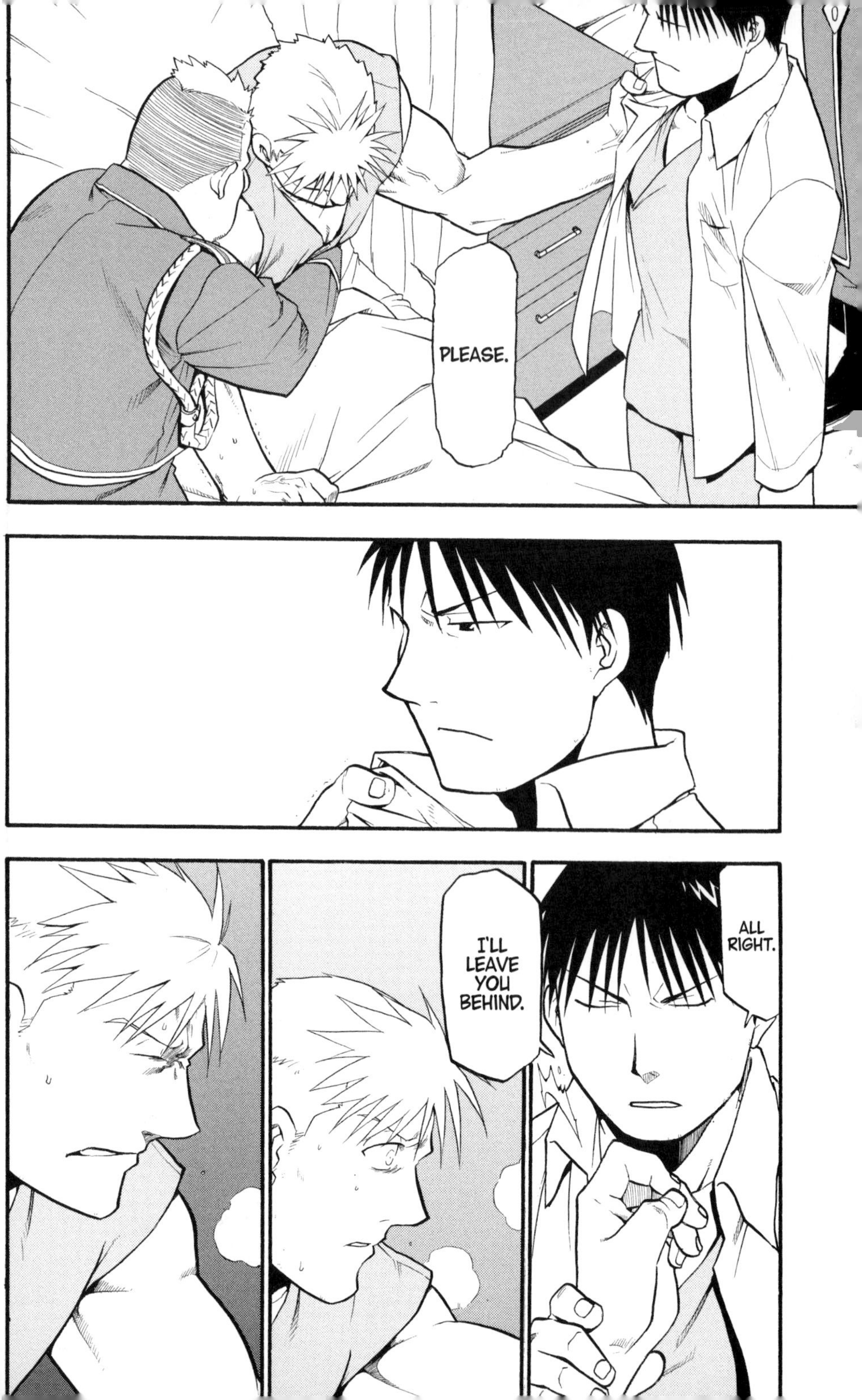
PLEASE.
ALL RIGHT.
I'LL LEAVE YOU BEHIND.

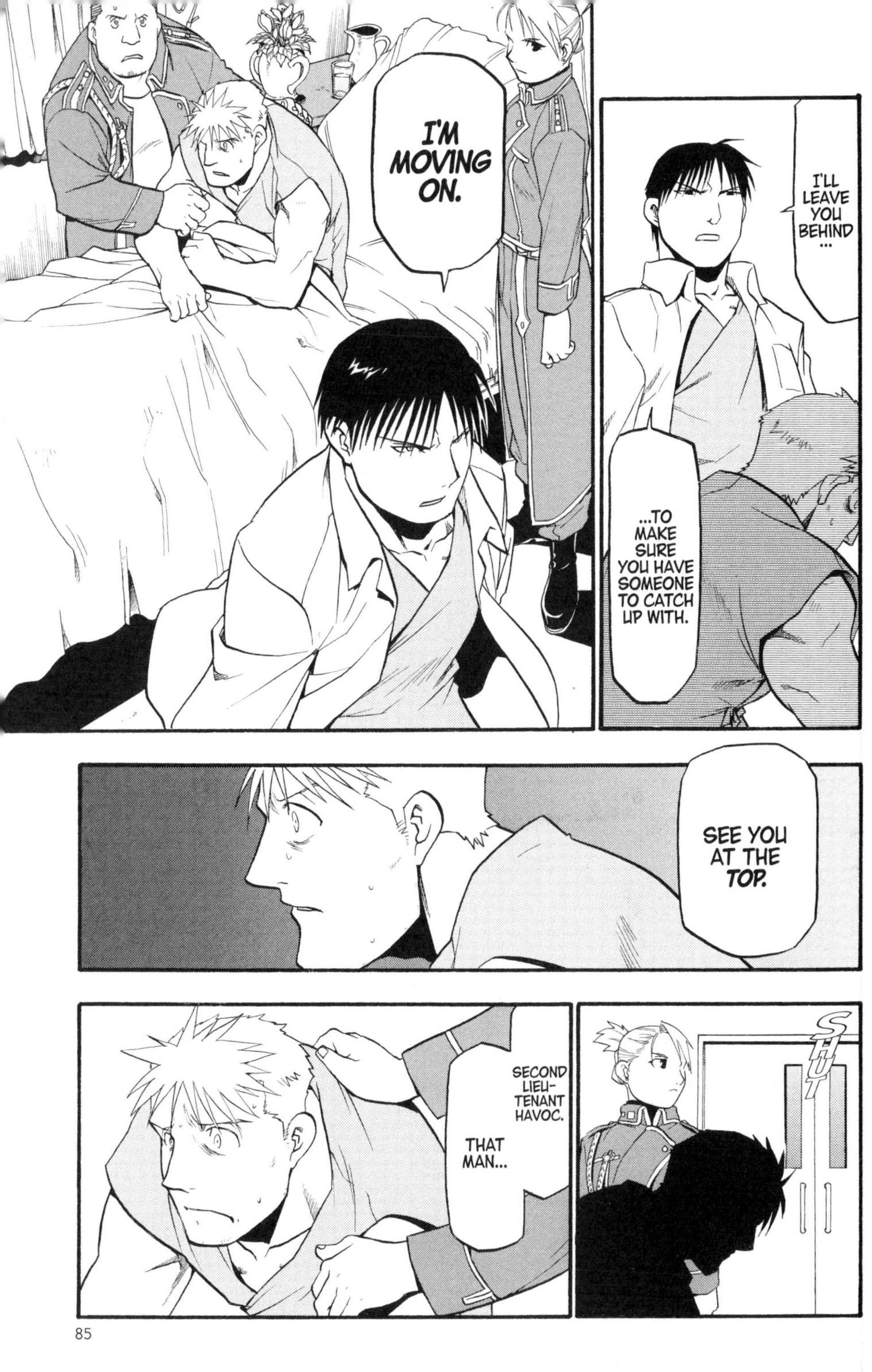
I'LL LEAVE YOU BEHIND ...
...TO MAKE SURE YOU HAVE SOMEONE TO CATCH UP WITH.
I'M MOVING ON.
SEE YOU AT THE *TOP.*
SHUT
SECOND LIEU-TENANT HAVOC.
THAT MAN...

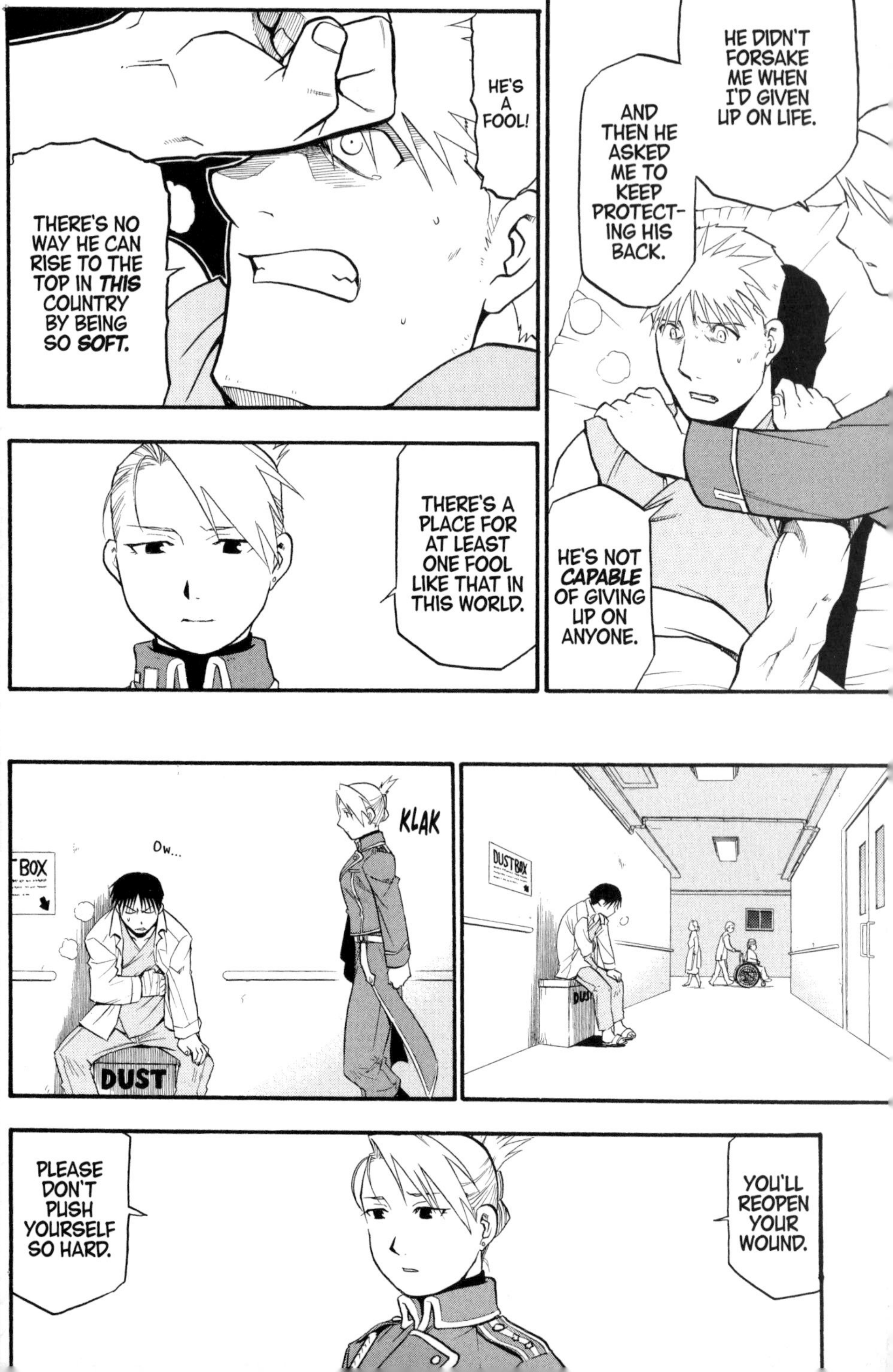
HE DIDN'T FORSAKE ME WHEN I'D GIVEN UP ON LIFE.
AND THEN HE ASKED ME TO KEEP PROTECTING HIS BACK.
HE'S NOT *CAPABLE* OF GIVING UP ON ANYONE.
HE'S A FOOL!
THERE'S NO WAY HE CAN RISE TO THE TOP IN *THIS* COUNTRY BY BEING SO *SOFT.*
THERE'S A PLACE FOR AT LEAST ONE FOOL LIKE THAT IN THIS WORLD.
DUSTBOX
KLAK
Ow...
BOX
DUST
YOU'LL REOPEN YOUR WOUND.
PLEASE DON'T PUSH YOURSELF SO HARD.

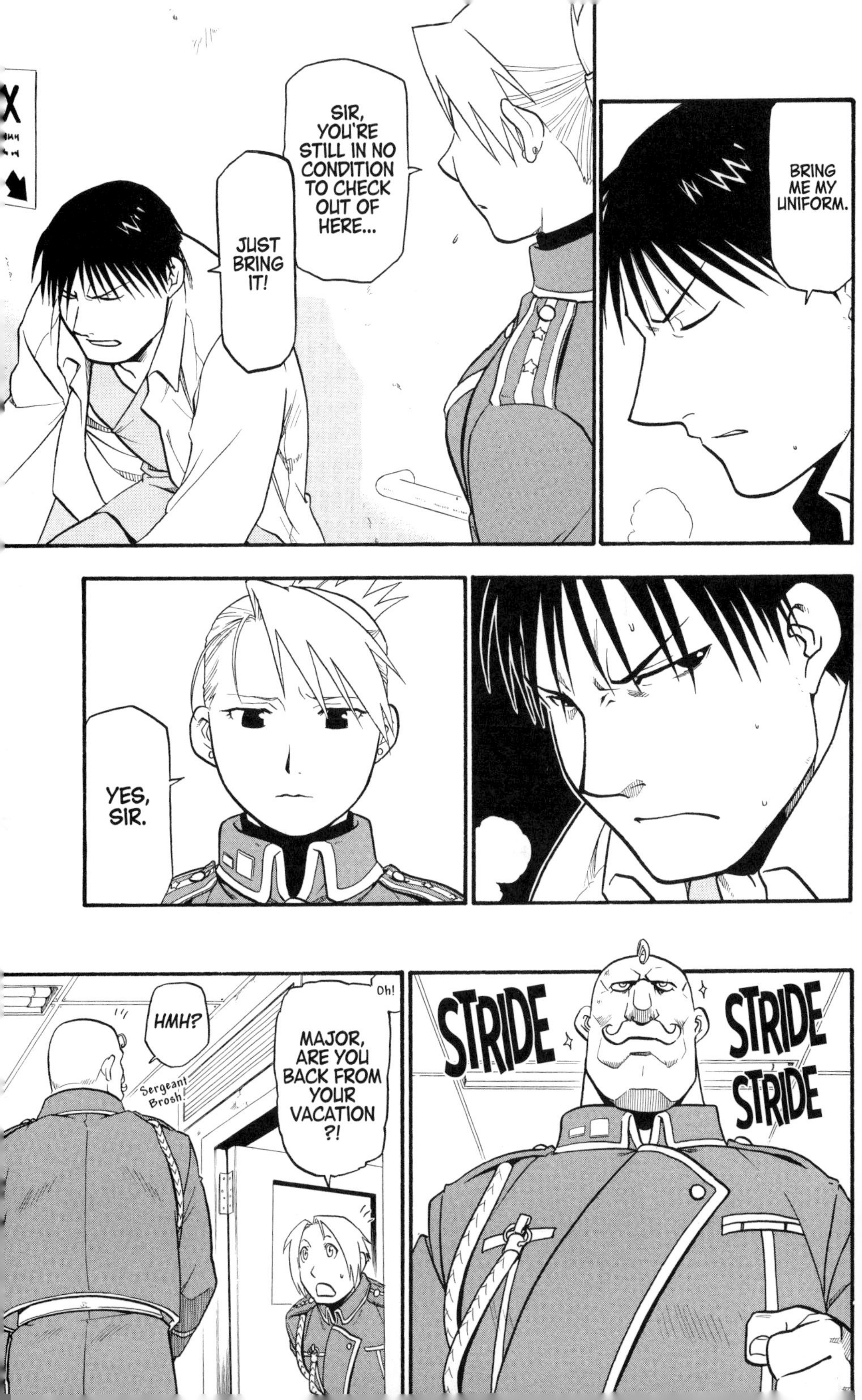
BRING ME MY UNIFORM.
SIR, YOU'RE STILL IN NO CONDITION TO CHECK OUT OF HERE...
JUST BRING IT!
YES, SIR.
STRIDE
STRIDE
STRIDE
Oh!
MAJOR, ARE YOU BACK FROM YOUR VACATION?!
HMH?
Sergeant Brosh!

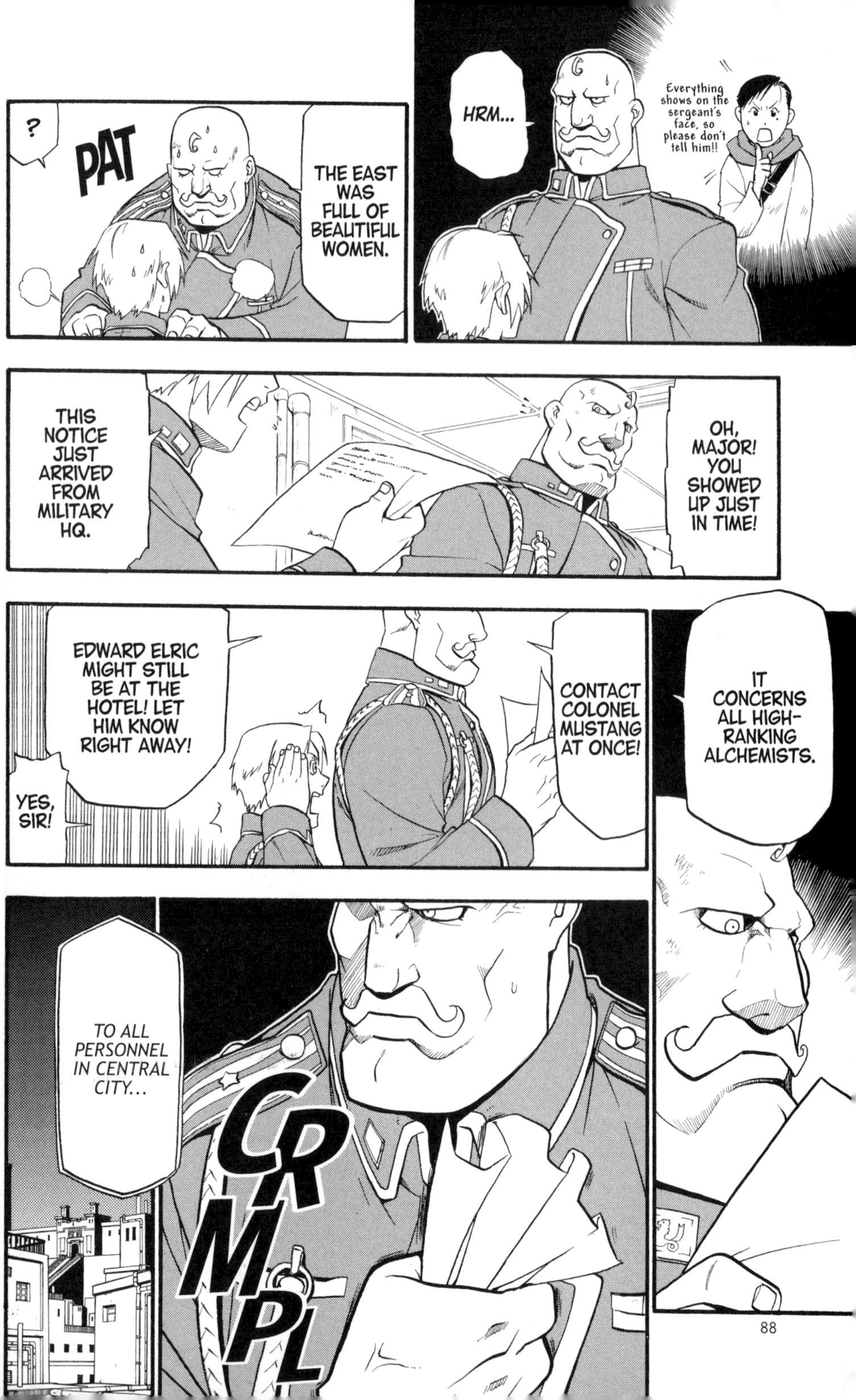
Everything shows on the sergeant's face, so please don't tell him!!
HRM...
THE EAST WAS FULL OF BEAUTIFUL WOMEN.
PAT
?
OH, MAJOR! YOU SHOWED UP JUST IN TIME!
THIS NOTICE JUST ARRIVED FROM MILITARY HQ.
IT CONCERNS ALL HIGH-RANKING ALCHEMISTS.
CONTACT COLONEL MUSTANG AT ONCE!
EDWARD ELRIC MIGHT STILL BE AT THE HOTEL! LET HIM KNOW RIGHT AWAY!
YES, SIR!
TO ALL PERSONNEL IN CENTRAL CITY...
CRMPL

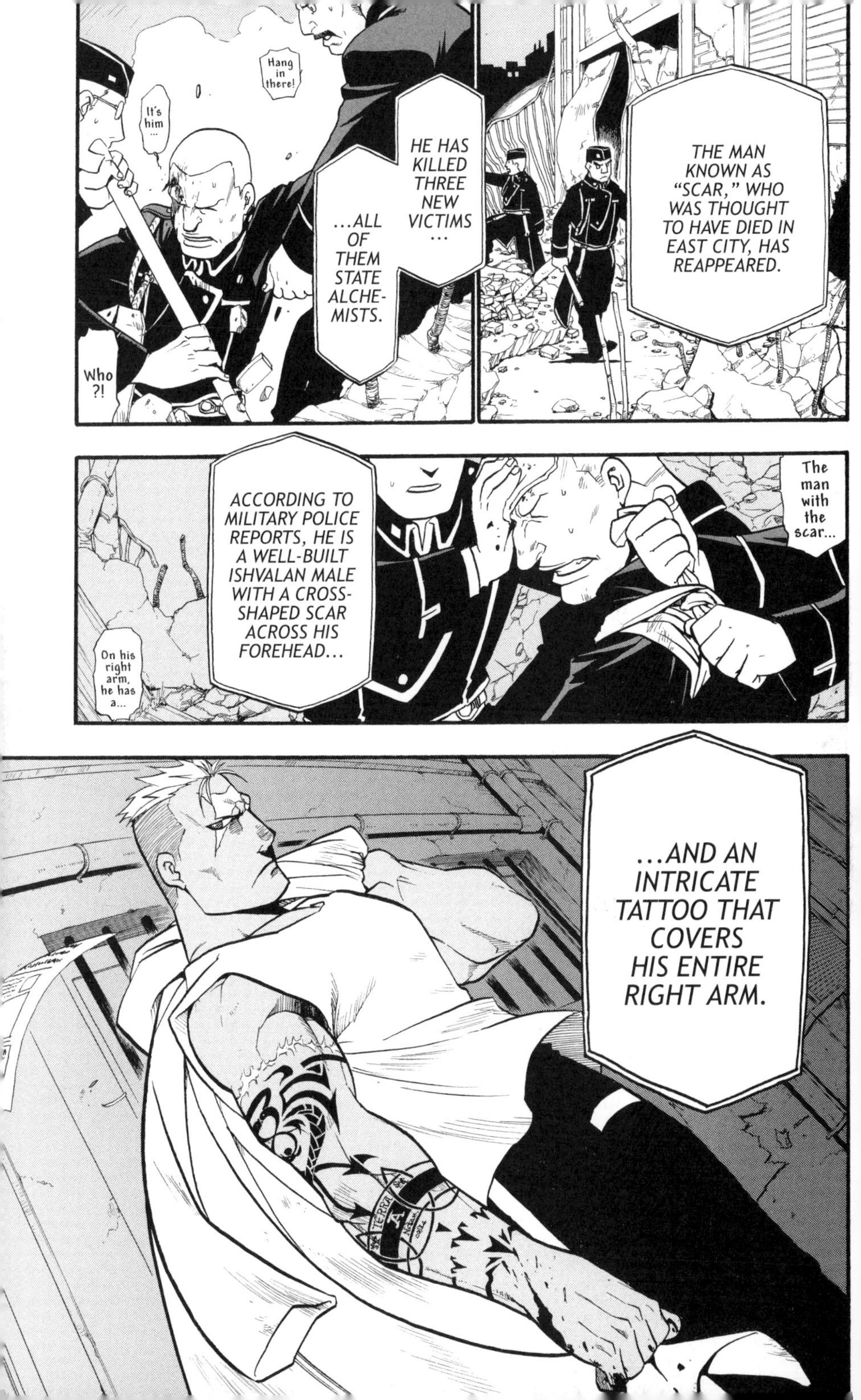
THE MAN KNOWN AS "SCAR," WHO WAS THOUGHT TO HAVE DIED IN EAST CITY, HAS REAPPEARED.
HE HAS KILLED THREE NEW VICTIMS…
…ALL OF THEM STATE ALCHEMISTS.
Hang in there!
It's him…
Who?!
The man with the scar…
ACCORDING TO MILITARY POLICE REPORTS, HE IS A WELL-BUILT ISHVALAN MALE WITH A CROSS-SHAPED SCAR ACROSS HIS FOREHEAD…
On his right arm, he has a…
…AND AN INTRICATE TATTOO THAT COVERS HIS ENTIRE RIGHT ARM.

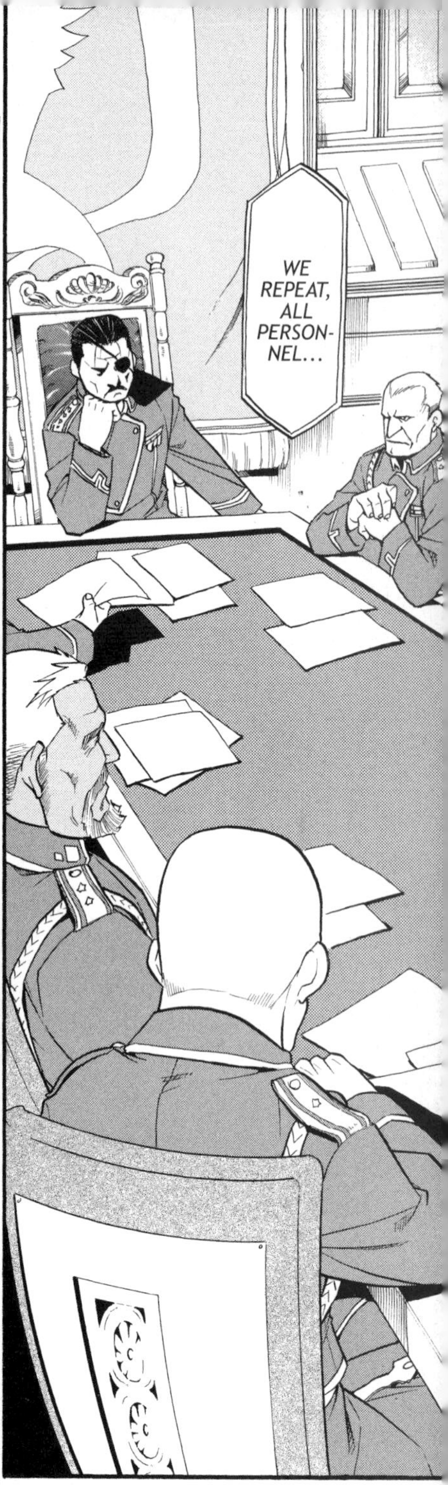
WE REPEAT, ALL PERSON-NEL...
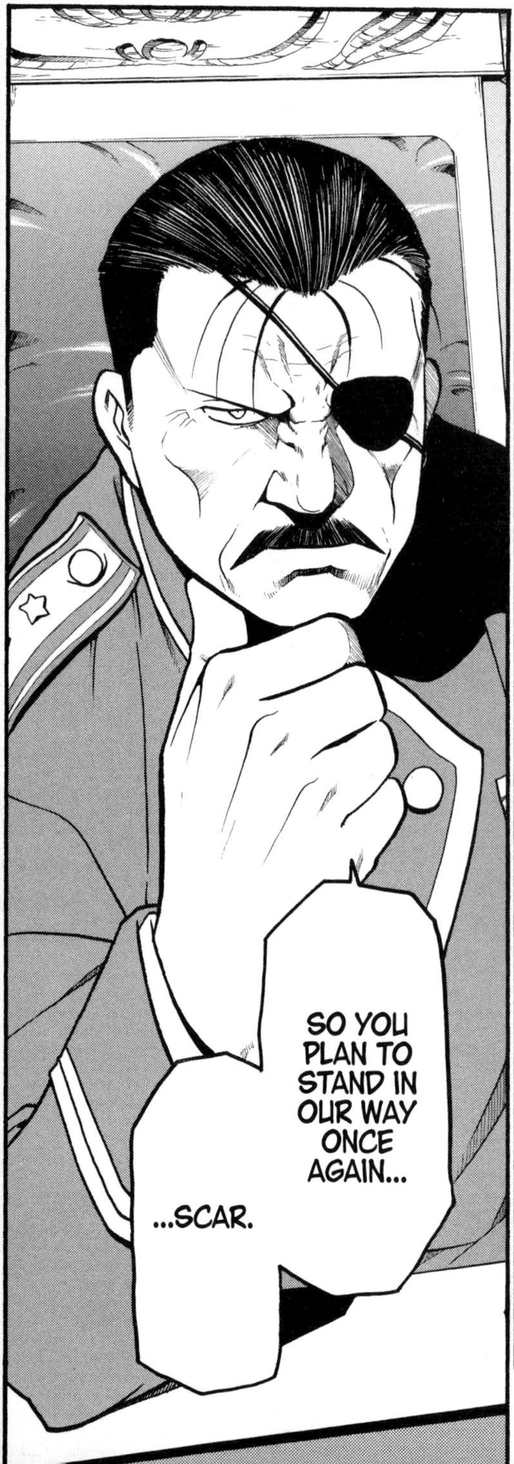
SO YOU PLAN TO STAND IN OUR WAY ONCE AGAIN...
...SCAR.

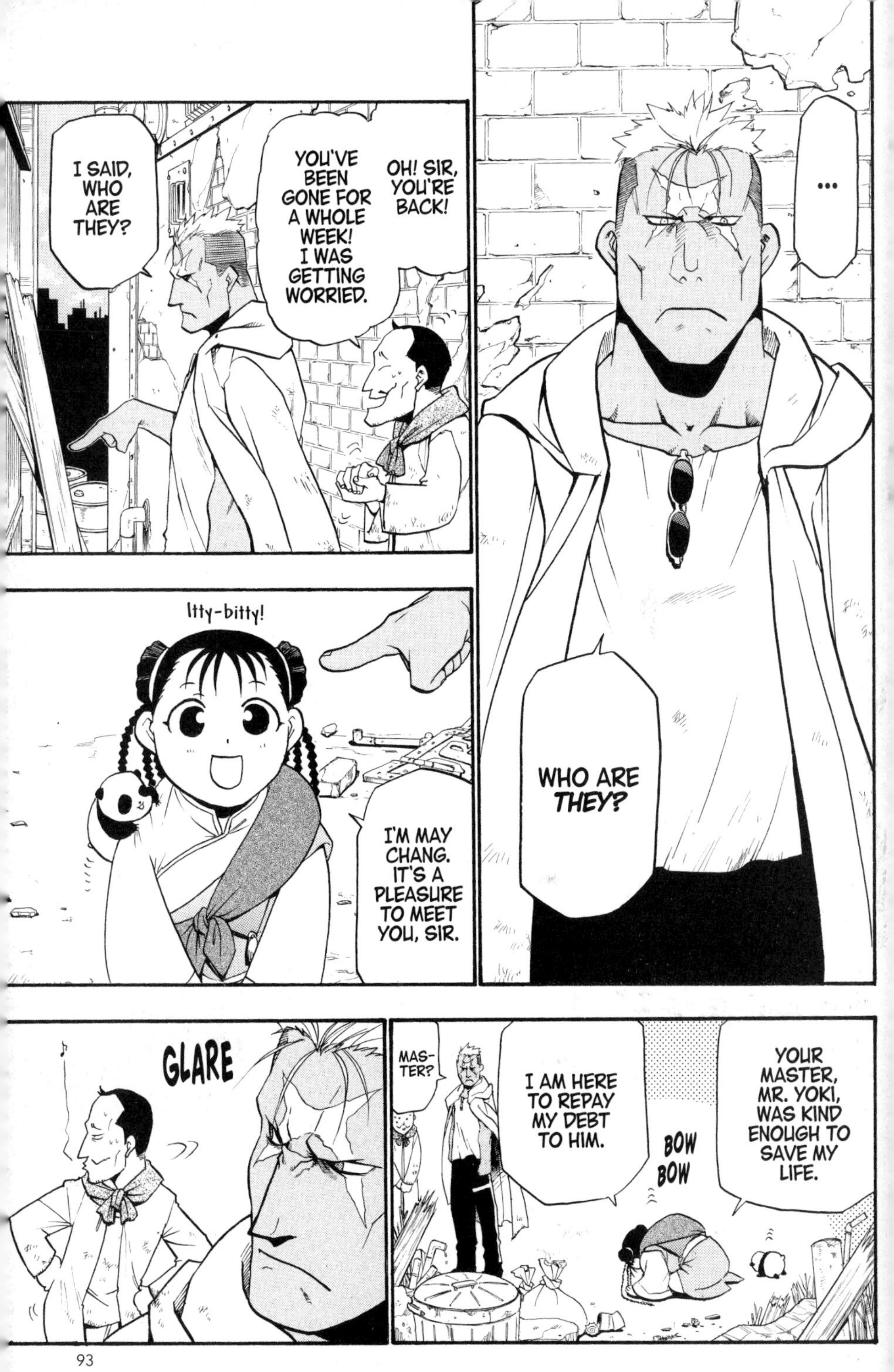
...
WHO ARE THEY?
OH! SIR, YOU'RE BACK!
YOU'VE BEEN GONE FOR A WHOLE WEEK! I WAS GETTING WORRIED.
I SAID, WHO ARE THEY?
Itty-bitty!
I'M MAY CHANG. IT'S A PLEASURE TO MEET YOU, SIR.
YOUR MASTER, MR. YOKI, WAS KIND ENOUGH TO SAVE MY LIFE.
BOW BOW
I AM HERE TO REPAY MY DEBT TO HIM.
MAS-TER?
GLARE

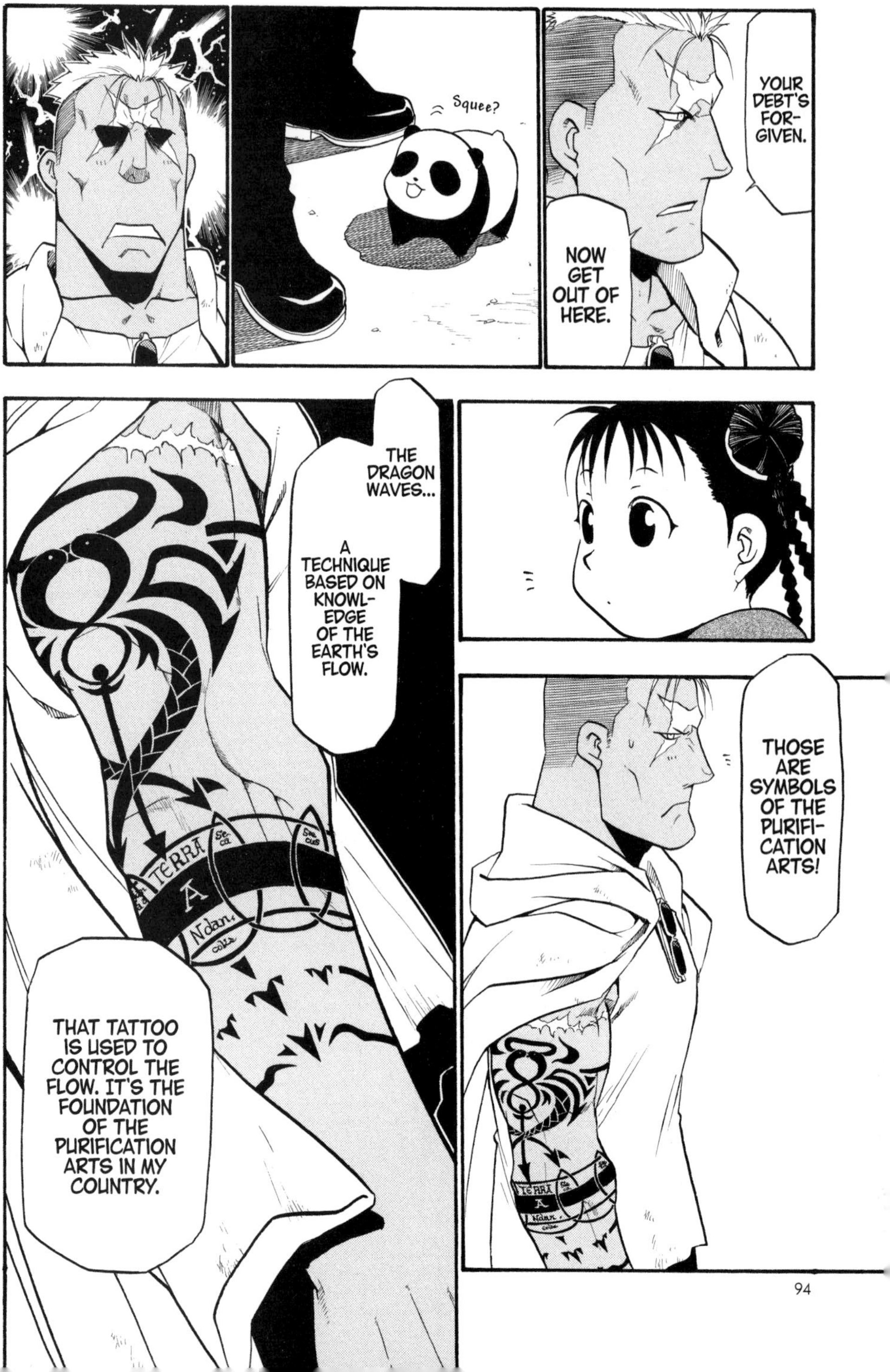
YOUR DEBT'S FOR-GIVEN.
NOW GET OUT OF HERE.
Squee?
THE DRAGON WAVES...
A TECHNIQUE BASED ON KNOWL-EDGE OF THE EARTH'S FLOW.
THOSE ARE SYMBOLS OF THE PURIFI-CATION ARTS!
THAT TATTOO IS USED TO CONTROL THE FLOW. IT'S THE FOUNDATION OF THE PURIFICATION ARTS IN MY COUNTRY.

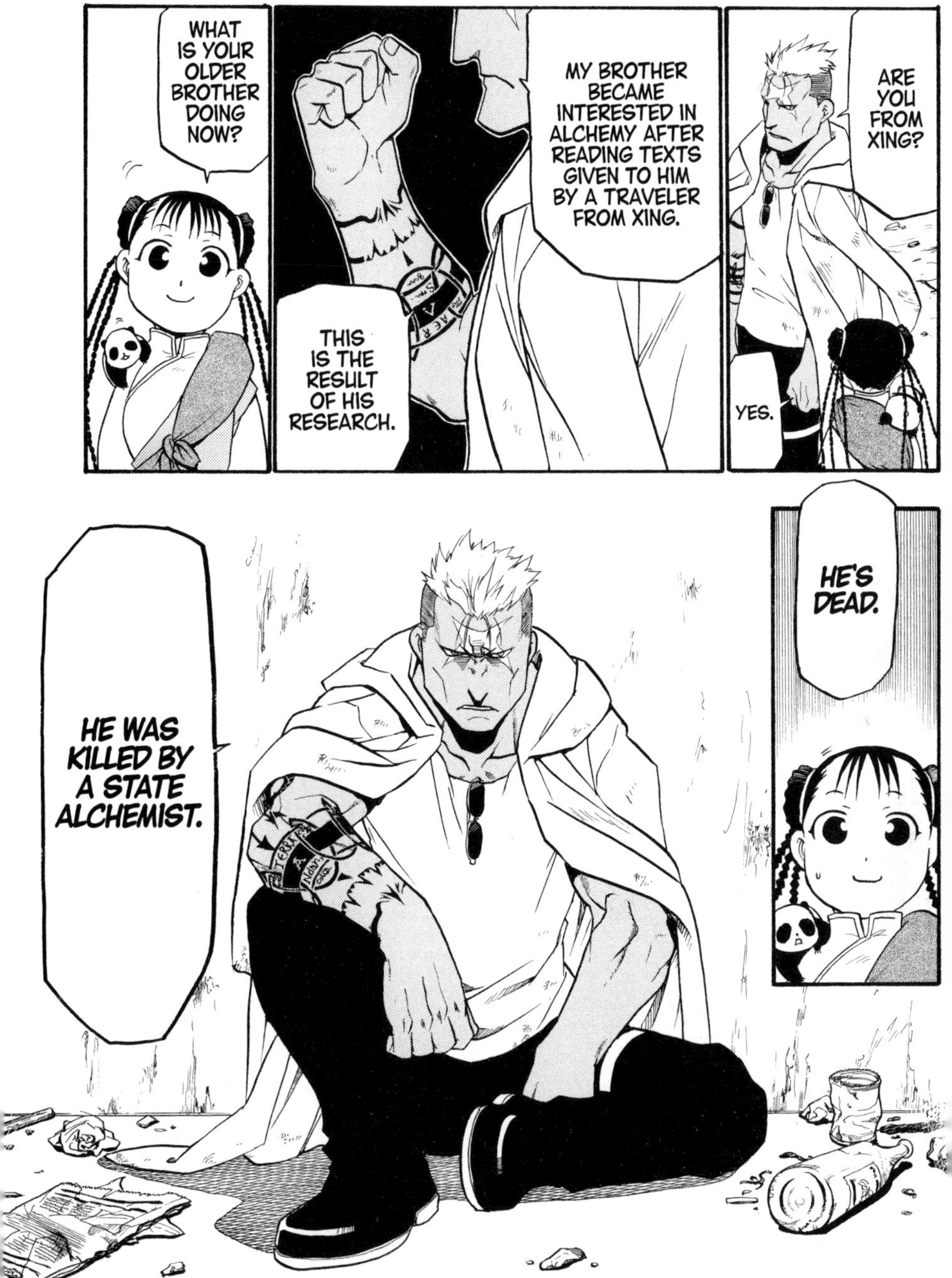
ARE YOU FROM XING?
YES.
MY BROTHER BECAME INTERESTED IN ALCHEMY AFTER READING TEXTS GIVEN TO HIM BY A TRAVELER FROM XING.
THIS IS THE RESULT OF HIS RESEARCH.
WHAT IS YOUR OLDER BROTHER DOING NOW?
HE'S DEAD.
HE WAS KILLED BY A STATE ALCHEMIST.

CHAPTER 45 SCAR'S RETURN

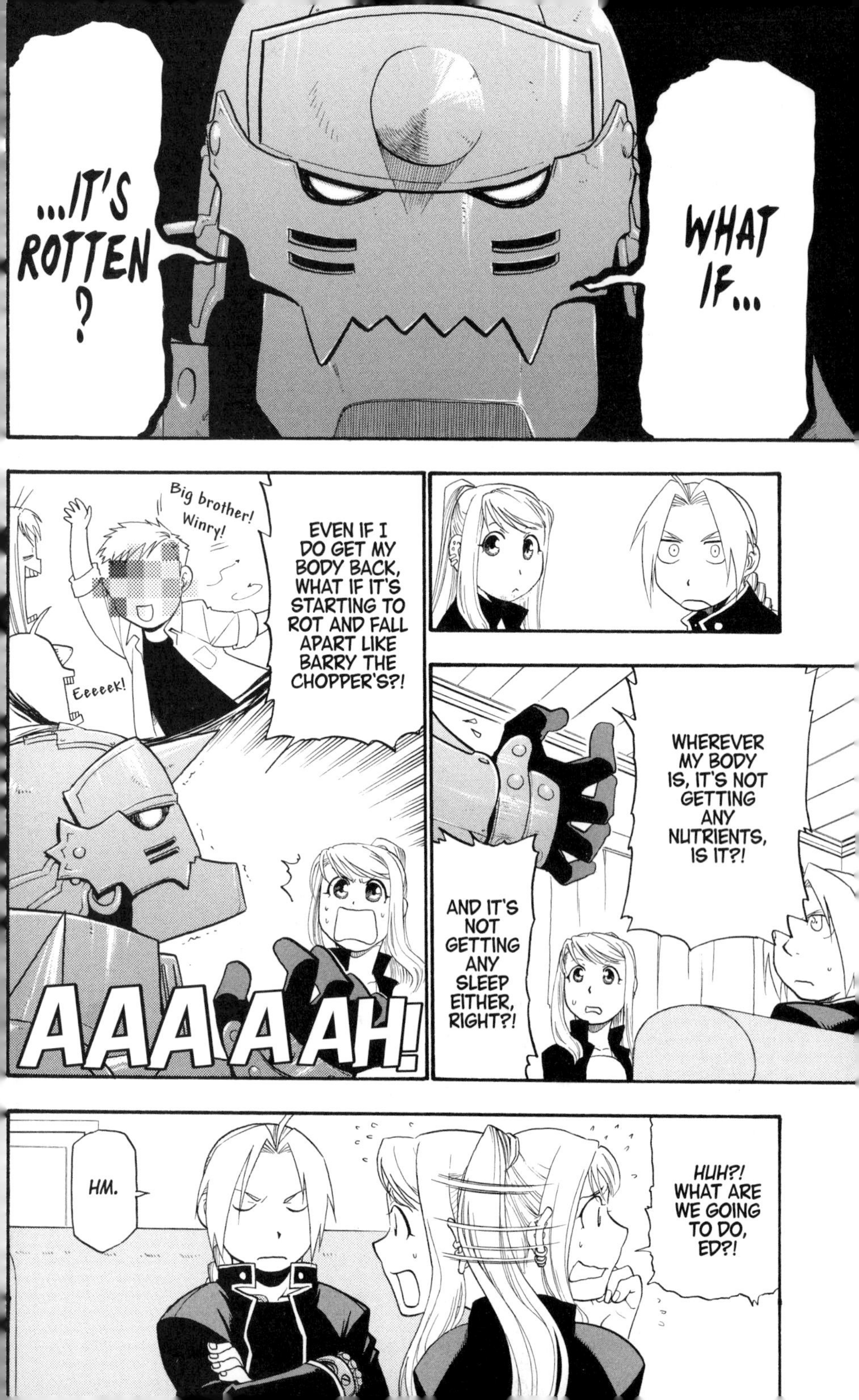
WHAT IF...
...IT'S ROTTEN?
WHEREVER MY BODY IS, IT'S NOT GETTING ANY NUTRIENTS, IS IT?!
AND IT'S NOT GETTING ANY SLEEP EITHER, RIGHT?!
EVEN IF I DO GET MY BODY BACK, WHAT IF IT'S STARTING TO ROT AND FALL APART LIKE BARRY THE CHOPPER'S?!
Big brother! Winry!
Eeeeek!
AAAAAH!
HUH?! WHAT ARE WE GOING TO DO, ED?!
HM.

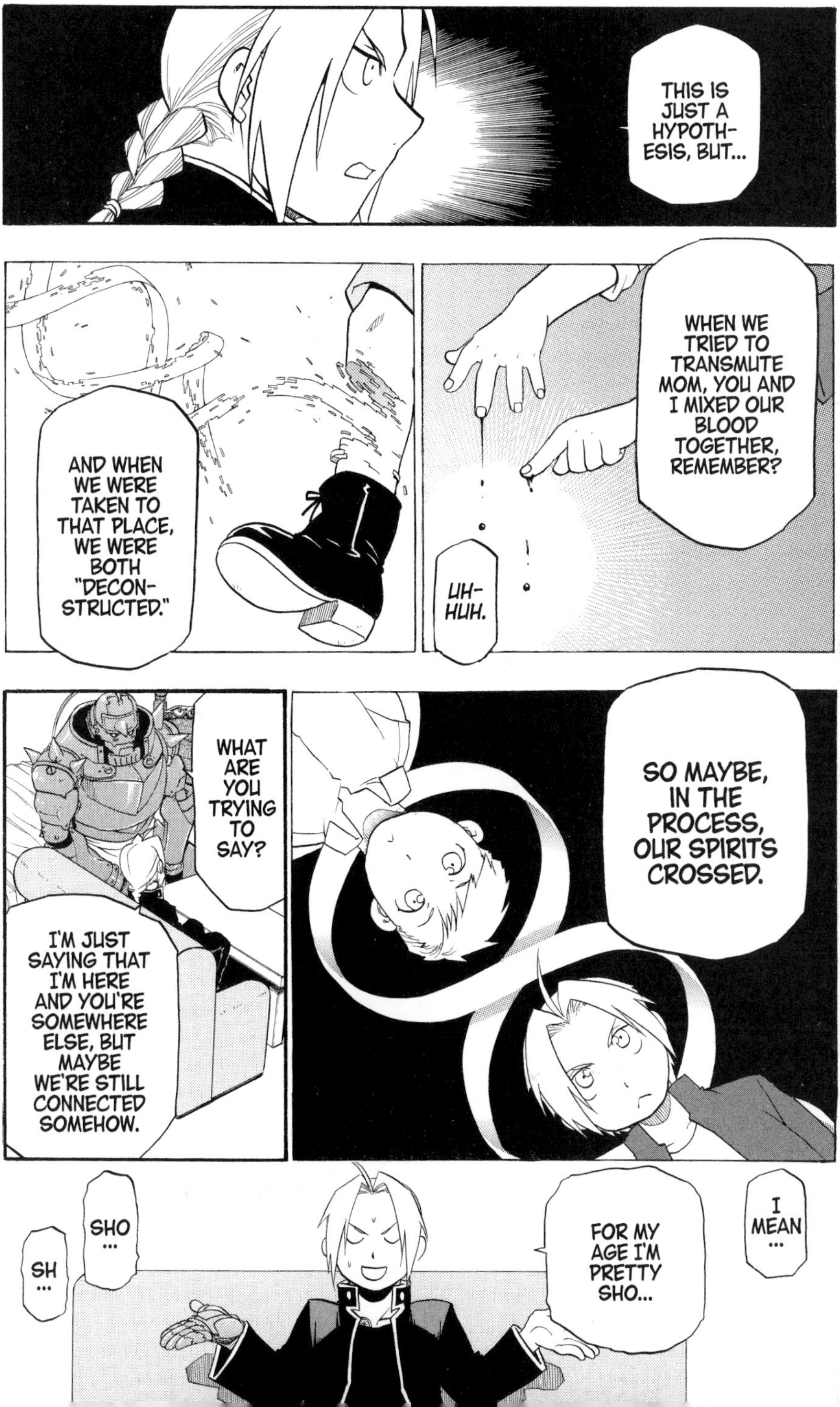
THIS IS JUST A HYPOTHESIS, BUT...
WHEN WE TRIED TO TRANSMUTE MOM, YOU AND I MIXED OUR BLOOD TOGETHER, REMEMBER?
UH-HUH.
AND WHEN WE WERE TAKEN TO THAT PLACE, WE WERE BOTH "DECONSTRUCTED."
SO MAYBE, IN THE PROCESS, OUR SPIRITS CROSSED.
WHAT ARE YOU TRYING TO SAY?
I'M JUST SAYING THAT I'M HERE AND YOU'RE SOMEWHERE ELSE, BUT MAYBE WE'RE STILL CONNECTED SOMEHOW.
I MEAN...
FOR MY AGE I'M PRETTY SHO...
SHO...
SH...

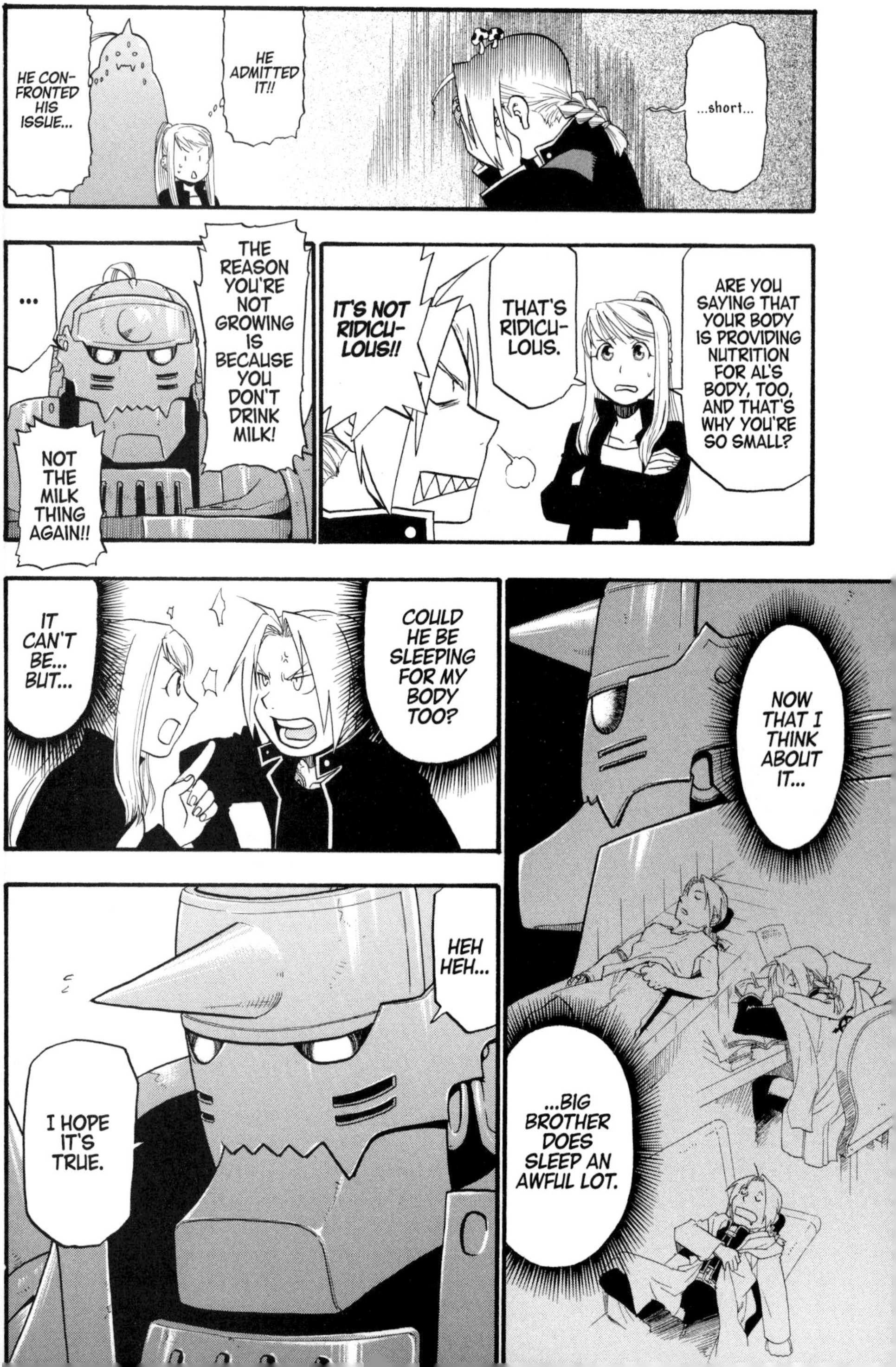
...short...
HE ADMITTED IT!!
HE CONFRONTED HIS ISSUE...
ARE YOU SAYING THAT YOUR BODY IS PROVIDING NUTRITION FOR AL'S BODY, TOO, AND THAT'S WHY YOU'RE SO SMALL?
THAT'S RIDICULOUS.
IT'S NOT RIDICULOUS!!
THE REASON YOU'RE NOT GROWING IS BECAUSE YOU DON'T DRINK MILK!
...
NOT THE MILK THING AGAIN!!
NOW THAT I THINK ABOUT IT...
...BIG BROTHER DOES SLEEP AN AWFUL LOT.
COULD HE BE SLEEPING FOR MY BODY TOO?
IT CAN'T BE... BUT...
HEH HEH...
I HOPE IT'S TRUE.

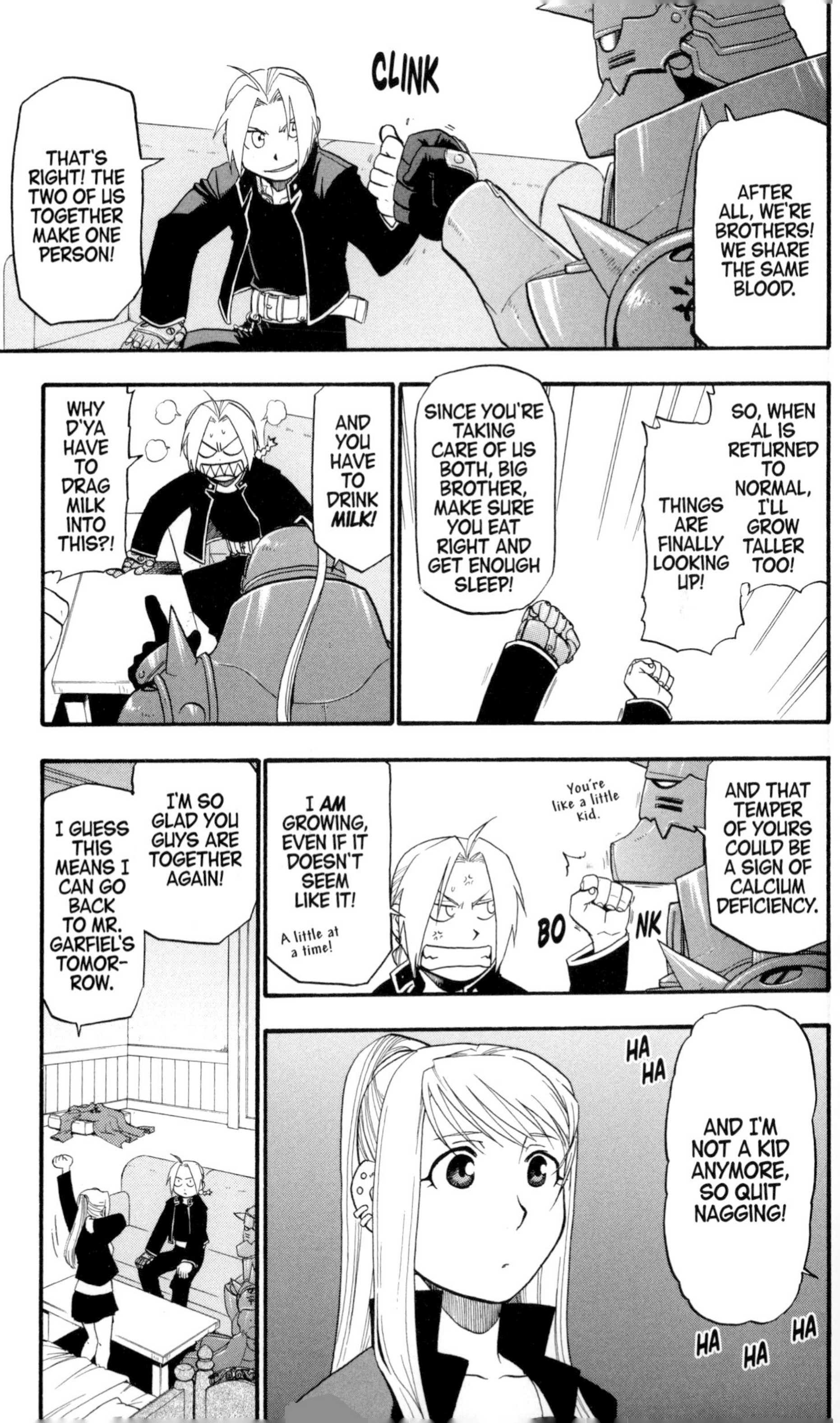
AFTER ALL, WE'RE BROTHERS! WE SHARE THE SAME BLOOD.
CLINK
THAT'S RIGHT! THE TWO OF US TOGETHER MAKE ONE PERSON!
SO, WHEN AL IS RETURNED TO NORMAL, I'LL GROW TALLER TOO!
THINGS ARE FINALLY LOOKING UP!
SINCE YOU'RE TAKING CARE OF US BOTH, BIG BROTHER, MAKE SURE YOU EAT RIGHT AND GET ENOUGH SLEEP!
AND YOU HAVE TO DRINK *MILK!*
WHY D'YA HAVE TO DRAG MILK INTO THIS?!
AND THAT TEMPER OF YOURS COULD BE A SIGN OF CALCIUM DEFICIENCY.
You're like a little kid.
BONK
I *AM* GROWING, EVEN IF IT DOESN'T SEEM LIKE IT!
A little at a time!
HA HA
AND I'M NOT A KID ANYMORE, SO QUIT NAGGING!
HA HA HA
I'M SO GLAD YOU GUYS ARE TOGETHER AGAIN!
I GUESS THIS MEANS I CAN GO BACK TO MR. GARFIEL'S TOMORROW.

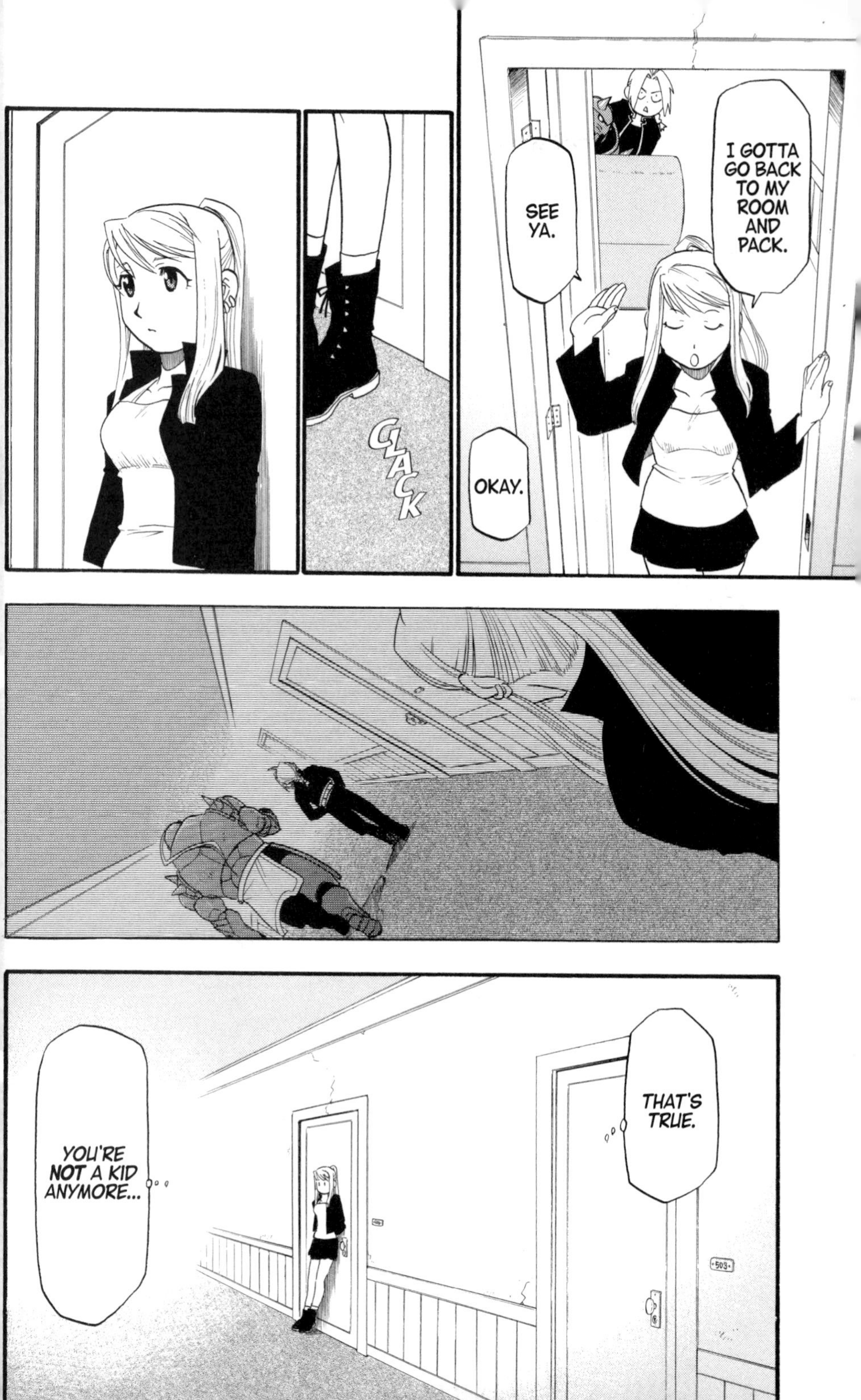
I GOTTA GO BACK TO MY ROOM AND PACK.
SEE YA.
OKAY.
CLACK
THAT'S TRUE.
503
YOU'RE NOT A KID ANYMORE...

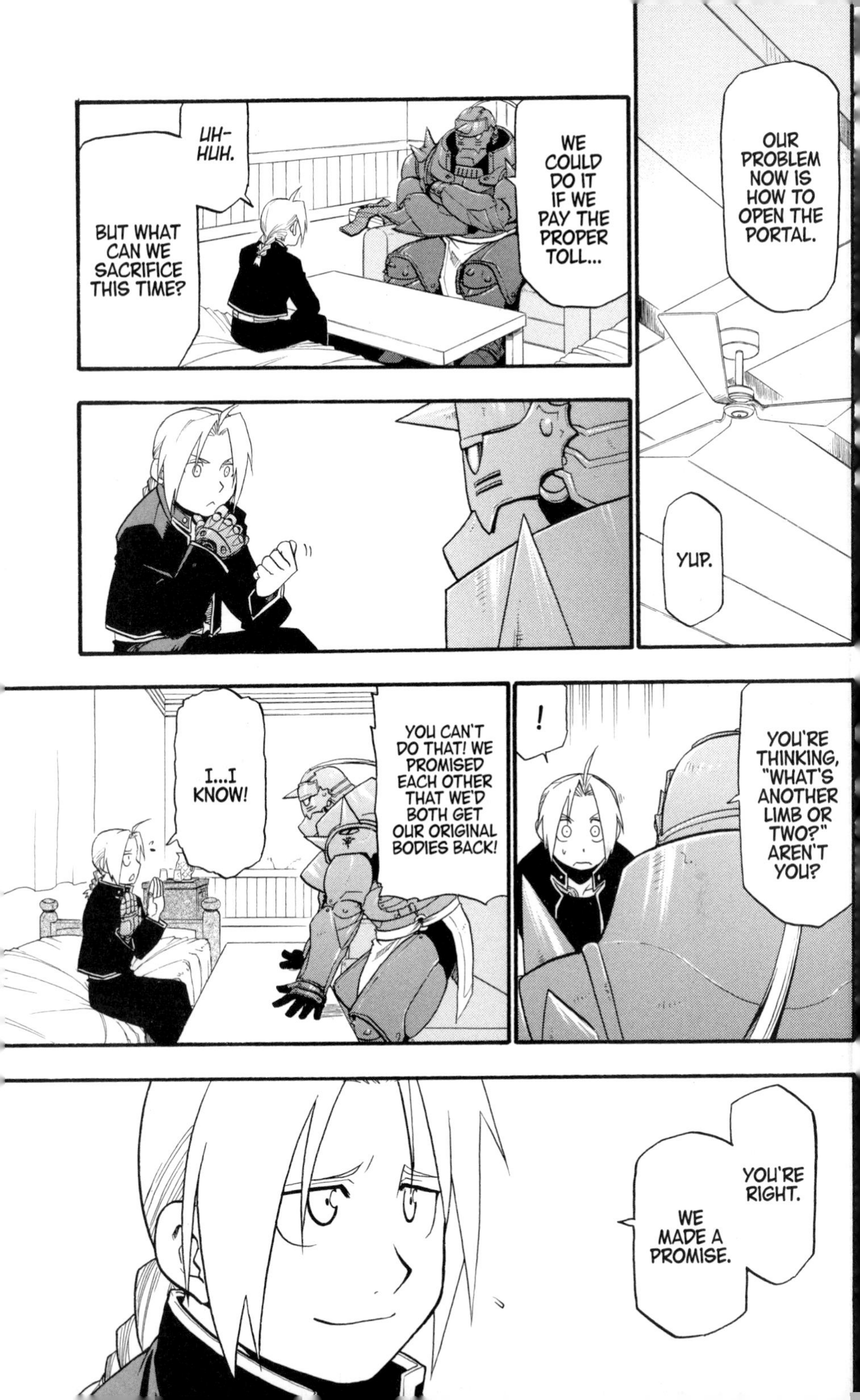
OUR PROBLEM NOW IS HOW TO OPEN THE PORTAL.
YUP.
WE COULD DO IT IF WE PAY THE PROPER TOLL...
UH-HUH.
BUT WHAT CAN WE SACRIFICE THIS TIME?
YOU'RE THINKING, "WHAT'S ANOTHER LIMB OR TWO?" AREN'T YOU?
!
YOU CAN'T DO THAT! WE PROMISED EACH OTHER THAT WE'D BOTH GET OUR ORIGINAL BODIES BACK!
I...I KNOW!
YOU'RE RIGHT.
WE MADE A PROMISE.

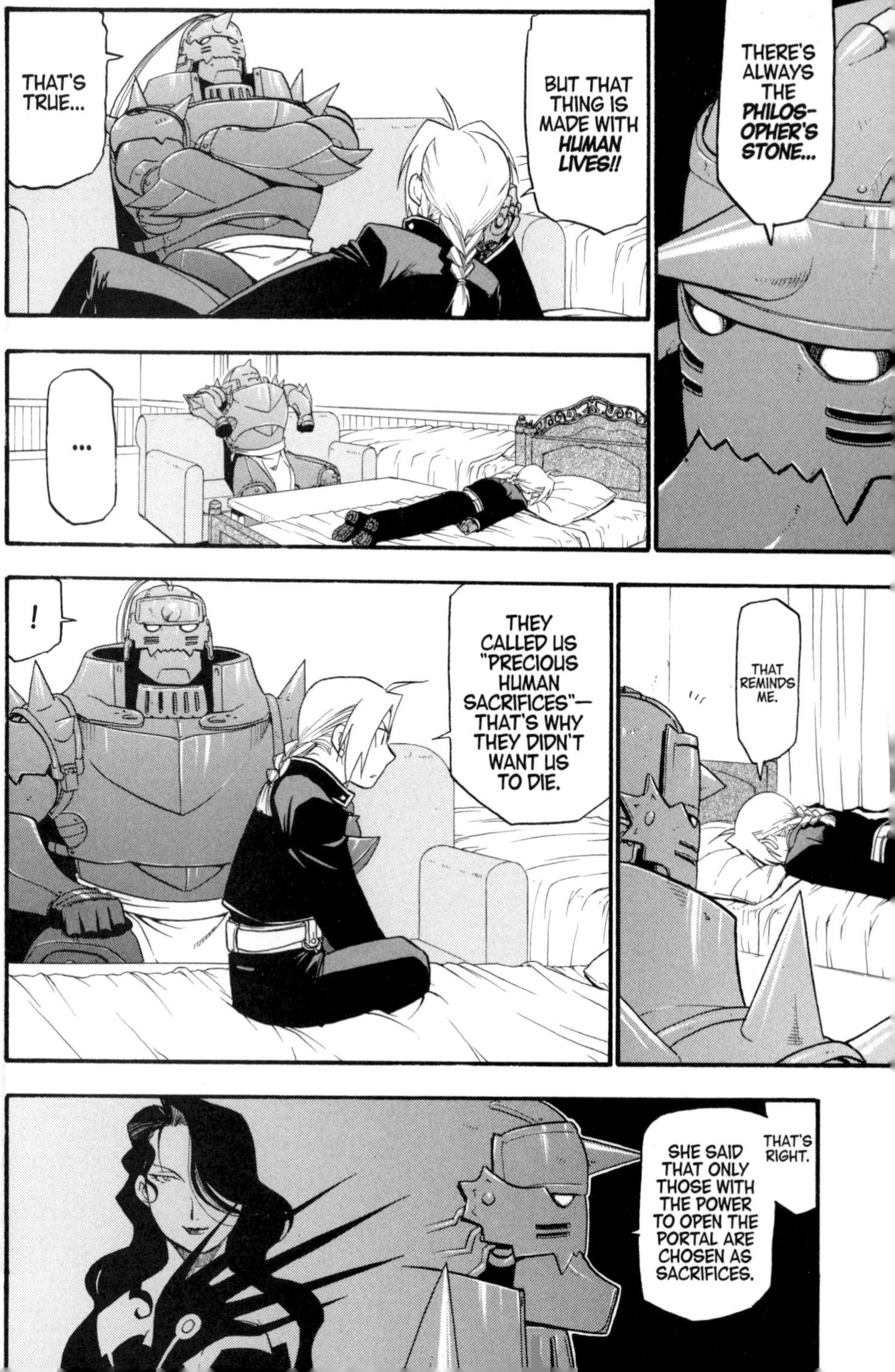
THERE'S ALWAYS THE PHILOSOPHER'S STONE...
BUT THAT THING IS MADE WITH HUMAN LIVES!!
THAT'S TRUE...
...
THAT REMINDS ME.
THEY CALLED US "PRECIOUS HUMAN SACRIFICES"—THAT'S WHY THEY DIDN'T WANT US TO DIE.
!
THAT'S RIGHT.
SHE SAID THAT ONLY THOSE WITH THE POWER TO OPEN THE PORTAL ARE CHOSEN AS SACRIFICES.

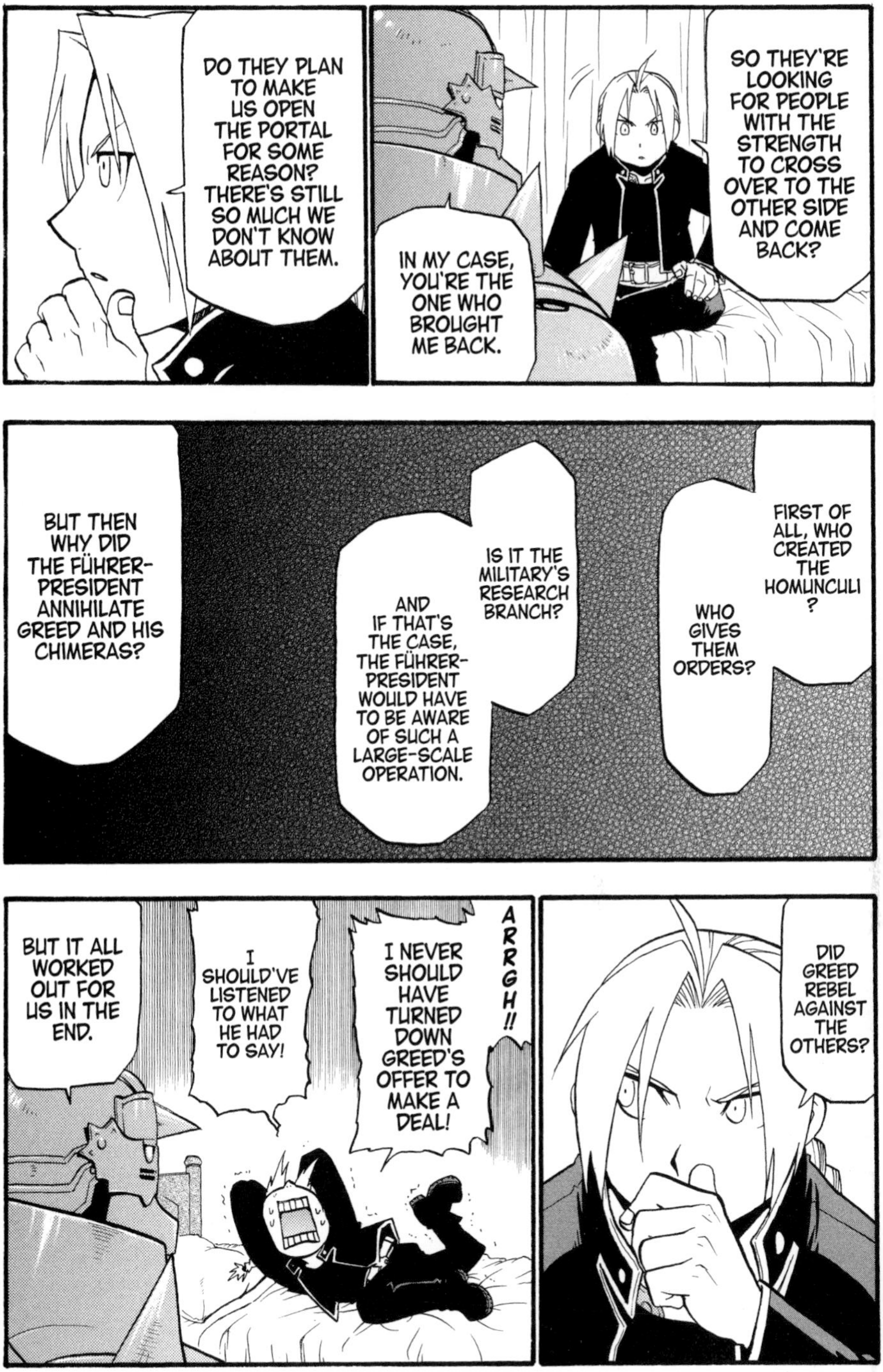
SO THEY'RE LOOKING FOR PEOPLE WITH THE STRENGTH TO CROSS OVER TO THE OTHER SIDE AND COME BACK?
IN MY CASE, YOU'RE THE ONE WHO BROUGHT ME BACK.
DO THEY PLAN TO MAKE US OPEN THE PORTAL FOR SOME REASON? THERE'S STILL SO MUCH WE DON'T KNOW ABOUT THEM.
FIRST OF ALL, WHO CREATED THE HOMUNCULI?
WHO GIVES THEM ORDERS?
IS IT THE MILITARY'S RESEARCH BRANCH?
AND IF THAT'S THE CASE, THE FÜHRER-PRESIDENT WOULD HAVE TO BE AWARE OF SUCH A LARGE-SCALE OPERATION.
BUT THEN WHY DID THE FÜHRER-PRESIDENT ANNIHILATE GREED AND HIS CHIMERAS?
DID GREED REBEL AGAINST THE OTHERS?
ARRGH!!
I NEVER SHOULD HAVE TURNED DOWN GREED'S OFFER TO MAKE A DEAL!
I SHOULD'VE LISTENED TO WHAT HE HAD TO SAY!
BUT IT ALL WORKED OUT FOR US IN THE END.

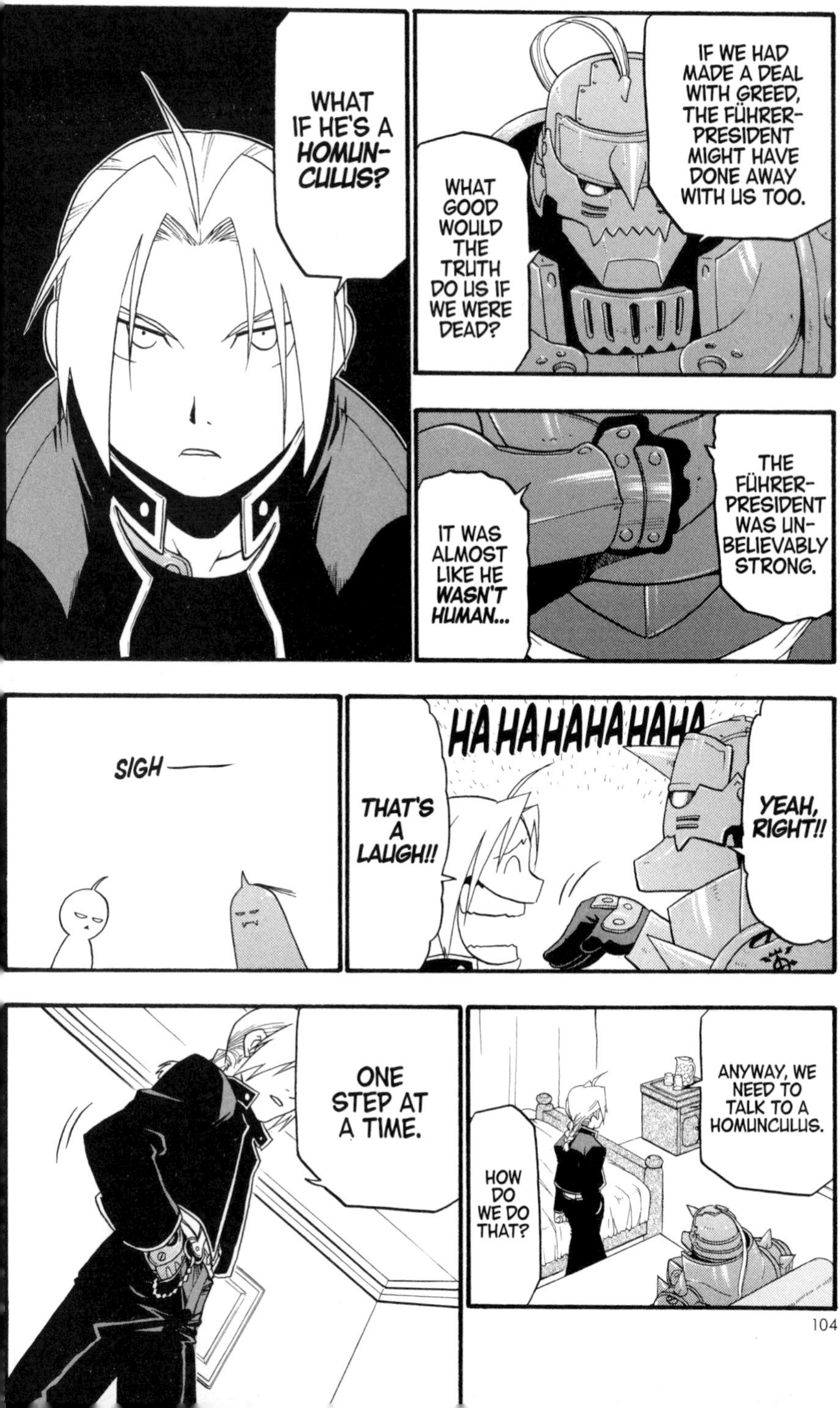
IF WE HAD MADE A DEAL WITH GREED, THE FÜHRER-PRESIDENT MIGHT HAVE DONE AWAY WITH US TOO.
WHAT GOOD WOULD THE TRUTH DO US IF WE WERE DEAD?
THE FÜHRER-PRESIDENT WAS UN-BELIEVABLY STRONG.
IT WAS ALMOST LIKE HE WASN'T HUMAN...
WHAT IF HE'S A HOMUN-CULUS?
HA HA HA HA HA HA
YEAH, RIGHT!!
THAT'S A LAUGH!!
SIGH—
ANYWAY, WE NEED TO TALK TO A HOMUNCULUS.
HOW DO WE DO THAT?
ONE STEP AT A TIME.

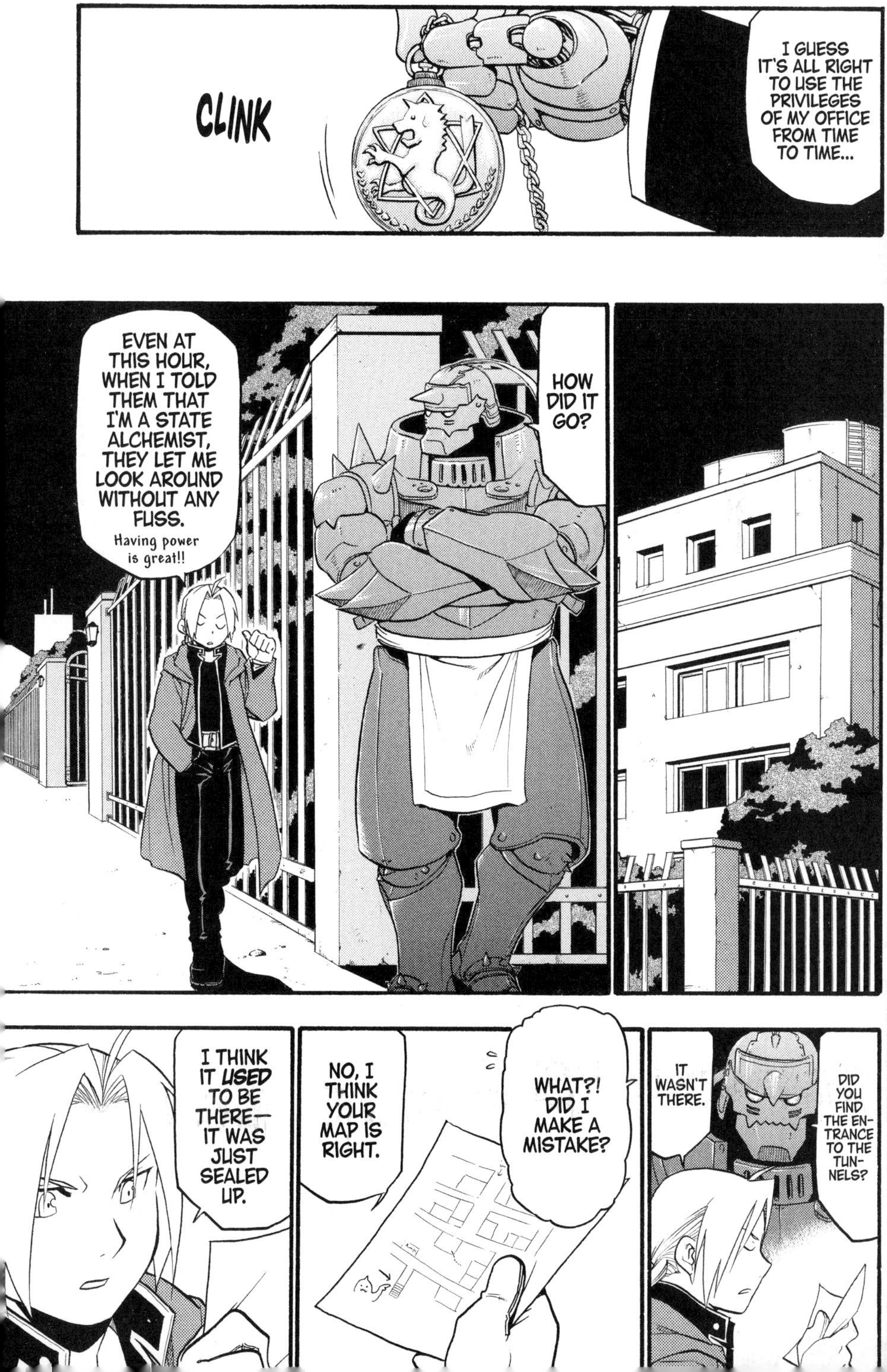
I GUESS IT'S ALL RIGHT TO USE THE PRIVILEGES OF MY OFFICE FROM TIME TO TIME...
CLINK
HOW DID IT GO?
EVEN AT THIS HOUR, WHEN I TOLD THEM THAT I'M A STATE ALCHEMIST, THEY LET ME LOOK AROUND WITHOUT ANY FUSS.
Having power is great!!
DID YOU FIND THE EN-TRANCE TO THE TUN-NELS?
IT WASN'T THERE.
WHAT?! DID I MAKE A MISTAKE?
NO, I THINK YOUR MAP IS RIGHT.
I THINK IT USED TO BE THERE—IT WAS JUST SEALED UP.

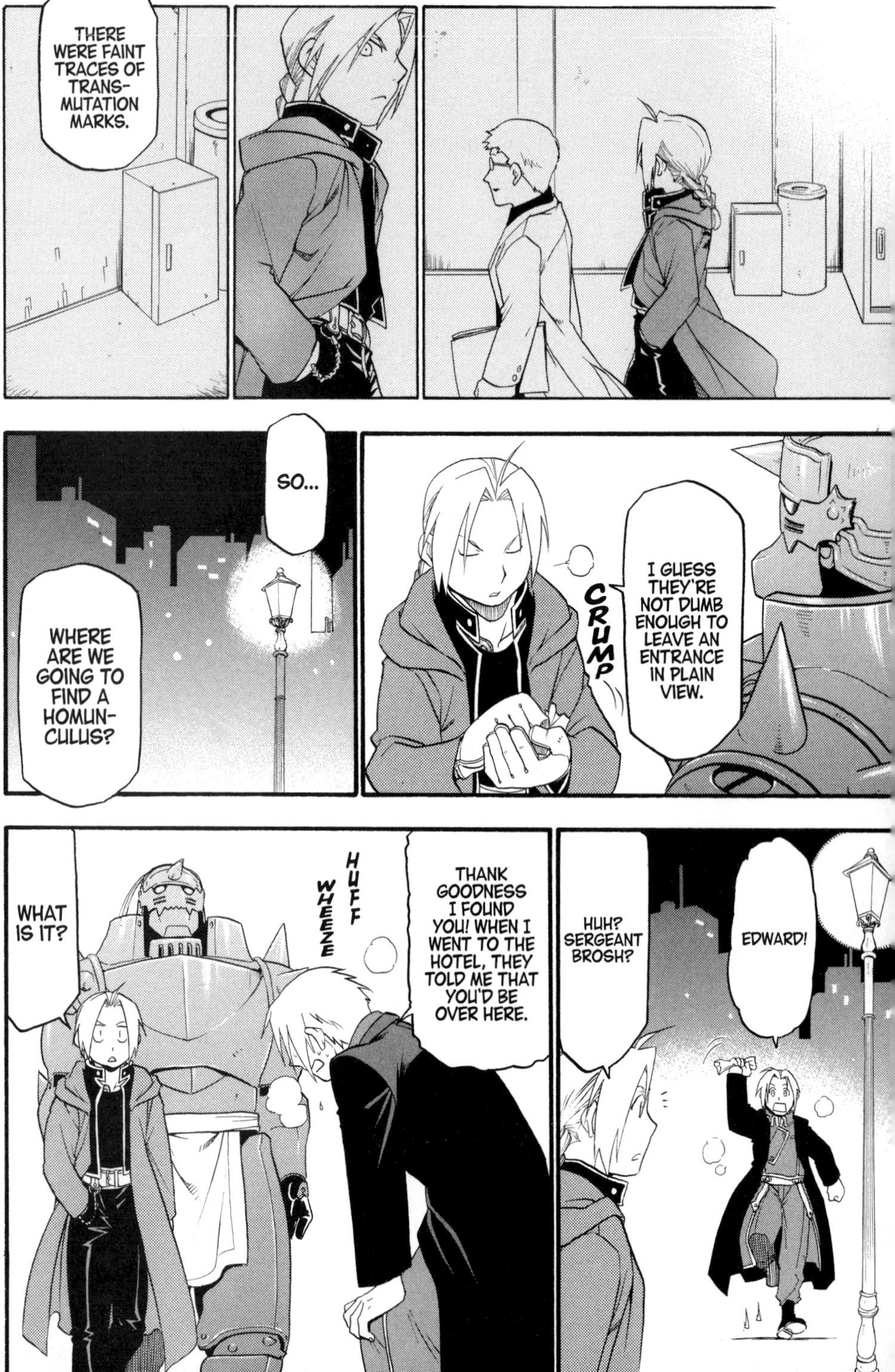
THERE WERE FAINT TRACES OF TRANS-MUTATION MARKS.
I GUESS THEY'RE NOT DUMB ENOUGH TO LEAVE AN ENTRANCE IN PLAIN VIEW.
CRUMP
SO...
WHERE ARE WE GOING TO FIND A HOMUN-CULUS?
EDWARD!
HUH? SERGEANT BROSH?
THANK GOODNESS I FOUND YOU! WHEN I WENT TO THE HOTEL, THEY TOLD ME THAT YOU'D BE OVER HERE.
HUFF
WHEEZE
WHAT IS IT?

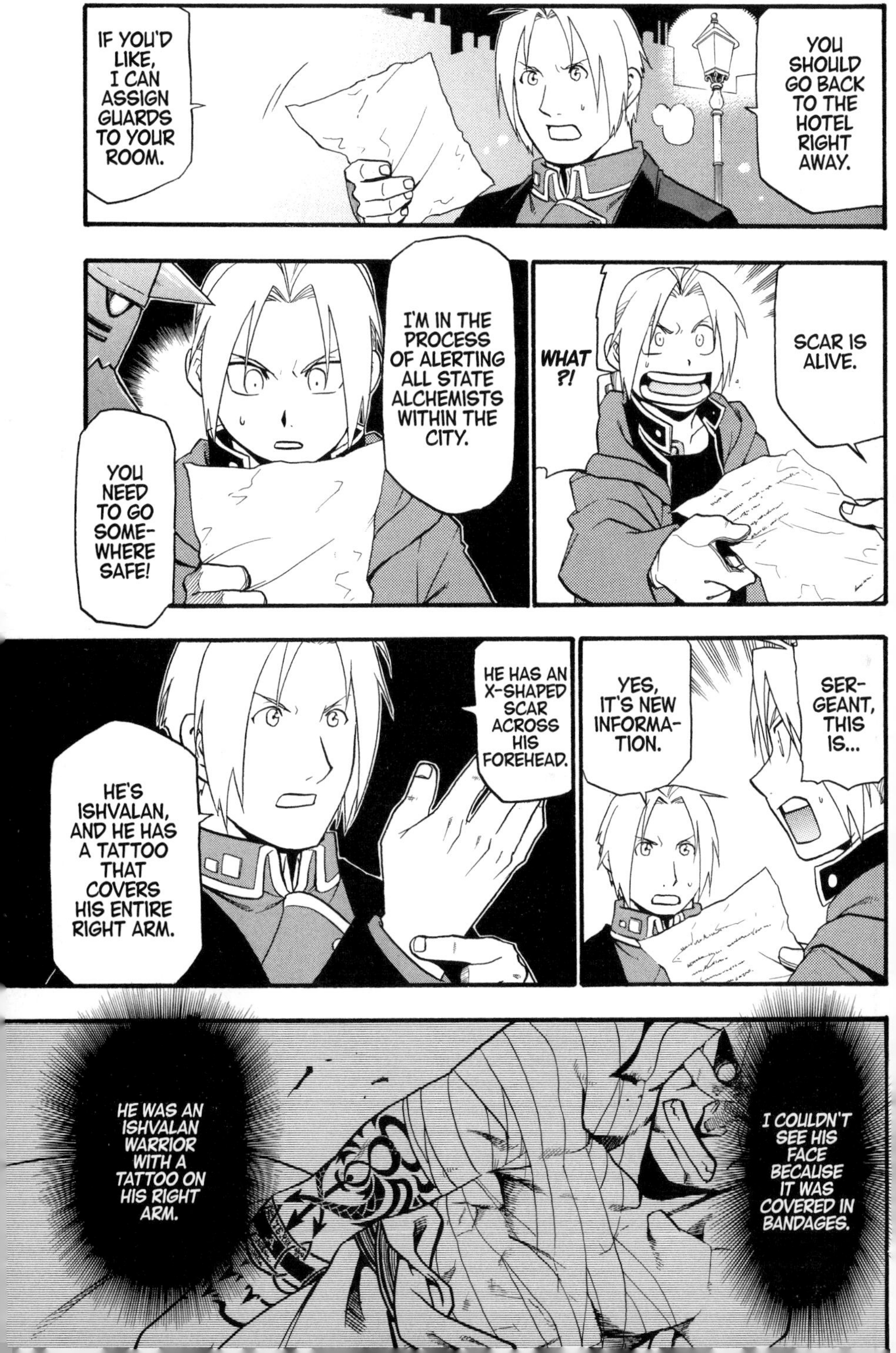
YOU SHOULD GO BACK TO THE HOTEL RIGHT AWAY.
IF YOU'D LIKE, I CAN ASSIGN GUARDS TO YOUR ROOM.
SCAR IS ALIVE.
WHAT ?!
I'M IN THE PROCESS OF ALERTING ALL STATE ALCHEMISTS WITHIN THE CITY.
YOU NEED TO GO SOME-WHERE SAFE!
SER-GEANT, THIS IS...
YES, IT'S NEW INFORMA-TION.
HE HAS AN X-SHAPED SCAR ACROSS HIS FOREHEAD.
HE'S ISHVALAN, AND HE HAS A TATTOO THAT COVERS HIS ENTIRE RIGHT ARM.
I COULDN'T SEE HIS FACE BECAUSE IT WAS COVERED IN BANDAGES.
HE WAS AN ISHVALAN WARRIOR WITH A TATTOO ON HIS RIGHT ARM.

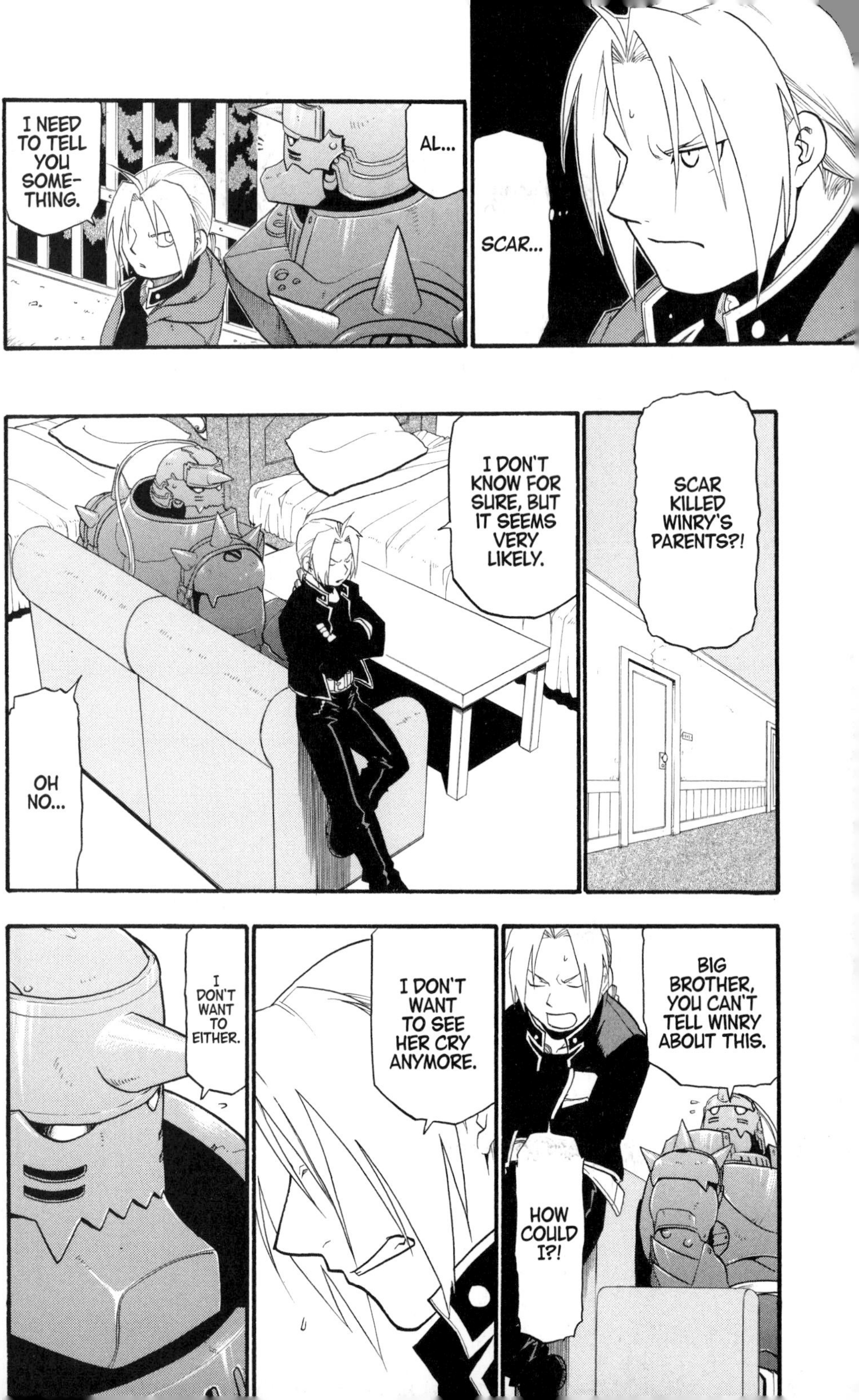
SCAR...
AL...
I NEED TO TELL YOU SOMETHING.
SCAR KILLED WINRY'S PARENTS?!
I DON'T KNOW FOR SURE, BUT IT SEEMS VERY LIKELY.
OH NO...
BIG BROTHER, YOU CAN'T TELL WINRY ABOUT THIS.
HOW COULD I?!
I DON'T WANT TO SEE HER CRY ANYMORE.
I DON'T WANT TO EITHER.

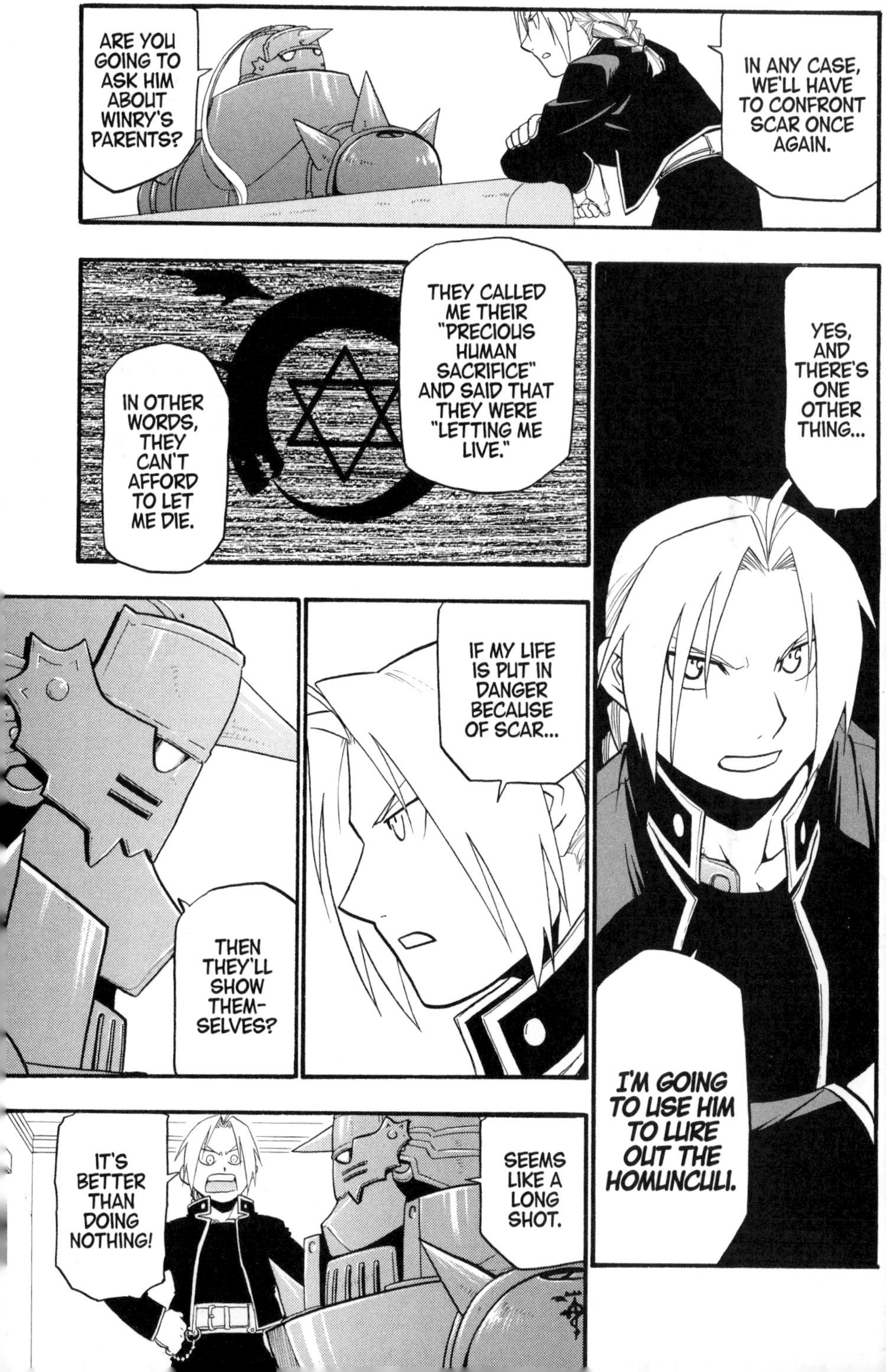

IN ANY CASE, WE'LL HAVE TO CONFRONT SCAR ONCE AGAIN.
ARE YOU GOING TO ASK HIM ABOUT WINRY'S PARENTS?
YES, AND THERE'S ONE OTHER THING...
I'M GOING TO USE HIM TO LURE OUT THE HOMUNCULI.
THEY CALLED ME THEIR "PRECIOUS HUMAN SACRIFICE" AND SAID THAT THEY WERE "LETTING ME LIVE."
IN OTHER WORDS, THEY CAN'T AFFORD TO LET ME DIE.
IF MY LIFE IS PUT IN DANGER BECAUSE OF SCAR...
THEN THEY'LL SHOW THEM-SELVES?
SEEMS LIKE A LONG SHOT.
IT'S BETTER THAN DOING NOTHING!

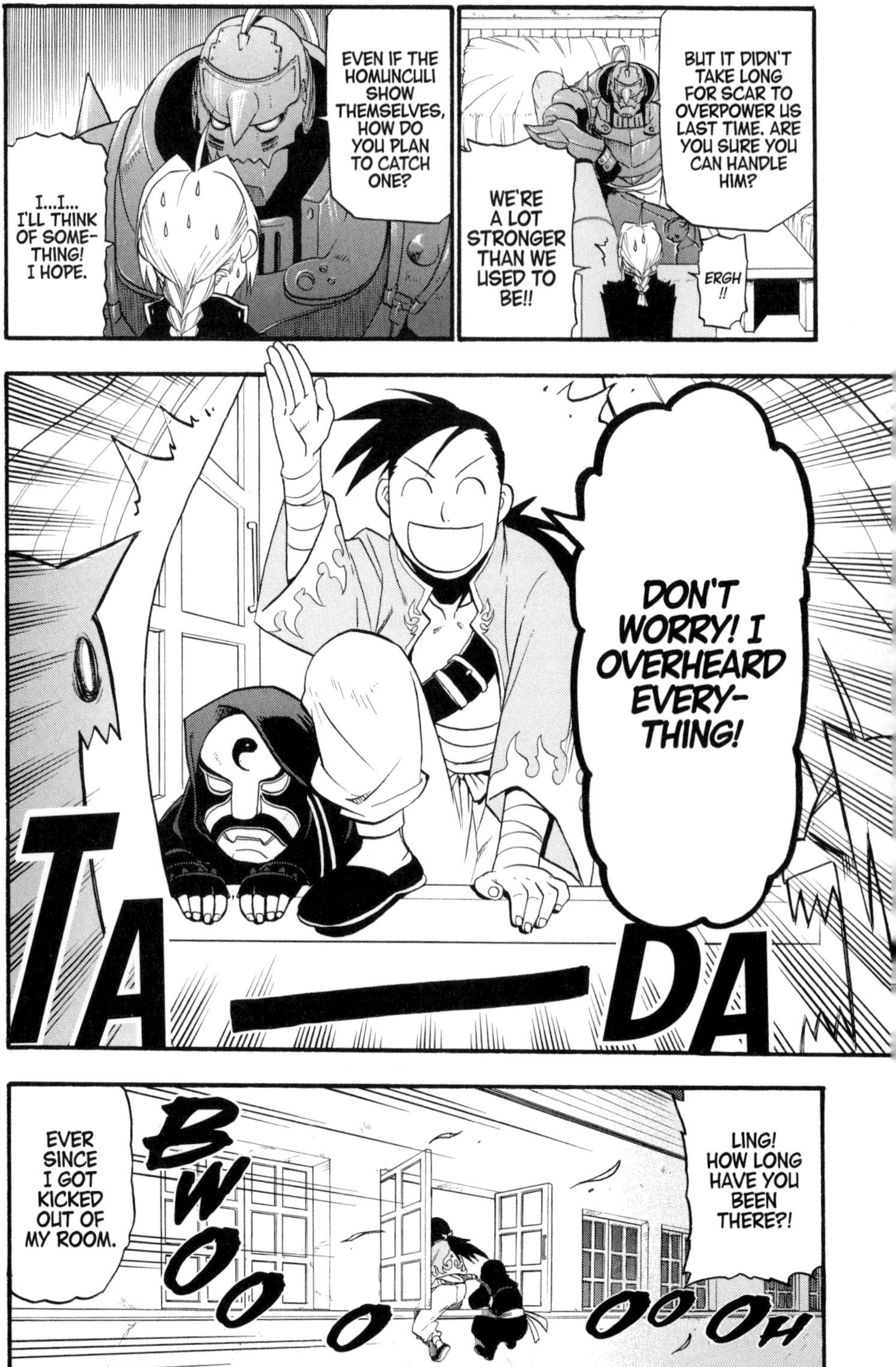
BUT IT DIDN'T TAKE LONG FOR SCAR TO OVERPOWER US LAST TIME. ARE YOU SURE YOU CAN HANDLE HIM?
WE'RE A LOT STRONGER THAN WE USED TO BE!!
ERGH!!
EVEN IF THE HOMUNCULI SHOW THEMSELVES, HOW DO YOU PLAN TO CATCH ONE?
I...I... I'LL THINK OF SOMETHING! I HOPE.
DON'T WORRY! I OVERHEARD EVERYTHING!
TA——DA
LING! HOW LONG HAVE YOU BEEN THERE?!
BWOOOOOOOH
EVER SINCE I GOT KICKED OUT OF MY ROOM.

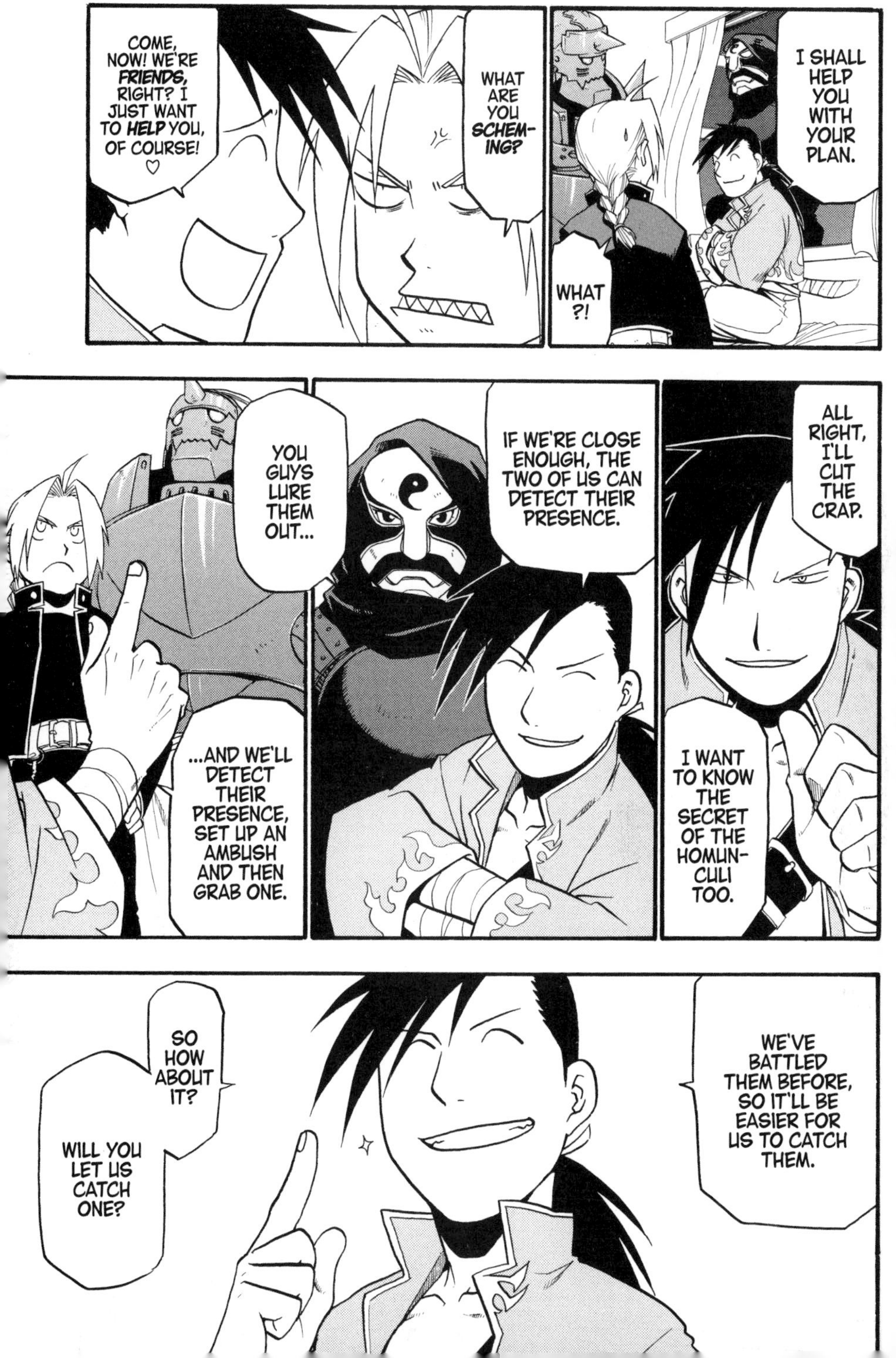
I SHALL HELP YOU WITH YOUR PLAN.
WHAT?!
WHAT ARE YOU SCHEMING?
COME, NOW! WE'RE **FRIENDS**, RIGHT? I JUST WANT TO **HELP** YOU, OF COURSE! ♡
ALL RIGHT, I'LL CUT THE CRAP.
I WANT TO KNOW THE SECRET OF THE HOMUNCULI TOO.
IF WE'RE CLOSE ENOUGH, THE TWO OF US CAN DETECT THEIR PRESENCE.
YOU GUYS LURE THEM OUT...
...AND WE'LL DETECT THEIR PRESENCE, SET UP AN AMBUSH AND THEN GRAB ONE.
WE'VE BATTLED THEM BEFORE, SO IT'LL BE EASIER FOR US TO CATCH THEM.
SO HOW ABOUT IT?
WILL YOU LET US CATCH ONE?

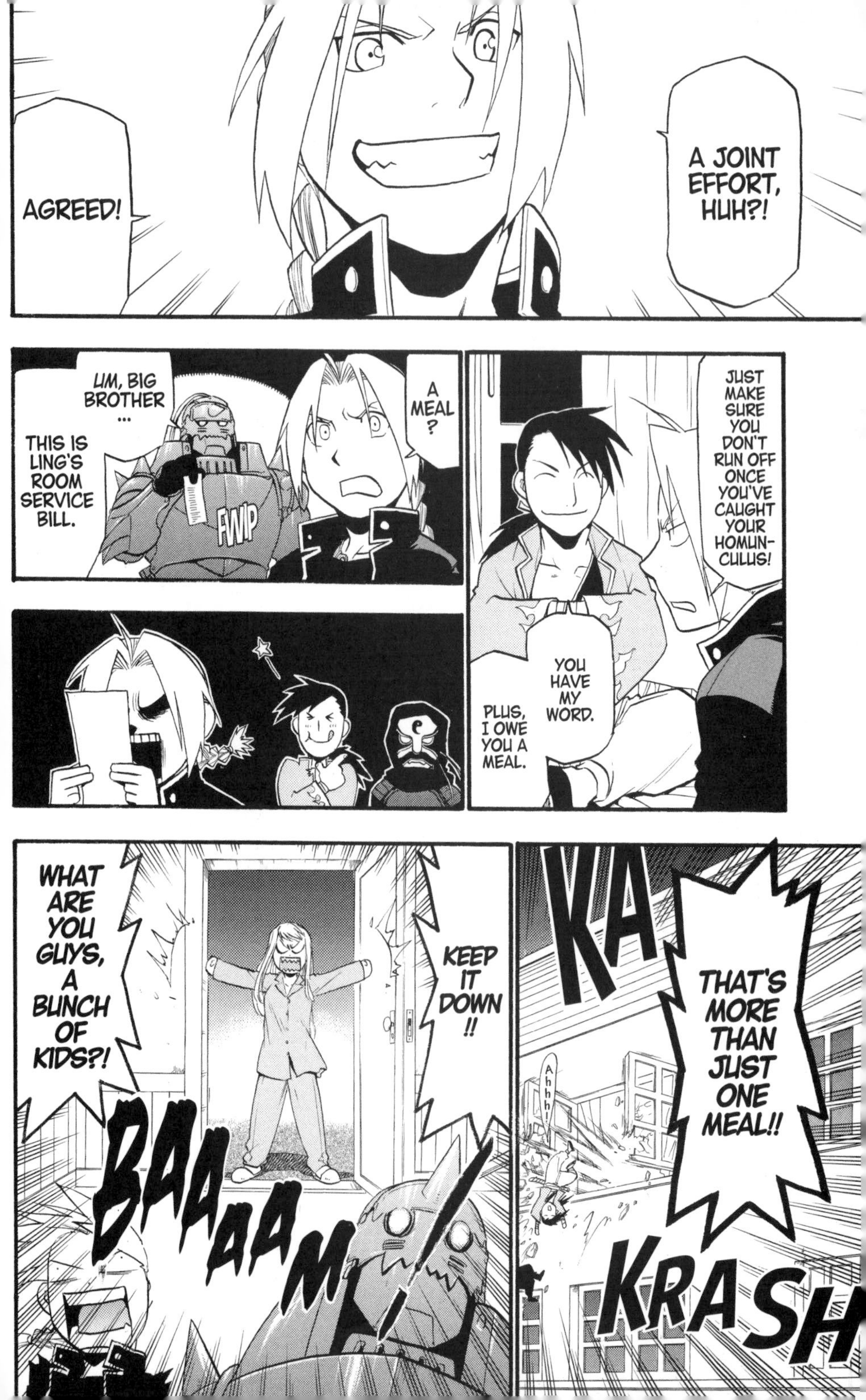
A JOINT EFFORT, HUH?!
AGREED!
JUST MAKE SURE YOU DON'T RUN OFF ONCE YOU'VE CAUGHT YOUR HOMUNCULUS!
YOU HAVE MY WORD.
PLUS, I OWE YOU A MEAL.
A MEAL?
UM, BIG BROTHER ...
THIS IS LING'S ROOM SERVICE BILL.
FWIP
KA
THAT'S MORE THAN JUST ONE MEAL!!
Ahhh!
KRASH
KEEP IT DOWN!!
WHAT ARE YOU GUYS, A BUNCH OF KIDS?!
BAAAAM!!

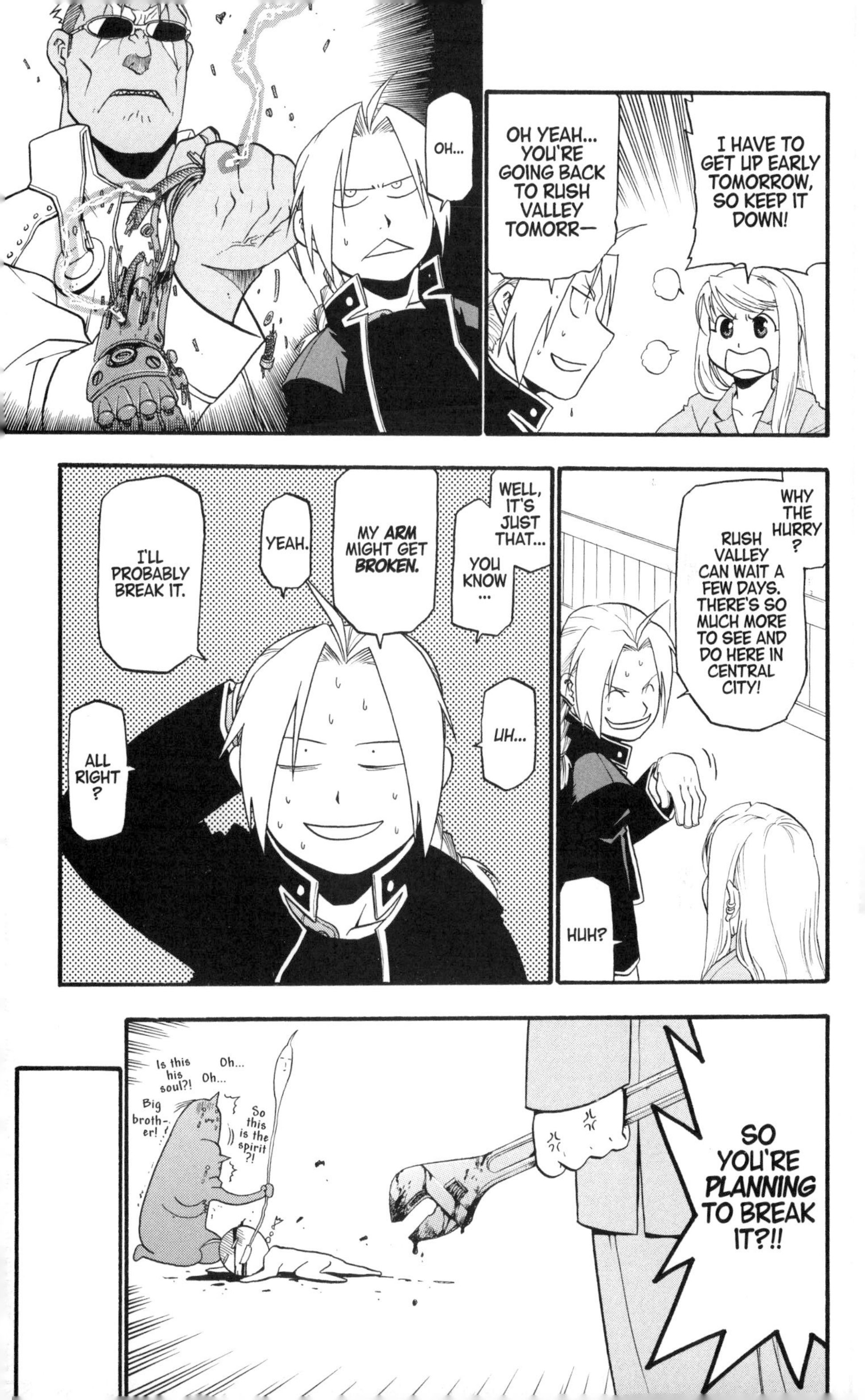
I HAVE TO GET UP EARLY TOMORROW, SO KEEP IT DOWN!
OH YEAH... YOU'RE GOING BACK TO RUSH VALLEY TOMORR—
OH...
WHY THE HURRY?
RUSH VALLEY CAN WAIT A FEW DAYS. THERE'S SO MUCH MORE TO SEE AND DO HERE IN CENTRAL CITY!
HUH?
WELL, IT'S JUST THAT...
YOU KNOW...
MY ARM MIGHT GET BROKEN.
UH...
YEAH.
I'LL PROBABLY BREAK IT.
ALL RIGHT?
SO YOU'RE PLANNING TO BREAK IT?!!
Oh... Oh...
Is this his soul?!
So this is the spirit?!
Big brother!

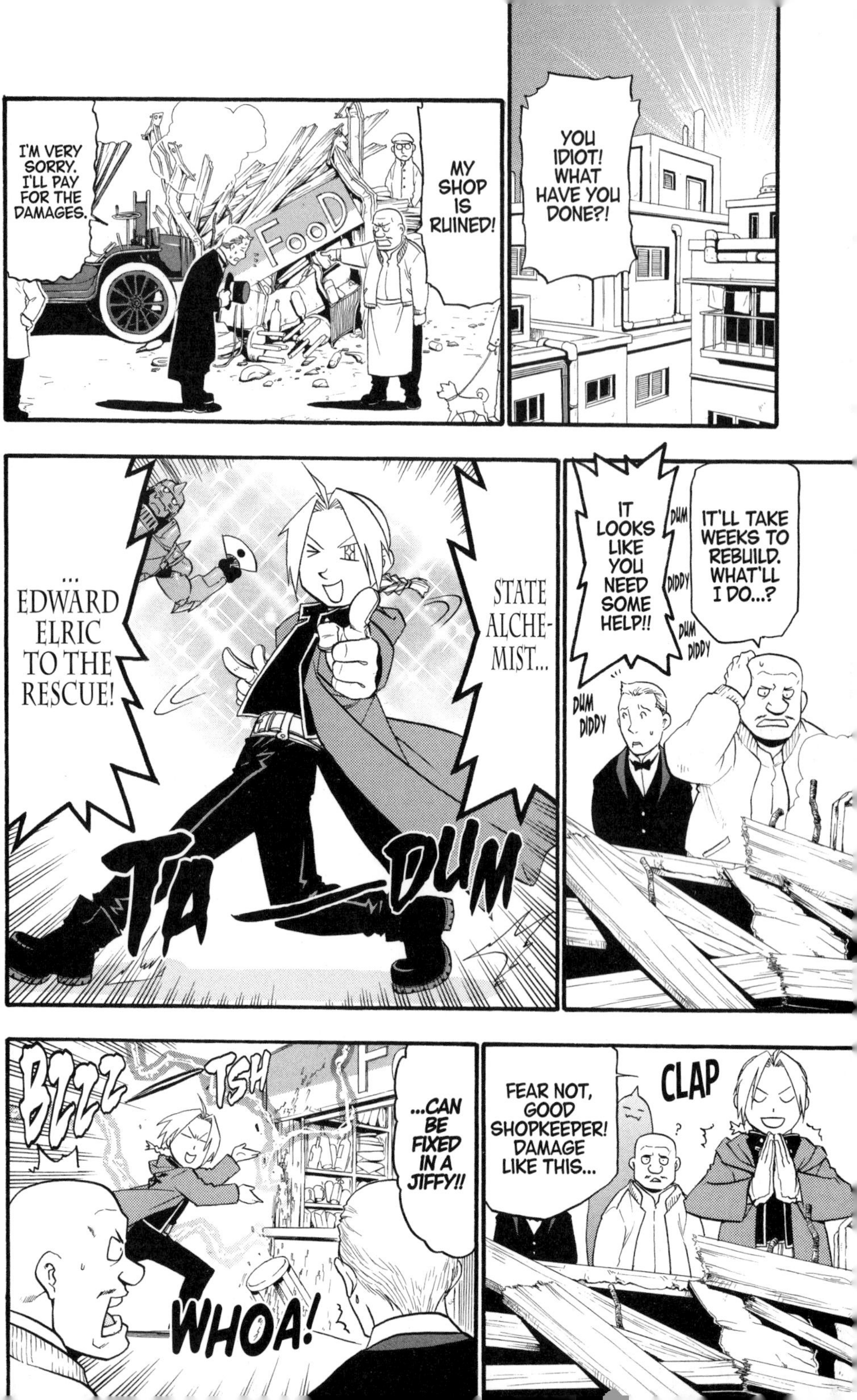
YOU IDIOT! WHAT HAVE YOU DONE?!
MY SHOP IS RUINED!
I'M VERY SORRY. I'LL PAY FOR THE DAMAGES.
IT'LL TAKE WEEKS TO REBUILD. WHAT'LL I DO...?
DUM DIDDY
DUM DIDDY
DUM DIDDY
IT LOOKS LIKE YOU NEED SOME HELP!!
STATE ALCHEMIST...
...EDWARD ELRIC TO THE RESCUE!
TA DUM
FEAR NOT, GOOD SHOPKEEPER! DAMAGE LIKE THIS...
CLAP
...CAN BE FIXED IN A JIFFY!!
TSH
BZZZ
WHOA!

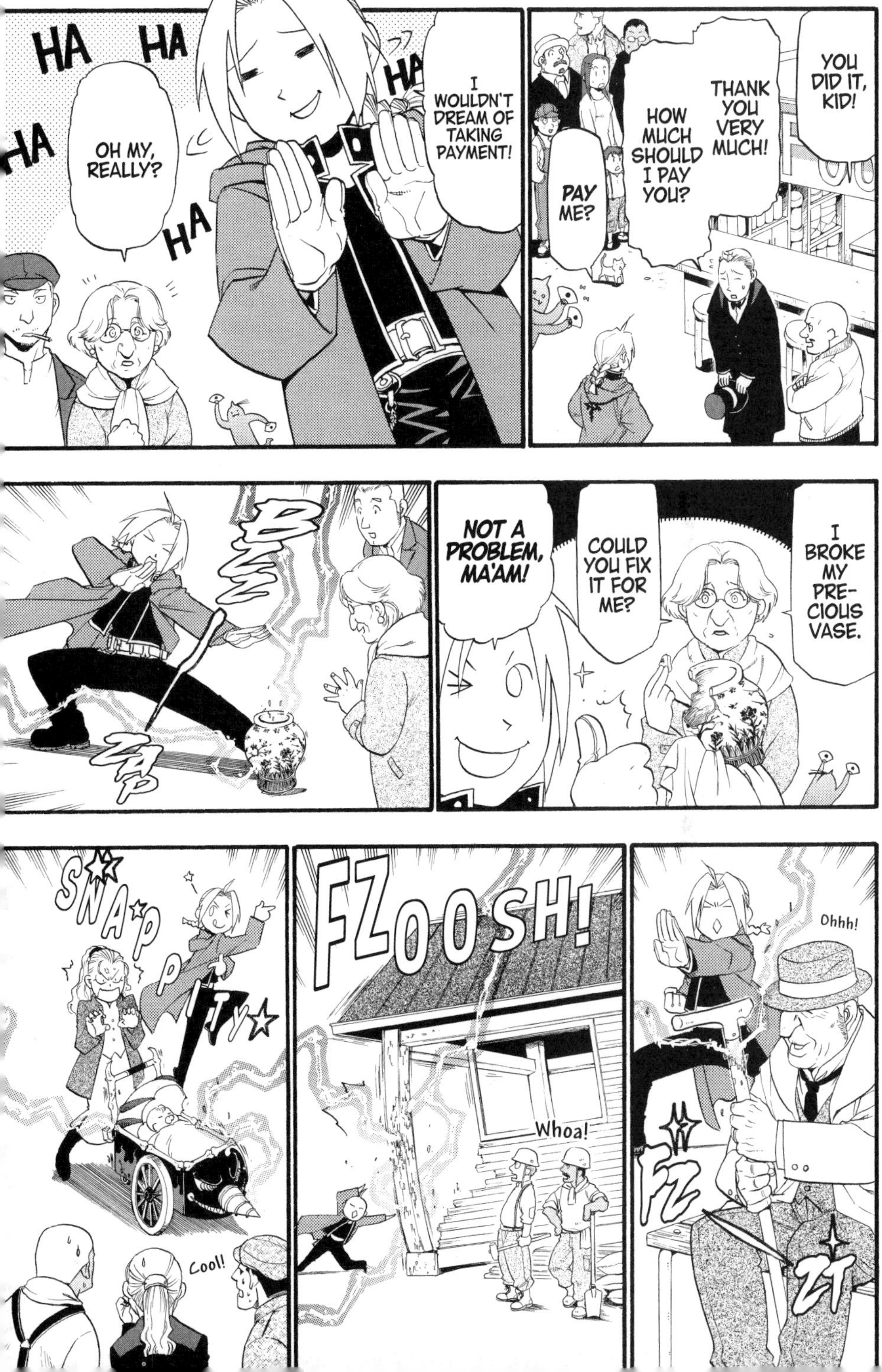
YOU DID IT, KID!
THANK YOU VERY MUCH!
HOW MUCH SHOULD I PAY YOU?
PAY ME?
I WOULDN'T DREAM OF TAKING PAYMENT!
HA HA HA HA HA
OH MY, REALLY?
I BROKE MY PRE-CIOUS VASE.
COULD YOU FIX IT FOR ME?
NOT A PROBLEM, MA'AM!
ZAP
Ohhh!
FZ
ZT
FZOOSH!
Whoa!
SNAPPITY
Cool!

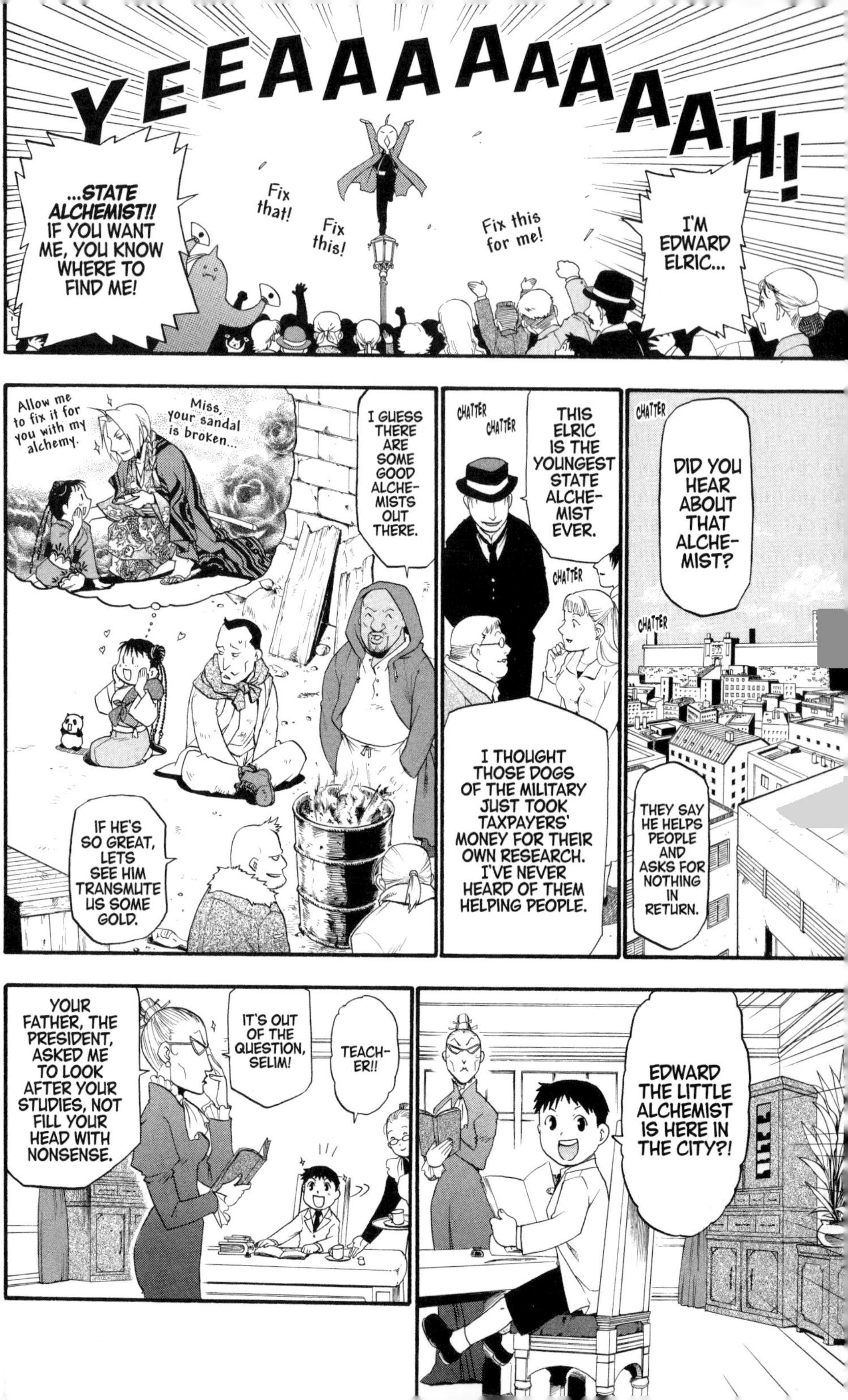
I'M EDWARD ELRIC...
YEEAAAAAAAAAH!
Fix this for me!
Fix this!
Fix that!
...STATE ALCHEMIST!! IF YOU WANT ME, YOU KNOW WHERE TO FIND ME!
CHATTER
DID YOU HEAR ABOUT THAT ALCHE- MIST?
CHATTER
THEY SAY HE HELPS PEOPLE AND ASKS FOR NOTHING IN RETURN.
CHATTER CHATTER
THIS ELRIC IS THE YOUNGEST STATE ALCHE- MIST EVER.
CHATTER
I THOUGHT THOSE DOGS OF THE MILITARY JUST TOOK TAXPAYERS' MONEY FOR THEIR OWN RESEARCH. I'VE NEVER HEARD OF THEM HELPING PEOPLE.
I GUESS THERE ARE SOME GOOD ALCHE- MISTS OUT THERE.
Miss, your sandal is broken...
Allow me to fix it for you with my alchemy.
IF HE'S SO GREAT, LETS SEE HIM TRANSMUTE US SOME GOLD.
EDWARD THE LITTLE ALCHEMIST IS HERE IN THE CITY?!
TEACH- ER!!
IT'S OUT OF THE QUESTION, SELIM!
YOUR FATHER, THE PRESIDENT, ASKED ME TO LOOK AFTER YOUR STUDIES, NOT FILL YOUR HEAD WITH NONSENSE.

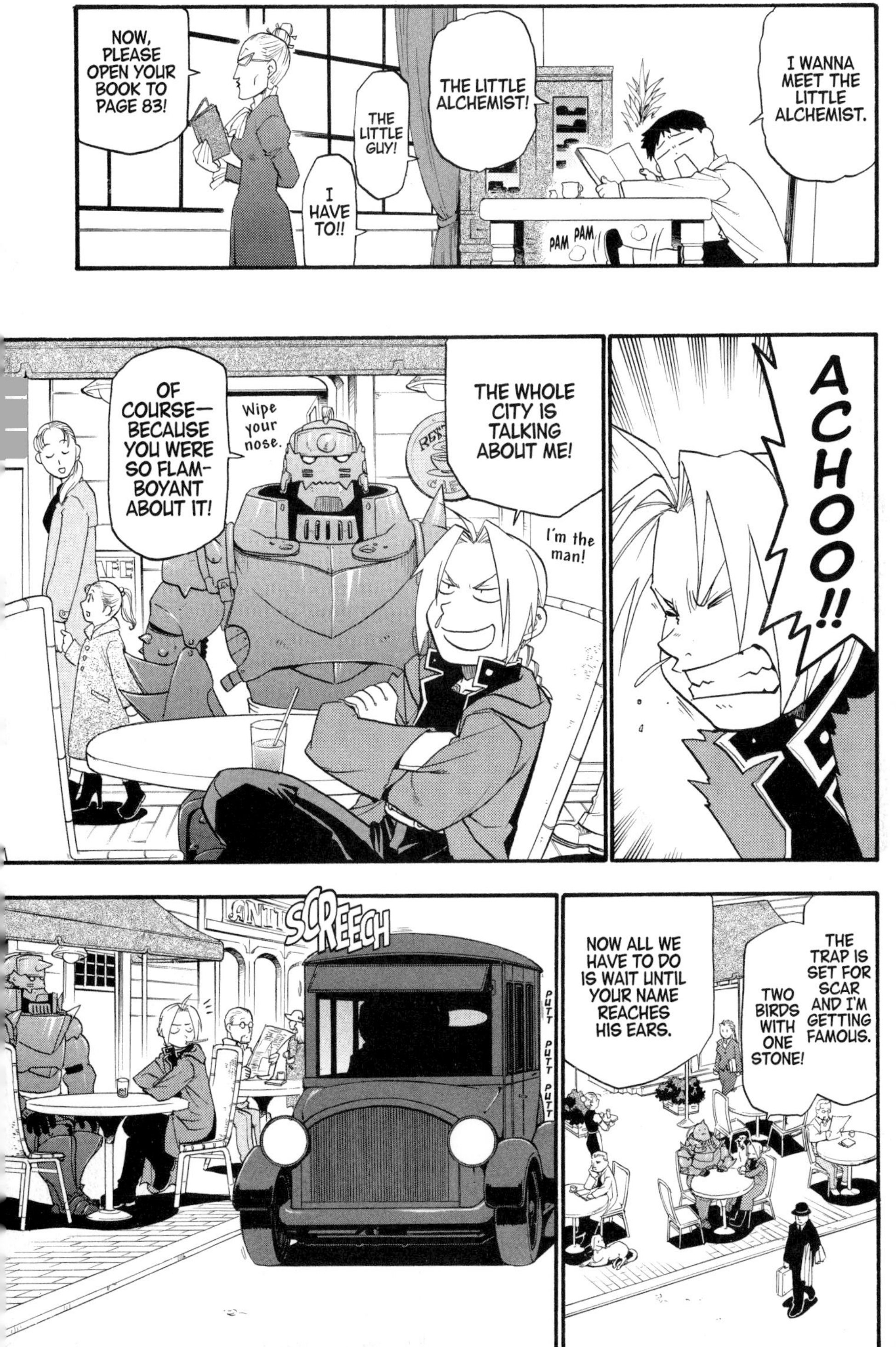
I WANNA MEET THE LITTLE ALCHEMIST.
THE LITTLE ALCHEMIST!
THE LITTLE GUY!
I HAVE TO!!
PAM PAM
NOW, PLEASE OPEN YOUR BOOK TO PAGE 83!
ACHOO!!
THE WHOLE CITY IS TALKING ABOUT ME!
I'm the man!
Wipe your nose.
OF COURSE— BECAUSE YOU WERE SO FLAM-BOYANT ABOUT IT!
THE TRAP IS SET FOR SCAR AND I'M GETTING FAMOUS.
TWO BIRDS WITH ONE STONE!
NOW ALL WE HAVE TO DO IS WAIT UNTIL YOUR NAME REACHES HIS EARS.
SCREECH
PUTT PUTT PUTT

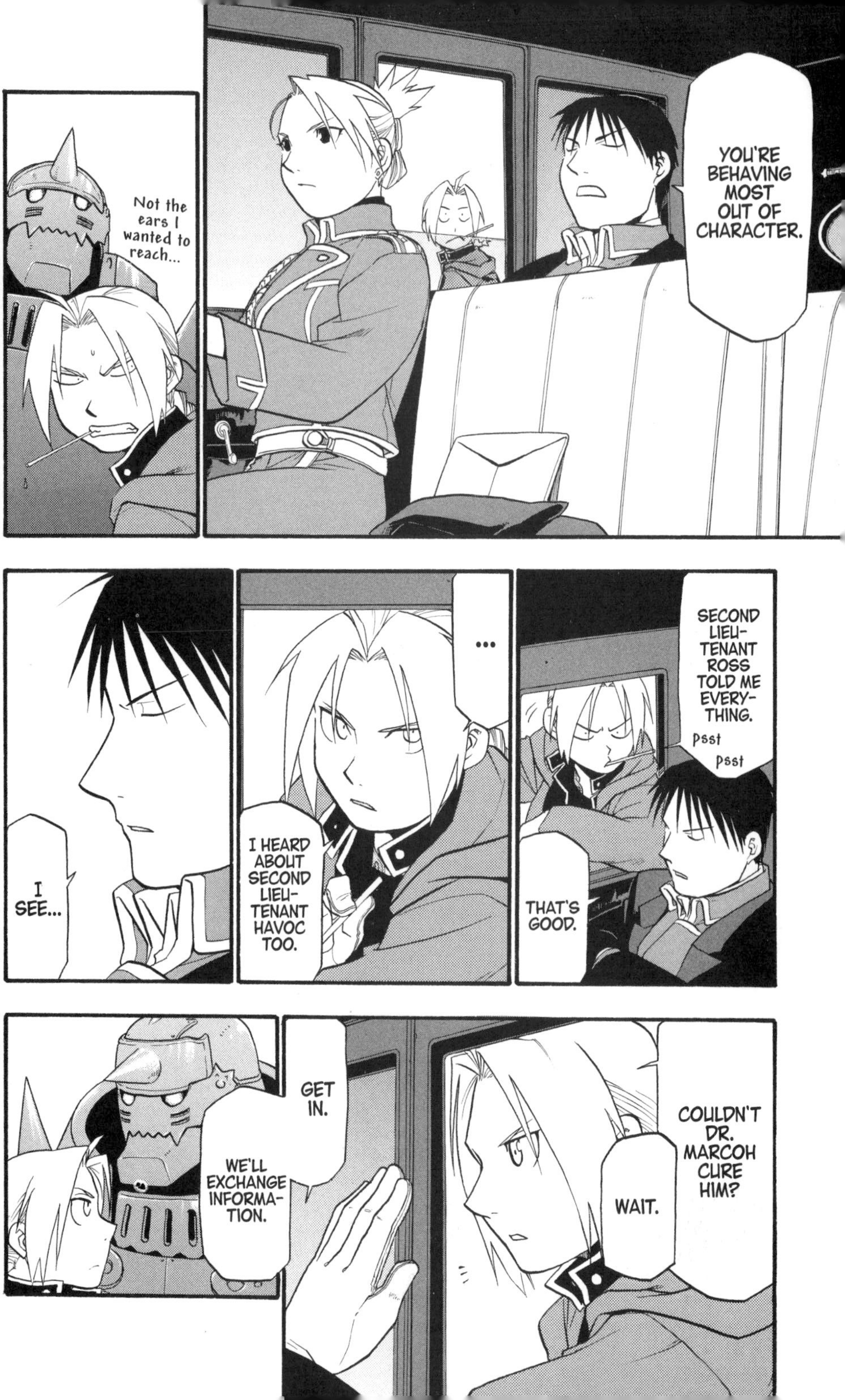
YOU'RE BEHAVING MOST OUT OF CHARACTER.
Not the ears I wanted to reach...
SECOND LIEU-TENANT ROSS TOLD ME EVERY-THING.
psst psst
THAT'S GOOD.
...
I HEARD ABOUT SECOND LIEU-TENANT HAVOC TOO.
I SEE...
COULDN'T DR. MARCOH CURE HIM?
WAIT.
GET IN.
WE'LL EXCHANGE INFORMA-TION.

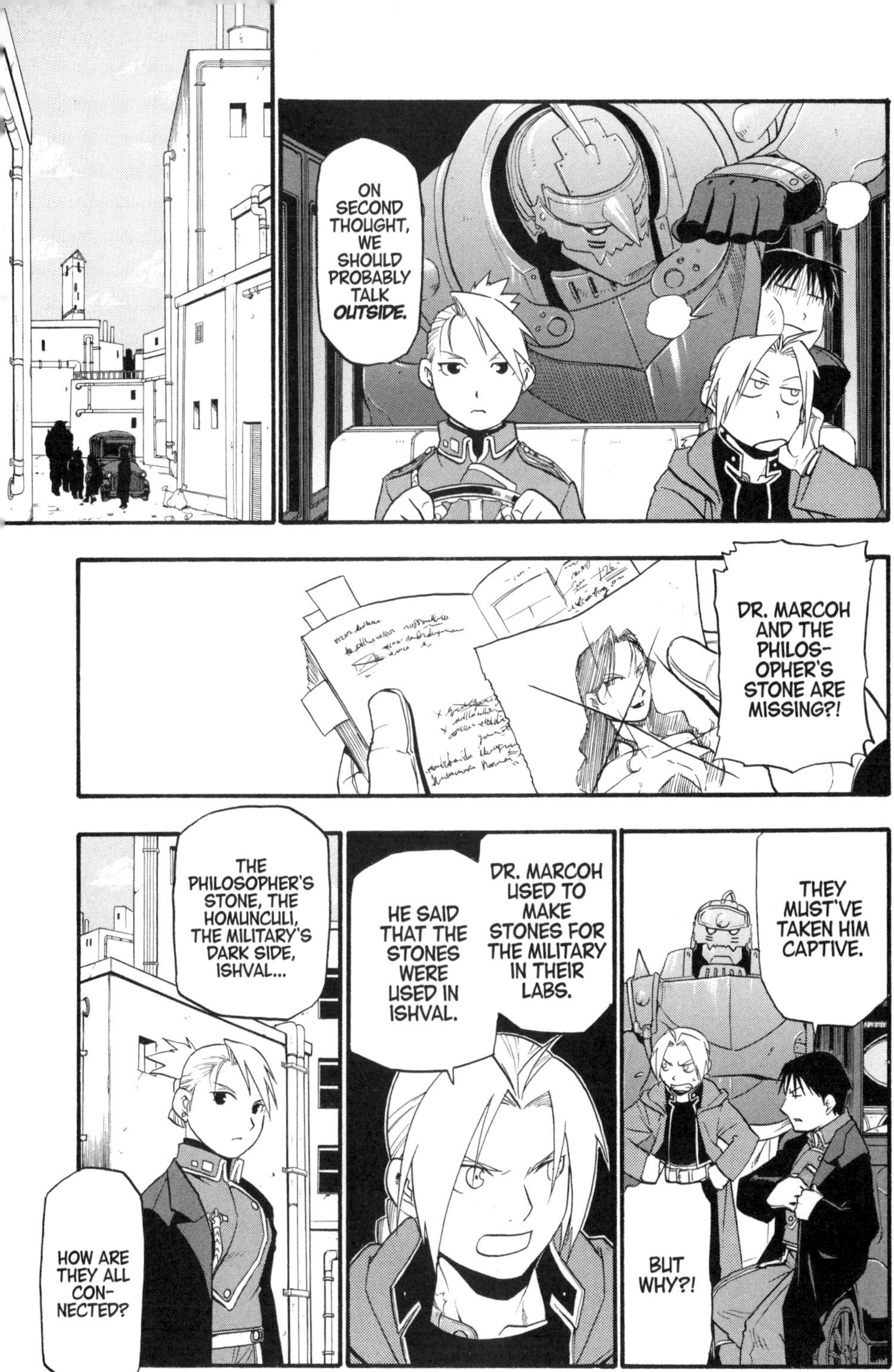
ON SECOND THOUGHT, WE SHOULD PROBABLY TALK OUTSIDE.
DR. MARCOH AND THE PHILOSOPHER'S STONE ARE MISSING?!
THEY MUST'VE TAKEN HIM CAPTIVE.
BUT WHY?!
DR. MARCOH USED TO MAKE STONES FOR THE MILITARY IN THEIR LABS.
HE SAID THAT THE STONES WERE USED IN ISHVAL.
THE PHILOSOPHER'S STONE, THE HOMUNCULI, THE MILITARY'S DARK SIDE, ISHVAL...
HOW ARE THEY ALL CONNECTED?

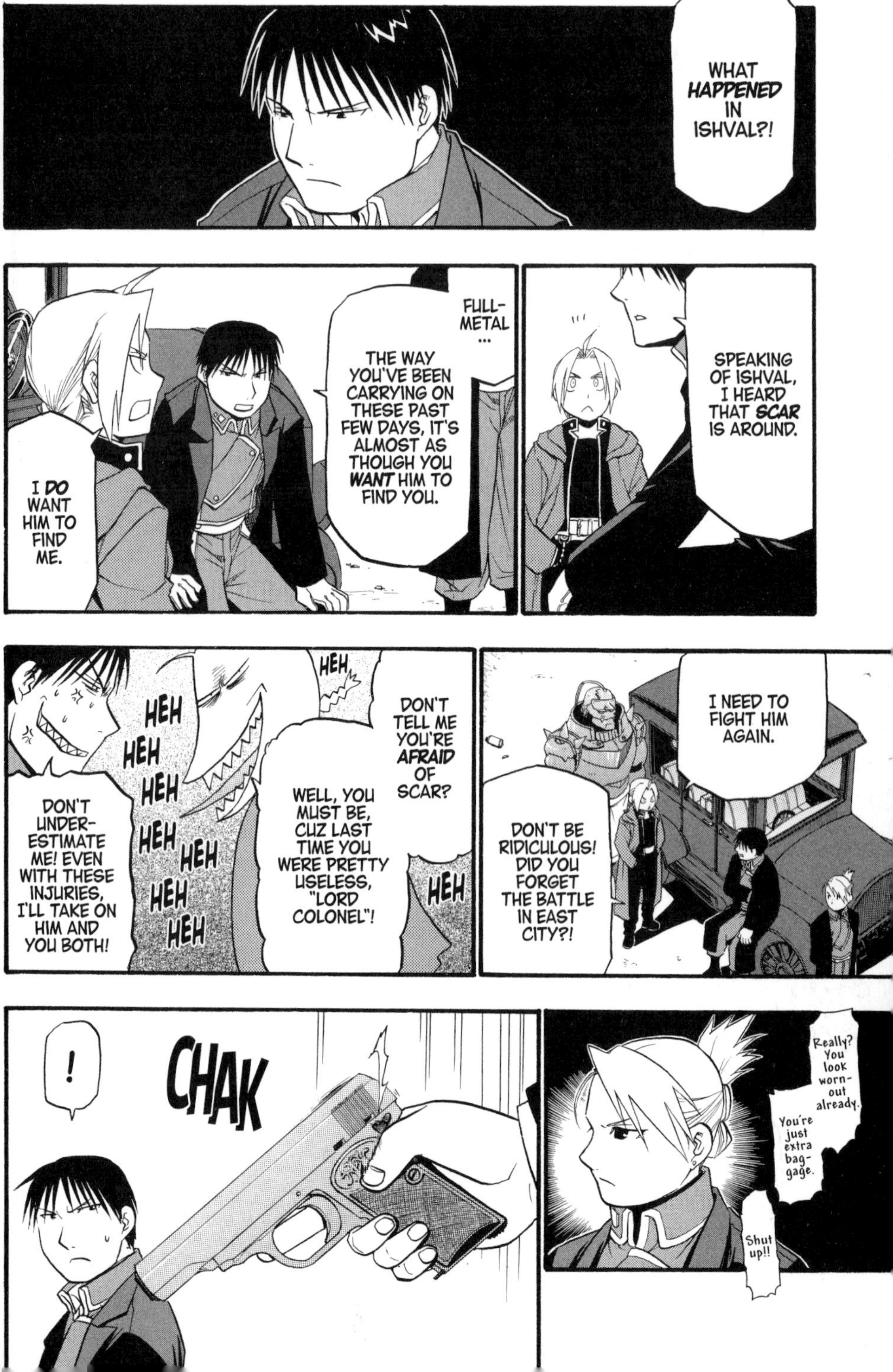
WHAT HAPPENED IN ISHVAL?!
SPEAKING OF ISHVAL, I HEARD THAT SCAR IS AROUND.
FULL-METAL...
THE WAY YOU'VE BEEN CARRYING ON THESE PAST FEW DAYS, IT'S ALMOST AS THOUGH YOU WANT HIM TO FIND YOU.
I DO WANT HIM TO FIND ME.
I NEED TO FIGHT HIM AGAIN.
DON'T BE RIDICULOUS! DID YOU FORGET THE BATTLE IN EAST CITY?!
HEH
DON'T TELL ME YOU'RE AFRAID OF SCAR?
WELL, YOU MUST BE, CUZ LAST TIME YOU WERE PRETTY USELESS, "LORD COLONEL"!
HEH
HEH HEH HEH HEH HEH HEH HEH
DON'T UNDER-ESTIMATE ME! EVEN WITH THESE INJURIES, I'LL TAKE ON HIM AND YOU BOTH!
Really? You look worn-out already.
You're just extra baggage.
Shut up!!
CHAK
!

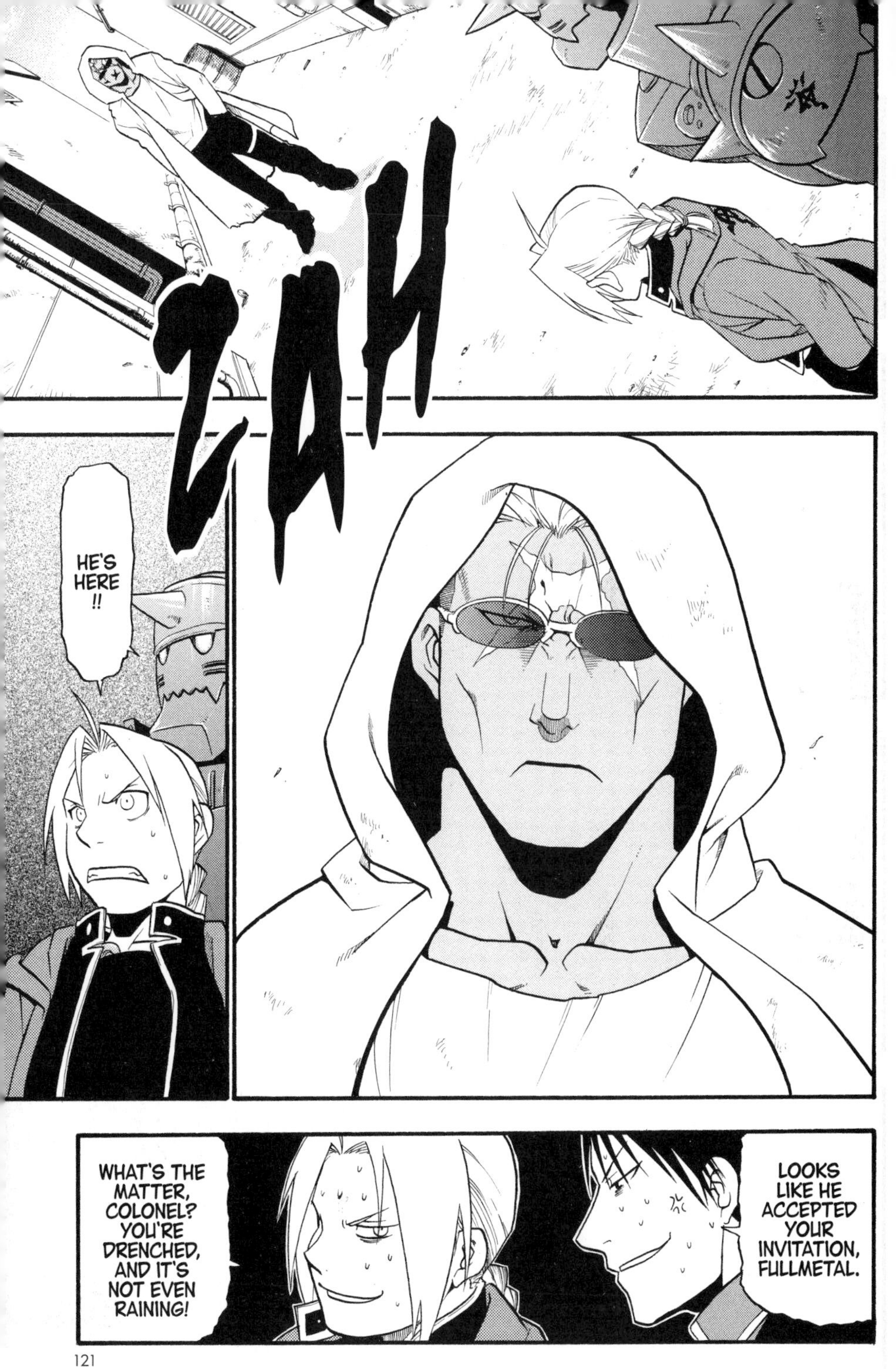
ZAH
HE'S HERE !!
LOOKS LIKE HE ACCEPTED YOUR INVITATION, FULLMETAL.
WHAT'S THE MATTER, COLONEL? YOU'RE DRENCHED, AND IT'S NOT EVEN RAINING!

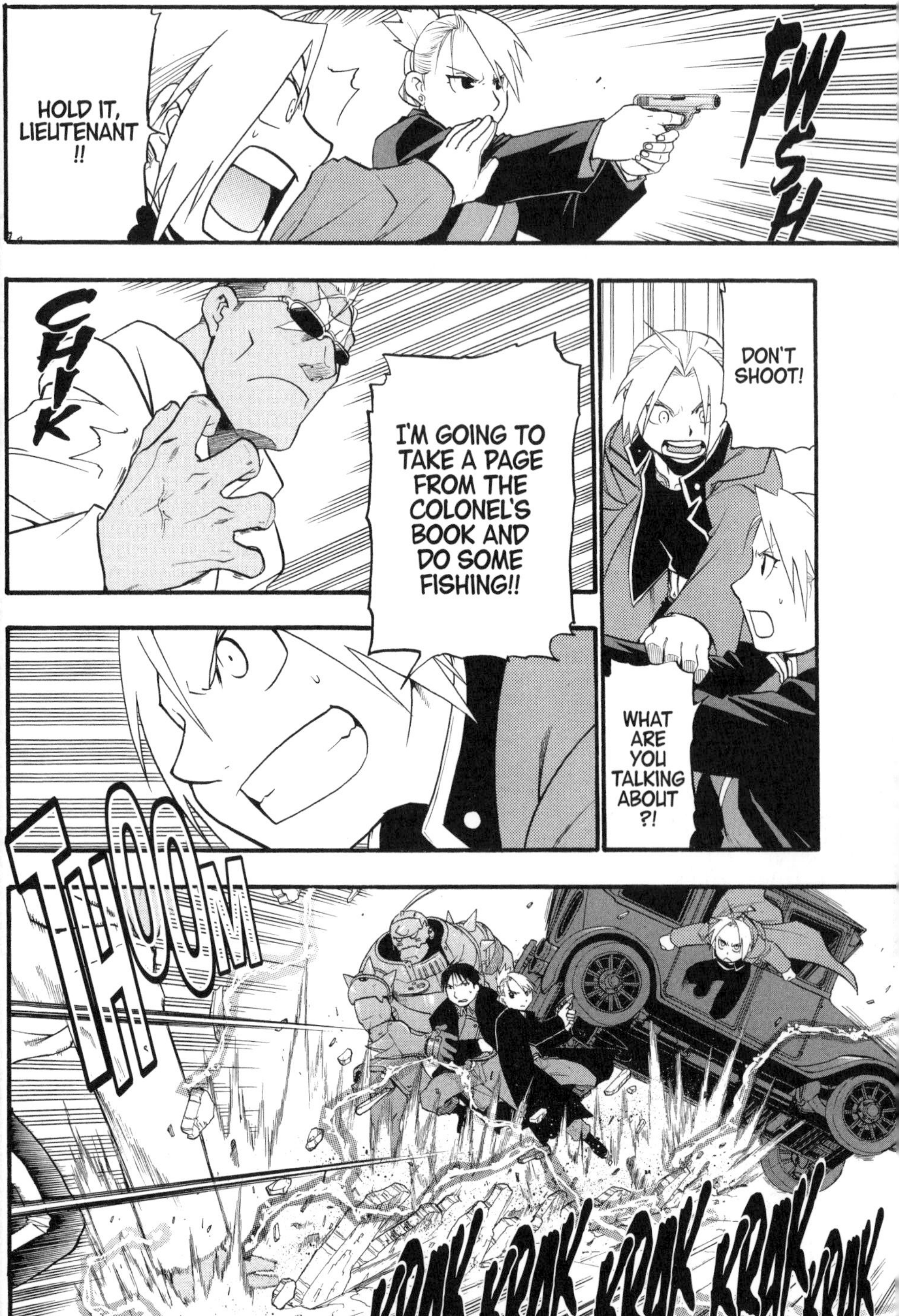
FWSH
HOLD IT, LIEUTENANT!!
DON'T SHOOT!
WHAT ARE YOU TALKING ABOUT?!
CHIK
I'M GOING TO TAKE A PAGE FROM THE COLONEL'S BOOK AND DO SOME FISHING!!
THOOM
KRAK KRAK KRAK KRAK KRAK

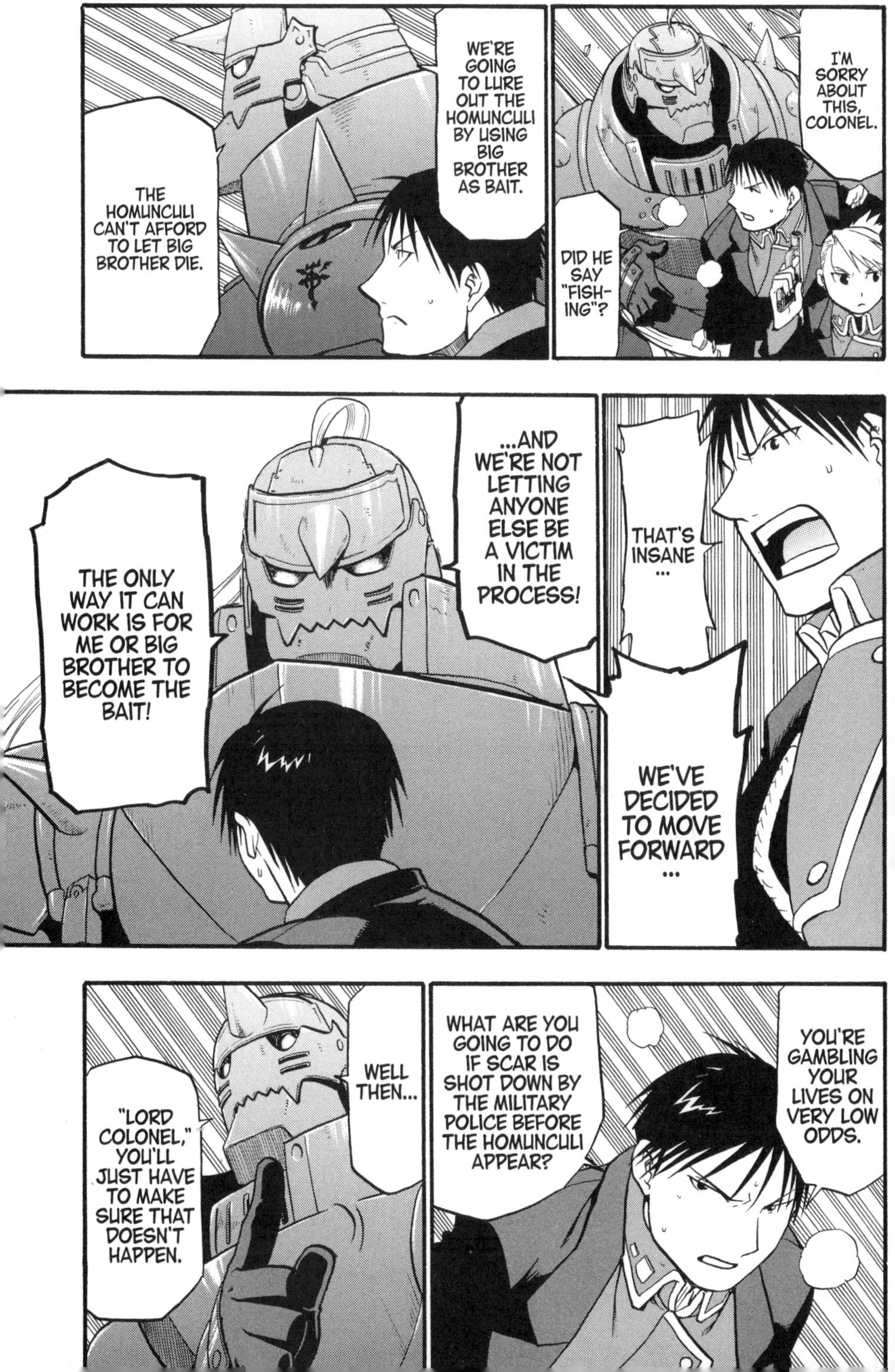
I'M SORRY ABOUT THIS, COLONEL.
DID HE SAY "FISHING"?
WE'RE GOING TO LURE OUT THE HOMUNCULI BY USING BIG BROTHER AS BAIT.
THE HOMUNCULI CAN'T AFFORD TO LET BIG BROTHER DIE.
THAT'S INSANE...
WE'VE DECIDED TO MOVE FORWARD...
...AND WE'RE NOT LETTING ANYONE ELSE BE A VICTIM IN THE PROCESS!
THE ONLY WAY IT CAN WORK IS FOR ME OR BIG BROTHER TO BECOME THE BAIT!
YOU'RE GAMBLING YOUR LIVES ON VERY LOW ODDS.
WHAT ARE YOU GOING TO DO IF SCAR IS SHOT DOWN BY THE MILITARY POLICE BEFORE THE HOMUNCULI APPEAR?
WELL THEN...
"LORD COLONEL," YOU'LL JUST HAVE TO MAKE SURE THAT DOESN'T HAPPEN.

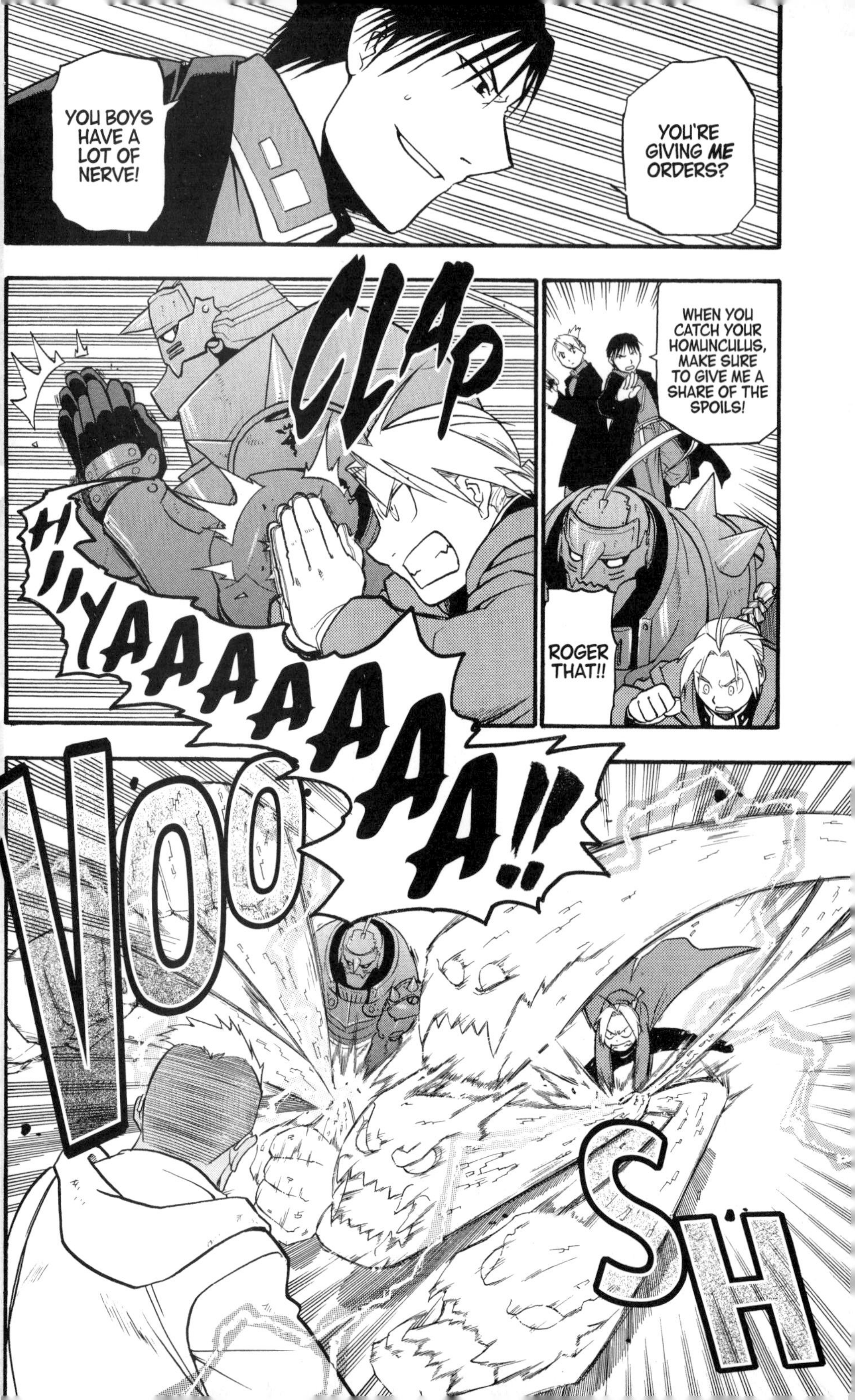

YOU'RE GIVING ME ORDERS?
YOU BOYS HAVE A LOT OF NERVE!
WHEN YOU CATCH YOUR HOMUNCULUS, MAKE SURE TO GIVE ME A SHARE OF THE SPOILS!
ROGER THAT!!
CLAP
HIYAAAAAAAAA!!
VOOSH

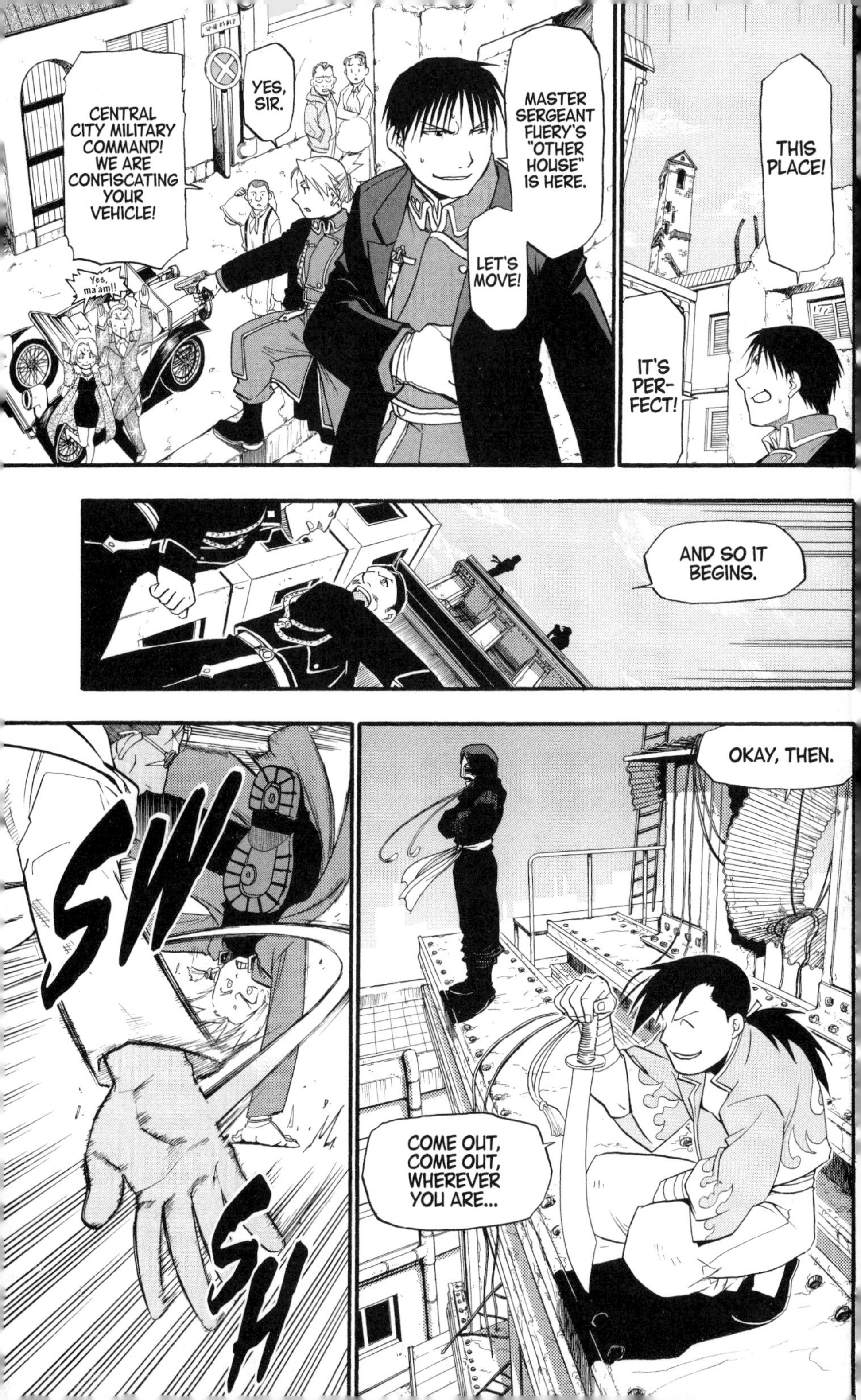
THIS PLACE!
IT'S PER-FECT!
MASTER SERGEANT FUERY'S "OTHER HOUSE" IS HERE.
LET'S MOVE!
YES, SIR.
CENTRAL CITY MILITARY COMMAND! WE ARE CONFISCATING YOUR VEHICLE!
Yes, ma'am!!
AND SO IT BEGINS.
OKAY, THEN.
COME OUT, COME OUT, WHEREVER YOU ARE...
SW
SH

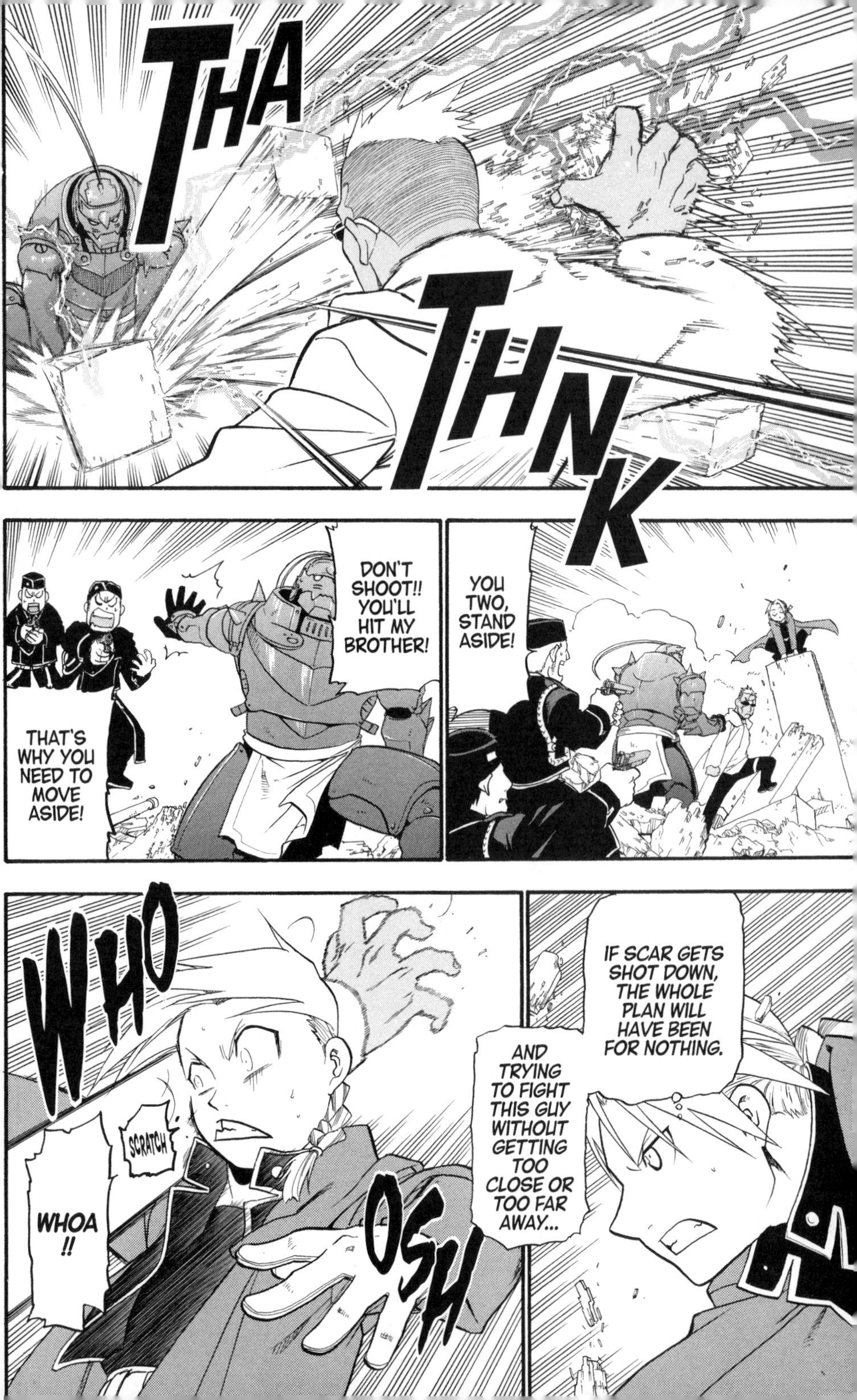
THA
THNK
YOU TWO, STAND ASIDE!
DON'T SHOOT!! YOU'LL HIT MY BROTHER!
THAT'S WHY YOU NEED TO MOVE ASIDE!
IF SCAR GETS SHOT DOWN, THE WHOLE PLAN WILL HAVE BEEN FOR NOTHING.
AND TRYING TO FIGHT THIS GUY WITHOUT GETTING TOO CLOSE OR TOO FAR AWAY...
WHOOSH
SCRATCH
WHOA !!

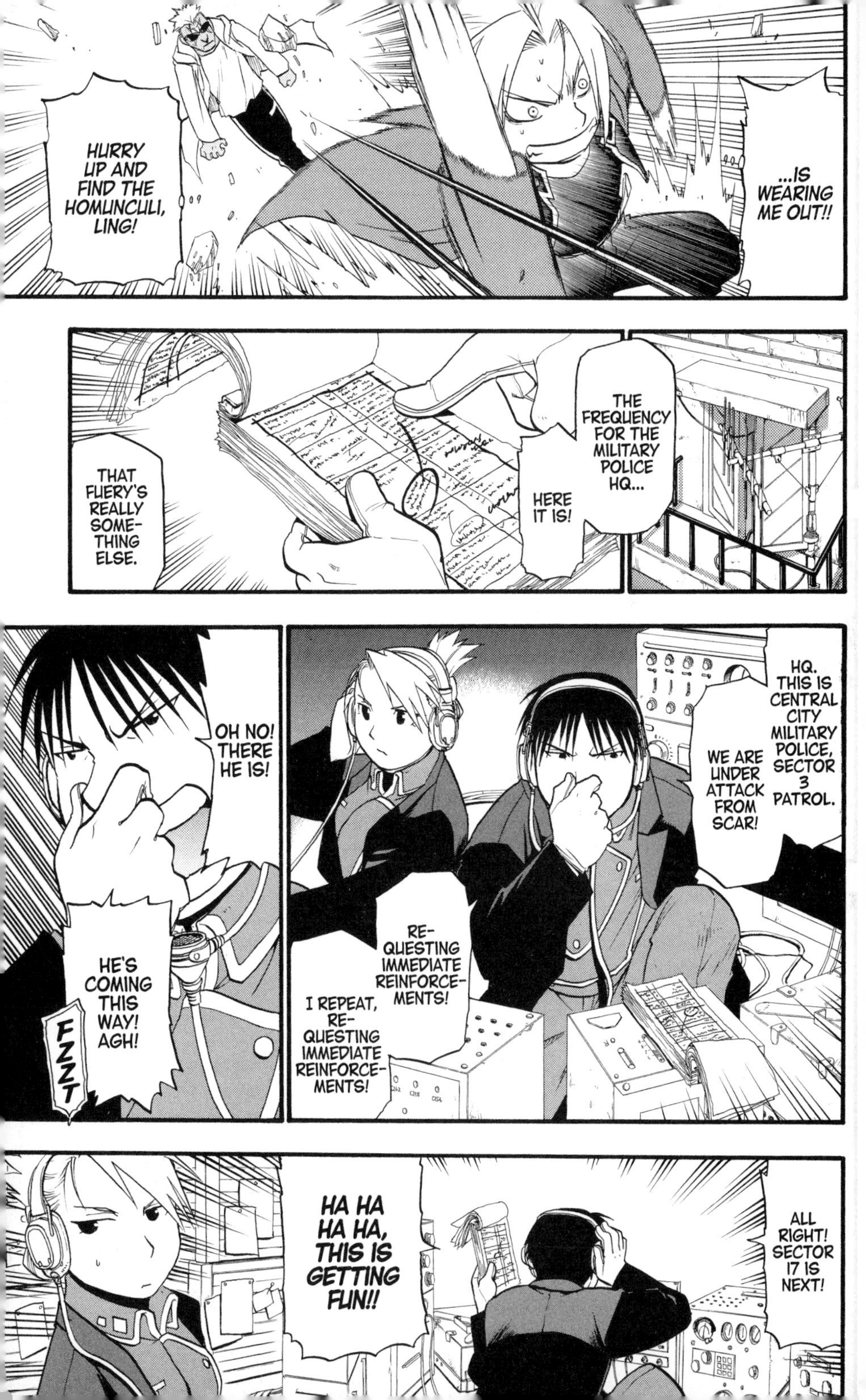

...IS WEARING ME OUT!!
HURRY UP AND FIND THE HOMUNCULI, LING!
THE FREQUENCY FOR THE MILITARY POLICE HQ...
HERE IT IS!
THAT FUERY'S REALLY SOMETHING ELSE.
HQ. THIS IS CENTRAL CITY MILITARY POLICE, SECTOR 3 PATROL.
WE ARE UNDER ATTACK FROM SCAR!
REQUESTING IMMEDIATE REINFORCEMENTS!
I REPEAT, REQUESTING IMMEDIATE REINFORCEMENTS!
OH NO! THERE HE IS!
HE'S COMING THIS WAY! AGH!
FZZT
ALL RIGHT! SECTOR 17 IS NEXT!
HA HA HA HA, THIS IS GETTING FUN!!

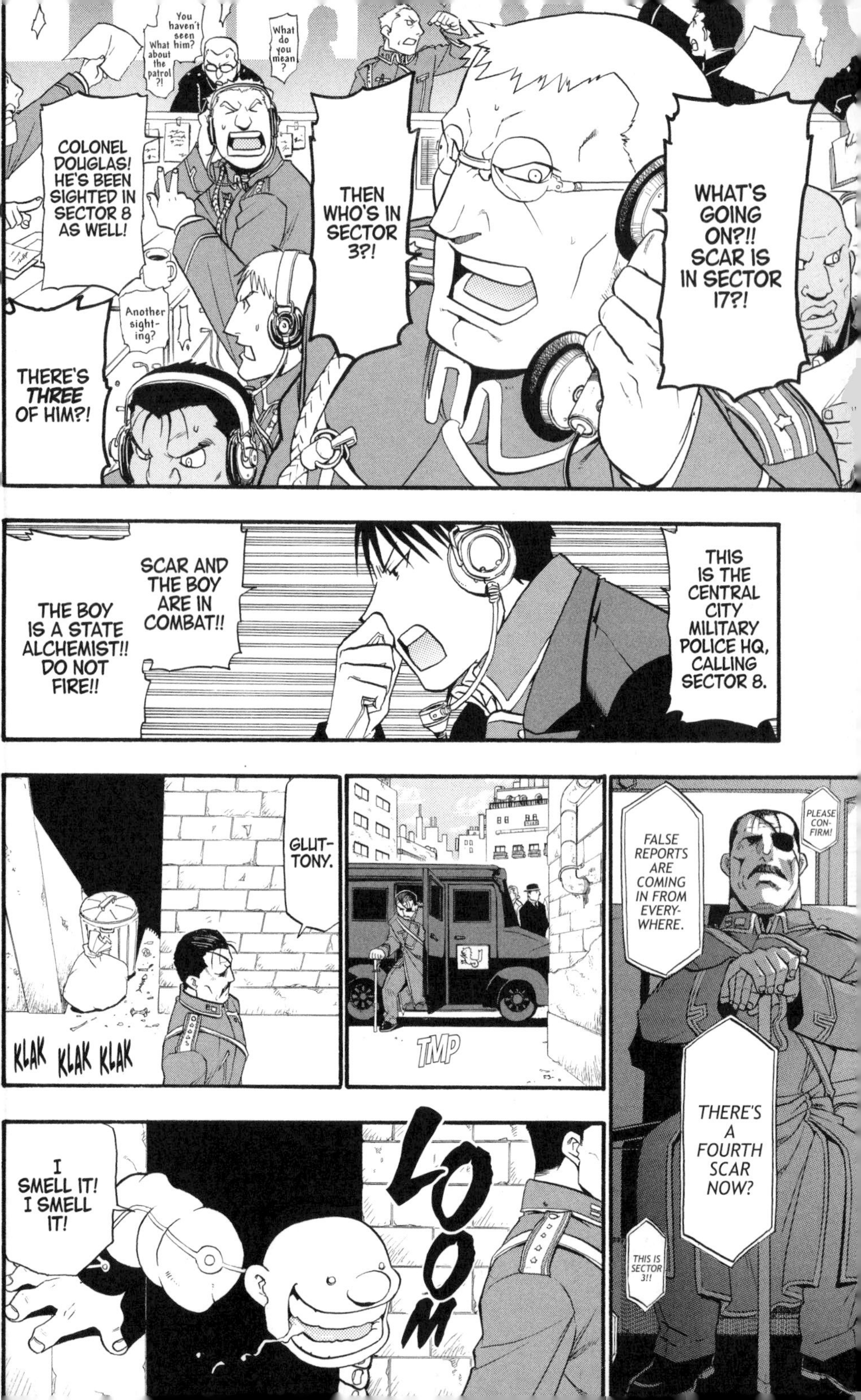
WHAT'S GOING ON?!! SCAR IS IN SECTOR 17?!
What do you mean?
THEN WHO'S IN SECTOR 3?!
You haven't seen him? What about the patrol?!
COLONEL DOUGLAS! HE'S BEEN SIGHTED IN SECTOR 8 AS WELL!
Another sighting?
THERE'S THREE OF HIM?!
THIS IS THE CENTRAL CITY MILITARY POLICE HQ, CALLING SECTOR 8.
SCAR AND THE BOY ARE IN COMBAT!!
THE BOY IS A STATE ALCHEMIST!! DO NOT FIRE!!
PLEASE CONFIRM!
FALSE REPORTS ARE COMING IN FROM EVERYWHERE.
THERE'S A FOURTH SCAR NOW?
THIS IS SECTOR 3!!
TMP
GLUT-TONY.
KLAK KLAK KLAK
LOOM
I SMELL IT! I SMELL IT!

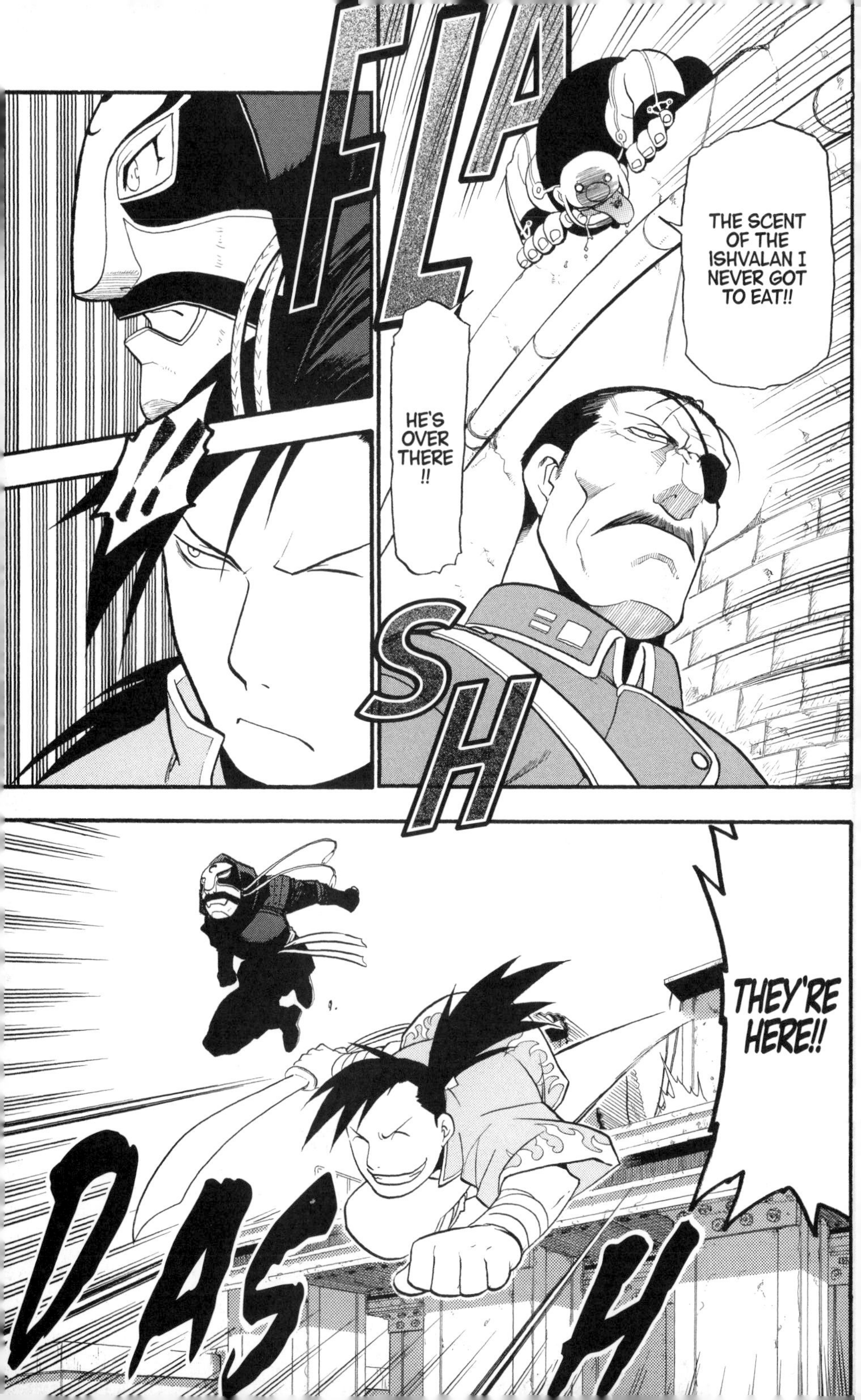
FLA
THE SCENT OF THE ISHVALAN I NEVER GOT TO EAT!!
HE'S OVER THERE!!
SH
THEY'RE HERE!!
DASH

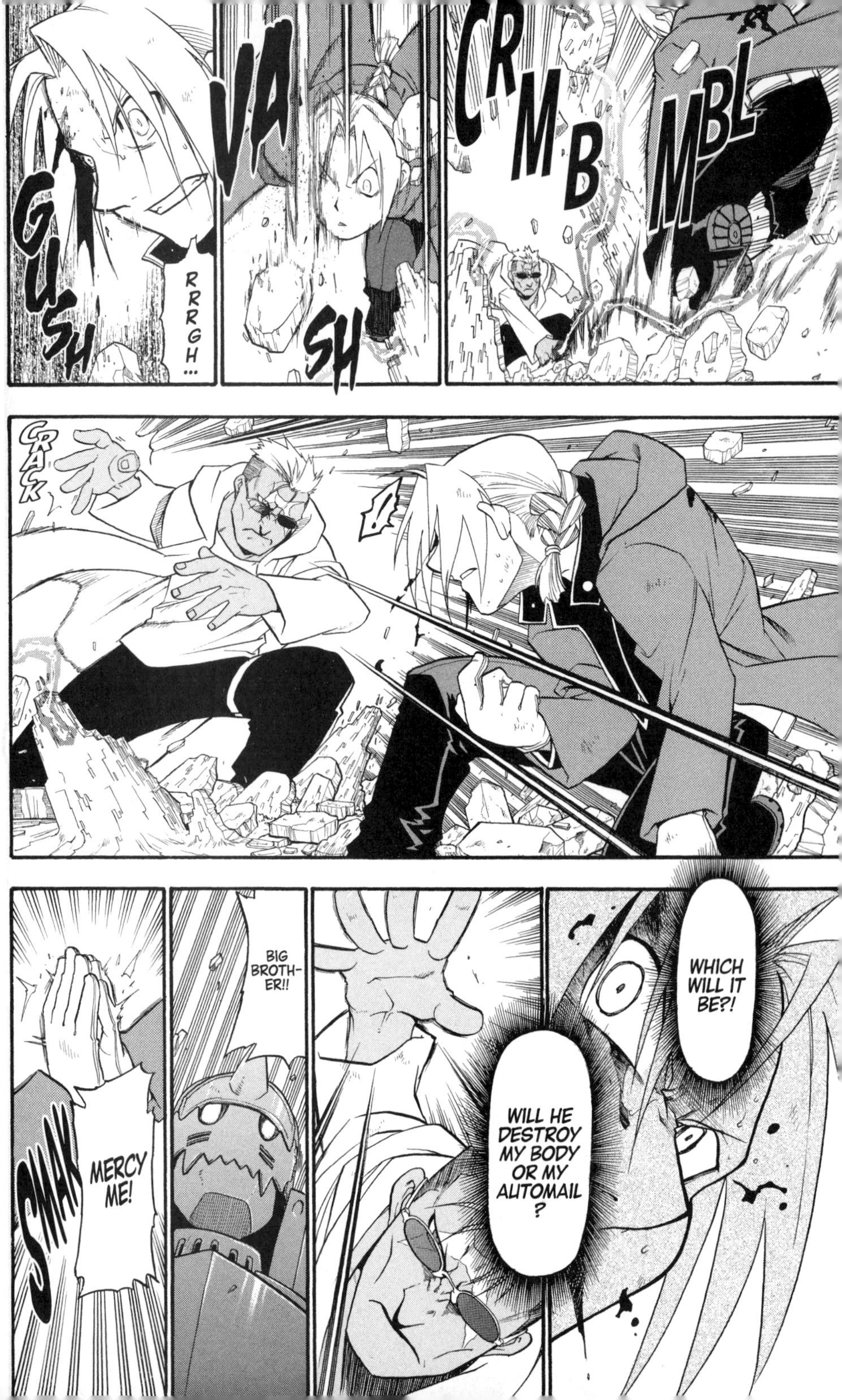
CRMB
MBL
VA
SH
GUSH
RRRGH...
CRACK
!
WHICH WILL IT BE?!
WILL HE DESTROY MY BODY OR MY AUTOMAIL?
BIG BROTHER!!
SMAK
MERCY ME!

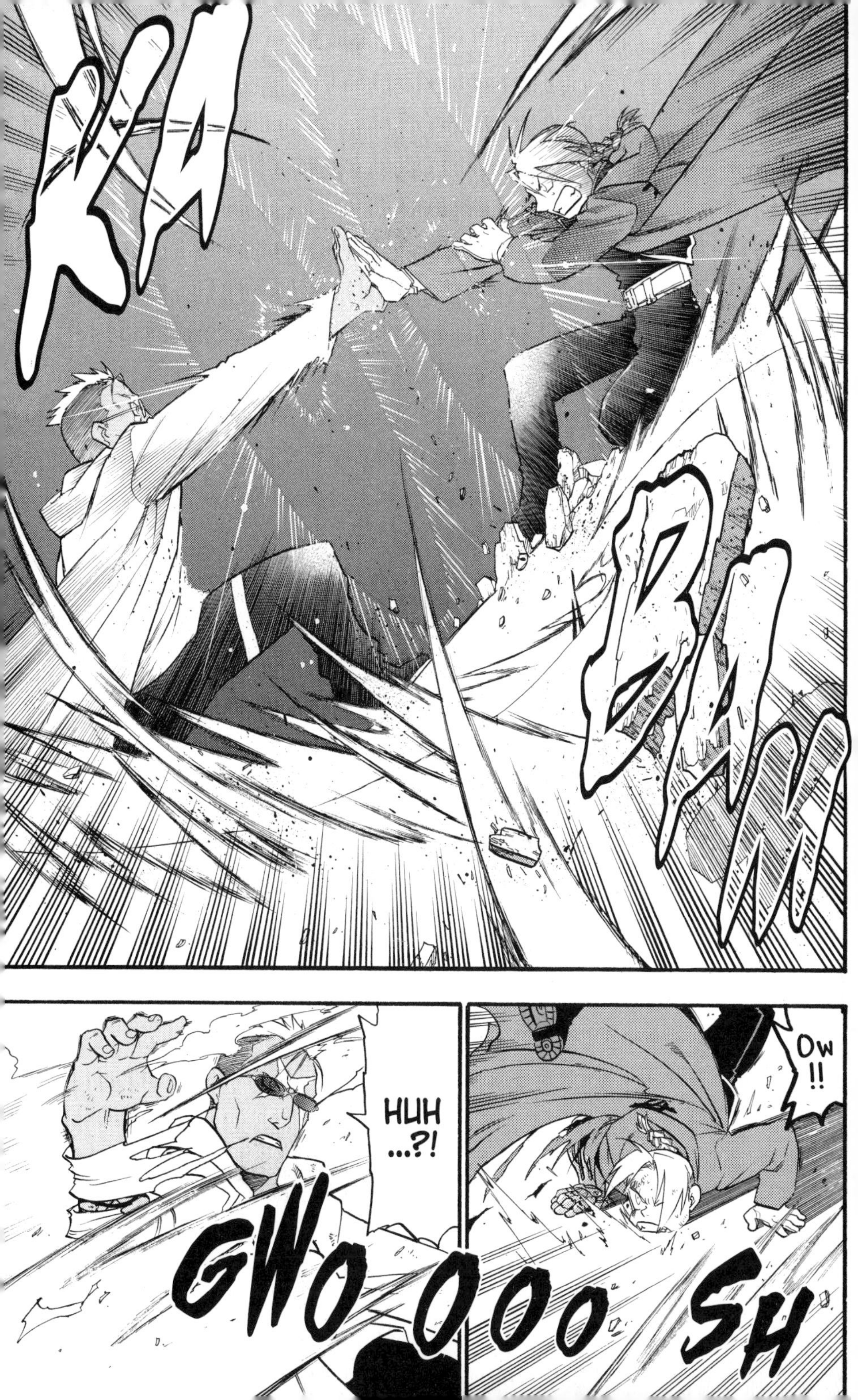
KRA
BAM
OW !!
HUH ...?!
GWOOOOSH

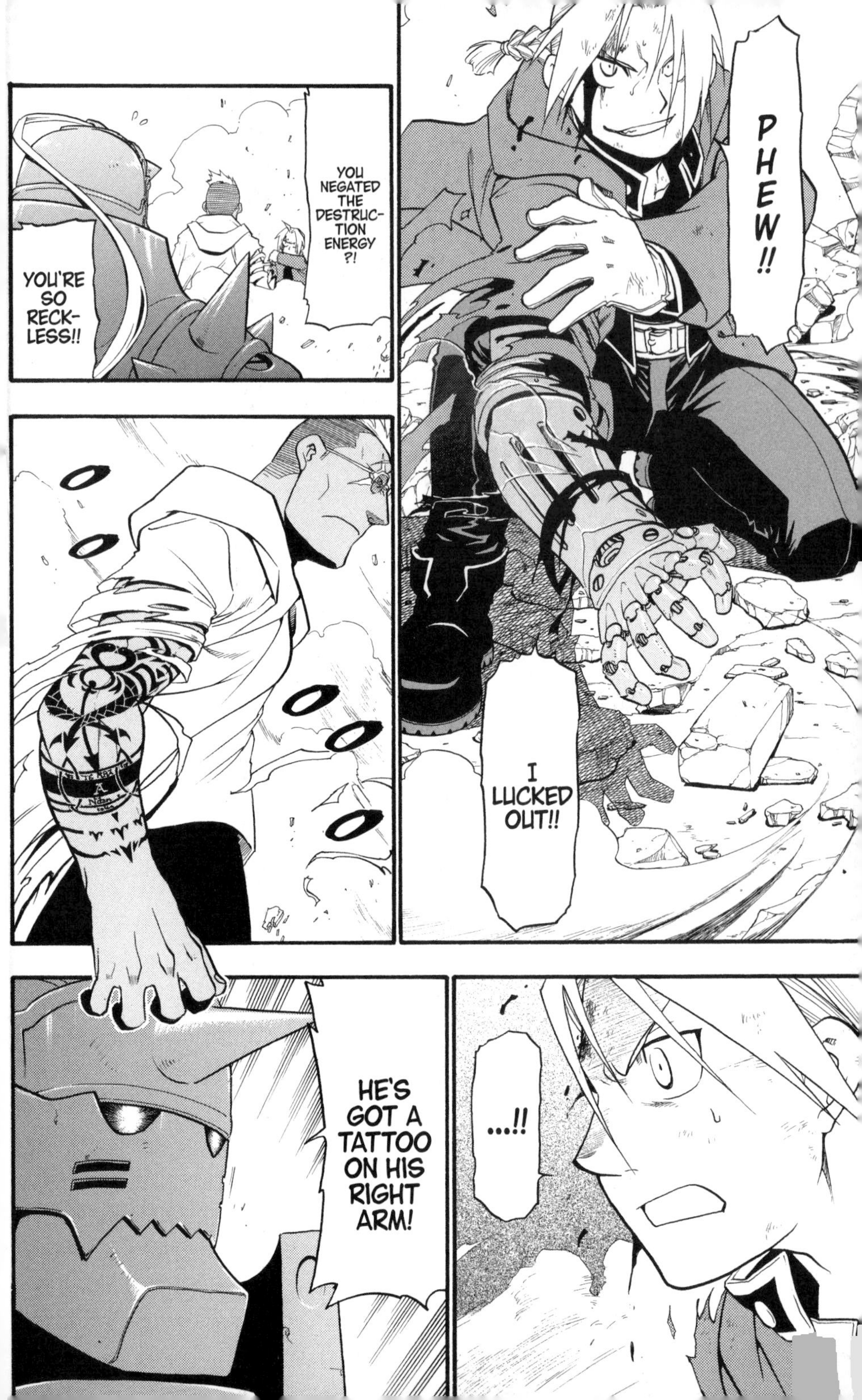
PHEW!!
I LUCKED OUT!!
YOU NEGATED THE DESTRUCTION ENERGY?!
YOU'RE SO RECKLESS!!
...!!
HE'S GOT A TATTOO ON HIS RIGHT ARM!

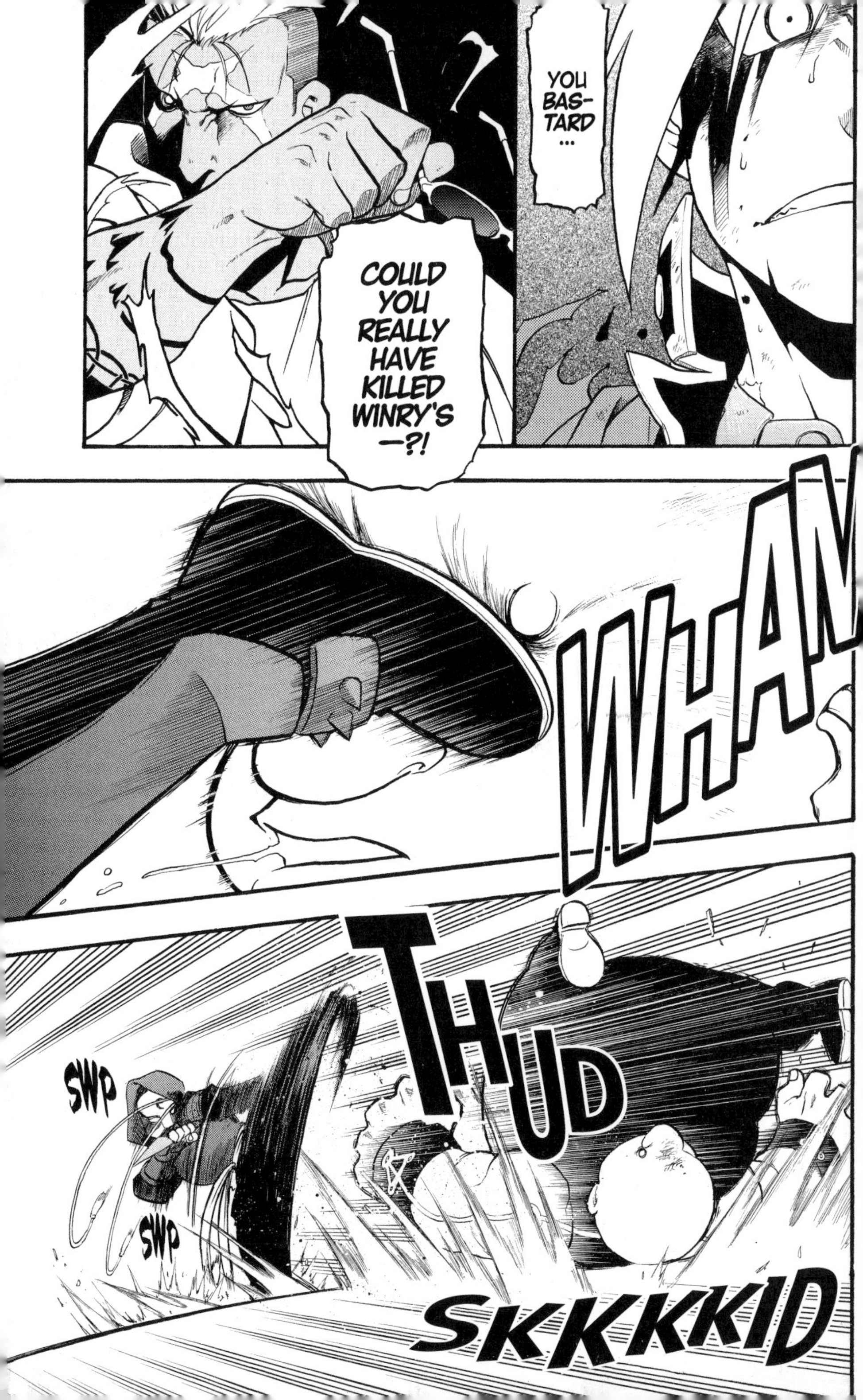
YOU BAS-TARD ...
COULD YOU REALLY HAVE KILLED WINRY'S —?!
WHAM
THUD
SWP
SWP
SKKKKID

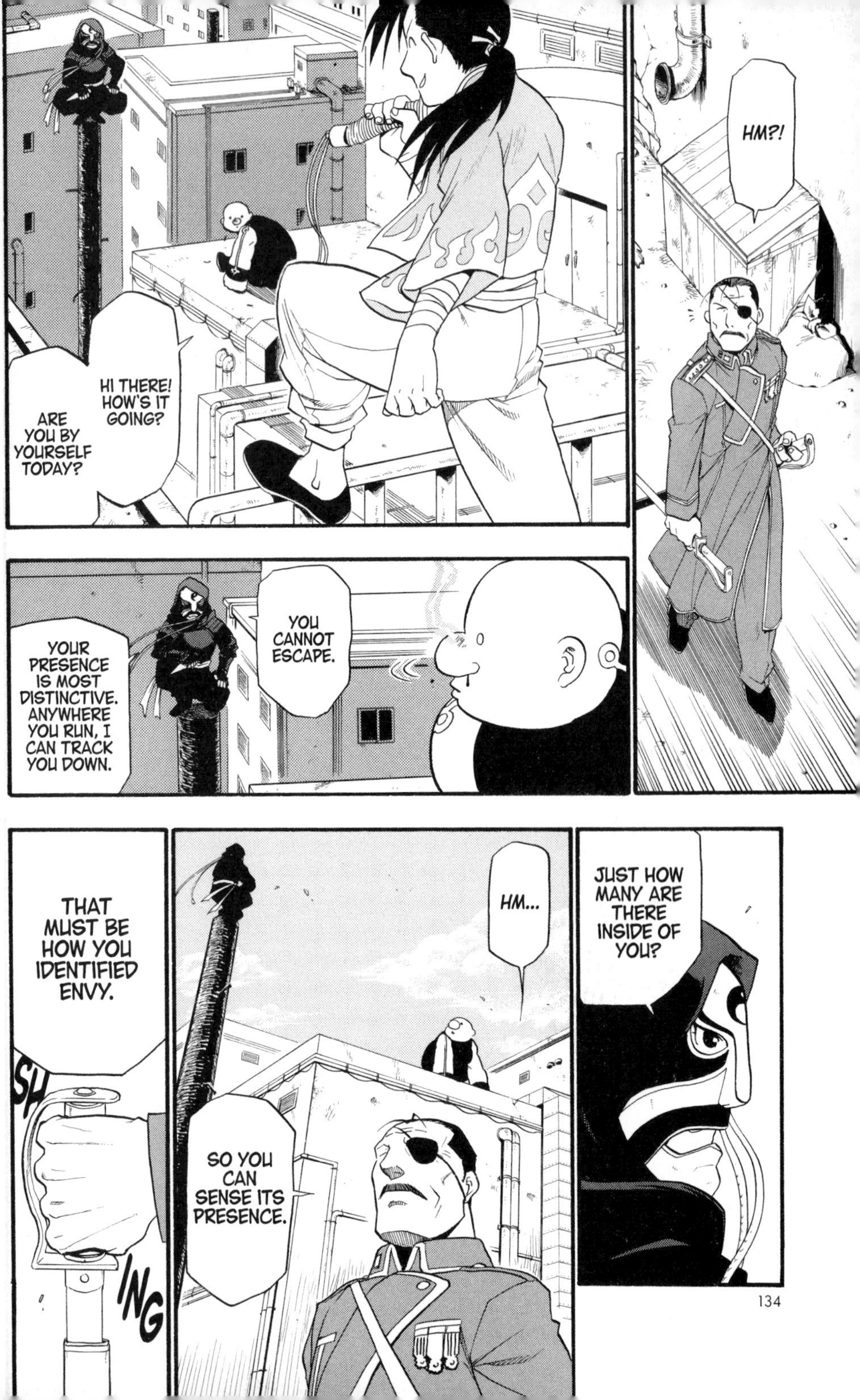
HM?!
HI THERE! HOW'S IT GOING?
ARE YOU BY YOURSELF TODAY?
YOU CANNOT ESCAPE.
YOUR PRESENCE IS MOST DISTINCTIVE. ANYWHERE YOU RUN, I CAN TRACK YOU DOWN.
JUST HOW MANY ARE THERE INSIDE OF YOU?
HM...
SO YOU CAN SENSE ITS PRESENCE.
THAT MUST BE HOW YOU IDENTIFIED ENVY.
SHING

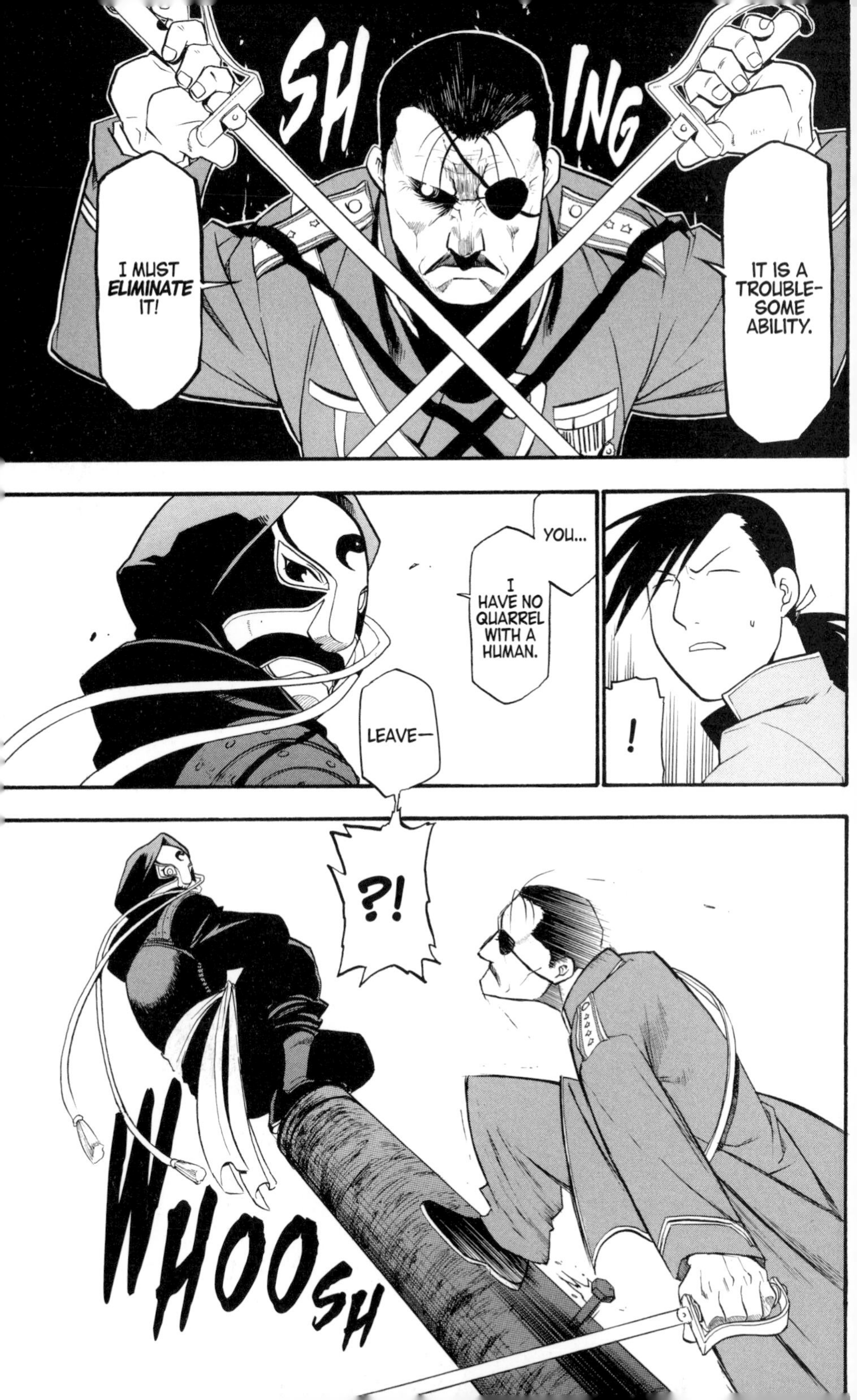
SHING
IT IS A TROUBLE-SOME ABILITY.
I MUST ELIMINATE IT!
!
YOU...
I HAVE NO QUARREL WITH A HUMAN.
LEAVE—
?!
WHOOSH

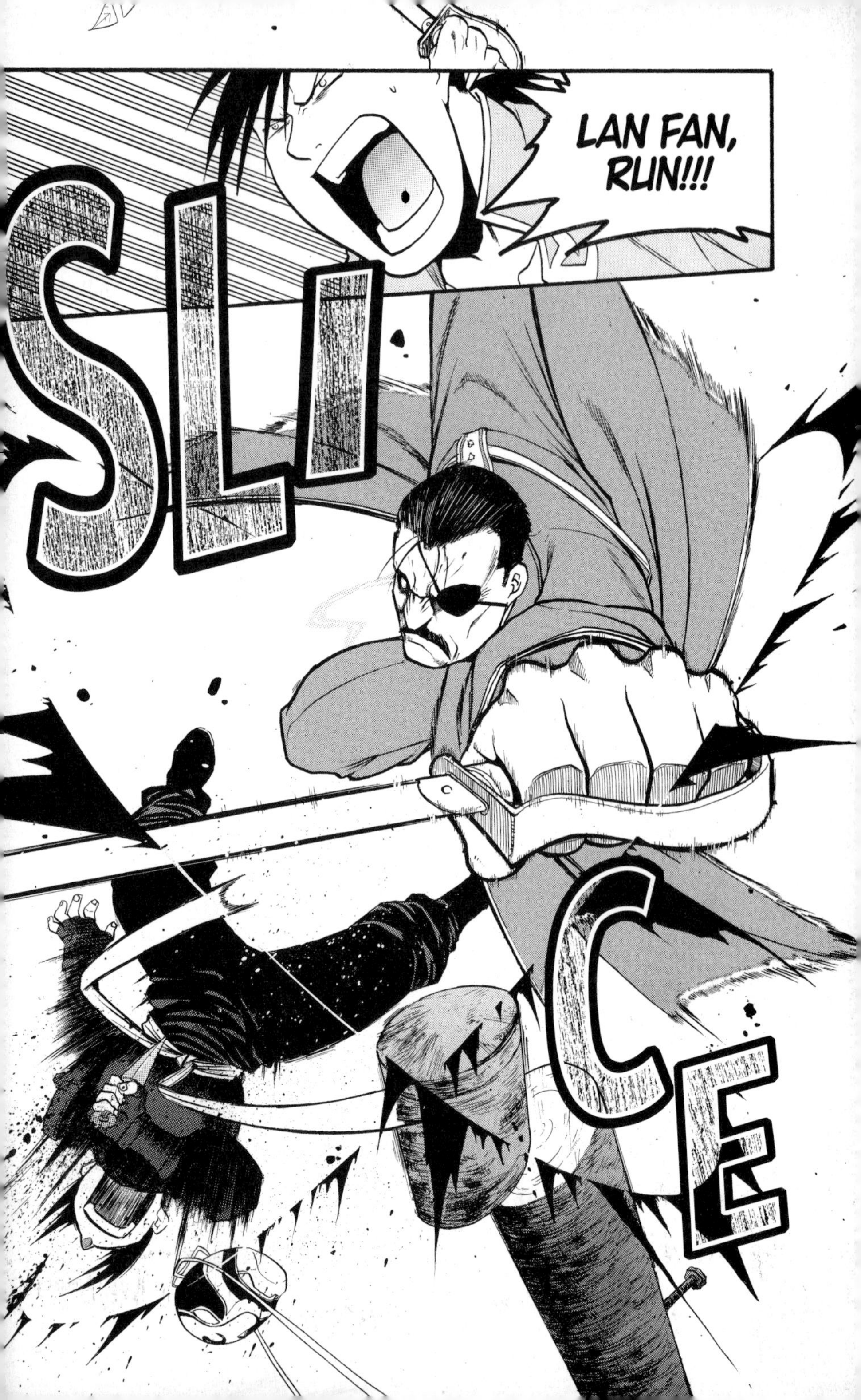
LAN FAN, RUN!!!
SLICE

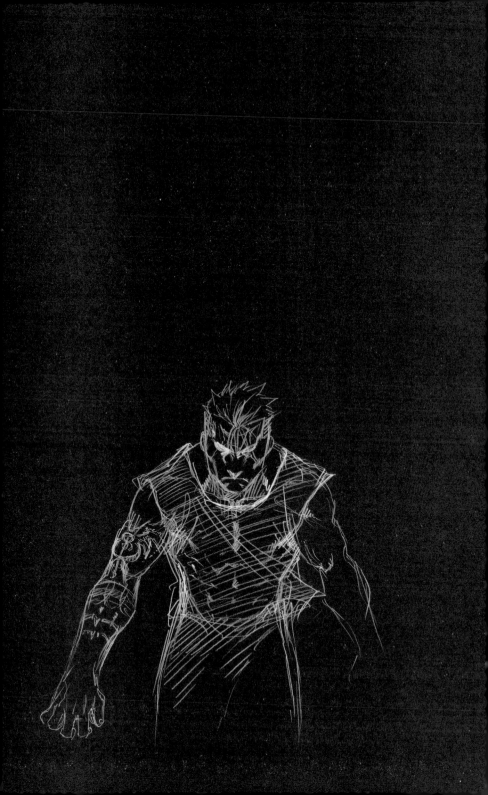

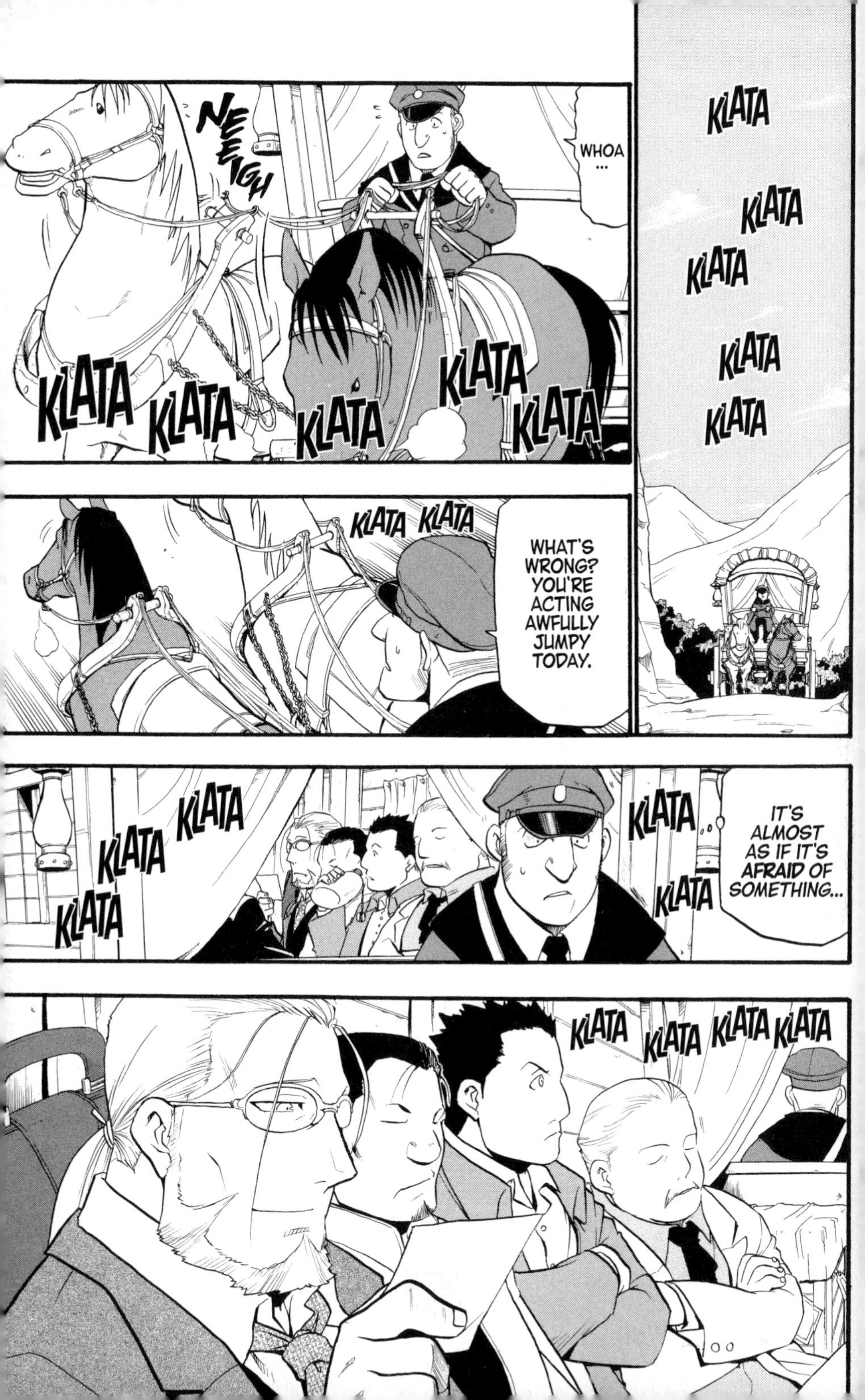
KLATA
KLATA
KLATA
KLATA
KLATA
WHOA ...
NEEIGH
KLATA
KLATA
KLATA
KLATA
KLATA
WHAT'S WRONG? YOU'RE ACTING AWFULLY JUMPY TODAY.
KLATA KLATA
IT'S ALMOST AS IF IT'S AFRAID OF SOMETHING...
KLATA
KLATA
KLATA
KLATA
KLATA
KLATA KLATA KLATA KLATA

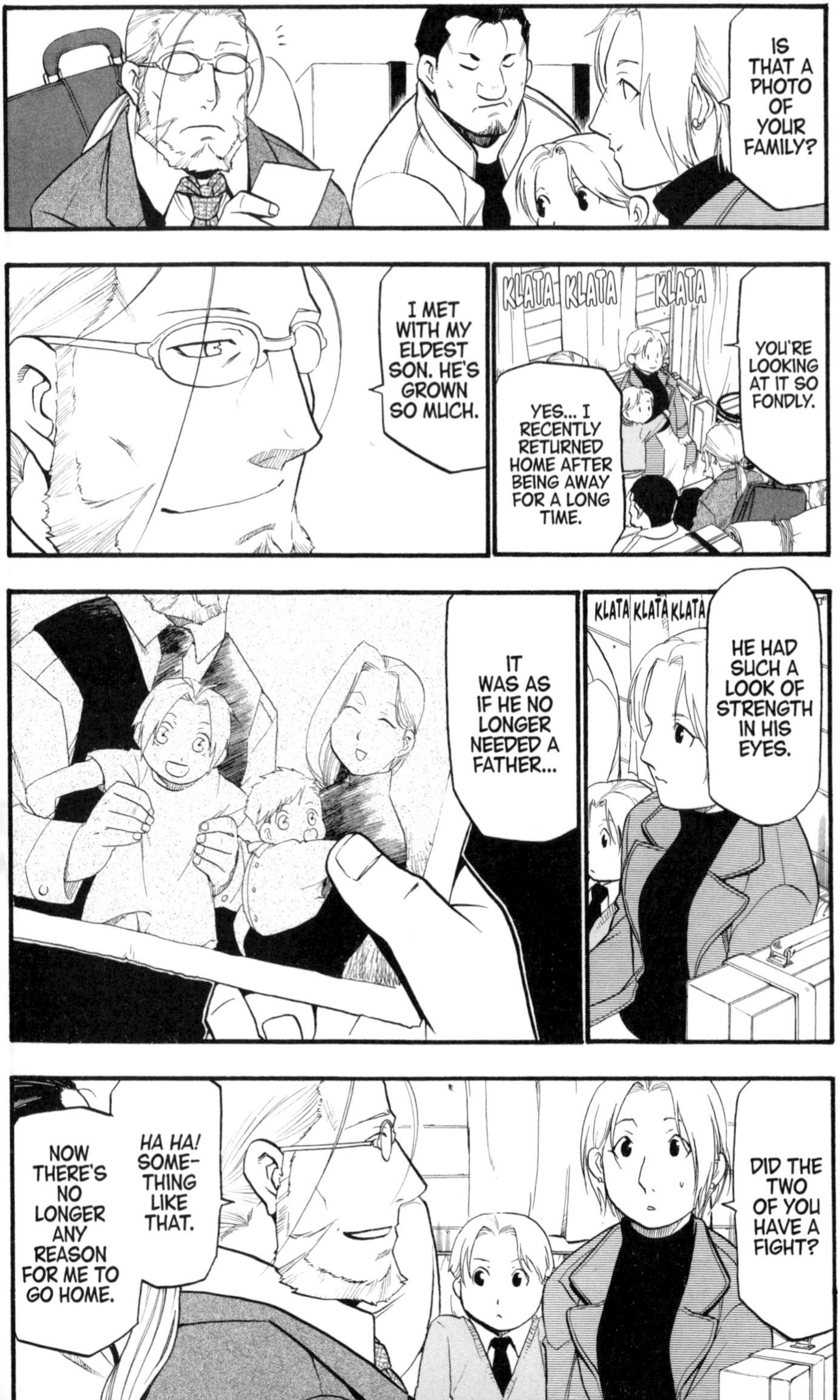
IS THAT A PHOTO OF YOUR FAMILY?
KLATA KLATA KLATA
YOU'RE LOOKING AT IT SO FONDLY.
YES... I RECENTLY RETURNED HOME AFTER BEING AWAY FOR A LONG TIME.
I MET WITH MY ELDEST SON. HE'S GROWN SO MUCH.
KLATA KLATA KLATA
HE HAD SUCH A LOOK OF STRENGTH IN HIS EYES.
IT WAS AS IF HE NO LONGER NEEDED A FATHER...
DID THE TWO OF YOU HAVE A FIGHT?
HA HA! SOMETHING LIKE THAT.
NOW THERE'S NO LONGER ANY REASON FOR ME TO GO HOME.

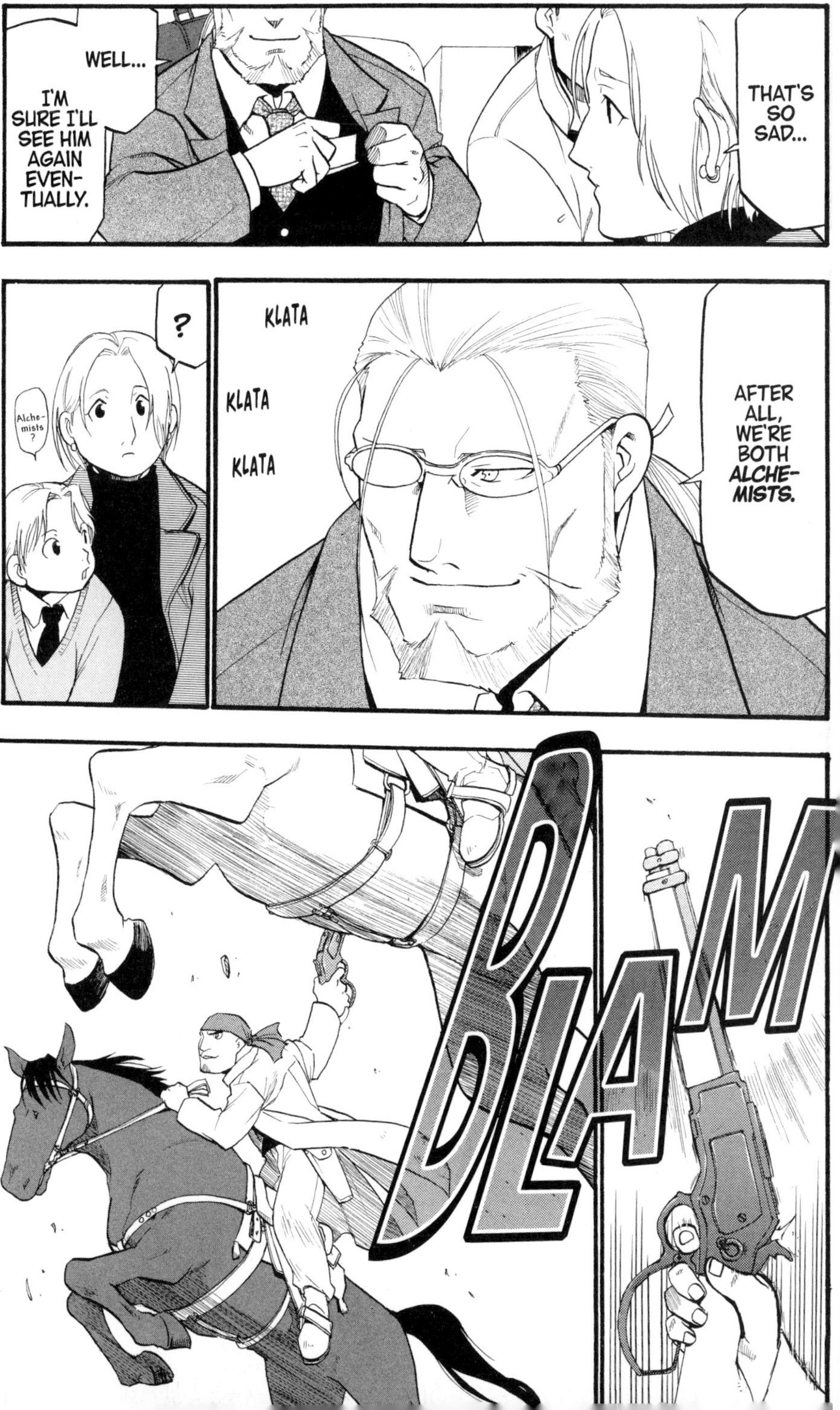
THAT'S SO SAD...
WELL...
I'M SURE I'LL SEE HIM AGAIN EVEN-TUALLY.
AFTER ALL, WE'RE BOTH ALCHE-MISTS.
KLATA
KLATA
KLATA
?
Alche-mists?
BLAM

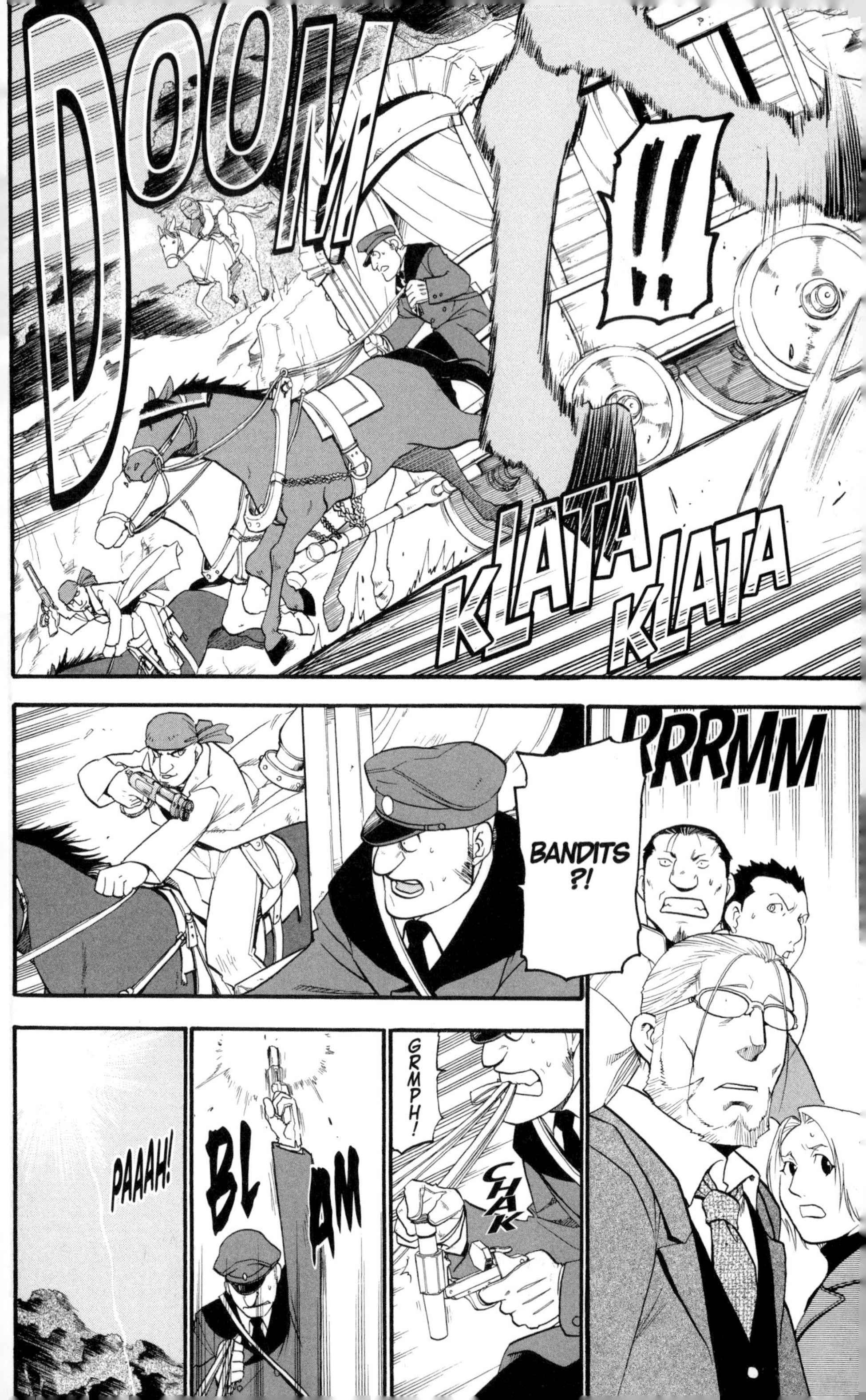
!!
DOOM
KLATA KLATA
RRRMM
BANDITS ?!
GRMPH!
CHAK
BLAM
PAAAH!

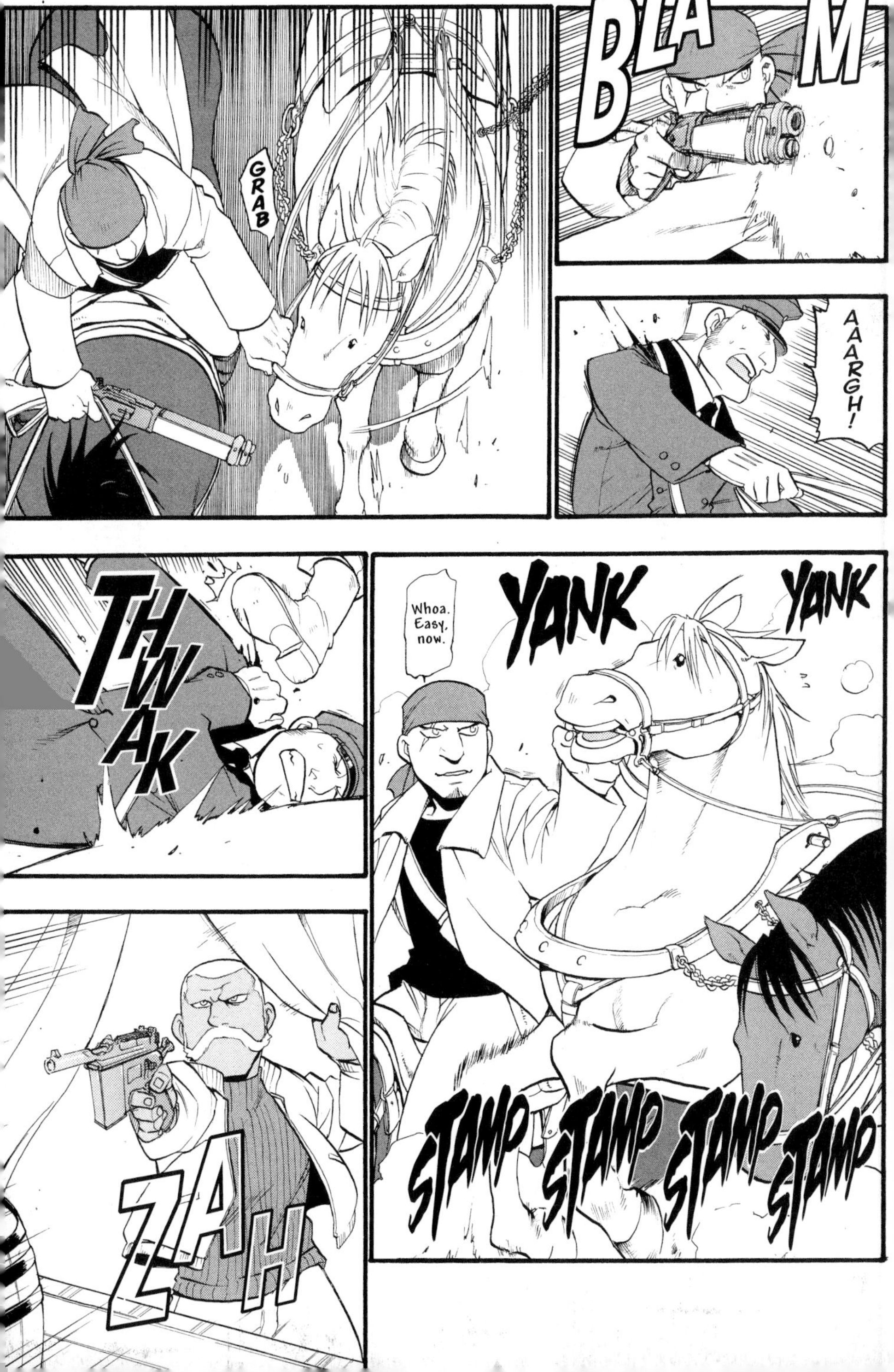
BLAM
AAAARGH!
GRAB
Whoa. Easy, now.
YANK YANK
STAMP STAMP STAMP STAMP
THWAK
ZAH

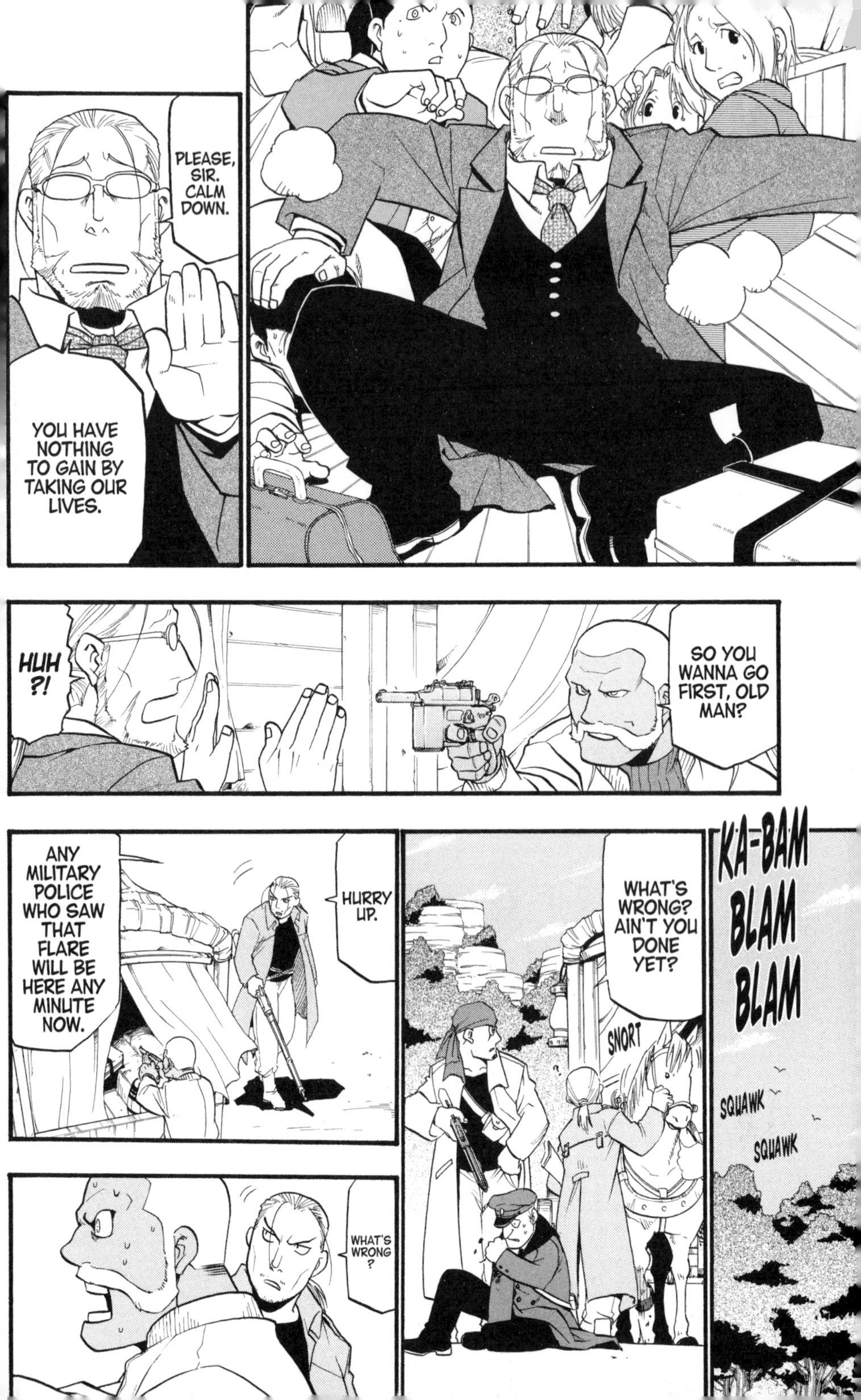
PLEASE, SIR. CALM DOWN.
YOU HAVE NOTHING TO GAIN BY TAKING OUR LIVES.
SO YOU WANNA GO FIRST, OLD MAN?
HUH?!
KA-BAM
BLAM
BLAM
SQUAWK
SQUAWK
WHAT'S WRONG? AIN'T YOU DONE YET?
SNORT
HURRY UP.
ANY MILITARY POLICE WHO SAW THAT FLARE WILL BE HERE ANY MINUTE NOW.
WHAT'S WRONG?

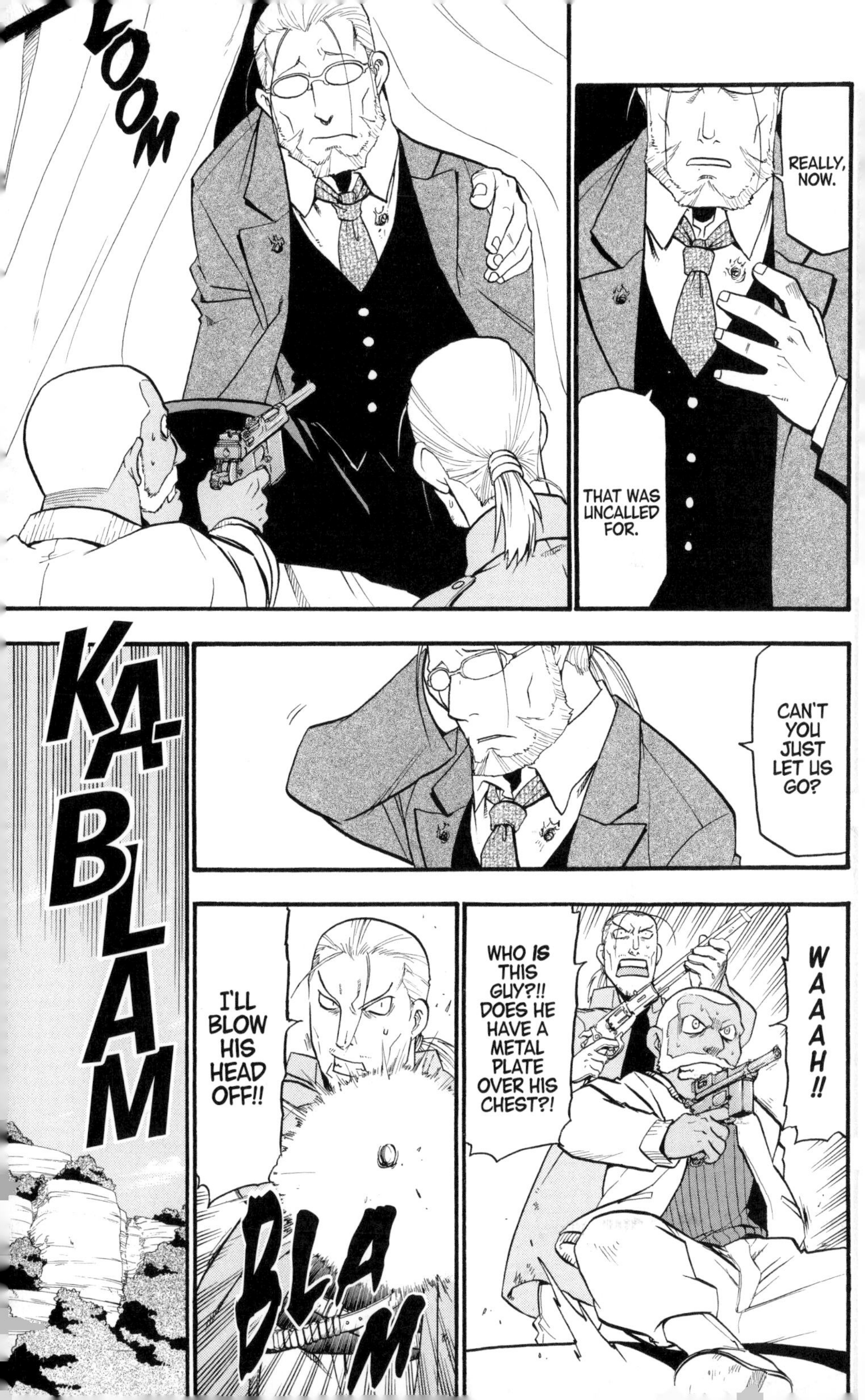
REALLY, NOW.
THAT WAS UNCALLED FOR.
VOOM
CAN'T YOU JUST LET US GO?
WAAAAH!!
WHO IS THIS GUY?!! DOES HE HAVE A METAL PLATE OVER HIS CHEST?!
I'LL BLOW HIS HEAD OFF!!
BLAM
KA-BLAM

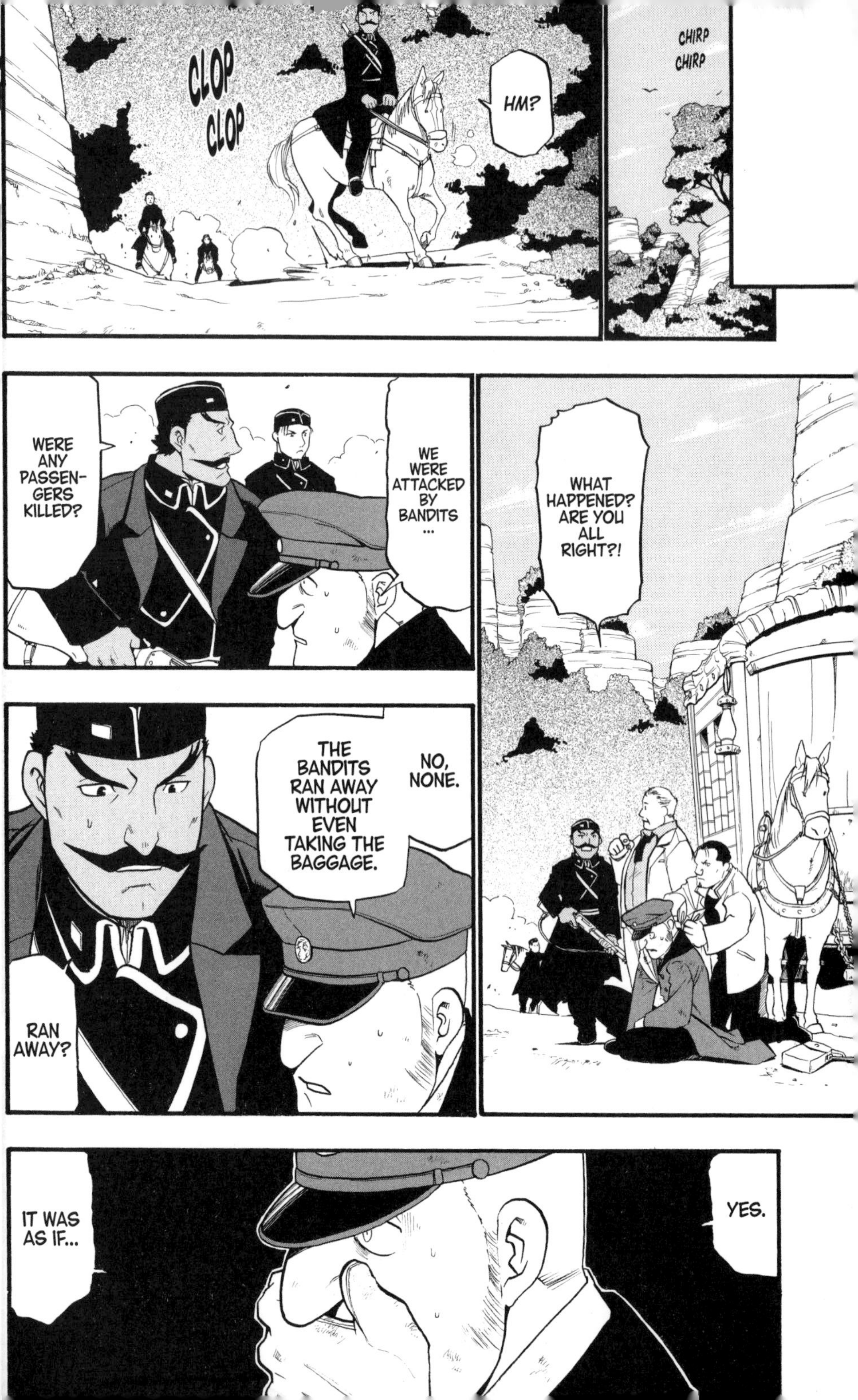
CHIRP CHIRP
CLOP CLOP
HM?
WHAT HAPPENED? ARE YOU ALL RIGHT?!
WE WERE ATTACKED BY BANDITS ...
WERE ANY PASSENGERS KILLED?
NO, NONE.
THE BANDITS RAN AWAY WITHOUT EVEN TAKING THE BAGGAGE.
RAN AWAY?
YES.
IT WAS AS IF...

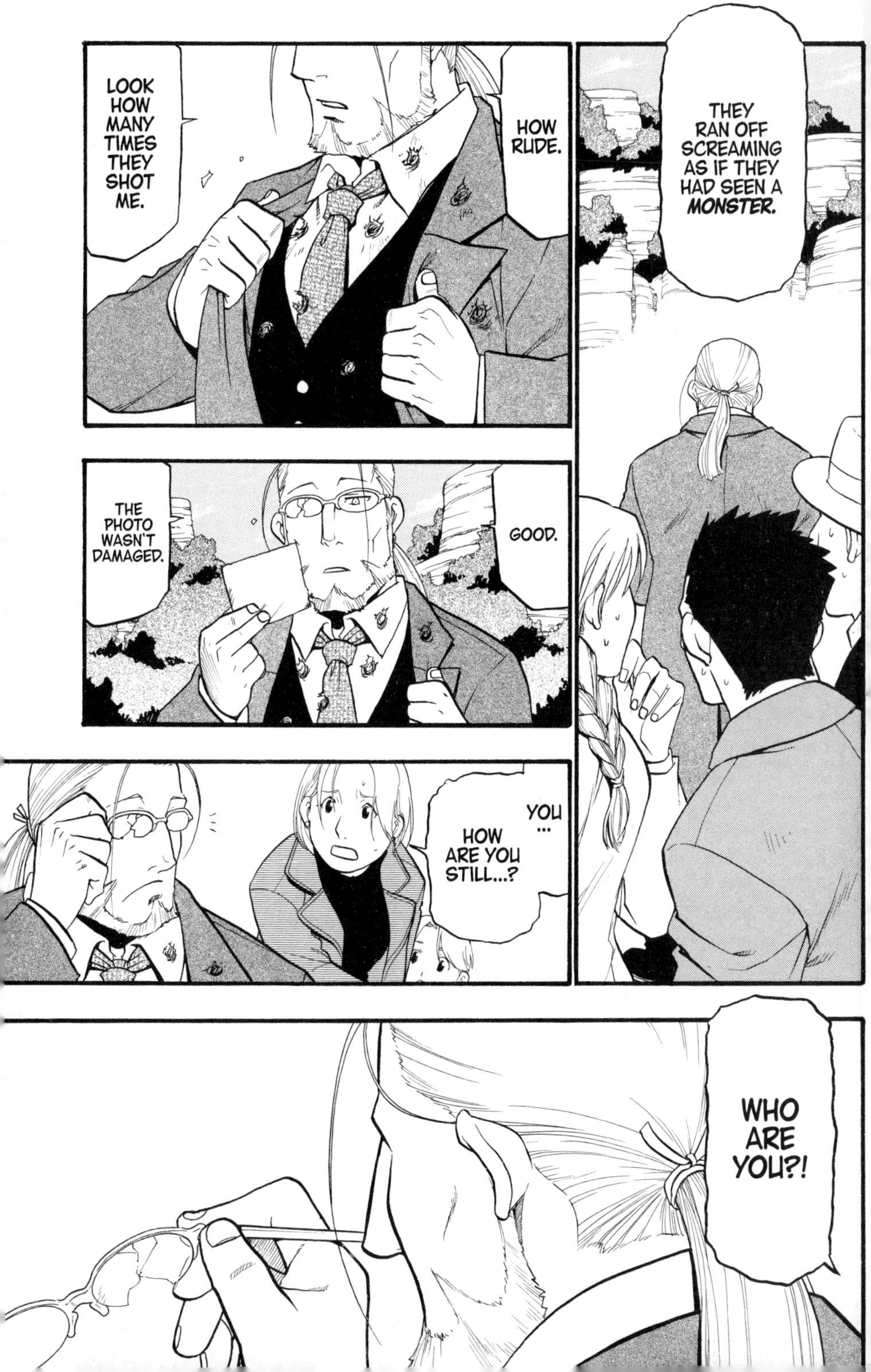
THEY RAN OFF SCREAMING AS IF THEY HAD SEEN A **MONSTER.**
HOW RUDE.
LOOK HOW MANY TIMES THEY SHOT ME.
GOOD.
THE PHOTO WASN'T DAMAGED.
YOU ...
HOW ARE YOU STILL...?
WHO ARE YOU?!

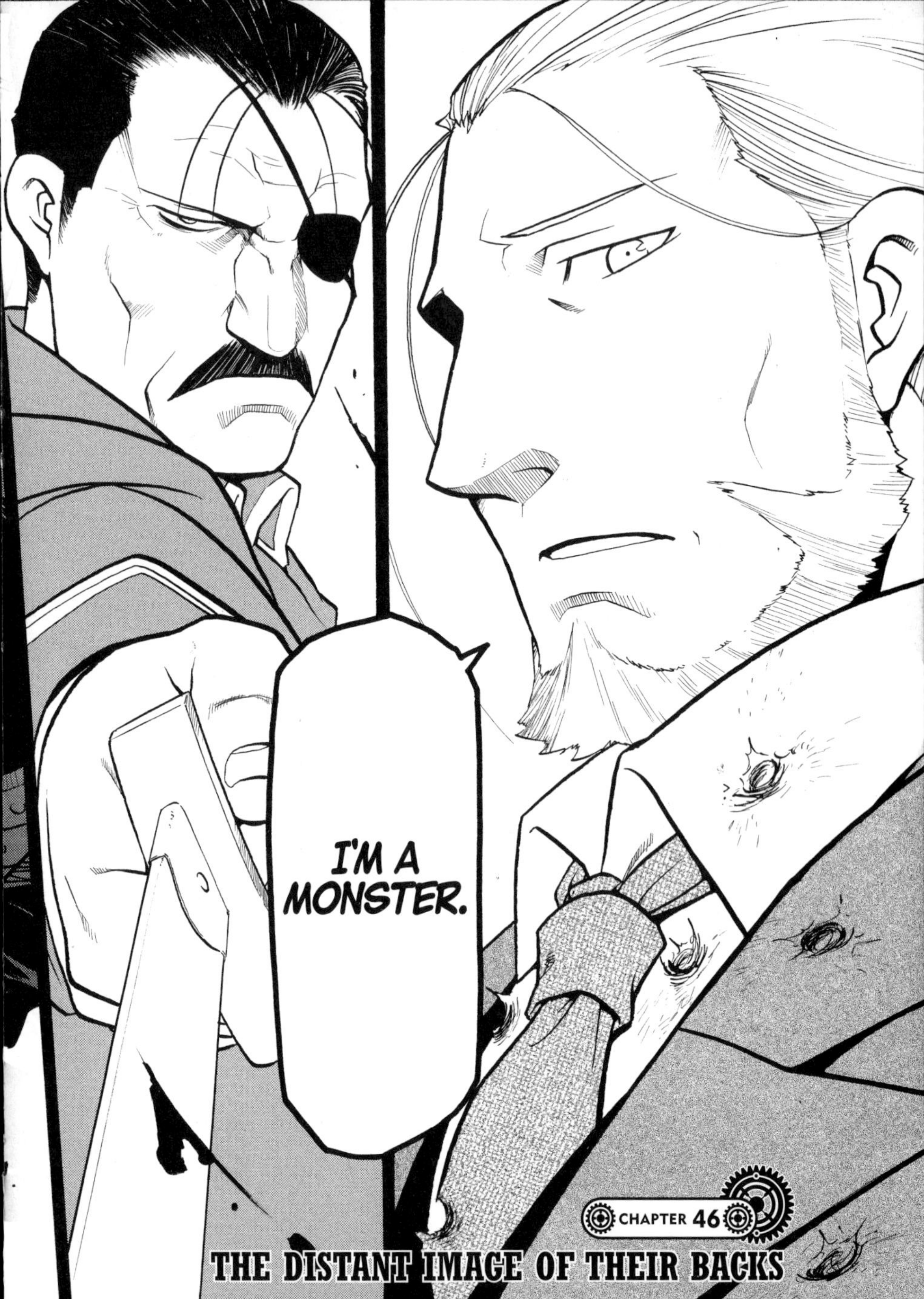
I'M A MONSTER.
CHAPTER 46
THE DISTANT IMAGE OF THEIR BACKS

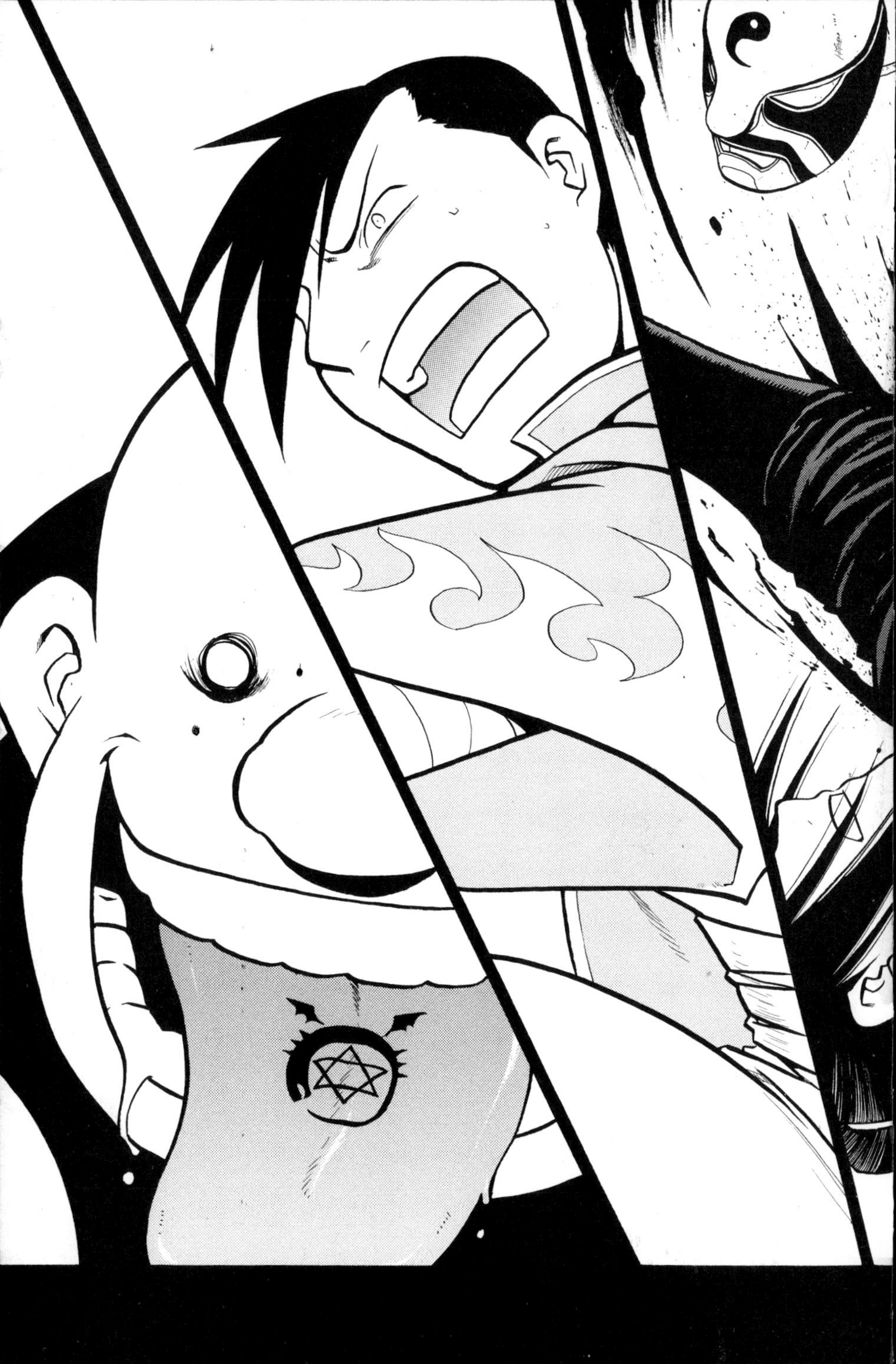

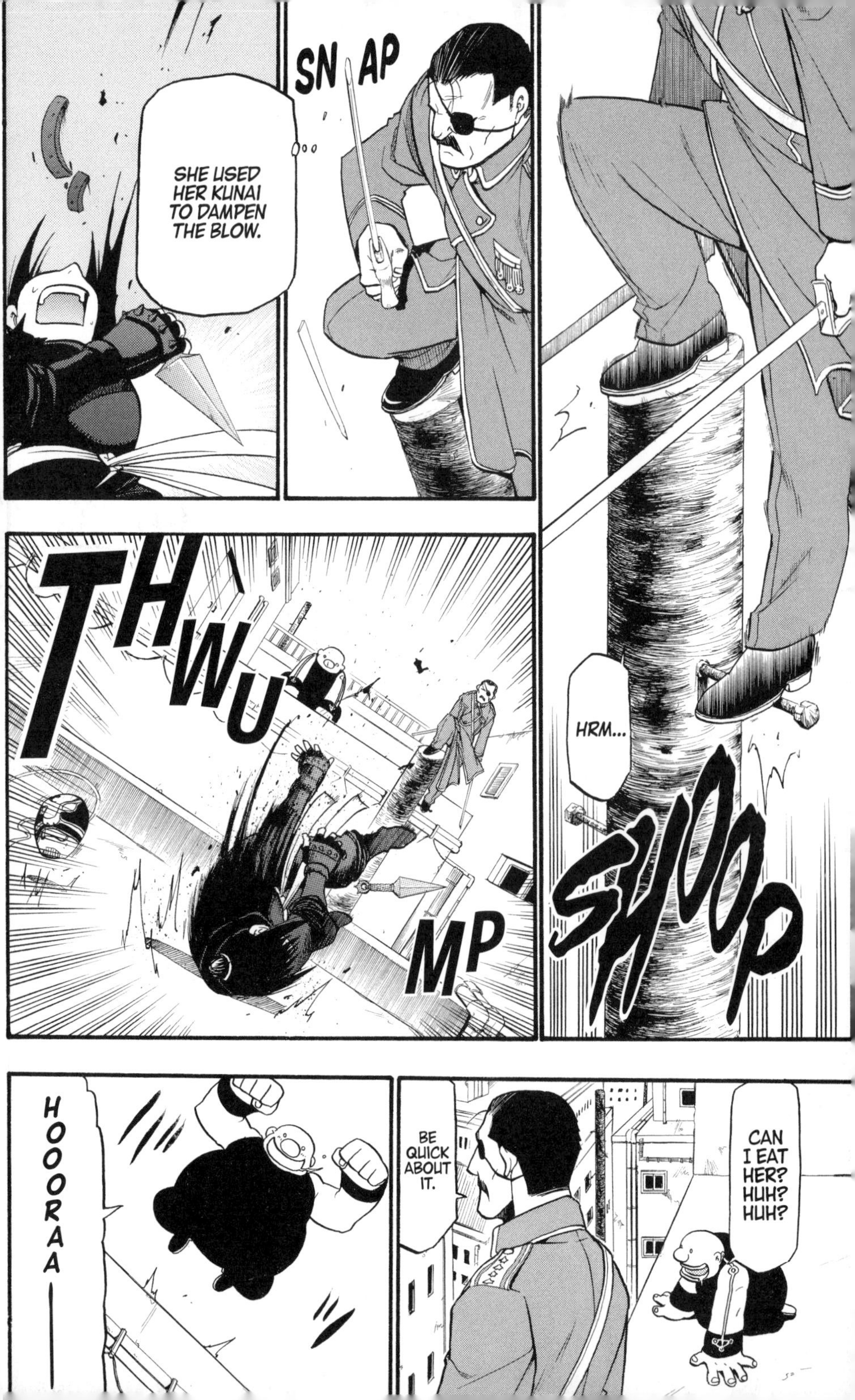
HRM...
SHOOP
SN AP
SHE USED HER KUNAI TO DAMPEN THE BLOW.
THWUMP
CAN I EAT HER? HUH? HUH?
BE QUICK ABOUT IT.
HOOORAA——

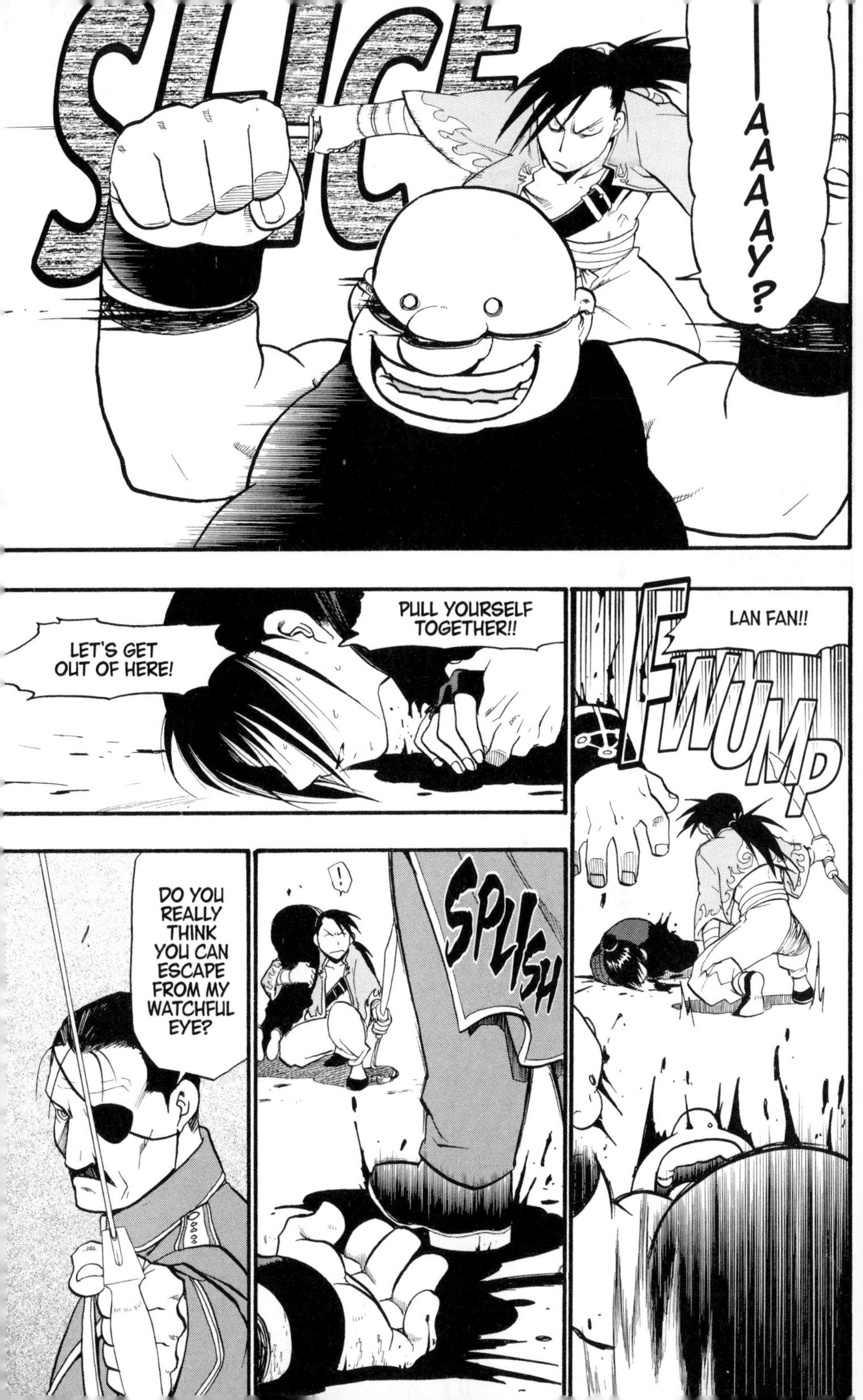
AAAAAY?
SLICE
LAN FAN!!
FWUMP
PULL YOURSELF TOGETHER!!
LET'S GET OUT OF HERE!
!
SPLISH
DO YOU REALLY THINK YOU CAN ESCAPE FROM MY WATCHFUL EYE?

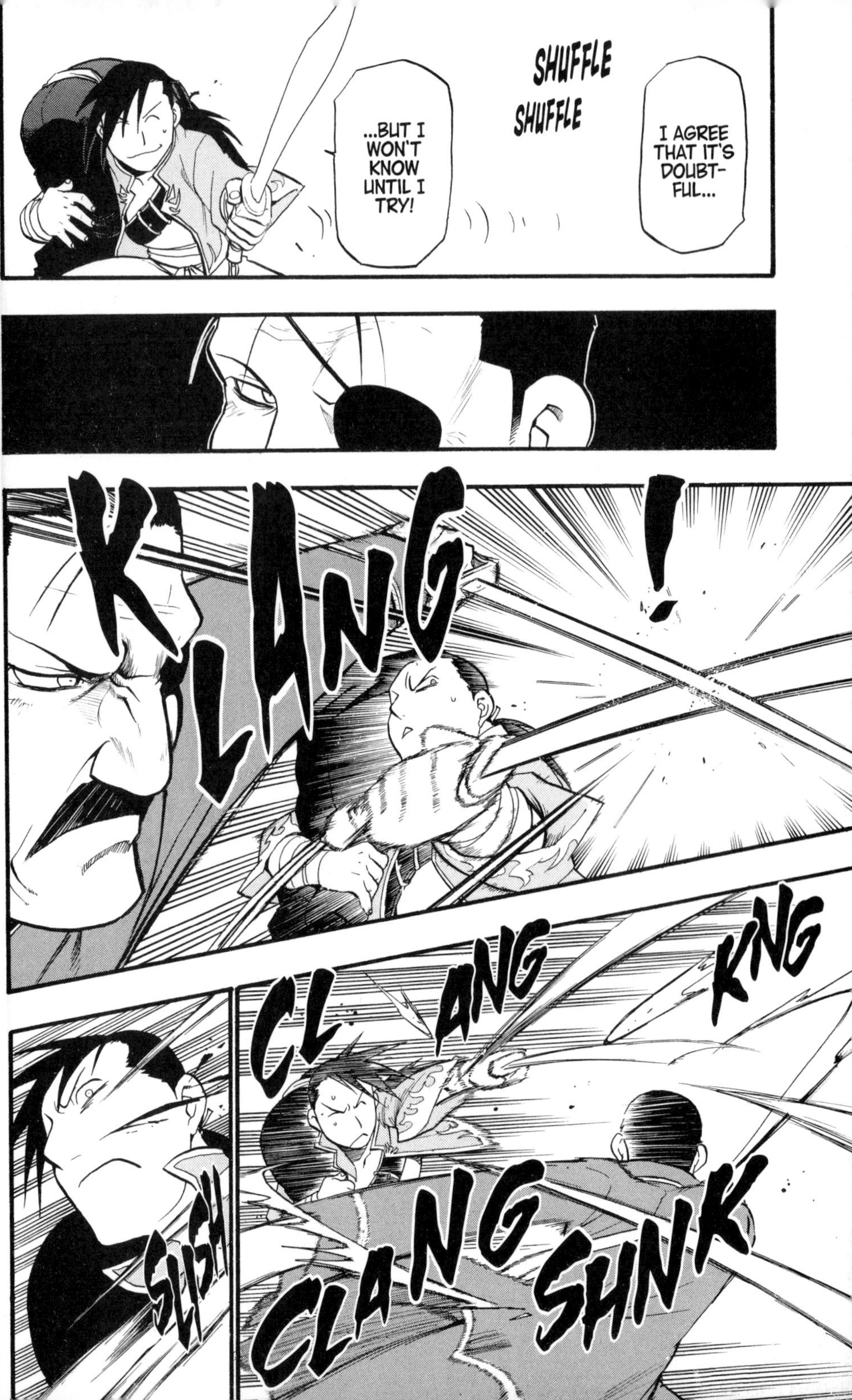
I AGREE THAT IT'S DOUBTFUL...
SHUFFLE
SHUFFLE
...BUT I WON'T KNOW UNTIL I TRY!
KLANG!
CLANG
KNG
CLANG
SHINK
SLISH

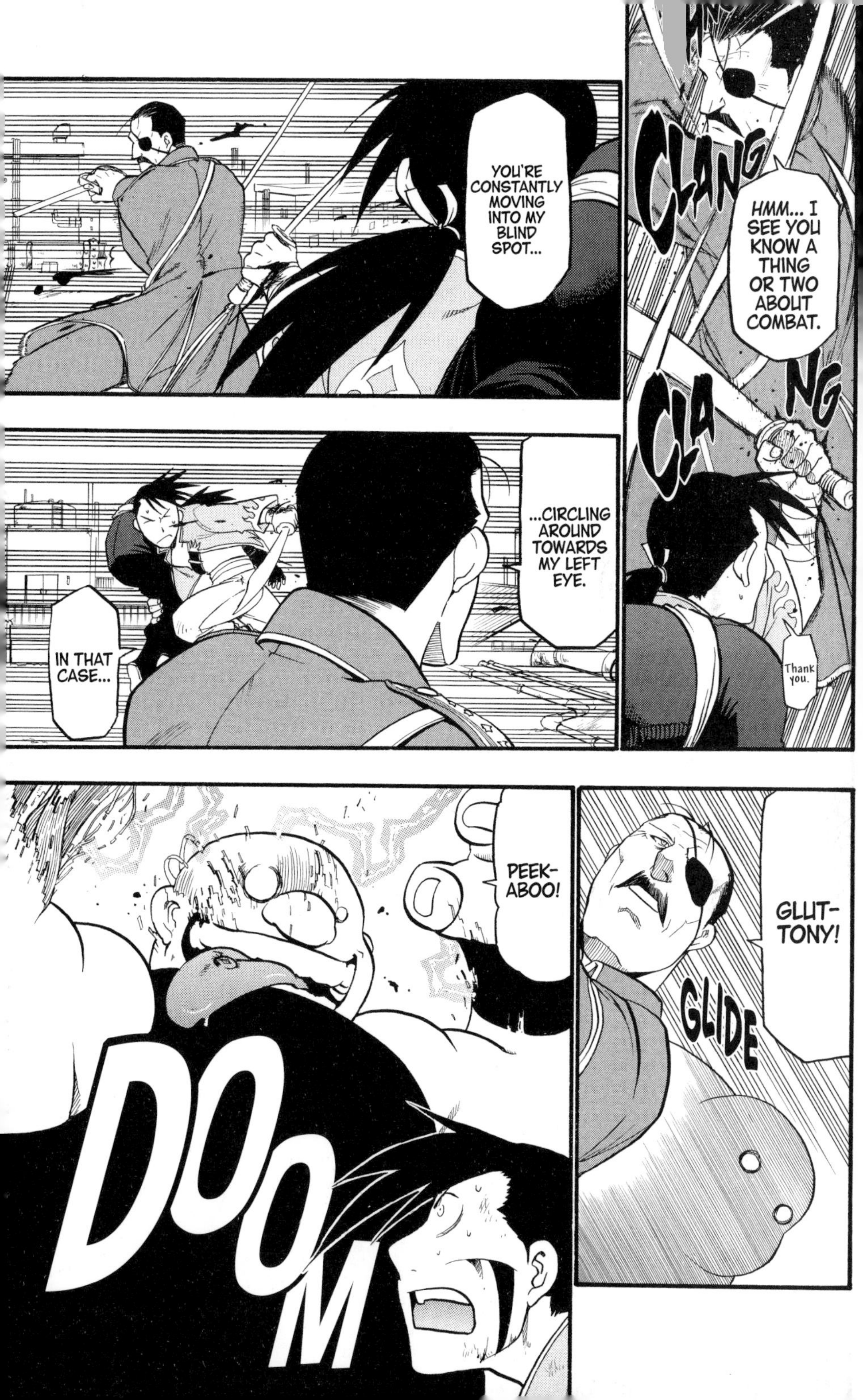
CLANG
HMM... I SEE YOU KNOW A THING OR TWO ABOUT COMBAT.
CLANG
Thank you.
YOU'RE CONSTANTLY MOVING INTO MY BLIND SPOT...
...CIRCLING AROUND TOWARDS MY LEFT EYE.
IN THAT CASE...
GLUTTONY!
GLIDE
PEEK-ABOO!
DOOM

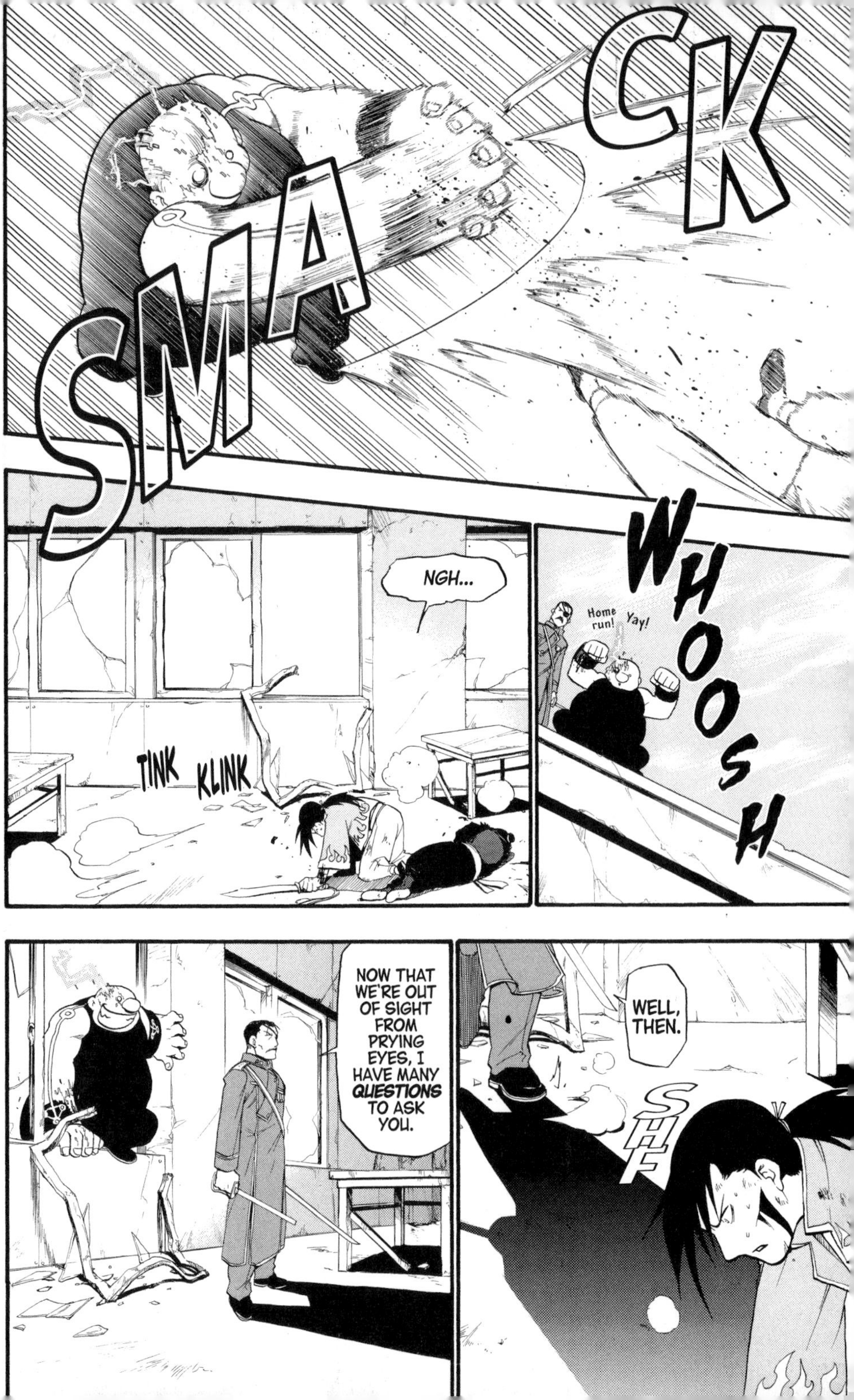
SMACK
WHOOSH
Home run!
Yay!
NGH...
TINK
KLINK
WELL, THEN.
SHF
NOW THAT WE'RE OUT OF SIGHT FROM PRYING EYES, I HAVE MANY **QUESTIONS** TO ASK YOU.

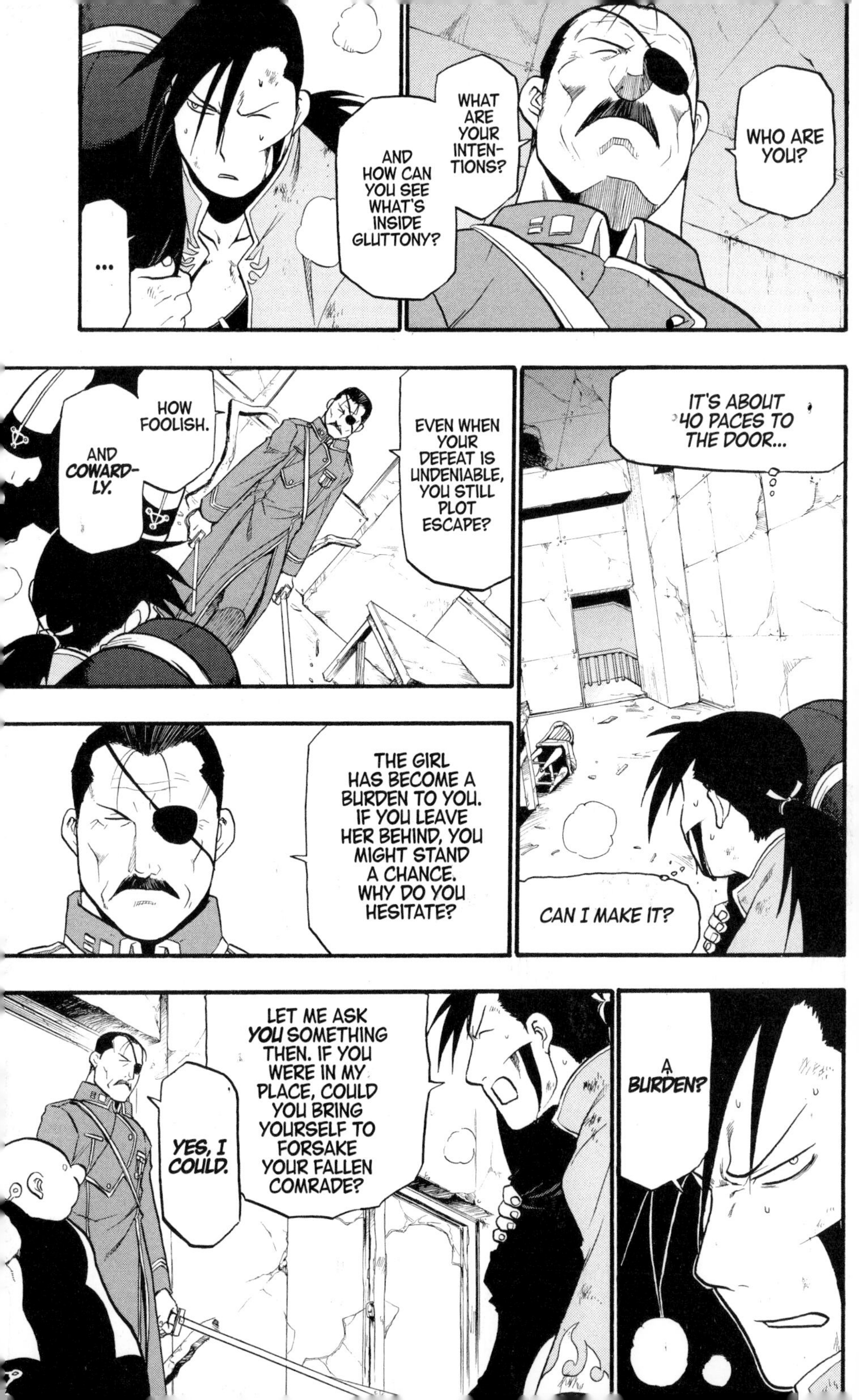
WHO ARE YOU?
WHAT ARE YOUR INTENTIONS?
AND HOW CAN YOU SEE WHAT'S INSIDE GLUTTONY?
...
IT'S ABOUT 40 PACES TO THE DOOR...
CAN I MAKE IT?
EVEN WHEN YOUR DEFEAT IS UNDENIABLE, YOU STILL PLOT ESCAPE?
HOW FOOLISH.
AND COWARDLY.
THE GIRL HAS BECOME A BURDEN TO YOU. IF YOU LEAVE HER BEHIND, YOU MIGHT STAND A CHANCE. WHY DO YOU HESITATE?
A BURDEN?
LET ME ASK YOU SOMETHING THEN. IF YOU WERE IN MY PLACE, COULD YOU BRING YOURSELF TO FORSAKE YOUR FALLEN COMRADE?
YES, I COULD.

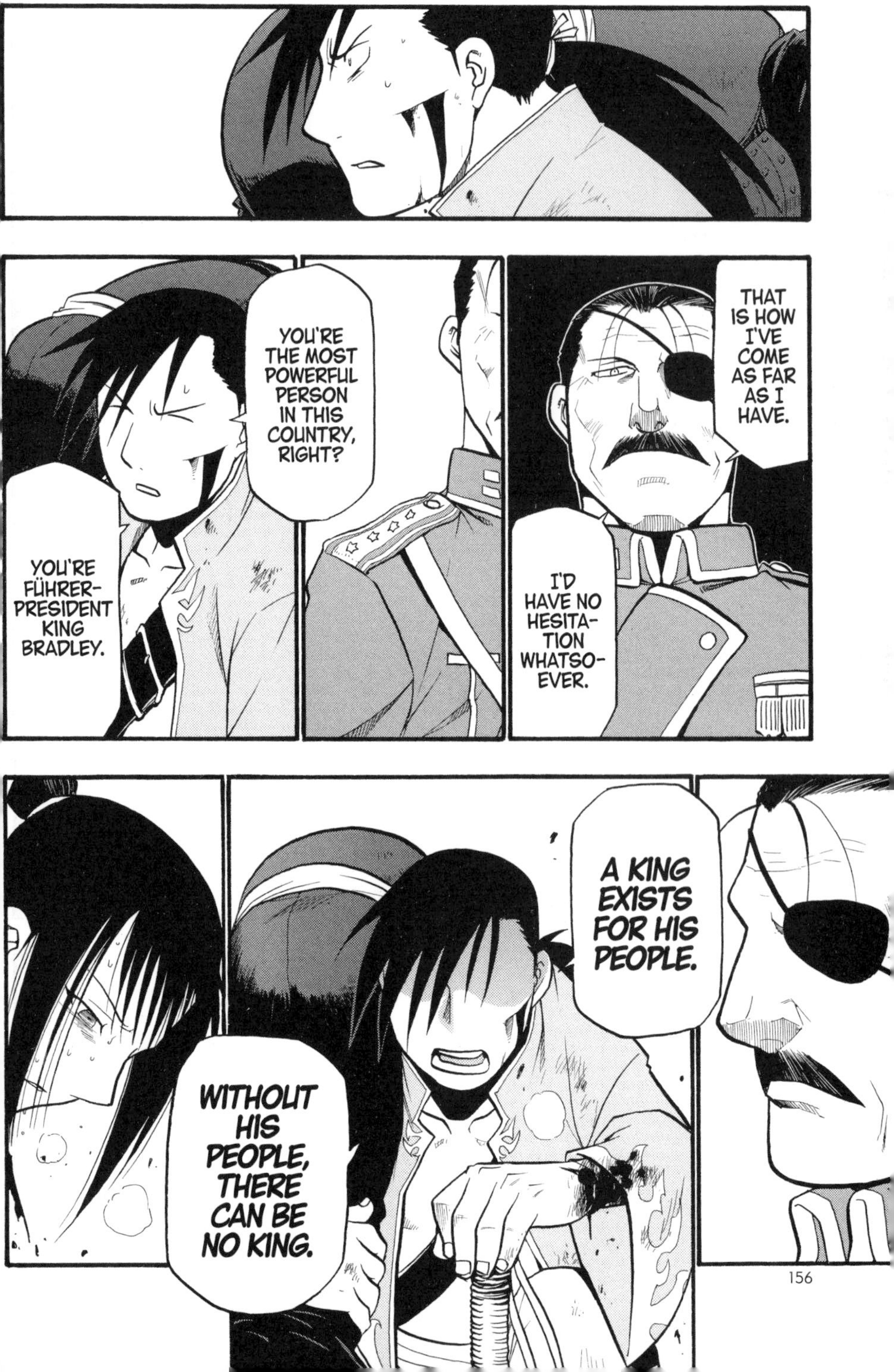
THAT IS HOW I'VE COME AS FAR AS I HAVE.
I'D HAVE NO HESITATION WHATSOEVER.
YOU'RE THE MOST POWERFUL PERSON IN THIS COUNTRY, RIGHT?
YOU'RE FÜHRER-PRESIDENT KING BRADLEY.
A KING EXISTS FOR HIS PEOPLE.
WITHOUT HIS PEOPLE, THERE CAN BE NO KING.

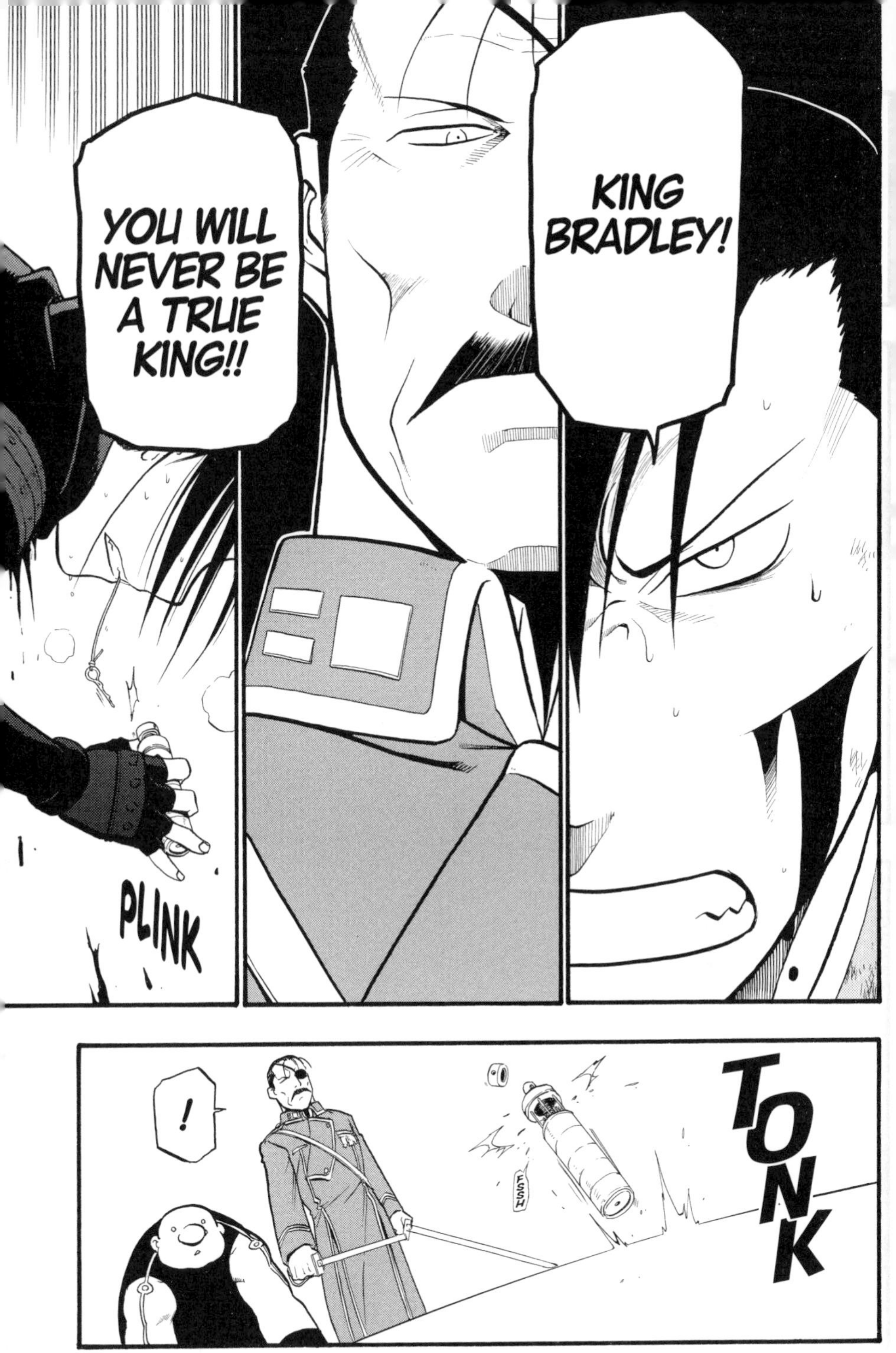
KING BRADLEY!
YOU WILL NEVER BE A TRUE KING!!
PLINK
TONK
FSSH
!

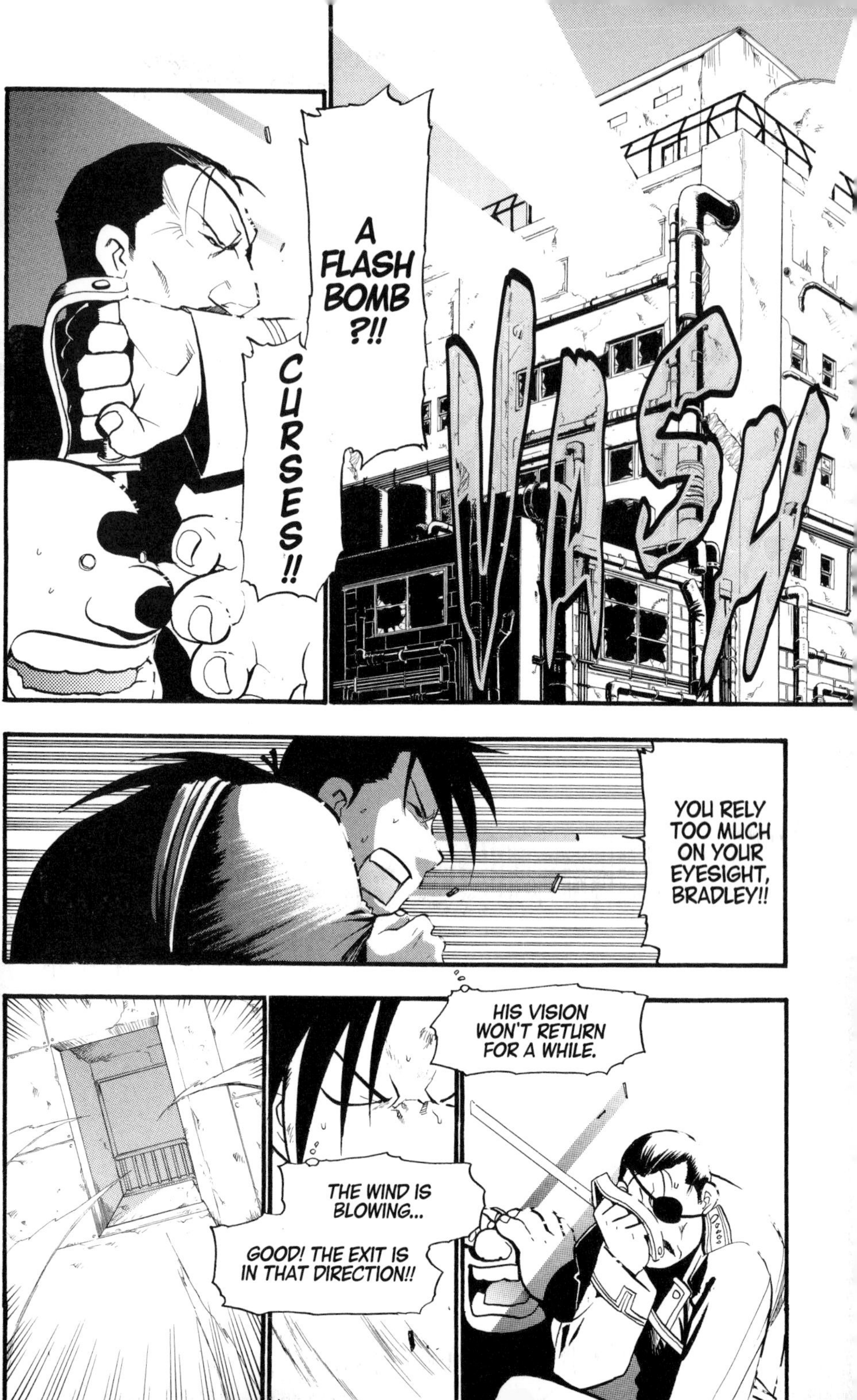
FLASH
A FLASH BOMB?!!
CURSES!!
YOU RELY TOO MUCH ON YOUR EYESIGHT, BRADLEY!!
HIS VISION WON'T RETURN FOR A WHILE.
THE WIND IS BLOWING...
GOOD! THE EXIT IS IN THAT DIRECTION!!

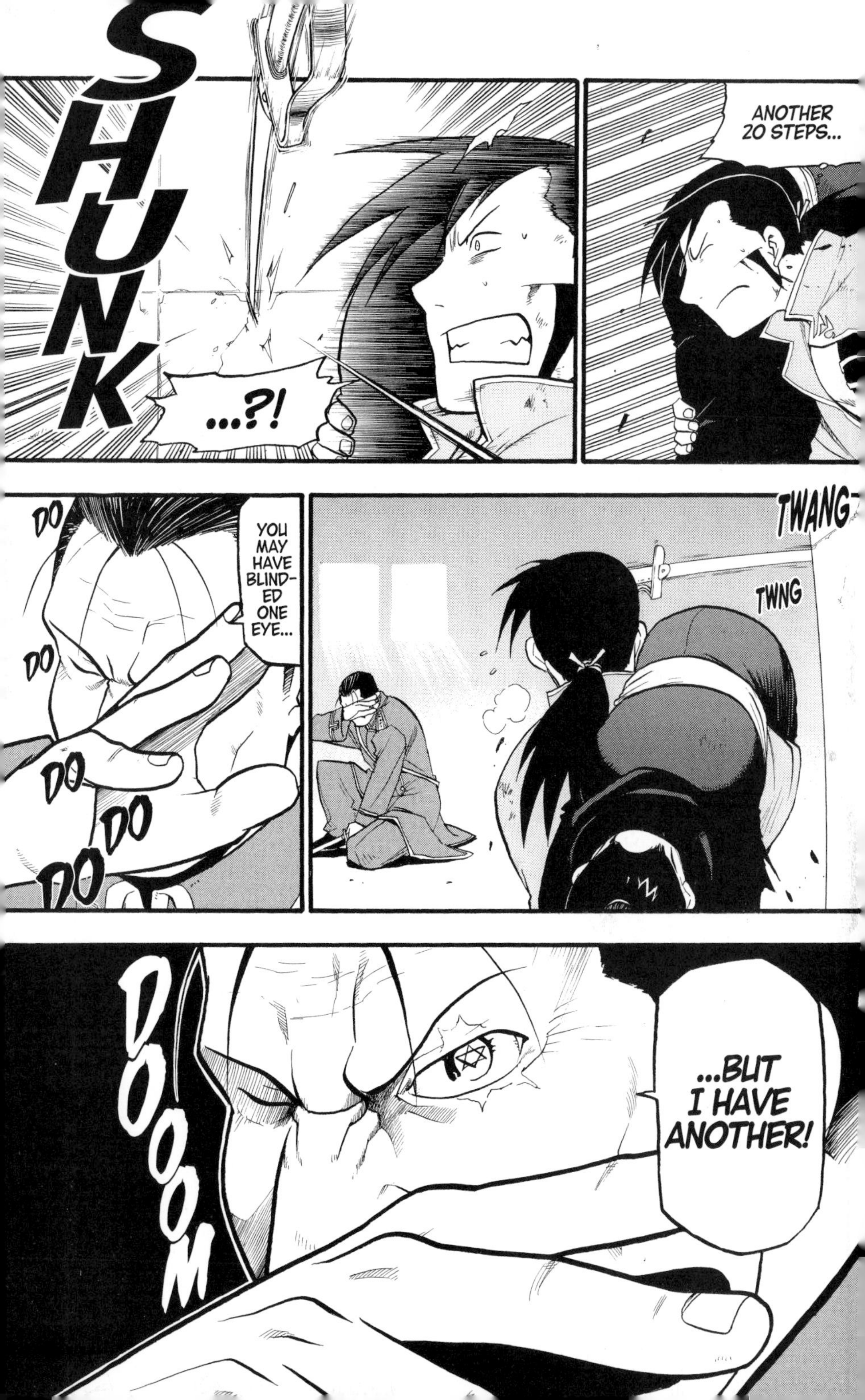
ANOTHER 20 STEPS...
SHUNK
...?!
TWANG
TWNG
YOU MAY HAVE BLIND-ED ONE EYE...
DO
DO
DO
DO
DO
...BUT I HAVE ANOTHER!
DOOOM

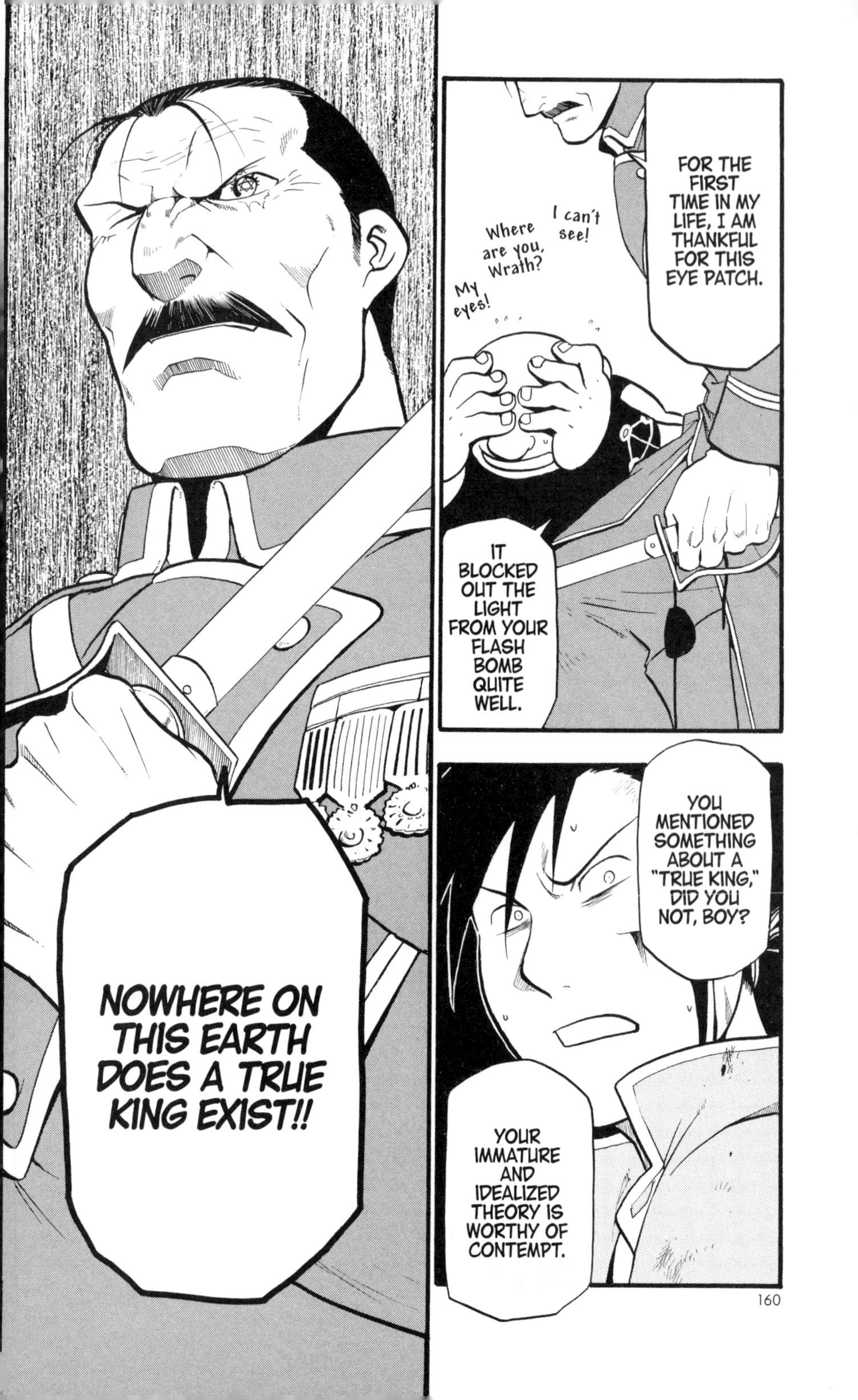
FOR THE FIRST TIME IN MY LIFE, I AM THANKFUL FOR THIS EYE PATCH.
I can't see!
Where are you, Wrath?
My eyes!
IT BLOCKED OUT THE LIGHT FROM YOUR FLASH BOMB QUITE WELL.
YOU MENTIONED SOMETHING ABOUT A "TRUE KING," DID YOU NOT, BOY?
YOUR IMMATURE AND IDEALIZED THEORY IS WORTHY OF CONTEMPT.
NOWHERE ON THIS EARTH DOES A TRUE KING EXIST!!

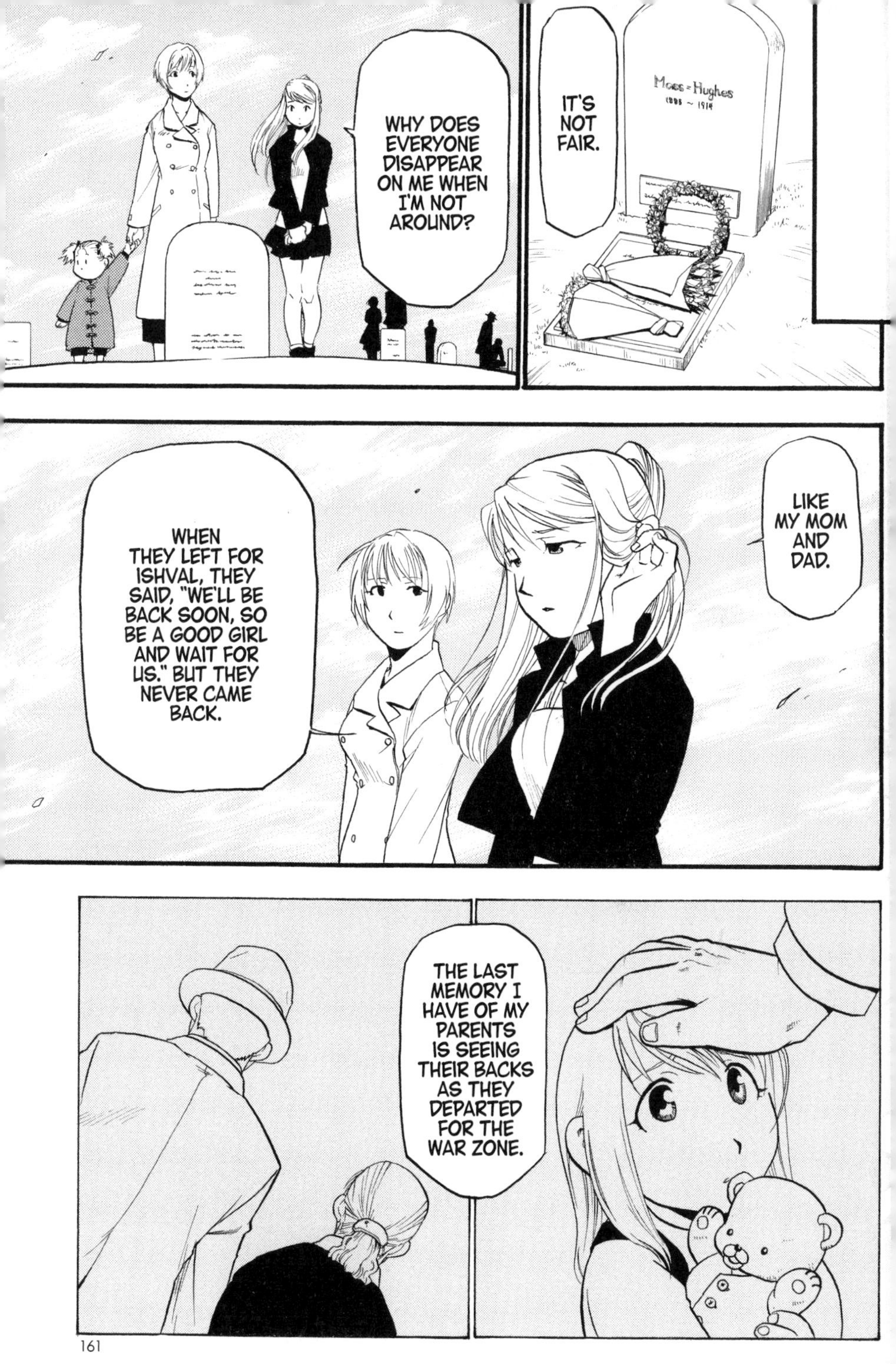
IT'S NOT FAIR.
Maes = Hughes
WHY DOES EVERYONE DISAPPEAR ON ME WHEN I'M NOT AROUND?
LIKE MY MOM AND DAD.
WHEN THEY LEFT FOR ISHVAL, THEY SAID, "WE'LL BE BACK SOON, SO BE A GOOD GIRL AND WAIT FOR US." BUT THEY NEVER CAME BACK.
THE LAST MEMORY I HAVE OF MY PARENTS IS SEEING THEIR BACKS AS THEY DEPARTED FOR THE WAR ZONE.

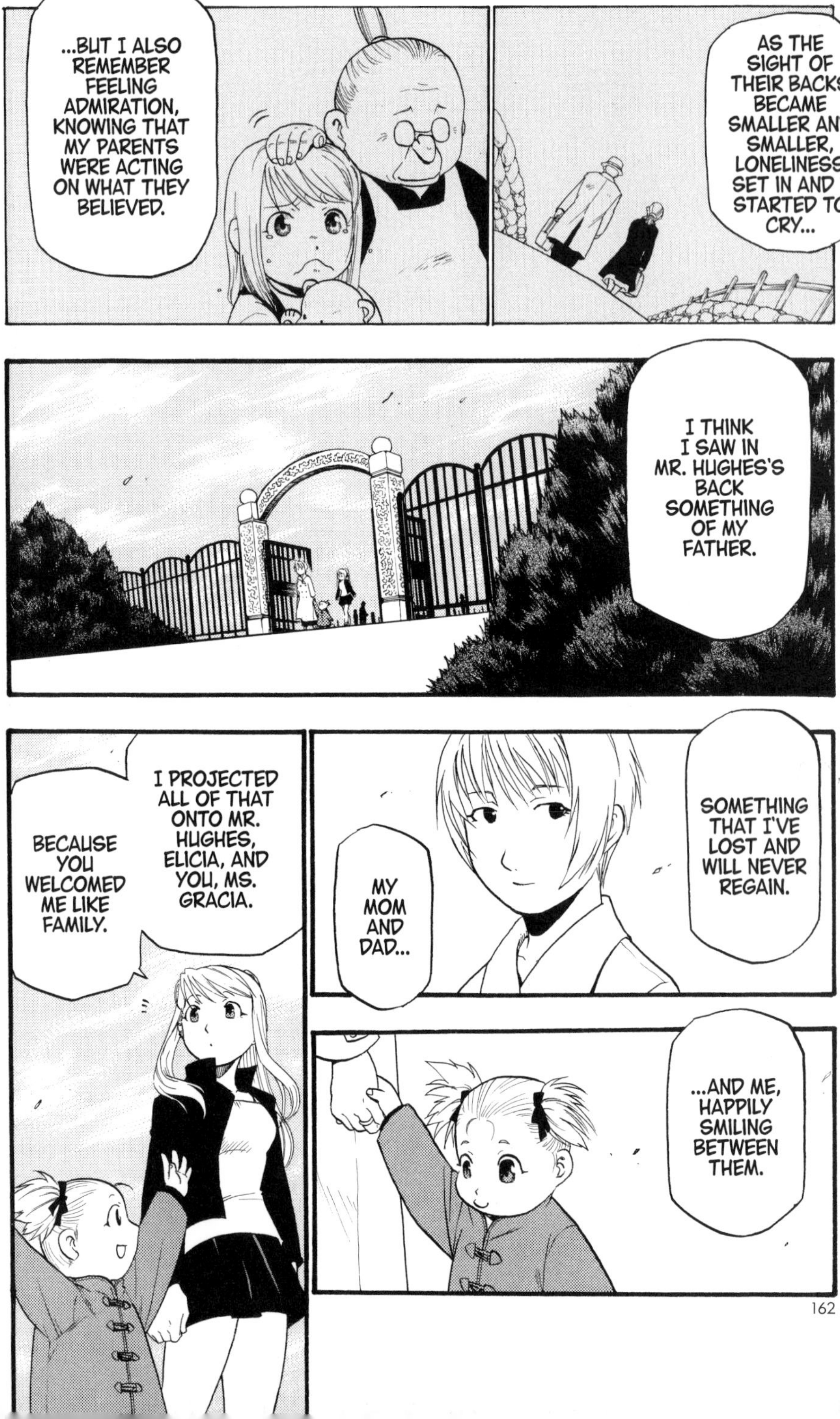
AS THE SIGHT OF THEIR BACKS BECAME SMALLER AND SMALLER, LONELINESS SET IN AND I STARTED TO CRY...
...BUT I ALSO REMEMBER FEELING ADMIRATION, KNOWING THAT MY PARENTS WERE ACTING ON WHAT THEY BELIEVED.
I THINK I SAW IN MR. HUGHES'S BACK SOMETHING OF MY FATHER.
SOMETHING THAT I'VE LOST AND WILL NEVER REGAIN.
MY MOM AND DAD...
...AND ME, HAPPILY SMILING BETWEEN THEM.
I PROJECTED ALL OF THAT ONTO MR. HUGHES, ELICIA, AND YOU, MS. GRACIA.
BECAUSE YOU WELCOMED ME LIKE FAMILY.

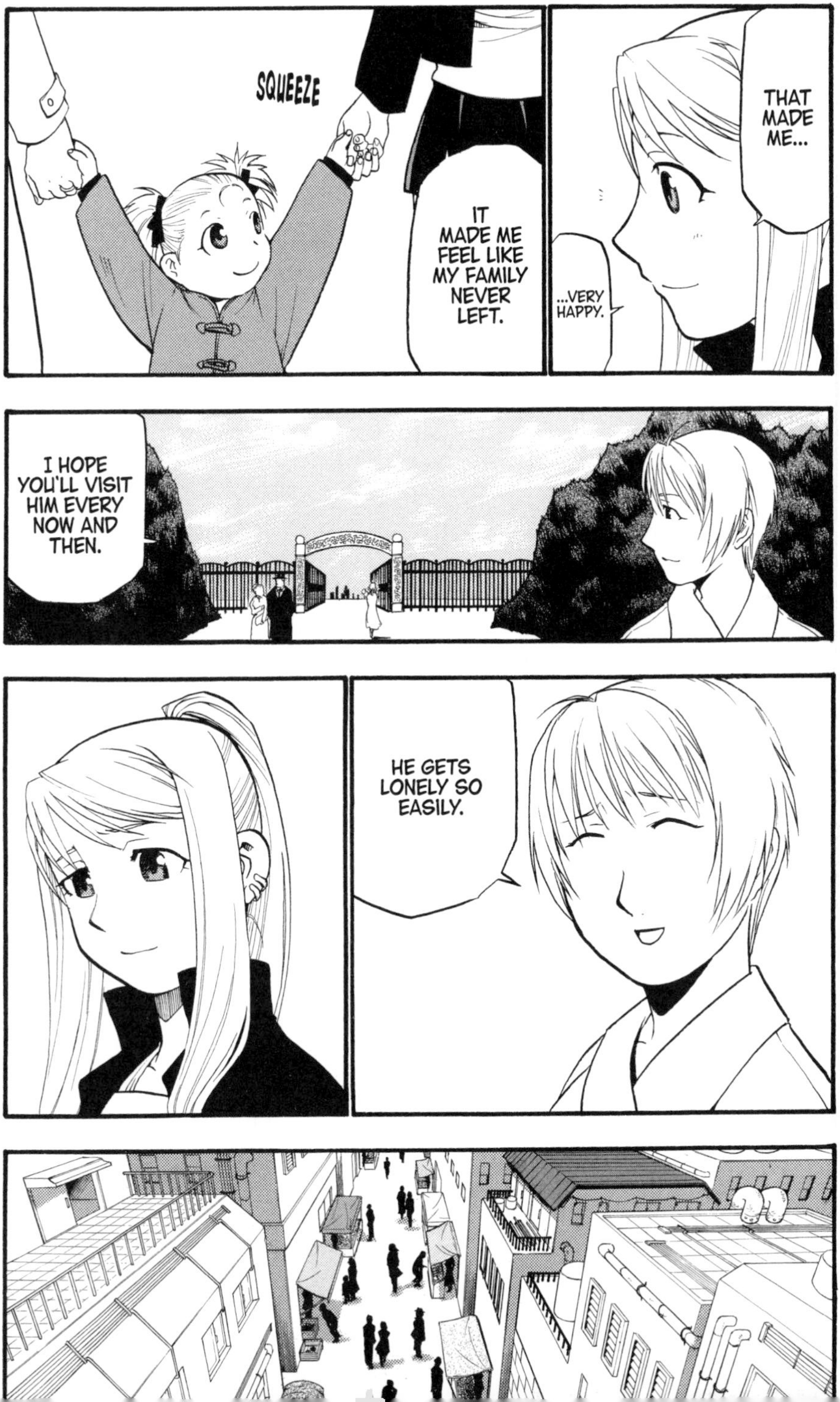
THAT MADE ME...
...VERY HAPPY.
SQUEEZE
IT MADE ME FEEL LIKE MY FAMILY NEVER LEFT.
I HOPE YOU'LL VISIT HIM EVERY NOW AND THEN.
HE GETS LONELY SO EASILY.

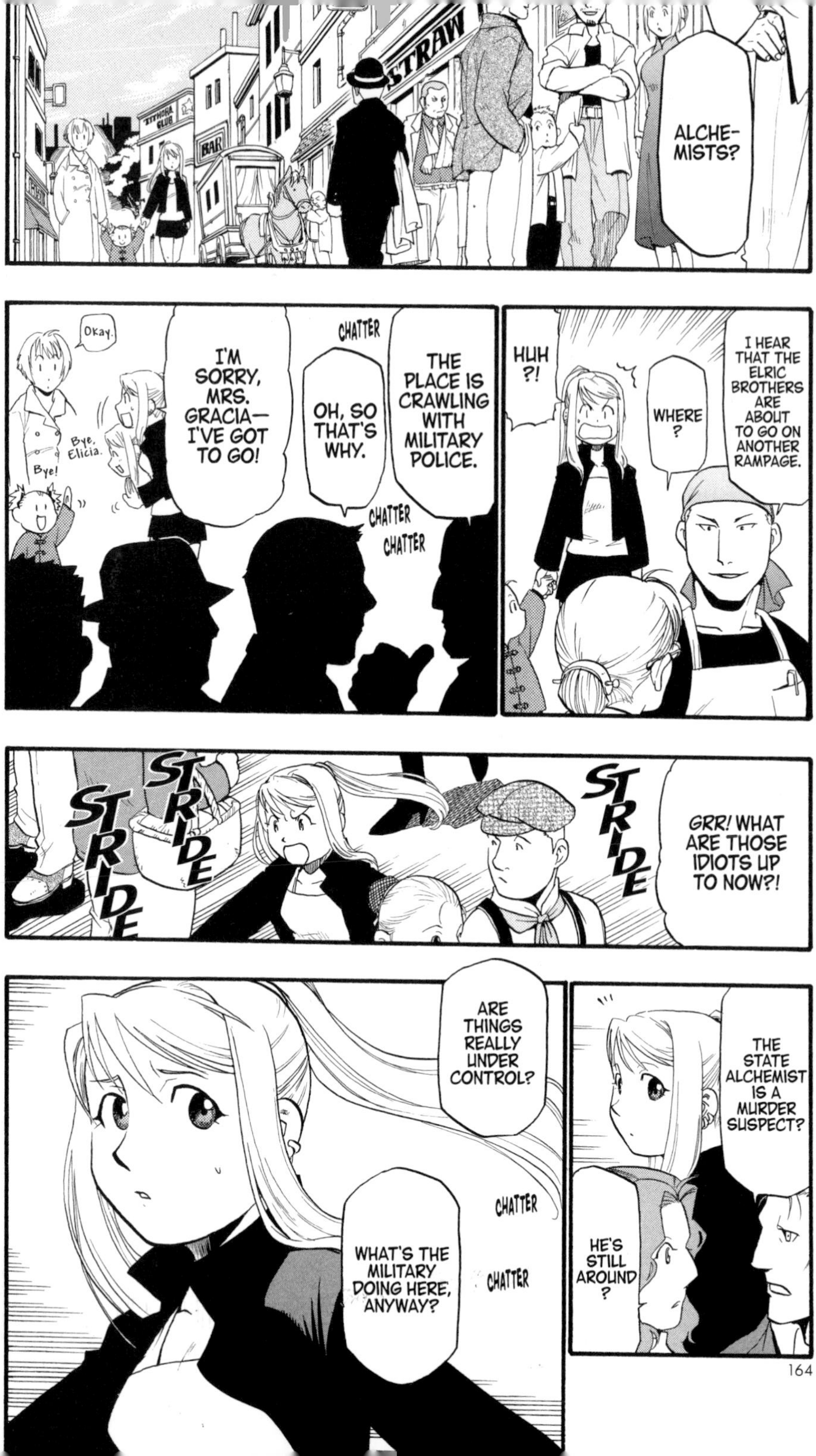
ALCHE-MISTS?
I HEAR THAT THE ELRIC BROTHERS ARE ABOUT TO GO ON ANOTHER RAMPAGE.
WHERE?
HUH?!
THE PLACE IS CRAWLING WITH MILITARY POLICE.
CHATTER
OH, SO THAT'S WHY.
CHATTER
CHATTER
I'M SORRY, MRS. GRACIA— I'VE GOT TO GO!
Okay.
Bye, Elicia.
Bye!
GRR! WHAT ARE THOSE IDIOTS UP TO NOW?!
STRIDE
STRIDE
STRIDE
THE STATE ALCHEMIST IS A MURDER SUSPECT?
HE'S STILL AROUND?
ARE THINGS REALLY UNDER CONTROL?
CHATTER
WHAT'S THE MILITARY DOING HERE, ANYWAY?
CHATTER

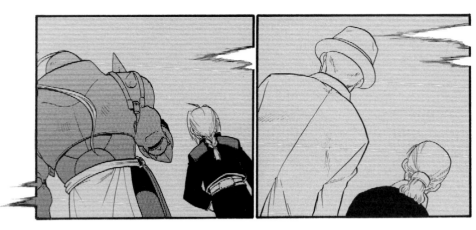

Oh
no...

DASH

WHY
ARE THEY
OVER-
LAPPING?!

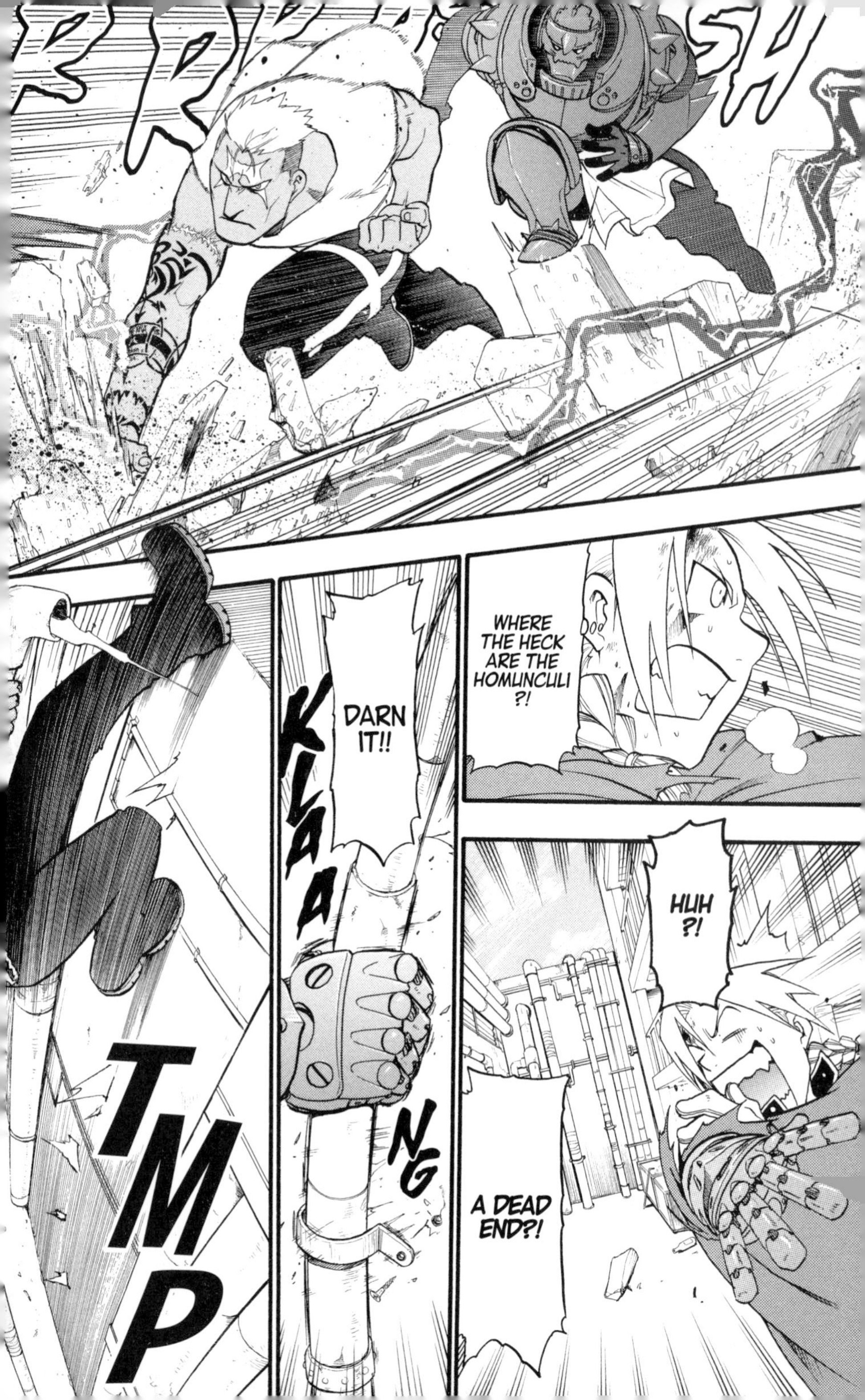
WHERE THE HECK ARE THE HOMUNCULI ?!
HUH ?!
A DEAD END?!
DARN IT!!
KLAANG
TMP

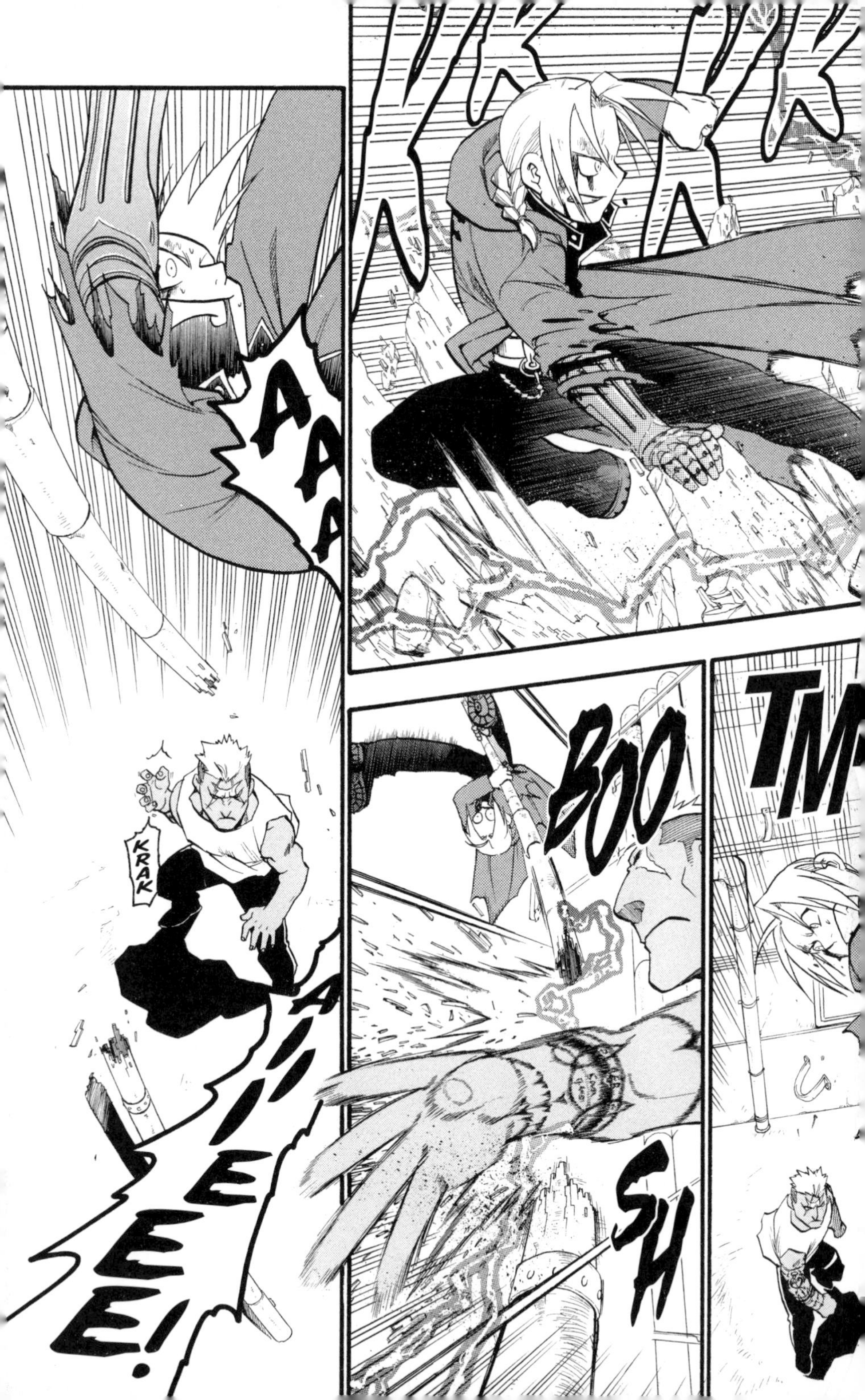
TMP
BOOSH
AAA
KRAK
AIIEEEEEE!

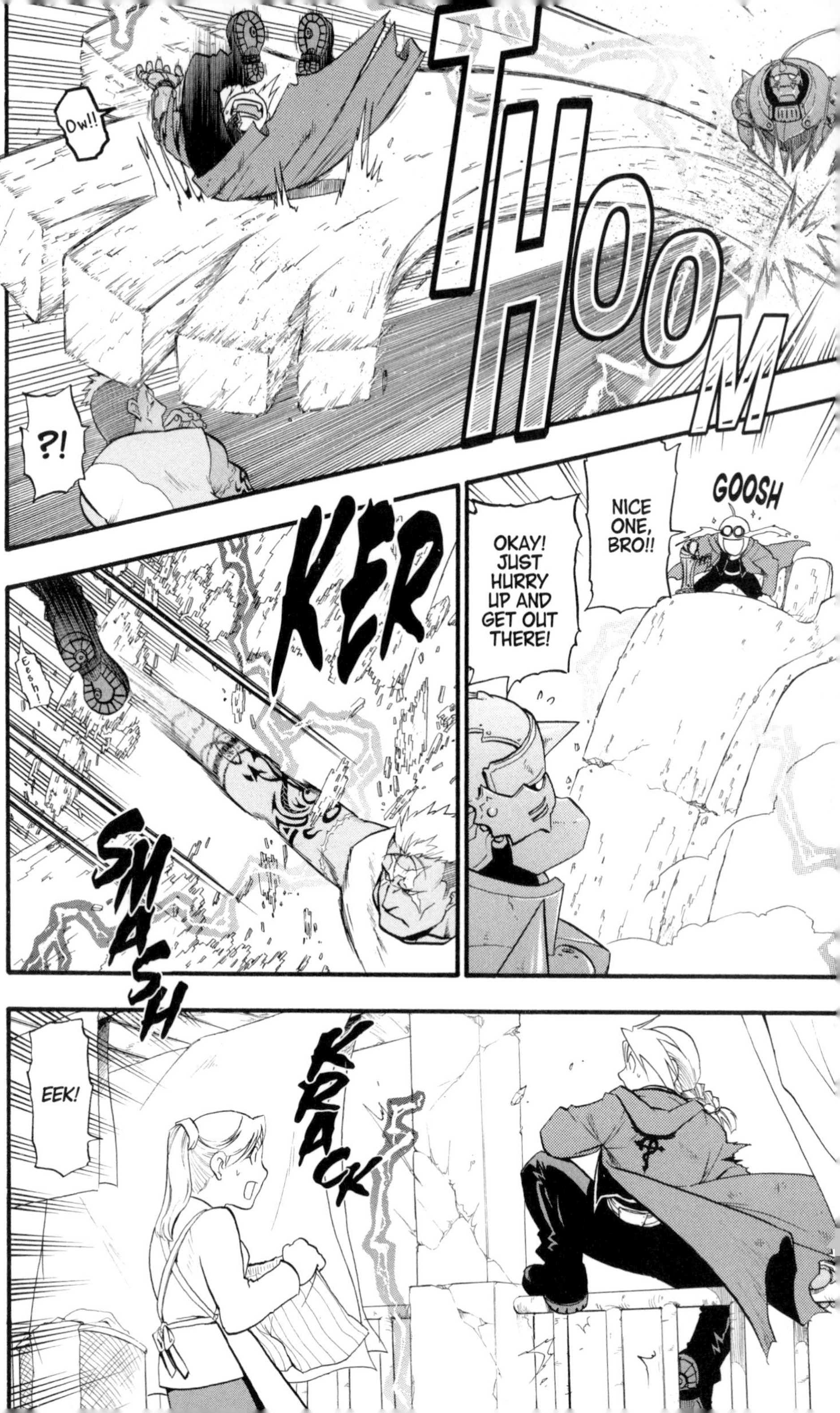
THOOM
Ow!!
?!
GOOSH
NICE ONE, BRO!!
OKAY! JUST HURRY UP AND GET OUT THERE!
KER
Eesh!
SMASH
KRACK
EEK!

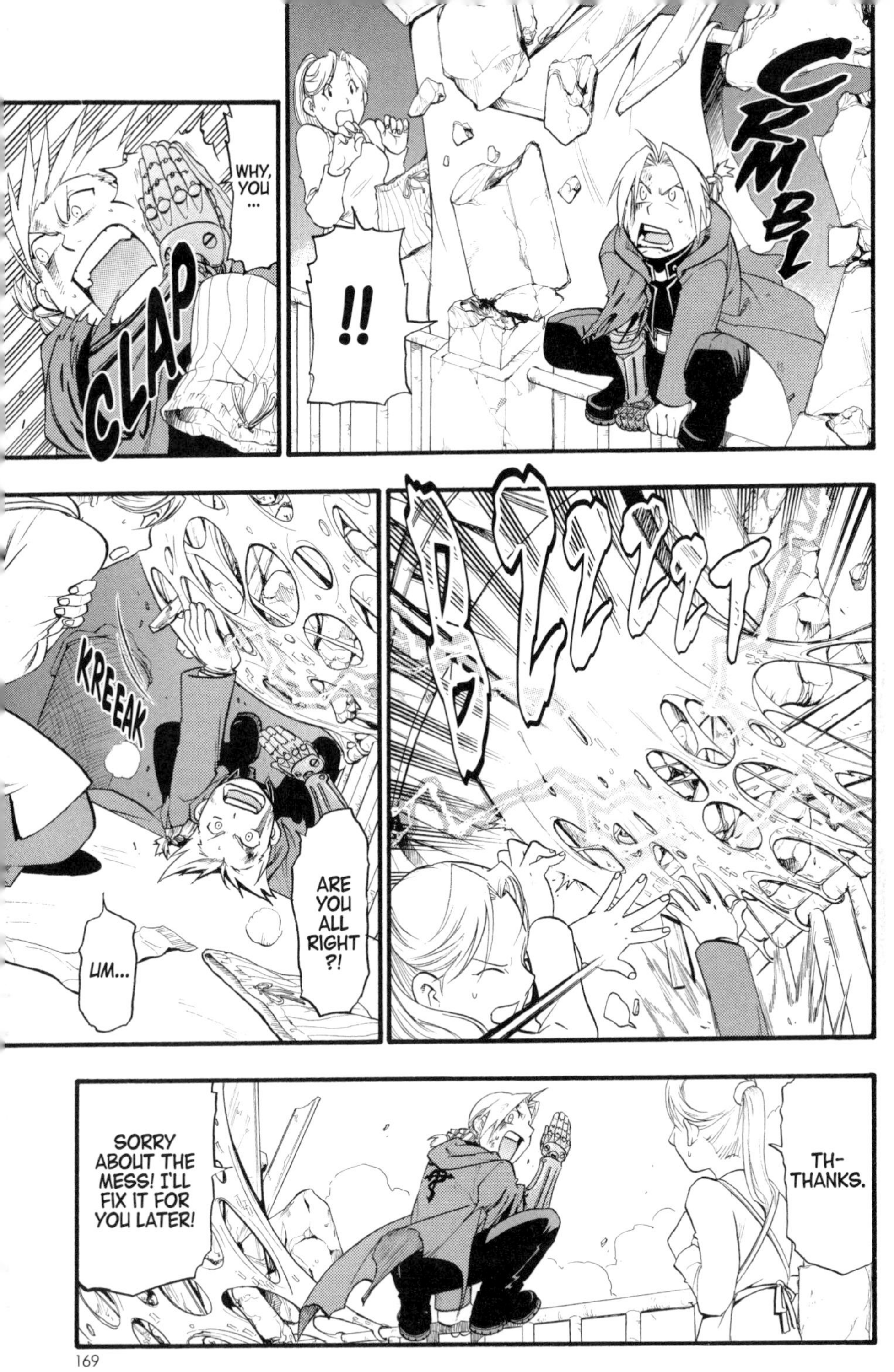
CRMBL
!!
WHY, YOU ...
CLAP
FIZZZZT
KREEAK
ARE YOU ALL RIGHT ?!
UM...
TH-THANKS.
SORRY ABOUT THE MESS! I'LL FIX IT FOR YOU LATER!

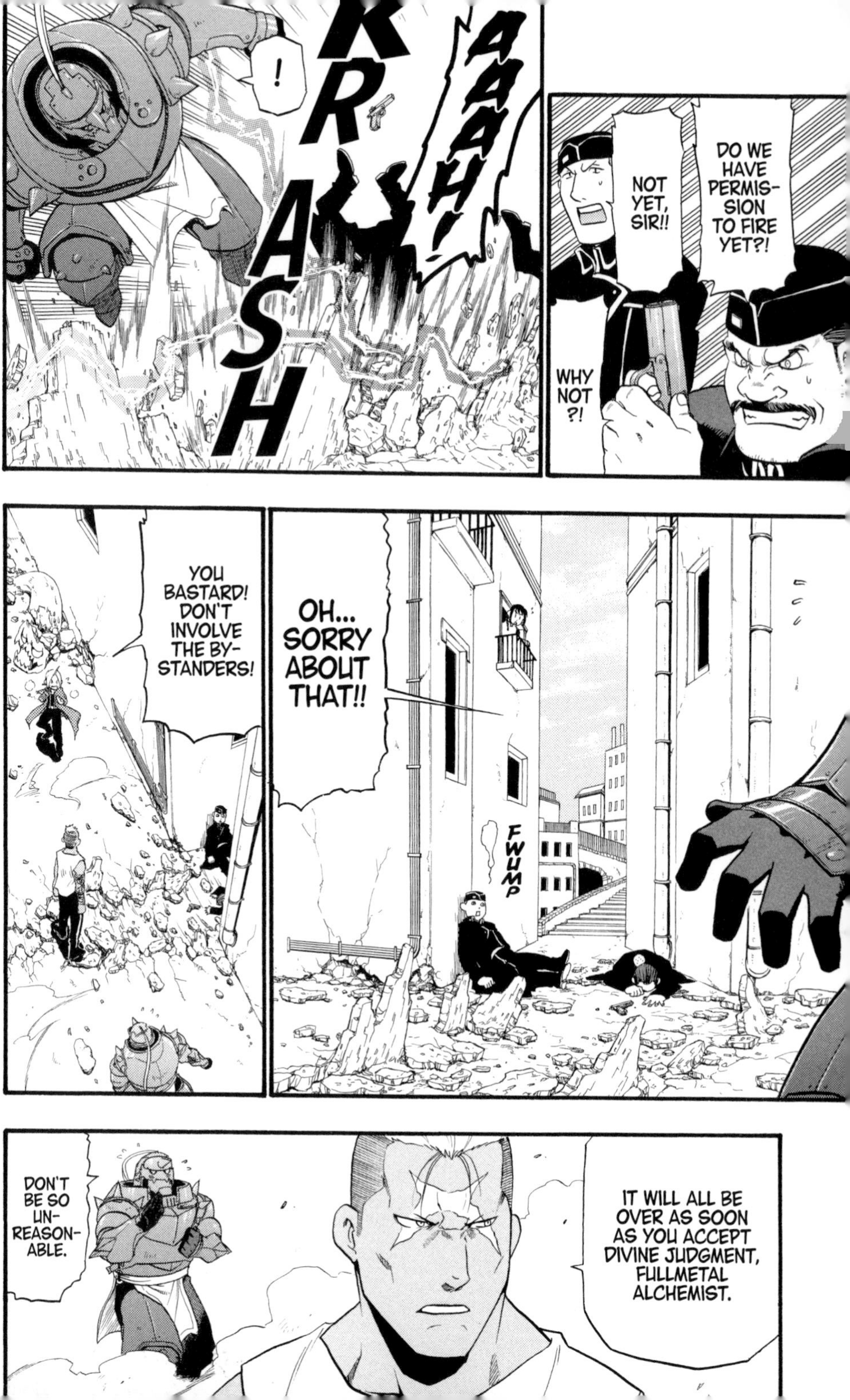
DO WE HAVE PERMISSION TO FIRE YET?!
NOT YET, SIR!!
WHY NOT?!
AAAAH!
KRASH
!
OH... SORRY ABOUT THAT!!
FWUMP
YOU BASTARD! DON'T INVOLVE THE BYSTANDERS!
IT WILL ALL BE OVER AS SOON AS YOU ACCEPT DIVINE JUDGMENT, FULLMETAL ALCHEMIST.
DON'T BE SO UNREASONABLE.

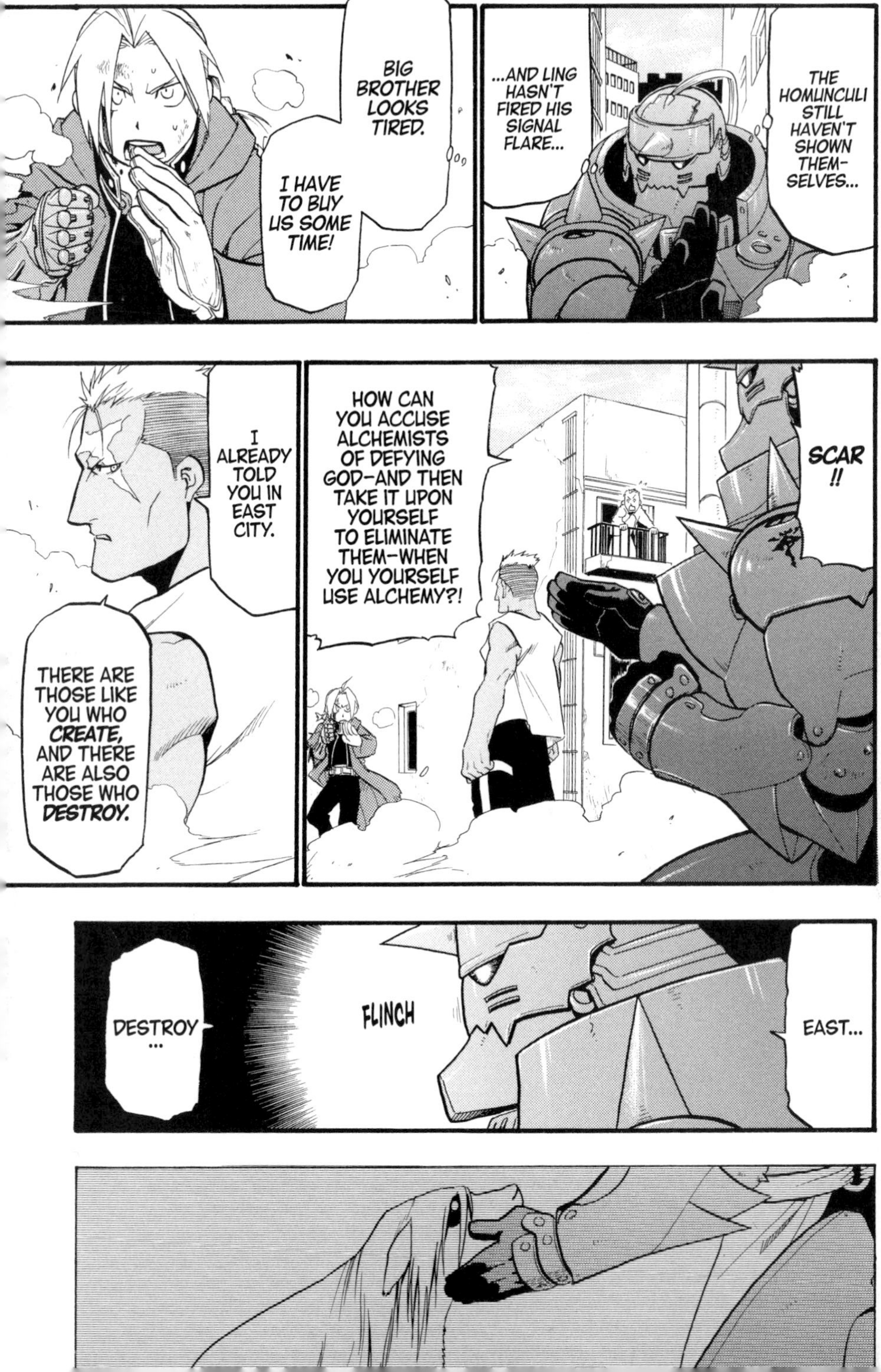
THE HOMUNCULI STILL HAVEN'T SHOWN THEMSELVES...
...AND LING HASN'T FIRED HIS SIGNAL FLARE...
BIG BROTHER LOOKS TIRED.
I HAVE TO BUY US SOME TIME!
SCAR!!
HOW CAN YOU ACCUSE ALCHEMISTS OF DEFYING GOD—AND THEN TAKE IT UPON YOURSELF TO ELIMINATE THEM—WHEN YOU YOURSELF USE ALCHEMY?!
I ALREADY TOLD YOU IN EAST CITY.
THERE ARE THOSE LIKE YOU WHO *CREATE*, AND THERE ARE ALSO THOSE WHO ***DESTROY.***
EAST...
FLINCH
DESTROY...

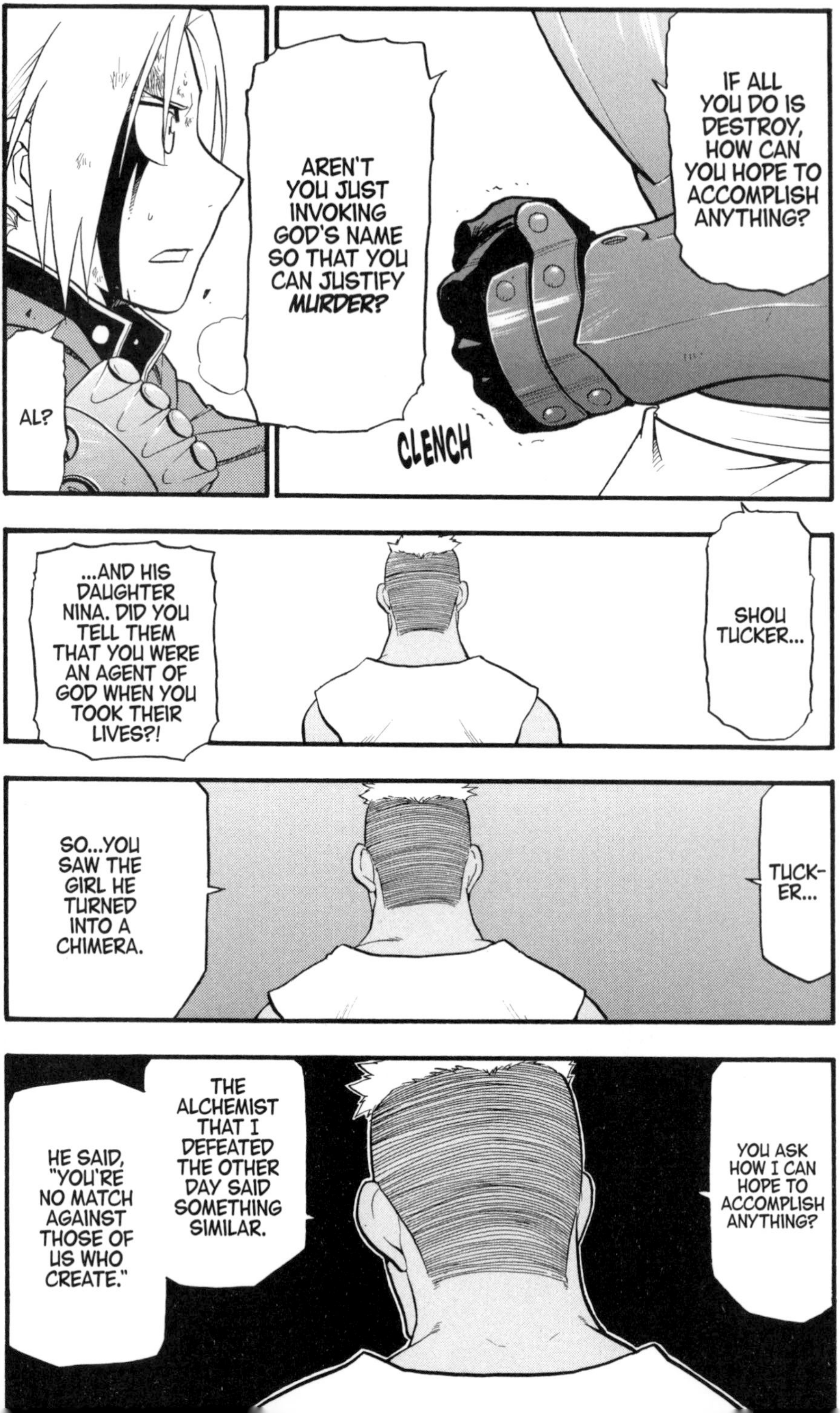
IF ALL YOU DO IS DESTROY, HOW CAN YOU HOPE TO ACCOMPLISH ANYTHING?
CLENCH
AREN'T YOU JUST INVOKING GOD'S NAME SO THAT YOU CAN JUSTIFY *MURDER?*
AL?
SHOU TUCKER...
...AND HIS DAUGHTER NINA. DID YOU TELL THEM THAT YOU WERE AN AGENT OF GOD WHEN YOU TOOK THEIR LIVES?!
TUCK-ER...
SO...YOU SAW THE GIRL HE TURNED INTO A CHIMERA.
YOU ASK HOW I CAN HOPE TO ACCOMPLISH ANYTHING?
THE ALCHEMIST THAT I DEFEATED THE OTHER DAY SAID SOMETHING SIMILAR.
HE SAID, "YOU'RE NO MATCH AGAINST THOSE OF US WHO CREATE."

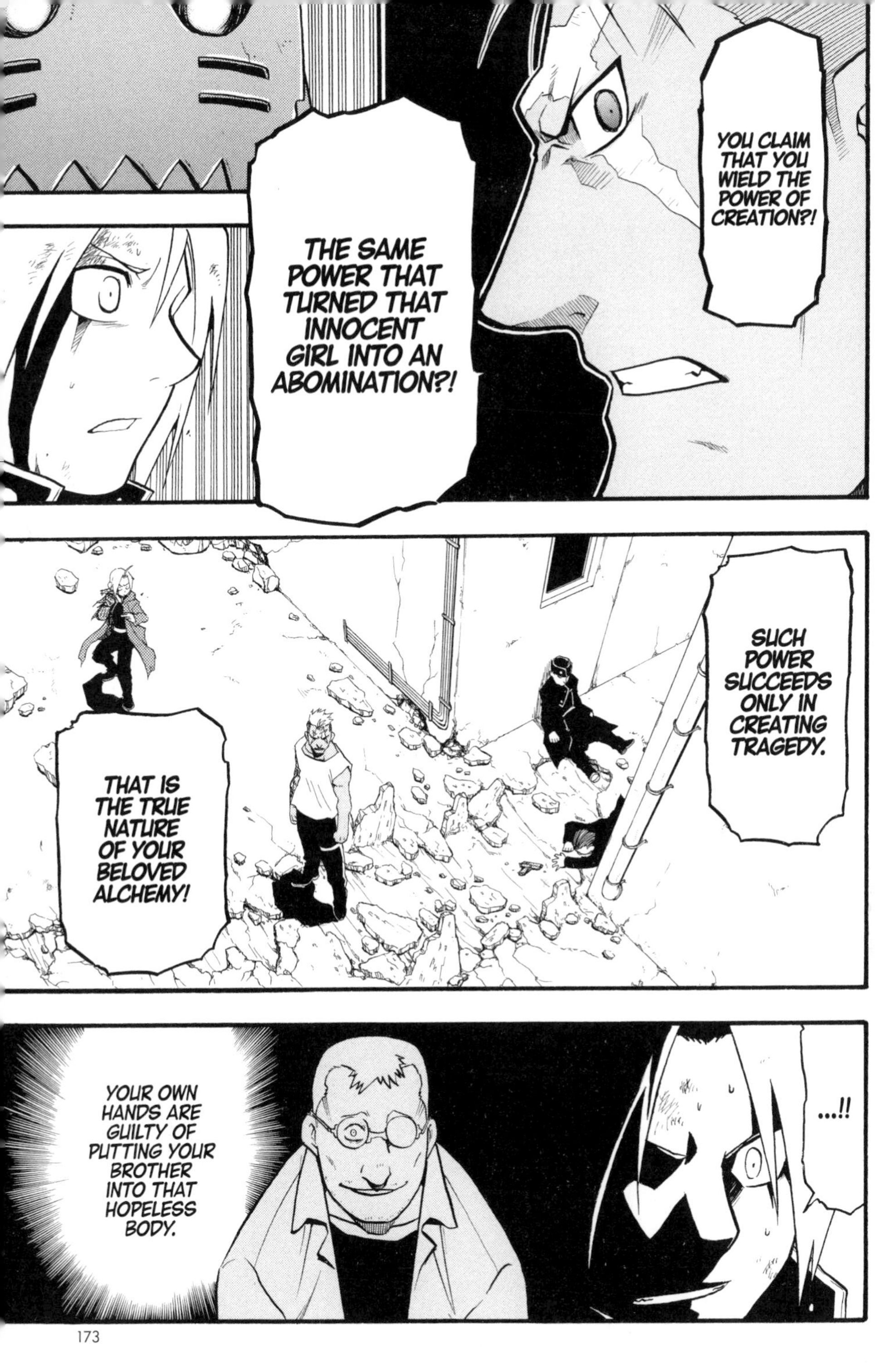
YOU CLAIM THAT YOU WIELD THE POWER OF CREATION?!
THE SAME POWER THAT TURNED THAT INNOCENT GIRL INTO AN ABOMINATION?!
SUCH POWER SUCCEEDS ONLY IN CREATING TRAGEDY.
THAT IS THE TRUE NATURE OF YOUR BELOVED ALCHEMY!
...!!
YOUR OWN HANDS ARE GUILTY OF PUTTING YOUR BROTHER INTO THAT HOPELESS BODY.

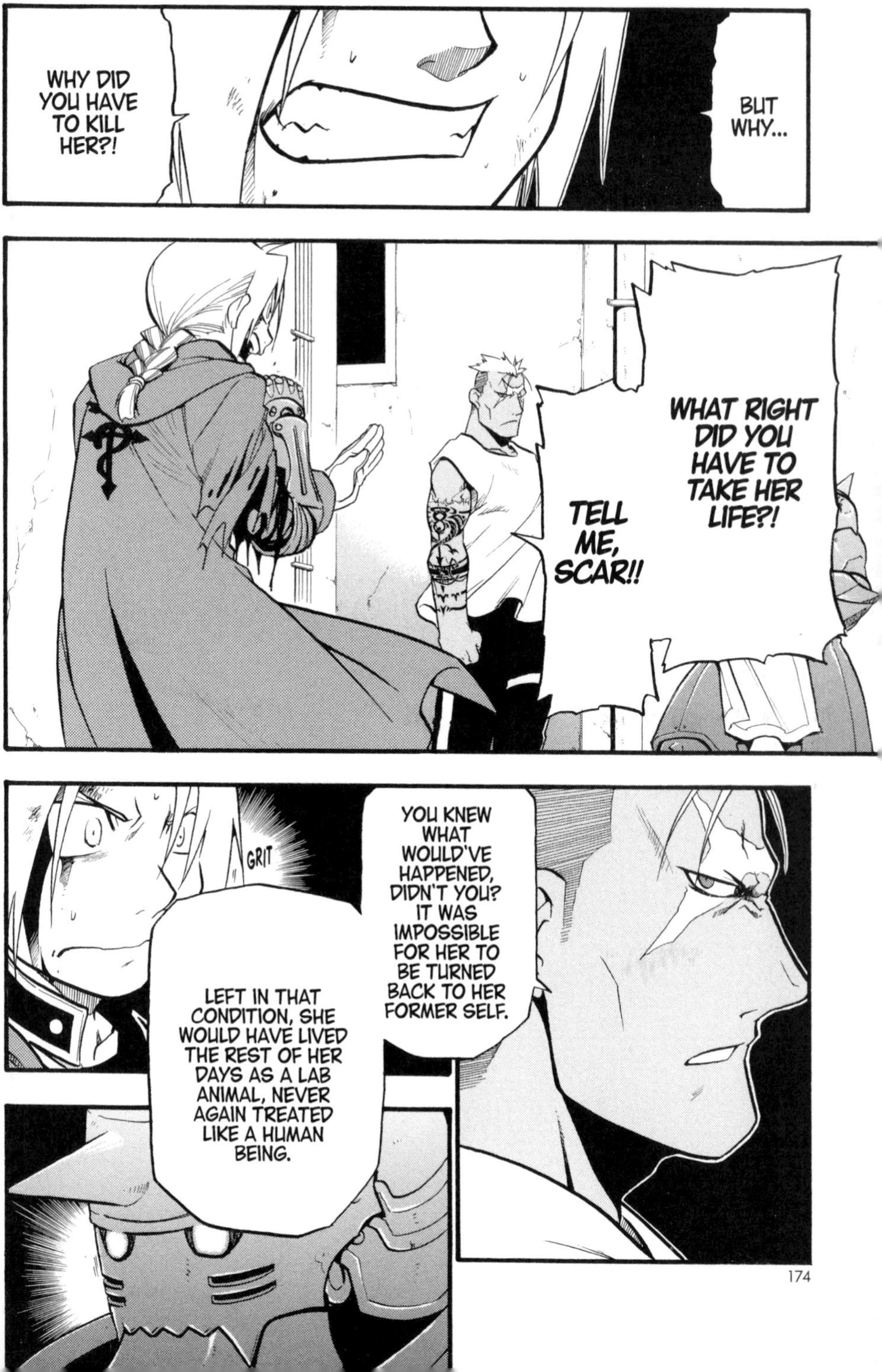
BUT WHY...
WHY DID YOU HAVE TO KILL HER?!
WHAT RIGHT DID YOU HAVE TO TAKE HER LIFE?!
TELL ME, SCAR!!
YOU KNEW WHAT WOULD'VE HAPPENED, DIDN'T YOU? IT WAS IMPOSSIBLE FOR HER TO BE TURNED BACK TO HER FORMER SELF.
LEFT IN THAT CONDITION, SHE WOULD HAVE LIVED THE REST OF HER DAYS AS A LAB ANIMAL, NEVER AGAIN TREATED LIKE A HUMAN BEING.
GRIT

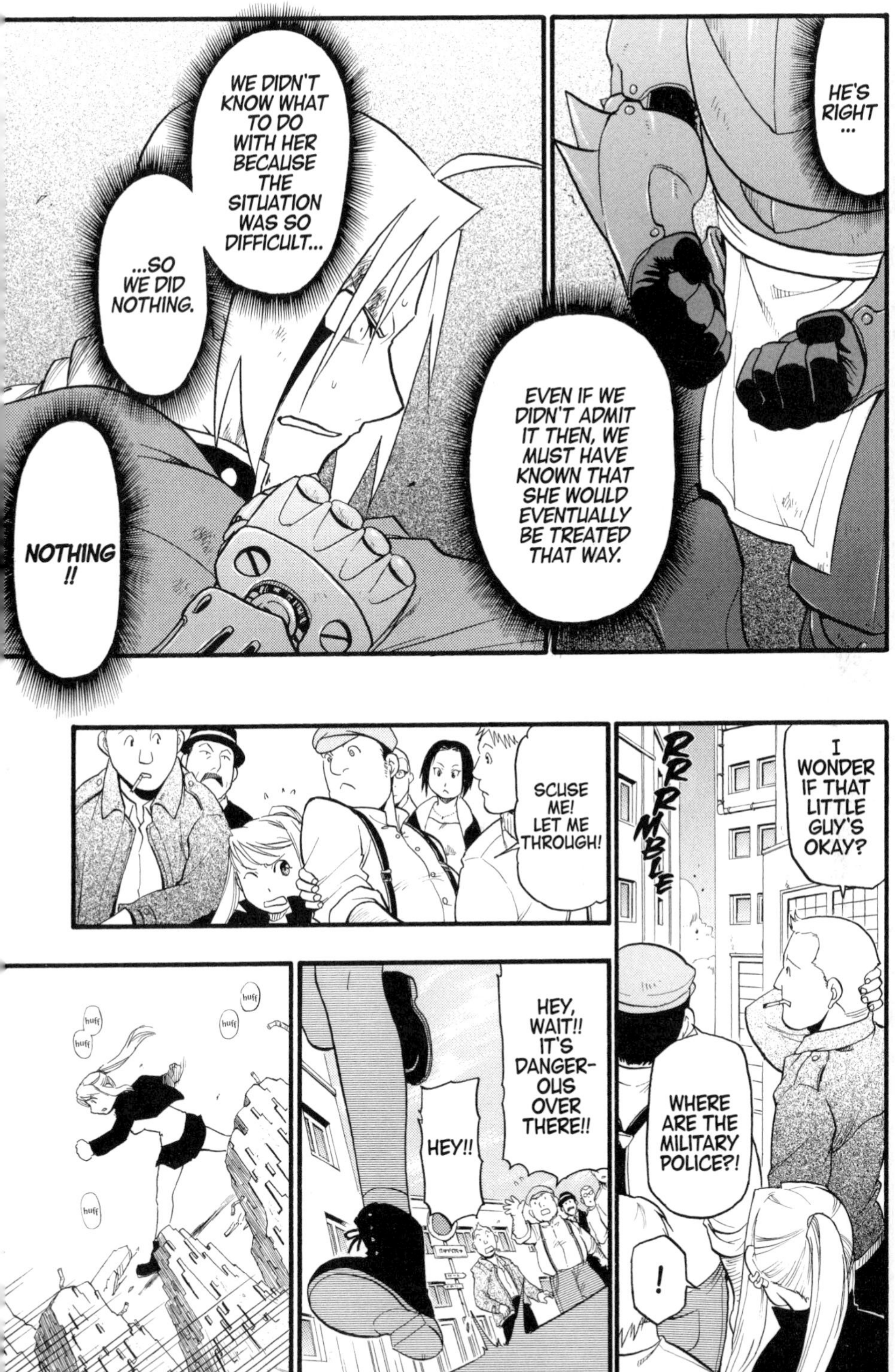
HE'S RIGHT...
EVEN IF WE DIDN'T ADMIT IT THEN, WE MUST HAVE KNOWN THAT SHE WOULD EVENTUALLY BE TREATED THAT WAY.
WE DIDN'T KNOW WHAT TO DO WITH HER BECAUSE THE SITUATION WAS SO DIFFICULT...
...SO WE DID NOTHING.
NOTHING!!
I WONDER IF THAT LITTLE GUY'S OKAY?
RRRMBLE
WHERE ARE THE MILITARY POLICE?!
!
SCUSE ME! LET ME THROUGH!
HEY, WAIT!! IT'S DANGER-OUS OVER THERE!!
HEY!!
huff
huff
huff
huff
huff
huff

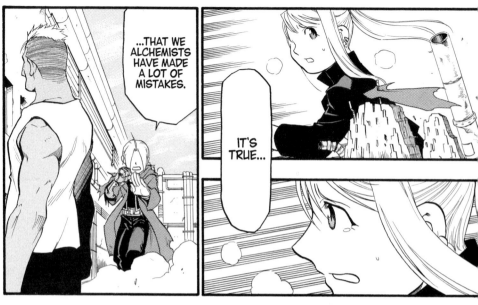

...THAT WE ALCHEMISTS HAVE MADE A LOT OF MISTAKES.

IT'S TRUE...

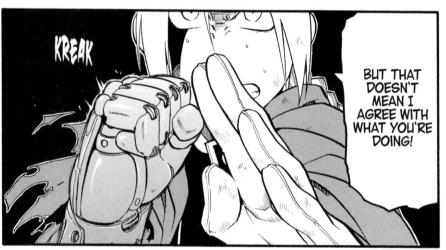

KREAK

BUT THAT DOESN'T MEAN I AGREE WITH WHAT YOU'RE DOING!

SCAR...

I HAVE TO ASK YOU.

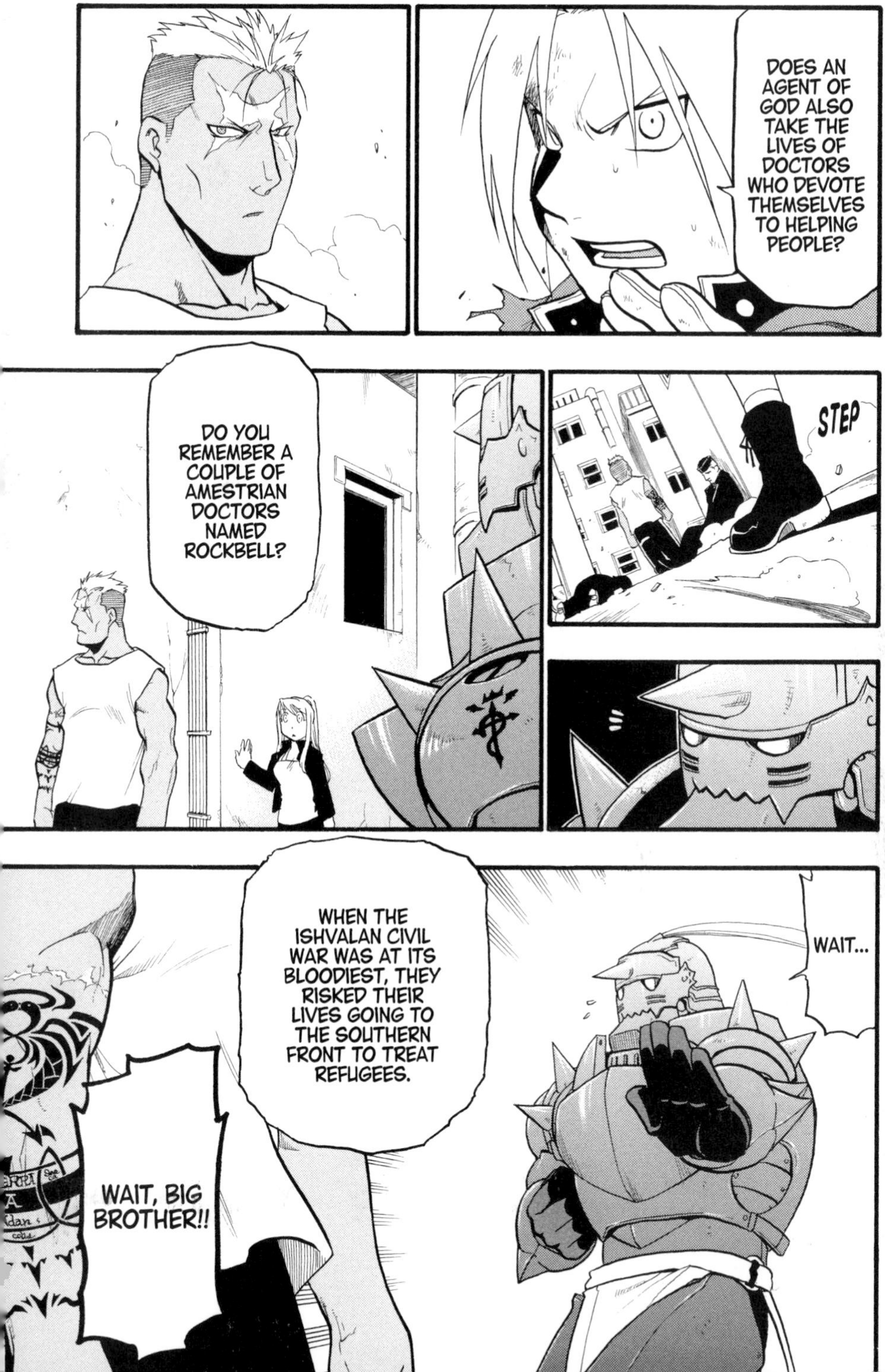
DOES AN AGENT OF GOD ALSO TAKE THE LIVES OF DOCTORS WHO DEVOTE THEMSELVES TO HELPING PEOPLE?
STEP
DO YOU REMEMBER A COUPLE OF AMESTRIAN DOCTORS NAMED ROCKBELL?
WAIT...
WHEN THE ISHVALAN CIVIL WAR WAS AT ITS BLOODIEST, THEY RISKED THEIR LIVES GOING TO THE SOUTHERN FRONT TO TREAT REFUGEES.
WAIT, BIG BROTHER!!

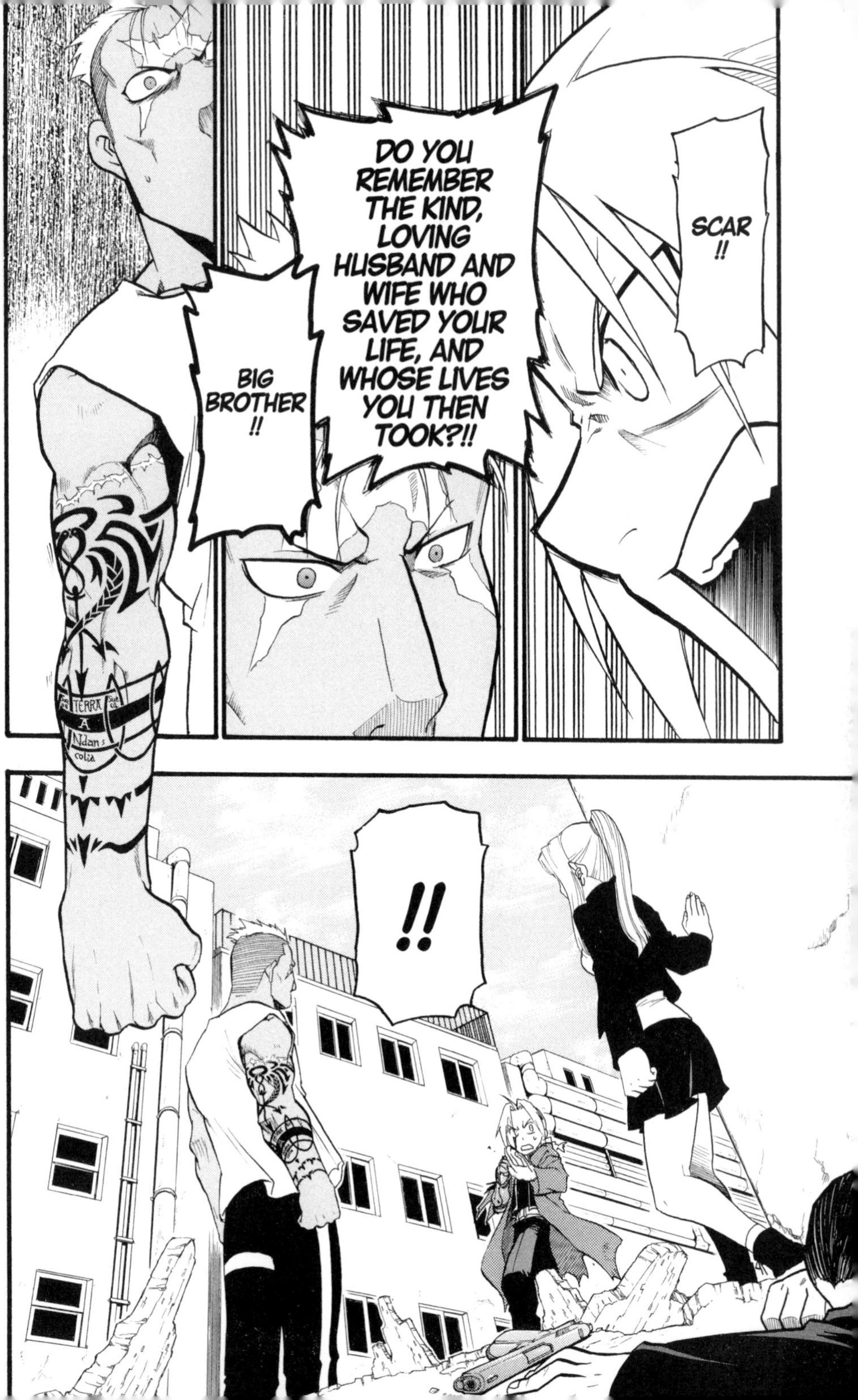
SCAR!!
DO YOU REMEMBER THE KIND, LOVING HUSBAND AND WIFE WHO SAVED YOUR LIFE, AND WHOSE LIVES YOU THEN TOOK?!!
BIG BROTHER!!
!!

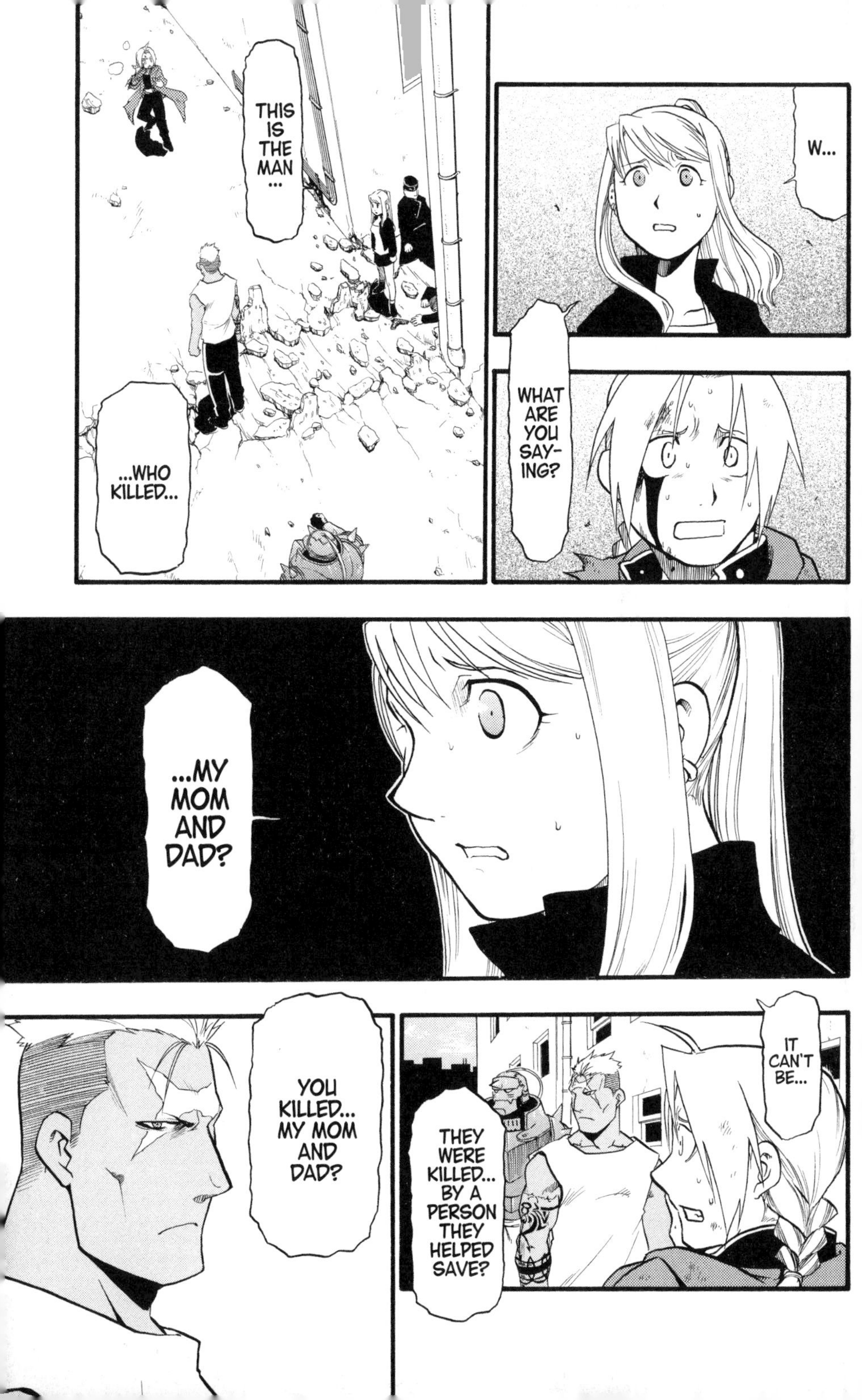
W...
WHAT ARE YOU SAYING?
THIS IS THE MAN...
...WHO KILLED...
...MY MOM AND DAD?
IT CAN'T BE...
THEY WERE KILLED... BY A PERSON THEY HELPED SAVE?
YOU KILLED... MY MOM AND DAD?

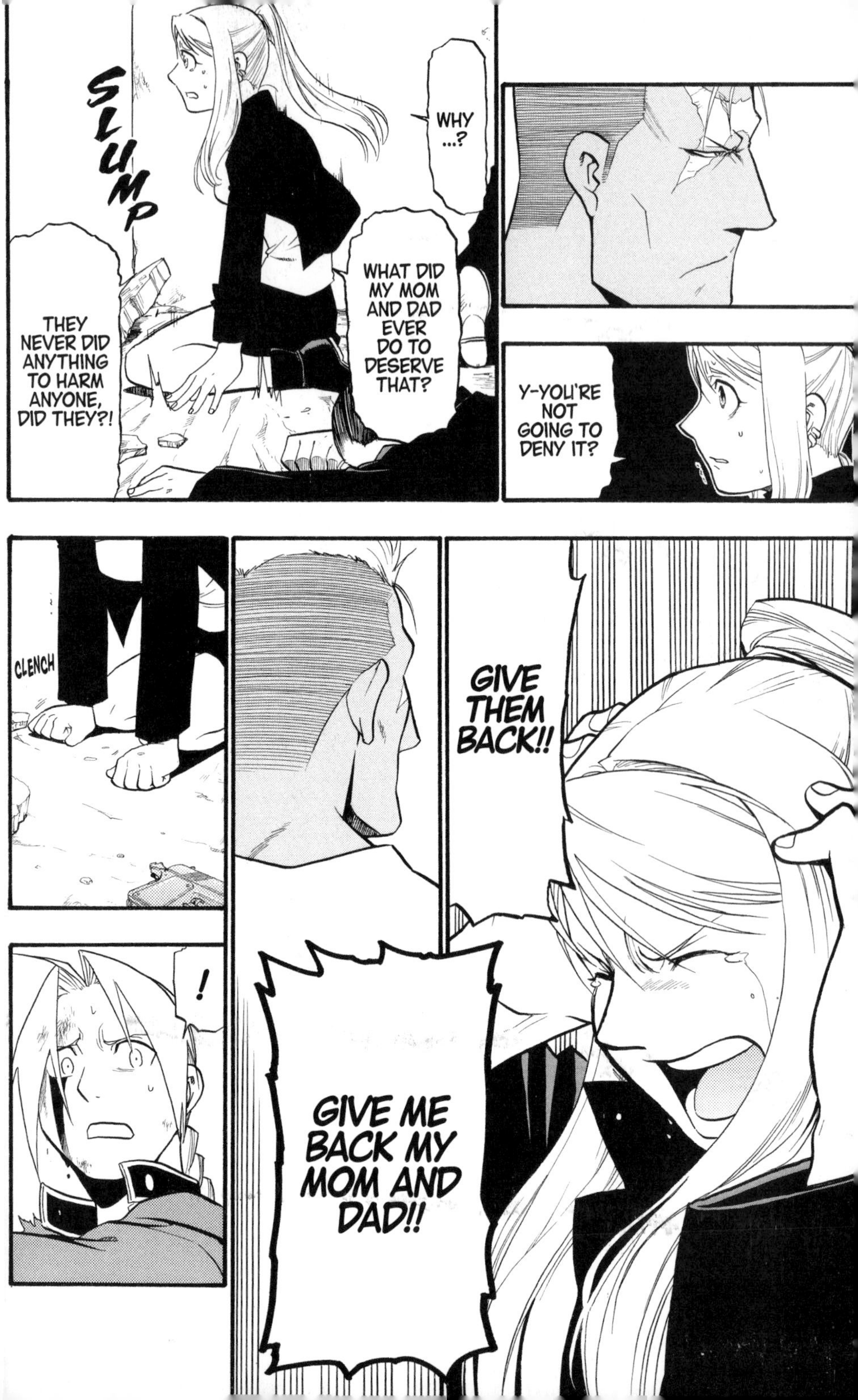
Y-YOU'RE NOT GOING TO DENY IT?
WHY ...?
SLUMP
WHAT DID MY MOM AND DAD EVER DO TO DESERVE THAT?
THEY NEVER DID ANYTHING TO HARM ANYONE, DID THEY?!
GIVE THEM BACK!!
GIVE ME BACK MY MOM AND DAD!!
CLENCH
!

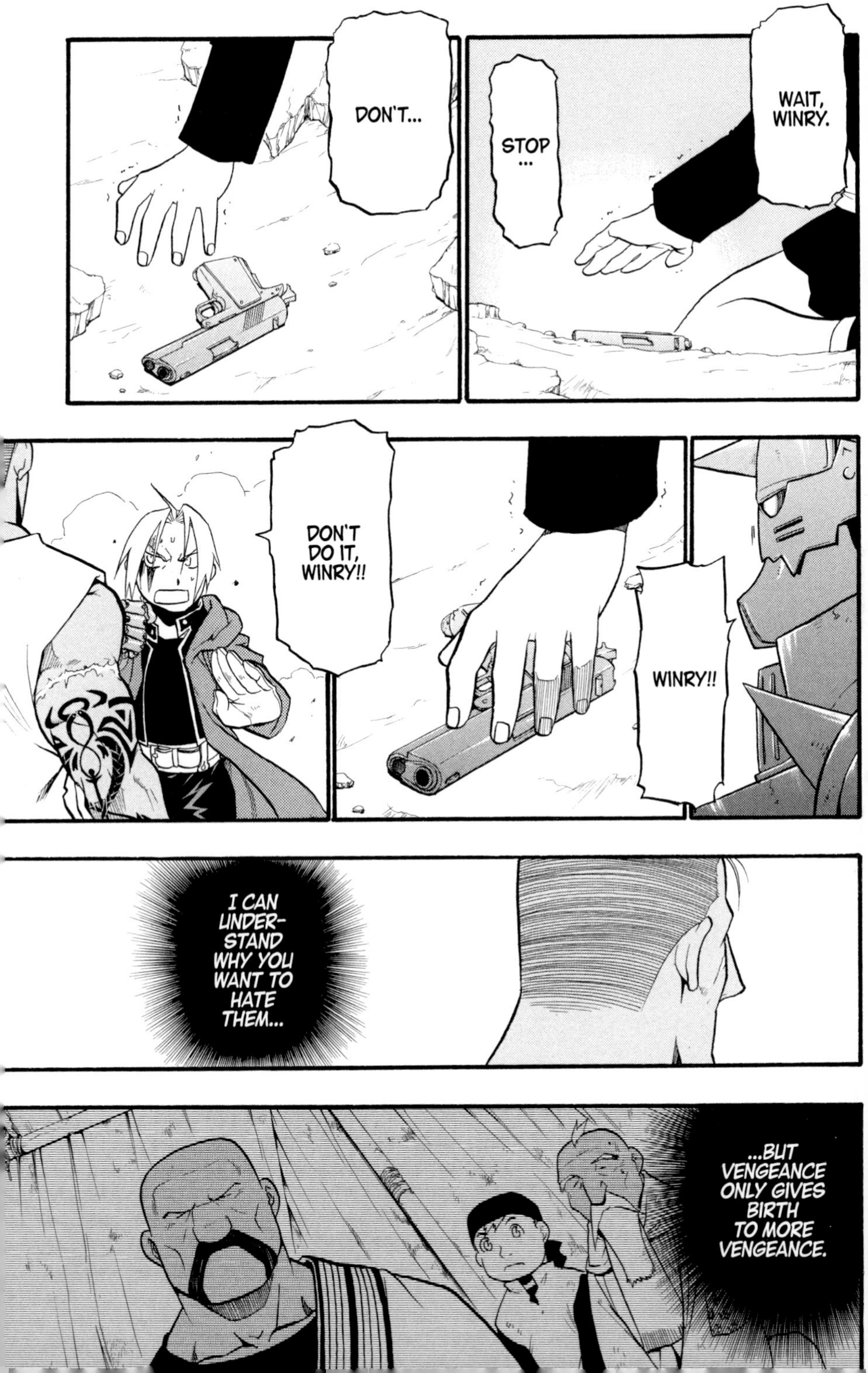
WAIT, WINRY.
STOP...
DON'T...
WINRY!!
DON'T DO IT, WINRY!!
I CAN UNDER-STAND WHY YOU WANT TO HATE THEM...
...BUT VENGEANCE ONLY GIVES BIRTH TO MORE VENGEANCE.

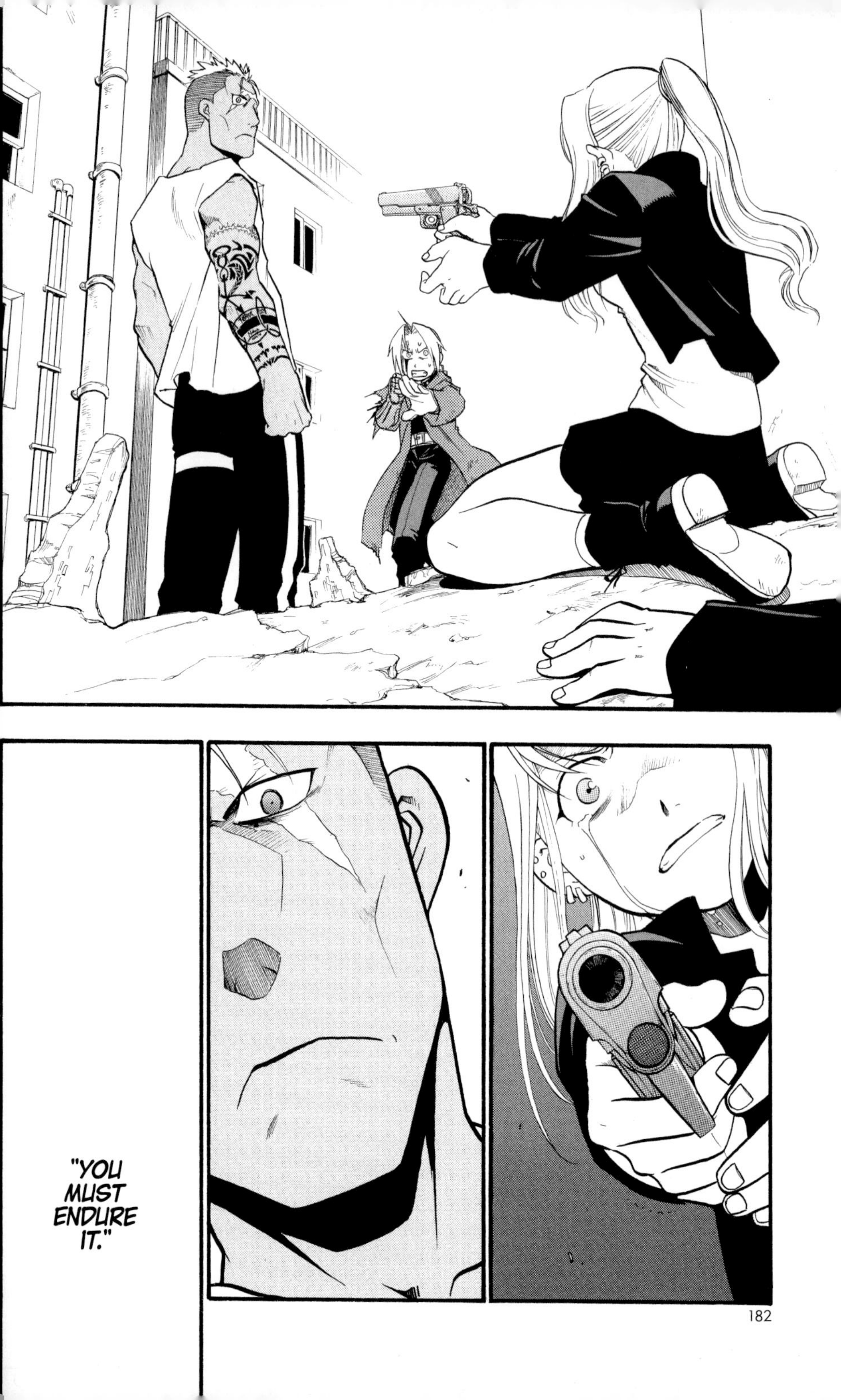
"YOU MUST ENDURE IT."

CHAPTER 47

A GIRL IN THE GRIP OF BATTLES PAST AND PRESENT

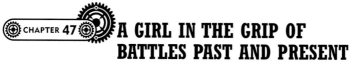

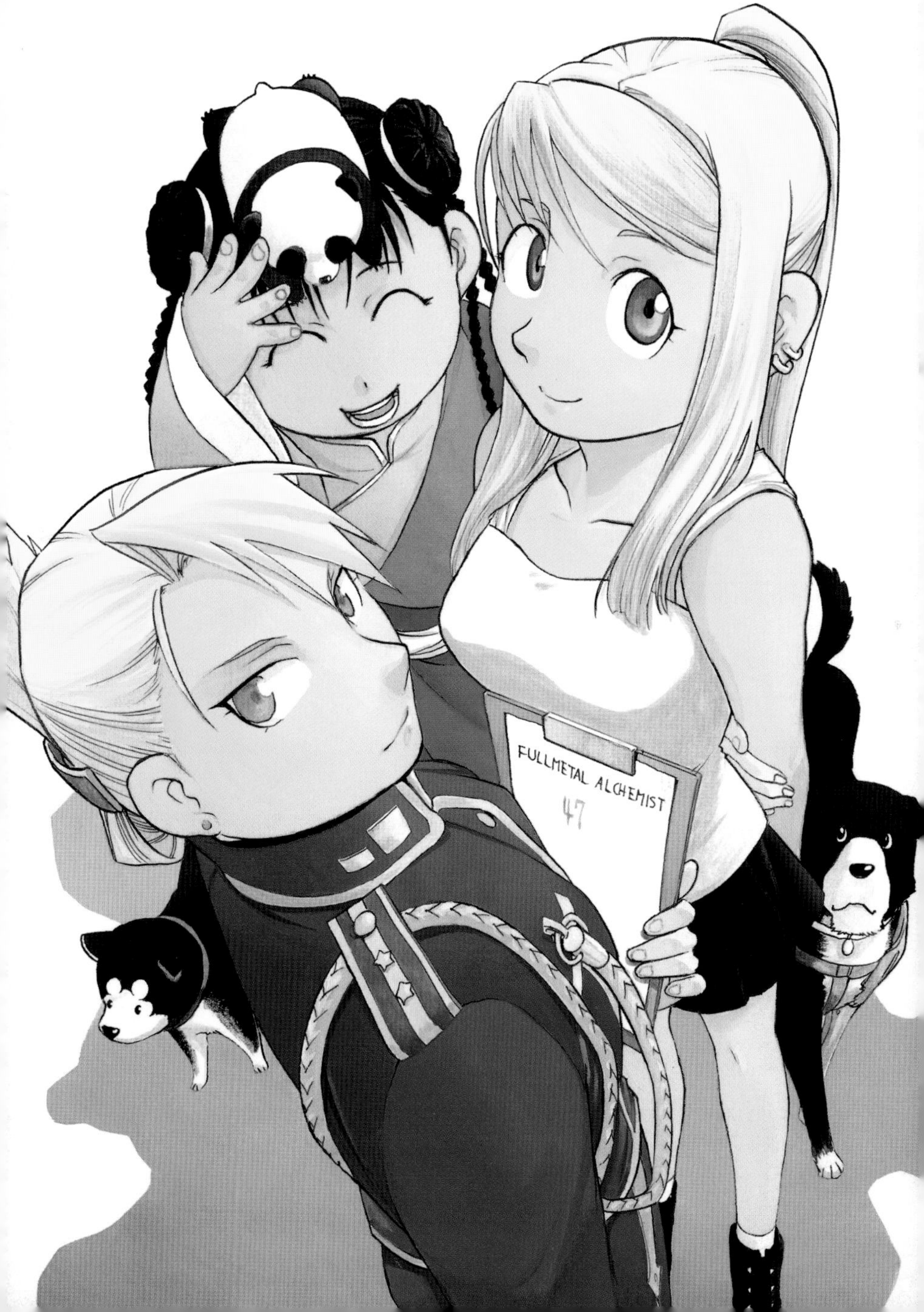
FULLMETAL ALCHEMIST
47

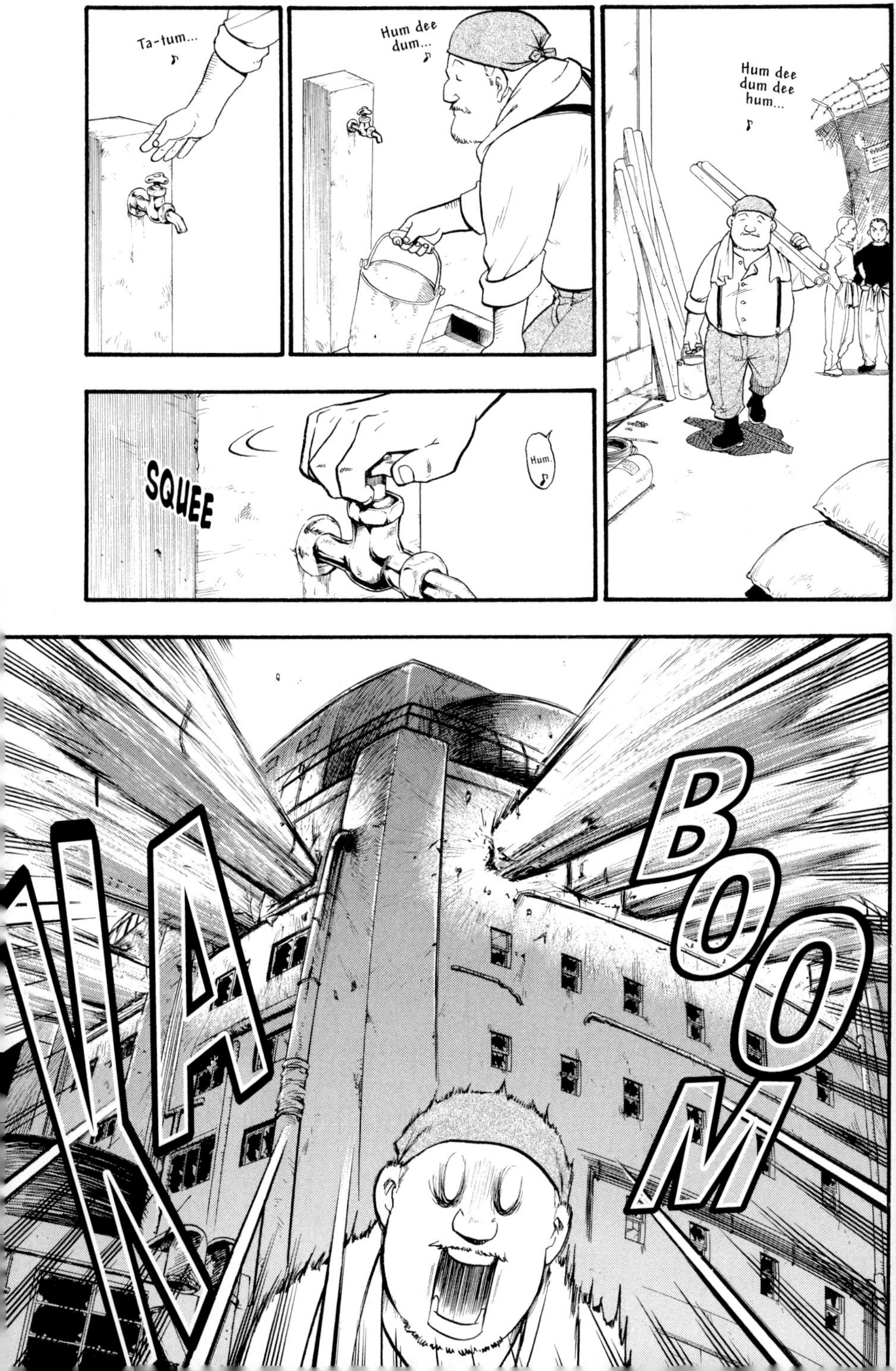
Hum dee dum dee hum...
Hum dee dum...
Ta-tum...
Hum.
SQUEE
BOOM
WA

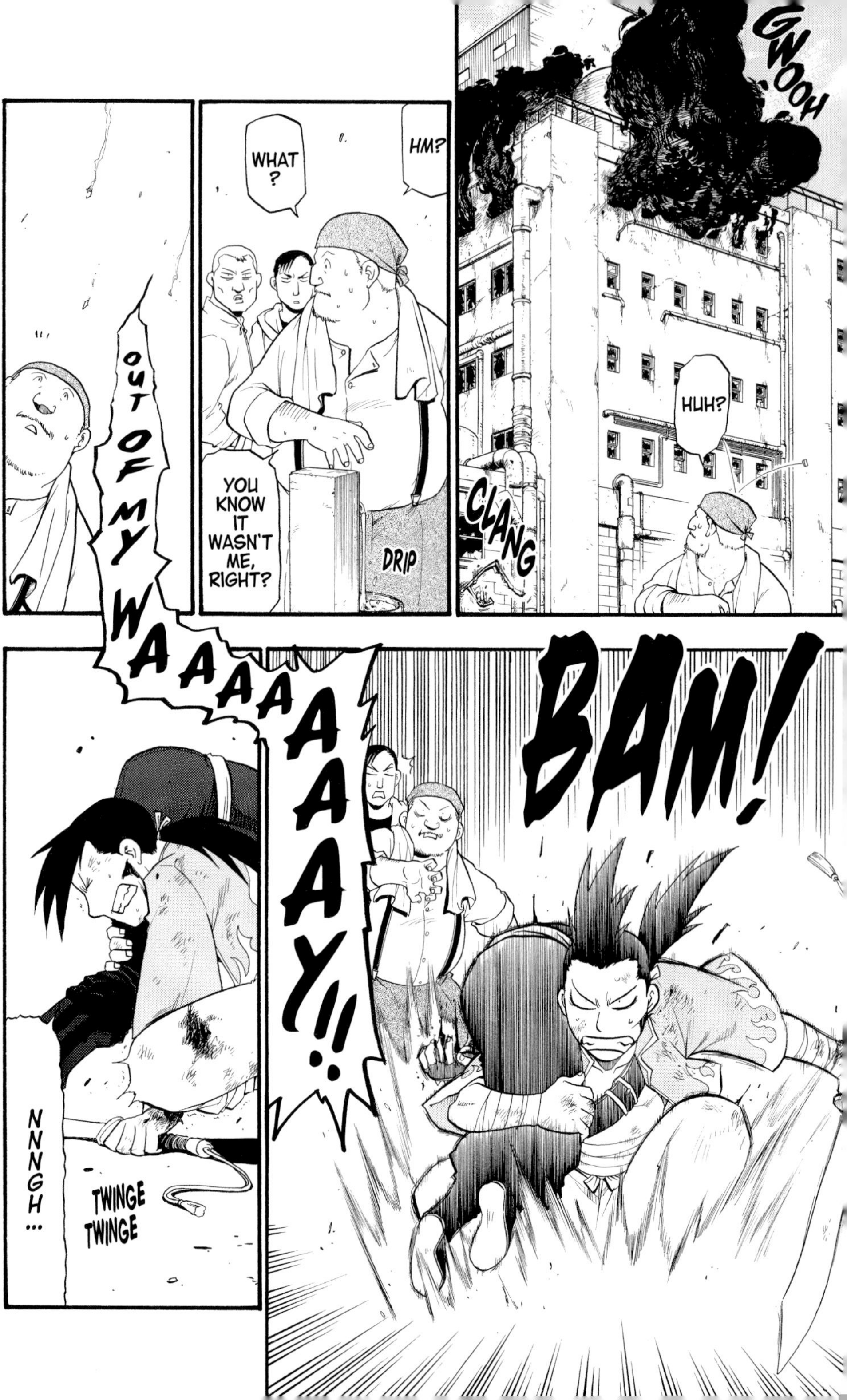
GWOOOH
HUH?
CLANG
HM?
WHAT?
YOU KNOW IT WASN'T ME, RIGHT?
DRIP
OUT OF MY WAAAAAAAY!!!
BAM!
NNNGH...
TWINGE TWINGE

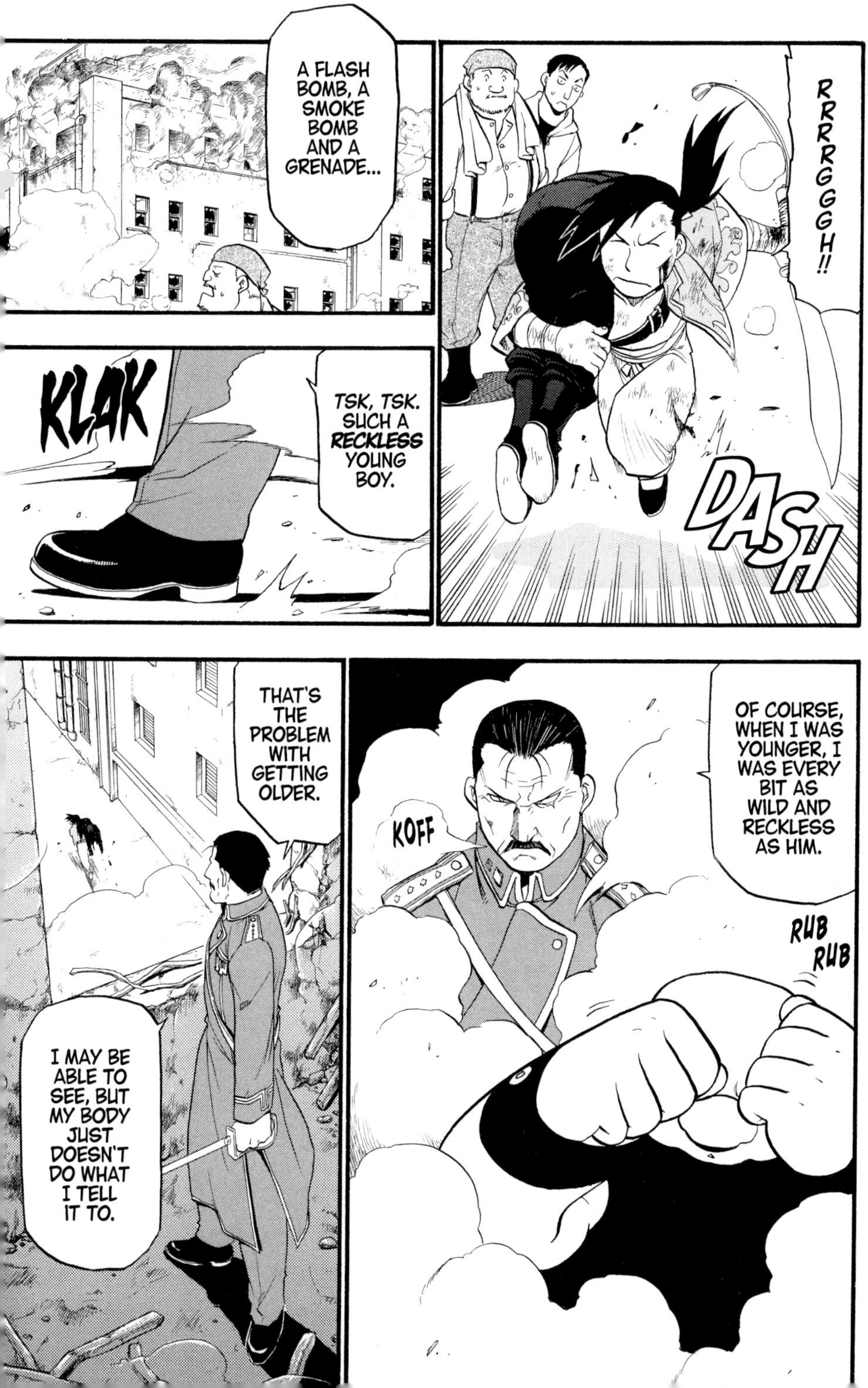
RRRRGGGH!!
DASH
A FLASH BOMB, A SMOKE BOMB AND A GRENADE...
KLAK
TSK, TSK. SUCH A RECKLESS YOUNG BOY.
OF COURSE, WHEN I WAS YOUNGER, I WAS EVERY BIT AS WILD AND RECKLESS AS HIM.
KOFF
RUB RUB
THAT'S THE PROBLEM WITH GETTING OLDER.
I MAY BE ABLE TO SEE, BUT MY BODY JUST DOESN'T DO WHAT I TELL IT TO.

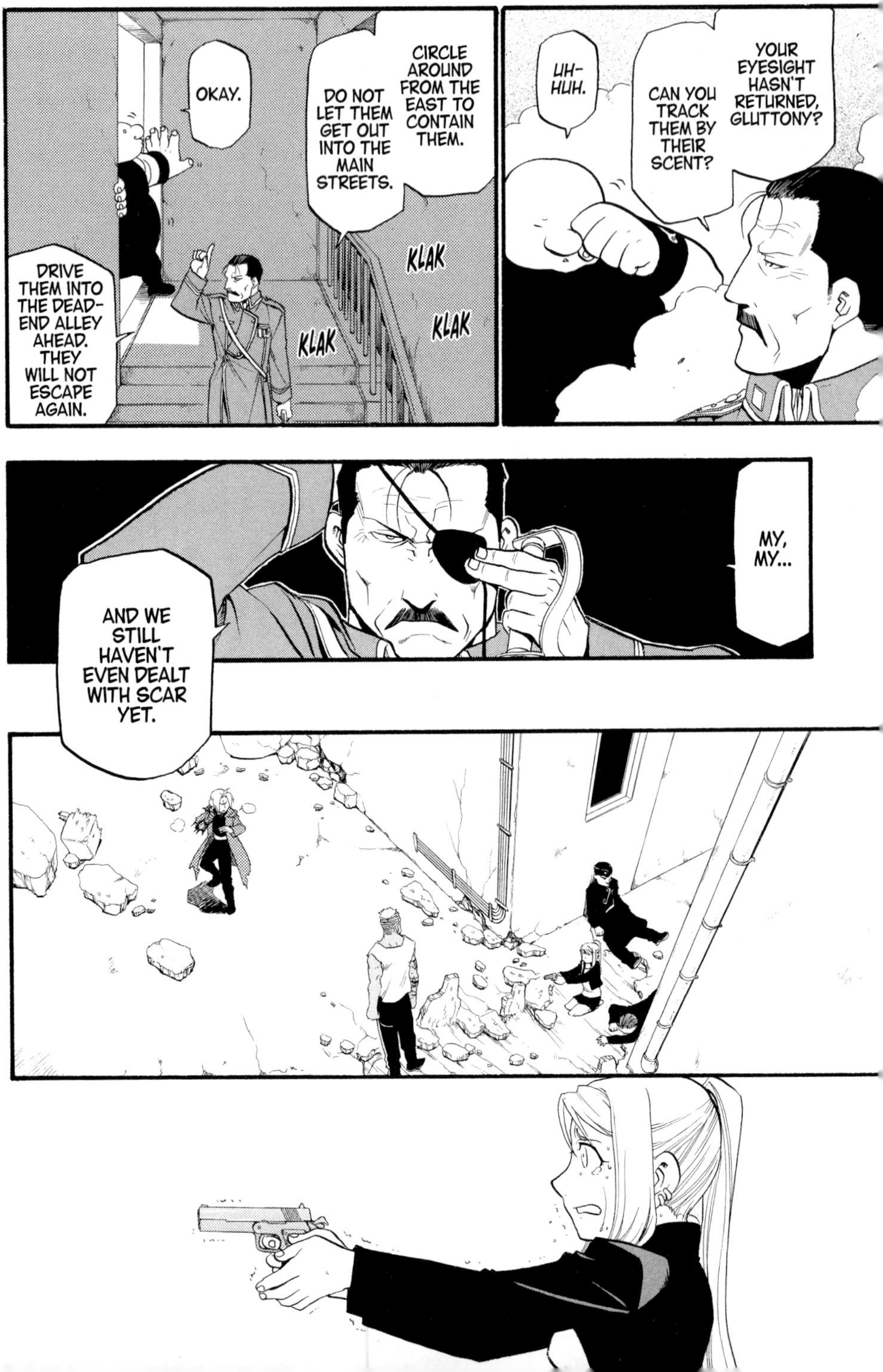
YOUR EYESIGHT HASN'T RETURNED, GLUTTONY?
CAN YOU TRACK THEM BY THEIR SCENT?
UH-HUH.
CIRCLE AROUND FROM THE EAST TO CONTAIN THEM.
DO NOT LET THEM GET OUT INTO THE MAIN STREETS.
OKAY.
KLAK
KLAK
KLAK
DRIVE THEM INTO THE DEAD-END ALLEY AHEAD. THEY WILL NOT ESCAPE AGAIN.
MY, MY...
AND WE STILL HAVEN'T EVEN DEALT WITH SCAR YET.

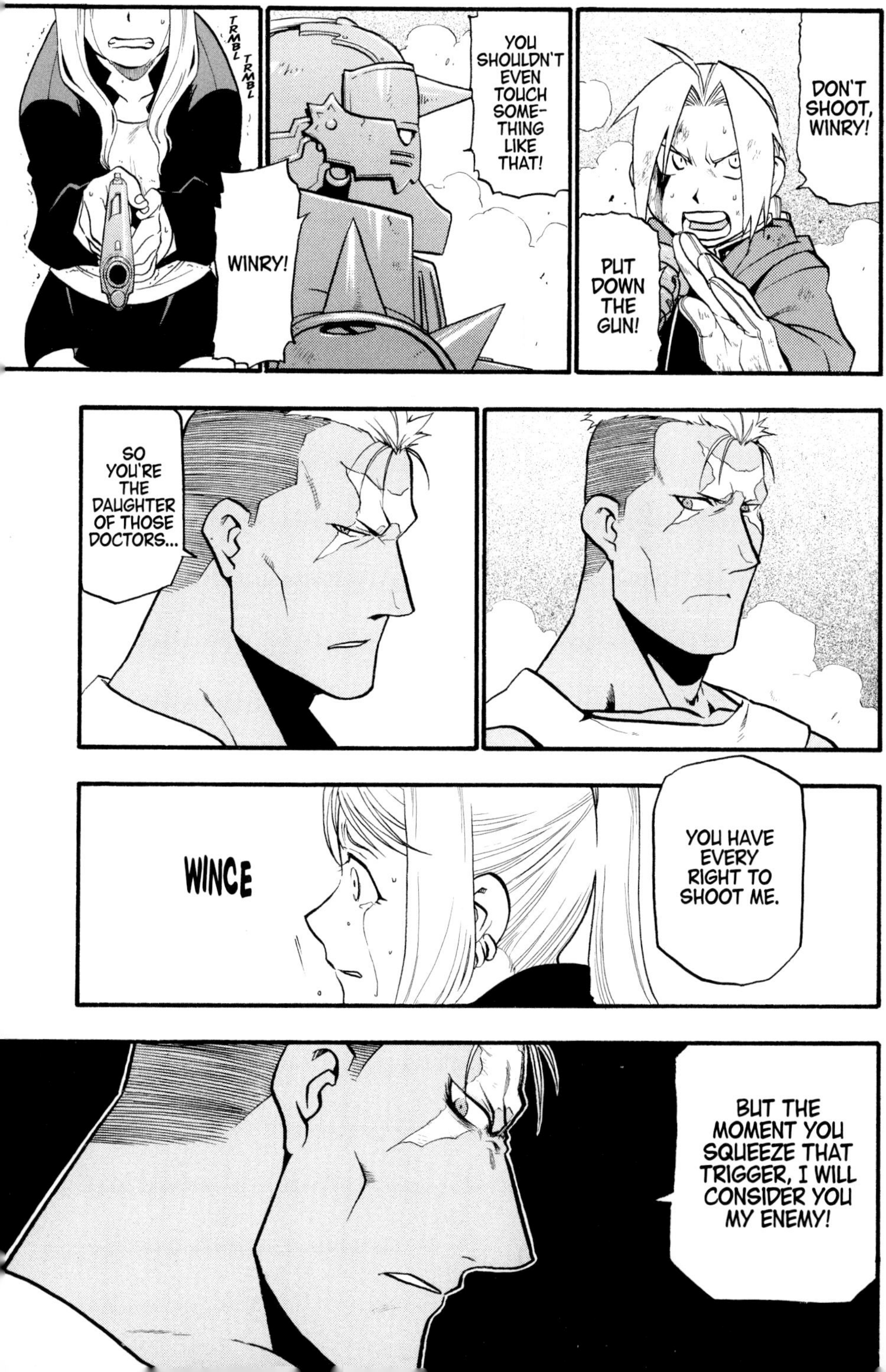
DON'T SHOOT, WINRY!
PUT DOWN THE GUN!
YOU SHOULDN'T EVEN TOUCH SOME-THING LIKE THAT!
WINRY!
TRMBL TRMBL
SO YOU'RE THE DAUGHTER OF THOSE DOCTORS...
YOU HAVE EVERY RIGHT TO SHOOT ME.
WINCE
BUT THE MOMENT YOU SQUEEZE THAT TRIGGER, I WILL CONSIDER YOU MY ENEMY!

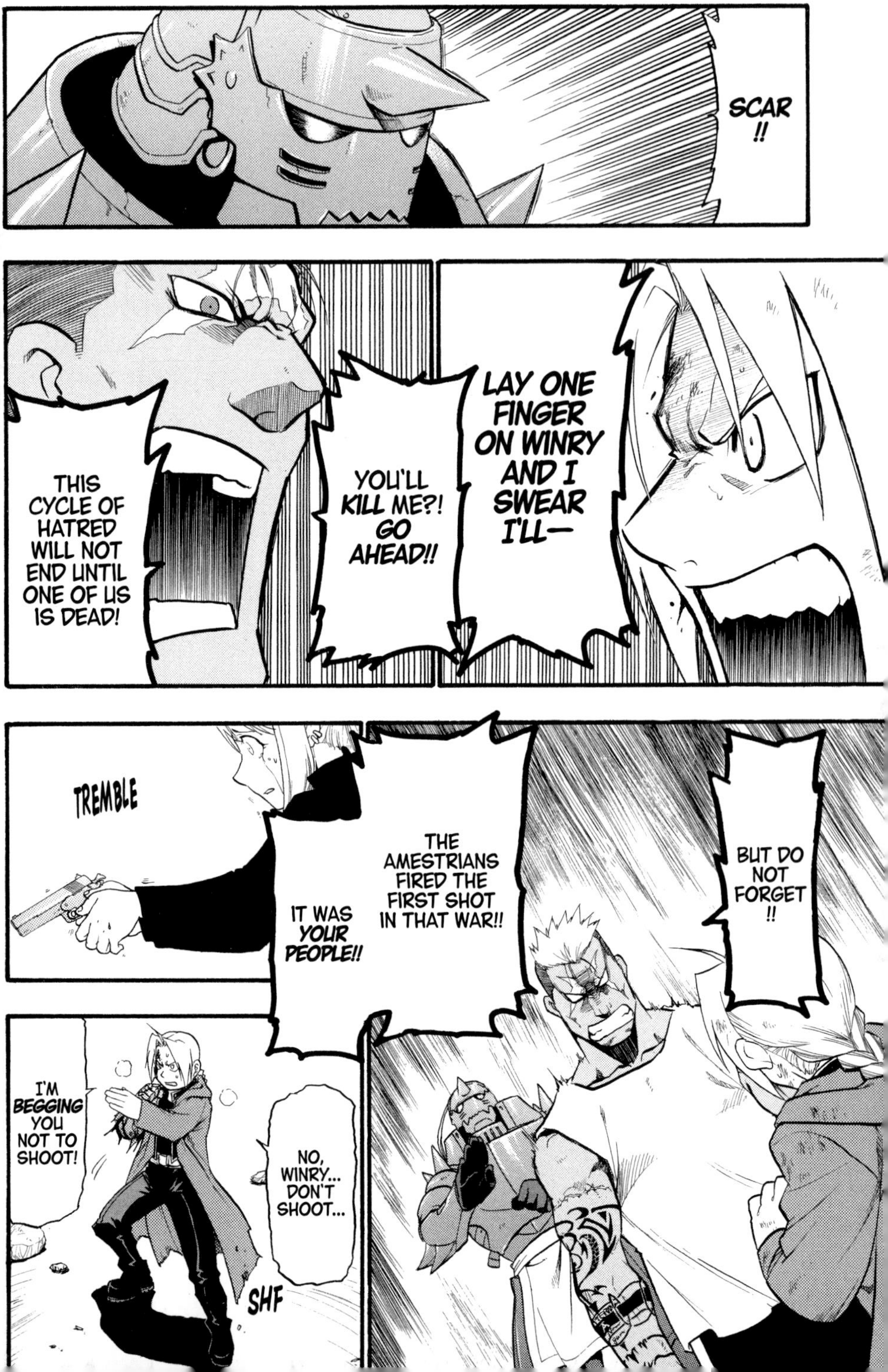
SCAR!!
LAY ONE FINGER ON WINRY AND I SWEAR I'LL—
YOU'LL KILL ME?! GO AHEAD!!
THIS CYCLE OF HATRED WILL NOT END UNTIL ONE OF US IS DEAD!
BUT DO NOT FORGET!!
THE AMESTRIANS FIRED THE FIRST SHOT IN THAT WAR!!
IT WAS YOUR PEOPLE!!
TREMBLE
NO, WINRY... DON'T SHOOT...
I'M BEGGING YOU NOT TO SHOOT!
SHF

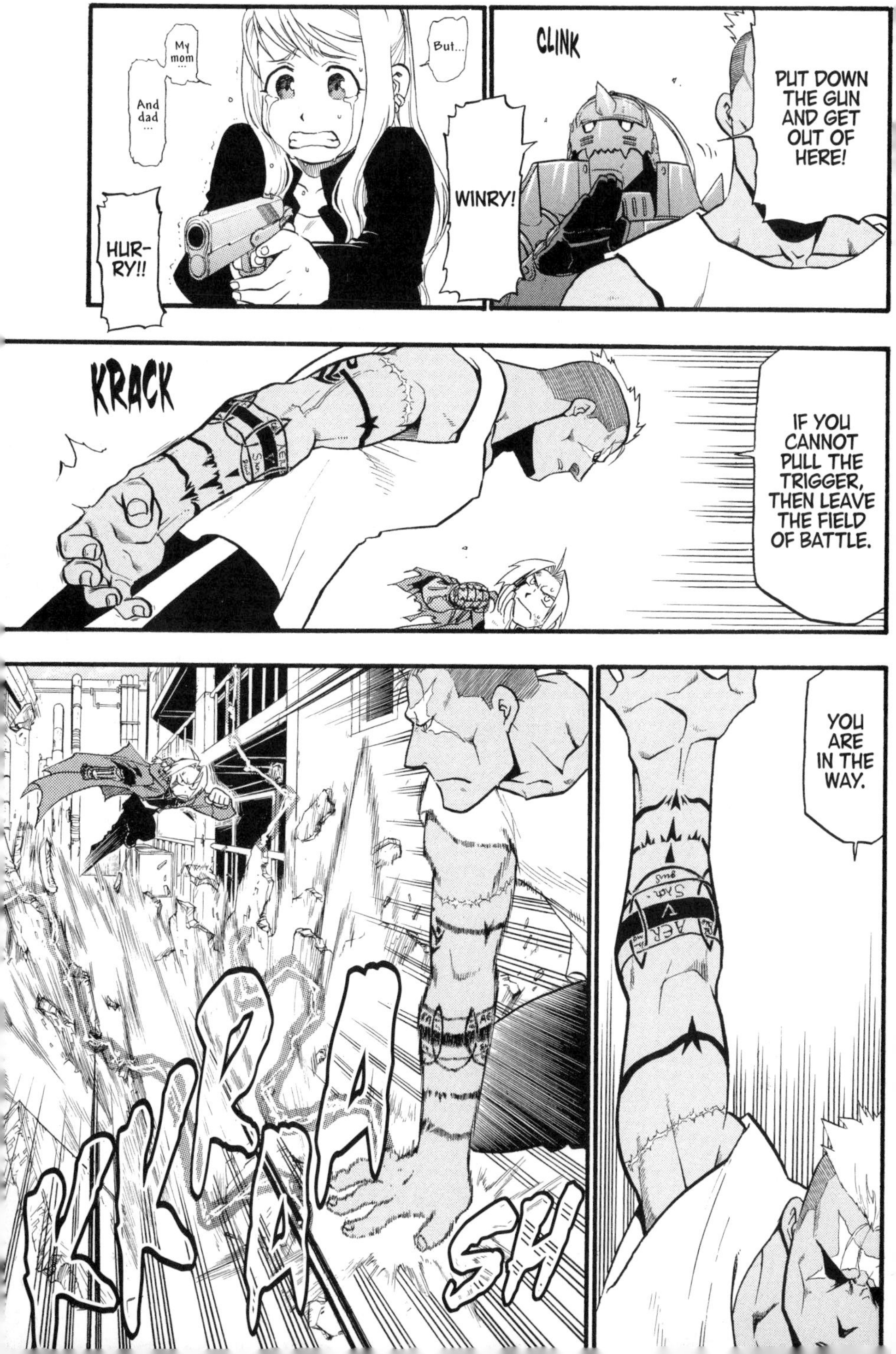
CLINK
PUT DOWN THE GUN AND GET OUT OF HERE!
WINRY!
But...
My mom...
And dad...
HURRY!!
IF YOU CANNOT PULL THE TRIGGER, THEN LEAVE THE FIELD OF BATTLE.
KRACK
YOU ARE IN THE WAY.
KRAAASH

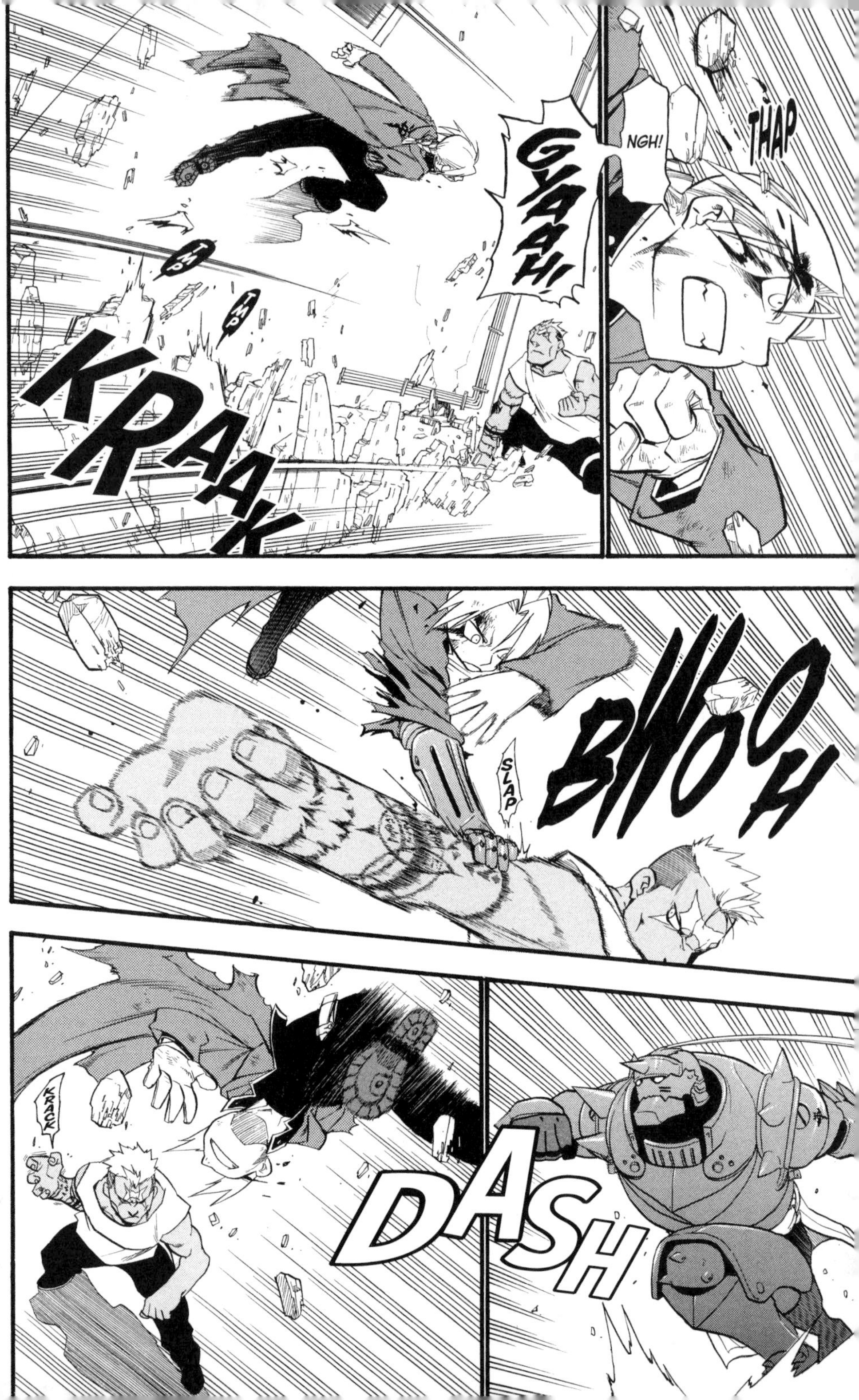
NGH!
THAP
GYAAAH!
TMP
TMP
KRAAK
BWOOOH
SLAP
DASH
KRACK

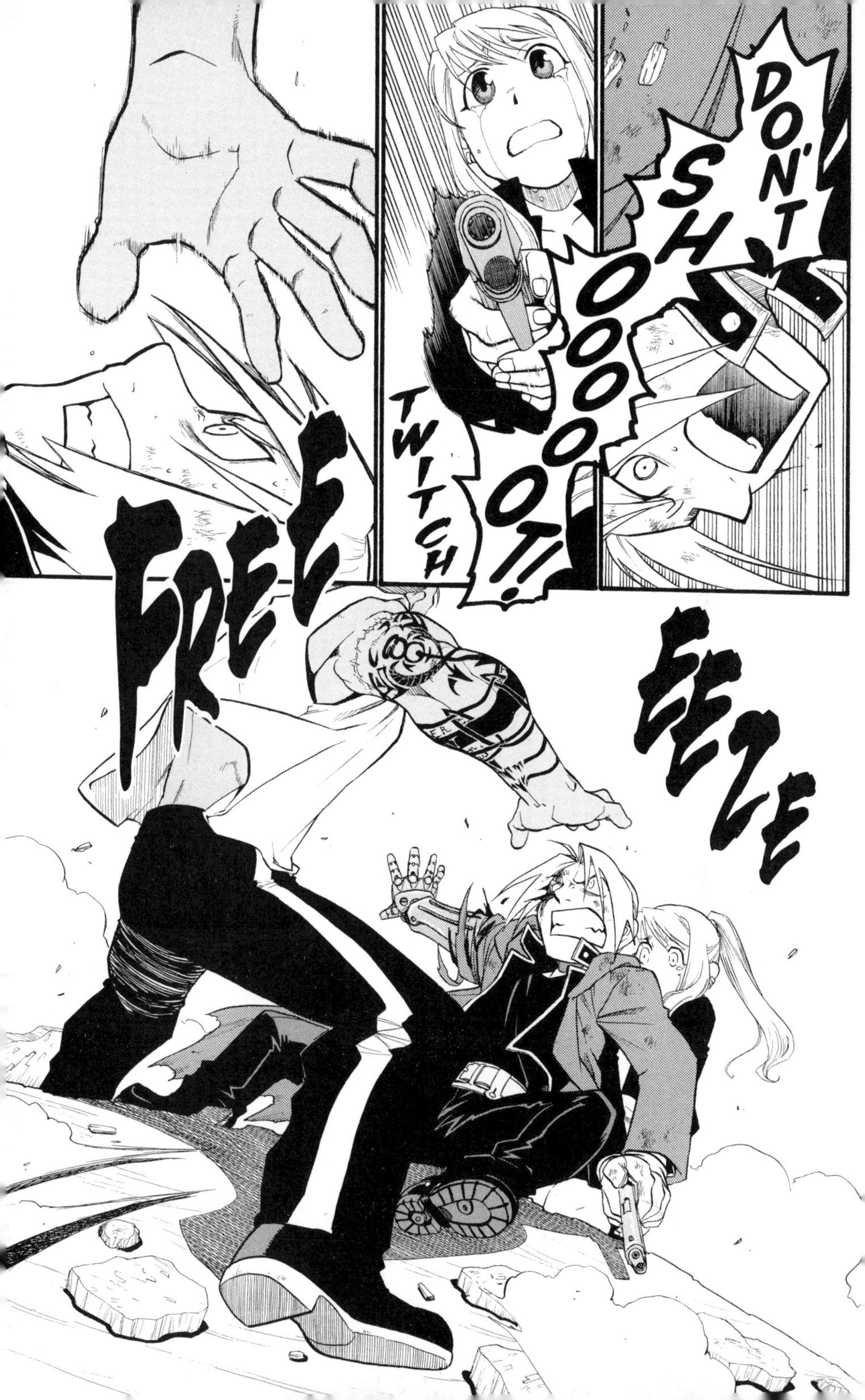

DON'T SHOOOOOOT!!
TWITCH
FREEEZE

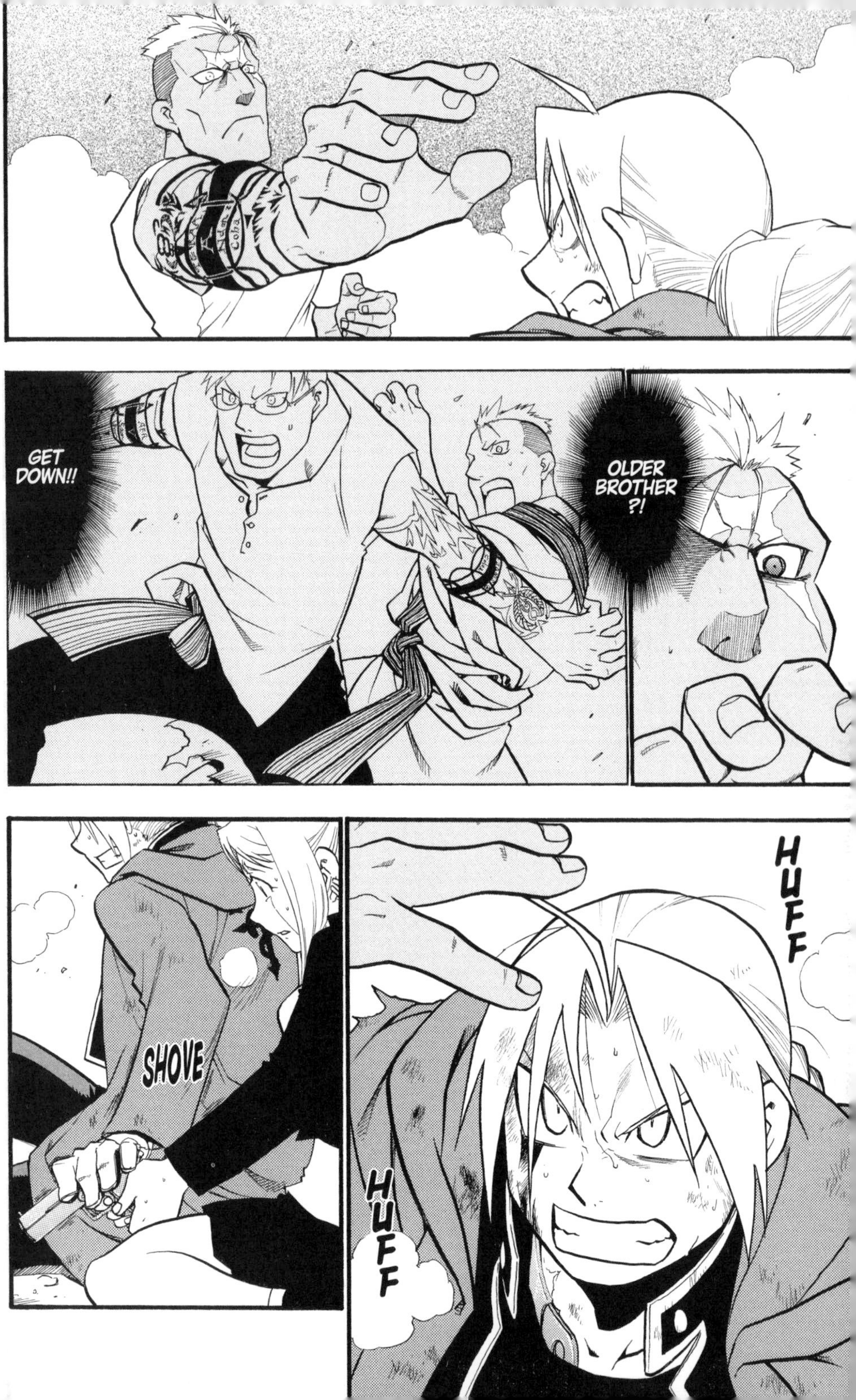
OLDER BROTHER ?!
GET DOWN!!
HUFF
HUFF
SHOVE

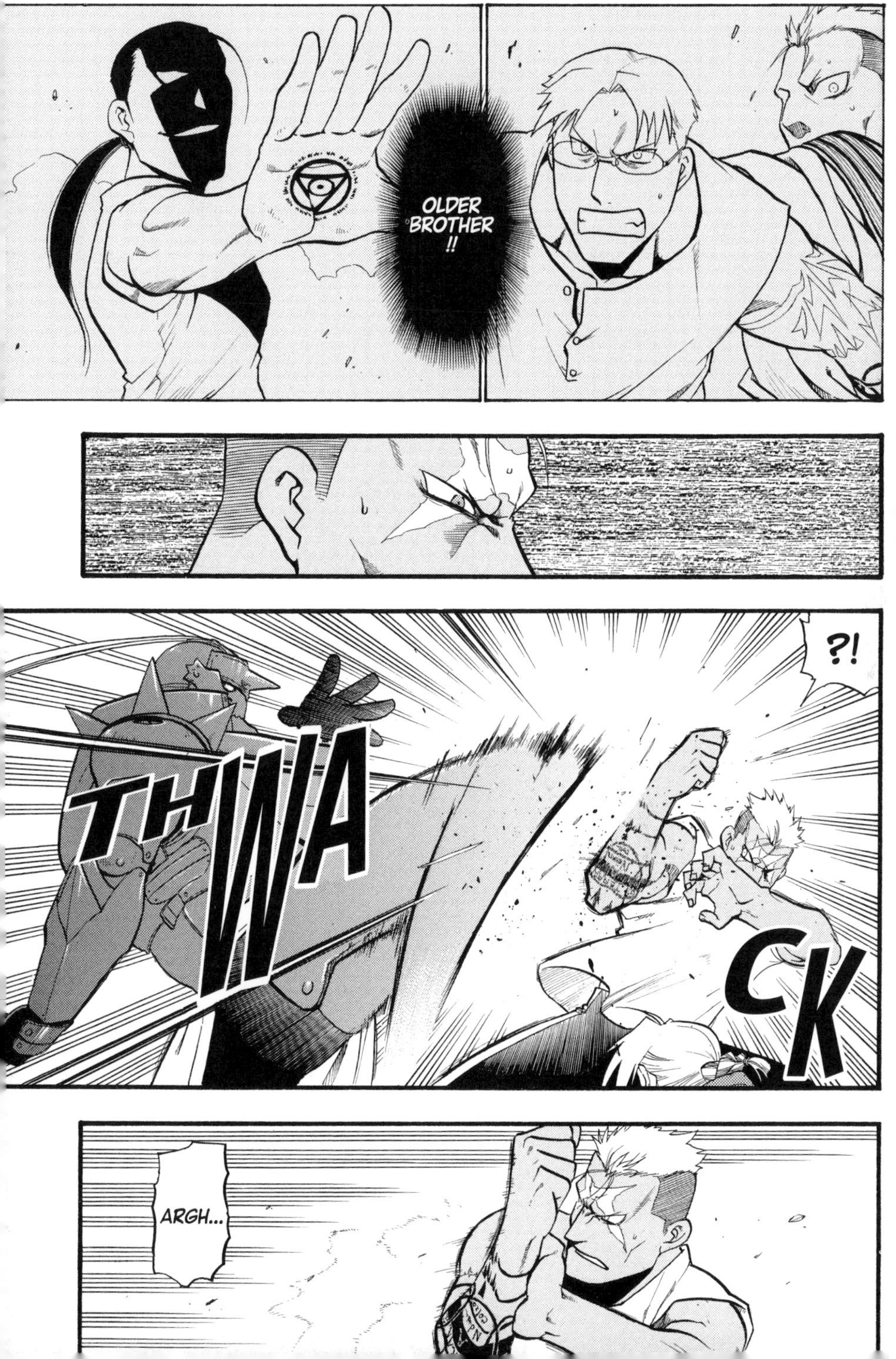
OLDER BROTHER !!
?!
THWA
CK
ARGH...

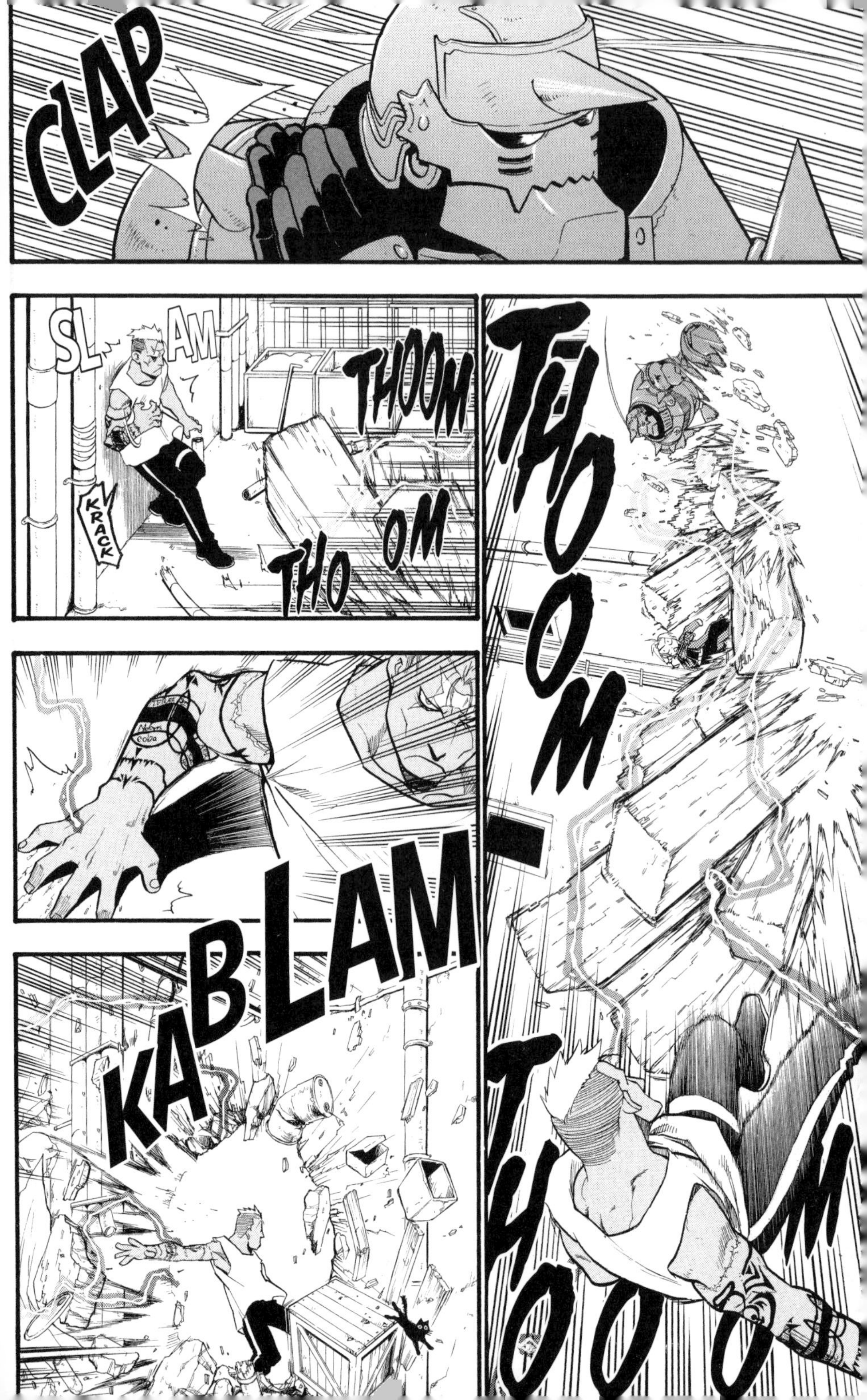
CLAP
THOOM-
THOOOOOM
SL AM
KRACK
THOOM
THO OM
KABLAM

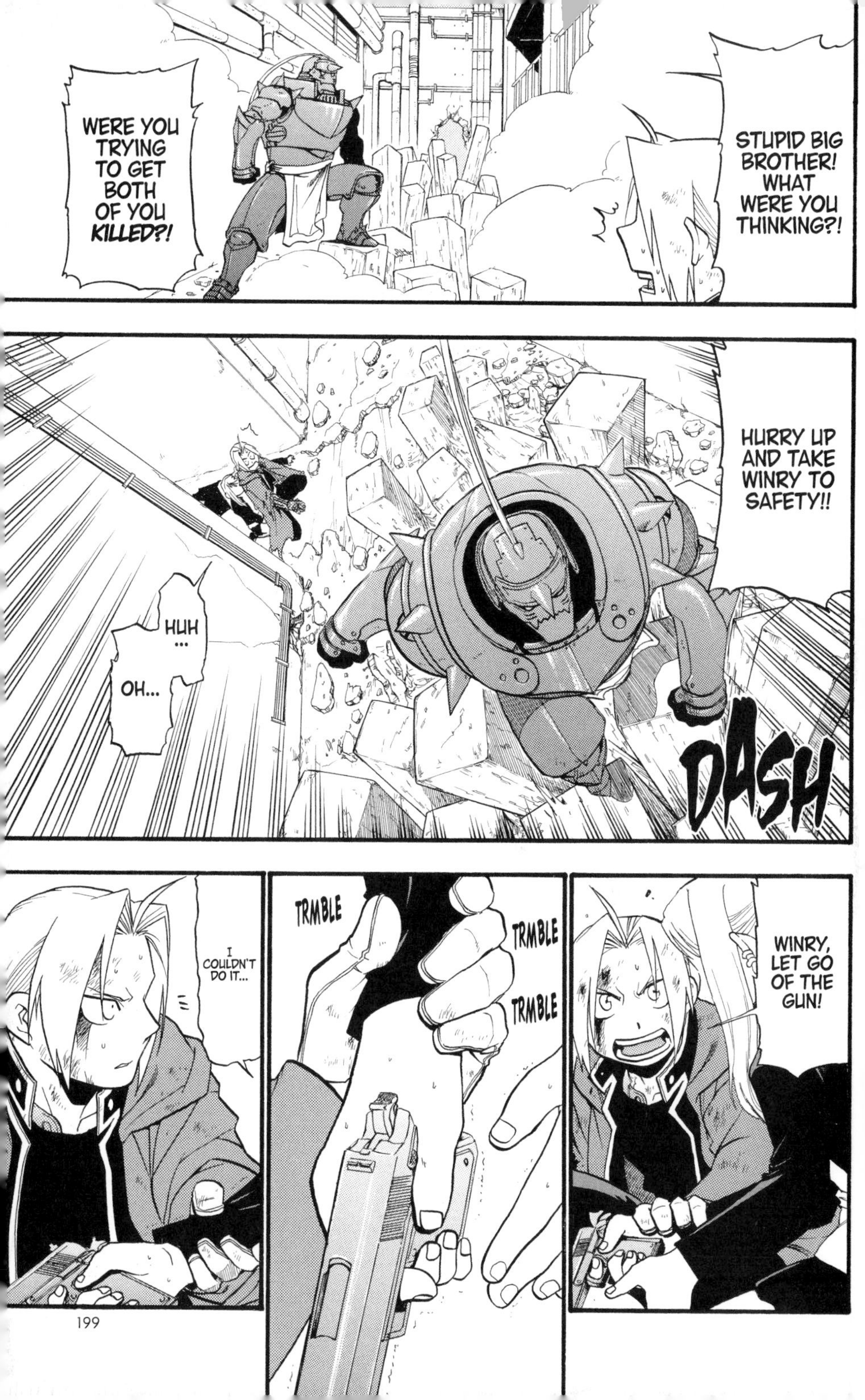
STUPID BIG BROTHER! WHAT WERE YOU THINKING?!
WERE YOU TRYING TO GET BOTH OF YOU KILLED?!
HURRY UP AND TAKE WINRY TO SAFETY!!
DASH
HUH...
OH...
WINRY, LET GO OF THE GUN!
TRMBLE
TRMBLE
TRMBLE
I COULDN'T DO IT...

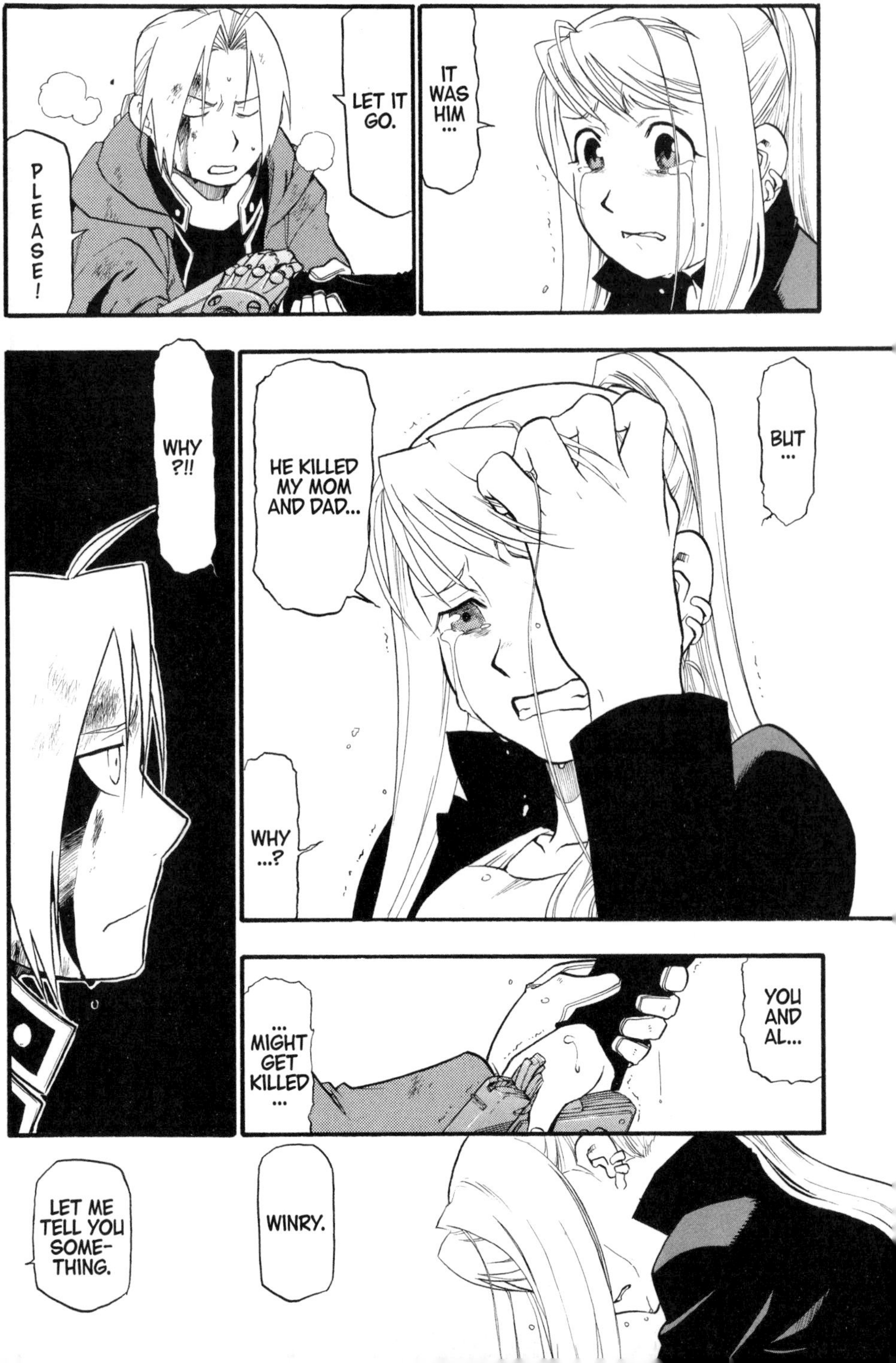

IT WAS HIM...
LET IT GO.
PLEASE!
BUT...
HE KILLED MY MOM AND DAD...
WHY...?
YOU AND AL...
...MIGHT GET KILLED...
WHY?!!
WINRY.
LET ME TELL YOU SOMETHING.

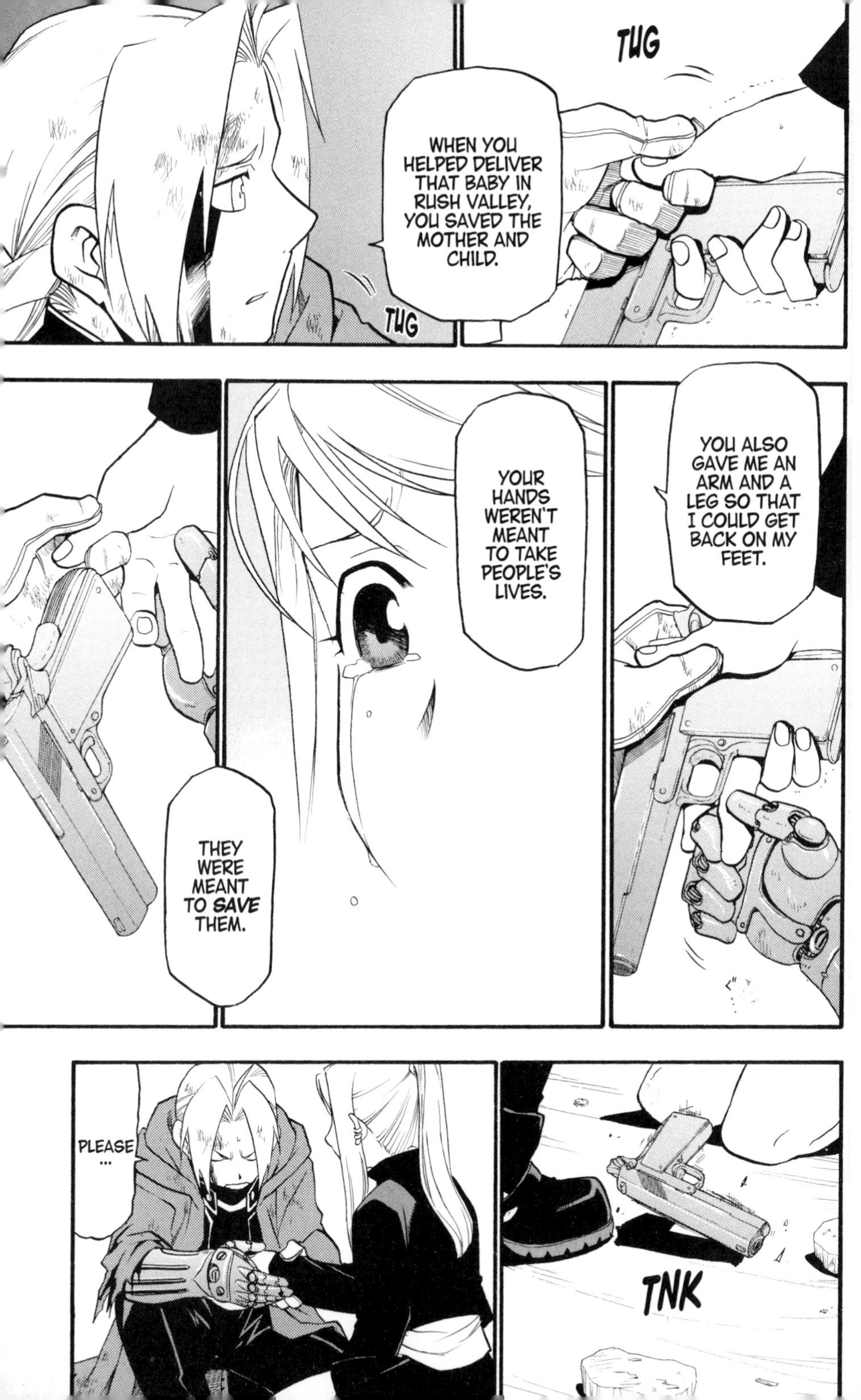
TUG
WHEN YOU HELPED DELIVER THAT BABY IN RUSH VALLEY, YOU SAVED THE MOTHER AND CHILD.
TUG
YOU ALSO GAVE ME AN ARM AND A LEG SO THAT I COULD GET BACK ON MY FEET.
YOUR HANDS WEREN'T MEANT TO TAKE PEOPLE'S LIVES.
THEY WERE MEANT TO **SAVE** THEM.
TNK
PLEASE ...

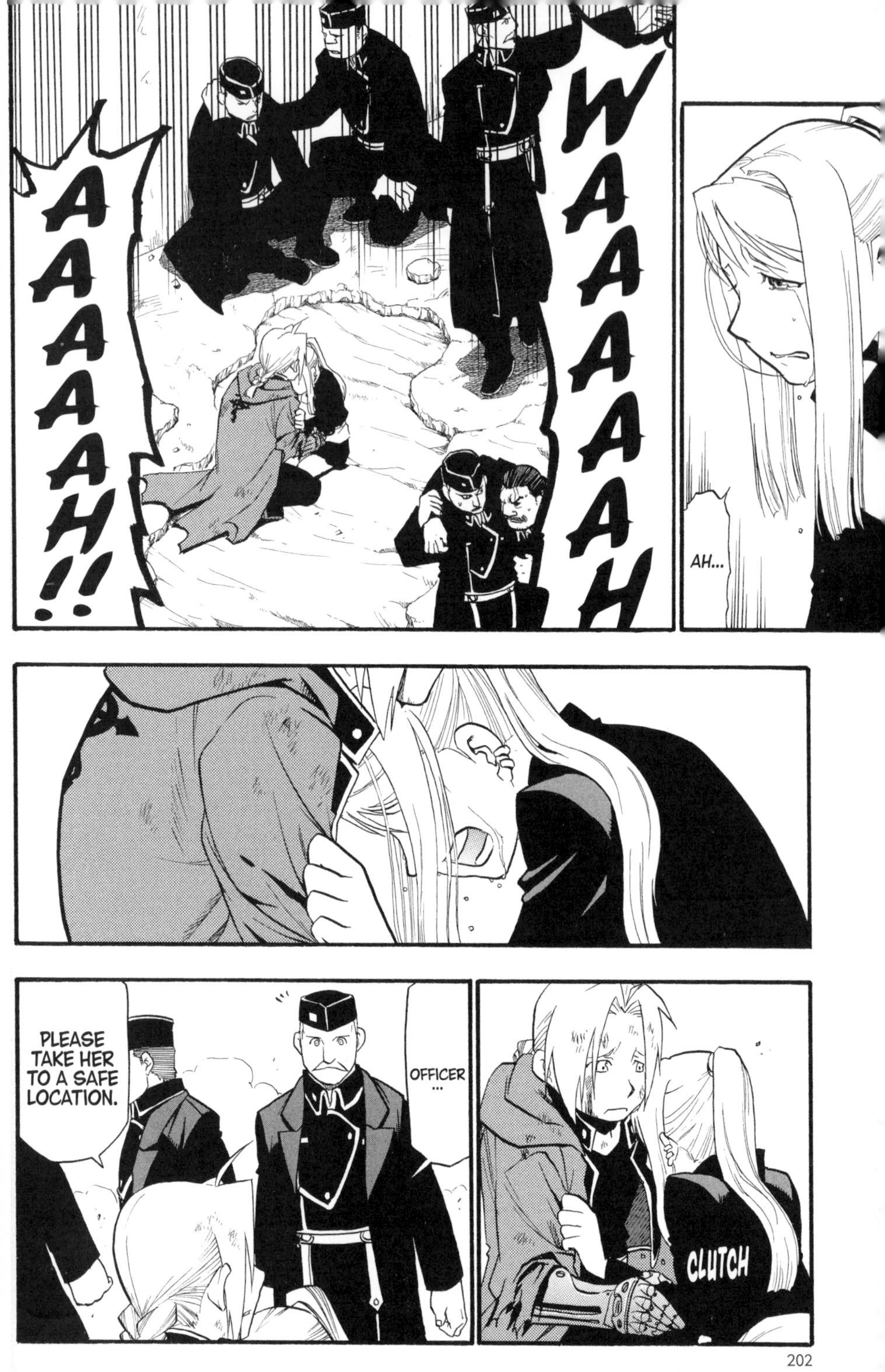
AH...
WAAAAAAH
AAAAAH!!
CLUTCH
OFFICER...
PLEASE TAKE HER TO A SAFE LOCATION.

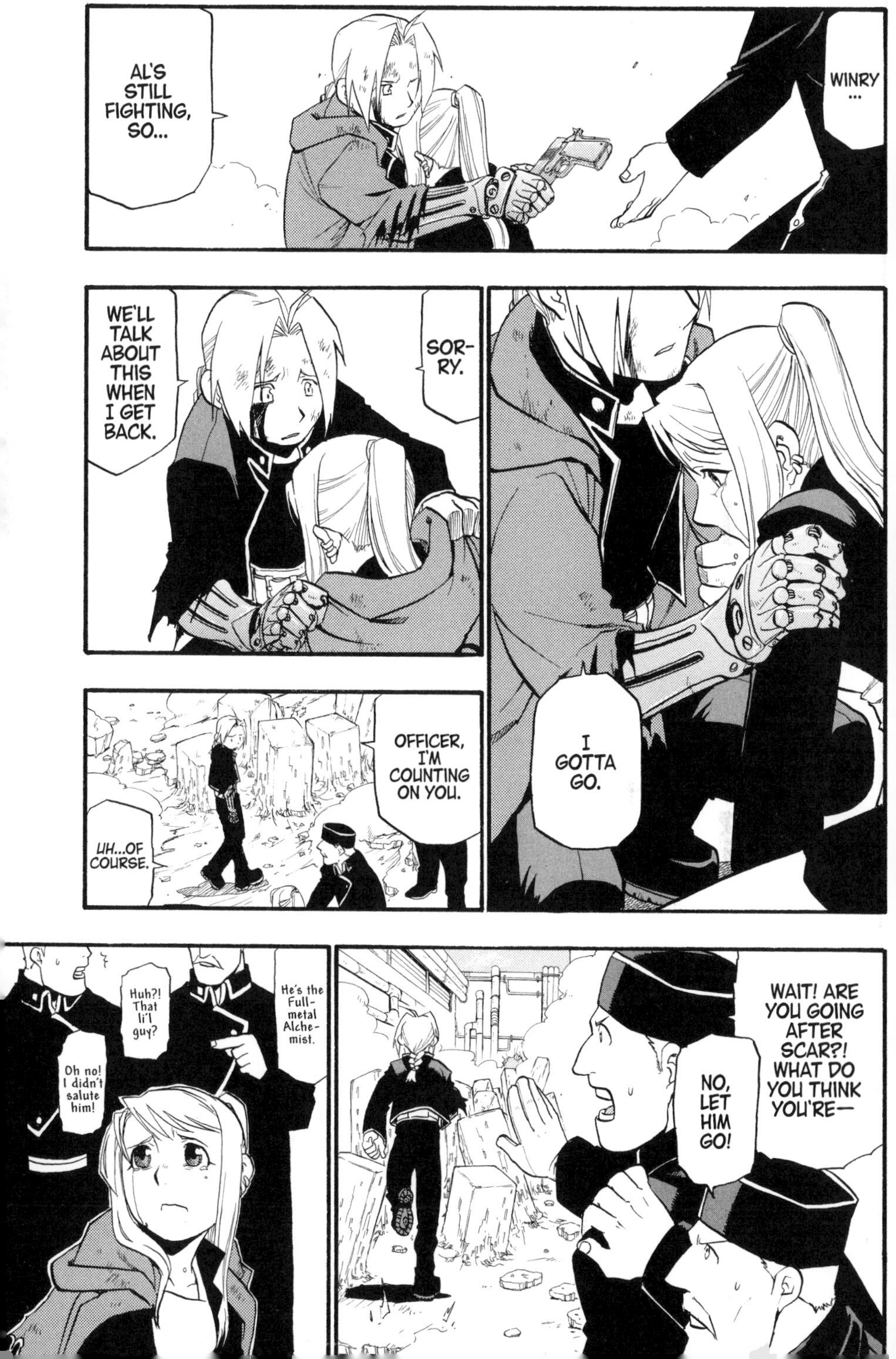
WINRY...
AL'S STILL FIGHTING, SO...
I GOTTA GO.
SOR-RY.
WE'LL TALK ABOUT THIS WHEN I GET BACK.
OFFICER, I'M COUNTING ON YOU.
UH...OF COURSE.
WAIT! ARE YOU GOING AFTER SCAR?! WHAT DO YOU THINK YOU'RE—
NO, LET HIM GO!
He's the Full-metal Alche-mist.
Huh?! That li'l guy?
Oh no! I didn't salute him!

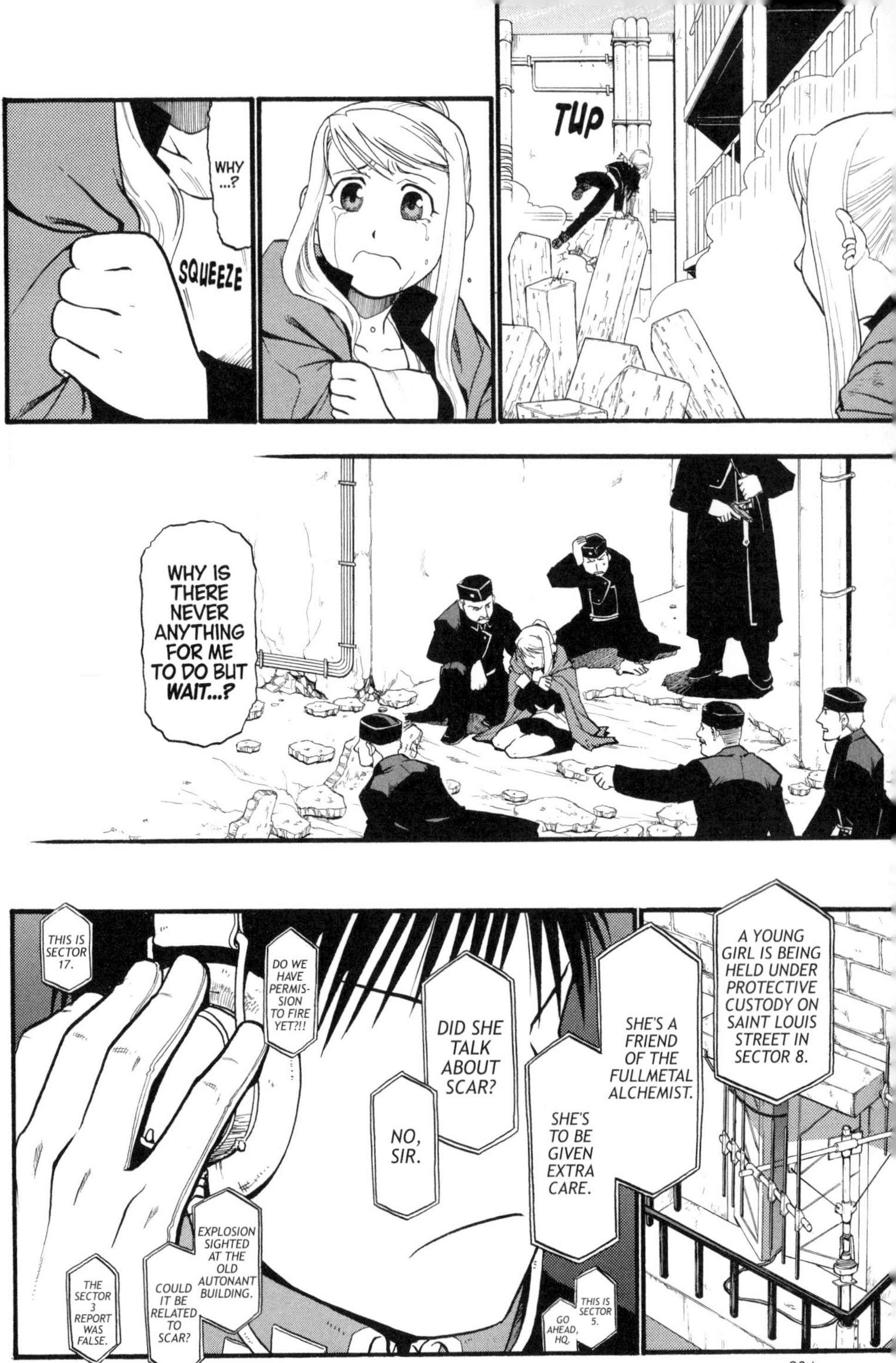

TUP
WHY ...?
SQUEEZE
WHY IS THERE NEVER ANYTHING FOR ME TO DO BUT WAIT...?
A YOUNG GIRL IS BEING HELD UNDER PROTECTIVE CUSTODY ON SAINT LOUIS STREET IN SECTOR 8.
SHE'S A FRIEND OF THE FULLMETAL ALCHEMIST.
SHE'S TO BE GIVEN EXTRA CARE.
DID SHE TALK ABOUT SCAR?
NO, SIR.
DO WE HAVE PERMISSION TO FIRE YET?!!
THIS IS SECTOR 17.
THIS IS SECTOR 5.
GO AHEAD, HQ.
EXPLOSION SIGHTED AT THE OLD AUTONANT BUILDING.
COULD IT BE RELATED TO SCAR?
THE SECTOR 3 REPORT WAS FALSE.

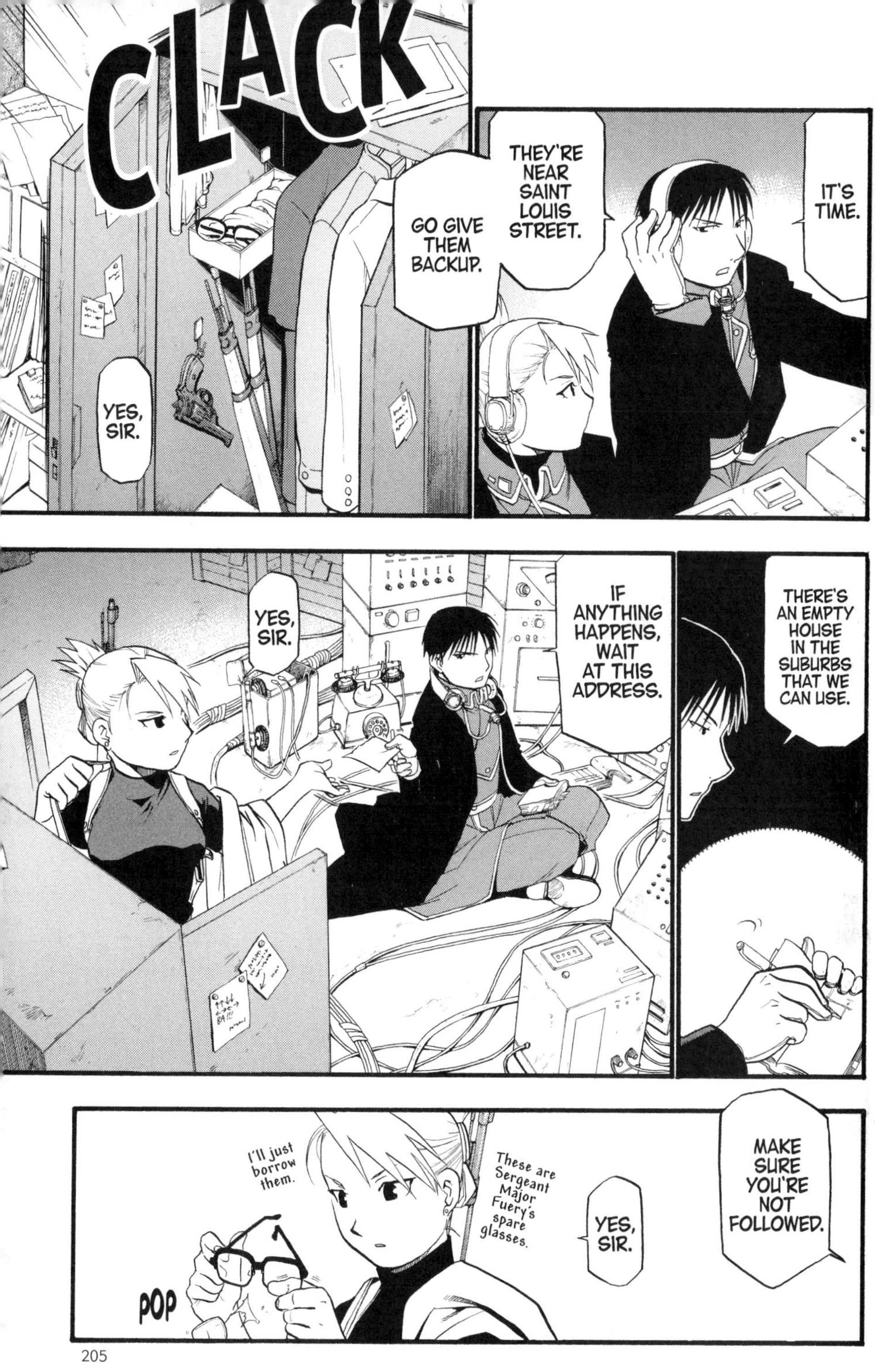
IT'S TIME.
THEY'RE NEAR SAINT LOUIS STREET.
GO GIVE THEM BACKUP.
CLACK
YES, SIR.
THERE'S AN EMPTY HOUSE IN THE SUBURBS THAT WE CAN USE.
IF ANYTHING HAPPENS, WAIT AT THIS ADDRESS.
YES, SIR.
MAKE SURE YOU'RE NOT FOLLOWED.
YES, SIR.
These are Sergeant Major Fuery's spare glasses.
I'll just borrow them.
POP

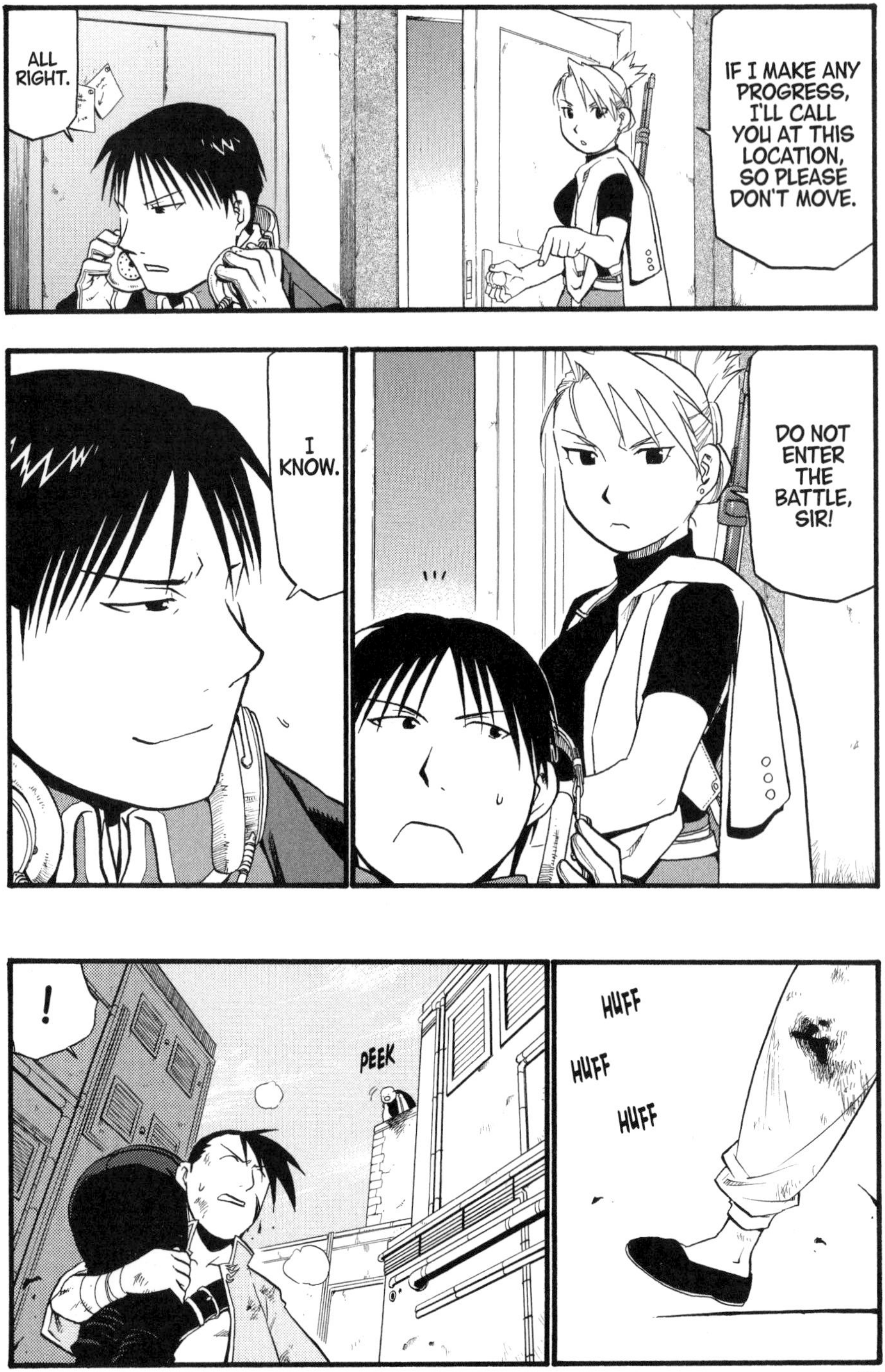
IF I MAKE ANY PROGRESS, I'LL CALL YOU AT THIS LOCATION, SO PLEASE DON'T MOVE.
ALL RIGHT.
DO NOT ENTER THE BATTLE, SIR!
I KNOW.
HUFF
HUFF
HUFF
PEEK
!

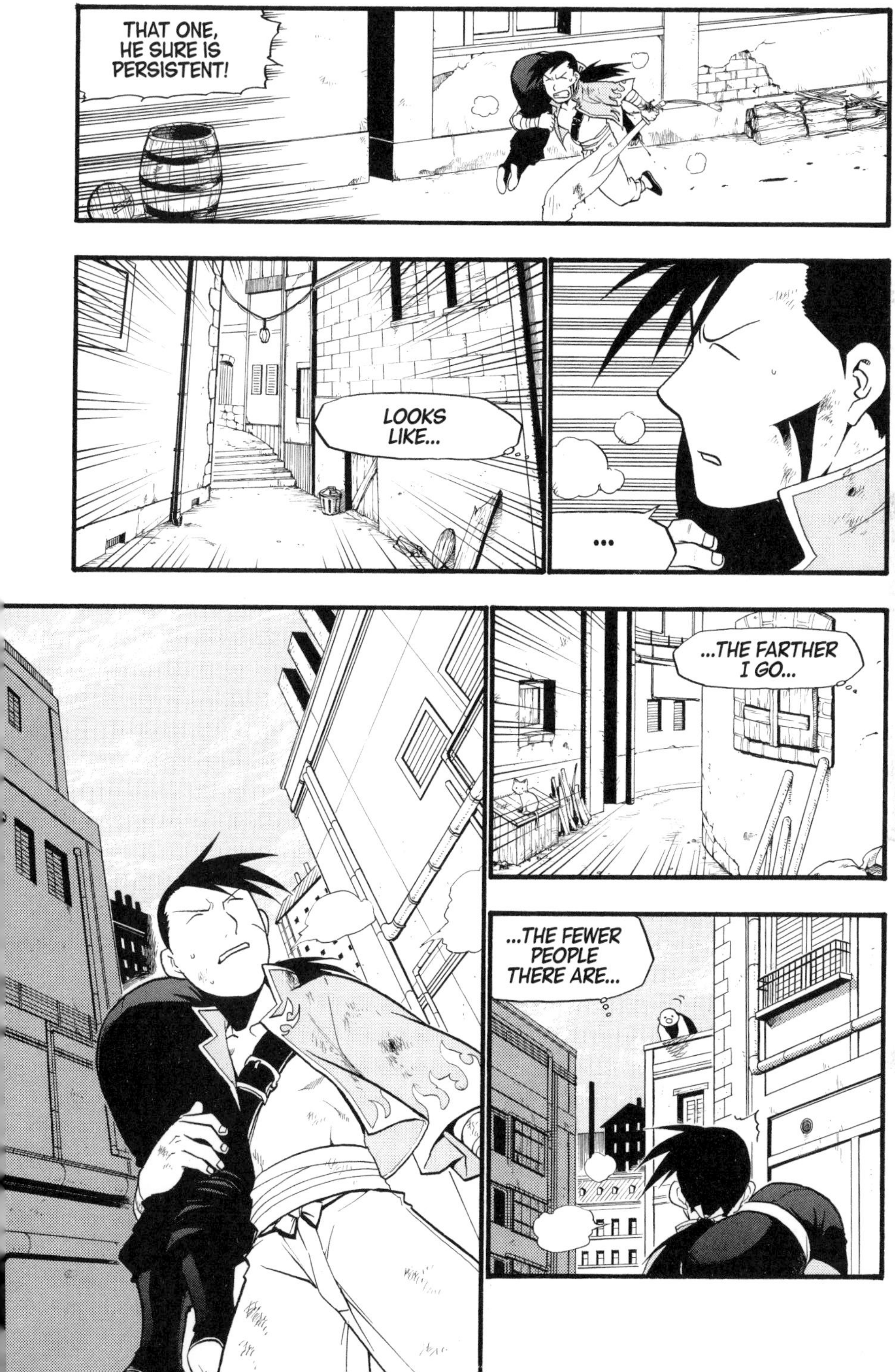
THAT ONE, HE SURE IS PERSISTENT!
...
LOOKS LIKE...
...THE FARTHER I GO...
...THE FEWER PEOPLE THERE ARE...

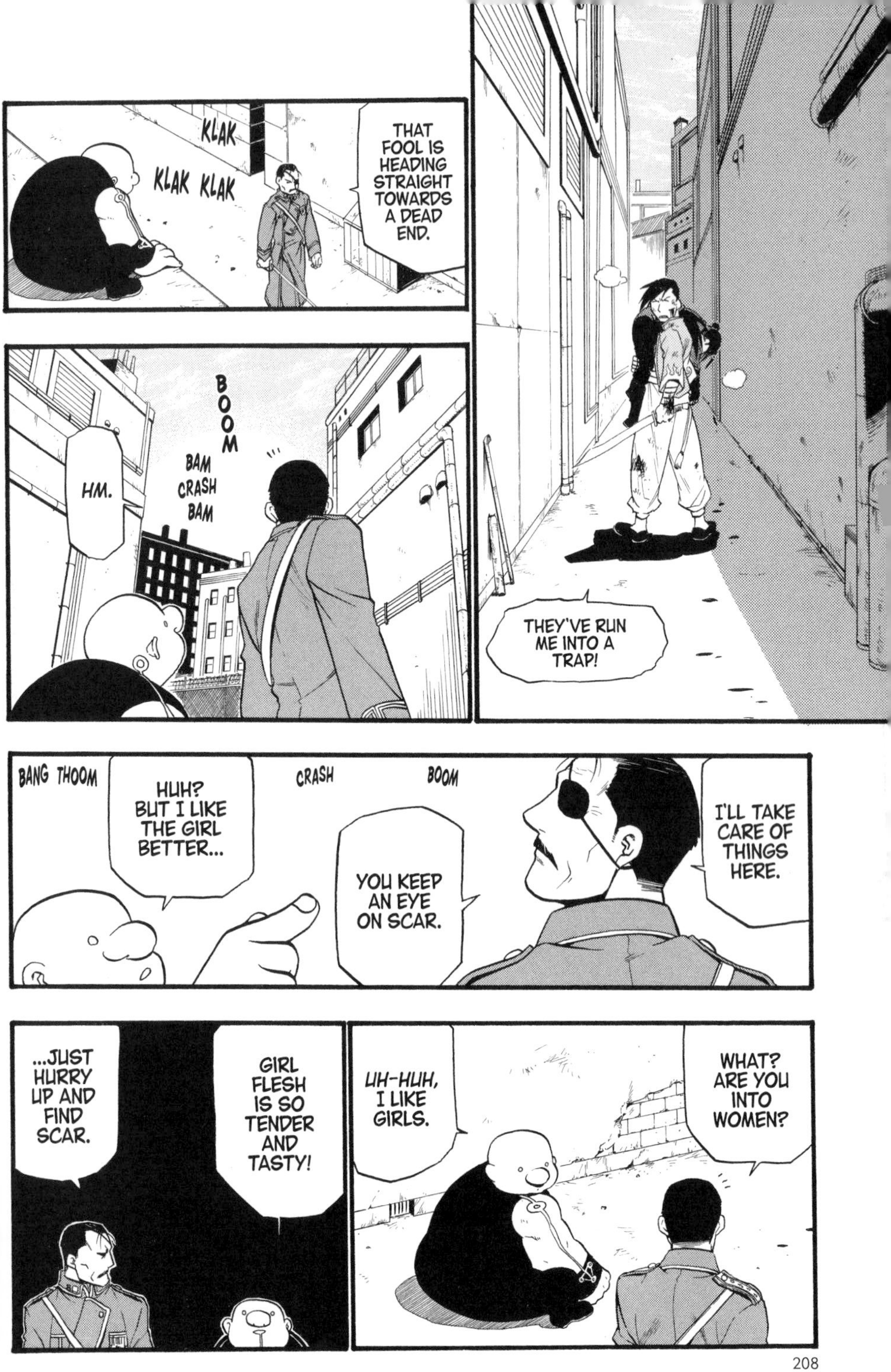
THEY'VE RUN ME INTO A TRAP!
THAT FOOL IS HEADING STRAIGHT TOWARDS A DEAD END.
KLAK
KLAK KLAK
BOOM
BAM CRASH BAM
HM.
I'LL TAKE CARE OF THINGS HERE.
BOOM
YOU KEEP AN EYE ON SCAR.
CRASH
HUH? BUT I LIKE THE GIRL BETTER...
BANG THOOM
WHAT? ARE YOU INTO WOMEN?
UH-HUH, I LIKE GIRLS.
GIRL FLESH IS SO TENDER AND TASTY!
...JUST HURRY UP AND FIND SCAR.

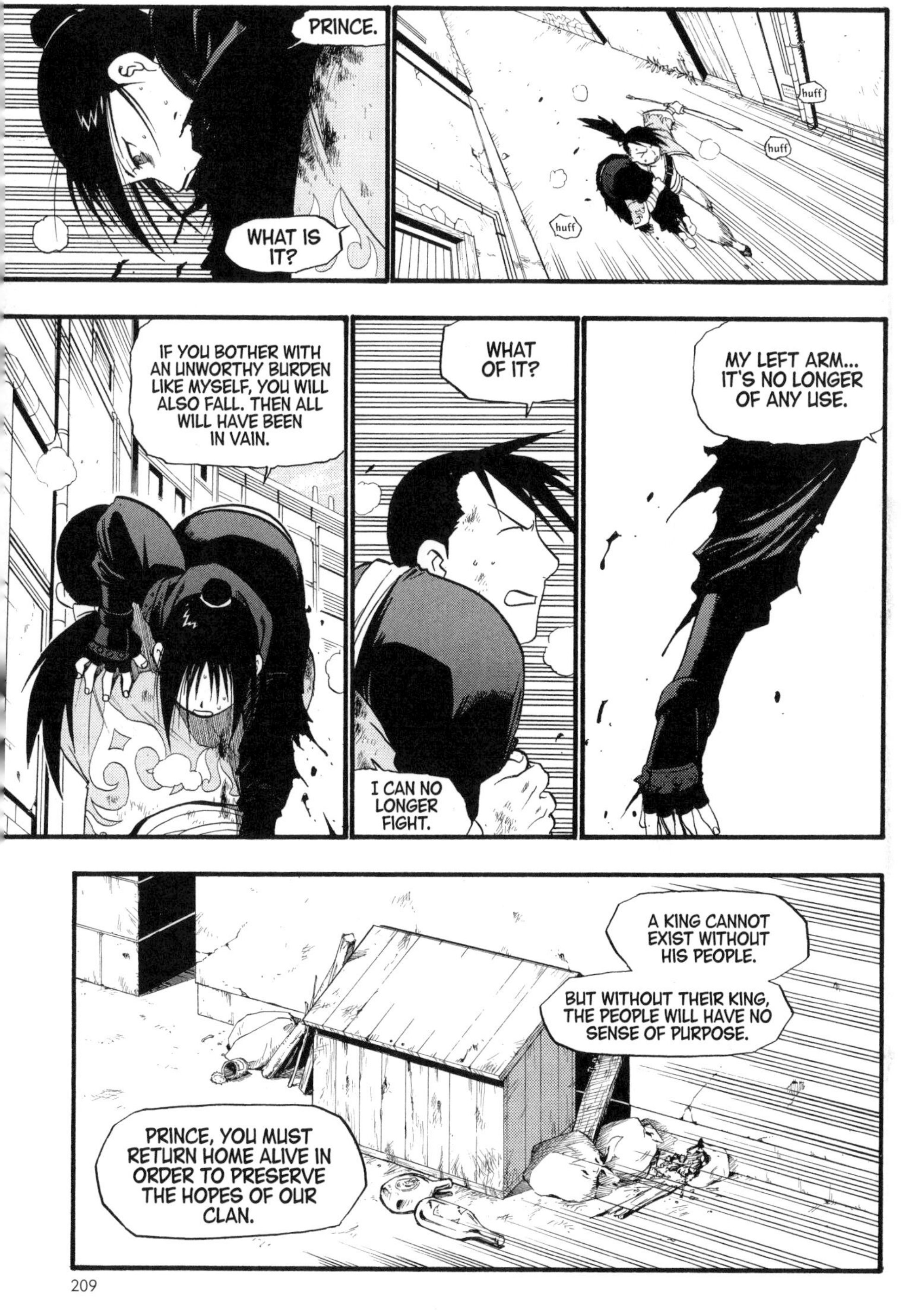
huff
huff
huff
PRINCE.
WHAT IS IT?
MY LEFT ARM... IT'S NO LONGER OF ANY USE.
WHAT OF IT?
I CAN NO LONGER FIGHT.
IF YOU BOTHER WITH AN UNWORTHY BURDEN LIKE MYSELF, YOU WILL ALSO FALL. THEN ALL WILL HAVE BEEN IN VAIN.
A KING CANNOT EXIST WITHOUT HIS PEOPLE.
BUT WITHOUT THEIR KING, THE PEOPLE WILL HAVE NO SENSE OF PURPOSE.
PRINCE, YOU MUST RETURN HOME ALIVE IN ORDER TO PRESERVE THE HOPES OF OUR CLAN.

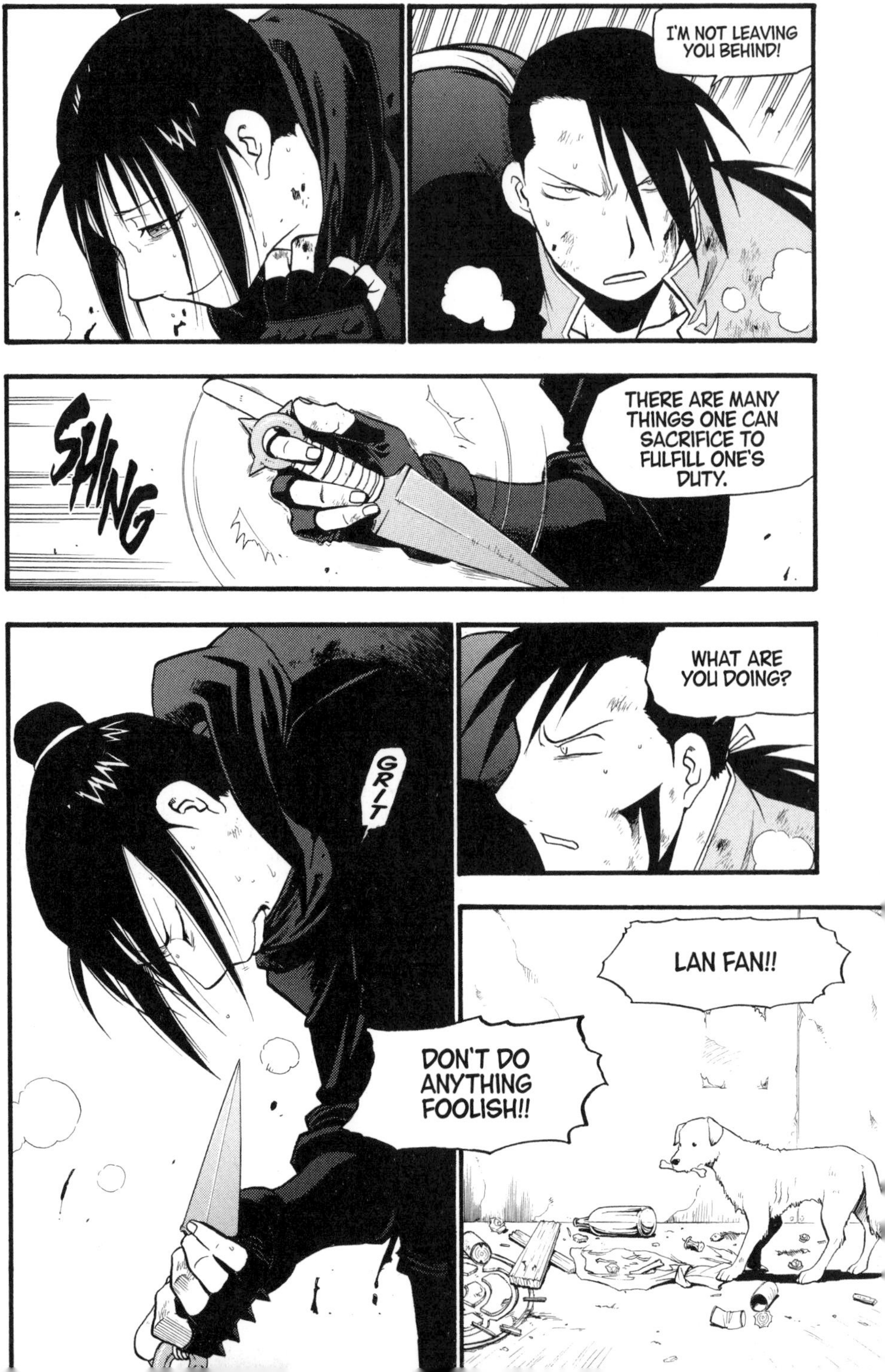
I'M NOT LEAVING YOU BEHIND!
THERE ARE MANY THINGS ONE CAN SACRIFICE TO FULFILL ONE'S DUTY.
SHING
WHAT ARE YOU DOING?
LAN FAN!!
GRIT
DON'T DO ANYTHING FOOLISH!!

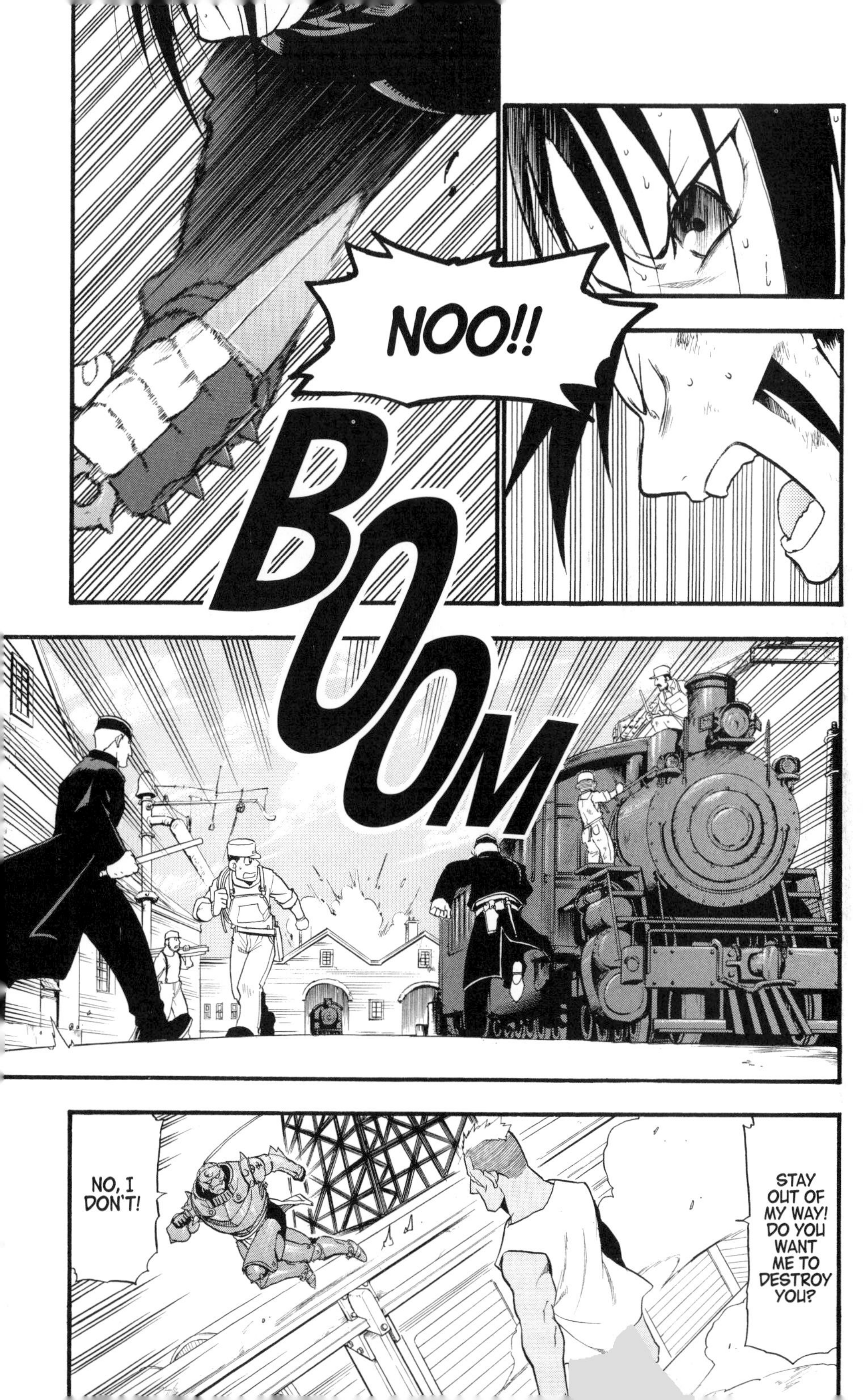
NOO!!
BOOM
STAY OUT OF MY WAY! DO YOU WANT ME TO DESTROY YOU?
NO, I DON'T!

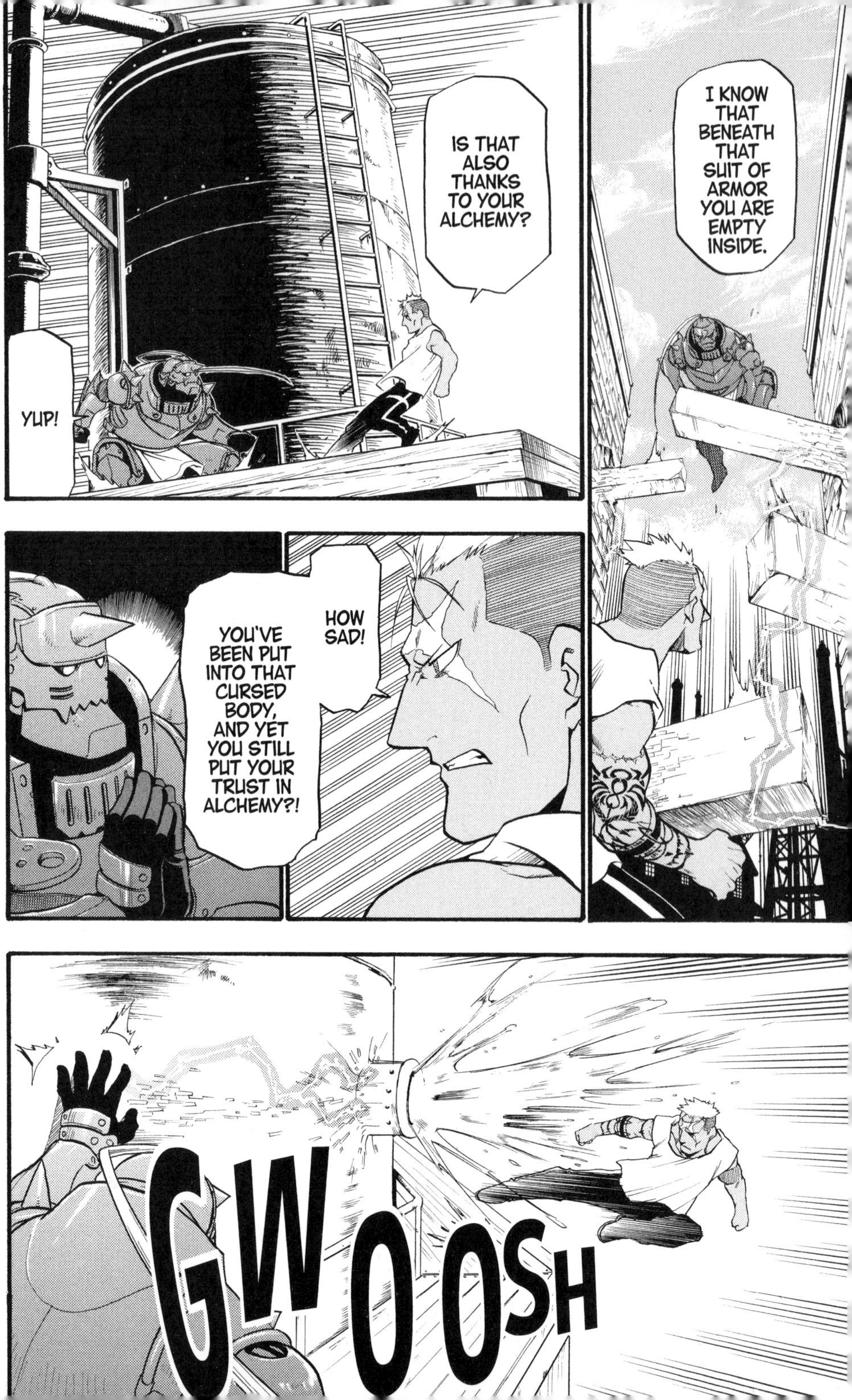
I KNOW THAT BENEATH THAT SUIT OF ARMOR YOU ARE EMPTY INSIDE.
IS THAT ALSO THANKS TO YOUR ALCHEMY?
YUP!
HOW SAD!
YOU'VE BEEN PUT INTO THAT CURSED BODY, AND YET YOU STILL PUT YOUR TRUST IN ALCHEMY?!
GWOOSH

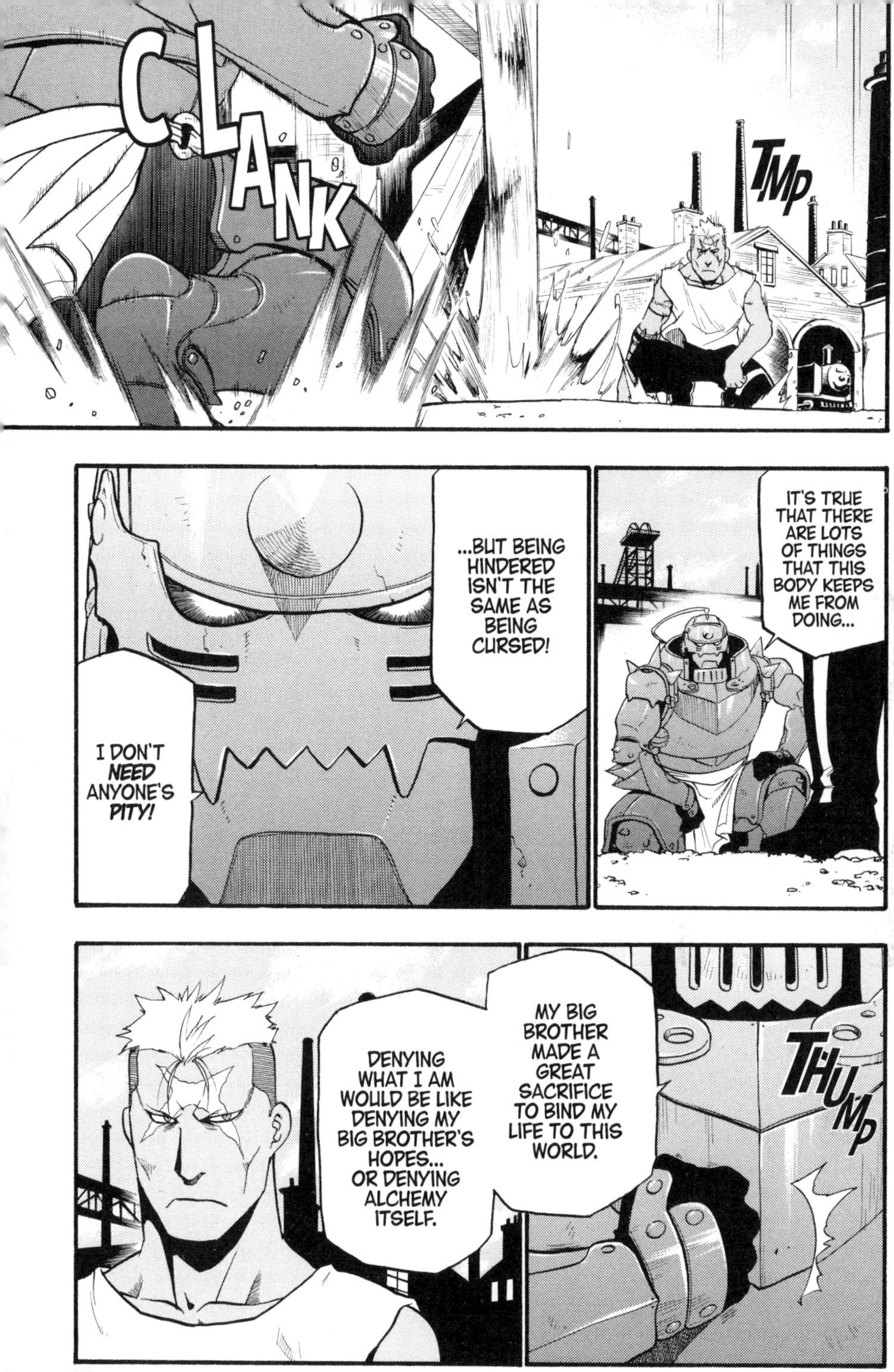
TMP
CLANK
IT'S TRUE THAT THERE ARE LOTS OF THINGS THAT THIS BODY KEEPS ME FROM DOING...
...BUT BEING HINDERED ISN'T THE SAME AS BEING CURSED!
I DON'T NEED ANYONE'S PITY!
THUMP
MY BIG BROTHER MADE A GREAT SACRIFICE TO BIND MY LIFE TO THIS WORLD.
DENYING WHAT I AM WOULD BE LIKE DENYING MY BIG BROTHER'S HOPES... OR DENYING ALCHEMY ITSELF.

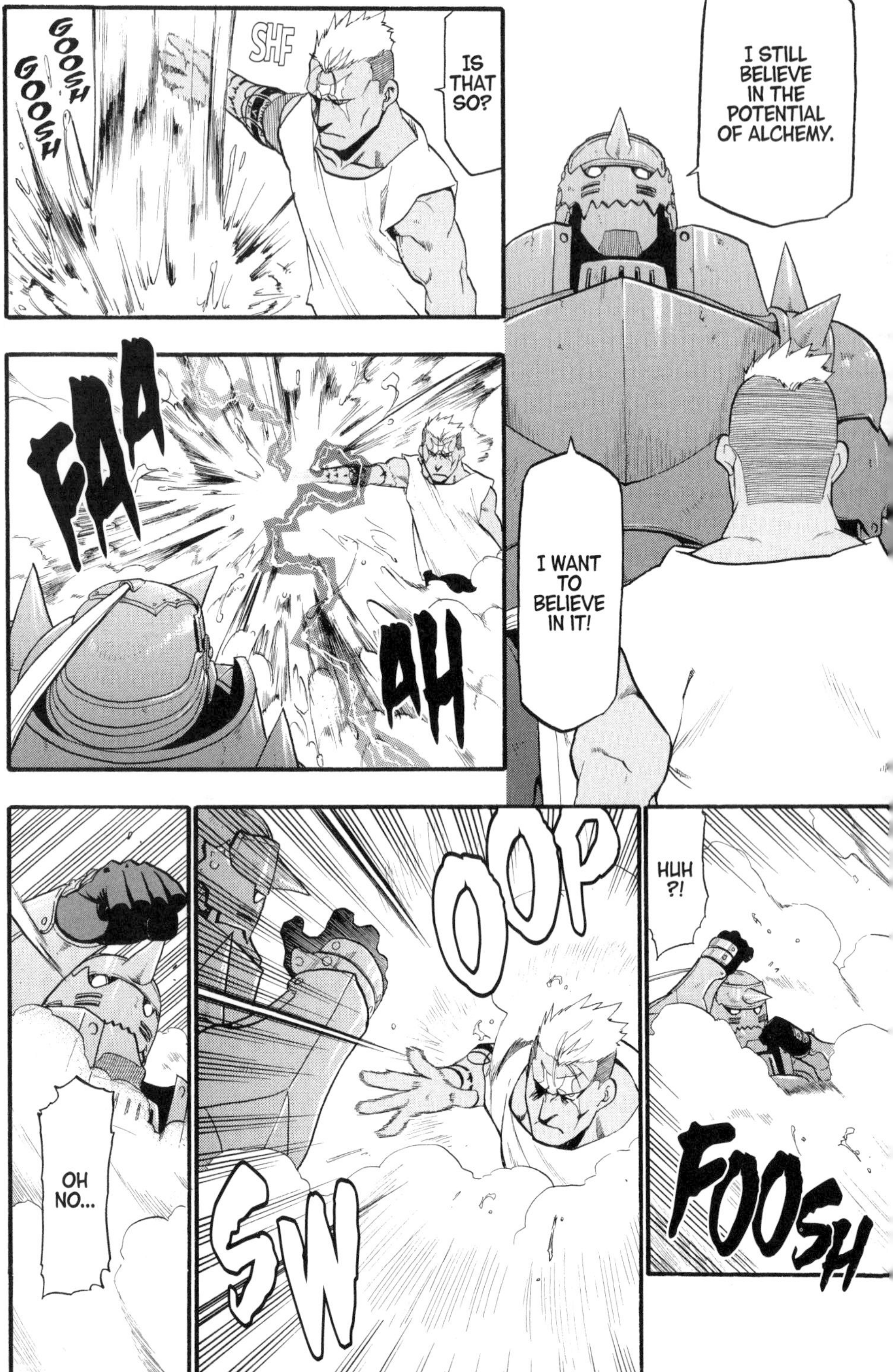
I STILL BELIEVE IN THE POTENTIAL OF ALCHEMY.
I WANT TO BELIEVE IN IT!
SHF
IS THAT SO?
GOOSH GOOSH
FAAA
AH
HUH?!
FOOSH
OOP
SW
OH NO...

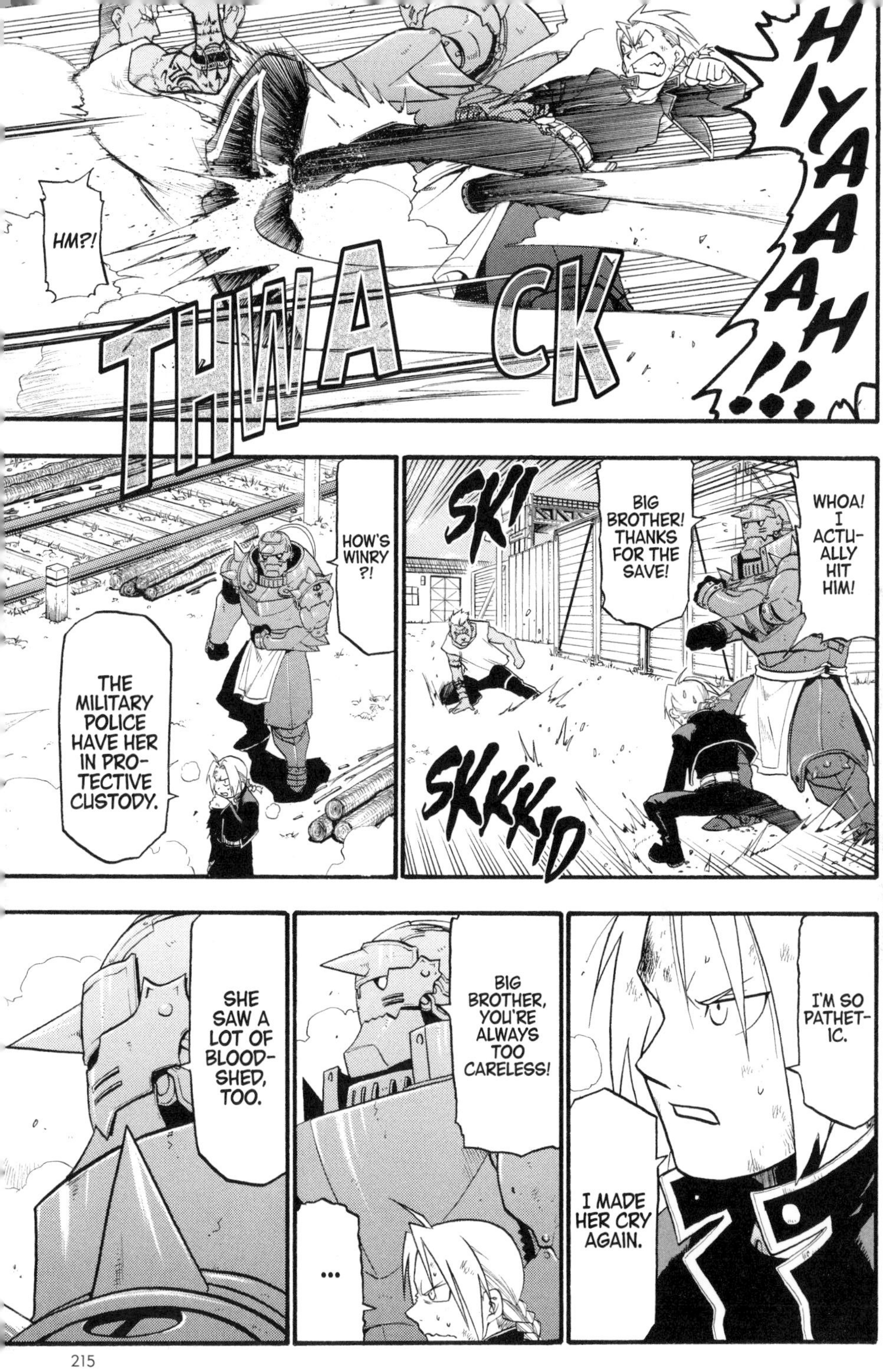
HIYAAAAH!!!
HM?!
THWACK
WHOA! I ACTUALLY HIT HIM!
BIG BROTHER! THANKS FOR THE SAVE!
SKI
SKKKID
HOW'S WINRY?!
THE MILITARY POLICE HAVE HER IN PROTECTIVE CUSTODY.
I'M SO PATHETIC.
I MADE HER CRY AGAIN.
BIG BROTHER, YOU'RE ALWAYS TOO CARELESS!
...
SHE SAW A LOT OF BLOODSHED, TOO.

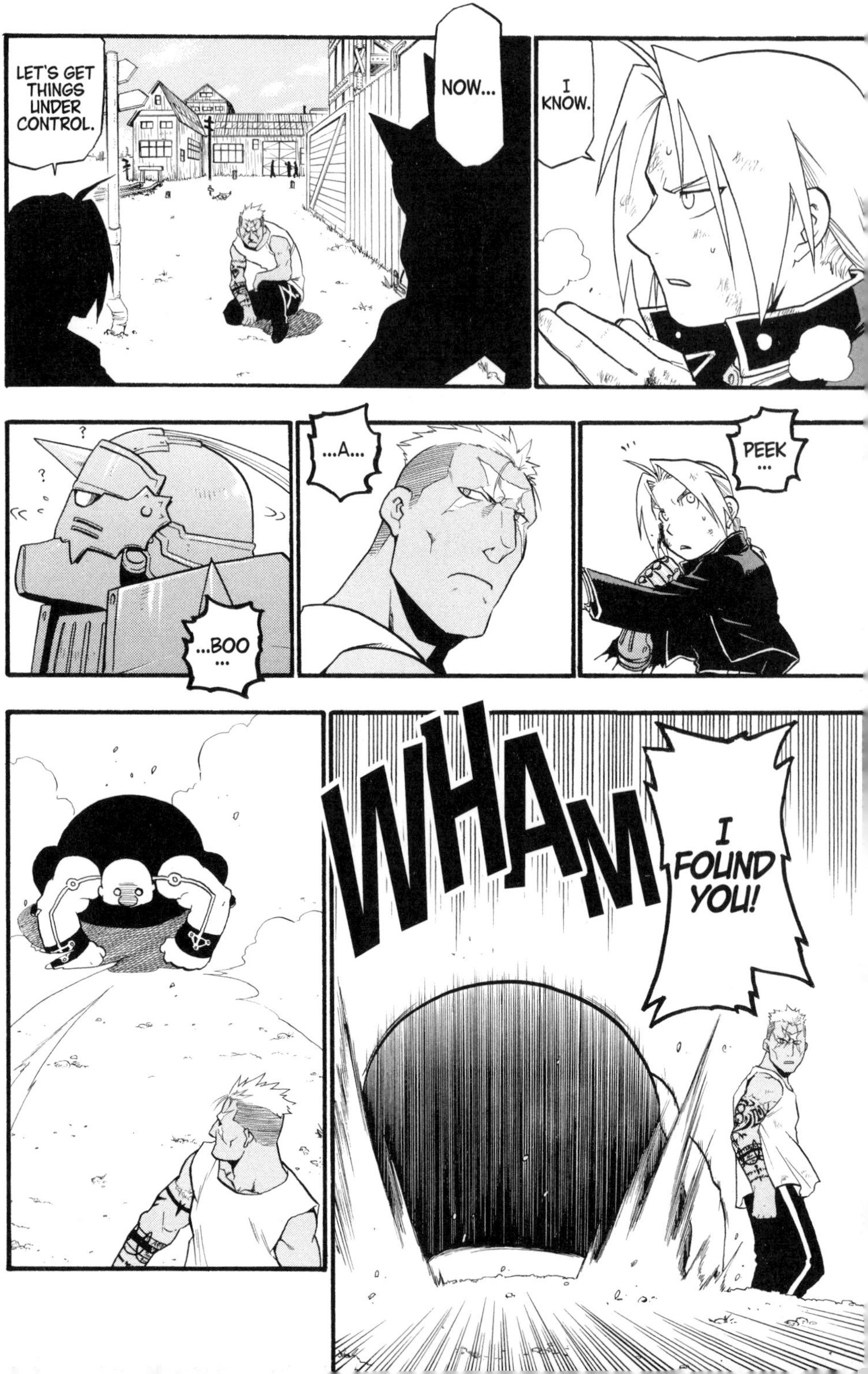
I KNOW.
NOW...
LET'S GET THINGS UNDER CONTROL.
PEEK...
...A...
...BOO...
WHAM
I FOUND YOU!

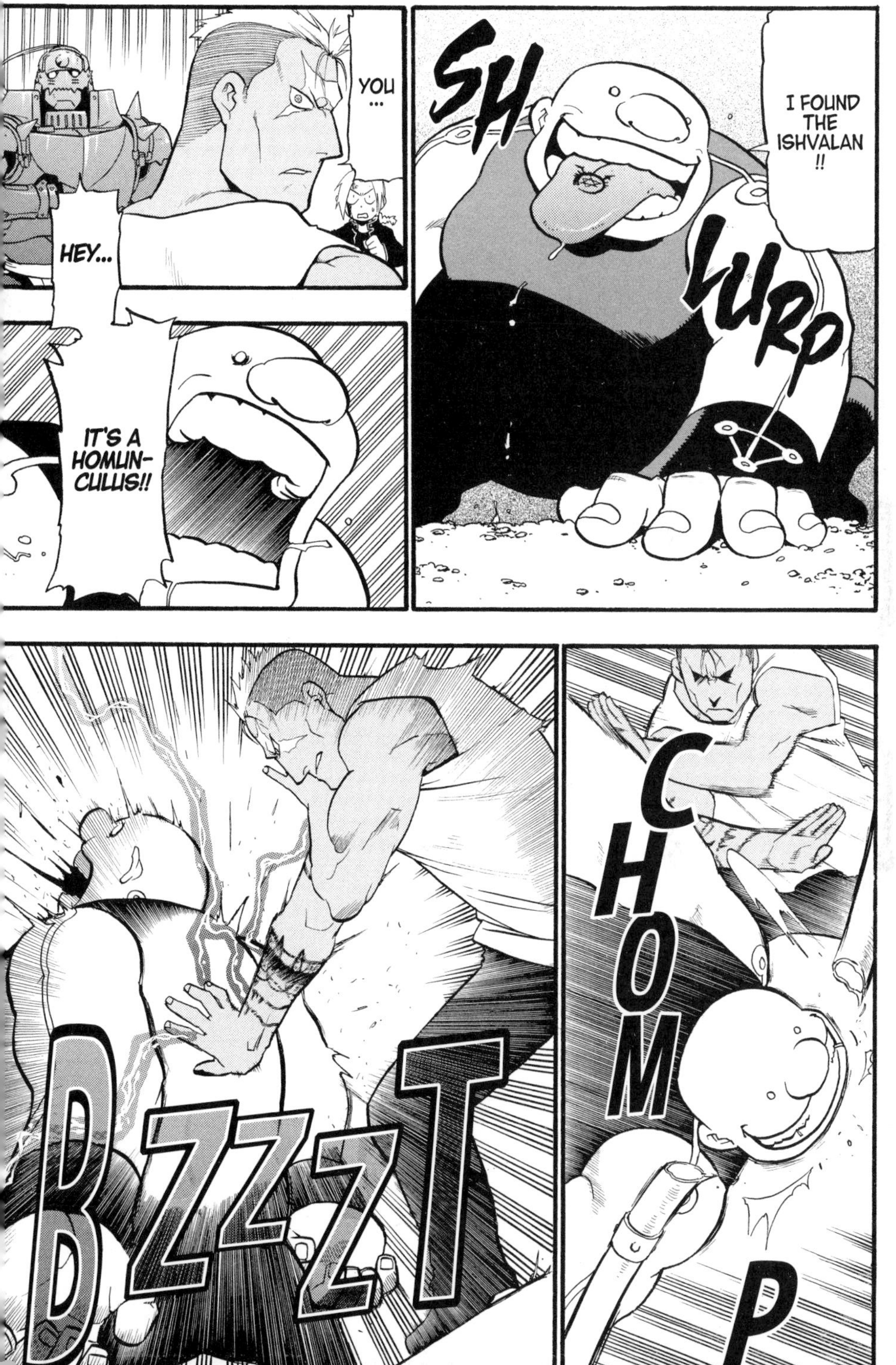
I FOUND THE ISHVALAN!!
SHLURP
YOU...
HEY...
IT'S A HOMUN-CULUS!!
CHOMP
BZZZT

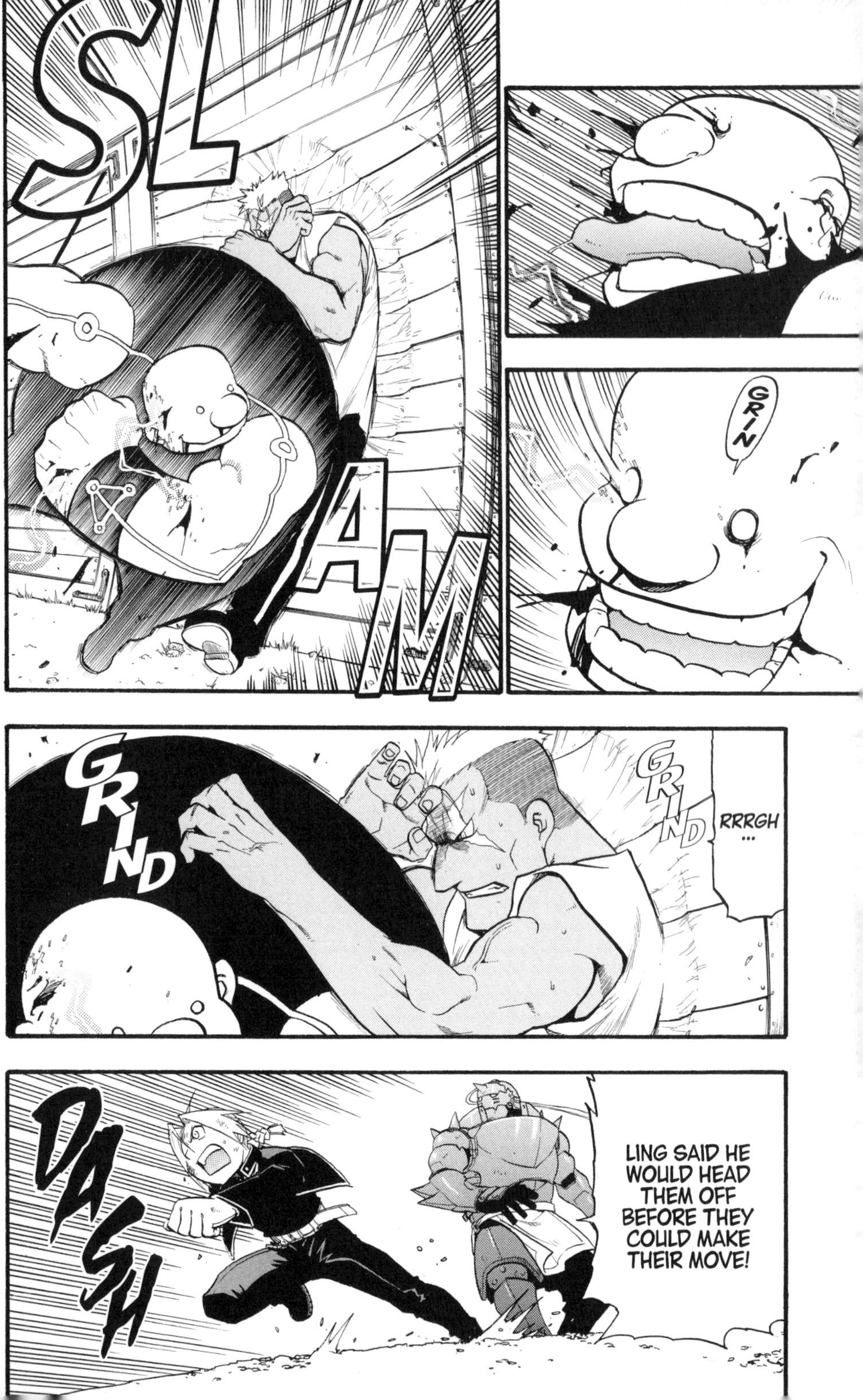
GRIN
SLAM
GRIND
RRRGH...
GRIND
LING SAID HE WOULD HEAD THEM OFF BEFORE THEY COULD MAKE THEIR MOVE!
DASH

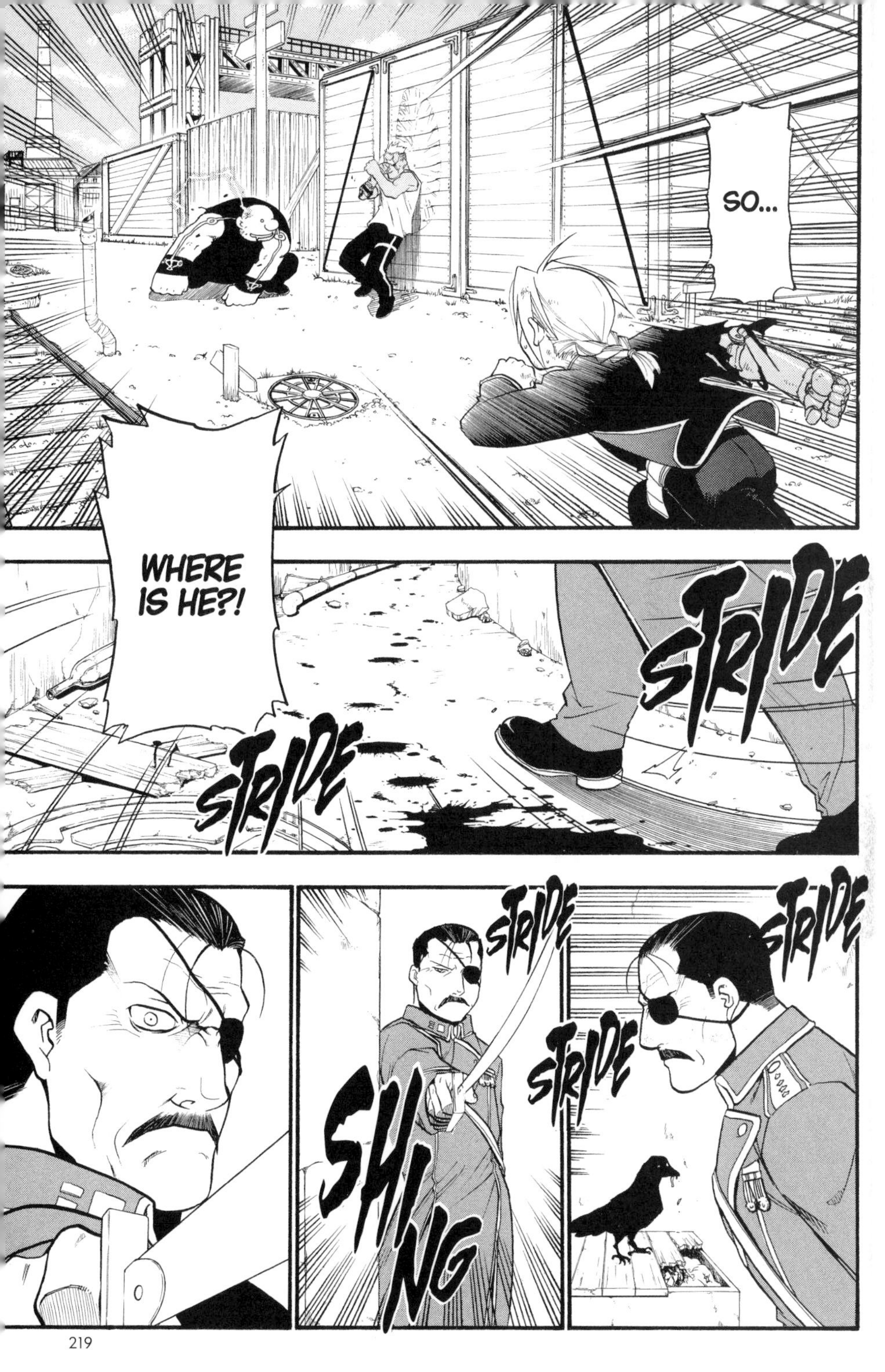
SO...
WHERE IS HE?!
STRIDE
STRIDE
STRIDE
STRIDE
STRIDE
SHING

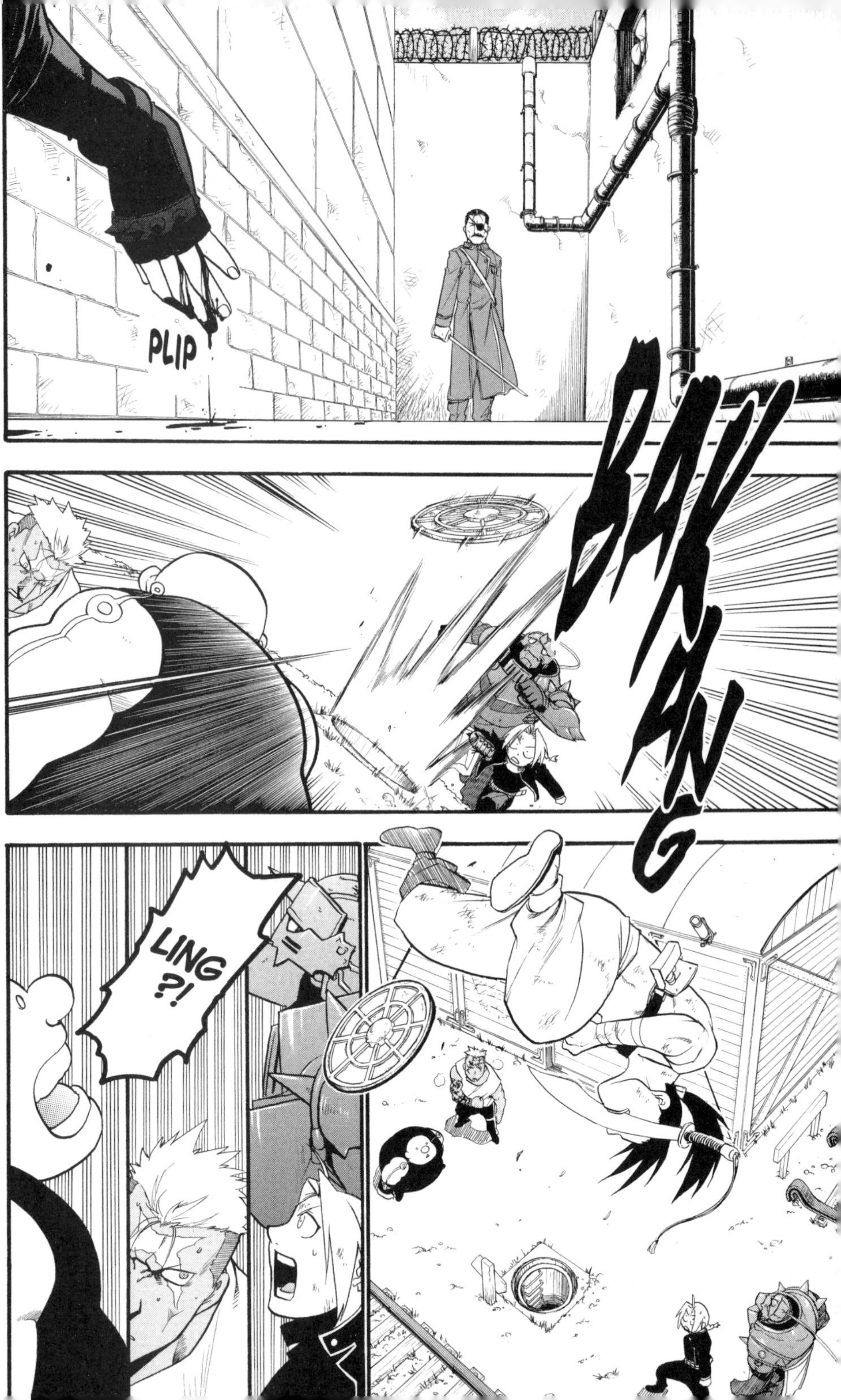
PLIP
BAKWANG
LING ?!

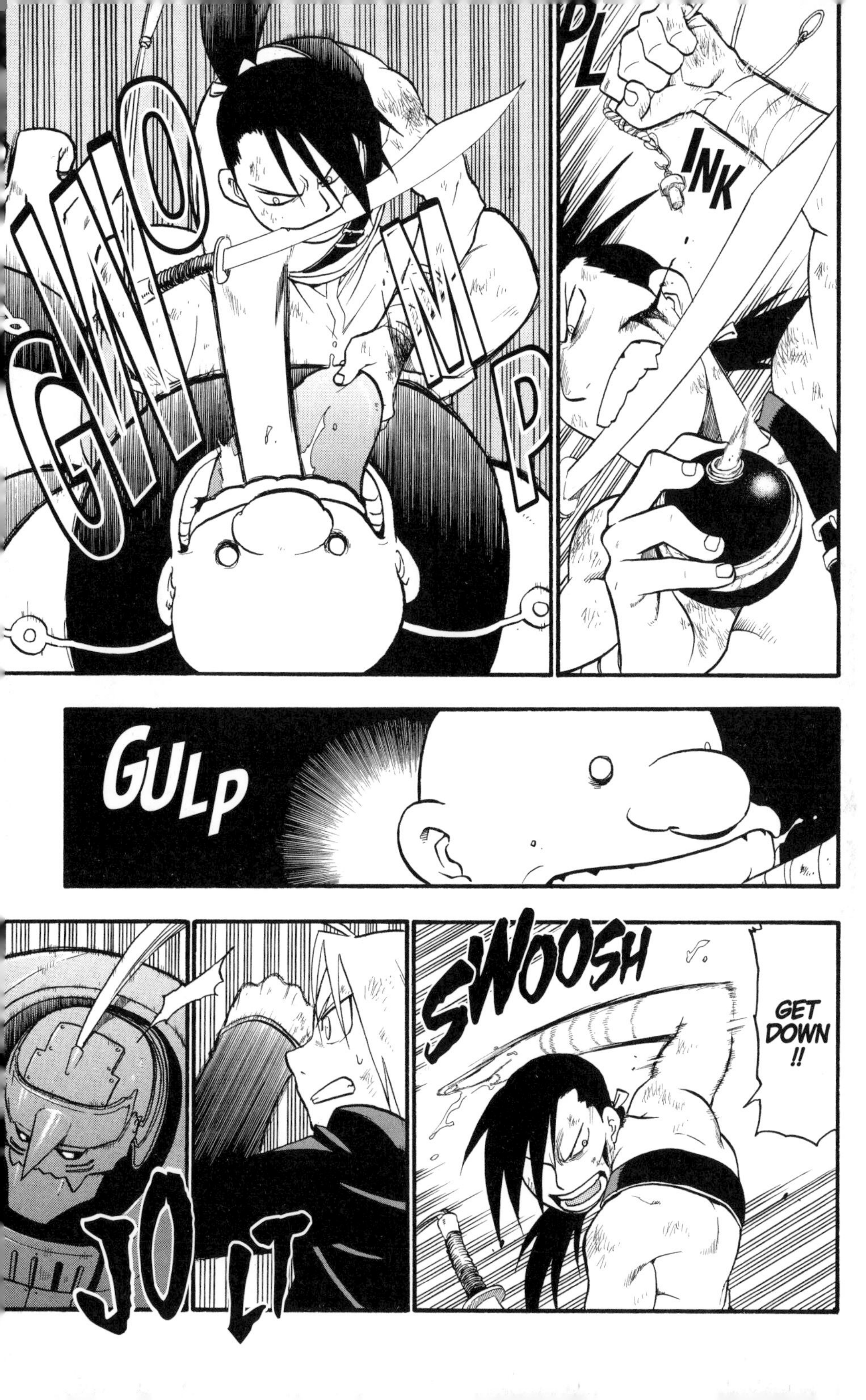
PL
INK
GWOMP
GULP
SWOOSH
GET DOWN !!
JOLT

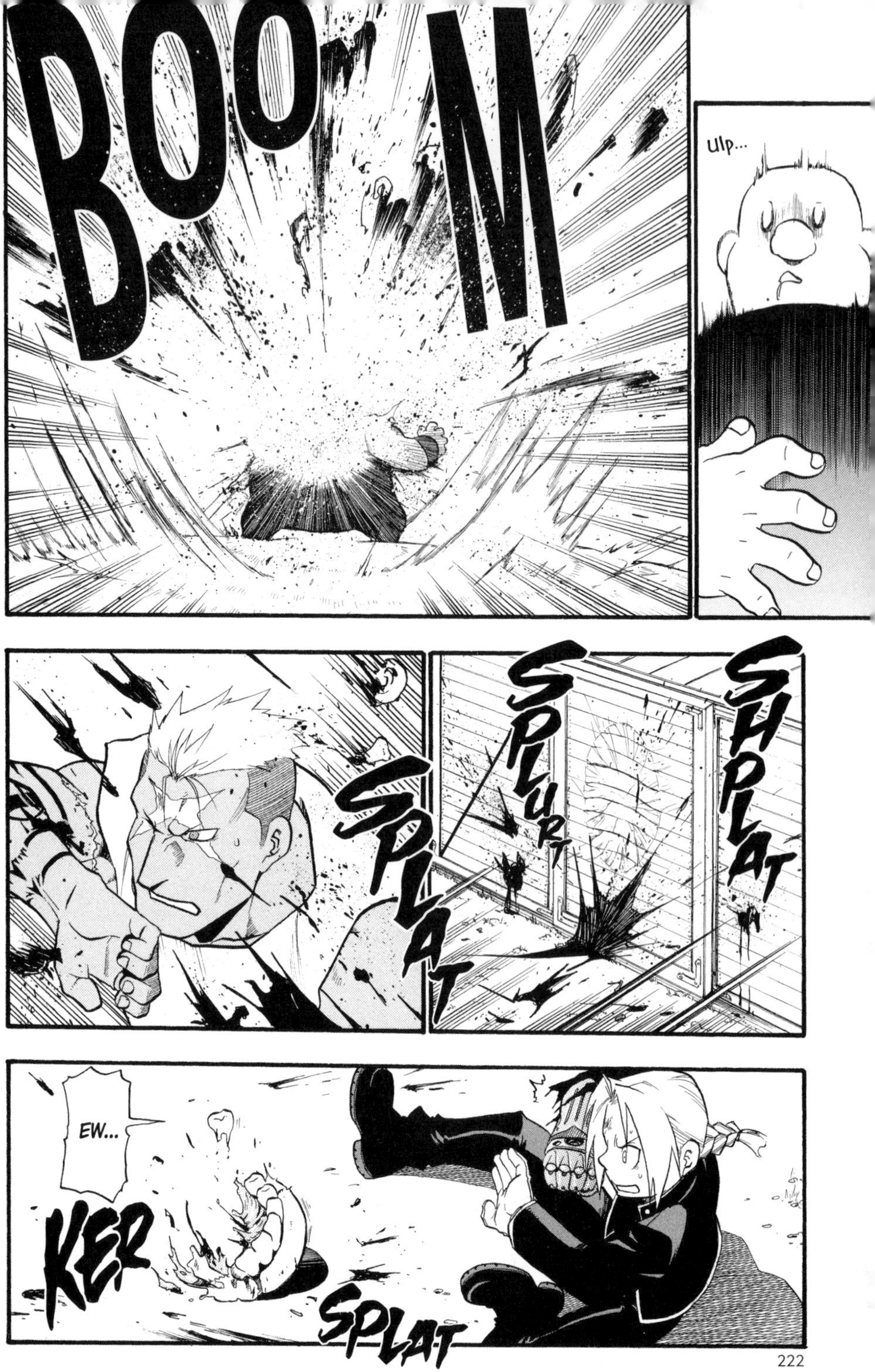
Ulp...
BOOM
SHPLAT
SPLURT
SPLAT
EW...
KER
SPLAT

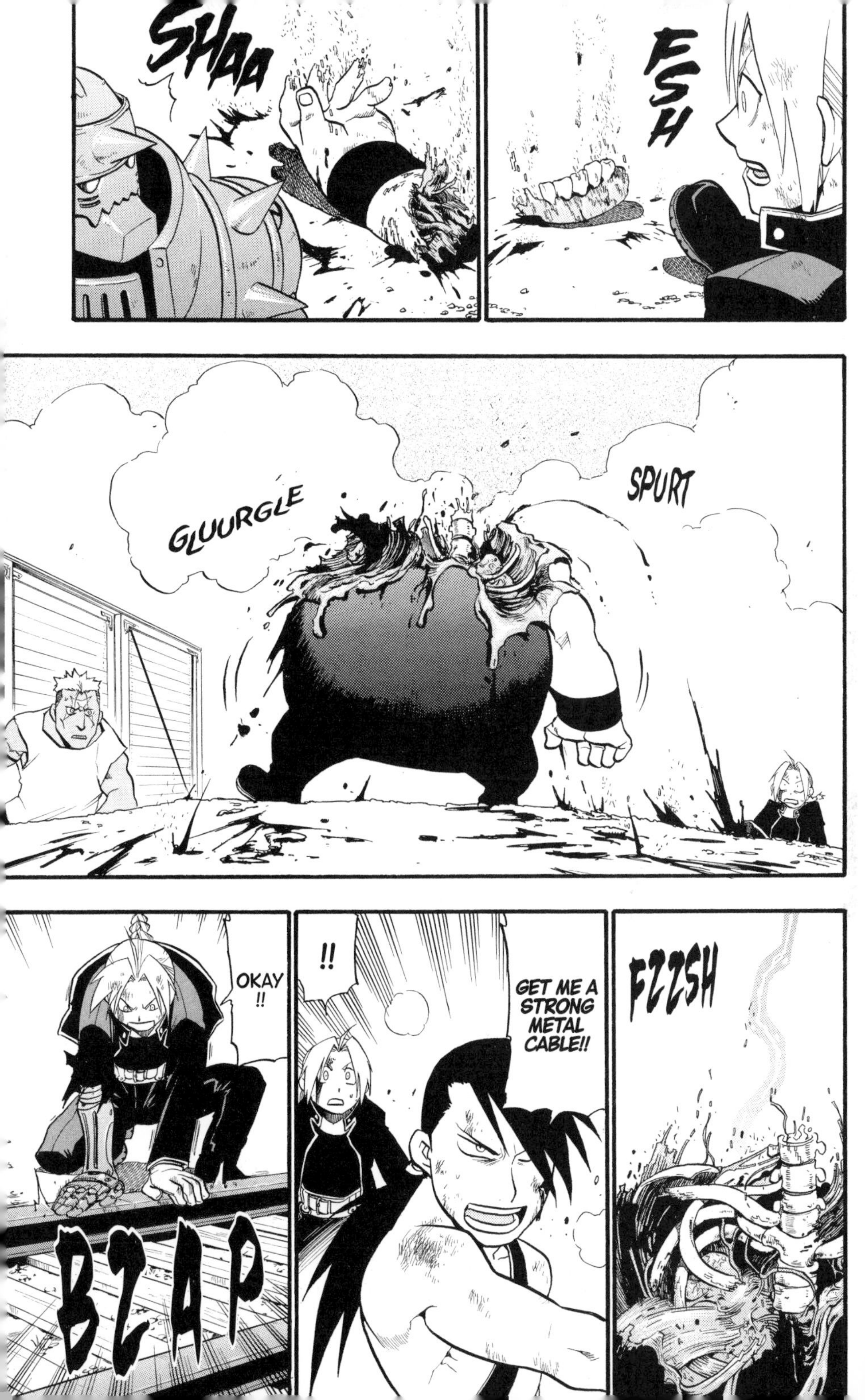
FSH
SHAA
SPURT
GLUURGLE
FZZSH
GET ME A STRONG METAL CABLE!!
!!
OKAY !!
BZAP

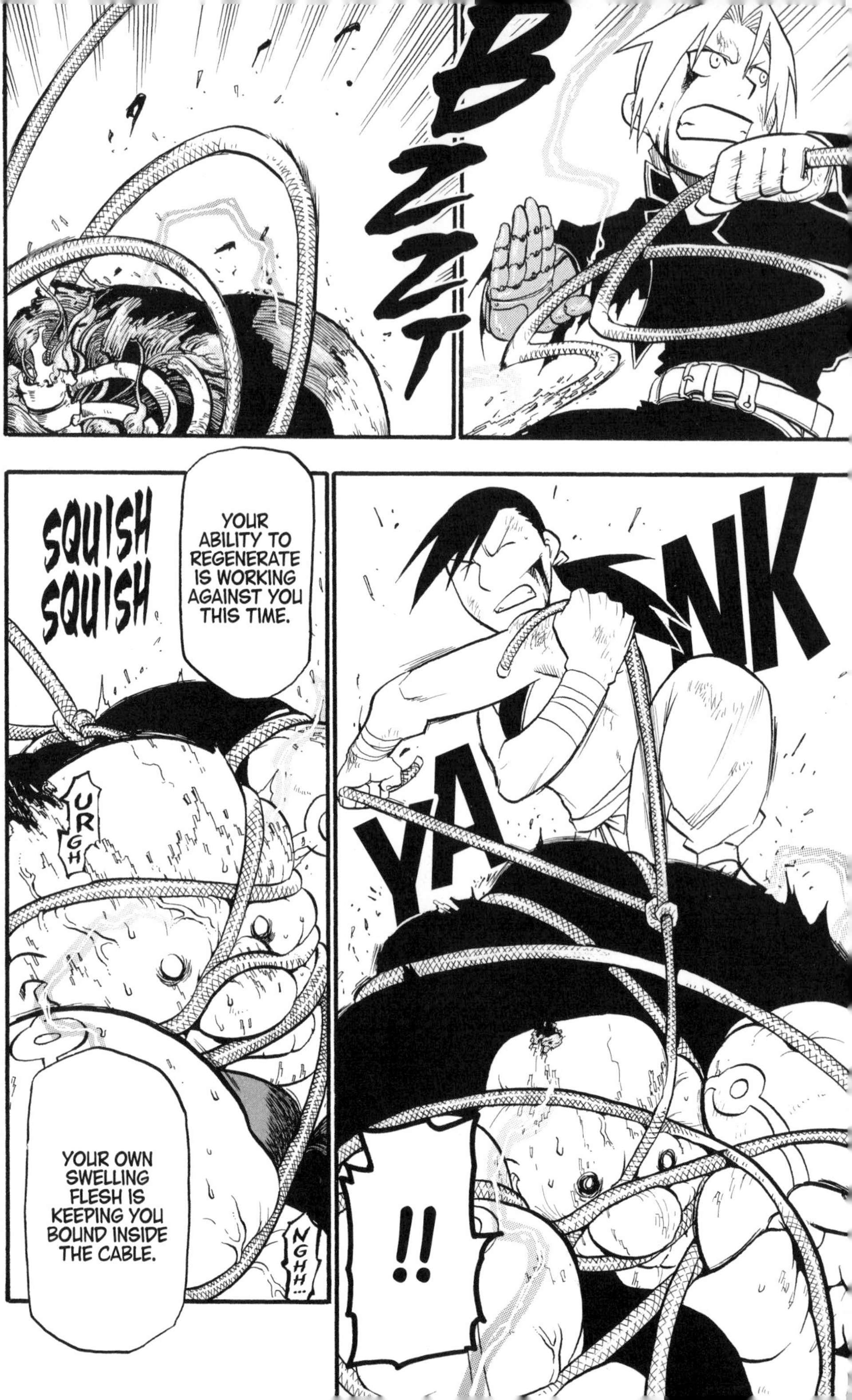
BZZZT
YANK
!!
SQUISH SQUISH
YOUR ABILITY TO REGENERATE IS WORKING AGAINST YOU THIS TIME.
URGH
YOUR OWN SWELLING FLESH IS KEEPING YOU BOUND INSIDE THE CABLE.
NGHH...

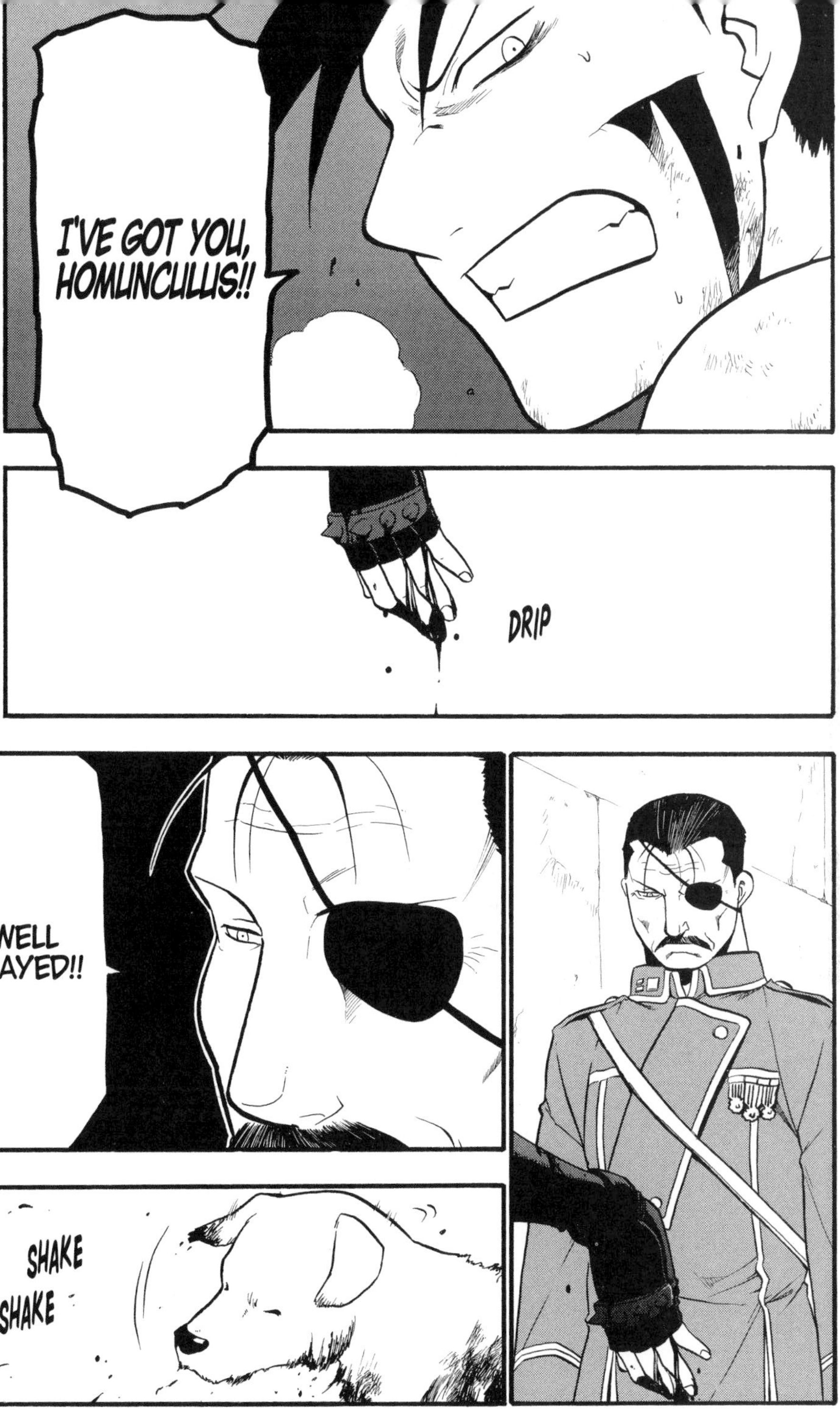
I'VE GOT YOU, HOMUNCULUS!!
DRIP
WELL PLAYED!!
SHAKE
SHAKE

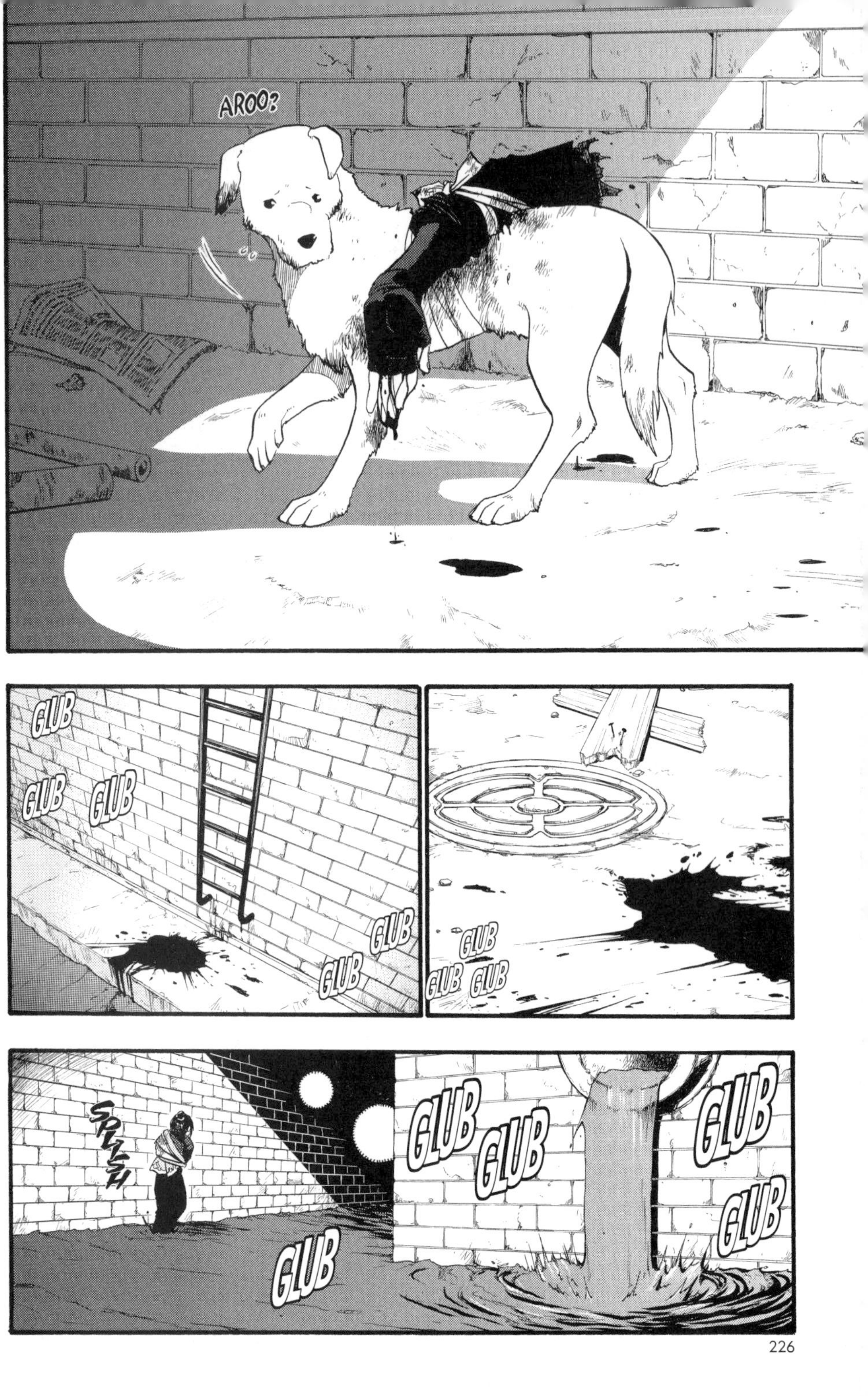
AROO?
GLUB
GLUB
GLUB
GLUB
GLUB
GLUB
GLUB
GLUB
GLUB
GLUB
GLUB
GLUB
GLUB
SPLISH

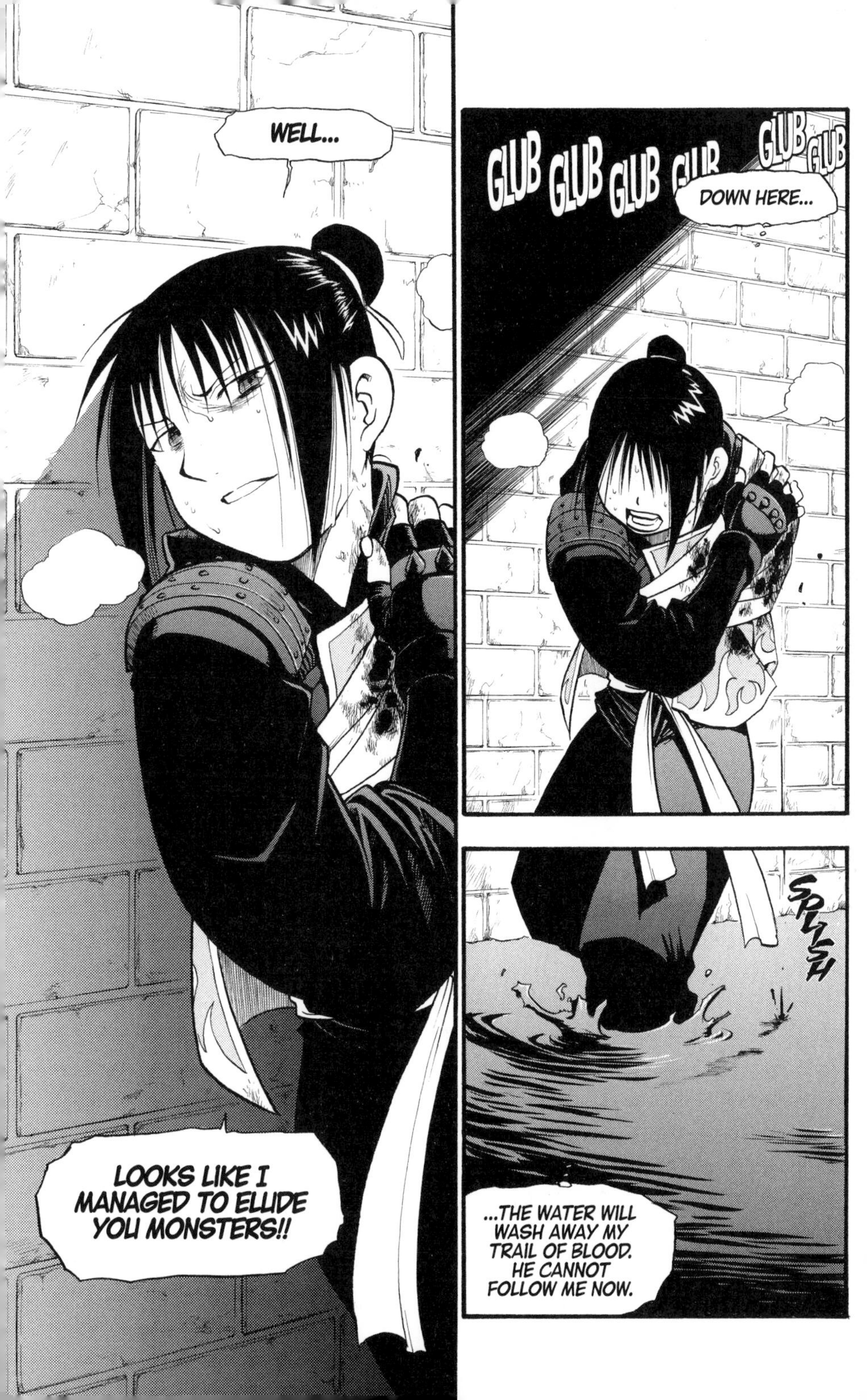
GLUB GLUB GLUB GLUB GLUB
DOWN HERE...
SPLISH
...THE WATER WILL WASH AWAY MY TRAIL OF BLOOD. HE CANNOT FOLLOW ME NOW.
WELL...
LOOKS LIKE I MANAGED TO ELUDE YOU MONSTERS!!

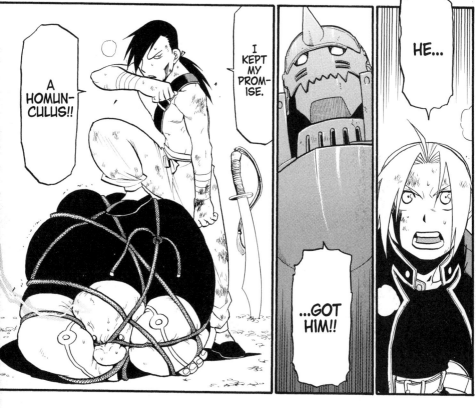

A HOMUN-CULUS!!

I KEPT MY PROM-ISE.

HE...

...GOT HIM!!

SKR SKR

SKR SKRAK

A HOMUN-CULUS ?!

WHAT'S GOING ON?

WHAT...

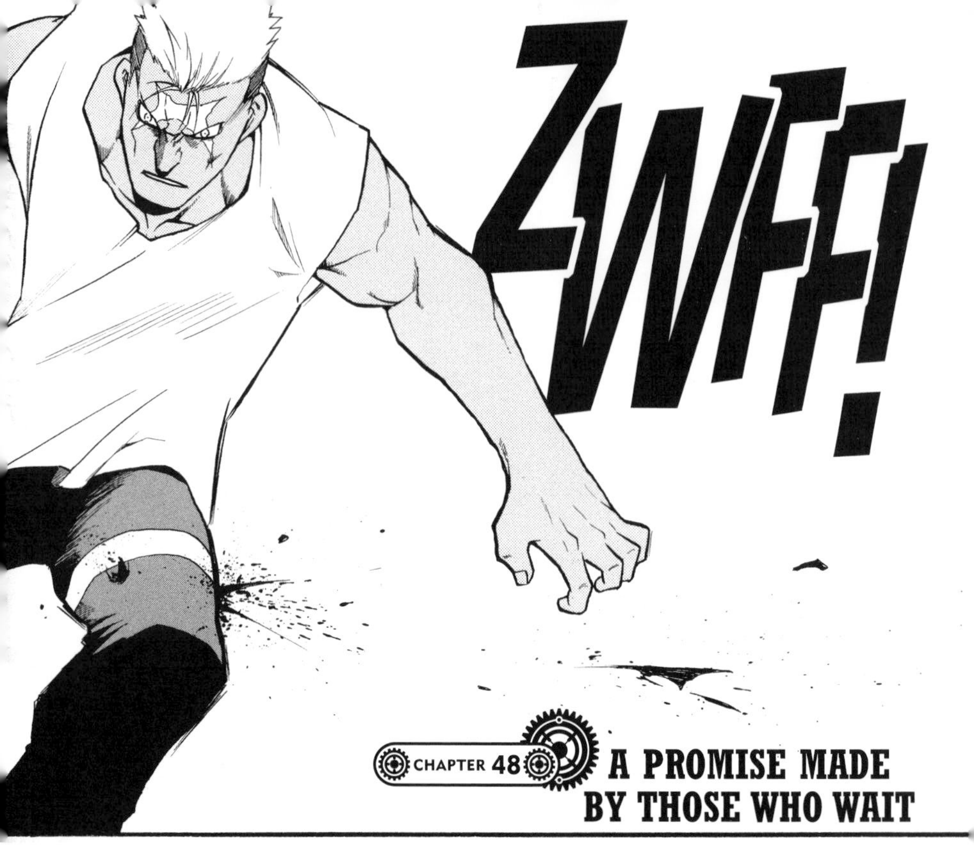
ZWFF!

CHAPTER 48 A PROMISE MADE BY THOSE WHO WAIT

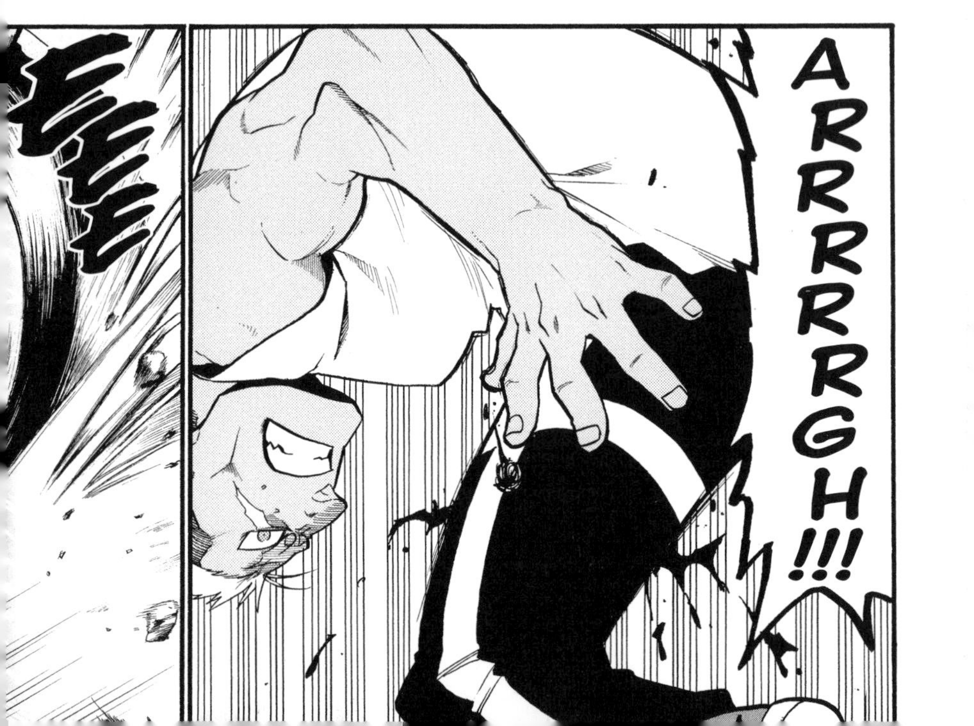
ARRRRRGH!!!

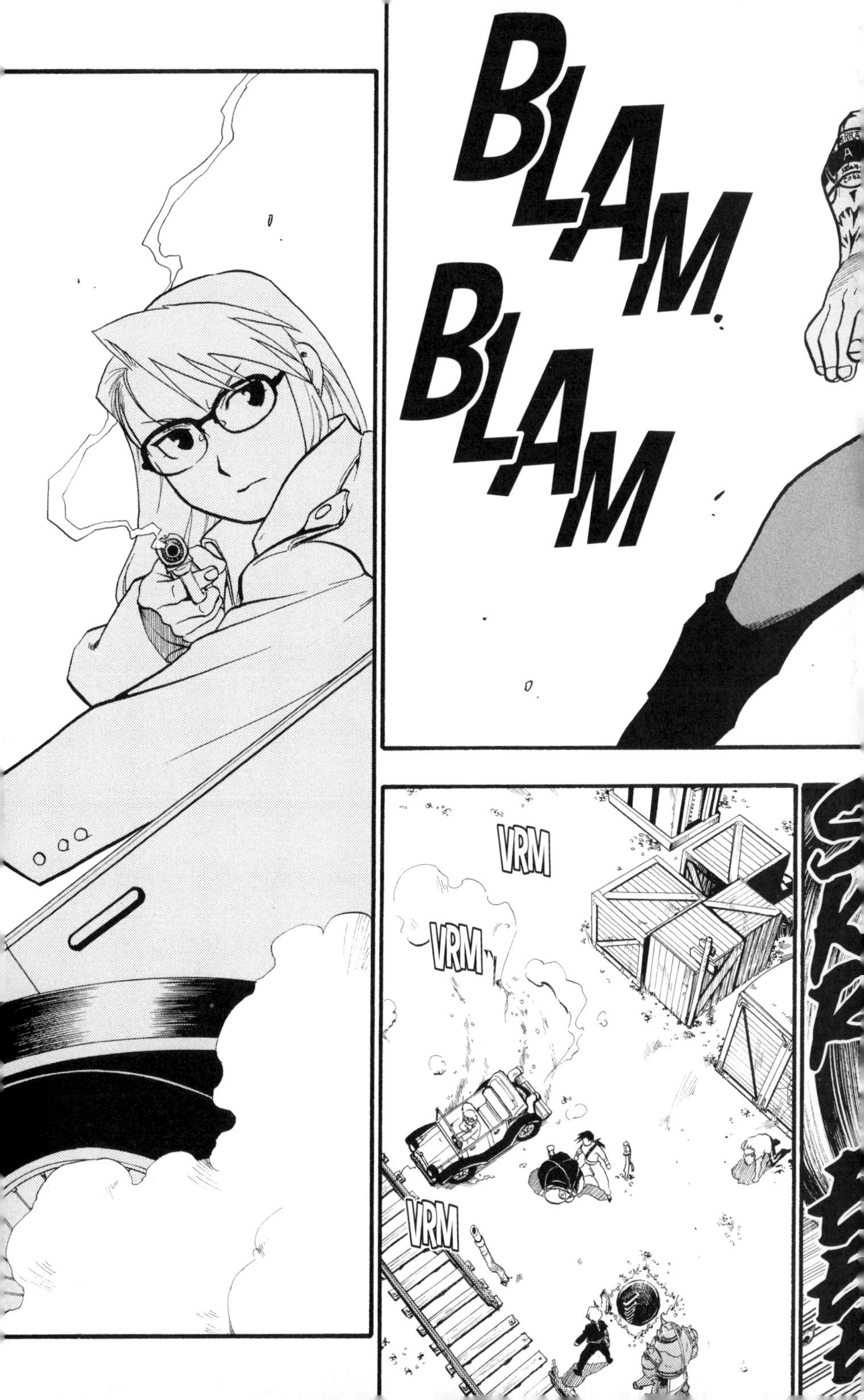
BLAM
BLAM
VRM
VRM
VRM

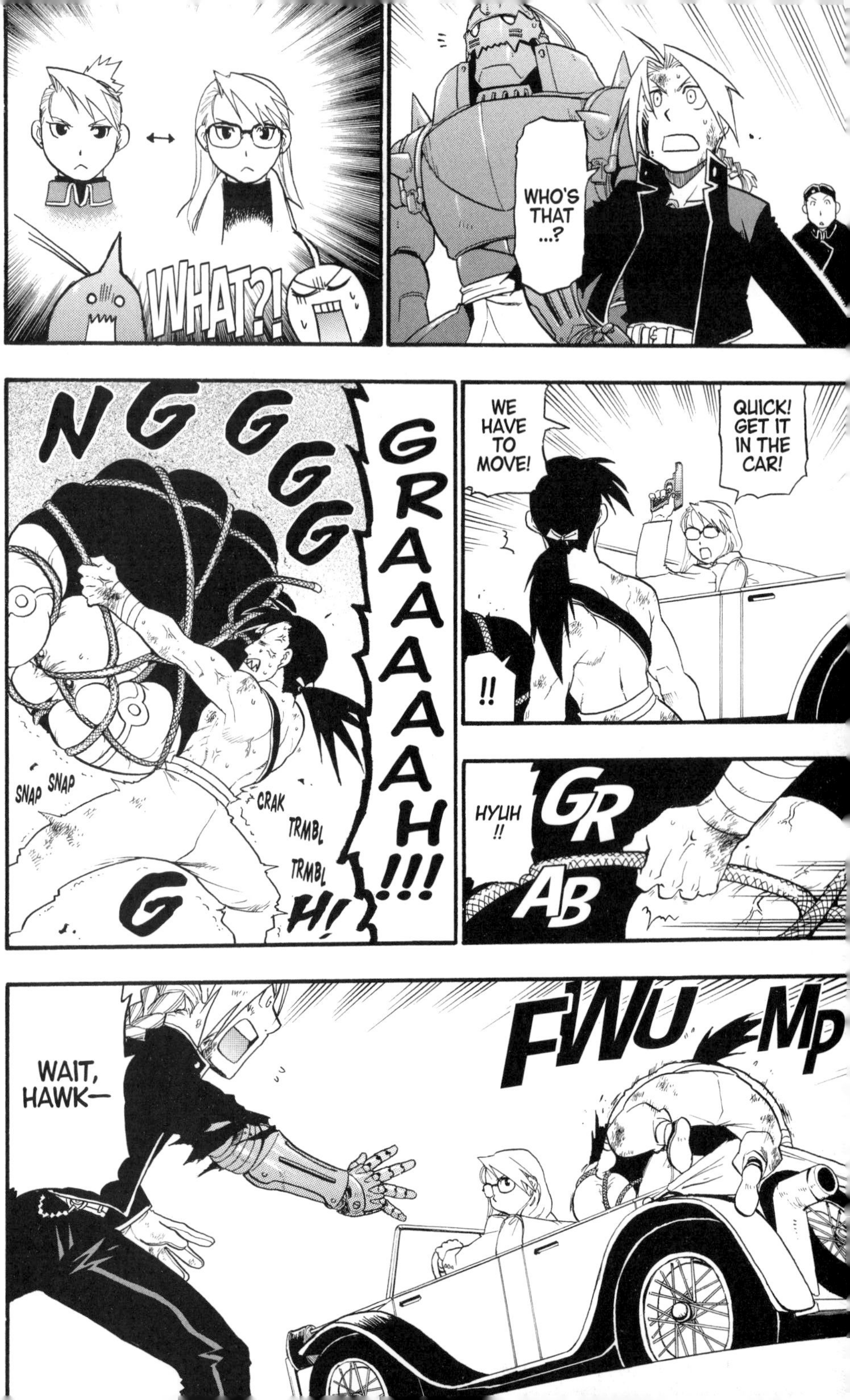
WHO'S THAT ...?
WHAT?!
QUICK! GET IT IN THE CAR!
WE HAVE TO MOVE!
!!
HYUH !!
GRAB
GRAAAAAH!!!
NGGGGGH!
CRAK
TRMBL TRMBL
SNAP SNAP
FWUMP
WAIT, HAWK—

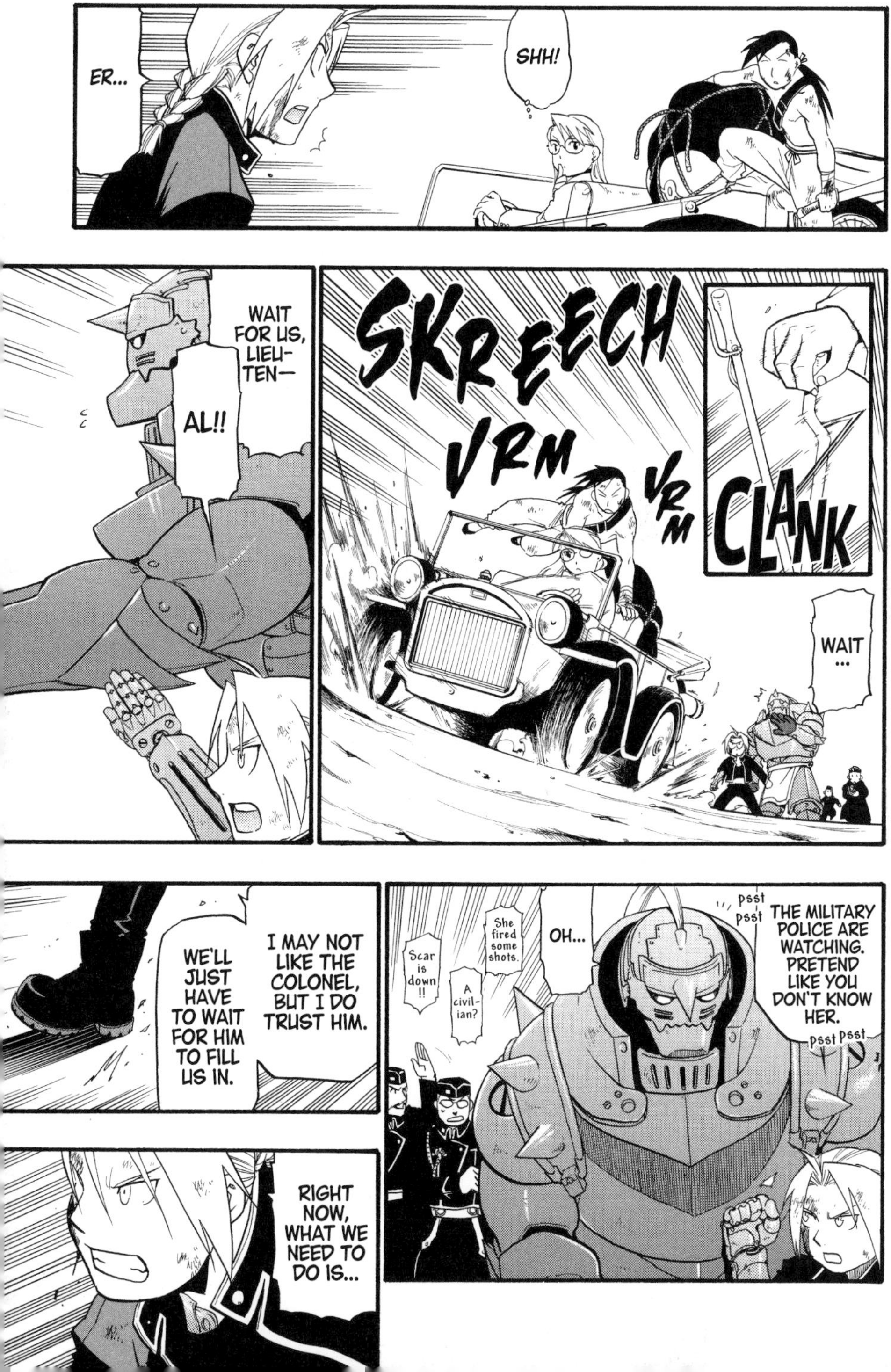

SHH!
ER...
CLANK
SKREECH
VRM
VRM
WAIT...
WAIT FOR US, LIEU-TEN—
AL!!
psst psst
THE MILITARY POLICE ARE WATCHING. PRETEND LIKE YOU DON'T KNOW HER.
psst psst
OH...
She fired some shots.
A civil-ian?
Scar is down!!
I MAY NOT LIKE THE COLONEL, BUT I DO TRUST HIM.
WE'LL JUST HAVE TO WAIT FOR HIM TO FILL US IN.
RIGHT NOW, WHAT WE NEED TO DO IS...

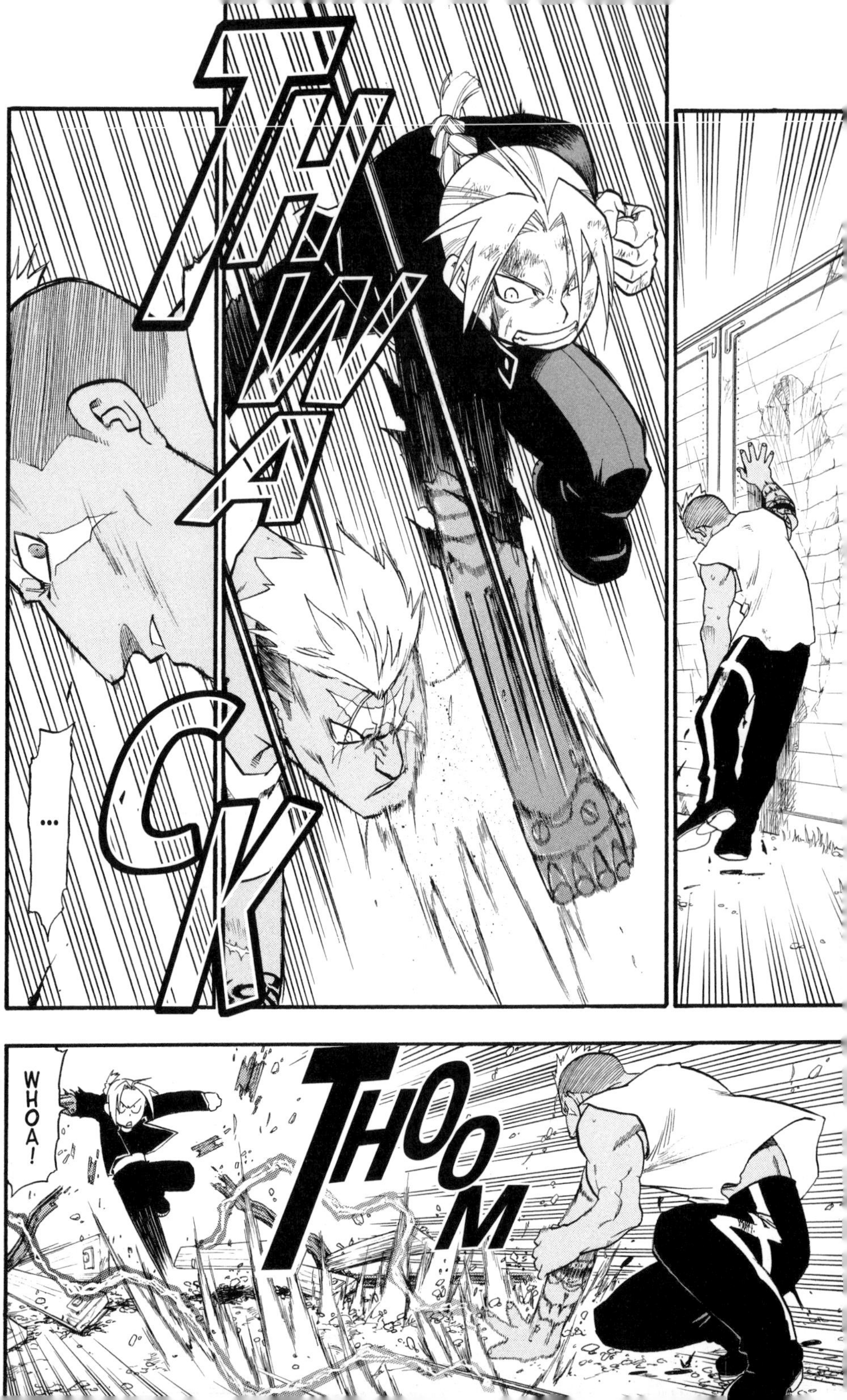
THWACK
...
THOOM
WHOA!

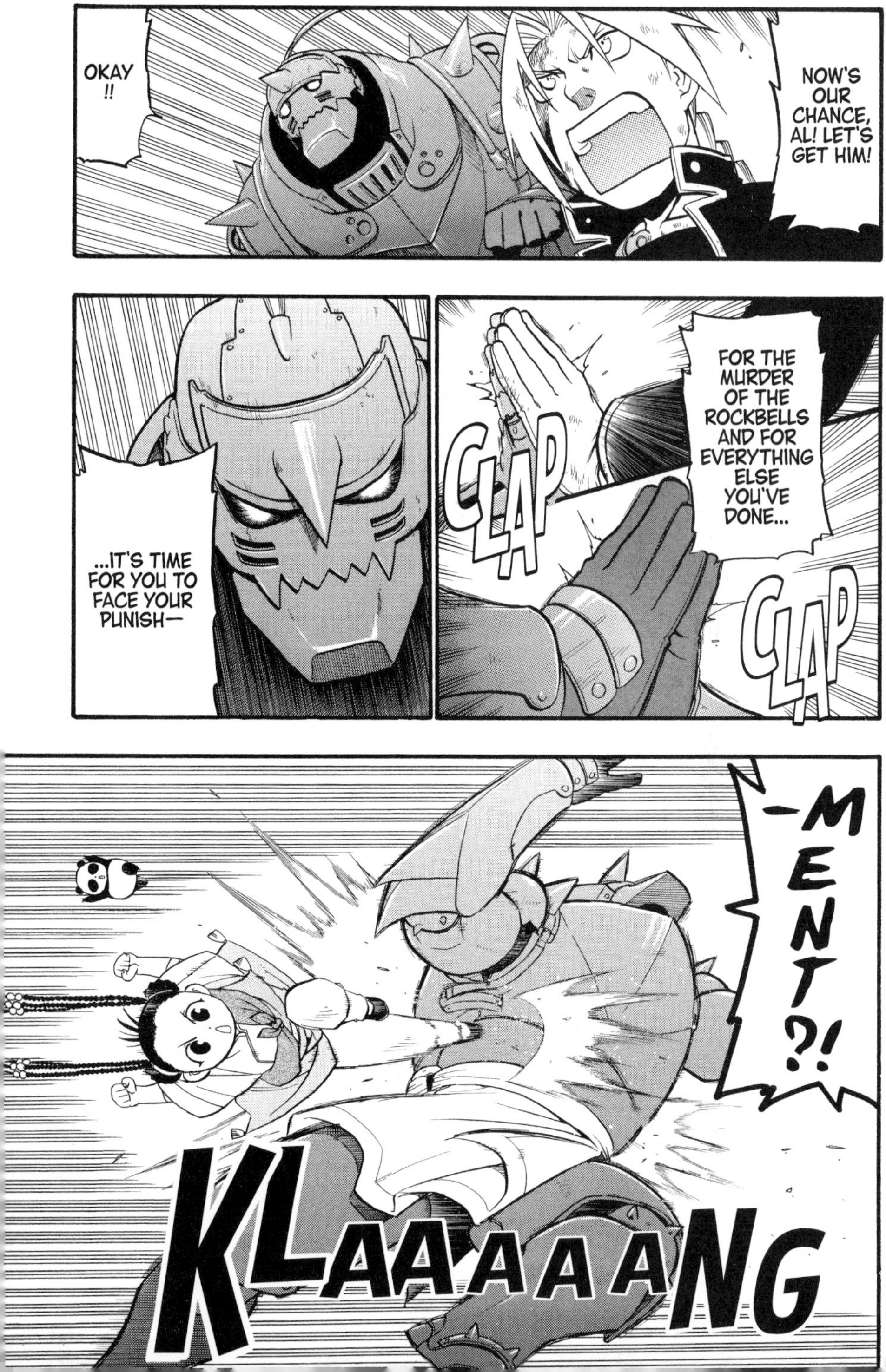
NOW'S OUR CHANCE, AL! LET'S GET HIM!
OKAY !!
FOR THE MURDER OF THE ROCKBELLS AND FOR EVERYTHING ELSE YOU'VE DONE...
CLAP
CLAP
...IT'S TIME FOR YOU TO FACE YOUR PUNISH—
—MENT?!
KLAAAAAANG

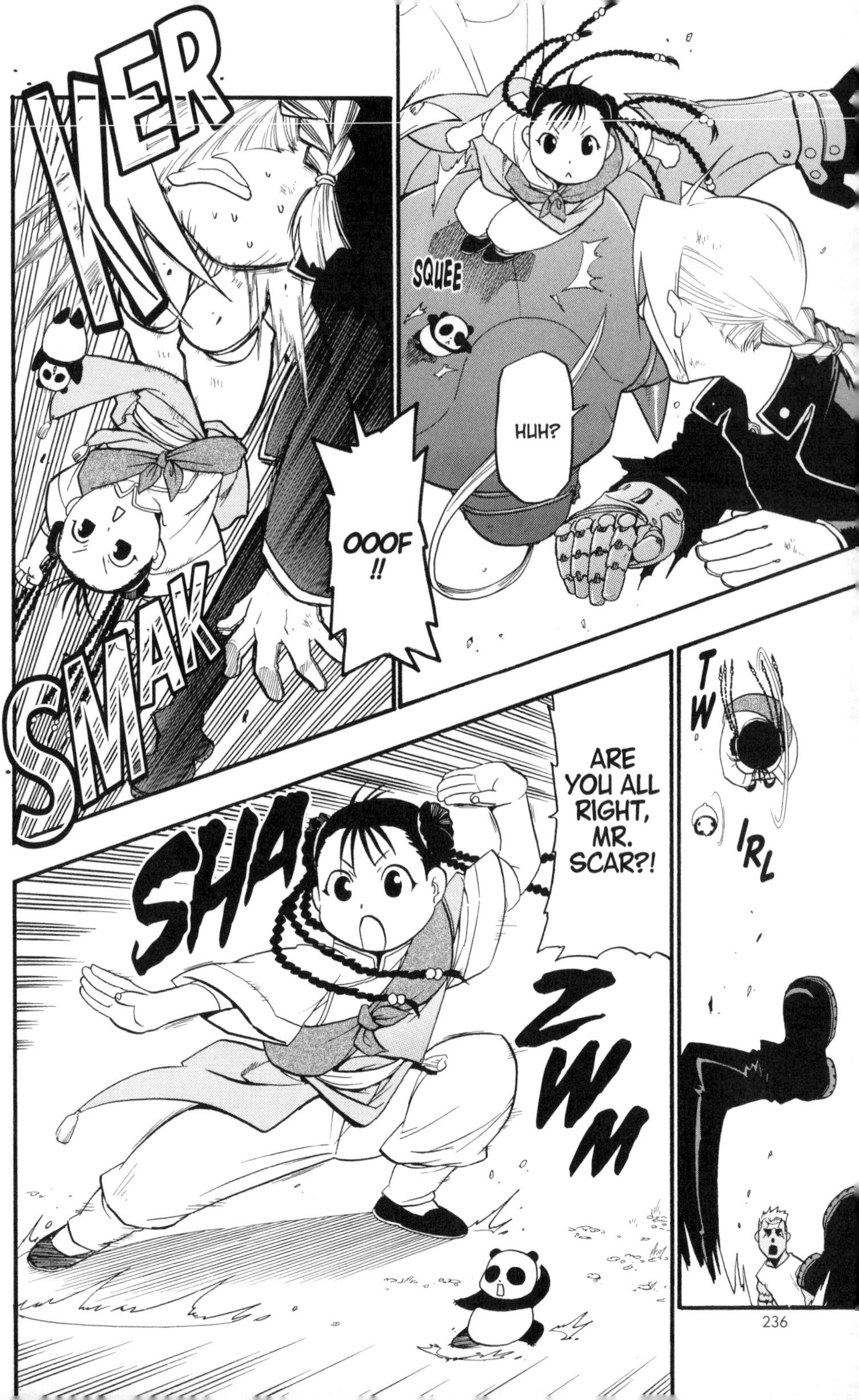
SQUEE
HUH?
KER
OOOF!!
SMAK
TW IRL
ARE YOU ALL RIGHT, MR. SCAR?!
SHA
ZWM

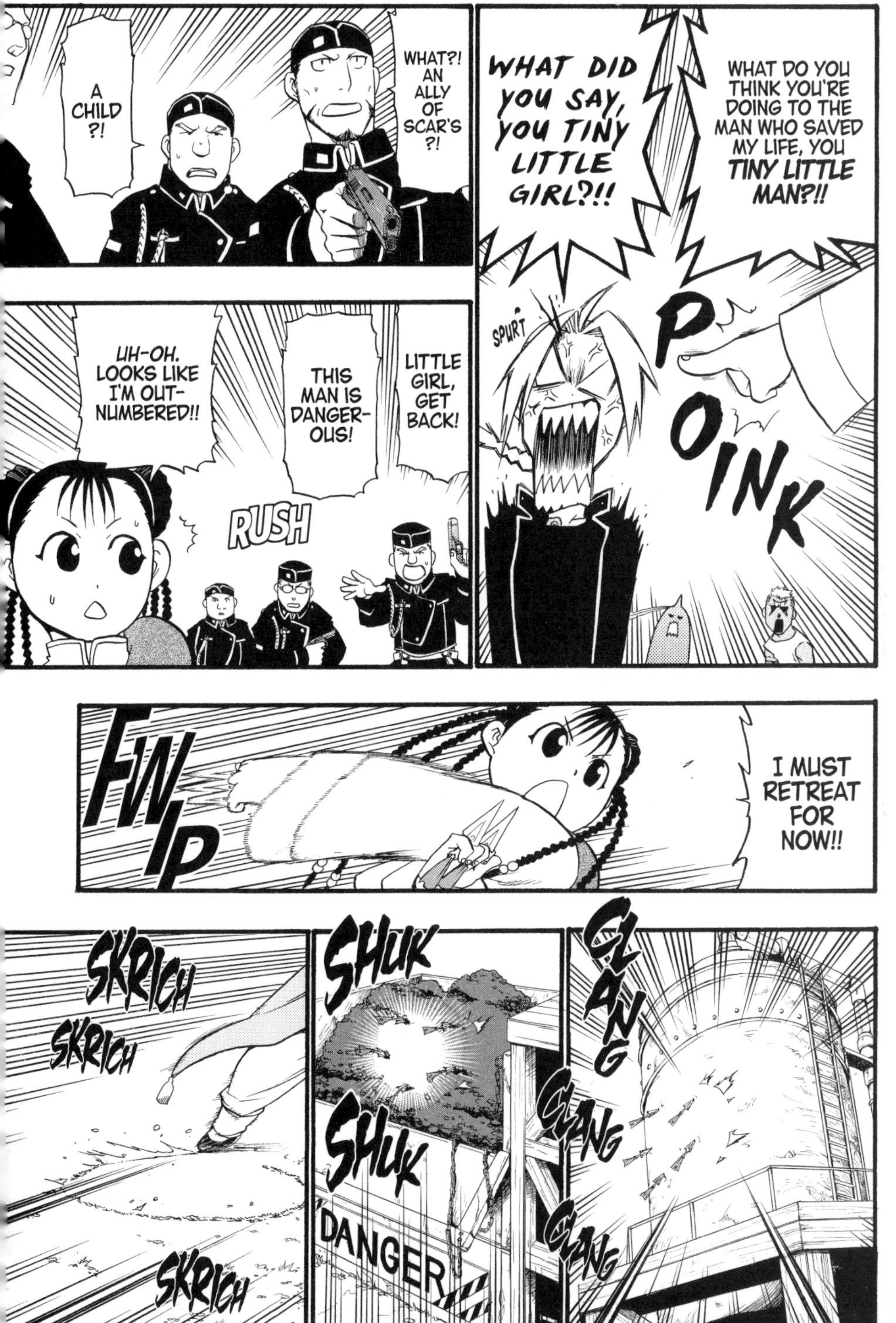
WHAT DO YOU THINK YOU'RE DOING TO THE MAN WHO SAVED MY LIFE, YOU TINY LITTLE MAN?!!
WHAT DID YOU SAY, YOU TINY LITTLE GIRL?!!
POINK
SPURT
WHAT?! AN ALLY OF SCAR'S?!
A CHILD?!
LITTLE GIRL, GET BACK!
THIS MAN IS DANGER-OUS!
UH-OH. LOOKS LIKE I'M OUT-NUMBERED!!
RUSH
I MUST RETREAT FOR NOW!!
FWIP
CLANG
CLANG
CLANG
CLANG
SHUK
SHUK
DANGER
SKRICH
SKRICH
SKRICH

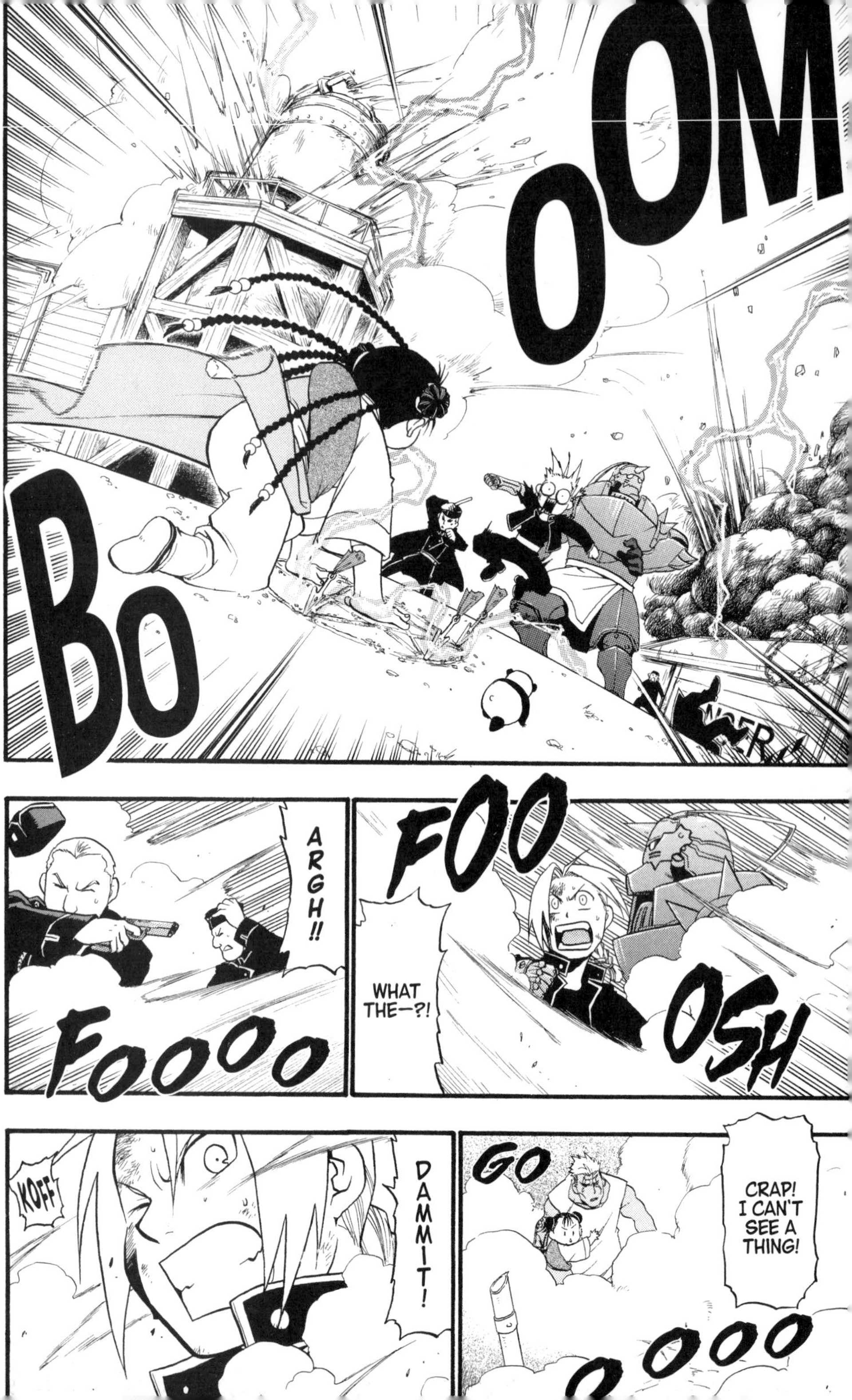
BO
OOM
FOO
WHAT THE—?!
OSH
ARGH!!
FOOOO
GO
CRAP! I CAN'T SEE A THING!
OOOO
DAMMIT!
KOFF

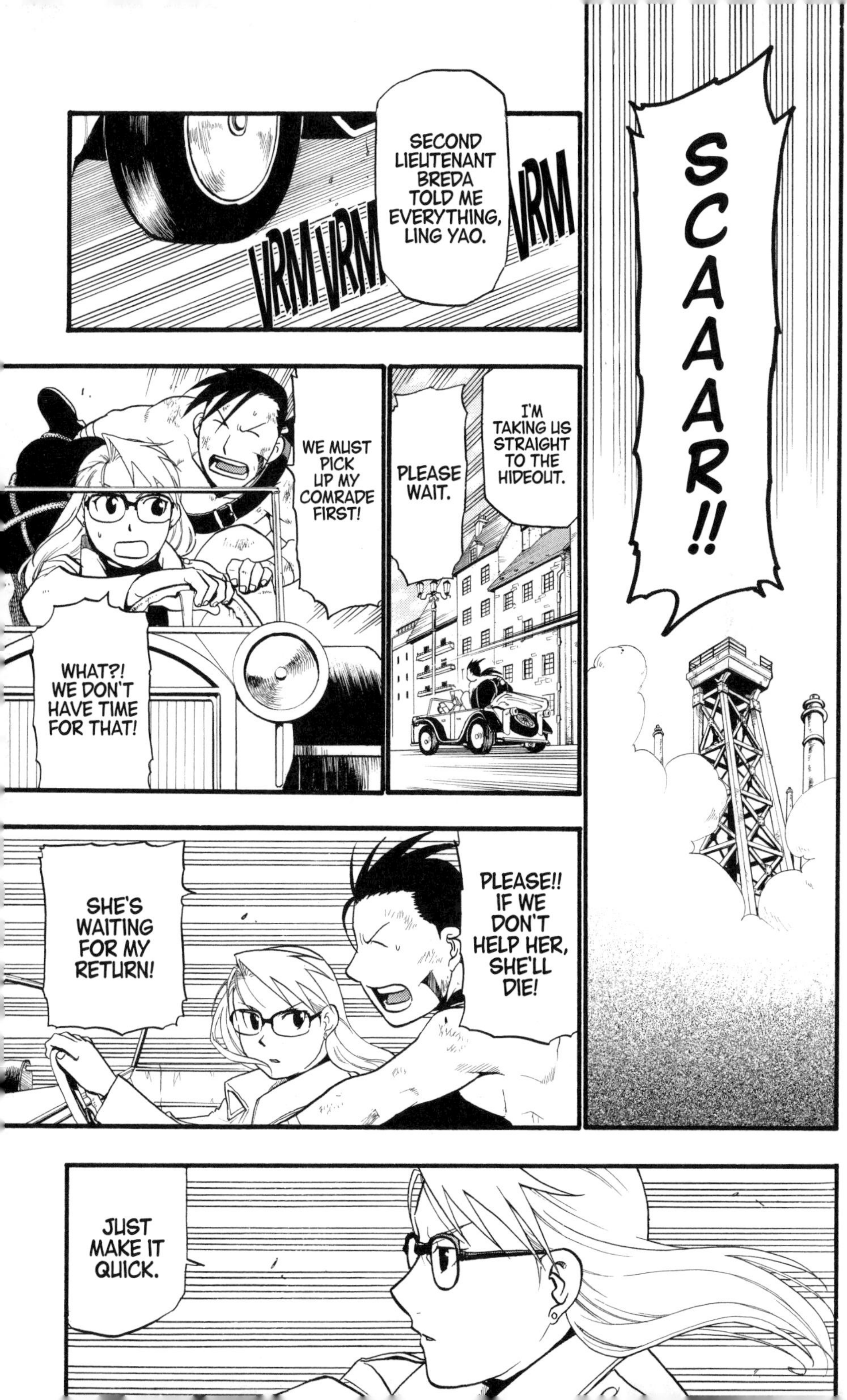
SCAAAR!!
VRM VRM VRM
SECOND LIEUTENANT BREDA TOLD ME EVERYTHING, LING YAO.
I'M TAKING US STRAIGHT TO THE HIDEOUT.
PLEASE WAIT.
WE MUST PICK UP MY COMRADE FIRST!
WHAT?! WE DON'T HAVE TIME FOR THAT!
PLEASE!! IF WE DON'T HELP HER, SHE'LL DIE!
SHE'S WAITING FOR MY RETURN!
JUST MAKE IT QUICK.

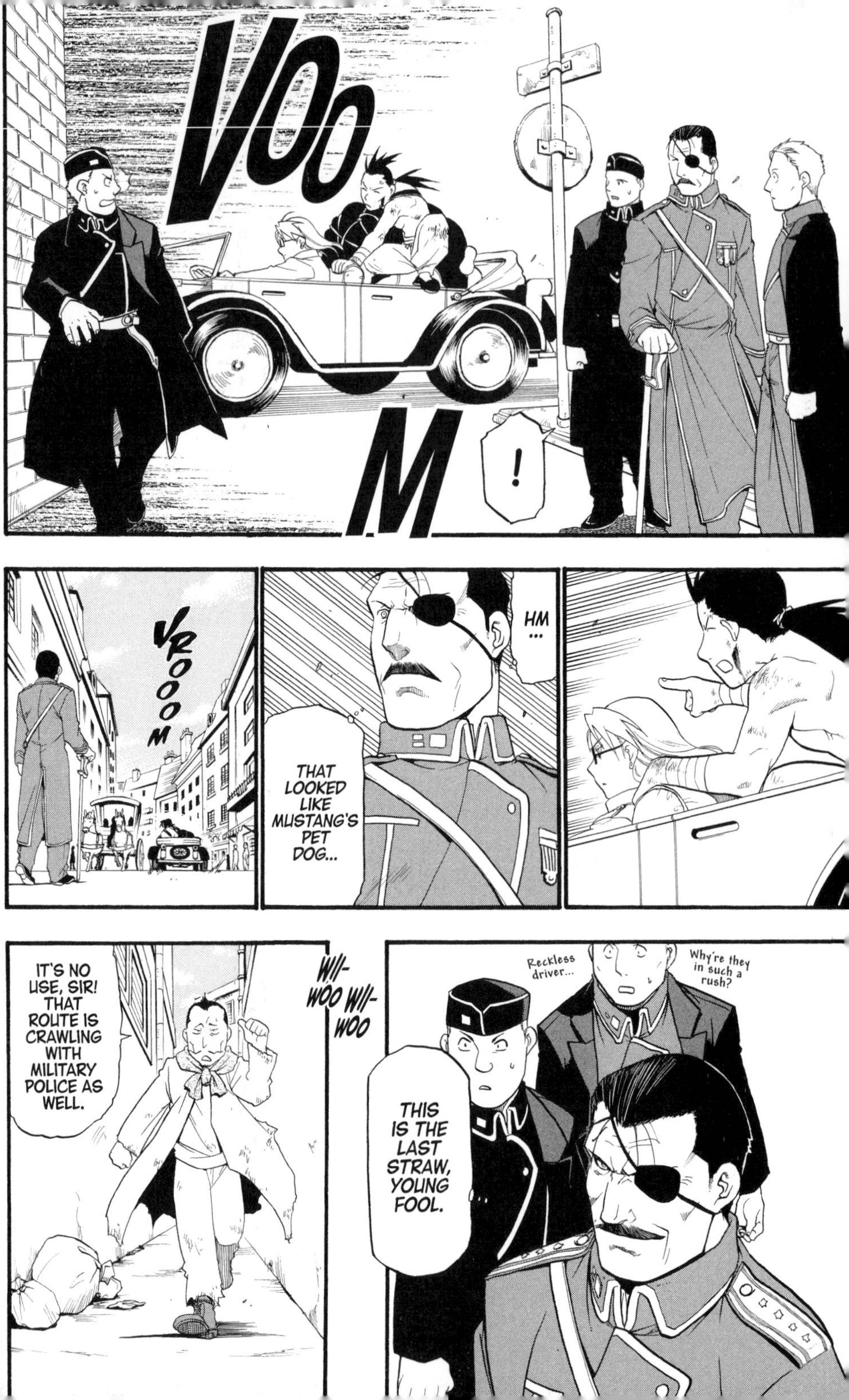
VOOM
!
HM ...
THAT LOOKED LIKE MUSTANG'S PET DOG...
VROOOOM
Why're they in such a rush?
Reckless driver...
THIS IS THE LAST STRAW, YOUNG FOOL.
WII-WOO WII-WOO
IT'S NO USE, SIR! THAT ROUTE IS CRAWLING WITH MILITARY POLICE AS WELL.

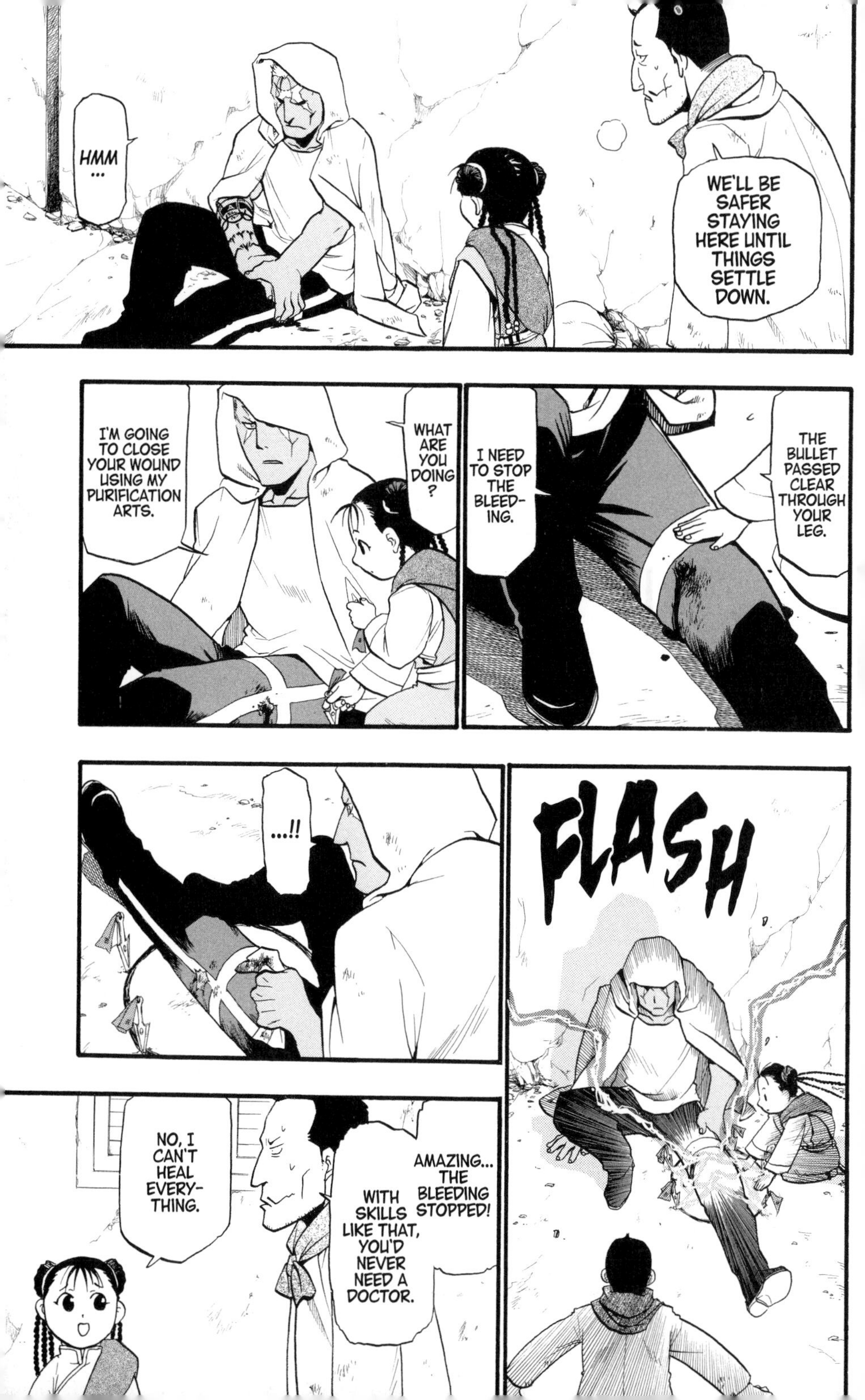
WE'LL BE SAFER STAYING HERE UNTIL THINGS SETTLE DOWN.
HMM...
THE BULLET PASSED CLEAR THROUGH YOUR LEG.
I NEED TO STOP THE BLEED-ING.
WHAT ARE YOU DOING?
I'M GOING TO CLOSE YOUR WOUND USING MY PURIFICATION ARTS.
FLASH
...!!
AMAZING... THE BLEEDING STOPPED!
WITH SKILLS LIKE THAT, YOU'D NEVER NEED A DOCTOR.
NO, I CAN'T HEAL EVERY-THING.

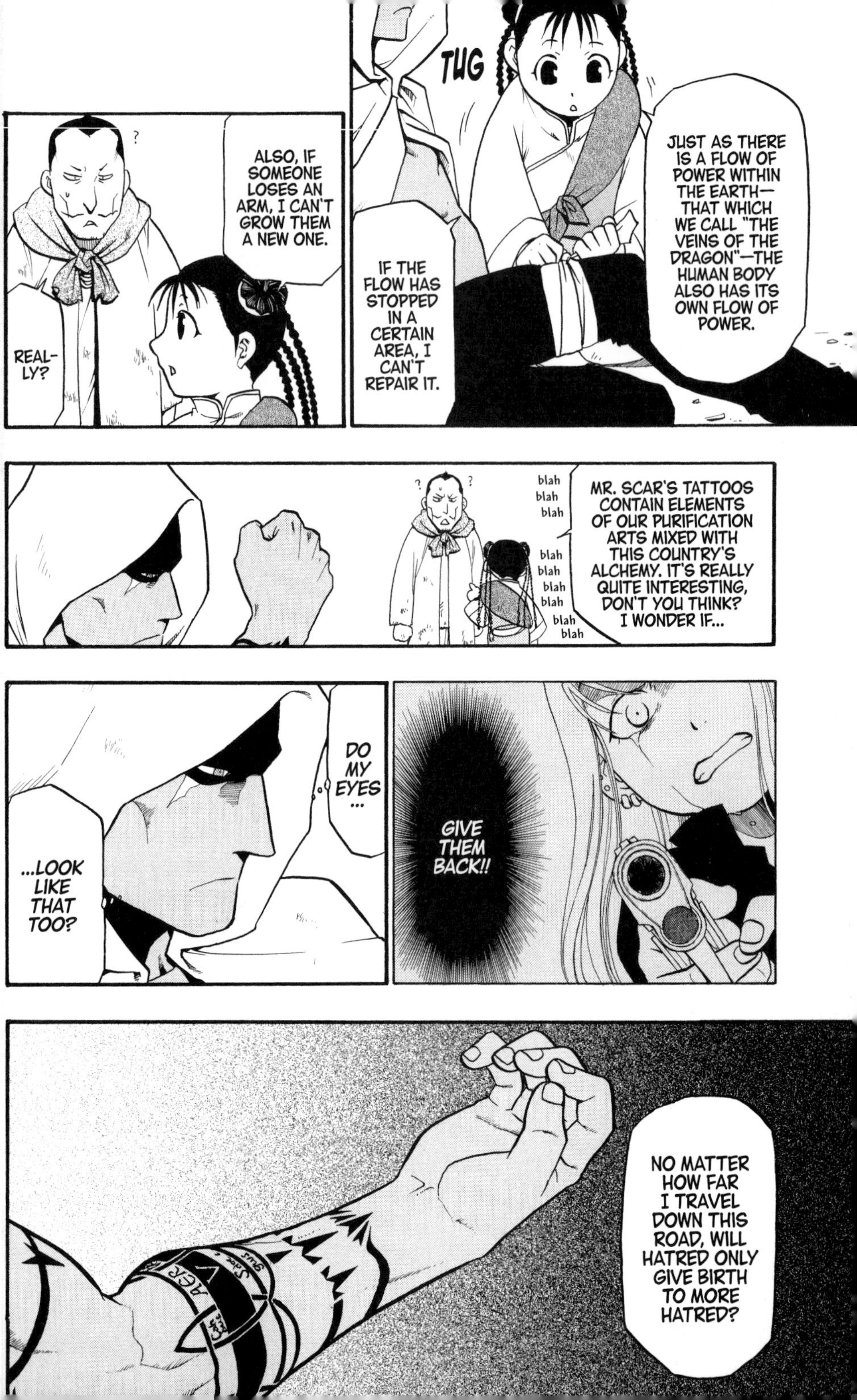
TUG
JUST AS THERE IS A FLOW OF POWER WITHIN THE EARTH—THAT WHICH WE CALL "THE VEINS OF THE DRAGON"—THE HUMAN BODY ALSO HAS ITS OWN FLOW OF POWER.
IF THE FLOW HAS STOPPED IN A CERTAIN AREA, I CAN'T REPAIR IT.
ALSO, IF SOMEONE LOSES AN ARM, I CAN'T GROW THEM A NEW ONE.
?
REALLY?
MR. SCAR'S TATTOOS CONTAIN ELEMENTS OF OUR PURIFICATION ARTS MIXED WITH THIS COUNTRY'S ALCHEMY. IT'S REALLY QUITE INTERESTING, DON'T YOU THINK? I WONDER IF...
blah blah blah
blah blah blah blah
blah blah
? ?
GIVE THEM BACK!!
DO MY EYES...
...LOOK LIKE THAT TOO?
NO MATTER HOW FAR I TRAVEL DOWN THIS ROAD, WILL HATRED ONLY GIVE BIRTH TO MORE HATRED?

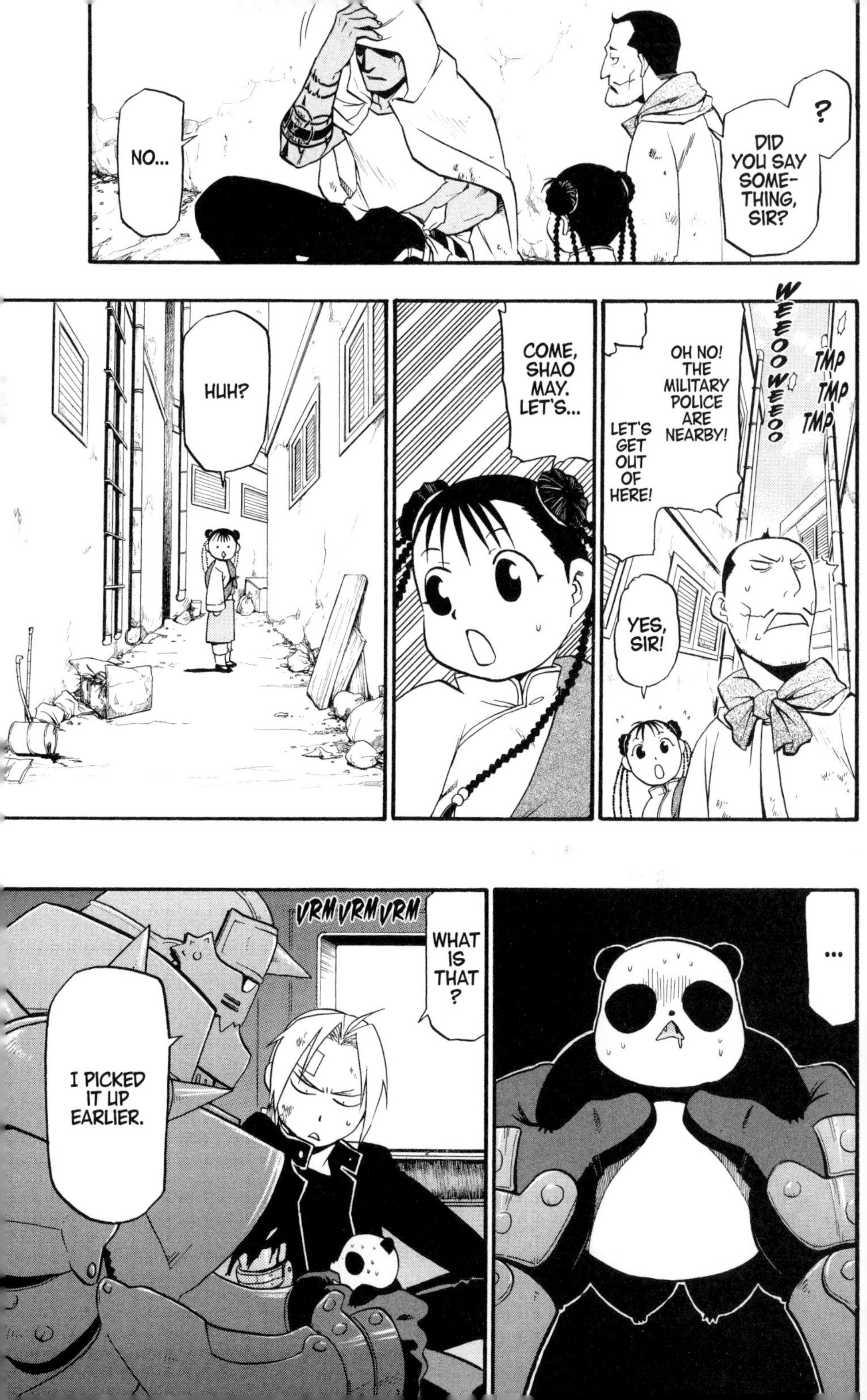
?
DID YOU SAY SOMETHING, SIR?
NO...
WEEOO WEEOO
TMP TMP TMP
OH NO! THE MILITARY POLICE ARE NEARBY!
LET'S GET OUT OF HERE!
YES, SIR!
COME, SHAO MAY. LET'S...
HUH?
...
VRM VRM VRM
WHAT IS THAT?
I PICKED IT UP EARLIER.

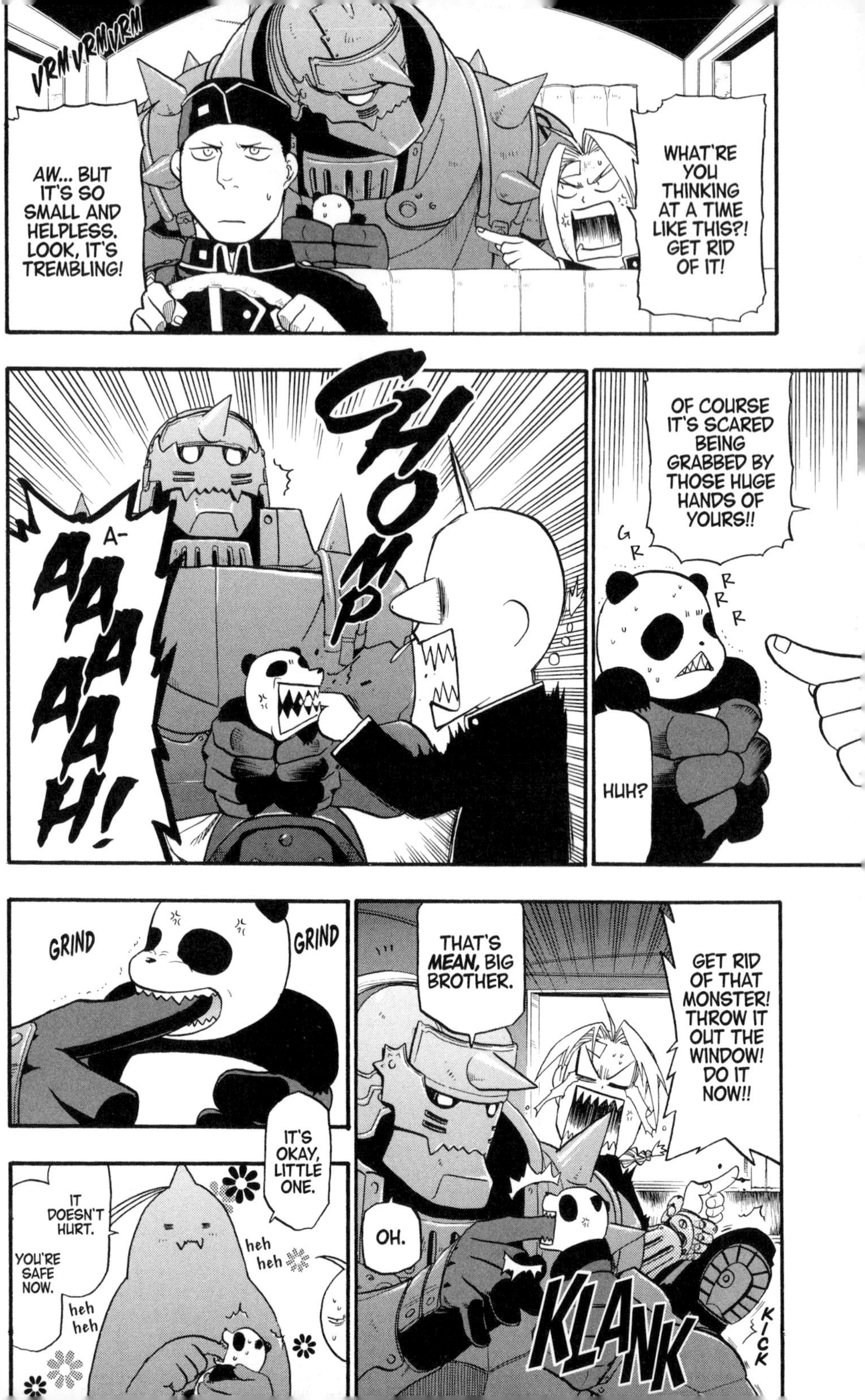
VRM VRM VRM
WHAT'RE YOU THINKING AT A TIME LIKE THIS?! GET RID OF IT!
AW... BUT IT'S SO SMALL AND HELPLESS. LOOK, IT'S TREMBLING!
OF COURSE IT'S SCARED BEING GRABBED BY THOSE HUGE HANDS OF YOURS!!
GRRRR
HUH?
CHOMP
A-AAAAAH!
GET RID OF THAT MONSTER! THROW IT OUT THE WINDOW! DO IT NOW!!
THAT'S MEAN, BIG BROTHER.
OH.
KICK
KLANK
GRIND
GRIND
IT'S OKAY, LITTLE ONE.
IT DOESN'T HURT.
YOU'RE SAFE NOW.
heh heh
heh heh

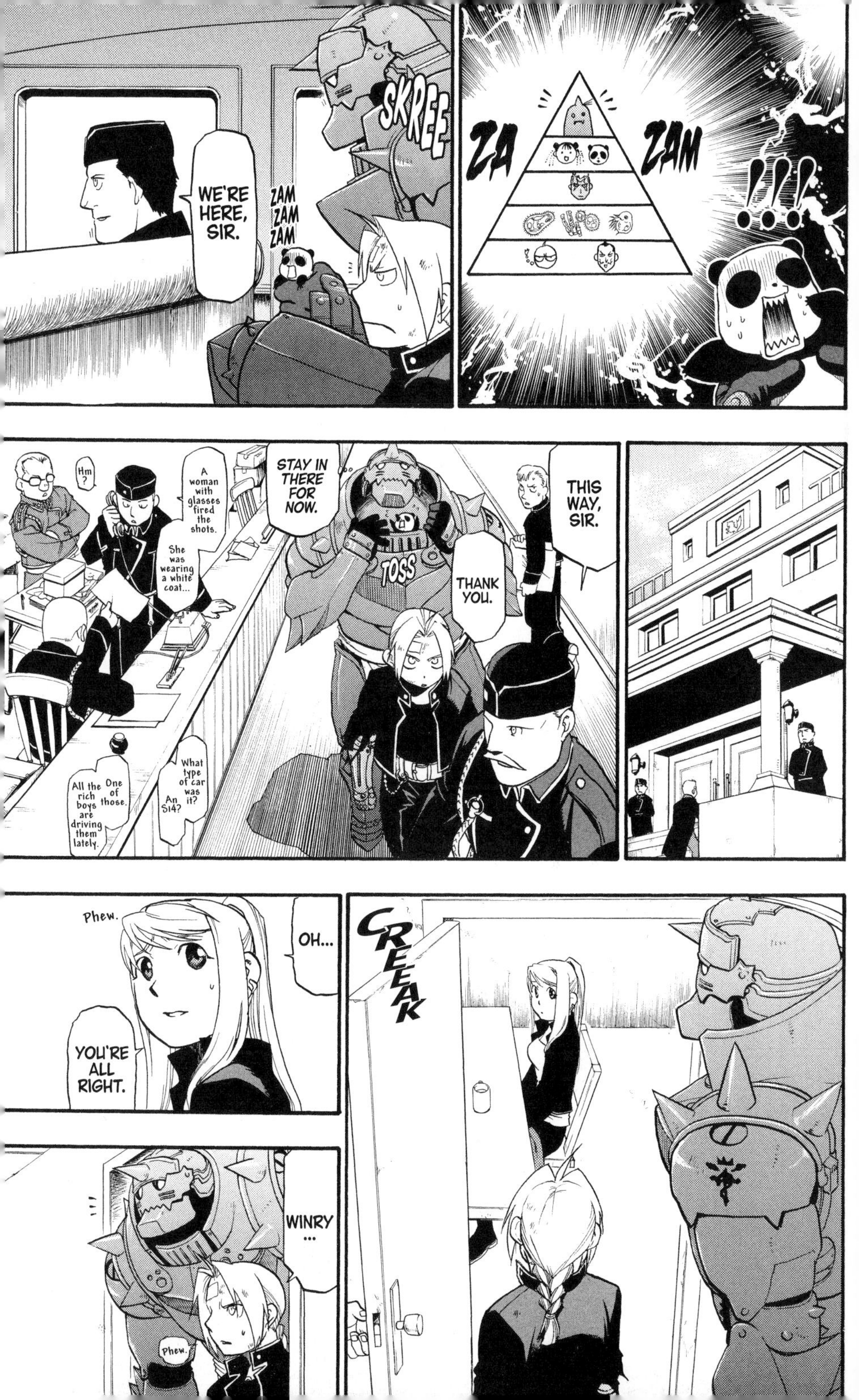
ZA
ZAM
!!!
SKREE
ZAM ZAM ZAM
WE'RE HERE, SIR.
THIS WAY, SIR.
THANK YOU.
STAY IN THERE FOR NOW.
TOSS
A woman with glasses fired the shots.
She was wearing a white coat...
Hm?
What type of car was it? An S14?
One of those.
All the rich boys are driving them lately.
CREEAK
OH...
Phew.
YOU'RE ALL RIGHT.
WINRY...
Phew.

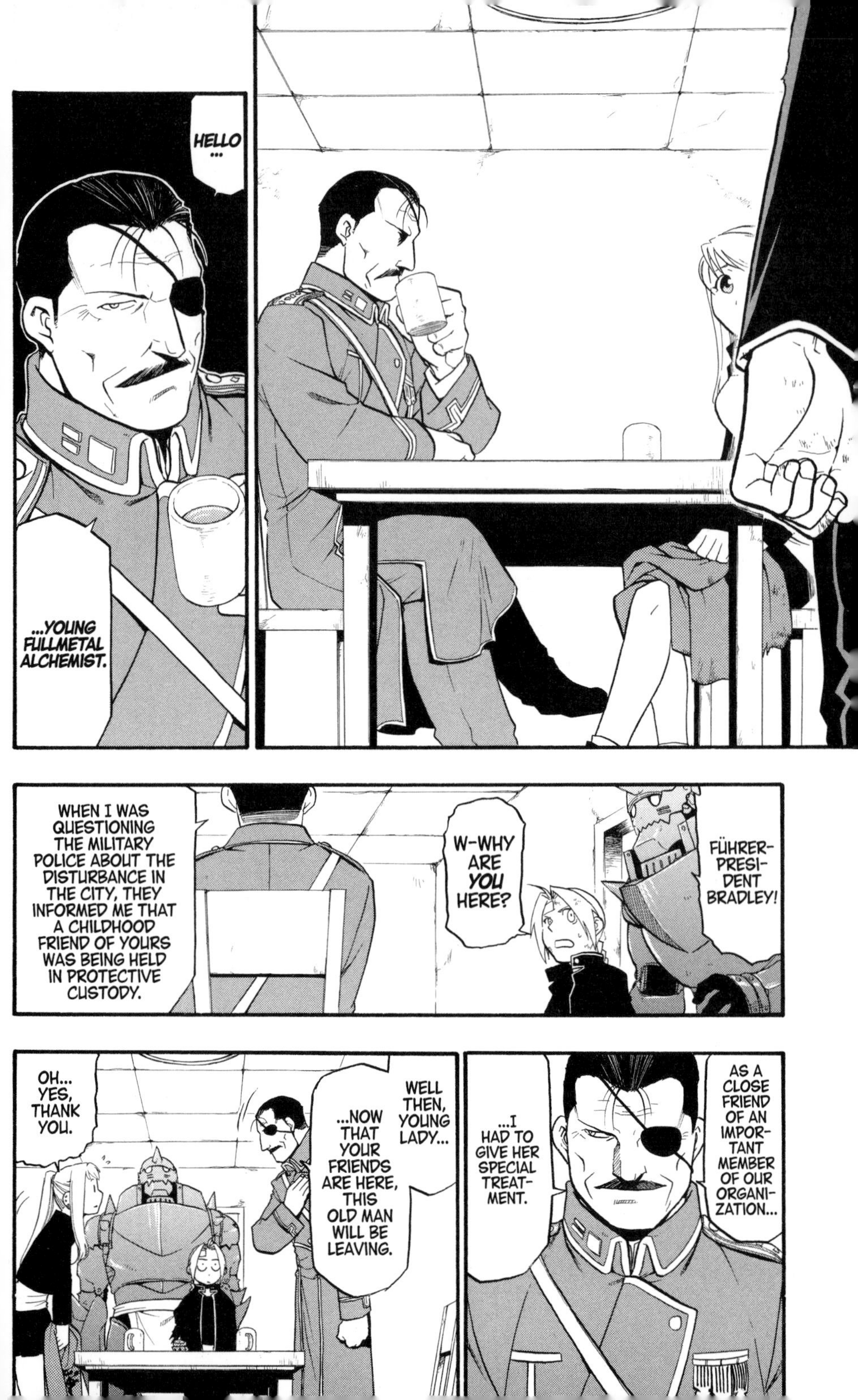
HELLO ...
...YOUNG FULLMETAL ALCHEMIST.
FÜHRER-PRESIDENT BRADLEY!
W-WHY ARE YOU HERE?
WHEN I WAS QUESTIONING THE MILITARY POLICE ABOUT THE DISTURBANCE IN THE CITY, THEY INFORMED ME THAT A CHILDHOOD FRIEND OF YOURS WAS BEING HELD IN PROTECTIVE CUSTODY.
AS A CLOSE FRIEND OF AN IMPORTANT MEMBER OF OUR ORGANIZATION...
...I HAD TO GIVE HER SPECIAL TREATMENT.
WELL THEN, YOUNG LADY...
...NOW THAT YOUR FRIENDS ARE HERE, THIS OLD MAN WILL BE LEAVING.
OH... YES, THANK YOU.

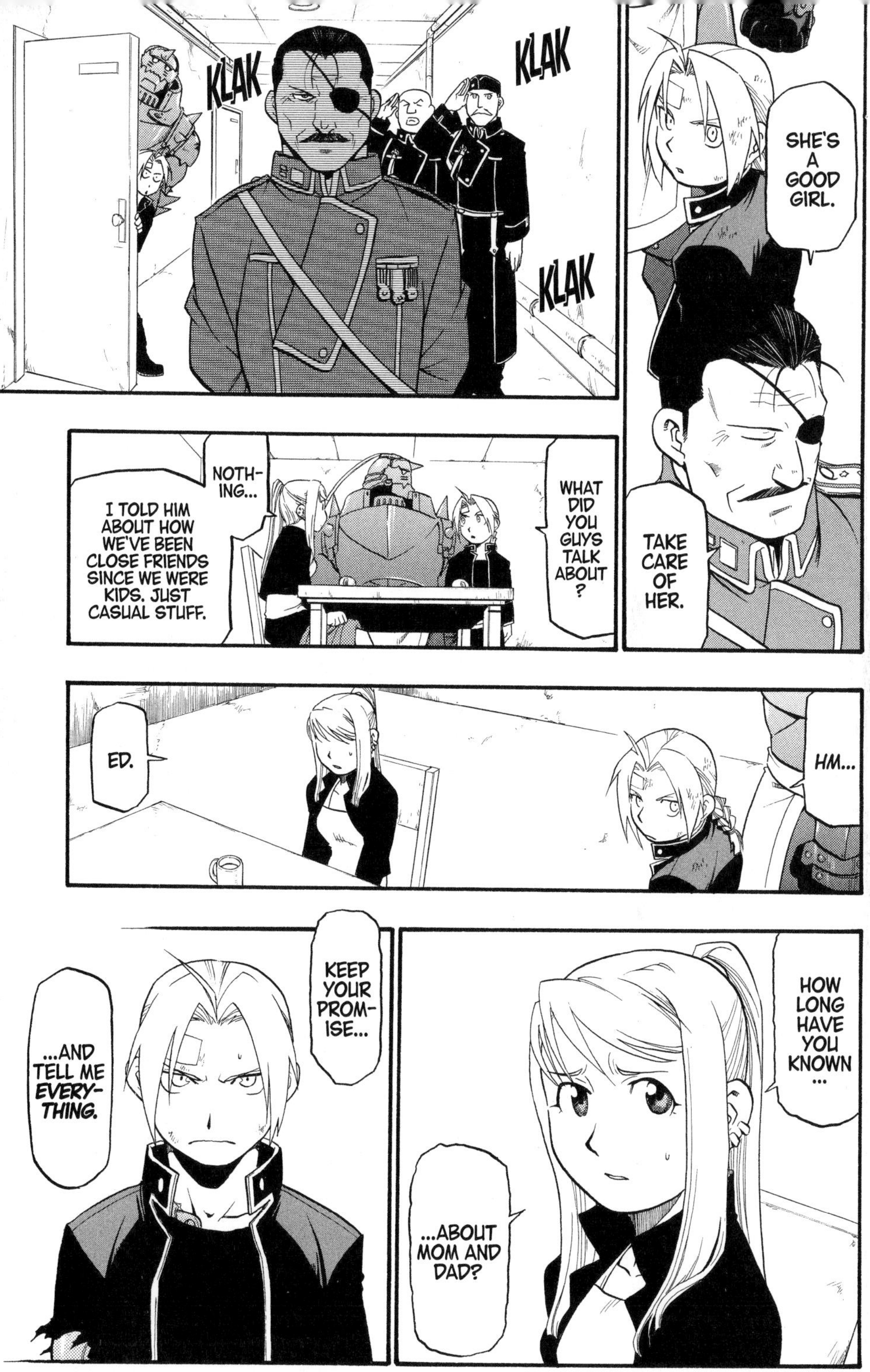
SHE'S A GOOD GIRL.
TAKE CARE OF HER.
KLAK
KLAK
KLAK
WHAT DID YOU GUYS TALK ABOUT?
NOTHING...
I TOLD HIM ABOUT HOW WE'VE BEEN CLOSE FRIENDS SINCE WE WERE KIDS. JUST CASUAL STUFF.
HM...
ED.
HOW LONG HAVE YOU KNOWN...
...ABOUT MOM AND DAD?
KEEP YOUR PROMISE...
...AND TELL ME *EVERYTHING.*

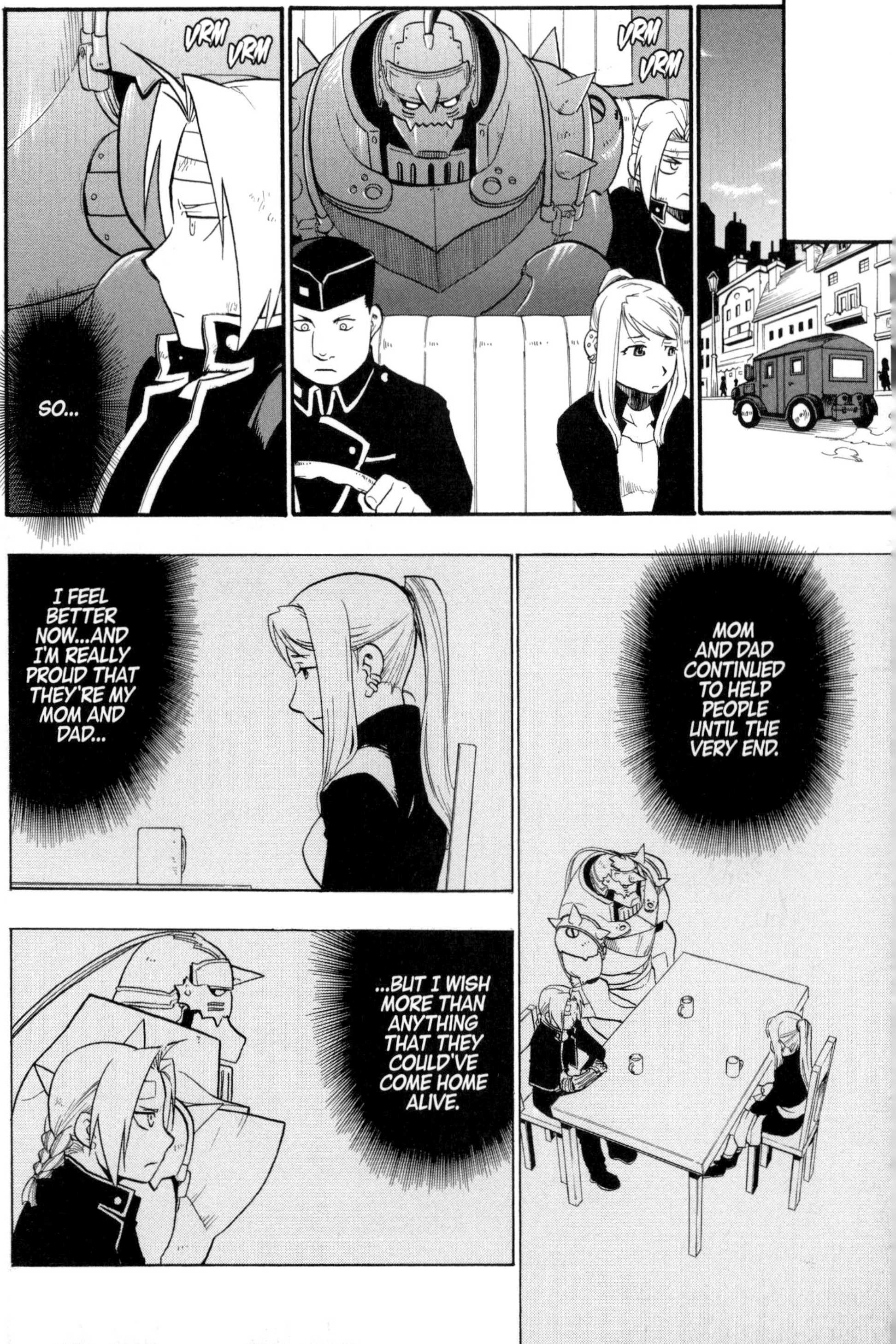
VRM
VRM
VRM
VRM
SO...
MOM AND DAD CONTINUED TO HELP PEOPLE UNTIL THE VERY END.
I FEEL BETTER NOW...AND I'M REALLY PROUD THAT THEY'RE MY MOM AND DAD...
...BUT I WISH MORE THAN ANYTHING THAT THEY COULD'VE COME HOME ALIVE.

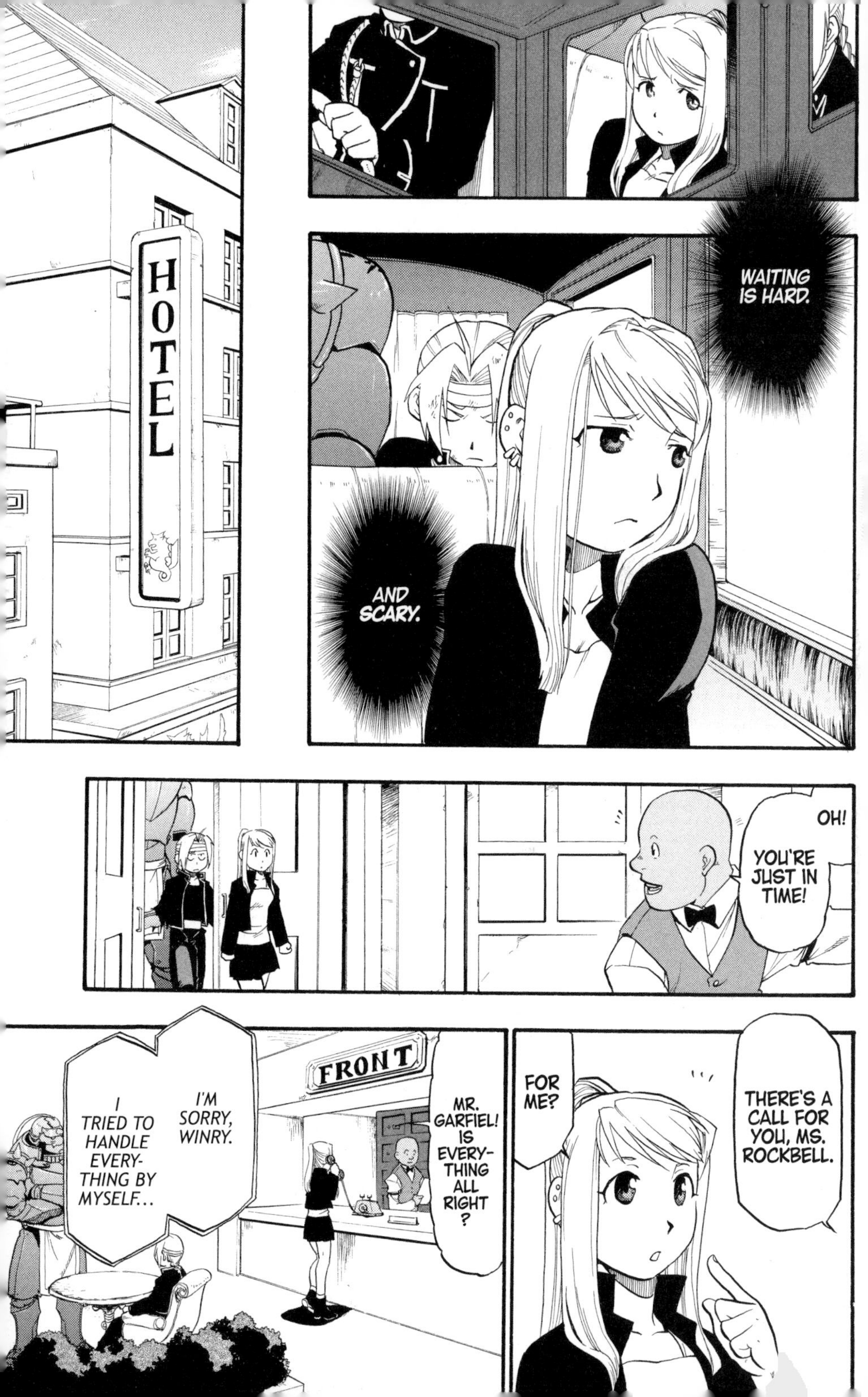
WAITING IS HARD.
AND SCARY.
HOTEL
OH!
YOU'RE JUST IN TIME!
THERE'S A CALL FOR YOU, MS. ROCKBELL.
FOR ME?
FRONT
MR. GARFIEL! IS EVERY-THING ALL RIGHT?
I'M SORRY, WINRY.
I TRIED TO HANDLE EVERY-THING BY MYSELF...

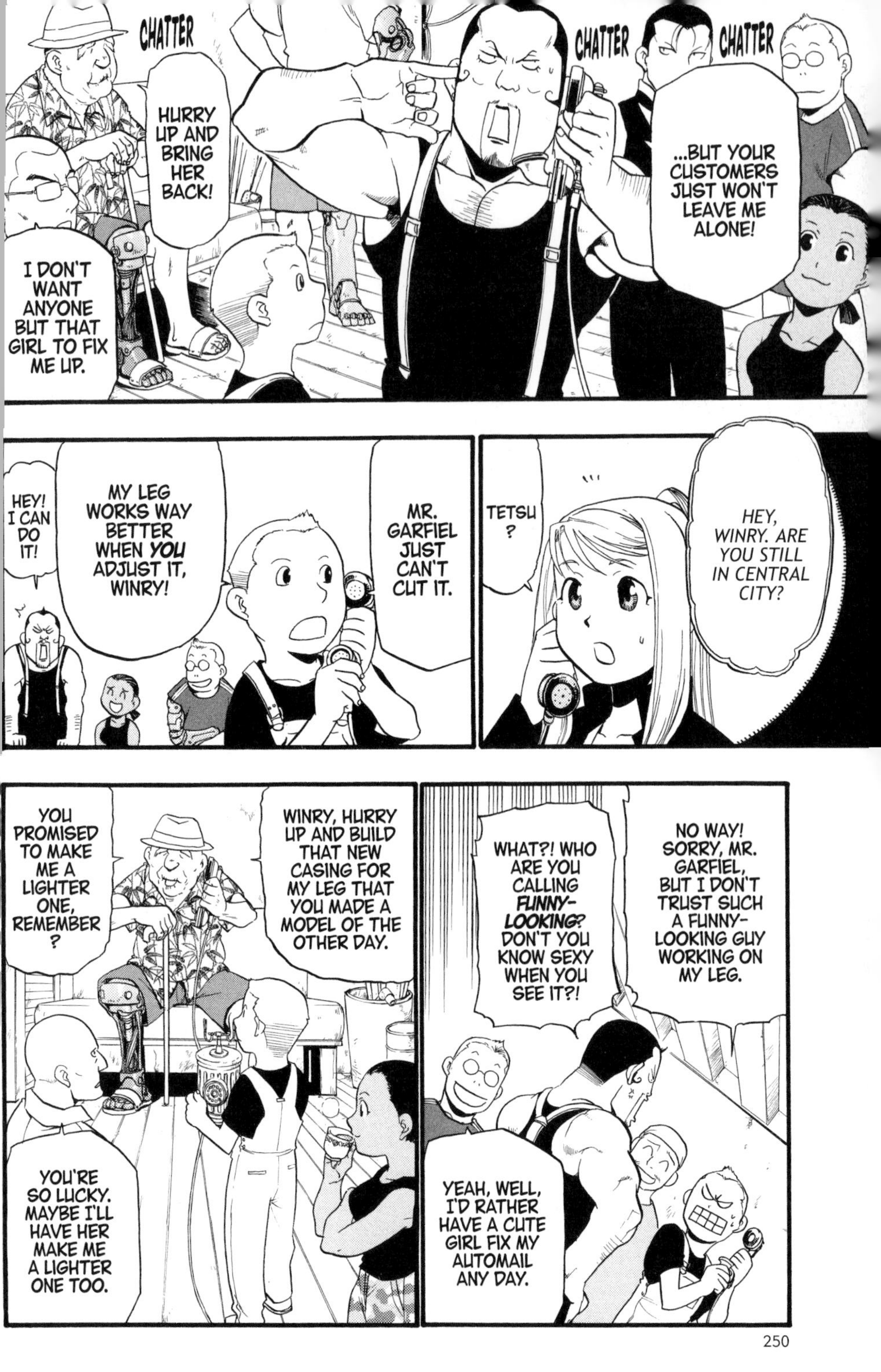
...BUT YOUR CUSTOMERS JUST WON'T LEAVE ME ALONE!
CHATTER
CHATTER
HURRY UP AND BRING HER BACK!
CHATTER
I DON'T WANT ANYONE BUT THAT GIRL TO FIX ME UP.
HEY, WINRY. ARE YOU STILL IN CENTRAL CITY?
TETSU?
MR. GARFIEL JUST CAN'T CUT IT.
MY LEG WORKS WAY BETTER WHEN *YOU* ADJUST IT, WINRY!
HEY! I CAN DO IT!
NO WAY! SORRY, MR. GARFIEL, BUT I DON'T TRUST SUCH A FUNNY-LOOKING GUY WORKING ON MY LEG.
WHAT?! WHO ARE YOU CALLING *FUNNY-LOOKING?* DON'T YOU KNOW SEXY WHEN YOU SEE IT?!
YEAH, WELL, I'D RATHER HAVE A CUTE GIRL FIX MY AUTOMAIL ANY DAY.
WINRY, HURRY UP AND BUILD THAT NEW CASING FOR MY LEG THAT YOU MADE A MODEL OF THE OTHER DAY.
YOU PROMISED TO MAKE ME A LIGHTER ONE, REMEMBER?
YOU'RE SO LUCKY. MAYBE I'LL HAVE HER MAKE ME A LIGHTER ONE TOO.

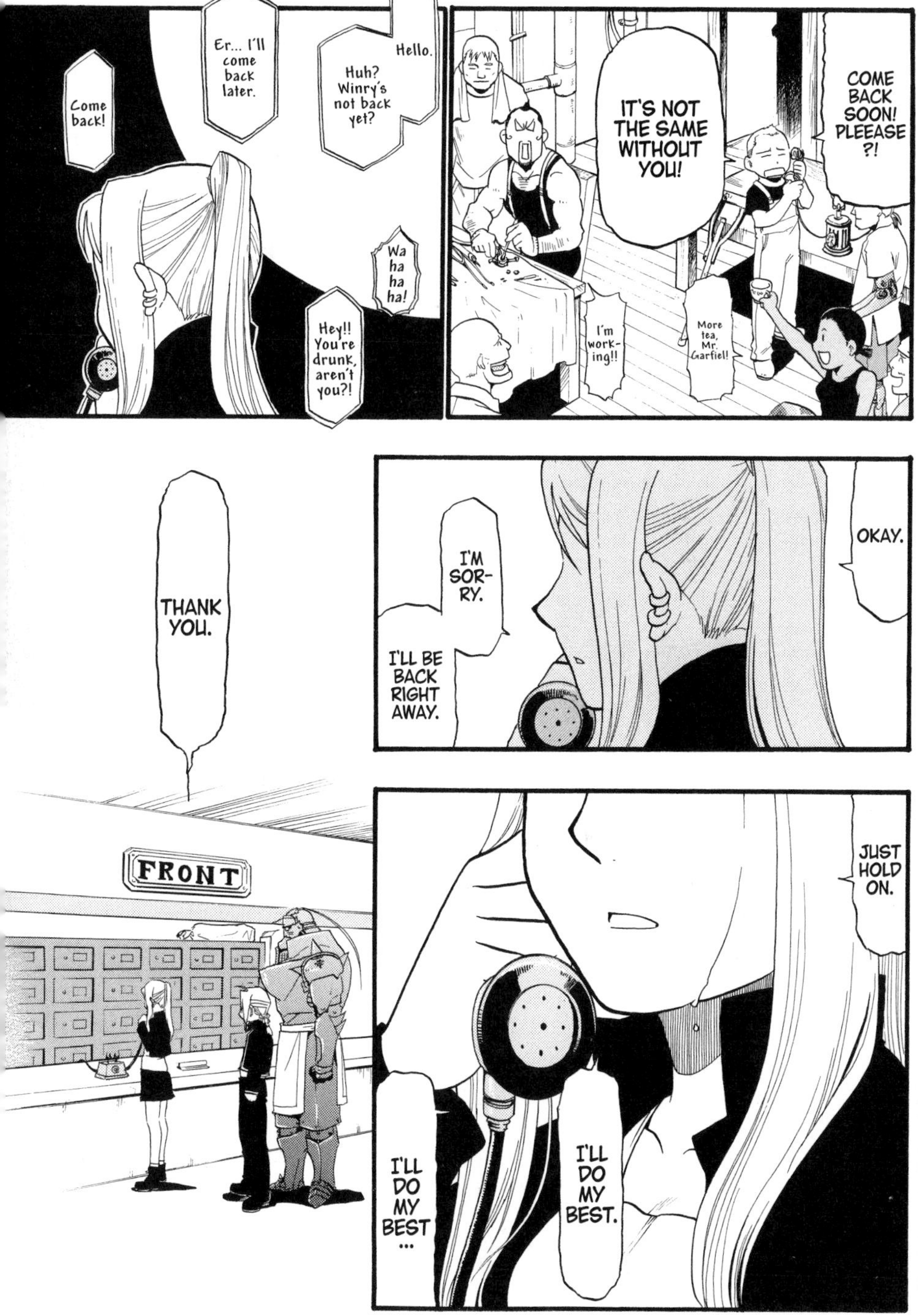
COME BACK SOON! PLEASE?!
IT'S NOT THE SAME WITHOUT YOU!
More tea, Mr. Garfiel!
I'm working!!
Hello.
Huh? Winry's not back yet?
Er... I'll come back later.
Come back!
Wa ha ha ha!
Hey!! You're drunk, aren't you?!
OKAY.
I'M SORRY.
I'LL BE BACK RIGHT AWAY.
JUST HOLD ON.
I'LL DO MY BEST.
I'LL DO MY BEST...
THANK YOU.
FRONT

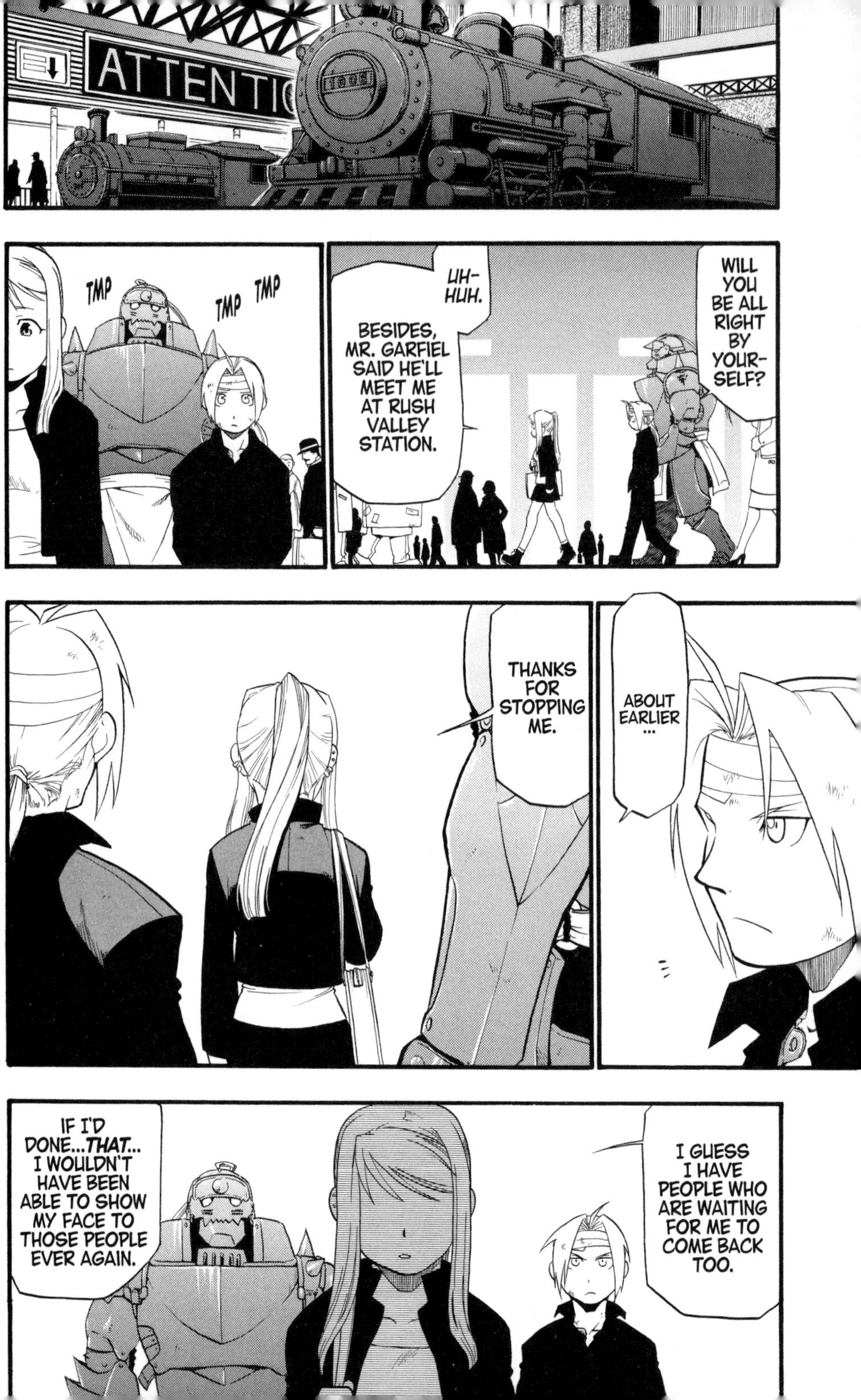
WILL YOU BE ALL RIGHT BY YOURSELF?
UH-HUH.
BESIDES, MR. GARFIEL SAID HE'LL MEET ME AT RUSH VALLEY STATION.
TMP TMP
TMP
ABOUT EARLIER...
THANKS FOR STOPPING ME.
I GUESS I HAVE PEOPLE WHO ARE WAITING FOR ME TO COME BACK TOO.
IF I'D DONE...*THAT*... I WOULDN'T HAVE BEEN ABLE TO SHOW MY FACE TO THOSE PEOPLE EVER AGAIN.

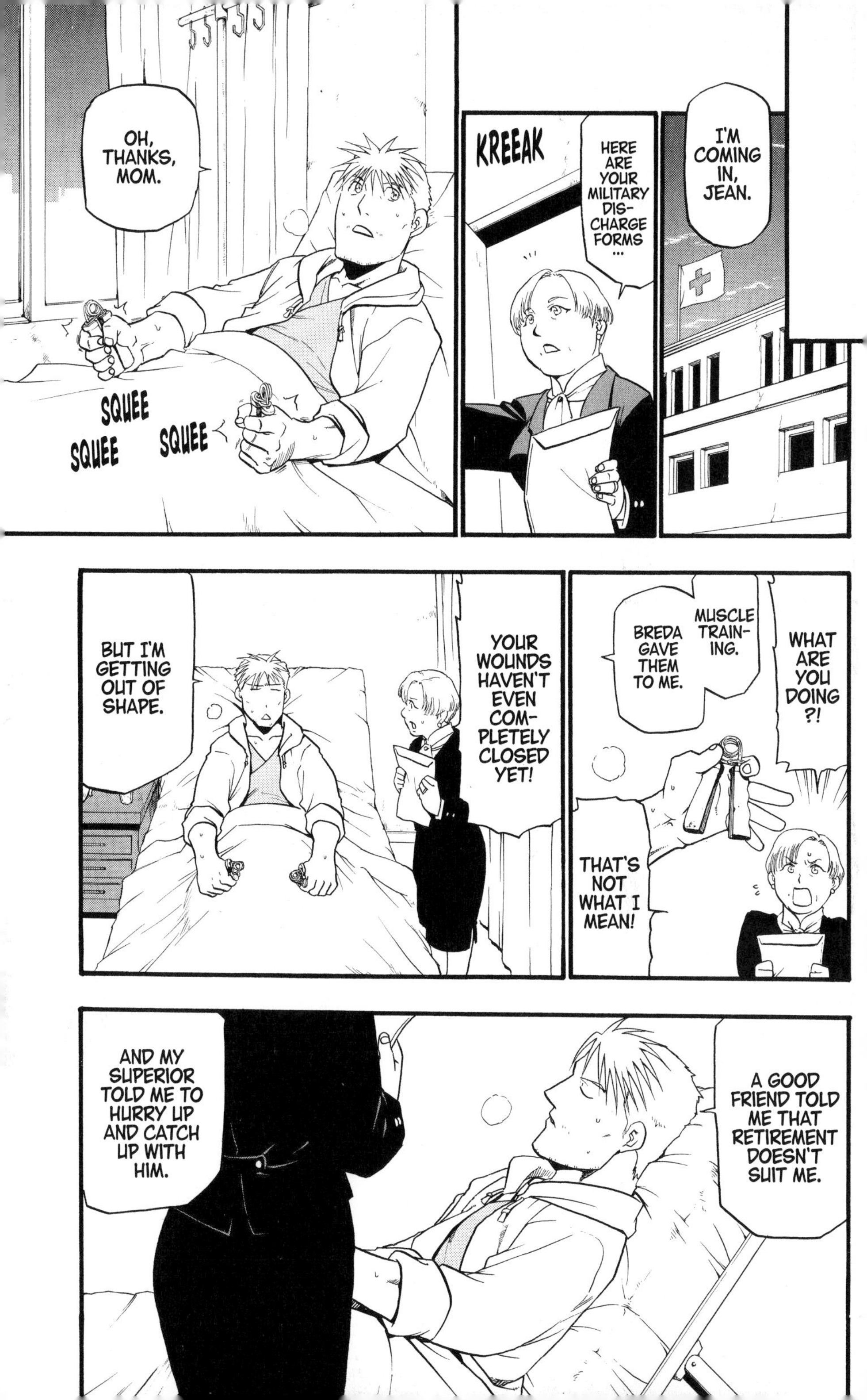
I'M COMING IN, JEAN.
KREEAK
HERE ARE YOUR MILITARY DISCHARGE FORMS ...
OH, THANKS, MOM.
SQUEE
SQUEE
SQUEE
WHAT ARE YOU DOING?!
MUSCLE TRAINING.
BREDA GAVE THEM TO ME.
THAT'S NOT WHAT I MEAN!
YOUR WOUNDS HAVEN'T EVEN COMPLETELY CLOSED YET!
BUT I'M GETTING OUT OF SHAPE.
A GOOD FRIEND TOLD ME THAT RETIREMENT DOESN'T SUIT ME.
AND MY SUPERIOR TOLD ME TO HURRY UP AND CATCH UP WITH HIM.

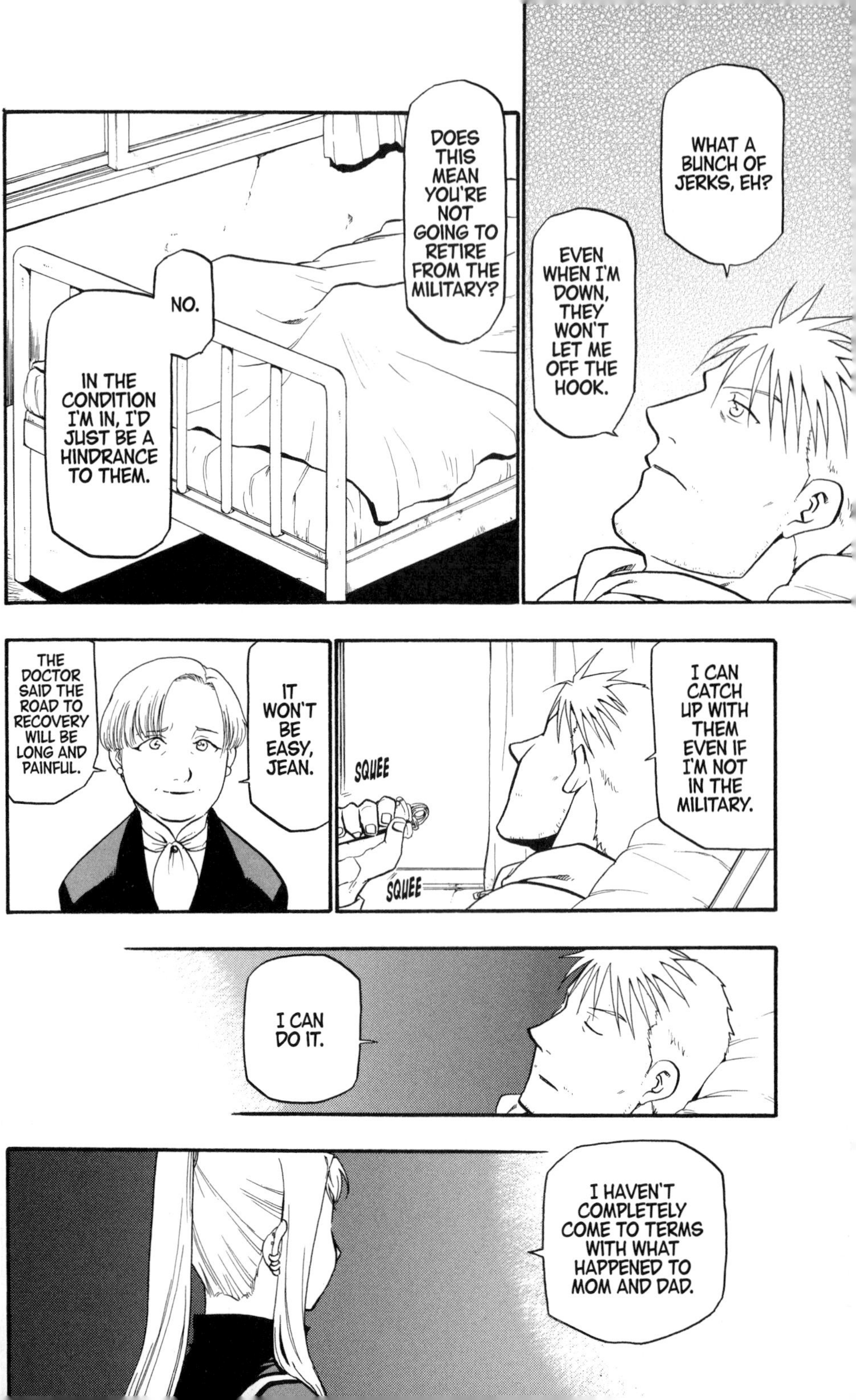
WHAT A BUNCH OF JERKS, EH?
EVEN WHEN I'M DOWN, THEY WON'T LET ME OFF THE HOOK.
DOES THIS MEAN YOU'RE NOT GOING TO RETIRE FROM THE MILITARY?
NO.
IN THE CONDITION I'M IN, I'D JUST BE A HINDRANCE TO THEM.
I CAN CATCH UP WITH THEM EVEN IF I'M NOT IN THE MILITARY.
SQUEE
SQUEE
IT WON'T BE EASY, JEAN.
THE DOCTOR SAID THE ROAD TO RECOVERY WILL BE LONG AND PAINFUL.
I CAN DO IT.
I HAVEN'T COMPLETELY COME TO TERMS WITH WHAT HAPPENED TO MOM AND DAD.

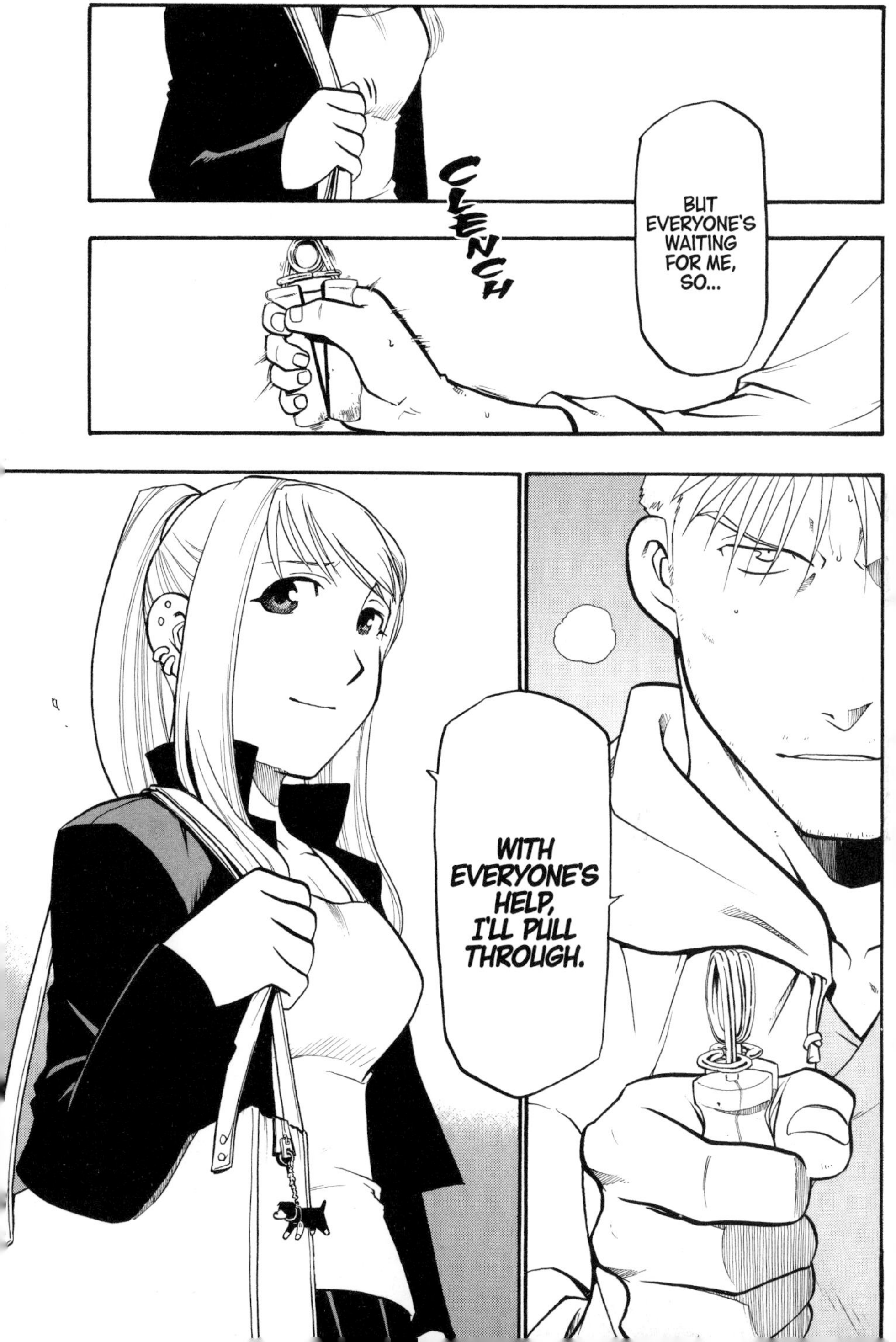
BUT EVERYONE'S WAITING FOR ME, SO...
CLENCH
WITH EVERYONE'S HELP, I'LL PULL THROUGH.

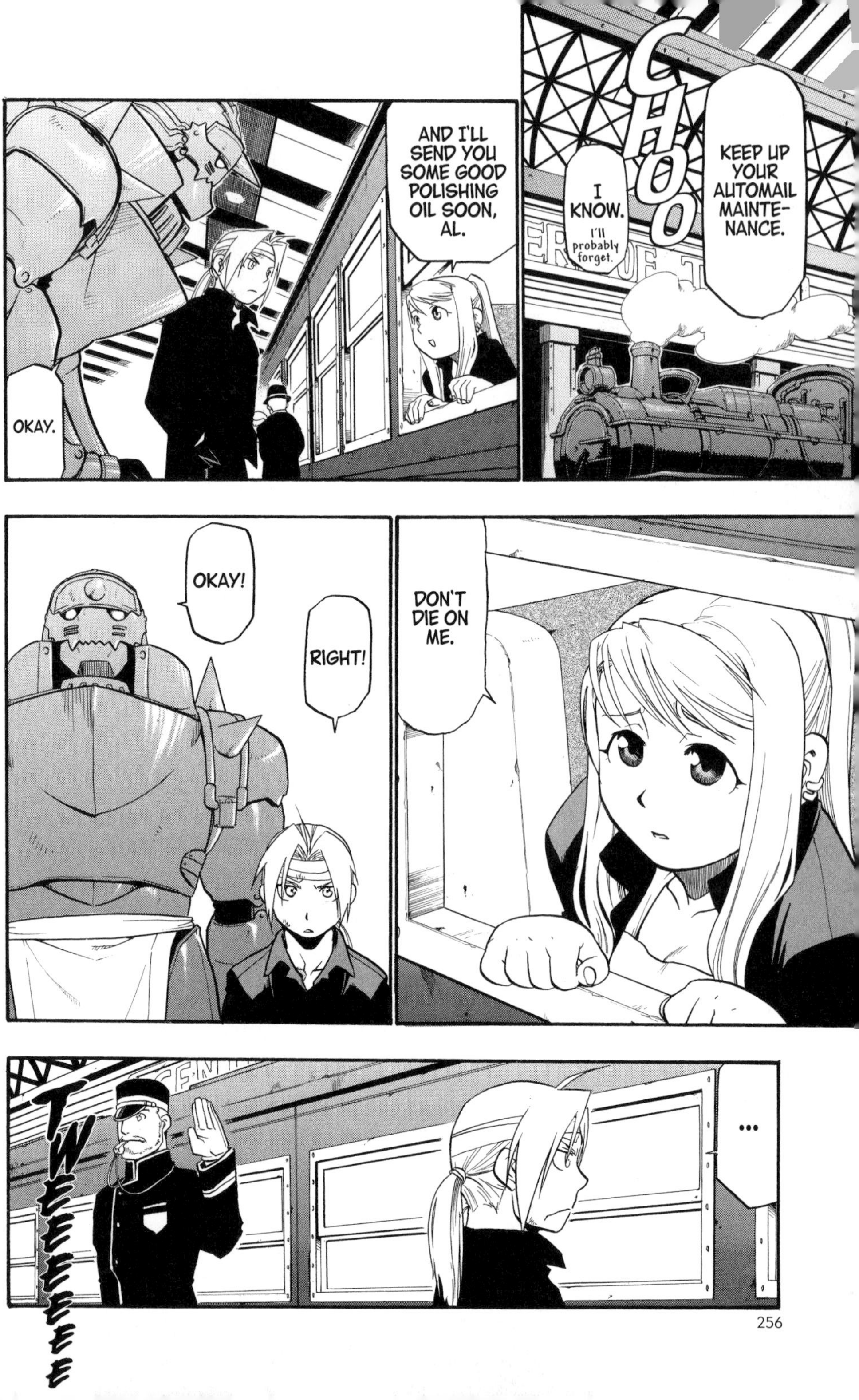
KEEP UP YOUR AUTOMAIL MAINTENANCE.
CHOO
I KNOW.
I'll probably forget.
AND I'LL SEND YOU SOME GOOD POLISHING OIL SOON, AL.
OKAY.
DON'T DIE ON ME.
OKAY!
RIGHT!
...
TWEEEEEEE

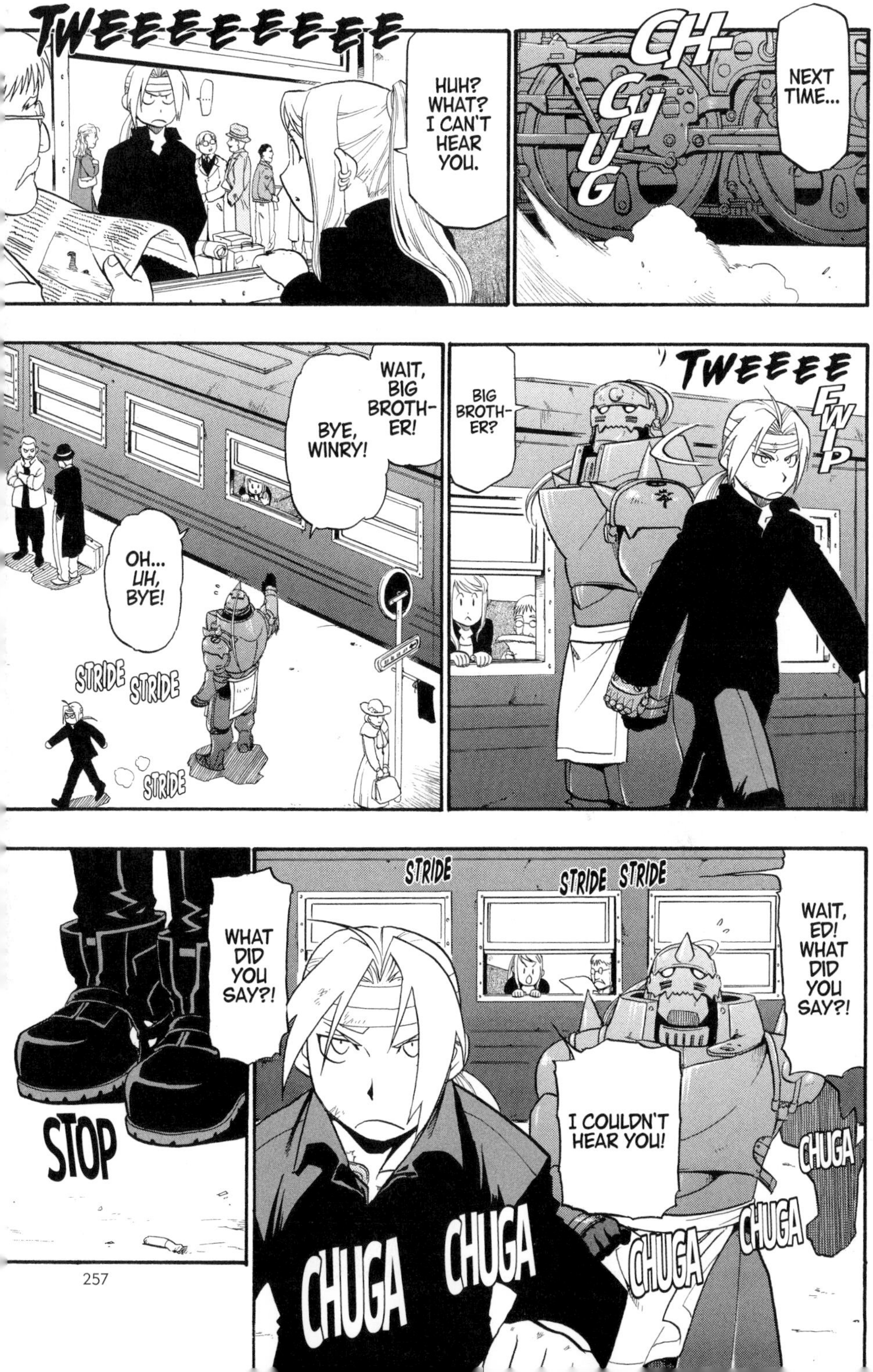
NEXT TIME...
CH-CHUG
TWEEEEEEEEEE
...
HUH? WHAT? I CAN'T HEAR YOU.
TWEEEEE
FWIP
BIG BROTHER?
WAIT, BIG BROTHER!
BYE, WINRY!
OH... UH, BYE!
STRIDE STRIDE
STRIDE
STRIDE
STRIDE STRIDE
WAIT, ED! WHAT DID YOU SAY?!
WHAT DID YOU SAY?!
I COULDN'T HEAR YOU!
CHUGA
CHUGA
CHUGA
CHUGA
CHUGA
STOP

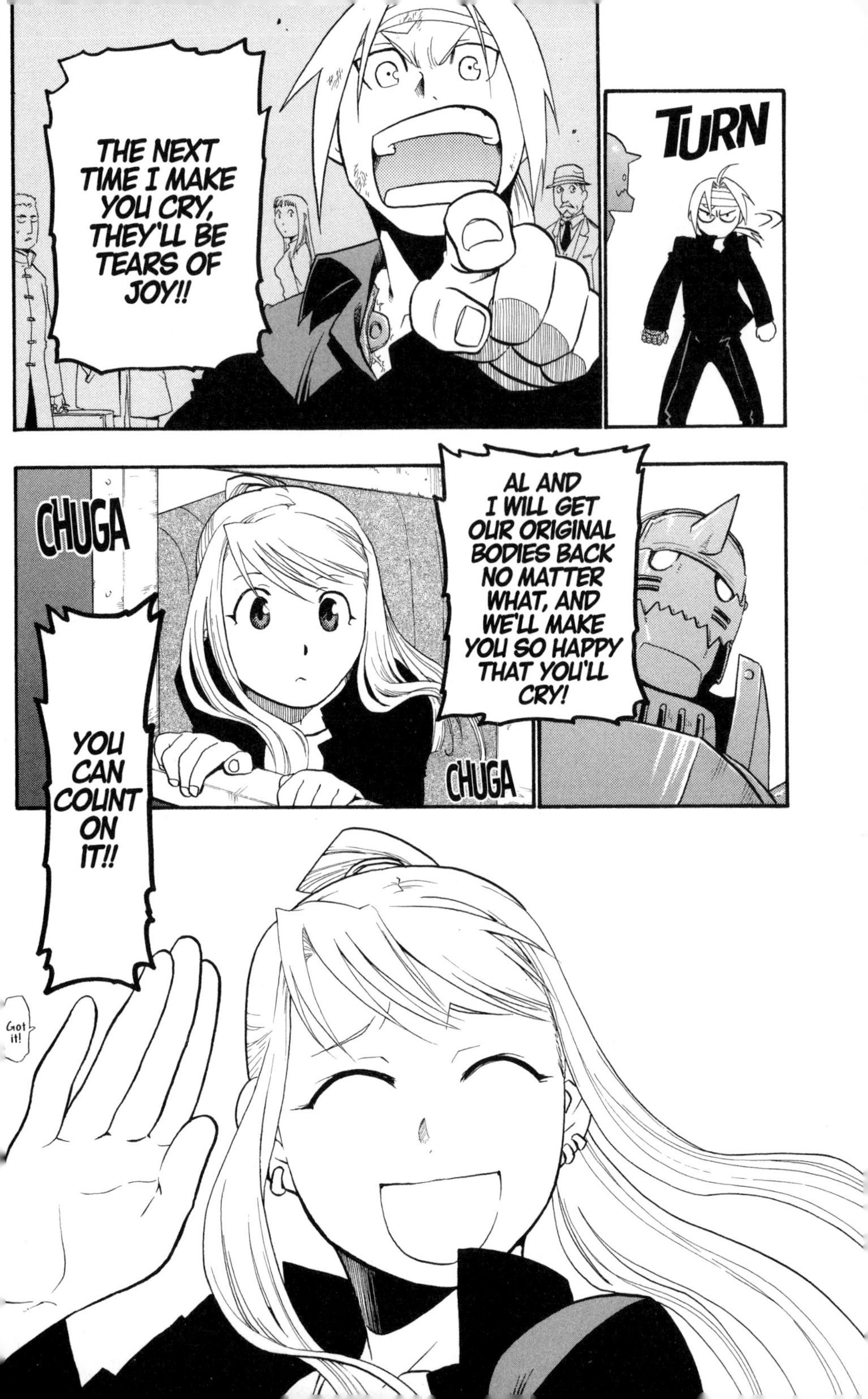
TURN
THE NEXT TIME I MAKE YOU CRY, THEY'LL BE TEARS OF JOY!!
AL AND I WILL GET OUR ORIGINAL BODIES BACK NO MATTER WHAT, AND WE'LL MAKE YOU SO HAPPY THAT YOU'LL CRY!
CHUGA
CHUGA
YOU CAN COUNT ON IT!!
Got it!

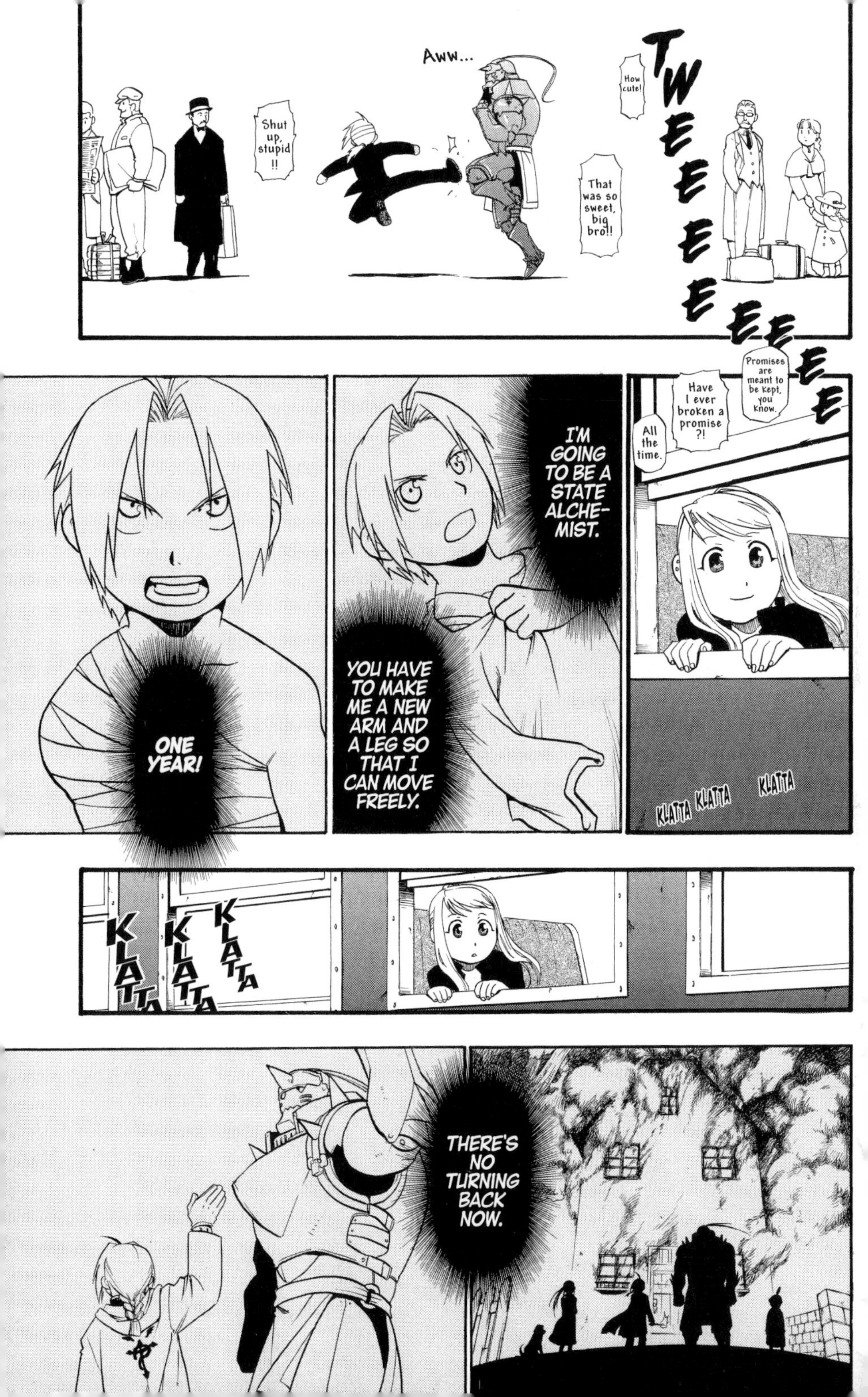

TWEEEEEEEEE
How cute!
Aww...
That was so sweet, big bro!!
Shut up, stupid!!
Promises are meant to be kept, you know.
Have I ever broken a promise?!
All the time.
KLATTA KLATTA KLATTA
I'M GOING TO BE A STATE ALCHEMIST.
YOU HAVE TO MAKE ME A NEW ARM AND A LEG SO THAT I CAN MOVE FREELY.
ONE YEAR!
KLATTA KLATTA KLATTA
THERE'S NO TURNING BACK NOW.

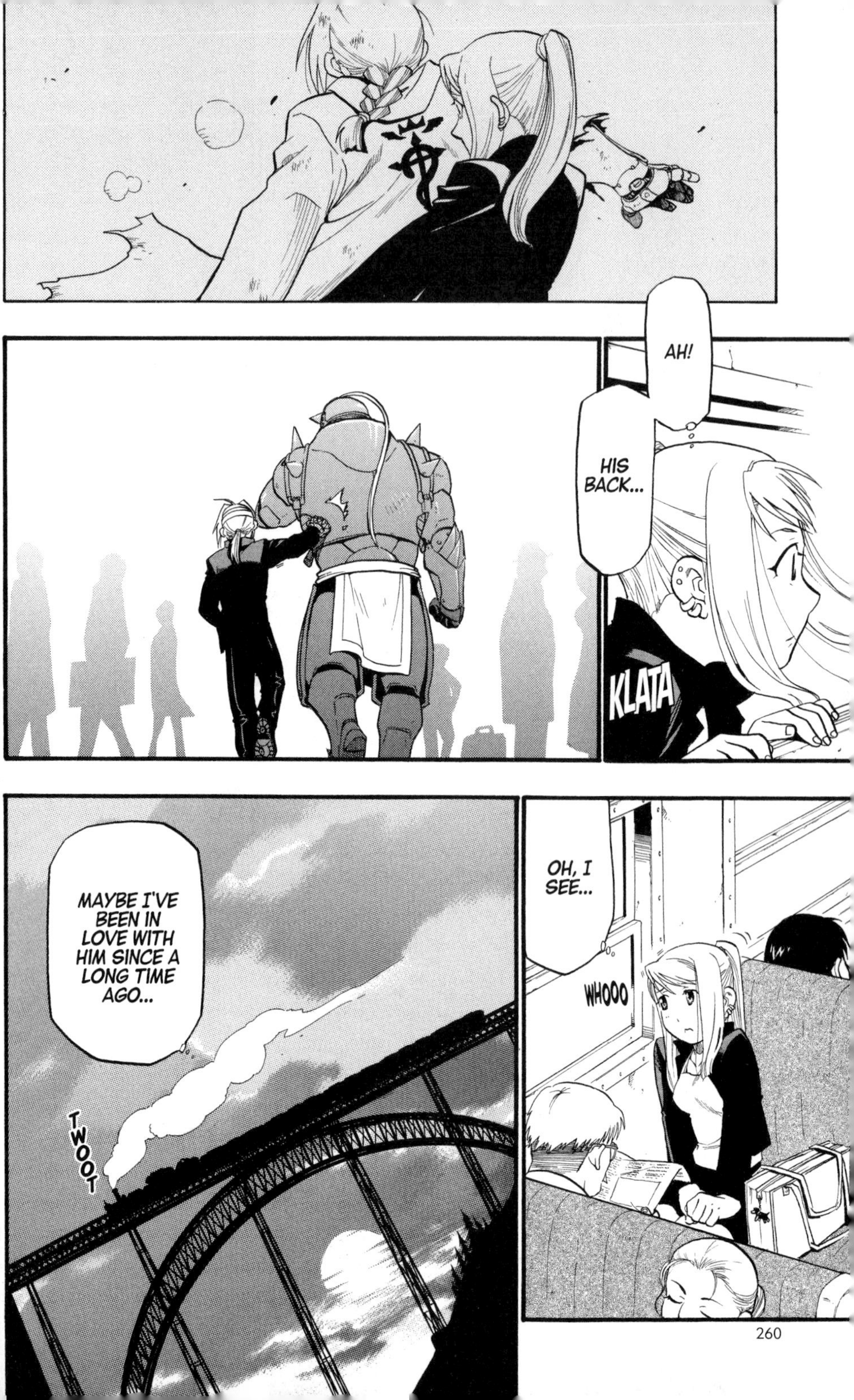
AH!
HIS BACK...
KLATA
OH, I SEE...
WHOOO
MAYBE I'VE BEEN IN LOVE WITH HIM SINCE A LONG TIME AGO...
TWOOT

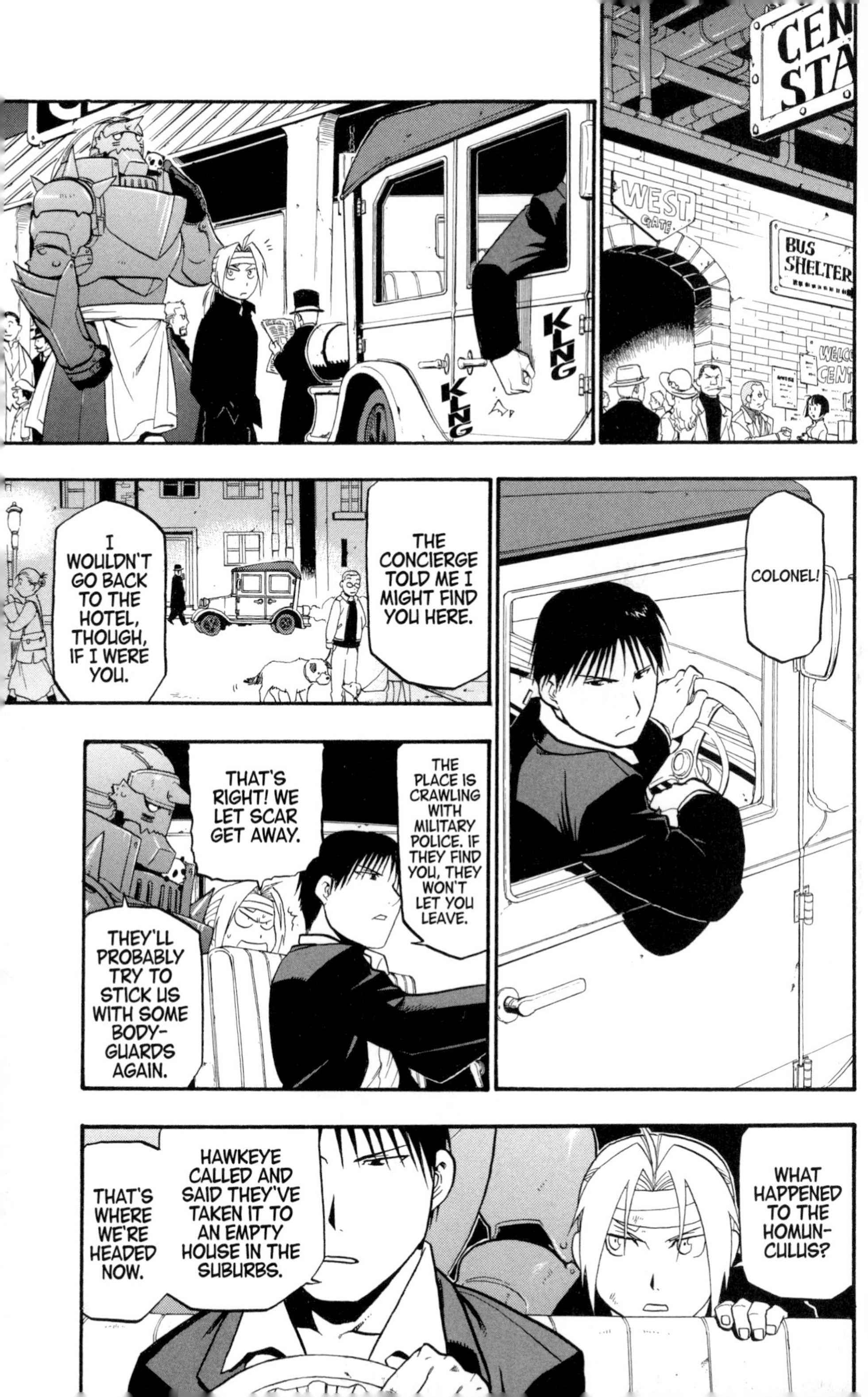
CEN
STA
WEST
GATE
BUS SHELTER
WELCO
CENT
KLNG
KLNG
COLONEL!
THE CONCIERGE TOLD ME I MIGHT FIND YOU HERE.
I WOULDN'T GO BACK TO THE HOTEL, THOUGH, IF I WERE YOU.
THE PLACE IS CRAWLING WITH MILITARY POLICE. IF THEY FIND YOU, THEY WON'T LET YOU LEAVE.
THAT'S RIGHT! WE LET SCAR GET AWAY.
THEY'LL PROBABLY TRY TO STICK US WITH SOME BODY-GUARDS AGAIN.
WHAT HAPPENED TO THE HOMUN-CULUS?
HAWKEYE CALLED AND SAID THEY'VE TAKEN IT TO AN EMPTY HOUSE IN THE SUBURBS.
THAT'S WHERE WE'RE HEADED NOW.

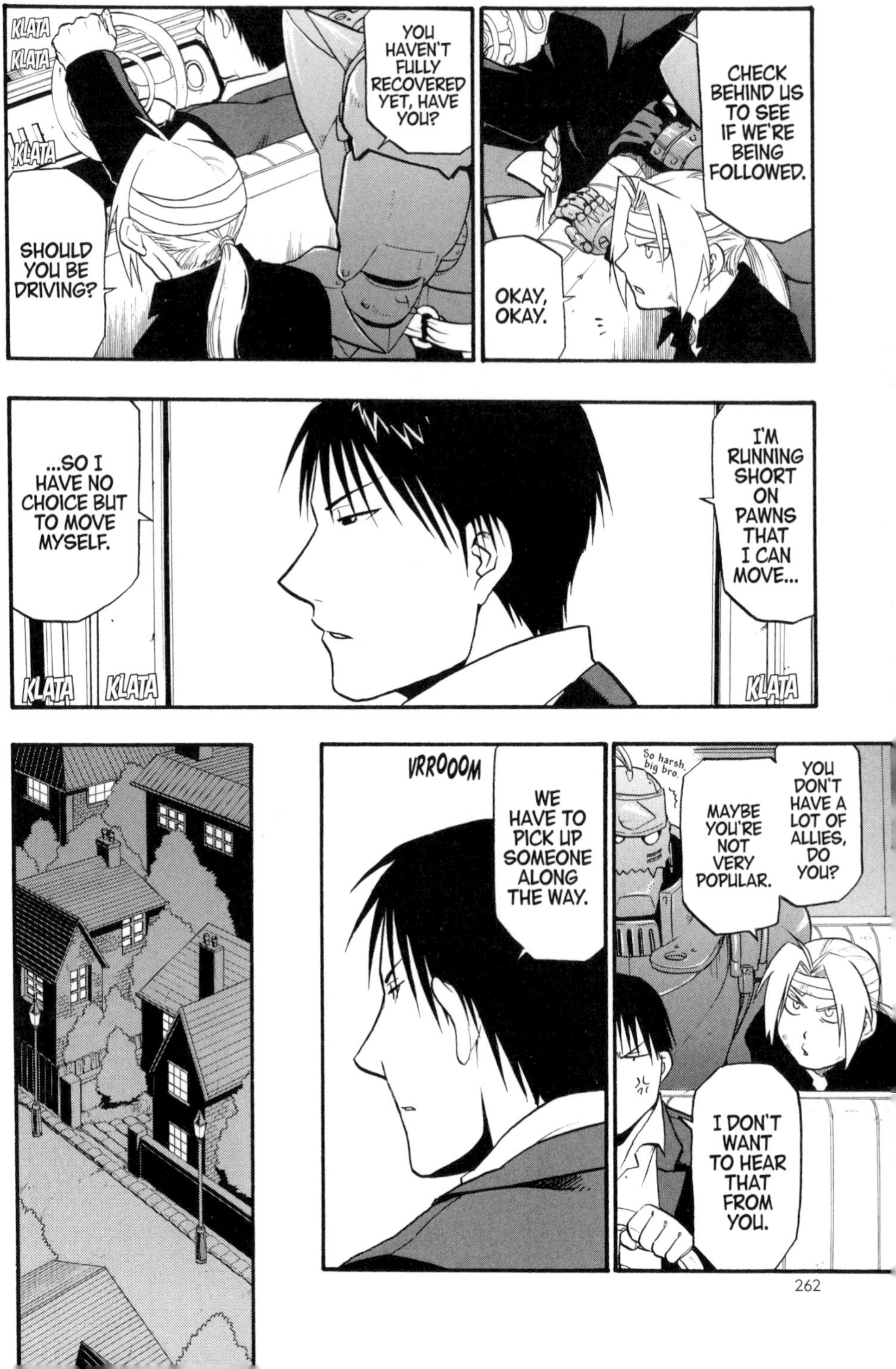
CHECK BEHIND US TO SEE IF WE'RE BEING FOLLOWED.
OKAY, OKAY.
KLATA
KLATA
YOU HAVEN'T FULLY RECOVERED YET, HAVE YOU?
KLATA
SHOULD YOU BE DRIVING?
I'M RUNNING SHORT ON PAWNS THAT I CAN MOVE...
KLATA
...SO I HAVE NO CHOICE BUT TO MOVE MYSELF.
KLATA
KLATA
YOU DON'T HAVE A LOT OF ALLIES, DO YOU?
MAYBE YOU'RE NOT VERY POPULAR.
So harsh, big bro.
I DON'T WANT TO HEAR THAT FROM YOU.
VRROOOM
WE HAVE TO PICK UP SOMEONE ALONG THE WAY.

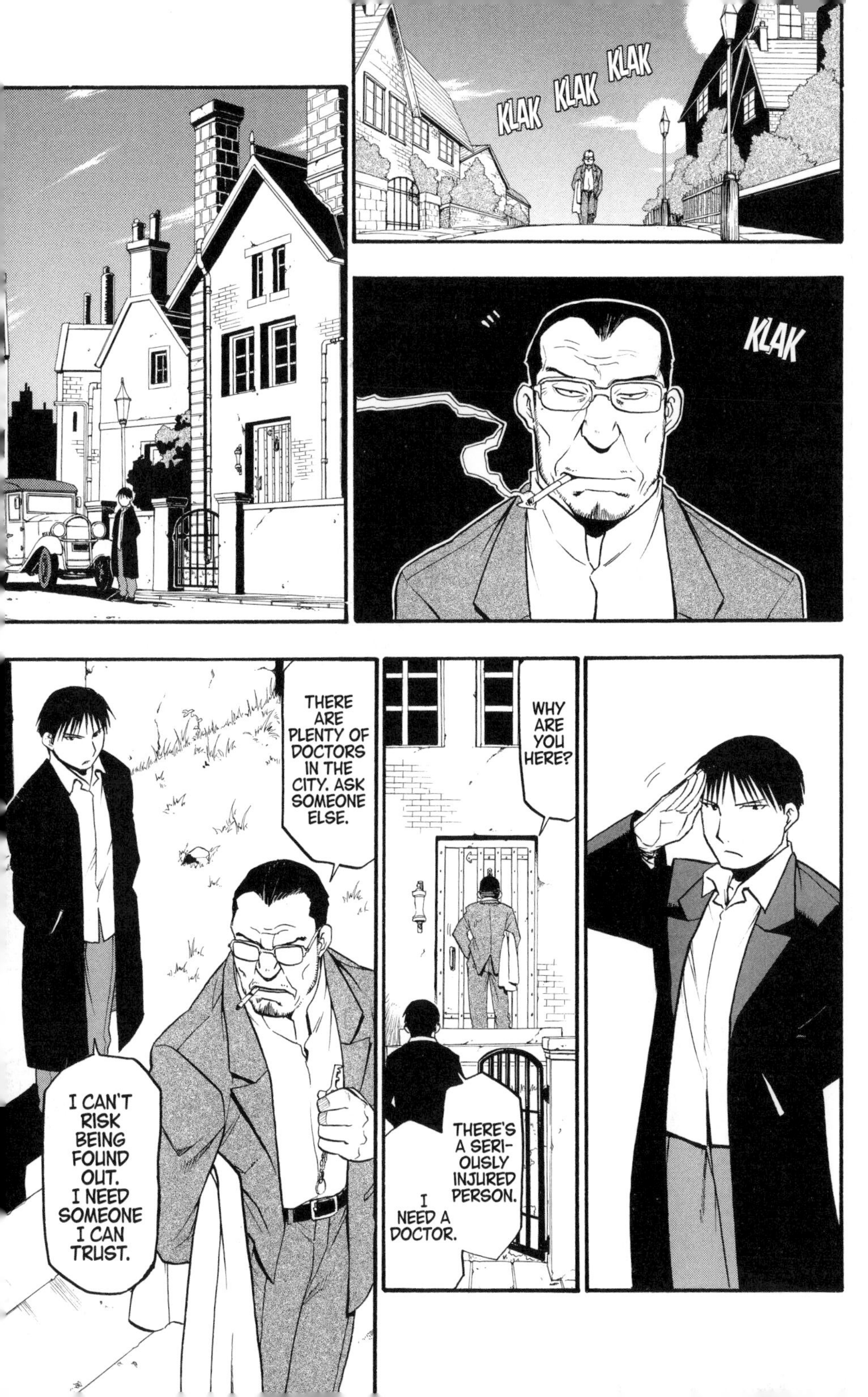
KLAK KLAK KLAK
KLAK
WHY ARE YOU HERE?
THERE'S A SERIOUSLY INJURED PERSON.
I NEED A DOCTOR.
THERE ARE PLENTY OF DOCTORS IN THE CITY. ASK SOMEONE ELSE.
I CAN'T RISK BEING FOUND OUT. I NEED SOMEONE I CAN TRUST.

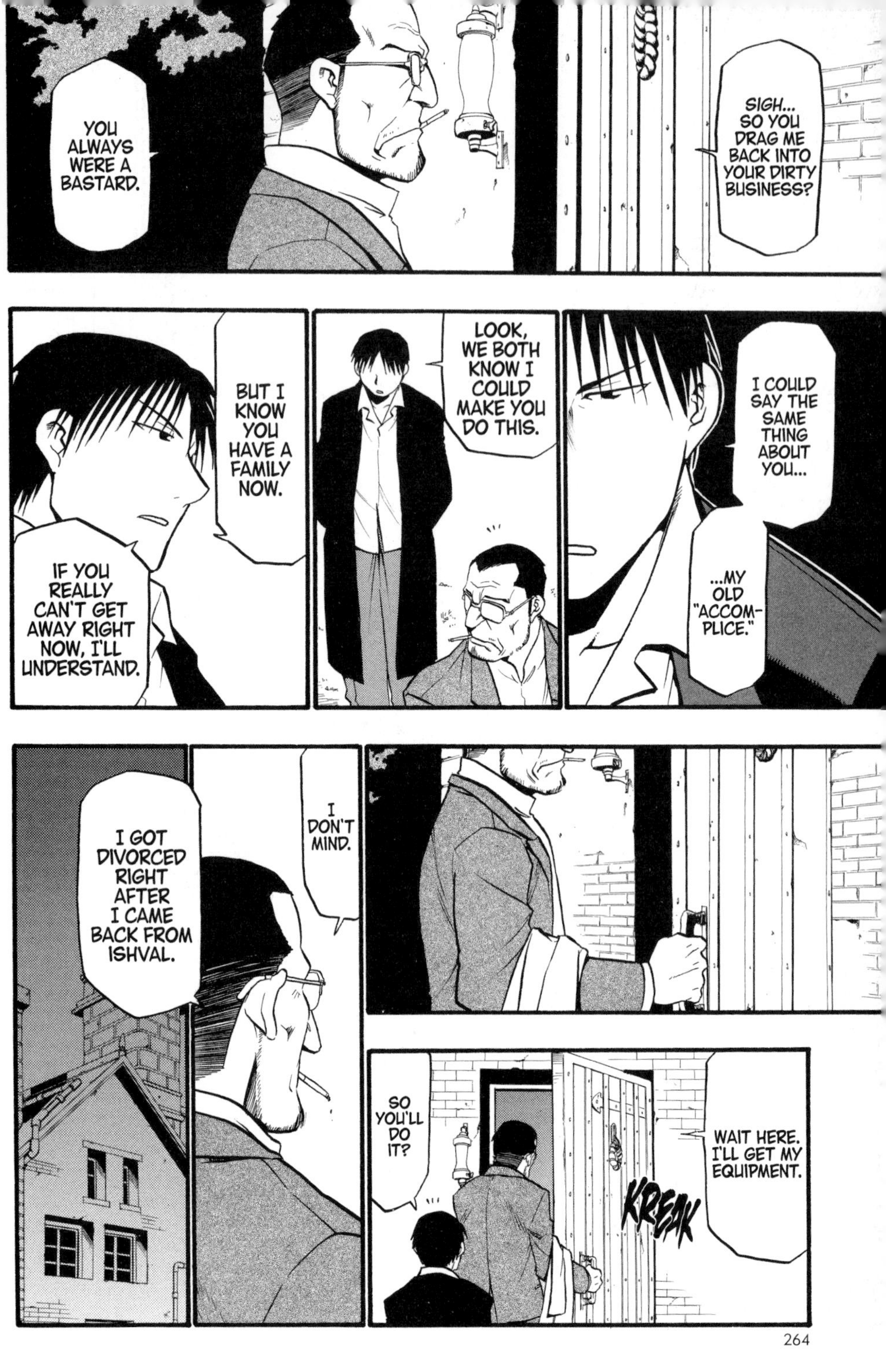
SIGH... SO YOU DRAG ME BACK INTO YOUR DIRTY BUSINESS?
YOU ALWAYS WERE A BASTARD.
I COULD SAY THE SAME THING ABOUT YOU...
...MY OLD "ACCOMPLICE."
LOOK, WE BOTH KNOW I COULD MAKE YOU DO THIS.
BUT I KNOW YOU HAVE A FAMILY NOW.
IF YOU REALLY CAN'T GET AWAY RIGHT NOW, I'LL UNDERSTAND.
WAIT HERE. I'LL GET MY EQUIPMENT.
KREAK
SO YOU'LL DO IT?
I DON'T MIND.
I GOT DIVORCED RIGHT AFTER I CAME BACK FROM ISHVAL.

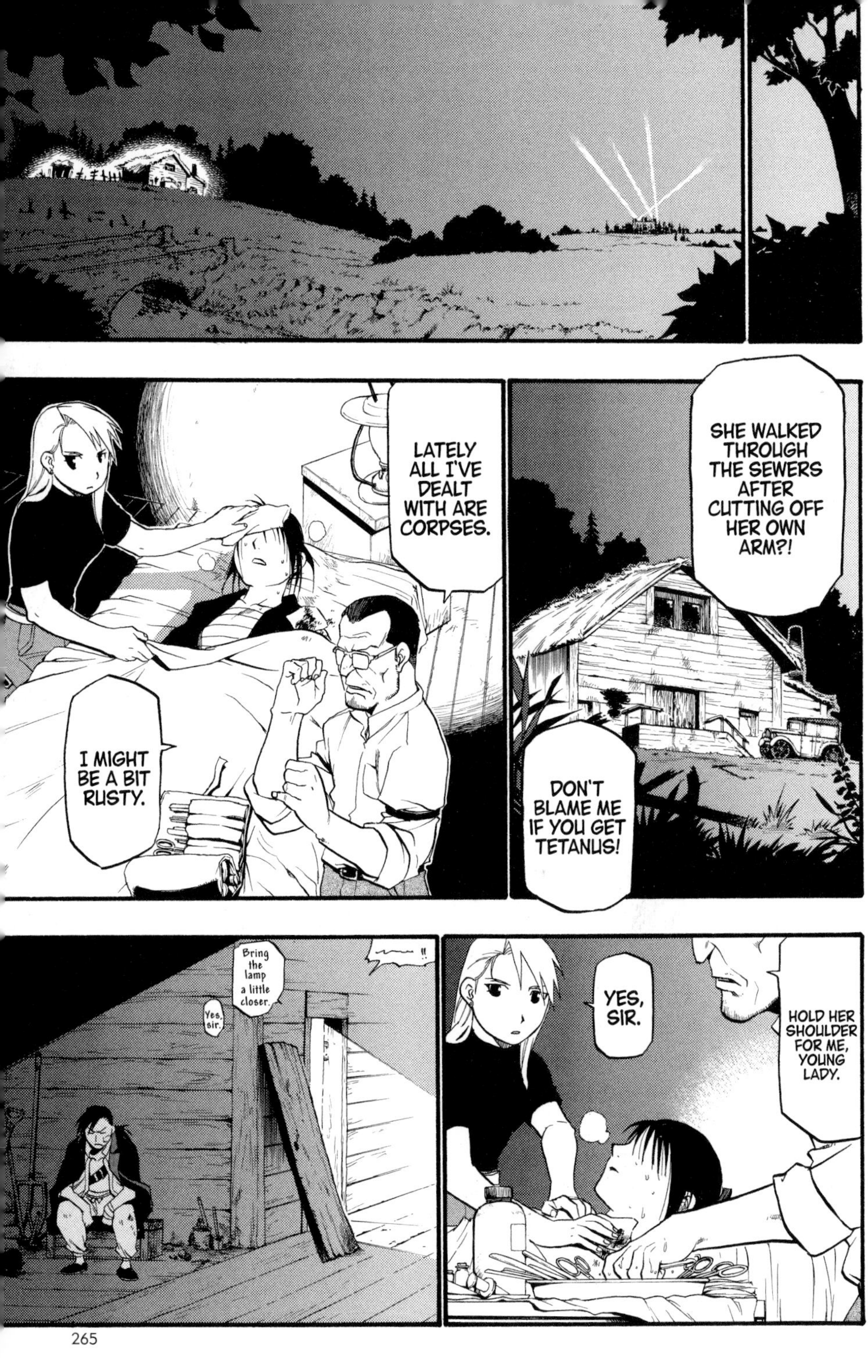
SHE WALKED THROUGH THE SEWERS AFTER CUTTING OFF HER OWN ARM?!
DON'T BLAME ME IF YOU GET TETANUS!
LATELY ALL I'VE DEALT WITH ARE CORPSES.
I MIGHT BE A BIT RUSTY.
HOLD HER SHOULDER FOR ME, YOUNG LADY.
YES, SIR.
——!!
Bring the lamp a little closer.
Yes, sir.

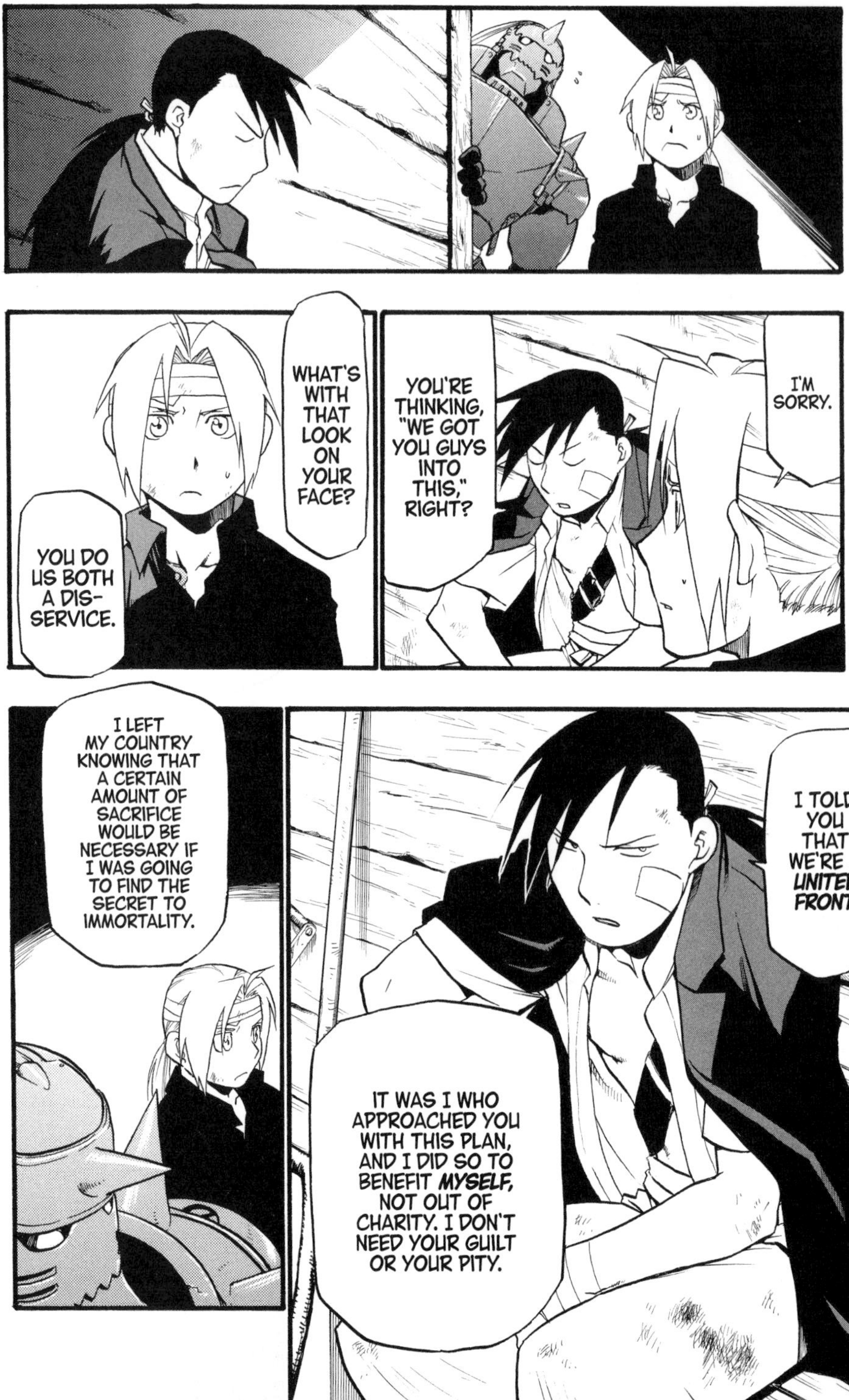
I'M SORRY.
YOU'RE THINKING, "WE GOT YOU GUYS INTO THIS," RIGHT?
WHAT'S WITH THAT LOOK ON YOUR FACE?
YOU DO US BOTH A DIS-SERVICE.
I TOLD YOU THAT WE'RE A *UNITED FRONT.*
IT WAS I WHO APPROACHED YOU WITH THIS PLAN, AND I DID SO TO BENEFIT *MYSELF,* NOT OUT OF CHARITY. I DON'T NEED YOUR GUILT OR YOUR PITY.
I LEFT MY COUNTRY KNOWING THAT A CERTAIN AMOUNT OF SACRIFICE WOULD BE NECESSARY IF I WAS GOING TO FIND THE SECRET TO IMMORTALITY.

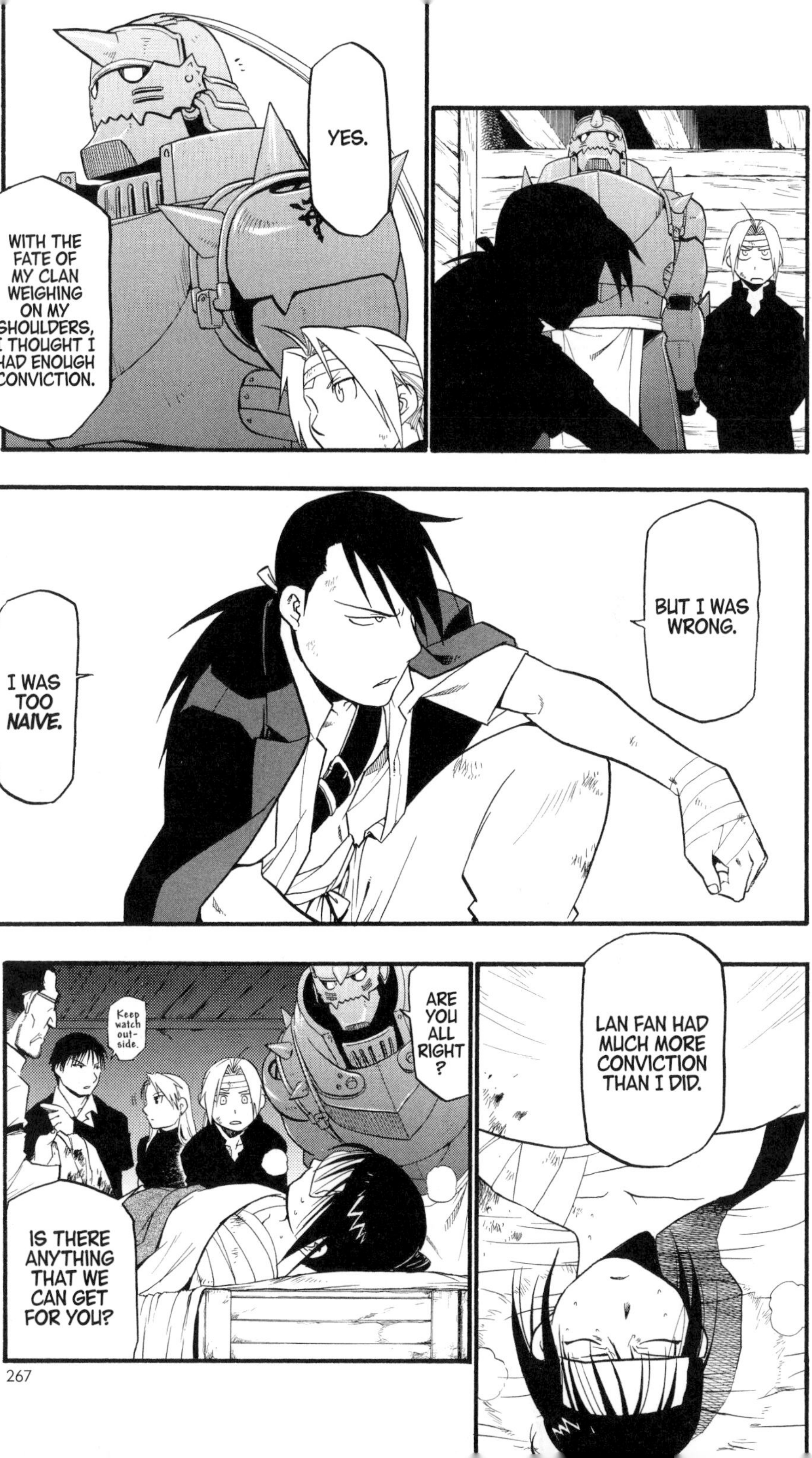
YES.
WITH THE FATE OF MY CLAN WEIGHING ON MY SHOULDERS, I THOUGHT I HAD ENOUGH CONVICTION.
BUT I WAS WRONG.
I WAS TOO *NAIVE*.
LAN FAN HAD MUCH MORE CONVICTION THAN I DID.
ARE YOU ALL RIGHT?
Keep watch outside.
IS THERE ANYTHING THAT WE CAN GET FOR YOU?

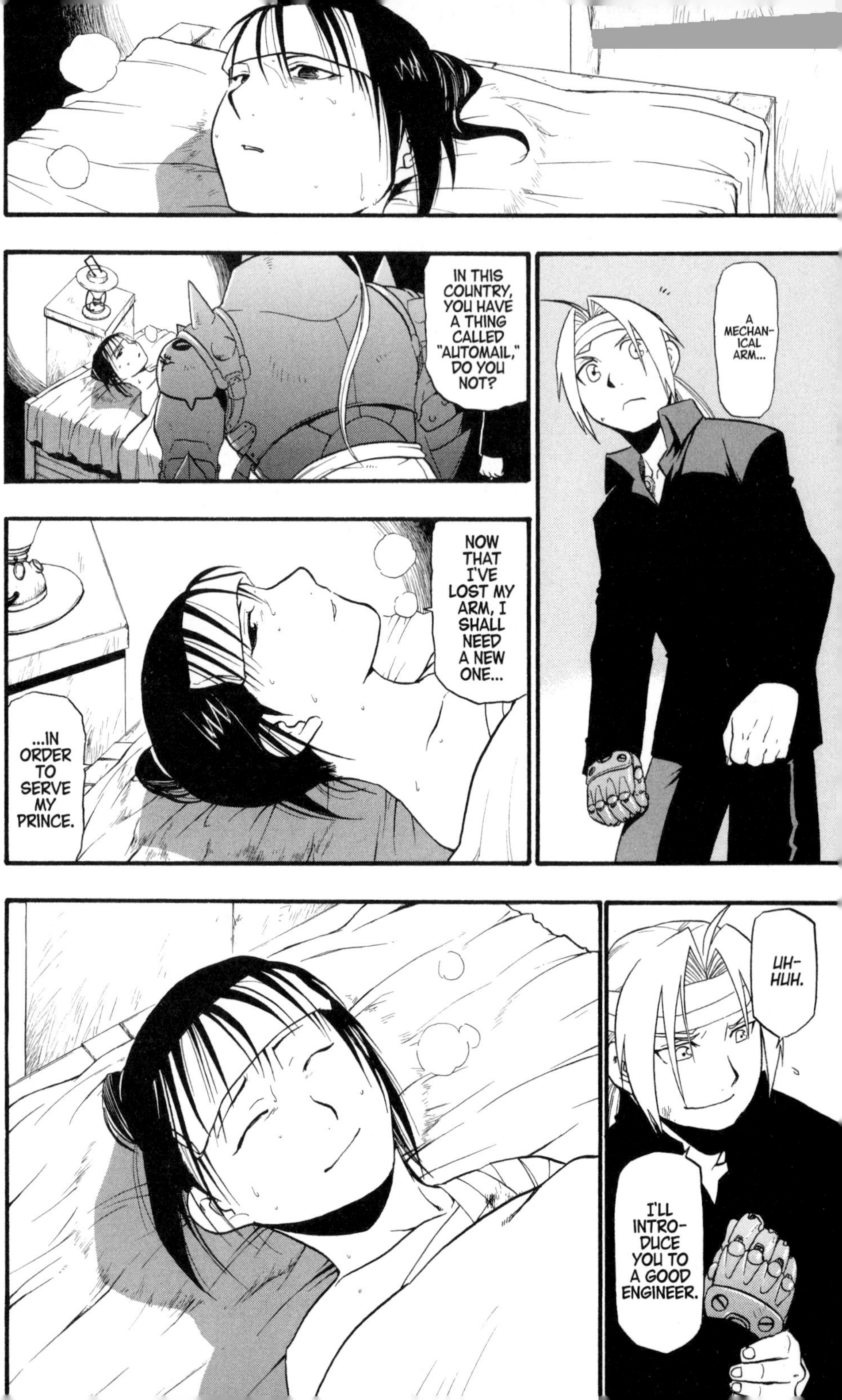
A MECHANICAL ARM...
IN THIS COUNTRY, YOU HAVE A THING CALLED "AUTOMAIL," DO YOU NOT?
NOW THAT I'VE LOST MY ARM, I SHALL NEED A NEW ONE...
...IN ORDER TO SERVE MY PRINCE.
UH-HUH.
I'LL INTRODUCE YOU TO A GOOD ENGINEER.

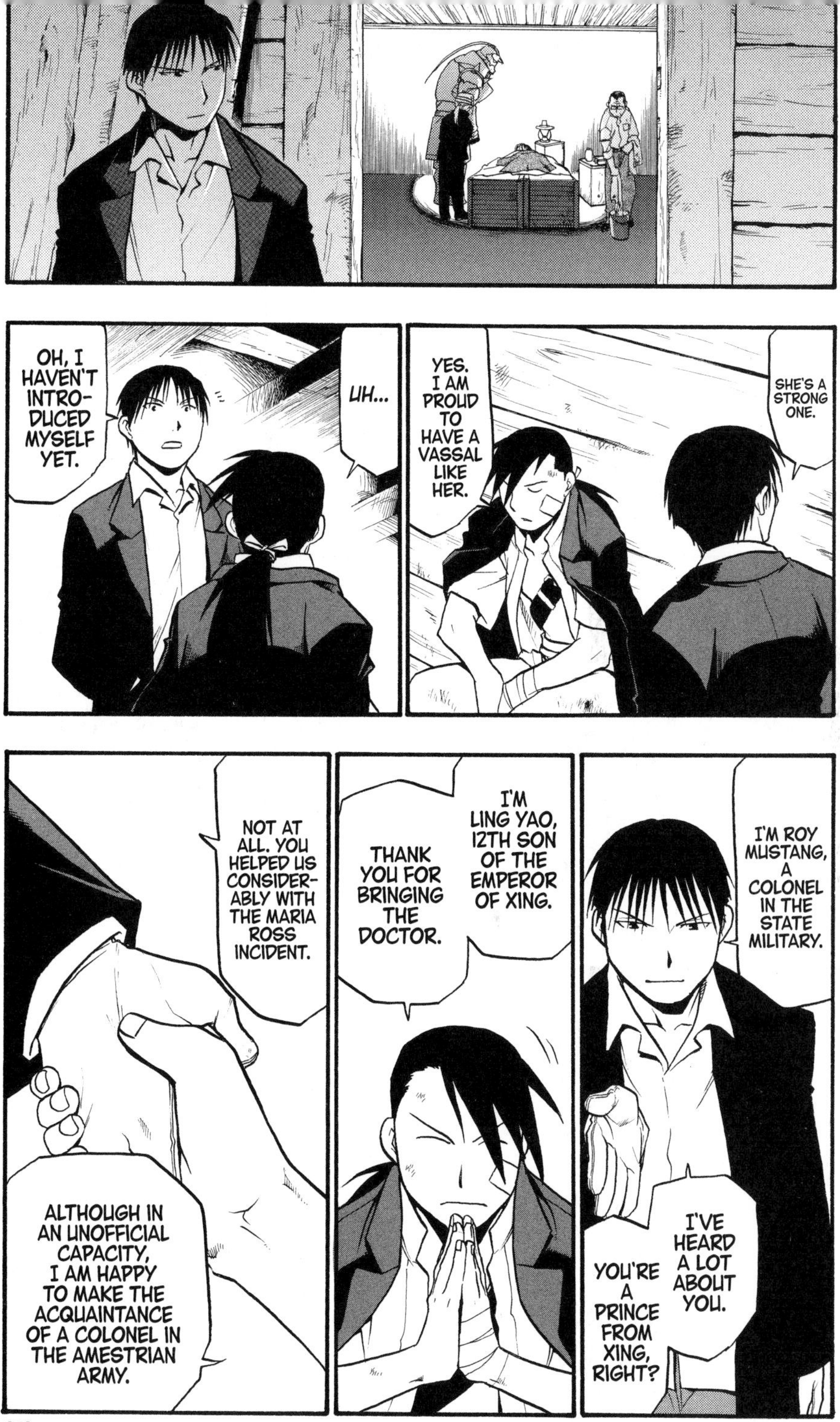
SHE'S A STRONG ONE.
YES. I AM PROUD TO HAVE A VASSAL LIKE HER.
UH...
OH, I HAVEN'T INTRODUCED MYSELF YET.
I'M ROY MUSTANG, A COLONEL IN THE STATE MILITARY.
I'VE HEARD A LOT ABOUT YOU.
YOU'RE A PRINCE FROM XING, RIGHT?
I'M LING YAO, 12TH SON OF THE EMPEROR OF XING.
THANK YOU FOR BRINGING THE DOCTOR.
NOT AT ALL. YOU HELPED US CONSIDERABLY WITH THE MARIA ROSS INCIDENT.
ALTHOUGH IN AN UNOFFICIAL CAPACITY, I AM HAPPY TO MAKE THE ACQUAINTANCE OF A COLONEL IN THE AMESTRIAN ARMY.

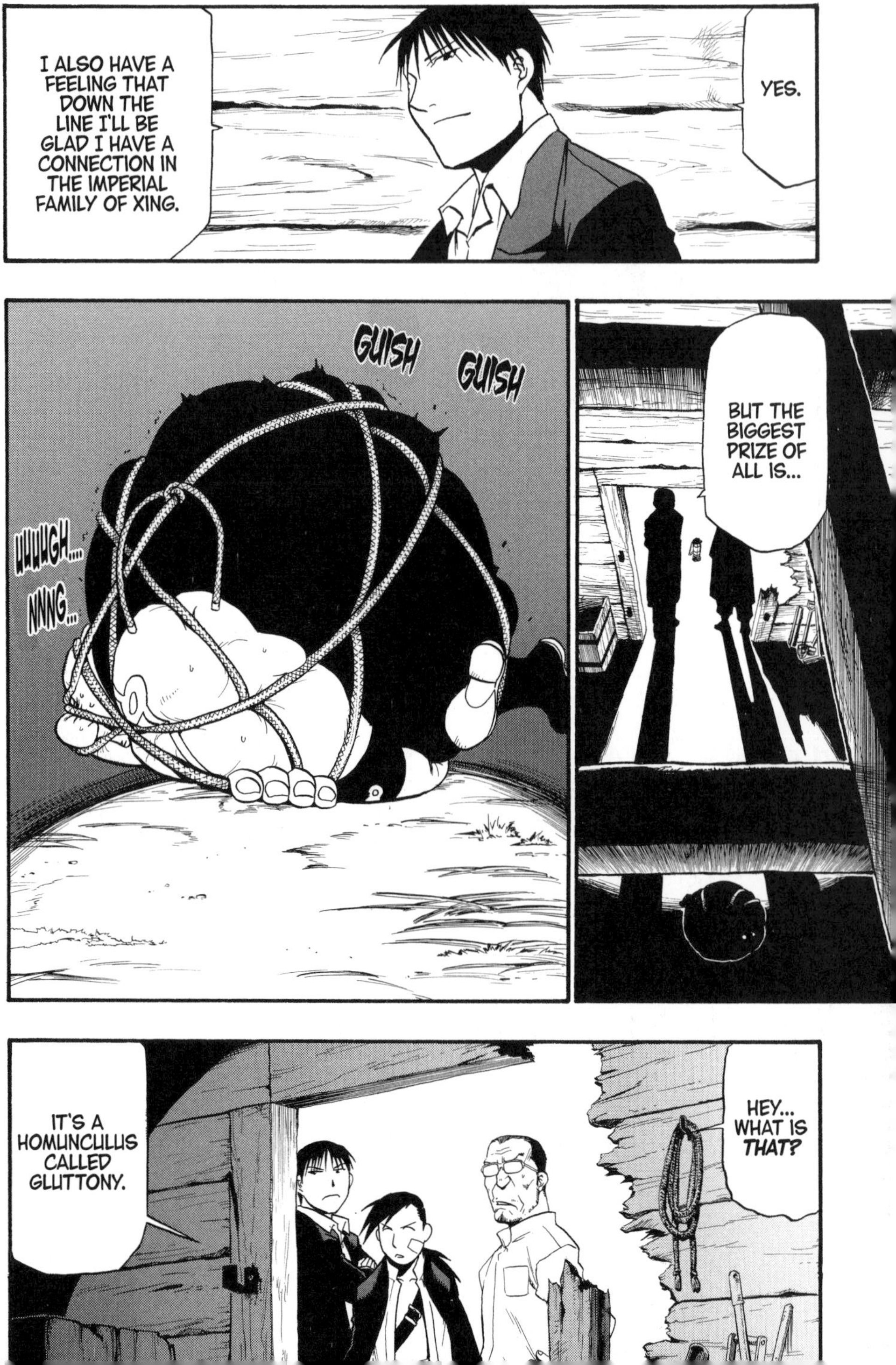
YES.
I ALSO HAVE A FEELING THAT DOWN THE LINE I'LL BE GLAD I HAVE A CONNECTION IN THE IMPERIAL FAMILY OF XING.
BUT THE BIGGEST PRIZE OF ALL IS...
GUISH
GUISH
UUUUGH...
NNNG...
HEY... WHAT IS *THAT?*
IT'S A HOMUNCULUS CALLED GLUTTONY.

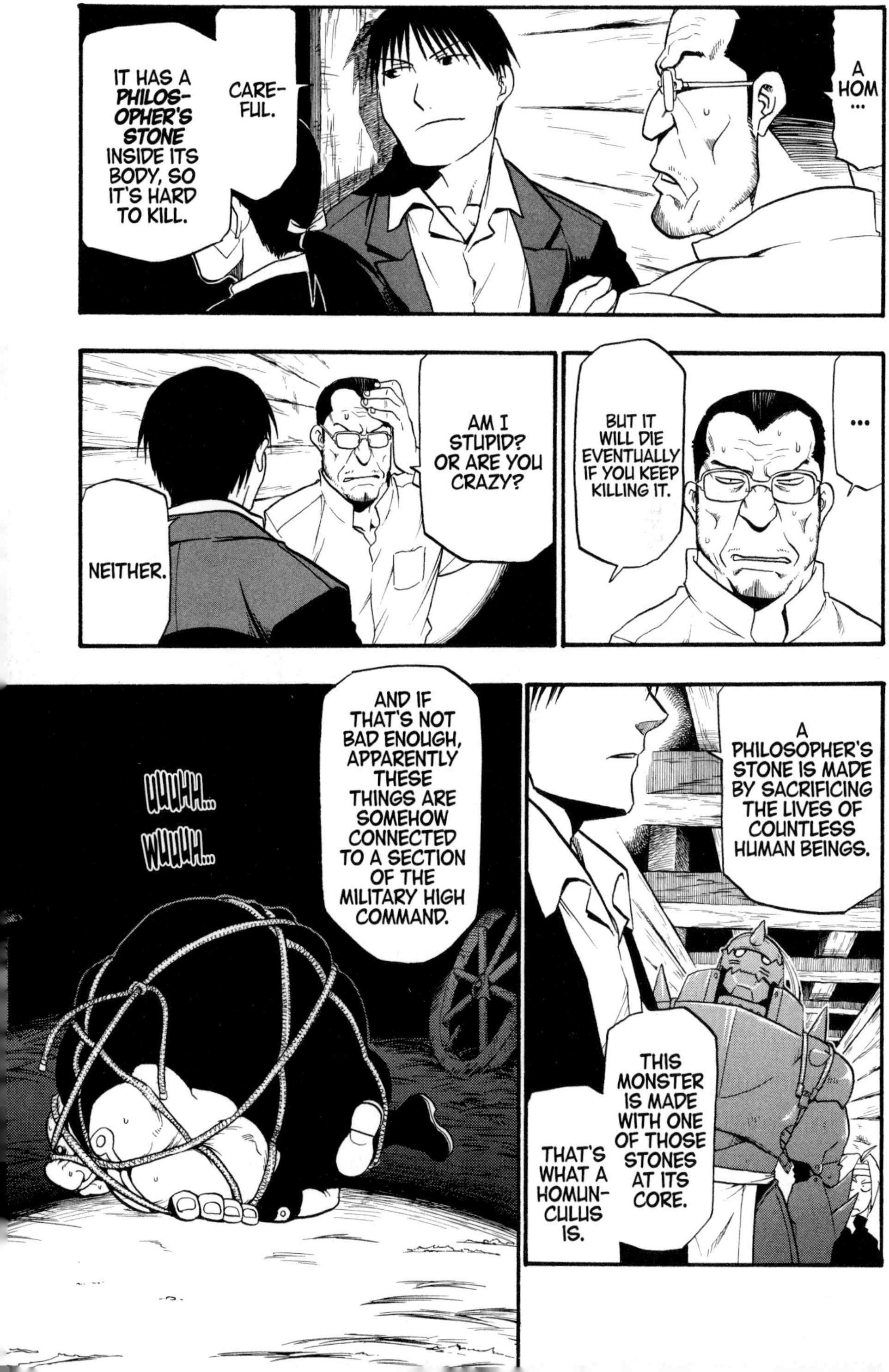
A HOM...
CAREFUL.
IT HAS A **PHILOSOPHER'S STONE** INSIDE ITS BODY, SO IT'S HARD TO KILL.
...
BUT IT WILL DIE EVENTUALLY IF YOU KEEP KILLING IT.
AM I STUPID? OR ARE YOU CRAZY?
NEITHER.
A PHILOSOPHER'S STONE IS MADE BY SACRIFICING THE LIVES OF COUNTLESS HUMAN BEINGS.
THIS MONSTER IS MADE WITH ONE OF THOSE STONES AT ITS CORE.
THAT'S WHAT A HOMUNCULUS IS.
AND IF THAT'S NOT BAD ENOUGH, APPARENTLY THESE THINGS ARE SOMEHOW CONNECTED TO A SECTION OF THE MILITARY HIGH COMMAND.

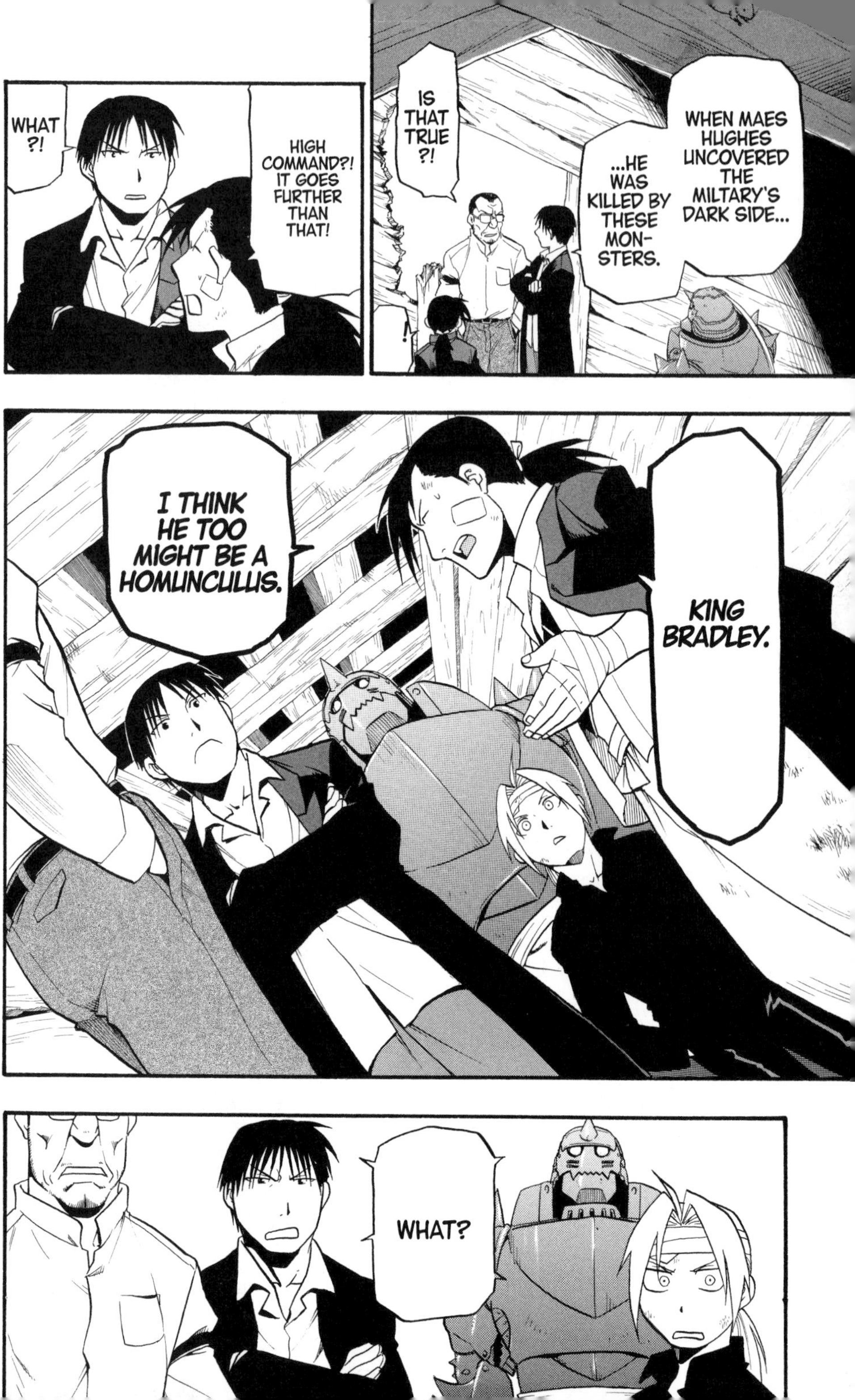
WHEN MAES HUGHES UNCOVERED THE MILTARY'S DARK SIDE...
...HE WAS KILLED BY THESE MON-STERS.
IS THAT TRUE?!
HIGH COMMAND?! IT GOES FURTHER THAN THAT!
WHAT?!
KING BRADLEY.
I THINK HE TOO MIGHT BE A HOMUNCULUS.
WHAT?

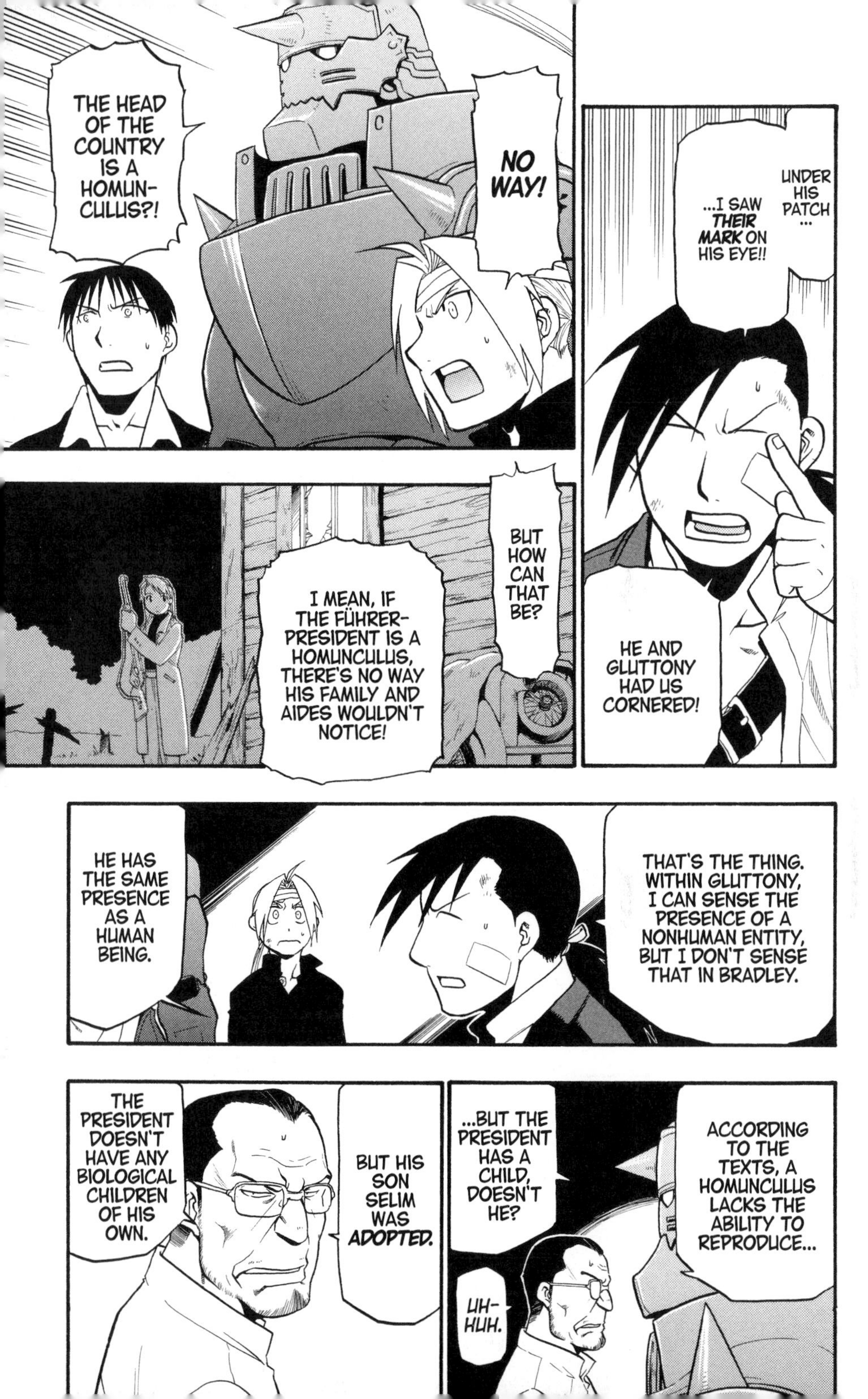
UNDER HIS PATCH...
...I SAW THEIR MARK ON HIS EYE!!
HE AND GLUTTONY HAD US CORNERED!
NO WAY!
THE HEAD OF THE COUNTRY IS A HOMUN-CULUS?!
BUT HOW CAN THAT BE?
I MEAN, IF THE FÜHRER-PRESIDENT IS A HOMUNCULUS, THERE'S NO WAY HIS FAMILY AND AIDES WOULDN'T NOTICE!
THAT'S THE THING. WITHIN GLUTTONY, I CAN SENSE THE PRESENCE OF A NONHUMAN ENTITY, BUT I DON'T SENSE THAT IN BRADLEY.
HE HAS THE SAME PRESENCE AS A HUMAN BEING.
ACCORDING TO THE TEXTS, A HOMUNCULUS LACKS THE ABILITY TO REPRODUCE...
...BUT THE PRESIDENT HAS A CHILD, DOESN'T HE?
UH-HUH.
BUT HIS SON SELIM WAS ADOPTED.
THE PRESIDENT DOESN'T HAVE ANY BIOLOGICAL CHILDREN OF HIS OWN.

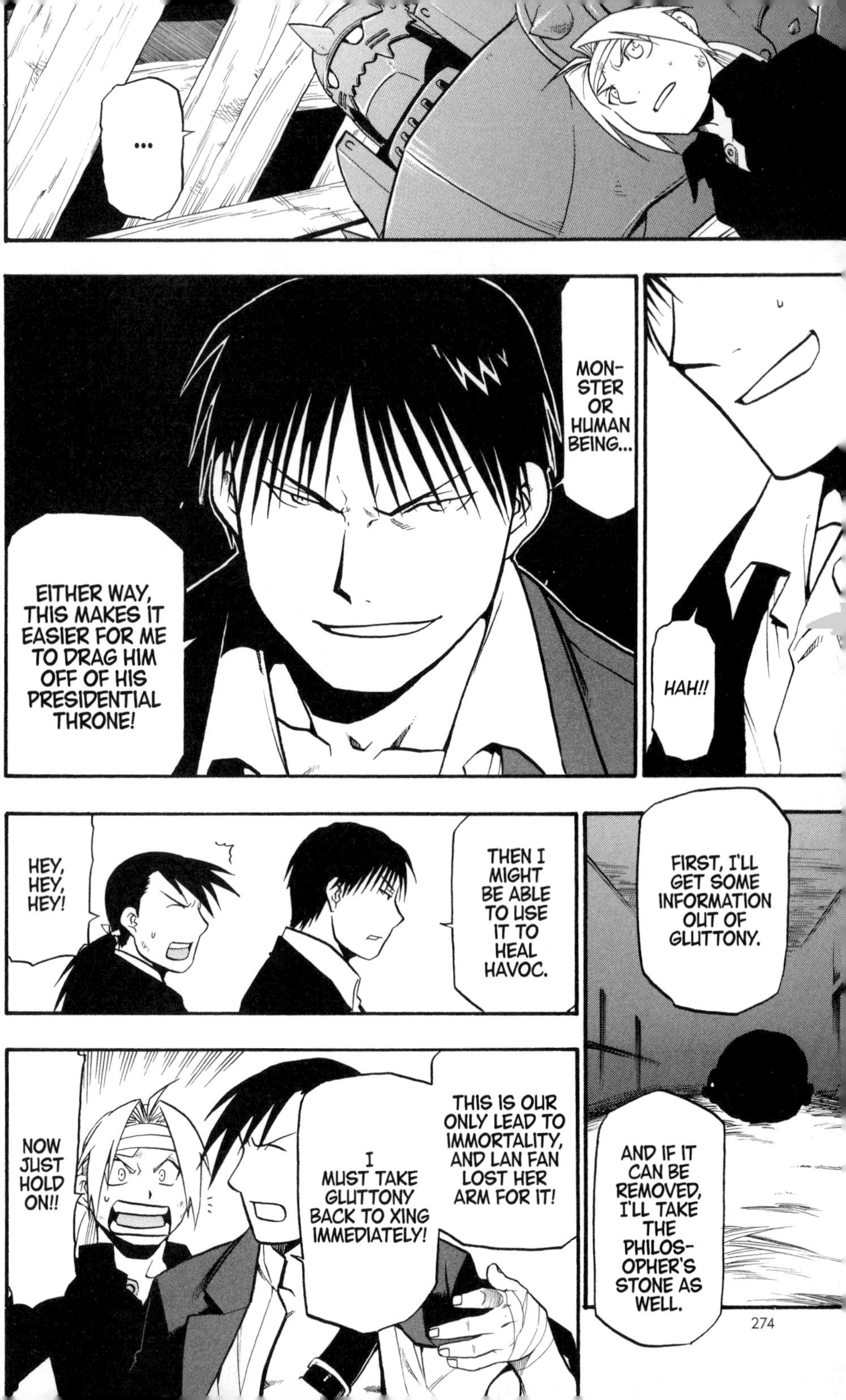
...
HAH!!
MON-STER OR HUMAN BEING...
EITHER WAY, THIS MAKES IT EASIER FOR ME TO DRAG HIM OFF OF HIS PRESIDENTIAL THRONE!
FIRST, I'LL GET SOME INFORMATION OUT OF GLUTTONY.
AND IF IT CAN BE REMOVED, I'LL TAKE THE PHILOS-OPHER'S STONE AS WELL.
THEN I MIGHT BE ABLE TO USE IT TO HEAL HAVOC.
HEY, HEY, HEY!
THIS IS OUR ONLY LEAD TO IMMORTALITY, AND LAN FAN LOST HER ARM FOR IT!
I MUST TAKE GLUTTONY BACK TO XING IMMEDIATELY!
NOW JUST HOLD ON!!

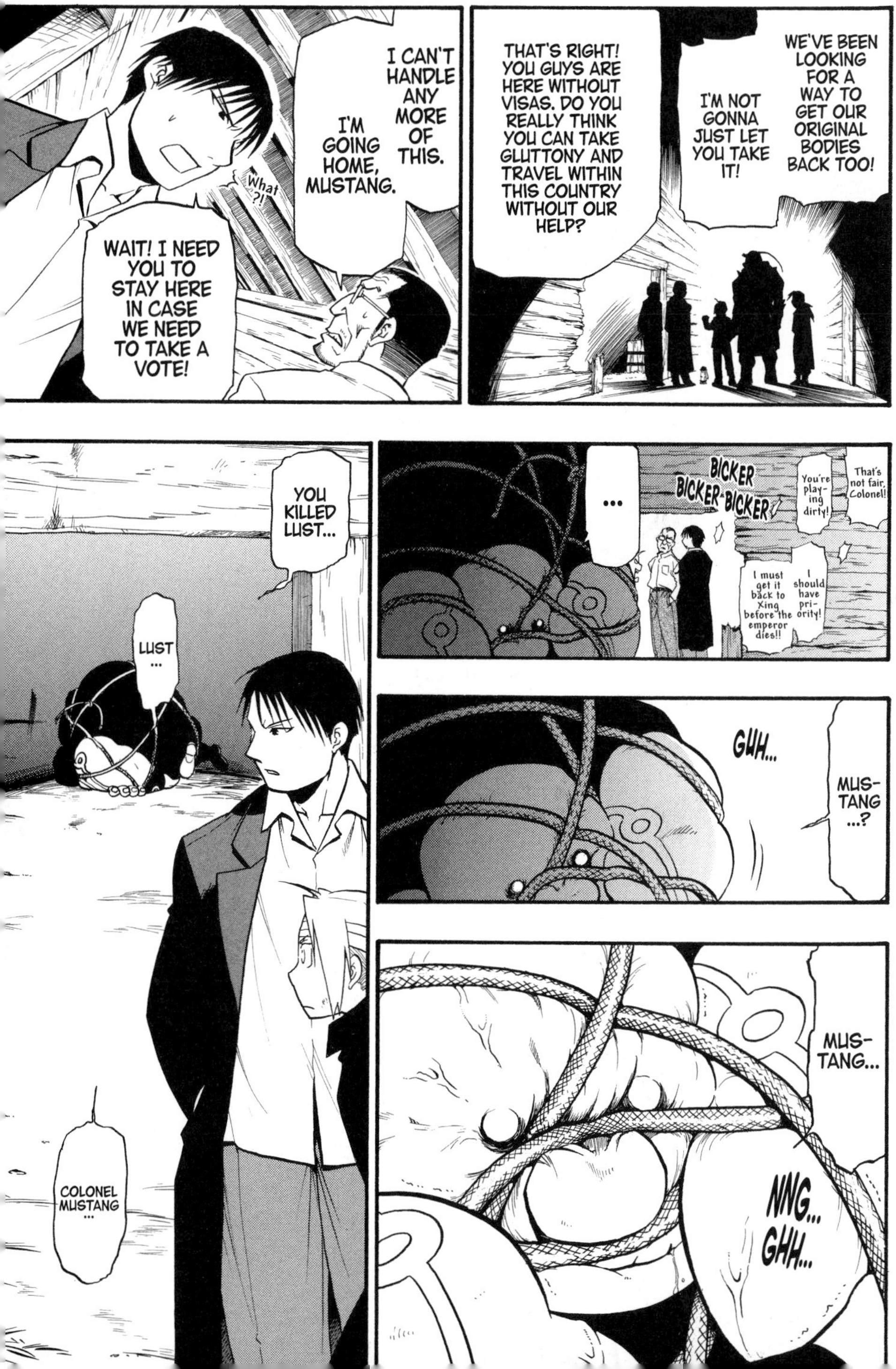
WE'VE BEEN LOOKING FOR A WAY TO GET OUR ORIGINAL BODIES BACK TOO!
I'M NOT GONNA JUST LET YOU TAKE IT!
THAT'S RIGHT! YOU GUYS ARE HERE WITHOUT VISAS. DO YOU REALLY THINK YOU CAN TAKE GLUTTONY AND TRAVEL WITHIN THIS COUNTRY WITHOUT OUR HELP?
I CAN'T HANDLE ANY MORE OF THIS.
I'M GOING HOME, MUSTANG.
What?!
WAIT! I NEED YOU TO STAY HERE IN CASE WE NEED TO TAKE A VOTE!
That's not fair, Colonel!
You're playing dirty!
BICKER BICKER BICKER
I should have priority!
I must get it back to Xing before the emperor dies!!
...
MUSTANG...?
GUH...
MUSTANG...
NNG... GHH...
YOU KILLED LUST...
LUST...
COLONEL MUSTANG...

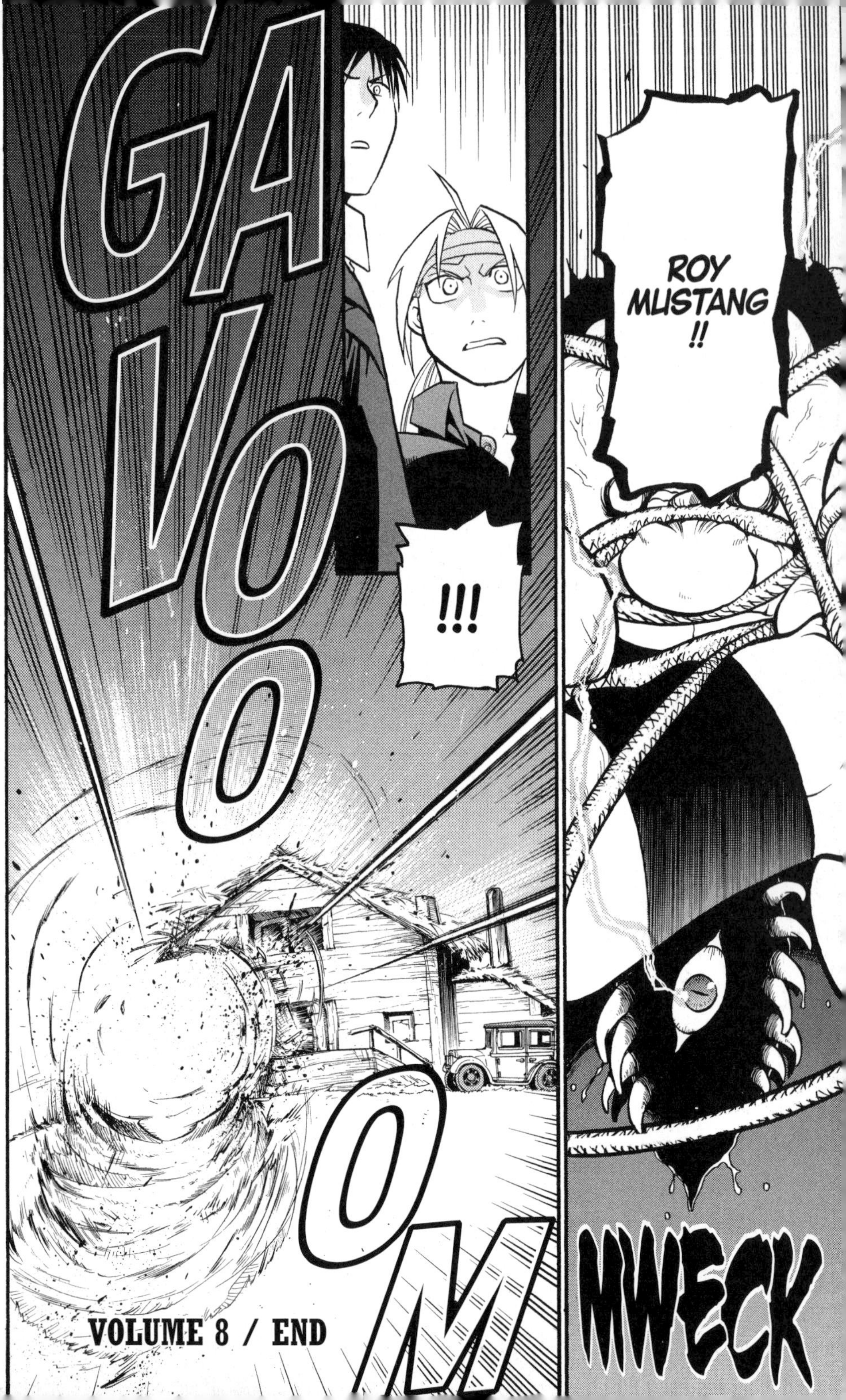
ROY MUSTANG !!
MWECK
!!!
GAVOOOM
VOLUME 8 / END

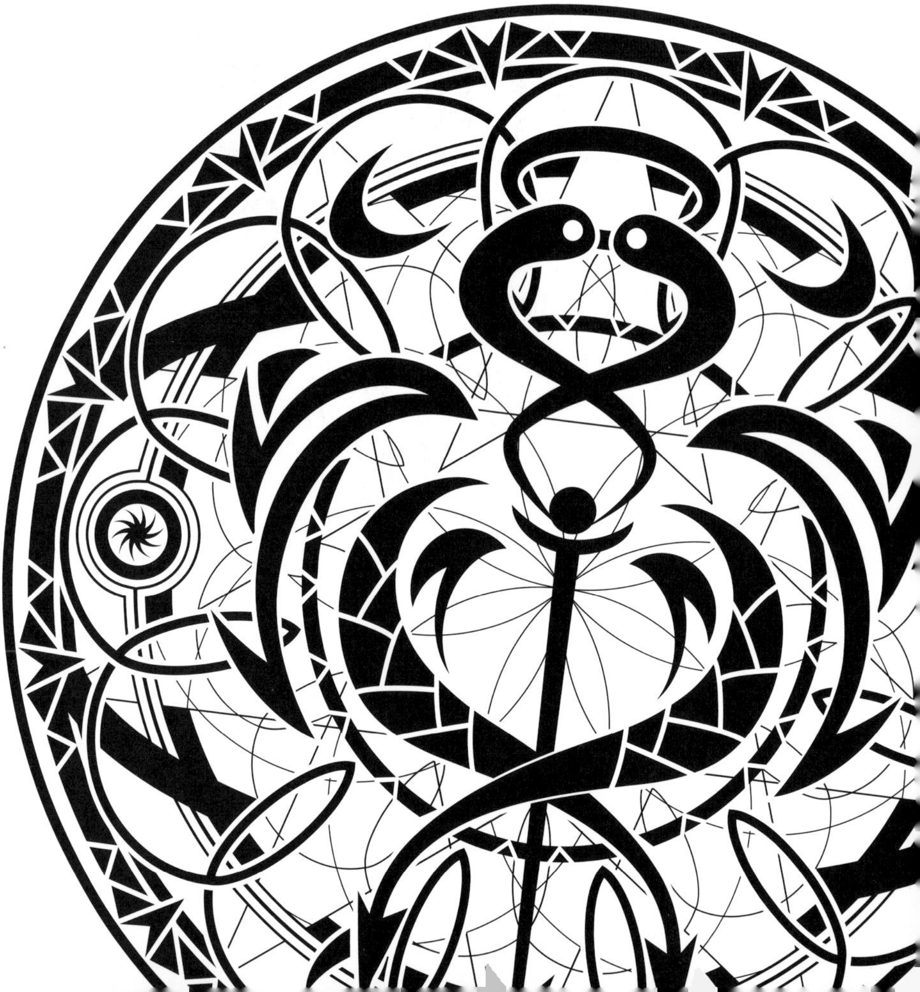

FULLMETAL ALCHEMIST

CONCEPT SKETCHES

08

スカー 初期案①

Scar Initial Design #1

決定案よりも、
感情を表に
出す人だったっ
ぽい。

More expressive than his final design.

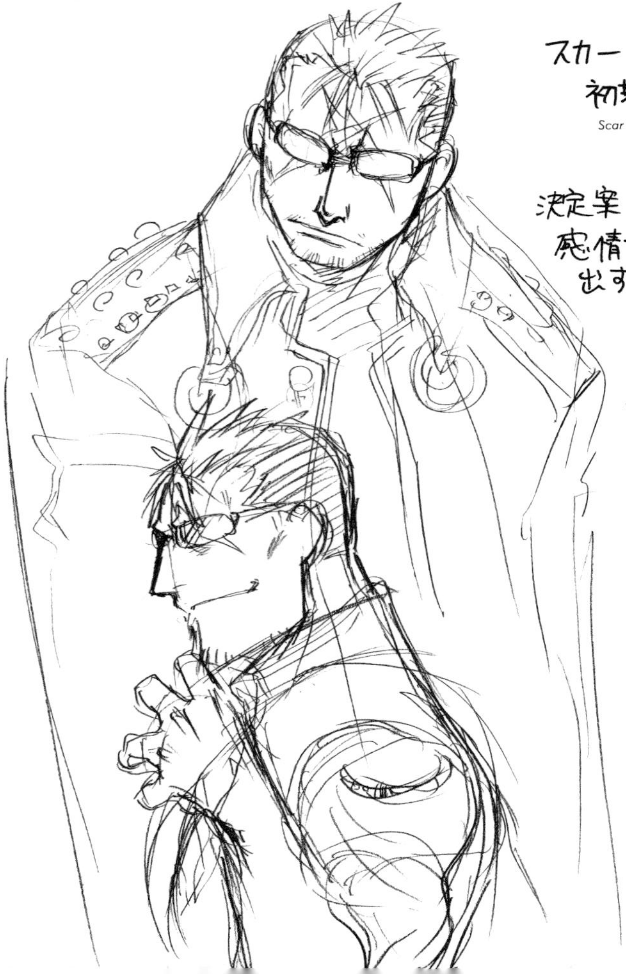

スカー 初期案②

Scar Initial Design #2

①より 感情豊かなイメージ。

タバコは ハボックがいるから
没になったのか?
つーか ピアスしてる!?

Even more expressive than the first version. I guess I ditched the cigarette because of Havoc? But more importantly, he had earrings?!

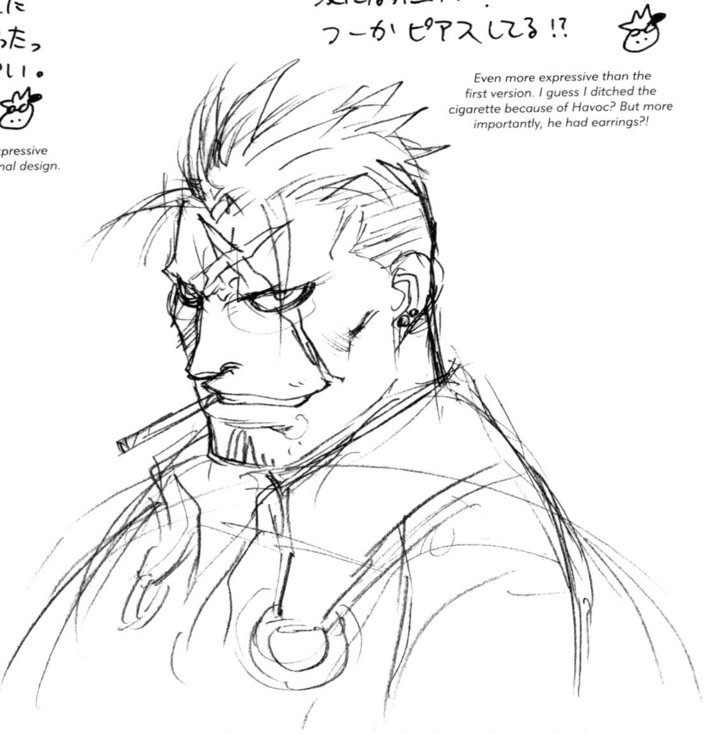

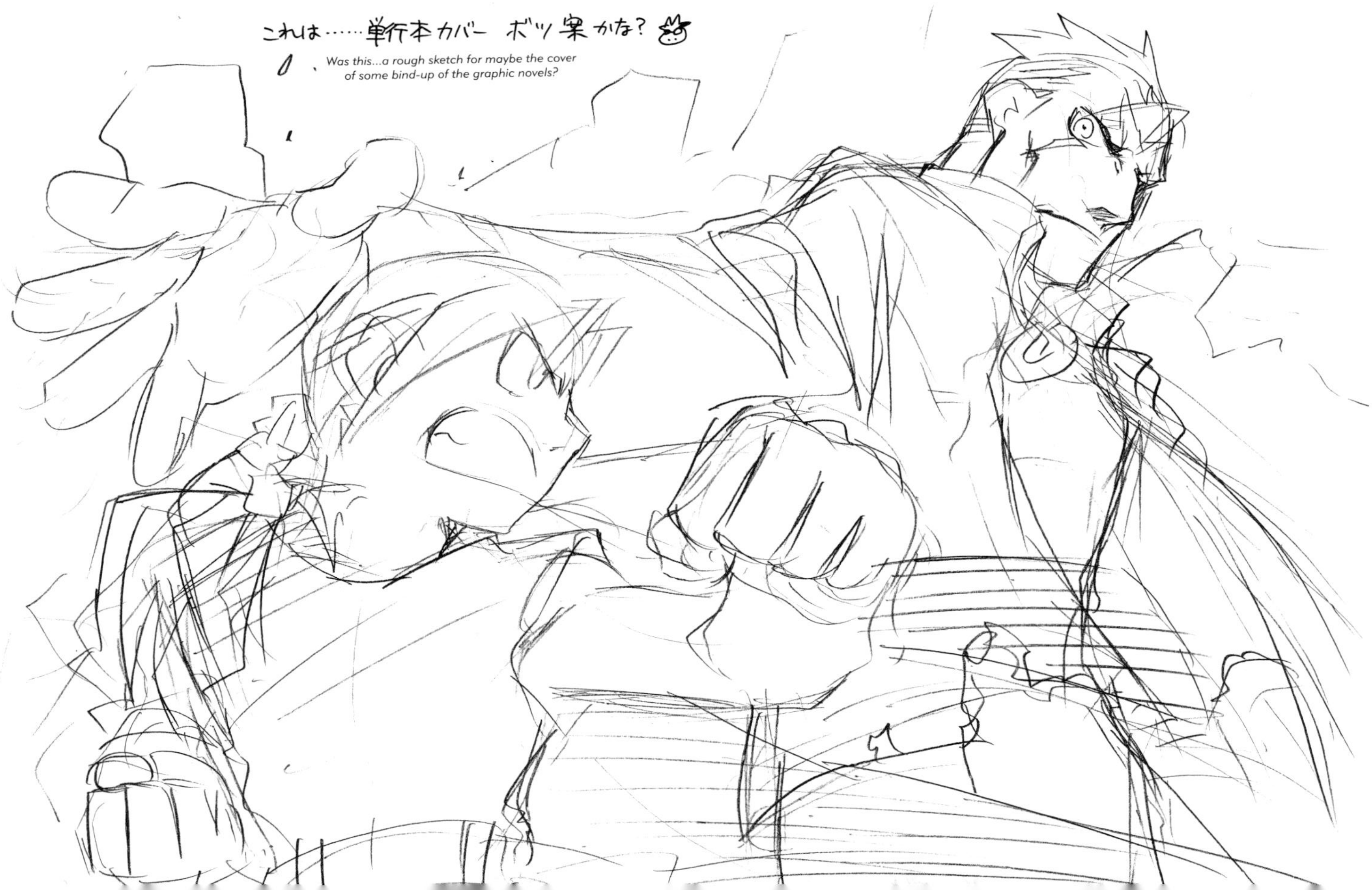
これは……単行本カバー ボツ案かな？
Was this...a rough sketch for maybe the cover
of some bind-up of the graphic novels?

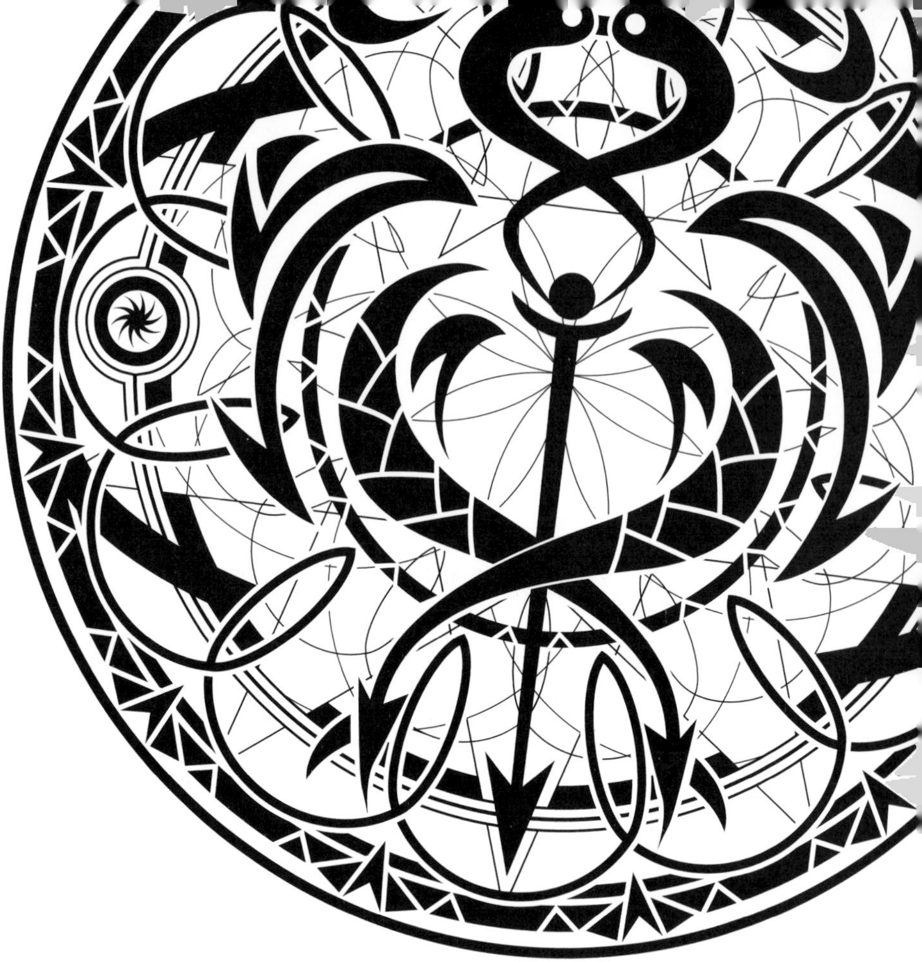

ABOUT THE AUTHOR

Born in Hokkaido, Japan, Hiromu Arakawa first attracted attention in 1999 with her award-winning manga *Stray Dog*. Her series *Fullmetal Alchemist* was serialized from 2001 to 2010 with a story that spanned 27 volumes and became an international critical and commercial success, receiving both the Shogakukan Manga Award and Seiun Award and selling over 70 million copies worldwide. *Fullmetal Alchemist* has been adapted into anime twice, first as *Fullmetal Alchemist* in 2003 and again as *Fullmetal Alchemist: Brotherhood* in 2009. The series has also inspired numerous films, video games and novels.

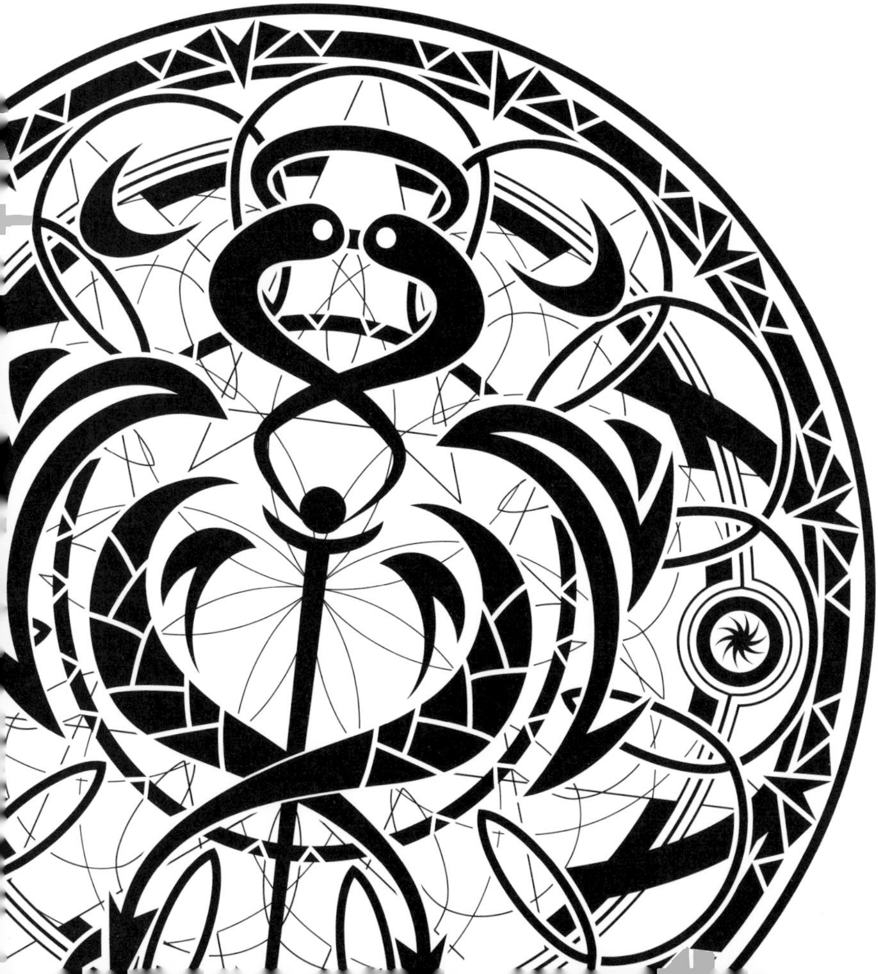

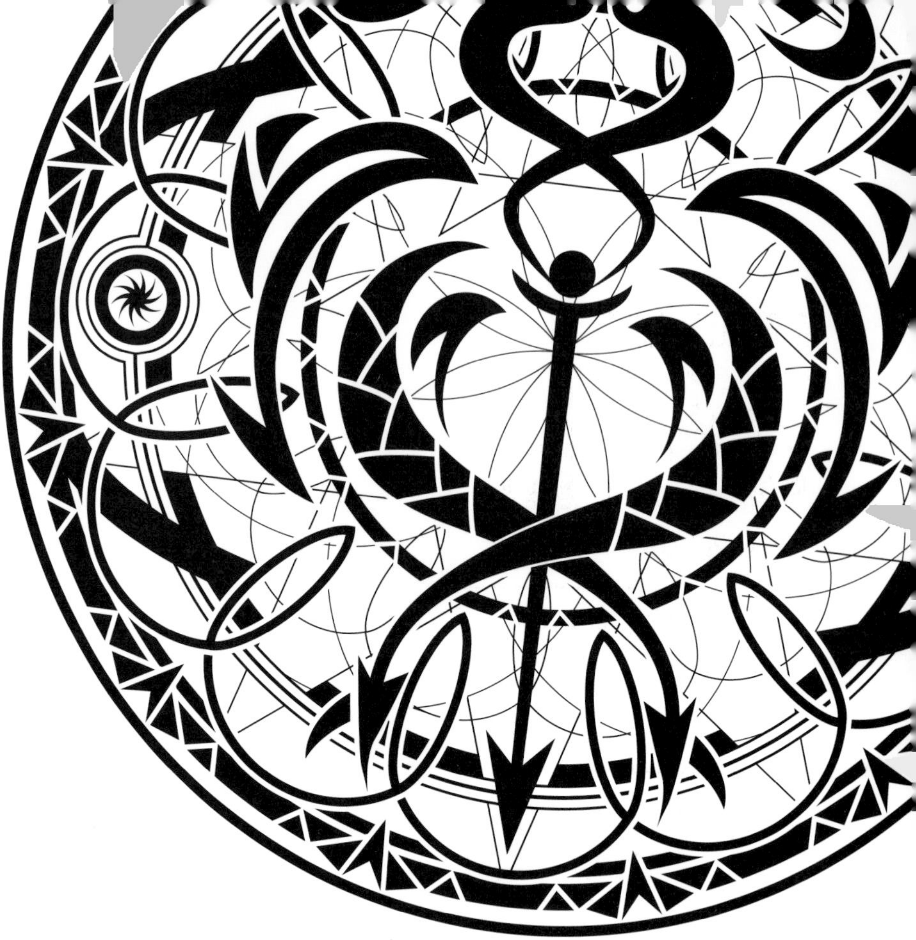

FULLMETAL EDITION
FULLMETAL ALCHEMIST
VOLUME 08

Story and Art by HIROMU ARAKAWA

Translation: AKIRA WATANABE
English Adaptation: JAKE FORBES
VIZ Media Edition Editor: ANDY NAKATANI
Touch-Up Art & Lettering: STEVE DUTRO
Design: ADAM GRANO
Editor: HOPE DONOVAN

FULLMETAL ALCHEMIST KANZENBAN vol. 8
© 2011 Hiromu Arakawa/SQUARE ENIX CO., LTD.
First published in Japan in 2011 by SQUARE ENIX CO., LTD.
English translation rights arranged with SQUARE ENIX CO.,
LTD. and VIZ Media, LLC. English translation © 2020 SQUARE
ENIX CO., LTD.

Printed in Canada

Published by VIZ Media, LLC
P.O. Box 77010
San Francisco, CA 94107

10 9 8 7 6 5 4 3 2 1
First printing, February 2020

viz.com

This is the last page.

Fullmetal Alchemist reads right to left.